Principles of Voice & Data Communications

Principles of Voice & Data Communications

Regis J. Bates
T.C. International Consulting, Inc.

Marcus Bates
T.C. International Consulting, Inc.

McGraw-Hill
Irwin

Boston   Burr Ridge, IL   Dubuque, IA   Madison, WI   New York   San Francisco   St. Louis
Bangkok   Bogotá   Caracas   Kuala Lumpur   Lisbon   London   Madrid   Mexico City
Milan   Montreal   New Delhi   Santiago   Seoul   Singapore   Sydney   Taipei   Toronto

PRINCIPLES OF VOICE & DATA COMMUNICATIONS

Published by McGraw-Hill/Irwin, a business unit of The McGraw-Hill Companies, Inc., 1221 Avenue of the Americas, New York, NY, 10020. Copyright © 2007 by The McGraw-Hill Companies, Inc. All rights reserved. No part of this publication may be reproduced or distributed in any form or by any means, or stored in a database or retrieval system, without the prior written consent of The McGraw-Hill Companies, Inc., including, but not limited to, in any network or other electronic storage or transmission, or broadcast for distance learning.

Some ancillaries, including electronic and print components, may not be available to customers outside the United States.

This book is printed on acid-free paper.

1 2 3 4 5 6 7 8 9 0 DOC/DOC 0 9 8 7 6

ISBN-13: 978-0-07-225732-8
ISBN-10: 0-07-225732-6

Editorial director   *Brent Gordon*
Executive editor   *Paul Ducham*
Managing developmental editor   *Jonathan Plant*
Editorial coordinator   *Lindsay Roth*
Marketing manager   *Sankha Basu*
Senior media producer   *Victor Chiu*
Project manager   *Bruce Gin*
Production supervisor   *Debra R. Sylvester*
Senior designer   *Adam Rooke*
Developer, Media technology   *Brian Nacik*
Cover design   *Jillian Lindner*
Typeface   *10/13 Times*
Compositor   *International Typesetting and Composition*
Printer   *R. R. Donnelley*

Library of Congress Cataloging-in-Publication Data

Bates, Regis J.
    Principles of voice & data communications / Regis J. Bates, Marcus Bates.
      p. cm.
    Includes index.
    ISBN-13: 978-0-07-225732-8
    ISBN-10: 0-07-225732-6 (alk. paper)
    1. Telecommunication.   I. Title: Principles of voice and data communications.   II. Bates, Marcus.   III. Title.
TK5101.B3153 2007
621.382--dc22

2005053374

About the Authors

Regis (Bud) Bates has more than 38 years of experience in telecommunications and management information systems (MIS). He oversees the operation of TC International Consulting, Inc., a full-service management-consulting organization. Bud has designed major global networks including LANs and WANs. His clients span the range of Fortune 100 to 500 companies and carriers alike. Bud also specializes in broadband wired and wireless communications, ranging from satellite installations to wireless LANs. He also has concentrated on the infrastructure of organizations that are growing and demanding more capacity and speed to satisfy their mission-critical applications.

Bud has written many books on the technologies, many of which have been "best sellers" for McGraw-Hill. As a consultant, he has worked with nearly every conceivable networking strategy in wireline and wireless networks. Using the combination of all wired and wireless services, Bud was instrumental in designing and laying out corporate networks that spanned the globe. His many projects have led to the acceptance of convergence of voice and data networks throughout the world. There is little that Bud has not touched in the industry when it comes to the overall layout and implementation of networks combining the wired and wireless worlds.

Regis J. (Bud) Bates Jr.,
TC International Consulting, Inc.
Phoenix, AZ

Marcus Bates has over nine years experience in the telecommunications field. Prior to his current assignment with TCIC, Marcus served five years with major communications' suppliers in the Chicago area, where he became involved with many wide-area data network implementations with Fortune 500 companies, many with worldwide presence. Marcus Bates's past experiences with AT&T Data Networking Sales help him to focus the importance of consistency in the implementation and delivery of his writing and presentations. His endeavors have brought him through the ranks of various organizations. Marcus has worked with many executive-level managers and operational supervisors in determining the return on investment (ROI) and the business gains from the services he provided.

His youthful approach to qualitative improvements allows Marcus to develop a rapport with many designers and project engineers alike. His technical savvy, combined with his managerial approach, have made Marcus extremely popular. Marcus has helped to create technology roadmaps on the emerging technologies to evaluate their strengths and weaknesses versus the current environment within the organization. This roadmap, combined with current assessments of their clients, allow Bud and Marcus to provide the best solutions and migration plans for businesses over the next five years.

Marcus is CTP-certified and an authorized CTP certified instructor. He is an adjunct professor at South Mountain Community College (SMCC) as an adjunct professor and, for three years, he has developed/taught Convergence, Wireless Technologies, and Transmission Systems.

Marcus D. Bates
TC International Consulting, Inc.
Phoenix, AZ 85076

Technical Editors and Peer Reviewers

Technical Editors:

William Kuglich	Benedictine University—Lisle, IL
Joseph Mayes	Bellevue Community College—Bellevue, WA

Peer Reviewers:

Tom Cavaiani	Boise State University—Boise, ID
Scott Quinn	Portland Community College—Portland, OR
Jung P. Shim	Mississippi State University—Mississippi, MS
Paul Wilson	DeVry University—Fremont, CA
Andy Borchers	Kettering University—Flint, MI
Joseph Mayes	Bellevue Community College—Bellevue, WA
Robert Chow	Robert Golden Gate University—San Francisco, CA
Jeff Boucher	Dyersburg State Community College—Dyersburg, TN
William Kuglich	Benedictine University—Lisle, IL

Contents at a Glance

Contents

Acknowledgments

The authors would like to take the opportunity to recognize several people who had a considerable influence on our ability to complete this project. One cannot produce a book or write the manuscript in a vacuum. Therefore, without the people who aided us, this book might not be a reality.

First, we have to readily acknowledge and thank all the folks at McGraw-Hill for their continued support and exceptional patience. Occasionally, we needed a push and, at other times, we needed to back off. Somewhere is an unwritten rule that authors are supposed to have unlimited time available and unmitigated commitment to completing the book early. Well, in our case, this was not true! Too many challenges and changes crept into our lives and postponed the inevitable completion of this project. Changes in the Telecommunications industry, changes in the publishing business, and changes in people all led to potential delays. As the radical changes and slowdowns in the industry cause major changes in the providers, the protocols, and the acceptance of any specific product, we had to juggle all the schedules to try to complete this manuscript. We put the McGraw-Hill people through the paces using all the resources at our disposal.

We also appreciate the efforts of all the folks we never saw or talked with, who remained in the background. These unsung heroes of the Production Department never get their credit, but we all should be grateful to them for their dedication and stick-to-it attitudes.

Beyond the folks at McGraw-Hill, is a list of reviewers who took their time to review our initial manuscript and made their valuable contributions and suggestions. These folks all had much to do with the successful production of this book and deserve credit for keeping us on our toes.

Several vendors and friends were supportive and helpful in garnering information for the development of this manuscript. We thank all of them, for they are too numerous to mention each individually. However, they know who they are and they can take silent comfort in knowing they got us here.

In many cases, the ideas of telecommunications for both voice and data are still emerging for some of the areas discussed herein. However, we hope we captured the spirit and the letter of the concept even before it truly develops. Enjoy this book as you would a version of a 101 series handbook.

Convergence is the name of our industry today, yet we must continue to seek new ways of providing the information and using the technology. As long as you, the reader, continue to demand high-speed services, reliability, and mobility we will have a job. And that job will be to seek the ways of describing and applying the technologies, so you can use them.

Good Luck and Happy Reading!

Preface

Before you begin to read this book, please take a moment to read these introductory comments. The title of the book may be misleading for many people:

For the engineering student, this may sound like the bible of voice and data networks and switching systems. Not so! This is not an engineering book and it will not dig into the gory details. It will help an engineering student to understand the marketplace for the products and services that will be introduced into the marketplace. This book will also show you the applications that the voice and data networks satisfy. As stated, however, this is not a highly technical book. Read it for what it is worth.

For the financial and business student, the title may have a tendency to scare you away, thinking it is a highly technical book. Please persevere and read on. This book was written for you, so you can understand the various developments and challenges in using and working with voice and data networks. We wrote this with the simplest of terms and with some storyboards to make concepts more understandable. We also spent a significant amount of time in developing and shaping the business market strategies. If you are a newcomer who needs to understand the future demand for voice and data communications, then this book, *The Principles of Voice & Data Communications,* is for you.

This book is about the process of using and implementing the technologies in a communications infrastructure. This book is part of a continuing series of books that are geared toward a specific market niche.

We certainly hope this book will aid you in understanding the technologies without the "Techno Geek" jargon that is so common in our industry.

Regis J. (Bud) Bates, Jr. and Marcus Bates
Authors

Chapter 1

Principles of Voice and Data Communications: An Introduction

LEARNING OBJECTIVES:

Once you complete this chapter, you will be able to:

Describe the communications process.

Understand what a network is.

Describe the use of voice in our everyday process.

Discuss the way we transmit voice and data in a network.

Discuss the purpose of the hierarchy of telecommunications.

Understand the various names of the technologies we use.

Introduction

Welcome to the Principles of Voice and Data Communications! This book introduces you to one of the most fascinating industries in the business community. If pursued as a lifetime career, telecommunications can be confusing, challenging, and rewarding, all at the same time. What other industry can offer such contradictions and complements? Because of these challenges and confusing issues, you should never be bored in this industry. So just what is telecommunications all about? Let's step through some of the topics that unfold in this book for you.

The Beginning

Chapter 1 discusses the buildup of telecommunications from its inception of a voice communications network. We do not start from the beginning of all telecommunications systems but, instead, from a jumping-off point when the telephone was invented. First, let's define telecommunications.

Telecommunications is the exchange of information between a sender and a receiver, over a distance, across a medium in a usable and understandable format.

The rest of this book deals with exactly the way we interpret, modify, or utilize this model of a definition. What are we saying here? It would be better to describe the pieces of the puzzle here, so we shall break the definition down into its basic components.

1. The exchange of information. Information can come in many forms.

    a. Information can include voice. When we speak to one another, we are exchanging information. This can be sports-related information, such as who won the game last night. Or it can be educational information, such as when we learn from the professor in a class and the professor imparts knowledge. Moreover, it can be intimate information as we swap some of our deepest secrets with a trusted individual. Regardless of the content, we are exchanging information by conversing. This was one of the first portions of the voice network when Alexander Graham Bell invented the telephone set. Bell's intent was to exchange information through voice means. We discuss the use of basic voice in Chapter 2.

    b. Information can also be data. Data evolved later in the telecommunications industry, although data capabilities were available in the form of the old telegraph and teletype networks, and even in the use of the postal system. In the telegraph networks, we found they were painfully slow in the way we had to prepare our message to an individual at the distant end. The telegraph key is shown in the following illustration. We wrote it on a sheet of paper. Then, on handing it to a specially trained individual, the message was then sent across a wired system through a series of electrical keying dots and dashes. A receiver at the far end, another suitably trained specialist, listened to the electrical- and mechanical-keyed information and transcribed it letter by letter until the sentence or the message was re-created at the far end. Then, a third party was dispatched to deliver the message to our door. This form of telegraphy was not interactive, was not private, and was tedious, but it did work. Later on, there was the use of a new invention, the teletype, whereby the specially trained individual was no longer needed because the invention of the teletype included a standard keyboard interface. This was slow, but it was certainly more user-friendly. Moreover, if you used a teletype, this could be more interactive, but this was limited data transmission. Later, in the 1960s, we began to align our data communications with information that could be exchanged between computers. We call this *data communications*. Interestingly, though, we used the voice network to carry the data information.

The telegraph key Samuel Morse used on his first line in 1844 was simple—a strip of spring steel that could be pressed against a metal contact.

We spend a few chapters discussing the use of data communications from the method of dial-up modem communications across the voice network, the use of packets across a network, xDSL and cable, and more, so you get a much wider view of data communications.

   c. Information can be images. Images can be in the form of a facsimile (fax) or a video picture. This was another innovation to exchange information, and it first occurred through the use of a fax machine. While the fax machine wasn't great, it certainly helped to fill a need to communicate when someone needed to see a document (and possibly an original signature) and the postal-service delivery mechanism took too long. Video communications also enjoyed a lot of hoopla in 1960 through 1980+. With techniques to add the fax or video image onto a telephone line and carry it across town or across the world, these innovations added to our dependence on telecommunications.

2. Information can be between a sender and a receiver. If we are to exchange information, we must assume a minimum of two parties are involved. What good is it to speak if no one is there to listen and receive our speech? Occasionally, we may talk to ourselves and, remarkably, we answer our own questions or respond to our own comments. Then, we are both the sender and the receiver! For the purpose of this book, though, we assume that the sender and the receiver are two different entities. We want to pass the information on to a new recipient. Our telecommunications methodology, therefore, must assume two entities are involved (this can be people, computers, terminals, fax machines, and so forth).

3. Information can be over a distance. The Greek word "tele" means from afar. The distances in a telecommunications world can be close proximity or far distances. When we send a page of text from our PC to a printer attached to the PC, it travels a matter of a few feet. When we dial up a connection on the long-distance network between New York and L.A., for example, then our communications travels 3,000 miles. So, regardless of the distance, the real message is that it must travel a distance (short or long).

4. Information can be across a medium. We need something to carry our information from the sender to the receiver. In the previous example of a computer and a printer, the distance may have been 3 to 6 feet, typical of a cable connecting PC and printer. Yet, if we add other communications capabilities, we can introduce a new medium. However, the medium can take on different forms:

   a. Copper wires, or what is referred to unshielded twisted pairs, are the carrier. So, in a telephony world, we may be using copper wires that can travel across the country. This is what Bell was trying to accomplish, albeit in localized communications.

   b. Radio has been used to carry information for decades now. The first radio transmitter created by Guglielmo Marconi in Italy in 1895 is shown in the following illustration. Long-distance microwave communications emerged back in the 1930–1940 era and is still in use today carrying calls across the country. Satellite communications emerged in the 1960s. The use of satellite communication is still as popular today as it was back then to carry signals across the world. Newer radio systems, such as wireless local area networks (WLANs), can carry information at shorter distances (typically up to 300 feet in a local area). Cellular phones got their foothold in the industry in 1984 and have never slowed down since then, giving us wireless access to the local and long-distance networks for calls around the world.

The first Marconi radio transmitter from Villa Grifone, Bologna (1895).

c. Fiber optics can be used to carry information across glass or plastic wires. The difference is optical fibers are typically used in the local telephone company and the long distance companies' networks to carry hundreds of thousands of calls and informational streams across the globe. The fiber is seen as a contrast to the bundle of wires in a twisted pair cable, as shown in the following Illustration.

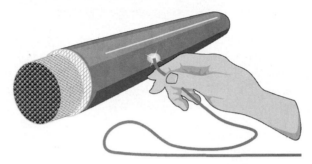

Fiber is smaller than a bundle of cables, but it carries many times the number of calls.

d. Coaxial cable is only a copper wire, but it is different. It was initially an invention during the 1950s–1960s to carry voice communications between telephone company offices. Then CATV was created to carry one-way video communications in the form of entertainment (TV) to us. This is still a sender-to-receiver transmission system. With later innovations, we saw that the same cable that once only carried one-way video now is enhanced to carry two-way Internet data at high (but asymmetrical) speeds, plus two-way voice communications. A representation of a coaxial cable is shown in the following illustration.

Coaxial cable can carry video and Internet access. Now, the CATV companies are offering voice telephony, which means the cable will carry voice, data, and video.

e. Power Lines. Yes, the electrical lines running from the electric company that carry the energy to power our lights, our PCs, and all our other communicating devices now can be used as a transmission medium. It is already a transmission medium, in the transmission of electricity. But now we have the methodology to carry our data traffic, high-speed Internet access, and, eventually, voice over the Internet (VoIP) across the same wires that are delivering our electricity. This is known as BPL and is an emerging technology, as shown in the following illustration.

The use of bypass filters allows the electric company to carry high-speed Internet access across the same wires as our electricity.

5. To communicate is to make common. We communicate information so that it is received and understood in a common format—what good would all this transmission be across various media over distances if we could not understand what is being sent? It must be sent in a usable and understandable format. For example, if we sent a fax to you halfway across the world and your fax machine was a different type than ours, it might not be acceptable or receivable. Worse yet, it might be received, but because of incompatibilities in the equipment, it could turn out as all gibberish. What is the value of this fax? We suspect your reply was a resounding zero! Receiving a fax that is totally unreadable has a zero value. The same holds true if I sent a TV broadcast from the U.S. to the United Kingdom. You are probably saying, "What's wrong with that?" In the U.S., we use a TV system that operates under what is defined as the National Television System Committee (NTSC) standard, which is the color TV standard developed in the U.S. in 1953 (this committee is now called the National Television Standards Committee). In the U.K., they use a standard called the Phase Alternating Line (PAL). The PAL TV standard was introduced in the early 1960s in Europe. These are two different standards that operate differently and are not directly interoperable. Let's try another one. Some of us may have a PC based on Microsoft's Windows operating system (OS), whereas others might be using a Macintosh machine. We all know that we cannot use programs that were written for OS on the other machine.

So, for all this to work the way it has to, we must transmit the information in a usable and understandable format to the device that is going to receive it. If we are sending a transmission to a PAL TV set, then the format of the transmission must somehow be placed in PAL format before the device can receive it. Otherwise, it doesn't work! That is the rule, and if you do not abide by the rule, things do not communicate with each other.

Structure

What we attempt to do throughout this book is to take the pieces apart—one at a time—and dissect them, so you can get a better understanding about what the technologies are, how they work, and what they will do for you. Let's start with a discussion of the invention of the telephone by Scottish-born inventor Alexander Graham Bell in 1874. Bell patented his invention in 1876 in the U.S. and, in 1877, in Canada. Bell's father, Melville, was assigned 75 percent of the Canadian telephone patent. Within two years, Melville Bell had sold off his share of the Canadian Bell patent to National Bell, the predecessor to AT&T.

The Bell Telephone Company was organized and licensed to promote telephone service throughout the United States on June 29, 1878.

Early in 1878, the powerful Western Union Telegraph Company entered the telephone business with transmitters by Thomas Edison and receivers by Elisha Gray, which Western Union claimed were superior to Bell's offerings. This situation brought the Bell Company to the brink of bankruptcy. In desperation, Bell sued Western Union for patent infringement. The suit was settled in 1879 with Western Union acknowledging the validity of Bell's patents and agreeing to stay out of the telephone business. The Bell System agreed to buy Western Union properties and abandon any interests in the telegraph field for those territories being served by its defeated competitor.

The Bell patents expired in 1893 and 1894. Within three years, more than 6,000 independent non-Bell telephone companies sprang up throughout the country. Most of them started servicing the rural areas that the Bell Company had avoided. Some companies ventured into more populated areas and competed with the Bell Company.

We saw this growth in the U.S. and Canada that amassed to over 1 billion users in the first 100 years. It took 100 years of evolution and expansion to install the first 1 billion wired phones worldwide. Remember this number combination because it shows that the growth of telephony was a long and tedious process. The telephone was, indeed, the device that revolutionized our world. Make no mistake about that.

The telephone set went through myriad changes in its form and format. In its early days, the original Bell telephone looked rather ominous, as you can see in the following illustration.

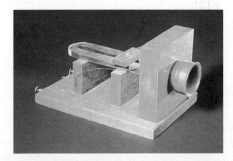

The original model of the Bell telephone invention looks rather awkward to use. The original phone had no handset, so it required some additional innovation.

The Network

The pictures of the various and evolutionary products are important to understand where we came from and what has been done to the components over the years. Can you imagine using these devices in today's environment? We would be stepping back 100 years and performing slow, tedious, and antiquated processes. Instead, you have the opportunity to learn about what is and what will be by selecting the telecommunications industry as your discipline!

The telephone set in itself is nothing, however, without a network of communications media connecting the points. From the first days of the telecommunications industry, the linkage was an absolute must. We needed a network of wires to link sites together and allow the passage of conversations across them. But what is a network?

A *network* is a series of interconnections that link the devices together. When we say "devices," we have to include a network of phones, phone switches, and computers along with many other devices that we see and use every day. This series of interconnections allows for the transport of information (voice, data, video, e-mail, messaging) across the connections. They may well be across the telephone company's local loop of twisted-pair wires, as seen in the following illustration.

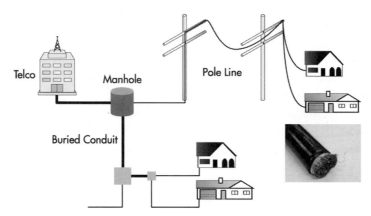

The telephone company uses its local loop to get to the consumer. This local loop is composed of unshielded twisted pairs of wires that may be up to 1,200 pairs (200 pairs are shown in the insert).

From the early days of telephony, in Chapter 3 we describe how the pieces came together to form the Public Switched Telephone Network (PSTN). The *PSTN* is a group of local telephone company networks, which began as the Bell Telephone System, that are interconnected to the long-distance telephone networks of AT&T, MCI, Sprint, and many others. PSTN is the world's collection of interconnected voice-oriented public telephone networks, both commercial and government-owned. It's also referred to as the Plain Old Telephone Service (POTS). The PSTN is the aggregation of circuit-switching telephone networks that has evolved from the days of Alexander Graham Bell ("Doctor Watson, come here!"). Today, it is almost entirely digital in technology, except for the final link from the central (local) telephone office to the user. What this means is the network is an amorphous cloud (which is how it always seems to be drawn) that enables us to access the services of the cloud. Once our voice, data, or anything else goes into the cloud, we do not know what happens inside (such as the routing it may take), but the information miraculously comes out at the far end in the form and format that it must. We have no idea how the information got to the distant end, only that it got there. This network has many owners, but it is considered one network overall because of the interoperability that makes this transparent. As you can see in the following illustration, the network of clouds lets us communicate to a distant end. The North American Numbering Plan (NANP) makes this possible by using an addressing scheme composed of 11 digits (the 1 for long distance and the 10-digit telephone number). You learn about the number of digits when we dissect the telephony networks in Chapter 2.

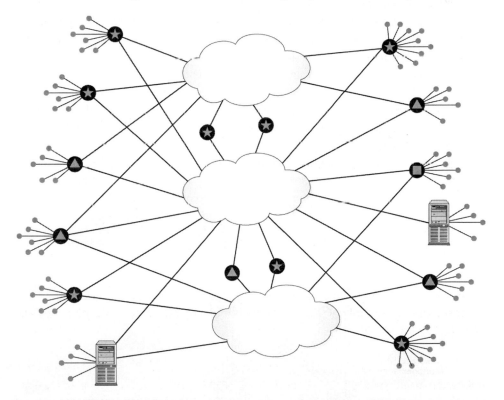

The PSTN is a series of clouds linked together through a myriad of technologies, but it enables us to get an end-to-end connection, regardless of where we are.

Call Control

In Chapter 4, we describe the way the networks communicate within and among themselves by describing the benefits of Signaling System 7 (SS7). This is an evolution of telephony networks that are now controlled by computer networks. Linking these sophisticated computer databases together, the telephone network can process our call requests (call setup) in subsecond timing. Moreover, this linkage is built as fully redundant, so that if one component fails along the way (or if 50 percent of the components fail), the calls will still be processed, albeit in a little more time. The PSTN is a lifeline service. That means if you have fallen and you can't get up, you may rest assured that when you dial 911 to get help, the call not only must get through to the emergency services (fire, police, ambulance), it should also display what number you are calling from, the street address of your phone number, and other critical information. That is where these databases come into play. If they did not, you might be on the floor for a long, long time!

As the network evolved, the signaling systems were also brought to the forefront to access the disparate databases of each of the network operators and to make them common. Thus, features, functions, and services available on one network can be formatted in a usable and understandable manner. Features were enhanced through the use of this sophisticated set of databases producing what we now call the Intelligent Network (IN) and the Advanced Intelligent Network (AIN). These proliferations of technology enable you, the user of the network, to access the features you want, when you want them, how you want them, and where you want them.

So, we can see the interlinkage of an SS7 network providing the necessary connections from end-to-end and delivering the necessary features. The following illustration is an example of the SS7 network using an interoperability solution to provide network intelligence.

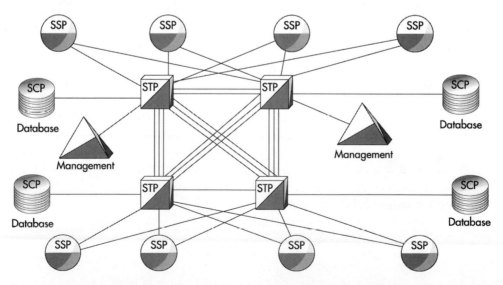

The SS7 network links the intelligence and databases together through its own network

1

Conversions

Our venture has to take you to new heights. In Chapter 5, for example, we describe the concept of analog and digital communications. The main thrust of this section is to familiarize you with the necessary terminology and conceptual techniques necessary to convert basic voice communications into data. Not data as you might think of it as being information in the computer, but data according to the format of voice becoming a string of ones and zeros. Our discussion describes the use of the T-carrier networks by all the network providers. These providers link their networks together with a digital carrier (it carries the information) that is more cost-efficient, higher quality, and even smoother than analog voice. Had Alexander Bell ever seen what might come of the network, he would certainly have been proud, but also most likely in awe at the same time. Who could imagine that on the same wires (that unshielded pair of copper wires we use for the voice conversation) we could multiply the number of users on the same pair of wires! *Multiplexing* is the name we give to this multiplication process. By multiplexing many conversations (24 to be more precise) onto a single pair of wires in each direction, the network achieved its next level in evolution. We saw the introduction of faster, better, and cheaper communications. Moreover, we started a revolution by gaining more information (voice or data) on fewer wires, so the evolution was far more efficient, while improved in terms of quality. What a concept! Better communications, fewer wires, cheaper cost, and more access all in one quick swoop. You want to pay particular attention to Chapter 5 because it describes the beginning of the digital revolution for the telecommunications industry. From every thought process, you will build this digital starting point from what we call a T1 to a T2 to a T3, each being just a method to develop the multiplexing specifications to get faster communications, more channels, and, hopefully, a lower cost.

If you were to look at the T1, it wouldn't be very exciting, but it does create a dilemma for some people. Back in the early 1960s when the T1 was first installed, it was strictly a service that carriers (telephone companies) used. User pressure on the telephone companies led them to create a service offering. In 1974, Bud installed his first T1 in a corporate environment from Boston, MA, to Santa Clara, CA. That circuit took over a year to install, and it carried a cost of $70,000.00 per month. You can imagine how few companies could afford that cost. But wait! We said the cost was supposed to be less expensive. That circuit installed between the two sites replaced 24 individual long-distance channels between the two sites that had an accumulated cost of $84,000.00. So you can see what we meant when we said it was better (digital is cleaner and less noisy than analog), faster (the channel operates at 1,544,000 bits per second compared to a telephone line back then that operated at less than 9,600 bps if you could afford the equipment), and cheaper. In the following illustration, you can see a typical T1 linkage with lots of pieces that are put together.

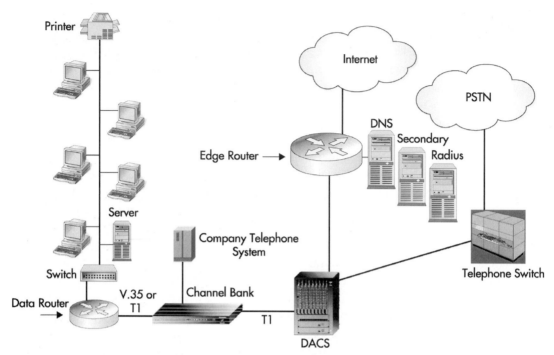

The T1 is used for voice and data access to the PSTN and the Internet.

By the way, if we were to order a T1 between Boston and Santa Clara today, it might take as little as a week to install and the cost would be less than $10,000 per month. This drives home the point that the networks are evolving quickly. Linking voice and data across the same access means the T1 allows more creativity in our telecommunications networks.

ISDN and SONET

With all the discussion of these high-speed communications on the T carrier, you have to stop and take a short breather. If everything changed to T1 right away, the standard dial-up telephone line described in Chapter 2 would become obsolete, and the consumers would be ripping out their telephone lines. Now you are thinking, "Where is this going?" Rightfully, it sounds as though we are talking in riddles. First, we talk about better, faster, and cheaper, and then we talk about people ripping out their telephone lines.

The point we need to make is this: the lifeline service must still be affordable to the masses or else no one will want a home line. What if the telephone company came to you tomorrow and stated that, effective immediately, it was going to change your dial-tone line (your cost probably averages between $25 and $35 per month) from analog (which it still is today) to a digital link? To do this, they are going to reconfigure the network to give you a T1 at your door.

The difference is that the local loop you currently use will now become a T1 at a cost of about $300 per month. That, by the way, only gets you access to the PSTN. Any calls you make may also bear a charge for long distance, which we discuss in Chapter 3. Wow! $300 every month just for the dial tone. Well, if the telephone company gave us a T1 to the door, that is only the starting price. It could run up to as much as $2,800 per month.

What is a telephone company to do? The evolution to a digital world led the industry standards bodies and all the providers to develop a new service that could be delivered less expensively, while still being better and faster than the analog network. So, the industry came up with a term called Integrated Services Digital Networks (ISDN), which is discussed in Chapter 6. This first step in digital to the door for residential and small business use could be delivered on a two-wire circuit (local loop) and use a lot of the older equipment. The ISDN basic service, called Basic Rate Interface (BRI), was just the ticket. It was offered at a mere $50 per month on average. Now we know you are probably squirming in your seat, ready to shout "50 dollars! That's still too much!" and you are correct. However, this $50 per month buys you two dial-tone lines (the equivalent thereof) and still gives you the capability to receive messages while on the phone. So, if you added two dial-tone costs of between $25 and $35 per month, that would be about right. The difference could be doing voice and data simultaneously on the same circuit (even though it appears to be two separate lines) and it would be all digital, so it should be much higher-quality voice and faster data. Check out this section for information on how ISDN works, but understand that ISDN is not all that popular in the U.S. It was heavily installed in Europe and many other parts of the world, but in the U.S. and Canada, ISDN was somewhat coolly accepted. It is good to know what it is and how it works, though, because some day we may have to deal with it. The *s* circuit is shown in its basic form in the following illustration.

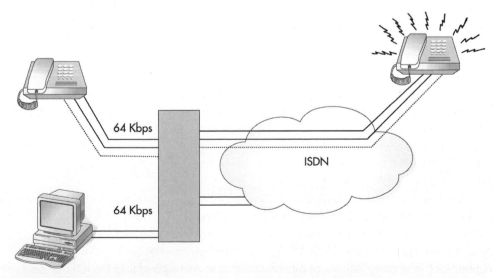

ISDN enables you to use two simultaneous connections on the same circuit; however, it is all digital.

Just when we thought it was okay to use the services of the T1 and ISDN to get better, faster, and cheaper communications, a new movement caught on in the industry. The use of optical networks began to explode. Using fiber is fine, but it requires an interface to convert our voice and data into an optical light and carry it down the glass or plastic wires. So we need some format and control over the use of the fibers. Additionally, one has to be aware that when we bundle all the individual telephone conversations of, say, 10,000 phone calls onto a single piece of glass, there must be a way of getting at the information. That way is synchronous optical networks (SONET), covered in Chapter 6.

To give you an idea of what SONET is all about, scribe the formatting and handling of the information that we can use on the fibers. Also, we go into the rates of speed that can be achieved on the fiber-based networks. What can be better than getting a comparison of the speeds, the format of how it all works, and a comparison of the North American speeds and those of the rest of the world? Today, we can handle telecommunications systems with speeds of billions of bits per second. Tomorrow, it will be trillions of bits of information per second. A basic layout of a fiber network is seen in the following illustration, which shows the optical connection into a core of the Internet.

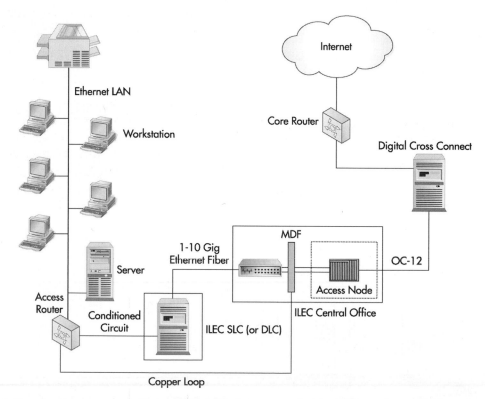

A fiber loop can carry billions of bits of information per second into the Internet and across our telephone networks.

Standards

One of the biggest problems and risks we have with all the pieces of this telecommunications network is the possibility of things not working together. In Chapter 7, we decided to delve into the standards-setting bodies and the role they played in developing the rules (which we call "protocols") on how and why things work. If all vendors build according to the standards, then this will be a simple network. However, greed, market position, and arrogance always present possible exclusions from the standards that we set. One example of a networking standard is what is called the Open Systems Interconnection reference model (OSI). This standard is a compilation of steps considered when you are attempting to connect or link different devices together across a network. Our OSI model lists several steps or layers that are adhered to, depending on what we are trying to accomplish. If all companies follow this model, then transparent communications among various manufacturers' and carriers' networks is achievable. Although this model has been around since 1984, it has never been fully implemented. It has, however, been adopted as a reference and people always ask, "What layer is this operating at?" This means that even though the OSI model has not been fully implemented, it is still used as a guideline. So we will look at the OSI as a comparative model. Then, we look at the model called Transmission Control Protocol/Internet Protocol (TCP/IP) and how it stands in reference to the overall industry. Although we still refer to the layered standards-based model of OSI, we are implementing the TCP/IP model far more prolifically. When we refer to the TCP/IP model, we usually refer to IP as a layer 3 protocol and it is, but we are drawing the comparison to OSI.

You have to understand that these internationally accepted standards (international standards like OSI are law in some parts of the world) and the de facto standard such as TCP/IP are required to keep harmony and protect the end user from obsolescence designed by manufacturers who can be unscrupulous. While we are not attempting to throw stones at the manufacturing community, we must be aware that in the past, it was a "buyer beware" world. The standards help to place some protection on the equipment investments that a user must suffer. The comparison of OSI to TCP/IP is shown in the following illustration, with OSI on the left and the TCP/IP layers on the right. Read Chapter 7 to understand the differences, as well as what each layer is designed to do.

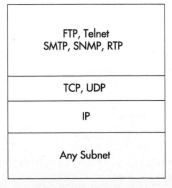

The OSI is a seven-layer protocol stack, whereas the TCP/IP stack is a four-layer stack.

Data Is Data!

After looking at the voice telephones, the carriers, and the evolution of the networks, you must understand that the telecommunications networks were built to carry voice. From 1876 until the early 1960s, that was pretty much the case. The network proliferated because of the use of voice communications. Then, a new world started to emerge: one that required the use of data transmissions. Computer technology began to move out of the computer room (also referred to as the "Glass House") to the desktop. With that move, users needed to access their information on these computers. To get the information locally posed a small challenge, but to get the information across town or across the country required more ingenuity. To provide this accessibility to our information, the data communications industry was born. We already had a voice network that spanned the globe, however, and it was somewhat ubiquitous. So, to make the information (now called "data") available, we began to use the telephone networks. All we had to do was make the data look like voice and things could work the same. Thus, in Chapter 8, we host a discussion of circuit-switched data communications. Chapter 8 explains how data is formed, how it moves across the network, and how it can be validated. The section also goes into a discussion of how we can take advantage of underused circuits by using multiplexing techniques to get more data on the wire. Not only can we handle the underutilized circuits, we can also accommodate an overutilized circuit by compressing the data (more or less squeezing the data down because of redundancy). Chapter 8 can help you understand how data works through the use of modems. Another comparison looks at leasing private (or dedicated) lines across the PSTN when the volume of data justifies the cost of such a dedicated circuit. A graphic representation of the modem communications through either a dial-up circuit or a leased line is shown in the following illustration. The intent here is to discuss how the rules for data communications can make the process work somewhat transparently on the voice network. This, of course, assumes that the modem is connecting the local terminal device to the wide area network (WAN).

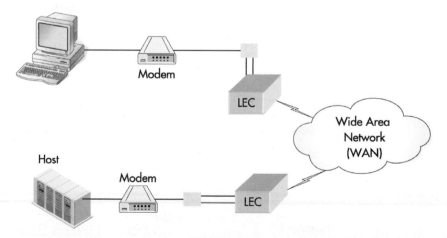

Modems let us use data across the voice network by making the data look like voice.

1

The Internet Emerges

With all the communications that evolved in the telephony network, we saw several implementations take place, and yet another network evolution was simultaneously being created. The Internet was an outgrowth of some government funding to transport data across a data network instead of across a voice network. Although this was happening at a snail's pace, the concept of opening the world to a data networking standard using TCP and IP is discussed in Chapter 7 in our coverage of standards. But just what is the Internet? The *Internet* is a network of networks, but that doesn't explain what we asked. Because we feel it is appropriate to discuss what the Internet does, rather than describing what it is, in Chapter 9 we cover the application of the Internet instead. The Internet is an enabling technology that lets us swap information (data) between disparate machines or networks. Remember how our discussion of standards explained the risks an end user faces with his or her purchases of equipment and network tools? The Internet makes most of these components transparent. In Chapter 7, we discuss the textual and graphical content that is possible on a shared basis across this transparent network.

Internet service providers (ISPs) emerged as competitors to the telephone companies, yet they used the telephone companies' circuitry to link computer technologies together. This ISP community offered dial-up connections into the amorphous cloud of the Internet or dedicated access into this cloud. What happens inside the cloud (much the same as the telephony networks) is not all that important, except that the data we send into the cloud comes out transparently at the other (correct) end. This is what the industry has evolved to—one of transparent communications at a reasonable cost. The Internet also changed the way we send data across the WAN. Instead of a dial-up connection end-to-end, we now dial into the closest node and pass the data across the Internet. This implies some cost efficiencies will be associated with this migration. A picture of the Internet is shown in the following illustration as a means of giving us a model to work with by using the data characteristics.

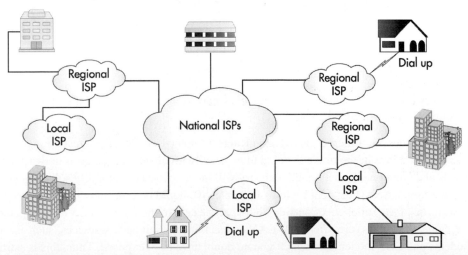

The Internet consists of many interconnected networks owned by various suppliers and provides both business and residential services.

Local Area Networks

When we began our discussion of data communications, we described it as a means of connecting to the WAN. Then we added Internet connectivity to carry data across the world. However, the data is created at the desktop and, many times, only needs to move within close proximity of the user. To this end, the industry created a data transmission system bounded geographically to less than a mile distance. Called a local area network (LAN), the evolution was to deliver high-speed data to a group of localized users who need to share resources. The resources shared may include files, printers, servers, and communications. Thus, a *LAN* is a localized data transmission system that moves data across a communications medium (cable or twisted pairs of wires, fiber, coax, and wireless) in a typically short distance.

Like any network, we stated that there must be a series of interconnections that link the services together so that they may be shared. Thus, connections are provided at megabit per second data rates (millions) compared to the dial-up telephone network that operates at kilobit per second data rates (thousands). In any office environment today, you can be assured that a LAN is present. Moreover, many homes and small offices have LANs as we connect them to high-speed internal services, and then connect them to high-speed external communications, allowing connectivity to the Internet or to the dial-up telephone network.

Chapter 10 leads you through the different forms and types of LANs, the typical connections used, the speeds achieved, and the distances covered. The following illustration shows a picture of an Ethernet LAN that indicates many of the connections and linkage.

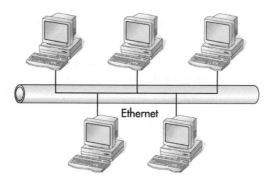

A wireless LAN allows connectivity from local and roaming users, and it extends coverage by connecting to the wired LAN.

After discussing Ethernets and Token Rings, Chapter 10 covers the latest arrangement, the WLAN. Let's face it, the future is going to be heavily involved with wireless networking. As speeds and components mature, the industry will move toward the mobility solutions afforded by a wireless LAN. Thus, your review of Chapter 10 should be especially important to you. Now, more of the suppliers of outside high-speed access to the Internet (CATV companies and telephone companies) are offering WLAN connections to their access devices, such as cable modems and DSL modems, to which you no doubt have been exposed. Thus, this is starting to bring some of the pieces together, such as LAN, wireless, and the Internet, all moving data in the enterprise or residential network.

Packets, Frames, and Cells

Now that we all understand the importance of data, the network suppliers are moving us closer to higher speed and broadband connection to move our data and WANs are being retrofitted to accommodate this data, so we should circle the wagons and discuss the means of moving data. With modem communications, which we describe in Chapter 8, the issue is sending data across the PSTN in a serial fashion. The serial data transfer was done because of the economics at the time of invention. If we could move the data differently, it might well be better for faster, better, and cheaper data transmission. Chapter 11 addresses just that issue. But what do you do to change the serial format? The first thing you can do is to create the data in different formats. In 1974, a standard called X.25 was created to format the data transfers into a highly reliable mechanism called *packets*. These X.25 packets were the first attempt to guarantee data transfer with integrity and reliability. However, the old saying "Pay me now or pay me later" rings true. If we need guaranteed delivery of our data, we pay the price in overhead, which translates into delay, less throughput, and more cost. Chapter 11 addresses the way the industry tried to overcome some of these issues by slicing the amount of data and packaging it into small packets, each with its own address information. We liken the packet (using X.25) to a certified envelope with a single sheet of paper inside. On the outside, we have all the addressing information needed to get the envelope where it needs to go. Also, we have the certification process that assures delivery because of special handling. Moreover, the certification process requires that the information be signed for and validated for accuracy. As you might imagine, all this special handling and validation will slow things down. The good news is that the guaranteed data delivery and the reliability make the delivery process almost a given.

After handling data packets for a number of years (1974–1992), the industry managed to eliminate some of the overhead associated with these small packets. How this was done involved many different principles. First, the packets were extended into much larger quantities of data called *frames*. These frames were larger, so the overhead proportionately was less. Next, the guaranteed checking every step of the way could be eliminated or minimized because the networks are more reliable, thanks to the widespread use of fiber optics, which we discuss in Chapter 6. If the errors can be reduced with a different delivery mechanism (the fiber), then the reliability can be assured with less overhead. Makes sense, don't you think? Well, if everything were perfect, this concept would work without flaws. However, this is an imperfect world and things do break. Thus, it was back to the drawing board looking for the next best way to do things.

The result of further investigation in the network was the creation of an asynchronous transfer mode (ATM) that was designed to operate faster, better, and cheaper. ATM marked a specific transport system, that being SONET (using the fiber optics that were deployed worldwide). Also, the packets were reduced to a fixed-sized cell, smaller than anything we had used before, creating more overhead. The ratio of overhead to data carried went up! This is opposite to what was being sought. The actual idea was that because the cells were smaller, they would move faster through the network, compensating for the extra overhead. The fiber was less prone to errors, and faster throughput speeds could be achieved. When all these pieces were combined, they were used to make cells (ATM) the latest craze.

What doesn't fit into the whole equation is the use of a different form of packets called IP datagrams. While the world was trying to create the latest and greatest, the industry pundits were quickly moving away from the X.25 packets, the frame relay frames, and the ATM cells by moving closer to an Internet packeting concept. These packets (IP) can be carried inside an X.25 packet. The IP packets are also carried inside frames, and the packets can be sliced and diced into small cells and then reassembled at the receiving end. What this means is the data can be carried across any medium, in any form, and with some high reliability factors.

Placing this all into some semblance of order, the data can also be carried across a LAN in a LAN frame, which is different from the WAN frames previously discussed. Also, the IP packets can be placed inside a LAN frame. So, we have packets that are carried inside frames or cells, depending on where the connections are. Does this sound confusing? Then pay particular attention to this grouping of concepts in Chapter 11 for a concise look at the ways we can carry data across the WAN. The WAN networks are shown in a graphic in the following illustration.

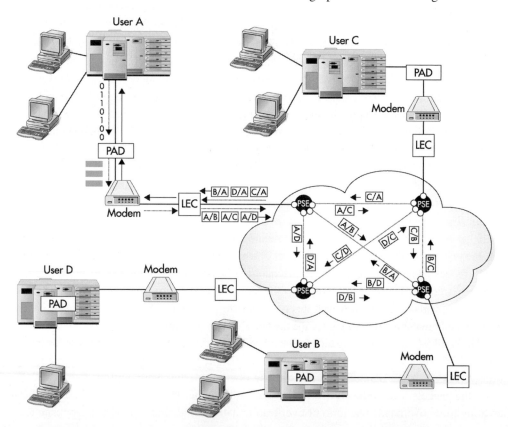

Packets, frames, and cells are different means of handling data transfer.

xDSL Worlds Colliding

Another area that is emerging, and yet maturing quickly, is digital subscriber line, in all its flavors addressed in Chapter 12. The telephone companies were certainly content with offering dial-up data services or leased line services to their consumers. When needed, they delivered fiber optics to large corporations to handle their high-speed data needs. Then, the Telecommunications Act of 1996 occurred and opened the door for competition. The CLEC business flourished as these telephone providers tried to carve out a market share. Although they were aggressive, they were not as prepared to fight the battle as they should have been. Yet, as these providers started to offer data communications, they posed a threat in a new arena, and the telephone companies were not prepared to lose market penetration. Therefore, the opportunity to offer new high-speed data services on the existing local loop (copper wires) digital subscriber line began a rocketing climb to popularity. You may be unaware that the telephone companies were not that astute in data communications, especially when the opportunity presented itself in this segment of the market. Consequently, the providers that people thought would be steadfast champions of data communications were just the opposite. Early installations were met with hardships to the consumer, with downtime as a regular occurrence. Mission-critical data could not be trusted on these links, even though it was Ma Bell maintaining the circuits. xDSL offers the capability to join together many of the technologies addressed thus far. The first means used is data using IP packets encapsulated in frames across a LAN, such as an Ethernet on the desktop. Added to the Ethernet data is a router device and a modem (usually in combination) where the modem uses ATM cells to carry the data on the same wires we use for our telephone calls. The difference here is this: the modem is built to operate in higher-frequency spectrum on the telephone wires, so we can simultaneously carry voice and high-speed data. The cells are then handled at the CO or some other point where they are then spread across a fiber link. The fiber link carrying the cells, which are small segments of the IP data packets, will then connect to the Internet. What more can we ask for?

You will want to pay particular attention to the way the infrastructure of that old copper wire is used in this new way. Essentially, this is data over voice (at least in the spectrum). Pay attention also to the way we modulate the data onto the wire in a spread of multiple channels, each of which carries the data. Also of note, you will see the different rates of speed available on the various modes of xDSL. What you will see is a change in the way the telephone companies now deliver their high-end digital services originally called T1. Now we call it HDSL or SDSL. So, what is old is new again! If you follow the overall thread of this development and see where xDSL is going, it lends itself to the telephone companies attempting to deliver the higher speeds to the consumer's door for voice, data, and video (entertainment). That opens the way for the carriers to provide fiber to the home (FTTH) or, at least, fiber to the curb (FTTC). An example of all the services that can be laid on this xDSL is shown in the following illustration.

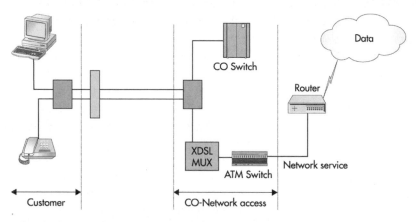

xDSL combines data and voice on a single copper pair and uses packets, frames, and cells on copper and fiber combined. More services will become available as technology matures.

Cable TV as a Telephony Medium

By now your head is probably spinning from the web we wove of various services, technologies, and players. But we are not quite done yet! The Telecommunication Act of 1996 opened the door for a new player to enter the market: the cable TV providers. These companies already had a form of copper to the door in coaxial cables. These cables were installed to carry many TV channels in a one-way direction from the CATV company to the consumer door. We discuss the evolution of the cable TV companies into telephone and data companies in Chapter 13. Traditionally, CATV was always a one-way service and strictly an entertainment medium. That was a posture designed around the regulatory landscape because the CATV could have been a two-way mechanism all along. Now, the addition of a cable modem offers us a two-way, high-speed data transmission system bringing us access to the Internet. Moreover, with limited changes, the CATV companies can also deliver digital telephony. Thus, on a single medium, they can deliver voice, data (high-speed Internet), and video in the form of TV. There was a change in the infrastructure of the cable networks by installing (upgrading to) fiber in the backbone and coax to the door. What more does a cable company need? Well, like the telephony industry trying to move into the data business, the cable companies had an equally difficult time moving into data and telephony fields that were previously foreign to them. Also, the telephone business is a lifeline service (meaning we have built networks that deliver 99.999 percent availability or better). Cable, on the other hand, was always considered an entertainment business (meaning 90 percent availability or less). If a cable goes out of service, the technicians repair it at their leisure. But if telephony is required, lives can be lost if extensive downtime occurs. Add mission-critical data from a home or small office and the devastation can be just as bad. So, the cable companies were fast to enter this business and began to outsell the telephone companies with their xDSL services. More homeowners were already on CATV, so the logical extension began with the Internet access, and then moved slowly to telephony.

A cable modem adds the services necessary to provide high-speed shared access on the equivalent of Ethernet to the door, and an Ethernet connection inside the home (or small office) to the desktop or PC. The difference here is that the CATV offers a 30-Mbps downstream data speed and only 1.5 Mbps upstream. This distribution system of fiber, coax services, and residential and enterprise networks is shown in the following illustration.

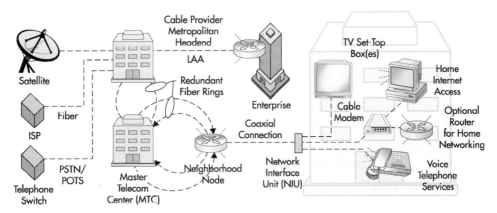

The cable TV service incorporates the services typical of a telephone company, a cable company, and an Internet service provider (ISP) for a neighborhood.

Wireless Networks

As much as all the pieces came together through several providers, the other side of the telephony industry, that being wireless telephony, began to blossom after the 1984 introduction of cellular communications. In Chapter 14, it is only logical to describe the secondary battle that is ongoing in the wireless side of the business. We try first to describe the concept of wireless, and then lead into infrastructure. Next, the use of access methods and multiplexing methods gets us more users on fewer frequencies (channels), while various methods of modulation also add depth to the telecommunications networks. Our service to Chapter 14 leads the way through the various generations of wireless communications. From analog to digital network, we also treat the various access methods of TDMA, CDMA, and GSM as the rival players in competing for your communications dollars. With the emphasis on the cellular communications, we look at how mobile communications works, and then what we can expect from this mobility. As the next generation of wireless networks rolls toward us, we are bracing for the introduction of better, faster, and cheaper wireless access. The third-generation wireless world will link untethered telephony, access to high-speed data, and Internet access. Moreover, we can also expect to see the LAN and WAN go wireless more than we have ever experienced in the past. Concentrate on the means and ways in which the providers are competing to implement the next generation. In their attempt to deliver high-speed access across the WAN at speeds of up to 2 Mbps, the WLANs are emerging in the metropolitan area network (MAN) and converging with the WAN. You can see that we must constantly stay on top of the latest developments in the industry; otherwise, in two years, everything we ever knew about the network will likely be obsolete. Chapter 14 is one of those chapters where we had fun working the details of voice, data, and Internet convergence where we want it, when we want it, and how we want it. You will be in the driver's seat if you spend time working in and around this industry. Even if you are a casual observer, you will be dragged into the technology because of the service offerings facing us in the next few years. We guarantee that!

A look at the wireless world of the future includes a look at the cellular/GSM services today offering data and voice. New and coming services include streaming video to our handset, in real time. Look at the following illustration and you can see the pieces coming together.

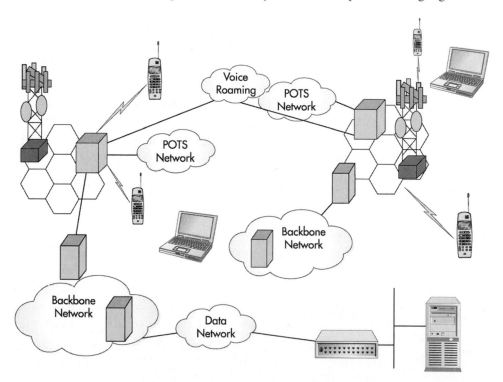

The voice and data networks are on a single wireless network today, but in the future, all the technologies will come together more tightly and more cohesively.

Now that we have most of the pieces, we can start overlaying the final pictures for this book as the wired and wireless opportunities continue to merge. This convergence will enable a user to have wired and wireless access at the door, using any one of the technologies already discussed. Moreover, the use of these services shown in the following illustration depicts what the inside of the home will look like, as well as the outside connectivity. Internet and intranet communications will all be possible when and where we desire a connection, making the cheaper, better, and faster argument much more of a reality. We truly believe that, by now, having read this introduction, you are equally excited and exhausted. And so it may well be! This is an overview of the principles of voice and data communications. The following illustration is only one of many that can be imagined for the future.

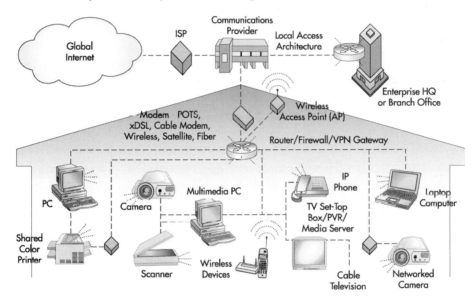

Wherever we are or need to be in the future, the wireless services will link us. Here, the local loop is supplemented with xDSL, CATV, fiber, satellite, or POTS with wireless access in the LAN, but also possibly in the MAN for the future.

The Disappointing News

We are sure you have heard the story of "good news and bad news." In our final chapter, Chapter 15, we discuss the unfortunate part of the telecommunications business: the risks to security. The disappointing part of this discussion is that once a company or a consumer chooses to use any technology we have discussed, others spend their free time trying to figure out how to disrupt that service or steal it from us. Many cases of industrial espionage have been recorded. Today, you cannot read a trade magazine without coming across some warning about a new computer virus being distributed across the networks or about some hacking penetration into a company network. It does not seem to matter what tool we choose to use, the risks are becoming exponential. A large degree of risk is in the data transmission across the WAN or the Internet. Thus, we would be doing a disservice if we did not express caution to you. In Chapter 15, we attempt to educate you regarding the types of risk, especially using IP. Then we weave a web around our data and voice communications as they travel across the networks. Using a tool called VPN, we discuss how you might secure your information while it is in transit across the networks. Chapter 15 should be a volume in itself, so please read it carefully. Although it is not all-encompassing, it is designed to give you a mini-tutorial on securing data. If you gain nothing more from Chapter 15 than an awareness of the risks, we will be satisfied.

Our intent is also a glossary of what might be issues that you will see in WLANs, such as the man in the middle attack, the hacker, cracker, and salami attacker. We are not trying to be poetic here, so do not mistake our intent. Another area we delve into is the crime triangle including motive, means, and opportunity. If you can break down the triangle, then you can disrupt the attack. We hope that this gives you a sense of urgency.

Finally, we want you to view the cases we have outlined to secure the data. At the end of this book and the course you are enrolled in, we believe you will have a fairly well rounded background on the principles that we laid out at the beginning of this book. Good luck and feel free to discuss these technologies and opportunities with your instructor and among your fellow students. This is a communications book that is intended to open that form of verbal communications.

Chapter 2

The Evolution of the Telephone Set

We are all familiar with using telephones to communicate with people near or far away, but what is actually happening when we place a call? This chapter explains the various components, features, and methods of carrying calls across the network, as well as services provided by modern devices. Our telephones are a direct interface to the phone company and the network called the Public Switched Telephone Network (PSTN). We cover how the PSTN is formed in Chapter 3, but it is important to understand the equipment at the customer site that lets us access this network. Various types of telephones exist now, ranging from a simple, single-line telephone set to large corporate systems supporting hundreds and even thousands of users. This chapter is devoted to the range of products and services provided by these different systems.

The Function of the Telephone Set

If you want to place a call on the PSTN, you need an interface device. That device is called a telephone set. The *telephone set* is designed to convert human speech into a form that the PSTN can deal with, and then convert the speech back into a form that a human can deal with. Using speech as our mechanism, the characteristics of voice play a key role in getting our speech across the network.

On average, the human voice creates sound waves that change at a rate varying from 100 to 5,000 times per second.[*]

These waves are composed of two variables: amplitude (think of this as the loudness of the voice) and frequencies (how many of these waves we create in a one-second period of time). Both the amplitude and the frequency are constantly changing. So, to place a call on the telephony network, the systems composing telephone sets and switching systems must accommodate the normal range of amplitudes and frequencies produced by the average conversation.

How then is the voice placed onto the telephone company's network and carried to the distant end of the line? The sound waves must travel along a pair of wires provided by the local telephone company. The challenge is to convert the human sound waves into something that the telephone network deals with: electricity. Yes, electricity is what runs across copper wires. The telephone company typically delivers a single pair of copper wires to our door for each telephone line we rent. The user then attaches a telephone set to those wires through a standard interface (a jack).

The primary function of the telephone set is to convert sound into electricity when we transmit voice onto the network. Thus, the telephone set is a change agent (see Figure 2-1).

At the receiving end, the telephone converts the electricity from the wires back to sound. Therefore, the telephone set must also function to convert this electricity back into sound.

---

[*]Although the average number of changes will range from 100 to 5,000, the human voice can range up to 8,000. An example is the use of *F* and *S* sounds, where the range could be as much as 7,200 to 7,600.

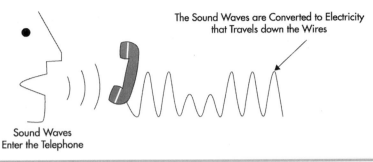

Figure 2-1 For your voice to transverse copper telephone wires, it must first be converted to electricity in the telephone set. The sound waves coming from the mouth enter the telephone and are converted into electricity, which runs down the wires.

The change process must work in two ways. The "from" and "to" functions are what the set must accomplish. Figure 2-2 is a representation of the reverse process.

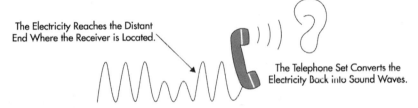

Figure 2-2 Once the electrical current reaches the party to whom you are talking at the distant end, the receiving telephone converts the electricity back to sound. Sound is what humans can understand.

Components of the Telephone Set

Despite the model or manufacturer, every telephone has two main parts: the base and the handset. Within these two parts, several other components and devices are incorporated. We describe these devices in the following segments.

Also important to realize is that as the telephone network evolved, all the Bell Telephone Companies (of which there were 23) were subsidiaries of AT&T. A separate subsidiary (Western Electric) manufactured all the telephone equipment used in the Bell network (including the Telephone Company Central Office equipment and the end-user telephone sets). In 1968, this all changed because a manufacturer of telephone interfaces sued the AT&T organization for the right to interconnect other equipment to the telephone lines. This was known as the "Carterphone Decision," which created the interconnect business. The courts were constantly scrutinizing AT&T for antitrust violations and were attempting to break apart this massive organization. In an out-of-court settlement, AT&T agreed to divest itself of its operating telephone companies as of

January 1, 1984. Prior to this divestiture, however, when customers ordered service, the phones were provided by the phone company for a nominal monthly fee.

NOTE

Prior to 1984, AT&T had a monopoly on telephone service and equipment across most of the United States. A customer using one of the Bell Telephone Companies could rent the equipment from the same Bell Telephone Company that provided the line.

This original mandate to use the Bell Telephone Company-provided equipment was to ensure compatibility. All maintenance was provided by the phone company as part of the monthly rental fee. Users were forbidden to open, look into, or work on the components themselves. Any tampering or alteration to the equipment might cause service to be suspended. This monopoly on hardware limited the types of telephones and features to those that the telephone companies wanted to provide. If they didn't make it, then you couldn't have it. Divestiture opened the hardware market to multiple vendors. With this decision, phone sets became more robust and more features were added as competition increased. Some of these

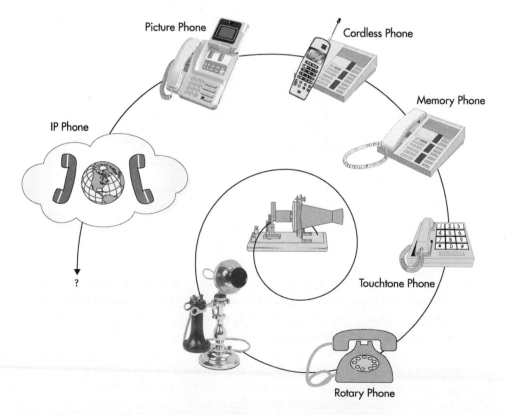

A full evolution of telephones has emerged from the changes over the years.

changes can be seen in the illustration on the previous page, showing the evolution from the basic rotary phone to a mix of features and functions combined in today's sets.

The Handset

The *handset* (see Figure 2-3) is the part of the telephone we speak into and from where we listen. The handset houses two separate components: the transmitter and the receiver. Today, the handset is ergonomically designed to fit the distance from the mouth to the ear.

The transmitter is located at the bottom portion of the handset, so it is logically positioned in front of the mouth when you hold the handset to your face. The mouthpiece holds the transmitter in place. The receiver is located at the top of the handset, so it rests against your outer ear when you hold the handset to your face. The earpiece holds the receiver in place.

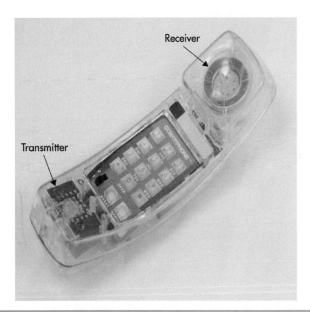

Figure 2-3 The two major parts of the handset are the transmitter and the receiver.

Handsets haven't always looked like the one shown in Figure 2-3. The first handsets consisted only of an ear mechanism; the transmitter was a stationary mount on the front of the base (see Figure 2-4). You had a choice of lifting the entire base of the phone to your mouth or leaving the base on a table and leaning down to speak into it. As you can tell, phones come in a myriad of different designs, but the basic functional parts, such as the transmitter and receiver, are always somewhere on the phone, even though they may not look the same from one phone to another.

Figure 2-4 The handset of one of the first telephones—the 1897 Deskset—consisted only of an ear mechanism. The transmitter was mounted on the front of the base.

NOTE

In this section, we are talking about telephones in which the earpiece and the mouthpiece are simply covers holding the transmitter and receiver in place. Otherwise, the handset serves no other active function. Modern handsets (such as the one shown in Figure 2-3) often have a dial pad integrated into the handset. This configuration is achieved through electronics. Devices with those features are covered in the section "Features of Newer Sets."

Figure 2-5 shows the handset with the transmitter and receiver wires indicated. Note that two pairs of wires are inside the handset. One pair of wires connects to the transmitter and one pair connects to the receiver. The wires carry the electricity created by the mouthpiece to the telephone set, where the electricity is then sent out to the telephone company network. The second set of wires carries the electricity from the network through the telephone set to the earpiece, where the electrical signal is converted back into sound.

Thus, the handset contains a **four-wire circuit**: two wires for the transmitter and two wires for the receiver. Each side of the function (transmit or receive) has its own two-wire electrical circuit at this point.

[handwritten annotations in top margin]

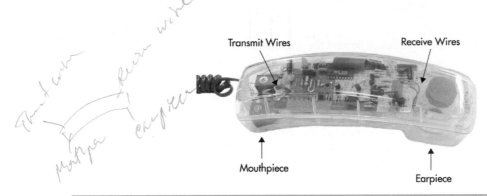

Transmit Wires   Receive Wires

Mouthpiece

Earpiece

Figure 2-5 This is a handset with a four-wire circuit. Note that two pairs of wires connect the transmitter and the receiver.

The modern-day functions of the following parts are still the same. Although newer solid-state components have replaced the pieces, they perform the same functions as the pieces described in the following paragraphs.

The Transmitter

The *transmitter* is the device responsible for the conversion of sound into an electrical signal. The transmitter houses some sophisticated components. The first portion of the transmitter houses a **diaphragm** just under the mouthpiece cover. The *diaphragm* is a sensitive membrane that vibrates with air pressure changes. When you speak into the mouthpiece of the telephone set, you are creating air pressure changes with your vocal cords. The sound pressure you create causes air pressure changes that move at the same frequency as the changes you produce by vibrating your vocal chords (see Figure 2-6). This figure is a view of the inside of the transmitter to represent the particles behind the diaphragm, and it is shown here separated so you can see the pieces. When the set is assembled, these pieces are closed together.

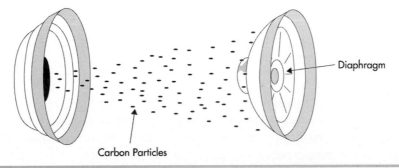

Diaphragm

Carbon Particles

Figure 2-6 The device responsible for converting sound to electricity is the transmitter. The transmitter is composed of a diaphragm and loosely packed carbon particles.

Carbon particles are loosely packed behind the diaphragm. When the diaphragm moves back and forth, it causes the carbon particles to move back and forth. This process produces an electrical resistance that occurs at the same frequency and amplitude as the sound pressure changes created by the voice. Therefore, the electric signal is created in the form of an analog sine wave. This *sine wave* is directly proportional to the frequency and amplitude of your voice. What really happens is the telephone set produces an electrical equivalent of your voice. This electrical energy is carried away from the transmitter across the wires behind the mouthpiece.

The electrical resistance created by the carbon particles also prevents the volume of your voice from creating a signal that is too strong for all the components and network elements. If the transmitter did not restrict the flow of the energy, your voice could create a signal so strong that it could cause damage to the equipment, not to mention what it could do to your eardrums.

The Receiver

Once the transmitter creates the electrical equivalent of your voice and transmits it over distance to another telephone, the electricity needs to be converted back to sound, so the listener can understand what was originally said. The *receiver* is the device in a telephone that performs the conversion from electricity back to sound. The wires behind the receiver are run up to an electromagnet that is mounted inside the receiver portion of the **handset** (see Figure 2-7).

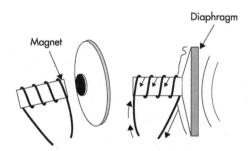

Figure 2-7 The receiver is made up of an electromagnet connected to a diaphragm. When the electrical signal comes to the magnet, it activates it, which pulls on the metal piece attached to the diaphragm. This pulling of the diaphragm is responsible for converting electricity to sound.

The electricity comes through the wires to the electromagnet and causes the electromagnet to vibrate at the same frequency as the received energy. As the electromagnet vibrates, it causes the membrane on the diaphragm to move back and forth. This back-and-forth motion causes air pressure changes (vibrations) that are at the same frequency as the transmitted energy. As the air pressure changes occur, they cause the air waves to bounce off the inner eardrum, which is what produces sound to your ears. See Figure 2-8 for the eardrum comparison.

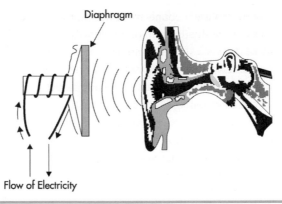

Diaphragm

Flow of Electricity

Figure 2-8 The receiver is the device responsible for converting electrical signals back into sound that can be heard by your ears.

The function of the transmitter and the receiver is to convert sound to electricity and electricity back to sound. We often refer to the handset functions as the **ear-and-mouth communications process (E&M)**. The E represents the direction of flow to the ear or to the receiver, and the M represents the direction of energy from the mouth or the transmitter.

The Connector or the Handset Cord

Extending from the handset and to the base of the telephone set is a coiled wire. An earlier version of the phone used a straight wire, but this was somewhat inflexible. The coiled wire compacts and expands as you use the telephone. This is a convenience factor that evolved over the years. Regardless of whether this is straight or coiled, four wires are still used. This connector is shown in the following illustration.

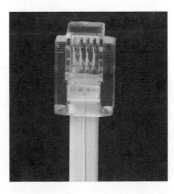

The cable and the RJ-11 male connector

The modern telephone sets use a connector called an **RJ-11C**, which is the four-wire connector that has a little spring-loaded clip on it to plug and unplug the connector into the female receptacle. An RJ-11C is a standard interface with four wires connected to pins inside the jack for the single-line telephone equipment. This standardization ensures that any replacement cord will work with your phone. The cord has a male RJ-11C connector on each end, which is a matter of convenience. For the most part, only one pair is used on the connector. A single-line telephone uses a transmit and a receive wire to get to the network.

Because the cords and the connectors are the most likely pieces to wear out, using a removable connector makes sense. Older versions of this cord used a screw-down connection, but this meant the telephone set had to be opened to get at the screw mounts.

When the cord is connected to the base of the telephone set, it is plugged into the female version of the RJ-11C (see Figure 2-9). Inside this jack, one of the transmitter wires and one of the receiver wires are connected to each other, as shown in Figure 2-10. This creates a loop-back arrangement of sorts. **Loop back** means that the transmitted sound is looped right back to the ear. This lets you hear what you are saying, as the sound is transmitted directly back through the earpiece. The remaining two wires continue into the set.

Figure 2-9 The RJ-11C jack is the standard connection for most telephones today. The RJ-11C houses four wires and pins to connect to the circuit.

The two main reasons for using this loop-back configuration are to create a **side tone** and to regulate the volume.

A *side tone* is a means of letting you know that an electrical connection across the network still exists. When you speak into a telephone during a conversation and you hear yourself, you know a connection still exists to the distant end. When you speak into the set and hear nothing or the sound is dead, you realize your connection has ended or was cut off.

The second purpose of the side tone is to let you regulate the volume of your conversation. When you hear yourself speak, you can regulate how softly or loudly you need to speak to maintain the conversation. This prevents a conversation at a level that is disturbing to the other party, unless this is your purpose, in which case you can then adjust your volume for that, too. Isn't this a nice feature?

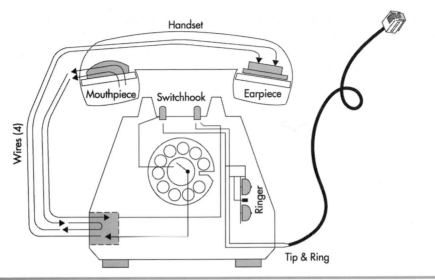

Figure 2-10 Loop-back configuration lets you hear a side tone and your conversation to monitor your volume in the conversation.

The Base

With the exception of the transmitter, the receiver, and the connection cord (unless it is wireless, and then there is no connection cord), all other components of the telephone are located inside the base unit.

NOTE

Although many modern home telephones provide the dialer in the handset, that feature is accomplished by use of solid state electronics. Prior to the 1980s, all dialers were located on the base. Today, phones are smaller, and, as with most devices, smaller is more convenient, so the dialer may be incorporated into the handset of modern phones. See the section "Features of Newer Sets."

The base unit provides protection to all the electrical and sensitive pieces of the phone. Base units are usually made of high-impact plastics and polymers to withstand the rigors put on the phone. These materials are designed to protect the components from impact due to dropping, slamming, and being knocked over. Additionally, because a phone is an electrical device, dust and liquids are catastrophic to both the user and the hardware, so the covering also serves to keep out foreign substances that accidentally come in contact with the base.

The wires meet up with a whole network of cross-connections inside the set, but we are only concerned with the two basic wires. The *transmit wire* is connected inside the set to the dial pad (whether rotary or tone dial). The *dial pad* is used as an addressing mechanism.

Telephone network addresses are made up of the digits from 1 to 0. We dial from seven to ten digits to reach the called party. The dial pad is used to send these digits out to the telephone company for delivery to the called party. The wire connected to the dial pad is also cross-connected to the **switchhook** (see the next section). This transmit wire continues on through the set to connect to another jack, which is connected to the outside world.

The second wire from the handset cord is connected through the network of wires to a ringer. The ringer can be in the form of a bell or a turkey warbler (electronic ringer), but the function is what is important here. The *ringer* is a receiver wire function. It is used to alert you that someone wants to speak to you.

If you do not have a ringer, you'd never know if anyone was on the line. This makes a ringer an essential part of the phone.

The Switchhook

Another feature that is just as important as the ringer is the switchhook function. The *switchhook* is a spring-loaded device housed beneath the buttons on the base. This is the portion of the set that gets the dial tone from the telephone company or, when you are through with the call, releases the dial tone. When the handset is in the cradle, the buttons are pressed down. When the handset is lifted from the cradle, the buttons pop up.

In reality, what happens is this: an electrical circuit, called the local loop, is physically connected from the telephone company office to your telephone set. The *local loop* is the normal two-wire circuit connected from the telephone company office to the customer's location. It provides access to the services offered by the telephone company, mainly the dial tone and the capability to make and receive calls.

You do not have a dial tone at your set. A dial tone is a service you must request. To request the service, you lift the handset off the switchhook. (See Figure 2-11 for a picture of the switchhook.) When you do this, the buttons pop up and complete a circuit. When the phone company's computer, located in the Central Office, sees a change across the wires, it recognizes that you are requesting a dial tone. This process is called going **off hook**, which is the process of acquiring a dial tone by lifting the handset off the switchhook.

When you go off hook and complete the circuit, you have connected the transmit and receive wires together. This creates a continual loop as the current flows from the telephone company (also called the *telco*) to the handset, and then it gets looped right back to the Central Office (CO). The *CO* is the site where the phone company maintains its switching and connection systems.

Switchhook

Figure 2-11 The switchhook is the part of the phone that springs up when the handset is lifted, creating the request for a dial tone from the telephone company.

NOTE

In early days, these offices were locations where the operators physically connected your calls with the switchboard; however, now this is all handled by computers.

This is how the CO recognizes the change in the state of the telephone set. We call this a **loop start circuit**. After you create the loop, the telco starts the process by providing you with the dial tone. If the dial tone is available, it will be provided immediately. In the time it takes you to go off hook and bring the handset up to your ear, the dial tone is there.

As you use the line and make calls, you will use the other components in the telephone set, but the CO computer will monitor the line (wires) to see if you are still using them. When you want to disconnect a call, you place the handset back into the cradle. This pushes the spring-loaded buttons back down and breaks the circuit. The phone company's computerized telephone switching system sees this change on the wires and ends the call. This releases the circuit at the CO, so other users can use this shared resource. For every ten telephone lines installed, the telephone companies have only one outgoing telephone connection to the rest of the world. Using statistical averages, the telephone companies determined that the 1:10 ratio was sufficient to meet the demands.

On certain occasions of unusually high phone traffic, this rule is not true, such as on holidays and during events like natural disasters. If too many people pick up the phone at the same time, either no dial tone is provided or a delay occurs before the dial tone is provided. This latter condition is called *slow dial tone*.

The Dial Pad

Now that you have a transmitter and an electrical connection to the telephone company, you need a mechanism to deliver addressing information about where you want your call placed. The *dial pad* is used to send the address to the network. Once you have your dial tone, you start dialing digits of the party to whom you want to speak. The CO switch reads these numbers and creates a path to the desired party. By default, every telephone line has its own unique telephone number (here in North America, that is a ten-digit telephone number).

As previously mentioned, the first telephone sets did not have a dial pad. This meant all connections had to be manually performed by the telephone company operators. If you needed to speak to someone, you got the operator by going off hook. The off-hook process created the circuit that lit a light or created a visual indication for the telephone company operator. The operator would answer and converse with you. At this point, you would pass on the name or number of the requested party, and the operator would provide the connection.

Although this process worked, as the number of calls increased, human involvement became inefficient. Let's face it, humans are much slower than switching systems, so as the volume of calls increased, the human operators were too slow to keep up with the demand. If the operators were busy, you could wait lengthy periods for an operator to become available.

The Ringer

As already discussed, the ringer serves the purpose of alerting you that someone has called. When a call is incoming, a high-voltage alternating electrical current is passed to your phone and activates the ringer, notifying you of the call. A *ringer* can either be a bell or an electronically produced sound. This is as simple as can be.

Rotary Dialing

In an effort to maximize customer satisfaction and network resources, the rotary dial was introduced, as shown in Figure 2-12. In *rotary dialing*, when the handset goes off hook, a tone is sent from the phone company to your telephone. Once the user received a dial tone

Figure 2-12 A rotary telephone is a device that uses the dial to create a series of electric pulses that represent the dialed number.

2

(a 48-volt current and tone), the user inserted his or her finger into a hole in the dialer and turned it to the stopper. When the dial was released, electric pulses were generated in a series of clicks (or on's and off's), which were received at the CO. The major change here is that instead of a physical operator, a device interpreted the pulses and routed the call automatically. The call was then routed to the appropriate caller. The idea of rotary dialing was to provide more accurate call routing and shorter call setup time.

Initially, rotary dialing was well received, but over time, it became a nuisance to the carriers. The rotary set is an electromechanical device. As you dialed the number, you would rotate the dial in a clockwise direction. When the dial was released, the counterclockwise return to the normal position created a series of electrical interrupts or pulses across the line to the telephone company office. The CO would interpret these pulses and make the necessary routing decisions. The reason this technology was such a nuisance is this: in days past, it could take as many as four attempts to complete a connection, either because of busy conditions or hardware misdials. This was both frustrating for the user and wasteful for the carriers' resources.

The pulses are generated at ten pulses per second (pps), which also created long call setup times because of the slowness of the dial pad. Although most localities are using touch-tone dialing, we mention rotary because as much as 10 to 15 percent of America *still* uses rotary service!

The carriers would like to eliminate pulse (rotary) service, but this hasn't happened yet for several reasons. Some of these are as follows:

- **Cost**—The cost of touch-tone dialing is typically $1 more per month (than rotary). Many people who make infrequent calls don't want to pay for a service they seldom use. Most of the carriers have buried the cost of the touch-tone in the monthly service charges. Although it is not shown as a line item on a bill, touch-tone is considered an added feature.

- **Technology**—Some independent (incumbent) local exchange carriers have old technology and have not yet upgraded their equipment, so the service is only rotary. In some parts of the country, the carriers serve small rural communities and do not have the funds to upgrade their equipment.

- **Gimmes**—A lot of folks who now own their own phones have subscribed to services and received free phones as a reward for signing up. These phones might have push buttons on the set. However, during dialing, the conversion from tone to pulse occurs inside the telephone set. The distinctive click-click in the ear identifies such phones as rotary sets.

Dual-Tone Multifrequency (DTMF) Dialing

The touch-tone phone was the second evolution of the dial pad. Instead of using the rotary dial to electromechanically produce the digits, this phone employed a tone-dialing sequence. Using a group of tones that fall into the spectrum of voice frequency, the tone dialer has a set of buttons that send out frequency-based tones instead of electrical impulses.

The touch-tone telephone set was created to speed dialing and call processing, reduce user frustration, increase productivity, and enable additional services through the dial pad. The touch-tones are a **Dual Tone Multiple Frequency (DTMF)** system. Each of the numbers represented on the dial pad has both an *X* and a *Y* matrix or cross-point. See Figure 2-13 for the tone dial pad and note the frequencies as they appear on the chart. When you press a number, two separate tones are generated and sent to the CO simultaneously. Each number on the dial pad has its own distinct set of dual tones, so the system recognizes each as a discrete number.

Figure 2-13 The DTMF keypad creates a dual-sequence tone to represent each digit dialed. The dual-tone frequencies prevent the system from mistaking a human voice for a number to be dialed.

The reasoning behind utilizing dual tones is this: the human voice could not generate a harmonic shift in frequency quickly enough to re-create these tones. Therefore, the telecommunications systems can recognize the tone shifts as dialed digits instead of conversational path information (voice). For the most part, this works, but from time to time, humans can generate these quick harmonics. This is rare, but it can be done.

In particular, a female voice generating more amplitude shifts will generate a quick shift in vocal pattern and create the digit 8, whereas the male voice generating more frequency shifts will create the digit 7. This, of course, is rare, but it does happen and it's called **talk off**. This will be important for you to remember when we discuss newer features, such as voice-messaging systems, where the digit 7 or the digit 8 means something to a computer system when a voice is being used.

This talk-off arrangement can be controlled through the use of voice band pass filters that can be acquired from most telecommunications suppliers. *Voice band pass filters* essentially strip off the human voice frequencies, allowing the true number dialed to be recognized.

Tone dialing is faster than rotary because the tones are generated at 23 pulses per second (pps), much quicker than the rotary set. As the tone dial was introduced, a 12-button pad was created, adding two extra numbers to the telephone. The older rotary set only had ten numbers (decimal). The two new buttons enabled new features and capabilities to be introduced in the telephone world, using the pound (#) and star (*) keys as delimiters when dialing into computers, and so on. The extra keys enable feature activation in various new systems (for example, to put a call on hold, dial #4; to retrieve the call, dial *4).

? Line Check 2-1

What was the first significant development that offloaded the need for human assistance in completing phone calls?

Was this development successful in achieving the desired goals or did it fail to meet the expectation?

One example of an improvement is the call setup time. Setup for a rotary call was as much as 43 seconds, whereas with tone dialing, the call can be set up in approximately 6 to 10 seconds. Other improvements, such as improved signaling systems, have reduced this setup time further, but the tones were the first big thrust in gaining time back from the network. Is this important? Sure it is!

Think about the hundreds of millions of calls placed in any given month. If you had a system that took 43 seconds for call setup (the older system tied up a line across the network for the setup period) and you could reduce it to 10 seconds, you would have reclaimed 33 seconds of line utilization (which was not billable time) per call for other users. This is big bucks, no matter how you look at it.

Think about this for a second:

You, as a user of the telephone network, have a rotary dial set. You want to place a call from Boston to San Francisco (approximately 3,000 miles). You place the call and tie up 3,000 miles of wire for as much as 43 seconds. This is nonbillable by the carrier. The clock only starts when the call is answered. So, now the carriers offer you the capability to speed the process by using a tone dialer. You are obviously going to be happy with this arrangement because you can dial so much faster. The carrier stands to save 33 seconds (remember that back then the cost per minute was $0.65) and get the call billing going that much faster. For this savings of approximately $0.30 to $0.35 per call that you make (that all rolls back into the carriers' profits), you have the privilege of paying $0.75 to $1 per month more on your phone bill for the convenience of tone dialing. Isn't this a wonderful industry?

So let's see what that might mean to us! Assume 200,000,000 calls made by 50,000,000 customers at $.35 savings per call and $1 per customer line cost for tone dialing.

(200,000,000 calls made in one-month * $.35 savings per call = $70,000,000 saved by the carrier) plus ($1.00 * 50,000,000 = $50,000,000) Total money to the carriers' pockets = $120,000,000 per month

Tip and Ring

"**Tip and ring**" is a phrase that telco installers or repairers use all the time. *Tip and ring* describes the two wires running from your phone set to the rest of the world. They call the transmit wire the "tip" and the receive wire the "ring." Tip and ring are nothing more than industry terms from the beginning of telephony when a switchboard operator manually plugged wires into the switch.

When the operator tested the line on a manual cord type switchboard, the tip of an RCA plug was used. If a call was already in progress on a line, after touching the tip of the plug against the jack, the operator would hear static on the line. An example similar to this is plugging a speaker into a stereo already turned on. There is a loud static sound letting you know the "circuit" is live.

If no conversation was in progress, the operator would then insert the plug into the designated extension port on the board. The operator then pressed a switch that would cause a ringing voltage to be generated across the wires and your phone to ring.

This system has all but disappeared here in the U.S., but in several other parts of the world, cord boards still exist (the old operator-plug switchboards). However, the telephone company installers never dropped the use of these terms (tip and ring) because they were comfortable with them, and they used the terms as part of their mystique over customers.

Features of Newer Sets

The telephone is a remarkable piece of equipment that evolved over time. There have been a few technology changes to the phone, and additional features offered, but it still provides the same overall service of the phones of the past.

Today's telephone sets provide far more functionality than just a plain old analog telephone did. Today's phones are solid-state, microprocessor-controlled sets that are digital. This means they perform the same functions with less voltage, provide higher quality of conversation, and even provide some basic switching options. Many of these added features are required at the Bell CO equipment or at the Customer Premises Equipment (CPE). *CPE* is equipment installed at the customer location for use by that company's employees. These come in various forms such as Key Telephone Systems, which are multiline, multifunction systems, or **Private Branch Exchanges (PBX)**. *PBXs* are private systems that mimic the telephone company's CO equipment with features and functions.

The newer sets come in all shapes and sizes, and they are feature-rich models. Anyone can now manufacture a telephone set, or system for that matter, as long as they abide by certain registration techniques and parameters. The production of a telephone system or set requires that the manufacturer meet an FCC specification before the equipment can be installed onto the PSTN. This is called the *FCC Part 68 specification*. A newer set is shown in Figure 2-14.

Figure 2-14 The newer telephone set has various features integrated into the telephone. These include large displays with directories, caller identification, call hold, call transfer, and so forth.

On this set, several added features that enhance the call placement process are incorporated into the telephone set, rather than being served by an external device. For example, some of the features that are now the norm are as follows:

Speed Dialing

Speed dialing is a feature designed to save a user time by enabling him or her to preprogram frequently used numbers into the phone. A user may preprogram from 1 to 100 numbers into the memory of the set, although, typically, only 10 to 15 numbers are used. Each speed number represents a ten-digit telephone number. An example for speed number 001 is 602-555-1212. In this case, you might dial *74 (the feature activation button for speed dialing) followed by 001 (which represents 602-555-1212).

When you use a feature button or a preprogrammed button on the set, the telephone will store and dial a much longer string of digits (usually up to 33 digits) and connect you with the requested party. Preprogramming a button with the numbers 001-49-41-02716-12345 is a sequence that may dial a number in Germany.

Call Hold

When you use the *call hold* feature, a visual indicator often alerts you that you have initiated this service. In the case of a hold, a flashing light lets you know that the call is still there, but on what is called a **hard hold**. The *hard hold* serves a mechanical function by keeping the link active, but it disengages the set until the line button is pressed again to reconnect the parties. Hard hold effectively turns off the transmitter while keeping the actual call intact. It provides a better function than simply covering the mouthpiece while the user does something else.

Other forms of call hold do not give you a visual indicator. This is particularly true when you have a single line set. When placing a call on hold, the system may give you an audio indicator.

Call Transfer

Call transfer, available at the CO (or PBX equipment), allows a call to be transferred to another line. This function is available in most central offices today. To activate call transfer, you must press the switchhook down and draw what is called a recall dial tone. Then you must dial the third-party number (the number transferred to) and wait for the line to ring. A good idea is to wait for the newly called party to answer and announce that the call is being transferred, and then hang up.

Occasionally, a problem occurs with activating this feature; it requires you to press the switchhook down for a short period (usually 100 to 200 milliseconds) to draw the recall dial tone. Knowing how people are today, you might expect one of two outcomes. First, many people are in such a hurry, they simply click too fast, and never get a dial tone. This phenomenon is called "skinny fingers" in the telephony world. Perhaps all the mouse clicking we do feeds this problem. Conversely, some people fail to react quickly enough and hold the switchhook down too long and disconnect the person who was being transferred (at least this is a convenient excuse to give them when they call back). In the telephony world, this is called "fat fingers," which should not be confused with "fat fingers" in an IT context where people try to type a character on a keyboard but hit two adjacent keys at the same time.

To prevent this problem, manufacturers have provided an automated feature called the flash key. The *flash key* automatically takes you off hook for the prescribed 150 milliseconds when pressed.

Conference Call

The *conference call* is similar to the transfer feature, but in this case, rather than transferring the call to a third party, the third party called will be added into the call. The conference feature enables the three parties to converse without worrying about cutting each other off. Most systems will allow three- or four-party conference calls. If more are needed, then an added piece of equipment called a *conference bridge* is needed. Some bridges will accommodate as many as 100 parties on a single call.

Last Number Redial

Sets with the *last number redial* feature have their own internal memory, so they can automatically store and dial the last number called, even if it is not a speed number. This is great when you encounter a busy tone on the network. The problem with last number redial comes into play when the call requires a string of digits longer than the normal 11 digits for a phone call. Pauses are required in some cases, but this feature will send the 11 digits, plus the credit card number and any other digits dialed in the last sequence. This can cause some confusion, but it is a time-saver.

Redial can also be a preprogrammed feature where some sets, on encountering a busy tone, will redial up to 99 times in a preset time period (over the next 60 to 90 minutes, for example). Not all sets will do this.

Built-in Speakerphone

Many sets have the capability to turn on a *built-in speakerphone* for hands-free, two-way communications. This can be *half-duplex,* which means that you must be careful not to talk over the other end. You have to wait for the other person to finish before you can talk because the device can't transmit and receive at the same time (this is called **overtalk**). If overtalk occurs, then the conversation becomes choppy because the set is bouncing between the transmitter and the receiver, cutting off words or syllables.

Some sets have a *full-duplex speakerphone,* which means that simultaneous talk and receiving can occur without cutting in and out. This duplex circuitry has separate paths for the transmitter and the receiver. Remember, the telephone has a complete circuit for transmit and a separate circuit for receive. Thus, with a full-duplex speakerphone, both parties could be talking at the same time without a problem. If you have ever spoken on a half-duplex speakerphone, you probably noticed that only one end could speak at a time. If both ends attempt to speak simultaneously, then the conversation probably will break up and be choppy.

Transmissions

Simplex and Duplex

Simplex *communications* refers to communications that are one-way only. Modern public announcement systems are an example of simplex communications.

Duplex *communications* means that a transmission path can support two-way conversations. Two types of duplex communications exist: half-duplex and full-duplex.

- *Half-duplex* communications is similar to walkie-talkie communications. Although a device can both transmit and receive, only one of those operations can be performed at a time. You must wait for the other party to stop talking before you transmit. This is also what happens with most of the speakerphones previously listed. They are half-duplex, so only one end can speak at a time.

- *Full-duplex* communications, on the other hand, means you can have two-way communications on the path at the same time. This is similar to face-to-face speech where both parties can talk and listen at the same time. Normal telephone conversations, although half-duplex, occasionally will have both ends speaking at the same time. This is possible because the two-wire circuit has both a transmit and a receive capability on separate wires.

 Try This

Simplex Demonstration

For a small experiment, we will experiment with simplex transmissions. You will need two empty tin cans, a hammer and nail, and a piece of string.

Begin by punching a hole in the end of the two empty tin cans with the hammer and nail, and then remove the nail.

Through the hole in one can, pass a long piece of string and knot the end, so it doesn't slip through. Repeat the same process with the other can, so the two cans are connected by the string.

Give one end to your partner and have him or her walk to the other side of the room. Make sure the string is taut, and then speak into one end of the can. Have your partner put the other can near his or her ear.

What happens? How this is simplex communications? What happens when both of you try to talk at the same time and have a full-duplex conversation? How could you have a duplex conversation? What would you need to accomplish this?

Hands-Free Dialing

Hands-free dialing lets a user go off hook by pressing the line button on the telephone set and then dialing. This frees the user's hands for other tasks while the connection is being made. Once the called party answers the phone, however, the caller must pick up the handset and converse. The speaker is strictly a speaker, not a two-way device. Many people get confused over this feature and assume they have a full speakerphone when, in fact, they do not.

Displays

When features are available in the CO, a display set can be used to show the incoming caller's telephone number (if you pay for the service, that is). Where the incoming caller display is not available or used, the display can still be used to:

- Display the number the caller dials
- Display the time of the call
- Show the elapsed time, which can be used for client billing and chargeback
- Show reminders of an upcoming meeting

How Calls Originally Progressed Through the Network

Now that we had a device to provide voice communications, several providers emerged to provide the medium for transmission. These telephone companies provided the physical connection (local loop), the twisted pair of wires to customers, and a means of connecting those wires to the desired party.

This means of connection, or switching of calls from one pair to another, was accomplished in the CO. That meant all switching of calls had to be manually performed by the telephone company operators. If you needed to speak to someone, you got the operator by going off hook. The off-hook process created the circuit that created a visual indication for the telephone company operator. The operator would answer and converse with you. At this point, you would pass on the name or number of the requested party, and the operator would provide the connection. Then, the electric current would pass down the wires to the destination you requested, causing the phone to ring. Once the called party answered, the circuit was completed and the conversation would flow.

What Do You Think?

As the numbers of subscribers increased, imagine trying to call someone with the last name of Smith or Johnson, for example. What problems might you expect? What kind of user experience could this cause?

Modern Devices

The invention of DTMF switching and keypads allowed for further advancements in telephone devices. Original single-line sets were an individual interface to the network, but modern systems provide support for multiple users and advanced features, many of which were listed previously. In reality, modern devices have occurred only recently in the history of telecommunications; they reflect the changing laws and regulations. What has happened is this: the network-switching equipment has moved further away from the carriers and has moved into the doors of the customers. Now devices that handle actual switching are located on some customers' premises.

Key Systems

Single telephone sets work fine for home use, but what happens when you move to the environment of a business office? Offices have a need for a larger number of phones for service, plus additional features that usually aren't required in homes.

Imagine the impact of needing to call a coworker and having to dial his or her complete phone number to reach that person. In this scenario, you make an outgoing call to the CO, where your call is routed back to your business, and then on to your coworker. Now you would need to install a second phone line for each user in your business to ensure customers can get through to the appropriate parties or to provide a dial tone to make a three-way call. This becomes an expensive proposition because, most of the time, only one line (if that) is used at a time. It is also wasteful of resources within the carrier's network.

Manufacturers saw this need, and they created a phone system that would enable users to share resources and provide these additional features to them. They created a **key system**, which is a form of the telephone typically used in smaller office environments. Essentially, a key system is a device for using outside telephone lines and sharing those lines among many users within an office.

A key system is more of a mechanical device, meaning that the users are responsible for making the selection and control of the individual calls/functions. And in a key system, the user must manually press or select a button to grab an outside line, and then get the dial tone. Users must look at the lights next to the buttons to make sure the individual line they are trying to select is not already in use. This procedure manually provides call pickup. Newer key system sets utilize electronics, although the premise is still the same. The user selects the line and function to be performed manually. Figure 2-15 illustrates a key telephone system.

Figure 2-15 The key telephone system lets the user manually select the outside line needed. It also allows intercom, conferencing, call transfer, and do not disturb functions.

Note the reference to lines in this example. The telephone company sees the system as an end-user connection in much the same way as a single-line telephone set. Lines connect the end user to the CO, whereas trunks connect switches together (CO to CO).

NOTE

Newer key systems utilize desk set telephones that are almost identical to those used with PBXs. Mechanical key systems are not as popular as they used to be because inexpensive PBXs have entered the market. That is not to say there aren't still hundreds of thousands of key systems in the workplace. These devices will be around for some time to come because, typically, they do not break easily. If they do not break, there is no motivation to replace them.

The advantage the key system provides is not requiring every individual telephone to require its own outside line. After all, many phones go unused for lengthy periods throughout the day.

Each key system contains the following components, regardless of the packaging. Some systems have electronic components that are integrated on cards, while others have distinct individual components:

- A **key service unit (KSU)** is the heart and brain of the telephone system. It is the point where the outside lines interface with the central interface.

- **Line cards** are the interfaces to the telephone company lines. They effectively provide the off-hook and on-hook signals to the CO in lieu of the individual telephone sets.

- **Station cards** are the cards that control the intelligence and interface to the end user's key system. The station card interfaces with the end user and the line cards for the access control of the system.

- **Intercom cards** are not always required. Some systems use an intercommunication card for internal connectivity, whereas others have this feature built into their functionality on the backplane of the system.

- Telephone sets are variable-user interfaces, whether they are single line or digital multiline sets. The telephone set controls the intelligence a user is allowed to access within the system.

- Power supplies and logic cards.

- The wiring infrastructure used to connect the sets to the KSU central processor unit (CPU), the brains of the system.

A key system is limited in its configuration to provide a certain number of internal stations, running to a maximum number of outside lines. A system is defined by a number. For example, 1648 would support 16 outside lines to 48 in-office telephone sets. Some newer key systems provide support of up to 200 users.

Station cards are then installed, which provide the intelligence to the individual telephone sets installed within the system. *Intercom cards* enable intercommunication from one inside set to another station set. This prevents outside lines from being tied up while internal offices carry on a conversation. The number of intercoms allowed will vary on each device and manufacturer.

From each station, or telephone set, wiring—called a *horizontal run*—connects to the KSU in the phone closet. Depending on the size of the system, the horizontal wiring may be a bundle of cable pairs in 25, 50, or 100 pairs. These cable pairs terminate on the wall on something called a **66 block**, which is the device (located in the phone closet) where the individual pairs get separated, and then punched down onto the ingress side of the block. On the egress side of the block, the connections are run to the key system, and then terminated on the appropriate line card or station card. A 66 block is shown in the following illustration. The 66 block can handle up to 25 pairs of wire per block, which, in turn, means that up to 25 outside circuits (lines) or 25 internal circuits (stations) can be accommodated. These blocks can be mounted vertically on a wall or horizontally on a rack, whichever is more convenient to the installer.

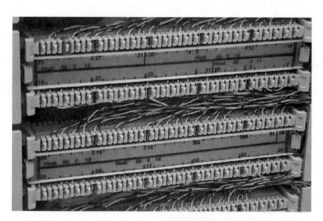

The 66 block connects up to 25 pairs of cables as shown.

A *station drop* is the point where the horizontal run is tapped and individual pairs are connected to the individual station set. These may come in a two-, three-, or four-pair wiring configuration.

Each key system requires a different number of wiring pairs to the station, which varies, depending on model and manufacturer. Even though some key systems require only one pair of wires to the desk, it is *always* recommended to run more pairs for future growth and additional devices to be connected to the system. A minimum of four pairs is recommended.

The termination of the four-pair wiring system is a plug called a RJ-45. It looks much like the plug from a single telephone set in your home, but it has more wires in it. This is a standard interface for both voice and data devices today.

❓ Line Check 2-2

What is the difference between a station card, a line card, and an intercom card?

Which of these is not essential for a key system to function?

Features of the Key System

When making a decision to use a key system, it often helps to understand what you will get for the additional money. Most key systems are feature-rich, providing the opportunity to enhance the telephone experience at the user's desk. Some of the many features that are common today include:

- Voice mail
- Station message detail recording
- Automated attendant
- Least-cost routing
- Data and voice simultaneously
- Automatic call distribution

As covered earlier, the systems approach has other advantages. For example, one advantage is the use of the intercommunications channel, called the intercom. The *intercom* frees the outside lines for incoming customer calls when two workers in the same office need to communicate.

Using the intercom, party *A* calls party *B* on the internal communications paths in the system. Some systems have a fixed number of intercom paths, whereas others have an unlimited number. This is a function of the manufacturer equipment. When using the alternate system (the non-key telephones), the choices are far more restrictive. If party *A* wants to talk to party *B,* the two outside telephone lines associated with these two individuals are busy. The customer calls coming into the building for either party are blocked until they terminate their conversation. The customer might become frustrated and take his or her business elsewhere if this is a constant occurrence.

Moreover, it is far easier to add features and services in the key telephone system than in the single-line telephone set. Users will like the features they can have in the key system, such as:

- Call transfer to another party

- Call hold by pressing a feature button—newer sets provide hold music or prerecorded announcements on the company

- Three-way or conference calling

- Consultation hold—a call can be placed on hold while the user confers with another user in the system

- Speed dialing on an individual or system basis

- Speakerphones

- Hands-free dialing—similar to speakerphone, but the user must manually pick up the phone when the call is connected; otherwise, you cannot hear the calling party

- Direct inward dialing—the ability to directly call an individual's desk, without passing through a receptionist

Private Branch Exchanges (PBXs)

Key systems work well for smaller office environments, but they aren't well suited for environments where there are hundreds of phones. As the number of users increases, the chance that users will be contending for outside lines also increases. It is impractical for each station or desk to have a console with hundreds of buttons for outbound lines from which to check and select. Therefore, hardware makers created the next evolution in phone systems: PBXs.

Let's start with a quick definition of a *private branch exchange.*

- Private—it belongs to an organization or individual; it is not a public service.

- Branch exchange—the telephone company defines a Central Office as a branch exchange. This is the point where the dial tone is provided. So the branch (think of it as the limbs of the network hierarchy tree) exchange offers a dial tone to the end user.

A private branch exchange (PBX) is the typical telephone system for large organizations. Note that PBXs are relatively expensive when compared to other phone systems. They can cost hundred of thousands of dollars, depending on size and functionality. The main difference between a key system and a PBX is this: the PBX acts like a CO and provides a dial tone through its direct connection to the PSTN. In this environment, an organization that is served a dial tone from the local exchange company might need the capacity of high-volume calling and handling services. Clearly, a single-line telephone set with a dial-tone line for each user could work, but it will not satisfy the needs of the organization, and it will be extremely expensive and wasteful. The single-line set limits what the user can do with the basic dial-tone service. Also, the single-line set does not allow for intercommunication between the users within the organization, unless they tie up their dial-tone lines as follows:

- Grab the dial tone by going off hook.

- When dial tone is received, dial the digits (seven or ten) of the desired internal party.

- When the party answers, conduct a conversation.

This completely ties up two outside lines for this conversation.

If a customer tries to call either of these two parties, the customer will get a busy tone unless the call hunts to some other number. *Hunting* is the term used to describe a preselected sequence that the call will go through if the dialed number is busy. If the call does hunt, then a third outside line is occupied while a message is taken at the rollover line. Customers can be denied access and can get frustrated.

All this can occur while the two parties could be talking to each other in the adjacent office. Note that however long the wires are that run back to the central office where the dial tone is provided, the call uses twice that to get the two conversationalists together. Clearly, this is not an optimal use of telecommunications services.

From the previous discussion, it should be obvious that larger organizations require the larger capacity and capability of a PBX. These systems are sometime called **Private Automated Branch Exchanges (PABX)**. A *PABX,* as its name entails, provides all PBX features, but the routing of incoming calls is automated, or the person dialing in gets voice prompts and chooses which department or user he or she wants to connect to. At that point, the PABX looks up users and automatically transfers the call.

A PBX is private (customer owned and operated) and, like a CO, switches and routes calls internally or externally, and it provides a dial tone to the internal users.

The PBX marketplace is inundated with acronyms and features, but all PBXs do similar things. They primarily process voice calls for the organization. These devices are computer systems that transmit voice messages, although now many also provide data communications and data access.

The components of the PBX are shown in Figure 2-16. These include the following:

- The central processor unit (CPU) is the computer inside the system—the brains.

- The memory—any computer needs some amount of memory.

- The stations, or telephone sets, are also called lines.

- The trunks are the telco CO trunks that terminate into a PBX.

- The network switches calls within the system.

- The cabinets house all the components.

- The information transfer or information bus carries the switching information to and from the computer.

- The console or switchboard enables the operator to control the flow of incoming calls.

- The common logic, power cards, and so forth, facilitate the system's operation.

- The battery backup ensures against power failures.

- The wiring infrastructure connects all the components together.

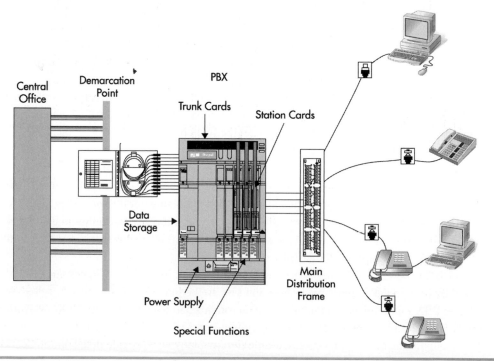

Figure 2-16 A PBX is composed of several components, all of which reside on the customer's premise.

The PBX is a stored-program, common-controlled device. As a telephone system, it is a resource-sharing system that provides the capability to access a local dial tone and outside trunks to the end user. This stored-program controlled system today is an all-digital architecture. A picture of a PBX is shown in Figure 2-17.

Figure 2-17 PBXs vary in size, depending on the number of users and applications needed, with several thousand telephones and outside connections (called trunks) shown here.

Further, all the wires come to a central point at the **main distribution frame (MDF)** where blocks are used to terminate the wires in a centralized location. The *MDF,* shown in Figure 2-18, is used as a central point connecting the telephone company entrance and the distribution to the rest of the organization. In many cases, other distribution frames are used throughout the building or campus. These are all referred to as distribution frames, but the nomenclature will change depending on the location. For example, intermediate distribution frames (IDF) are used between the MDF and the end user, such as in closets on individual floors. The term "building distribution frame" or BDF is used in a campus environment as the entrance to an individual building separate from the main location where the telephone company connections arrive. The point is that each facility has several options and various naming conventions are used in describing these.

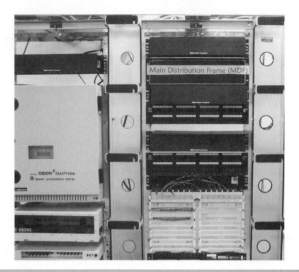

Figure 2-18 The MDF is the central point where all the wires integrate, and then run to the desks. Or, going the other way, they go to the main PBX and then to the outside world.

Digital PBX

All newer systems are digital. As a computer architecture (all PBXs today are computers), the system processes the information in its digital format. A digital coder/decoder (codec) in the telephone set converts the analog voice conversation into a digital format. The digital signals are then carried down the wires to the PBX heart (the CPU) for processing. The PBX is responsible for making any conversion needed to process the call in a usable format for the outside world. In the case where the call will be traversing the telephone company's CO links on an analog circuit, the PBX must format the information for the outside link. In this case, a digital-to-analog conversion will take place, as shown in Figure 2-19.

A variant of a digital PBX utilizes a computer screen as the display for the phone. The actual phone system is integrated into the Personal Computer (PC) system, and software allows all previous functions described to be performed with the click of a mouse. This hybrid PBX and computer is called Computer Telephony Integration (CTI). *CTI* is best suited to applications where inbound calls are linked to the customer purchasing database and all relevant account information literally "pops" onto the screen. CTI is an evolving hybrid arrangement that is becoming more prevalent in businesses. Its future is promising because it integrates telephone and computer functionality into a single device (combining voice and data into one network).

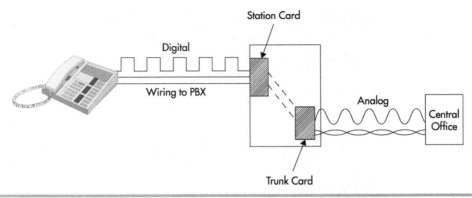

Figure 2-19 Because newer PBXs are digital, they are responsible for all formatting of the signal to traverse the PSTN. If the public network trunks are analog, the digital PBX converts the in-house digital signal into an analog signal, which can be sent over the public network.

 ## Telecomm Careers

PBX Administrator

Organizations that own PBXs need to have staff to maintain them or purchase a maintenance contract from the hardware vendor. PBX administrators are responsible for programming moves, adds, and changes within the hardware switch. (These changes are made when an employee moves from one office to another within the building. Typically, the number follows the employee to the new office.) In addition, they also set up and maintain voice-mail systems that are attached to the PBX. Because PBXs are smaller versions of CO switches, their functionality needs to be programmed, and this computer needs to be updated with the latest software packages for routing. The administrator may oversee these changes or let users handle updates themselves.

Different reports (uptime, call duration, call termination, number of inbound calls, number of outbound calls, and so forth) can be printed from the machine. These management reports of the PBX are utilized in planning for future growth through several calculations. Individual departments within an organization may also ask for information from these reports. For example, advertising may want to know how many calls came from a certain area where an ad was run. This information may have some bearing on when to run the next ad or how many additional ads should be placed. All this information comes from the telecommunications department. Organizations usually hire a couple of people who assist the PBX administrator in all these functions.

(continued)

To become an administrator, you are usually hired and trained on the job, or you come from a PBX vendor. When we mentioned that PBX vendors offer service contracts, the vendors' staff performs maintenance functions. Several books are available on PBX maintenance programming, and classes are offered by some hardware vendors. PBX administrators are well advised to learn data communications as well. The next generation phone services will be voice over data networks. This is VoIP, and it is covered in Chapter 9.

Note that hardware configurations differ from manufacturer to manufacturer. Being able to administer one product does not guarantee being able to administer a PBX from a different manufacturer. Care should be taken when choosing which system you learn—choose the most generic system available. A little research can identify which manufacturers lead the way in terms of sales, and this will assist you in determining on which system(s) you want to be trained.

PBX administrators can earn anywhere from $35,000 to $70,000 annually, depending on their experience.

Central Office Centrex

An alternative to the purchase of a PBX is **Centrex**. *Centrex* is a service originally offered by incumbent local exchange carriers (ILEC), formerly Bell companies, and now it's offered by all providers who offer dial-tone service.

Centrex stands for "central exchange" or PBX services provided from the CO (exchange). The ILECs—either the Bell Telephone Companies or the independent telephone companies—all have a service offering. The *Centrex* service is a partition inside the carrier's CO switch, which provides telephone service on a private basis to businesses (see Figure 2-20). Centrex provides all the functionality of key systems or PBXs without requiring you to buy,

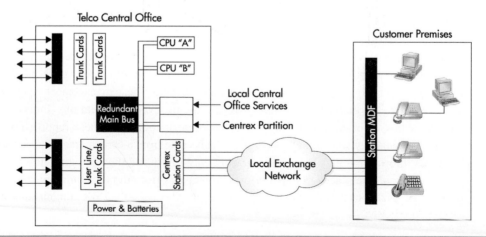

Figure 2-20 Centrex is a service where the features of a PBX are supplied from the CO switching equipment.

maintain, and wire the components of a phone system into your business. You still need to provide your own telephone sets, but single-line phones can be supported by Centrex service. Note that although these services mirror key systems and PBXs, the interface on how you apply these features can be slightly more cumbersome. And remember, when discussing the dial pad on phones, the * and # keys were added for Centrex service.

The components of a Centrex are as follows:

- Central office, which is the serving office
- Central Processing Unit or computer
- Station cards
- Switching network
- Line cards
- Memory
- Common logic and power cards
- Bus to carry information to and from the CPU

Centrex Service Providers

The primary suppliers, as already stated, are the ILECs. They provide the service as part of the CO function. A list of Centrex providers includes but is not limited to:

- **Regional Bell Operating Companies (RBOCs)**—The four Regional Bell Operating Companies (SBC, Qwest, Bell South, and Verizon) are the largest sellers of Centrex (ILECs).
- **Independent Operating Companies**—These are companies such as ConTEL, GTE (now owned by Verizon), Centel, and Commonwealth.
- **Resellers of Centrex service**—Many arrangements have been made with resellers around the country.
- **Bell authorized agents**—These are authorized agents of the ILEC, but are not employees of the company.
- **CATV companies**
- **CLECs**—KMC Telecom, McLeod, and Focal (this example is not an exhaustive list of the CLECs)
- **Electric companies**

Centrex service was typically created in North America. However, it is now available in 34 countries.

Peripheral Devices

The list of peripheral devices for the key systems, PBX, and Centrex markets is virtually unlimited. The devices range from items as simple as an external bell to sophisticated management systems. The pieces are too numerous to list here (and they change too frequently), but a lot of negotiating room still exists for any component you might need.

Some of the devices that might appear in the picture are as follows:

- Automatic call distribution

- Voice mail

- Automated attendant

- Call detail recording

- Modem pools

- Multiplexers

- Head sets

- Display sets (telephones)

- Paging systems

- Least cost call routing

- Network management systems

- Design tools

- Voice over IP devices

- Answering machines

Chapter 2 Review

Chapter Summary

Now that you have completed this chapter, you should be able to do the following:

Identify the Components of the Telephone and Describe Their Function

- Despite the model or manufacturer, every telephone has two main parts: the base and the handset.

- The handset houses the transmitter and receiver.

- The handset contains a four-wire circuit: two wires for the transmitter and two wires for the receiver. Each side of the function (transmit and receive) has its own two-wire electrical circuit at this point.

- The functions of the transmitter and the receiver are to convert sound to electricity and electricity back to sound. We often refer to the handset functions as E&M, or the ear-and-mouth communications process.

- The switchhook is the portion of the set that gets the dial tone from the telephone company or, when we are through with the call, gives the dial tone back.

- The dial pad uses the set to address the network.

- Tip and ring describes the two wires running from your phone set to the rest of the world. They call the transmit wire the "tip" and the receive wire the "ring."

Describe Features Provided in Newer Sets

- Speed dialing is a feature designed to save the user time by pre-programming the number into the phone. A user can preprogram from 1 to 100 numbers into the memory of the set.

- Call Hold is a feature that effectively turns off the transmitter while keeping the actual call intact.

- Call Transfer is a feature that (assuming this feature is available at the CO [or PBX equipment] within your area) enables a call to be transferred to another line.

- Conference call is similar to the transfer feature, but in this case, rather than transferring the call to a third party, the third party called will be added into the call.

- Redial last number. Sets with this feature have their own internal memory, so they can automatically dial the last number called, even if it is not a speed number.

- Built in speakerphone. Many sets have the capability to turn on a speakerphone for hands-free, two-way communications.

- Hands-free dialing. Without picking up the handset to the face, a user can go off hook electronically by pressing the line button or an on button, and then dialing. However, once the called party answers the phone, the caller must pick up the handset and converse.

- Displays. Where features are available in the CO, a display set can be used to show the incoming caller identification. Where the incoming caller display is not available or used, the display can still be used to display the number that the caller dials, or length of call.

Explain How Calls Originally Progressed Through the Network

- Telephone companies provide the physical connection (local loop) and a means of connecting those wires to the desired party. The means of connection or switching of the calls from one pair of wires to another is accomplished in the CO.

- Originally, all call switching was manually performed by the telephone company operators.

- As the number of calls increased, human involvement became a bottleneck and required some changes.

- The first attempt to offload human assistance was the creation and use of the rotary telephone set.

- The touch-tone telephone set was created to speed dialing and call processing, reduce user frustration, increase productivity, and enable additional services.

- Tone dialing helps to get the call through the network more quickly because the tones are sent at a much faster rate than rotary pulsing.

Describe the Need for, Features of, and Benefits Achieved by Modern Devices in Telephony

- Original telephone sets were an interface to the network, but modern systems provide support for multiple users and advanced features.

- Now, network-switching equipment has moved further away from the carriers and into the customer's door.

- A key system is a form of the telephone typically used in smaller office environments.

- A key system was a mechanical device. Users are responsible for making the line selection and controlling the individual calls/functions.

- Key systems work well for smaller office environments, but they aren't quite suited where hundreds of phones exist. As the number of users increases, the chance that users will be fighting for the outside lines increases. A private branch exchange (PBX) is the typical telephone system for large organizations. The main difference between a key system and a PBX is this: the PBX acts like a CO and provides a dial tone through its direct connection to the PSTN.

- All newer systems are basically digital. The PBX is responsible for making any conversion needed to process the call in a usable format for the outside world.

- An alternative to the purchase of a telephone system is called Centrex. Centrex stands for central exchange, or PBX services provided from the CO (exchange).

- Centrex provides all the functionality of key systems and PBXs without the need to buy, maintain, and wire the components of a phone system into your business.

Key Terms for Chapter 2

66 Block *(52)*
Centrex *(60)*
Diaphragm *(33)*
Dual Tone Multiple Frequency (DTMF) *(42)*
Duplex *(47)*
Ear-and-Mouth Communications Process (E&M) *(35)*
Four-Wire Circuit *(32)*
Handset *(34)*
Hard Hold *(45)*
Intercom Card *(51)*
Key System *(50)*
Key Service Unit (KSU) *(51)*
Line Card *(51)*
Loop Back *(36)*
Loop Start Circuit *(39)*
Main Distribution Frame (MDF) *(57)*
Off Hook *(38)*
Overtalk *(47)*
Private Automated Branch Exchanges (PABX) *(55)*
Private Branch Exchanges (PBX) *(44)*
RJ-11C *(36)*
Side Tone *(36)*
Simplex *(47)*
Station Card *(51)*
Switchhook *(38)*
Talk Off *(42)*
Tip and Ring *(44)*

Key Term Quiz

1. In an _____ process, _____ represents the flow to the ear or receiver and _____ represents the flow of electricity from the mouth or transmitter.

2. When you speak into a telephone and you hear yourself, you recognize there is still a connection to the distant end. This is called a _____.

3. The _____ is the portion of the set that gets the dial tone from the telephone company or, when you are through with the call, gives the dial tone back.

4. _Tip & ring_ describes the two wires running from your phone set to the rest of the world. They call the transmit wire the tip and the receive wire the ring.

5. The _touch tones_ are a dual-tone multifrequency (DTMF) system.

6. In a _Key System_, the user must manually press, or select, a button to grab an outside line, and then get the dial tone.

7. The main difference between a key system and a PBX is this: the PBX acts like a _CO_ and provides a dial tone through its direct connection to the PSTN.

8. A _key service Unit_ is the heart and brain of the key system.

9. _Station cards_ are the cards that control the intelligence and the interface to the end user's key system.
   station cards

10. _Line Cards_ are the interfaces to the telephone company lines.
    line cards

11. _Centrex_ provides all the functionality of key systems and PBXs without needing to buy, maintain, and wire the components of a phone system into your business.

Multiple-Choice Quiz

1. How many wires are used in the telephone handset?

   a. Two

   b. Three

   c. Four

   d. Five

2. How does the telephone company CO know when you want to make a phone call?

   a. You dial the digits

   b. You lift the handset and go off hook

   c. You enter in a credit cart number

   d. None of the above

3. How many wires are normally used in an RJ-11?

   a. 4

   b. 25

   c. 2

   d. 8

4. The purpose of the telephone set is to convert _____ to _____, so it can be sent down the wires (to the party on the other end) where the _____ is converted back to _____.

   a. Sound, electricity, electricity, sound

   b. Electricity, sound, sound, electricity

   c. Sound, electricity, sound, electricity

   d. Electricity, sound, electricity, sound

5. The dial pads can take on two forms. The original dial sets were _____, and newer sets are_____ sets.

   a. Single line, multiline

   b. Rotary, touch-tone

   c. Single line, touch-tone

   d. Rotary, multiline

6. The telephone set converts human sound into what format?

   a. Impulses

   b. Binary

   c. Electricity

   d. The set does not convert your voice into anything

7. In the old days, how long could it take to set up a phone call when you used a rotary phone?

   a. 13 seconds

   b. 23 seconds

   c. 33 seconds

   d. 43 seconds

8. _____ is the process when the human voice creates problems by generating a harmonic that sounds like a touch-tone digit.

   a. Off hook

   b. Overtalk

   c. Talk off

   d. Volume regulation

9. What does PBX stand for?

   a. Private Branch Telephone

   b. Public Branch Exchange

   c. Private Branch Exchange

   d. Private Bell Exchange

10. Who are the primary users of a PBX?

   a. Bell Systems

   b. CLECs

   c. Residential user

   d. Corporate users

11. PABX stands for:

   a. Private Analog Branch Exchange

   b. Public Analog Branch Exchange

   c. Public Automatic Branch Exchange

   d. Private Automatic Branch Exchange

12. The main providers of the PBX arc:

   a. ILECs

   b. Manufacturers

   c. CLECs

   d. CATV companies

13. Centrex is an alternative to buying a PBX. True or False

14. The following is not a prime candidate for using a key telephone system.

   a. Corporate headquarters

   b. Small accounting firm

   c. Auto dealership

   d. Home office

15. A KTS is used as a _____.

   a. Telephone company offering

   b. Regional telecommunications service

   c. Resource-sharing device

   d. Dedicated system for a user

16. The brain of the key system is called:

   a. Brain

   b. KTS

   c. KSU

   d. Memory

Essay Quiz

1. What are the main components of a telephone set? How do these pieces connect together to make the phone work?

2. If you are thinking of opening your own business, you will need to invest in office space, supplies, and a phone system. Your business will employ around 40 people: some will answer telephones for inbound orders; others will handle customer service and billing. You expect you will need to transfer calls between departments in the future as business picks up. What are your options to service your business without investing a large amount of your working capital in equipment? Which would be the best long-term solution for the business? Why?

3. If touch-tone service is so much better then rotary service, why is 15 percent of America still using rotary service?

4. What is the reason for using a DTMF pattern in touch-tone service?

5. Whether you use a KSU or a PBX, the vendor will ask you how many intercom cards you want. What is the function of an intercom card and what benefit does it provide?

Lab Projects

Lab 1.1 Take Apart a Telephone and Identify the Components.

For this demonstration, the class should be given some telephones. Because damage may occur, it is strongly recommended that these phones be used for demonstration purposes only. Telephones can be easily and cheaply obtained through local secondhand stores, electronic stores, or over the Internet at various retailers.

Allow the students to take the phone apart into its main components and identify them. The main parts and their locations should be noted. Components include the following: handset, mouthpiece, earpiece, transmitter, diaphragm, receiver, base, 4-wire E&M circuit, dial pad, ringer, RJ-11 jack, switchhook, and handset cord. This exercise could be used to perform a practicum or to have students identify the individual parts on a diagram. Students should know the names, location, and function of all the structures.

Items needed:

● Rotary telephone set, touch-tone phone

● Screwdrivers: Phillips and flathead. Smaller sizes are encouraged as telephones utilize small fasteners.

On a sheet of paper, answer the following questions about the phone.

1. Look at the telephone in front of you and look at its components. Who is the manufacturer and what model is the telephone? It is usually identified underneath the base.

2. Look at the connector cord. Is it integrated into the handset and base, or does it use a RJ-11?

3. Remove the mouthpiece and the earpiece. These are usually removed by turning them in a counterclockwise direction. (For touch-tone phones, the handset is usually two pieces screwed together by two fasteners located on the inside of the handset. Find the transmitter and the receiver underneath the corresponding pieces. If removable, can you see the diaphragm? Is it integrated into the transmitter? Is the receiver removable? How does it connect to the telephone? Is it hard wired?

4. Take the base and turn it over. You should notice several screws underneath that keep it intact. Remove these screws and separate the base. Note that sometimes the rotary dial is fastened through its center to the base. If this is the case, remove the rotary dial by removing the center cap. (It should come off like a hubcap.) A thin, flathead screwdriver should accomplish this.

5. Once the phone is separated, identify the major structures: ringer, four-wire circuit from the handset, switchhook, and connection to the wall jack. Identify the wires going to and coming from these devices.

6. Inspect the dialer (which you have already removed in a rotary phone) and notice the "ticking" when turned. In a touch-tone phone, notice the connections to the dialer. What is happening here?

7. Noting the construction of these devices, which do you think were the parts that caused the most problems and why?

8. Reassemble the telephone in the reverse order that you took it apart. You should not have any screws or parts left over.

Students should be allowed to work in pairs to "dissect" both types of telephones. They should notice how the technology has changed, and how devices have become smaller and more reliable.

Once both devices are examined, students should compare and contrast the devices in a two-page report indicating their findings and observations. This should be turned in to the instructor for grading.

This exercise may be used to administer a practicum for the components of the phone. Phones may be disassembled and individual parts labeled as *A*, *B*, *C*, and so forth. The students are given a minute at each station. They have to identify the individual parts or write the function of each part.

This could be supplemented by placing a diagram or picture on an exam showing the individual parts labeled as *A*, *B*, *C*, and so forth. Students should be able to name the individual part, as well as to identify where each individual part resides in the phone and to tell what the function is of each part.

Lab 1.2

In this lab, students should be taken to the campus phone switch and given a tour of the PBX at that location. Tours could be set up through the MIS/Technology department with instructor permission.

Students should note the manufacturer, the size of the PBX in terms of numbers of phone extensions, outside lines, call capacity of the system, routing capabilities, and its availability to support emerging applications. Call detail reports can be generated and shown to the students to show where calls are terminated, how adequate outside lines are supplied given the current call volume, and the busiest times of day.

Students should be instructed on the average uptime of this hardware, the number of people maintaining it, and how intensive it is to perform moves, adds, and changes.

During the tour, encourage students to ask questions on the system, its age, end-of-life timetable, and so forth.

After the tour, students should be given an assignment of summarizing the configuration and evaluating its effectiveness given the size of the student body. Is the system maxed out or can it handle the growth of the university? Student-body size can easily be obtained through the registrar's office. Students should also be able to predict when this hardware will need to be replaced given the previous variables. Students should visit Internet sites from the various BPX manufacturers and identify a new system that would replace the current system. This exercise enables students to see careers in an MIS department, know the hardware currently deployed and its configuration, and get an estimate of what systems cost.

Once you complete this two-page assessment, turn it in to your instructor.

Chapter 3

Introduction of the Carriers and Regulation in the Industry

LEARNING OBJECTIVES:

Once you complete this chapter, you will be able to:

Describe the initial formulation of the carrier network.

List the major legal battles and regulation, and their effects on the industry.

Explain what the Public Switched Telephone Network (PSTN) is and know about its addressing mechanisms.

Define RBOCs and their formulation.

List the main points of the Telecomm Act of 1996.

Define the various types of carriers and the services they provide.

In Chapter 2, you learned about the various components, features, and methods of carrying calls across the network, as well as services provided by modern devices. In this chapter, you learn about the initial formulation of the carrier network and explain the addressing mechanisms of the **Public Switched Telephone Network (PSTN)**. Because the telecommunications industry has been regulated extensively, the roles of the carriers, as well as their structure, have changed. We discuss these legal battles in depth and their effect on the industry to the present day. Understanding their past is important because it explains certain constraints and limitations on some carriers today. This chapter explains how the service providers have changed from the initial rollout of telephone service to become the robust providers they now are. Regulation of the industry continues to be an area of rapid change and further reform. If you pay special attention to the headlines in today's newspapers, you will see additional changes being suggested and implemented. These changes are being discussed and studied on at least a monthly basis. Events in this arena are critical to future trends and to opportunities available in the telecommunications field.

The Importance of the Telephone

It is important to realize how communications took place prior to the inventions mentioned in Chapter 2. Try to imagine how people stayed informed before the advent of telephones.

Within a community, people physically went to gathering places, or residences, to speak in person to others. Contact with other people outside your city was extremely limited, and other states must have seemed a world apart.

Information was disseminated primarily through newspapers, the U.S. Postal Service, and then the telegraph. Radio and newscasts did not exist. They became popular in the 1930s.

Imagine how people felt as the entire world began to open up for them with the availability of the telephone. Distance no longer mattered, as you could have a two-way conversation with someone miles away from your home. It is easy to see why the telephone was so well received; it opened the door to almost unlimited opportunities.

Almost immediately, everyone wanted to have this device. It wasn't long before companies began to spring up all over the place to provide service and get in on the market of this revolutionary invention.

The Initial Formulation of the Carrier Network

As you learned in Chapter 2, Alexander Graham Bell was awarded the patent for the telephone in 1876. Bell had sought financial backing to make this invention profitable and to capitalize on its opportunity. At first Bell approached Western Union, the largest telegraph company, with his patent. He offered it to them for the sum of $100,000. Western Union officials were unimpressed. They thought the telephone was a toy or a fad for the rich, and they quickly turned down this offer.

Bell remained determined about the potential of his device and acquired financial backing from two private investors: Gardiner Hubbard and Thomas Sanders. With this investment, they drew up the plans to create a company to provide the first telephone service. On July 1, 1877, the Bell Telephone Company was formed. For the next six months, the Bell Telephone Company began producing several phones and provisioned wires in New Haven, Connecticut. In 1878, the first services were provided in Connecticut. The Bell Telephone Company continued expanding and opening offices in the major cities in the Northeast.

3

Shortly after rejecting Alexander Graham Bell's offer for the telephone, Western Union realized it had made a terrible mistake in dismissing Bell and his telephone. The company realized it was losing out on this invention and all the future revenue associated with it. Western Union approached two other inventors to create their own version of the telephone.

Western Union used Dr. Elisha Gray's patent for the receiver, and then went to Thomas Edison for the transmitter. After Bell patented the telephone, Edison had developed a transmitter that was superior and improved the quality of the set. In addition, Edison's experience with the distribution of electricity was used to assist in the wiring of residential and corporate sites. Edison had designed a series of electrical distribution grids, and he now began applying these ideas to the telephone system.

At this point, Western Union created the American Speaking Telephone Company (ASTC) and used the Gray/Edison device to provide service.

The Bell Company was furious that Western Union entered the telephone business, and they challenged ASTC's legitimacy based on the Bell patents. In 1878, Bell filed suit against ASTC for patent right infringement and, eventually, prevailed in the courts. The settlement of this case came a year later when Western Union gave up all rights of telephone service and products, and even their network. In short, Western Union left the telephone industry. For giving up their place and the Edison/Gray patent, Western Union would receive a percentage of all the telephone rentals the American Bell Telephone Company made (until the Bell patent expired). In return, the American Bell Telephone Company agreed not to infringe into the telegraph manufacturing business. However, this didn't prohibit the American Bell Telephone Company from infringing on the telegraph industry. Over the next 25 years, they would buy a controlling interest in Western Union and would also absorb Western Electric, the former manufacturing arm of Western Union.

The American Bell Telephone Company decided to create a sibling company in 1885—called American Telephone and Telegraph (AT&T)—to address this void in long-distance communications. AT&T was responsible for creating and maintaining a long-distance voice and telegraph network.

Shortly thereafter, the American Bell Telephone Company decided to buy a controlling interest in the Western Union Company for the purpose of making Western Union the provider of AT&T hardware (telephones).

Also, around the same time as ASTC, the New England Telephone Company was formed. It assisted in the development of the two previously mentioned companies by both building telephones and providing additional network services. This meant that the New England Telephone Company was in direct competition with the American Bell Telephone Company.

With several providers now in the mix, customers were in a dilemma. Which carrier should they use? Were they all the same?

Each company was not the same. In fact, if you subscribed to one of these three individual companies, you couldn't communicate with a neighbor or business connected to another company's network. **Interconnectivity** didn't exist. For example, if a businessman needed to speak to three different businesses that used the services of the three different operating companies, three separate telephone lines and three different telephone sets would be required. This may be difficult to imagine, but it accurately represents the situation at that time.

Each of these small companies provided only local service. Without a connection from one city to another, long-distance communication was impossible. Still, there continued to be a demand to communicate with others who were some distance away.

Things were good for the American Bell Telephone Company up until 1894, when the patent on Bell's invention expired. The patent had allowed the American Bell Telephone Company, its subsidiaries, and its licensees to be the only legal provider of services in the United States. That meant every device and network was the property of the American Bell Telephone Company.

In 1899, AT&T had sustained such profitability and growth that it bought the assets of American Bell Telephone Company and incorporated it into its operations. What resulted was the creation of one of the largest, most influential companies ever. The sheer power of this organization became a force that took almost a century of rule and regulation to break up. This is not to say that AT&T wasn't necessary at the time, but in the long run, its sheer size and power became a hindrance.

With the expiration of this patent, new providers began to spring up everywhere. By 1920, over 9,000 local providers existed. AT&T did not welcome this competition; it saw its market share being taken by these small upstarts. AT&T decided it would not allow competitors to connect with their long-distance network, in an effort to ensure its position in the marketplace.

As with any new service, government regulatory control was lacking and true economics prevailed. Because there was such a tremendous start-up cost to become a long-distance provider, AT&T began to strangle out the competition.

Eventually, when these smaller companies began to lose subscribers (after all, who wants service where you can't talk with friends, businesses, and relatives outside your locality?) and became financially stressed, AT&T swooped in and bought them, increasing its overall network. From 1920 to1943, AT&T practiced this procedure until the total number of competitors was down to around 1,500. This wasn't totally a bad thing, as people using AT&T got what they always wanted: the ability to talk to people anywhere (as long as they were hooked up to AT&T).

However, AT&T still wasn't satisfied and pushed the envelope even further. AT&T enjoyed the position of being the largest provider with the largest network, and it began to put the pressure on the marketplace. They undercut competitors' prices and literally forced out all the competition, leaving customers in many areas with no local service at all.

As public outrage over AT&T grew, lawmakers began investigating the practices employed by AT&T.

Legal Battles and Regulation

When a new industry emerges, it is a new phenomenon and not widely understood by the masses. When dealing with technology, it is imperative that these businesses flourish and allow their products to benefit the public. In any business free market, without checks and balances, however, one company will eventually rise to the top and dominate the marketplace. This process has been repeated time and time again in various industries (oil, manufacturing, software, and so forth). We will now focus on the major regulations, acts, and legal battles that have shaped and changed this industry. Some of these laws were interim solutions, whereas others changed the landscape in telecommunications forever.

Sherman Antitrust Act of 1890

The federal government passed the Sherman Antitrust Act in 1890 to deal with monopolies and price fixing. This act made every contract, combination (in the form of trust or otherwise), or conspiracy in restraint of interstate and foreign trade illegal. The Sherman Antitrust Act authorized the federal government to start proceedings against trusts (or companies) to dissolve them in the name of public interest. Although the Sherman Laws originally dealt with Standard Oil, their significance cannot be understated.*

---

*Standard Oil was a company owned by John D. Rockefeller. Standard Oil, the largest oil company in the United States in the 1800s, engaged in price fixing. It laid the foundation of government regulation in the telecomm arena.

Kingsbury Commitment

AT&T had become a tremendously powerful entity that had dictated the marketplace in communications. Its practices were investigated by the government under the Sherman Antitrust Laws. Fearing that Congress would dissolve AT&T (which would have hurt tens of thousands of customers), AT&T decided to change its stance, settle the suit, and make changes. This was known as the **Kingsbury Commitment**.

In 1913, AT&T's Vice President Kenneth R. Kingsbury made a statement that AT&T would immediately make the following changes:

- Relinquish its holdings in Western Union (over a period of years, AT&T had purchased a controlling interest in its former competitor).

- Stop the practice of acquiring the independent telephone companies, unless authorized by the Interstate Commerce Commission (ICC).

- Allow the independent telephone companies to interconnect to the AT&T network.

1914 Clayton Antitrust Act

Although the Sherman Antitrust Laws created some change in the direction of AT&T and the communication industry, officials felt that the laws needed further reform to provide better monitoring of the industry. Knowing further regulations were needed, they supplemented the Sherman Laws further and created an overseeing agency for trust regulation. In 1914, the Sherman Act was supplemented by the **Clayton Antitrust Act**.

The main outcome of the Clayton Antitrust Act was the creation of the Federal Trade Commission (FTC), an independent presiding body of the federal government chartered to oversee competition of American businesses as part of a free and fair market. The Clayton Antitrust Act was part of the reforms to prevent the growth of monopolies and to preserve competition in the marketplace.

Despite the best efforts of this legislation, the issues of the communications industry were unique. The resources needed to provide free and fair competition in long-distance service was prohibitive. (After all, it took almost 20 years to get the AT&T network to its current state, and its network was underutilized.) Trying to provide another option would cost tens of millions of dollars, decades of time, and a talent pool that was employed by AT&T. The leaders at AT&T, therefore, began petitioning lawmakers about the idea of only having one long-distance carrier. Their logic was that creating such an expansive network was so costly and difficult that they should be given exclusive rights because they were allowing others to interconnect with it. Congress looked into these claims, agreed with them, and passed legislation in 1921 to address the issue.

Graham-Willis Act

The **Graham-Willis Act of 1921** established the telephone system as a natural monopoly. The Graham-Willis Act allowed AT&T to be a monopoly under the condition that it promise to cable up the entire country. AT&T's exclusive place as a long-distance carrier was protected if the company kept the commitment to connect all parts of the country to its network. Although this seemed acceptable at the time, what it did was to make AT&T temporarily exempt from the Sherman Antitrust Laws.

What Do You Think?

1. Was it beneficial for Congress to pass the Graham-Willis Act of 1921 or do you think it was a mistake to guarantee AT&T's position as a monopoly? How do you think the industry might be different if the Graham-Willis Act had never been passed? What might have been the effect on communications in this country?

2. The U.S. was the only major country with a private network instead of a PTT (Post, Telephone, Telegraph) as the practice was in almost every other country at the time. Which is better, a private network or a government network?

The Radio Act of 1927

Another communications invention—the radio—became available to the public in the 1920s. The first radio stations formed to provide content shows for the airwaves. These radio stations were regulated with the passing of the **1927 Radio Act**, which gave the Department of Commerce and the Interstate Commerce Commission the responsibility of regulating this new form of communication. See Figure 3-1 for the breakdown of government agencies. The consumer side, presided over by the **Federal Communications Commission (FCC)**, has four bureaus. The National Telecommunications and Information Administration (NTIA) presides over the government and the military. Note that these agencies receive their authority from Congress, under the Department of Commerce.

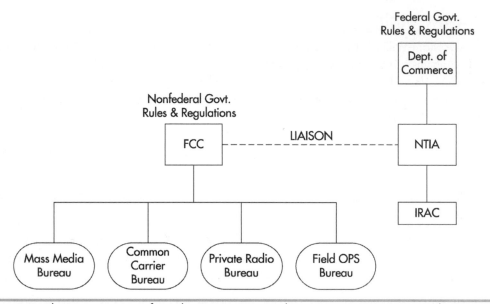

Figure 3-1 The organization of regulating agencies in the communications arena. The consumer side is presided over by the FCC; the NTIA presides over the government and military.

Communications Act of 1934

By 1934, there was pressure for one organization to regulate all telecommunications services, both wireless and wired. The *1934 Communications Act* enabled the creation (under the Department of Commerce) of the FCC. The function of the *FCC* is to be an independent government agency responsible for regulating both interstate and international communications over radio, television, wire lines, satellite, and cable media. Today, the FCC is the agency responsible for regulating all commercial communication services. It serves as the liaison between the consumer and the government.

Note: the government has its own agency to regulate governmental functions in its communications needs. For years, AT&T had dominated the industry through its long-distance service monopoly and its Western Electric manufacturing subsidiary. It provided all telephone equipment and service through its normal distribution channels, the telephone companies.

The network was untouchable, with only AT&T products and services allowed for interconnection to the networks. This was an appeasement to AT&T, which stated the connection of a foreign piece of equipment on the network would disrupt the network and decrease its efficiency, as well as jeopardize national security. The government agreed and continued allowing only AT&T devices to be used for communication.

 **Try This**

Explore the FCC's Web Site

Visit the FCC's web site and research the current issues before the industry. The FCC's web site is located at http://www.fcc.gov.

1. Enter the URL http://www.fcc.gov into your computer's web browser. Spend some time exploring the various aspects of the site.

2. Halfway down the left side of the page is a menu titled Consumer Center. Click Consumer Alerts and Fact Sheets.

3. Next click Charges on your Phone Bill. A document will open that provides a quick reference of charges that appear on your phone bill. Look at a copy of your own phone bill and identify the charges that are described with an acronym.

Navigate the site and find out the following information:

1. What is the purpose of the USF charge?

2. What is 7-1-1 service?

This stance was modified somewhat after World War II when the FCC permitted the connection of certain customer-owned and -provided recorders to the telephone lines, so long as a protection device was used. This *protection device* was a piece of hardware that electrically isolated the non-AT&T equipment from the telephone network. (The isolation equipment, of course, had to be leased from AT&T.)

Hush-a-Phone

In the 1950s, an innovation known as the **Hush-a-Phone**, an acoustically coupled device designed to eliminate noise and increase privacy, was tested before the FCC. Although this sounds impressive, the Hush-a-Phone was nothing more than a rectangular metal box-like cone that could be placed over a mouthpiece. Users spoke into the cone, and their conversation would be kept private from others in public places. Prior to this invention, users would have to "cup" their hands over the mouthpiece to accomplish the same thing. Everyone wanted his or her own Hush-a-Phone! Well over a hundred thousand units were sold before AT&T found out about it. Immediately, AT&T sued Hush-a-Phone because it had not approved this device for the public network. They had been granted exclusive rights for the public network and, clearly, this device was attached to the AT&T phone, causing a violation of the regulations. The FCC agreed with AT&T's position and moved to prevent "foreign" devices from being connected to the telephone network, even though this device was only a mechanical privacy cone and was not electrically connected to the network in any way.

An appeals court later overturned this decision because the acoustic coupler was a nonelectrical device. Therefore, the court ruled it would pose no threat to the integrity of the network. However, the legal battle and costs associated with it forced the Hush-a-Phone company out of business, leaving AT&T to lose the battle but win the war, creating a chilling effect for others who would consider challenging its dominance.

The U.S. Department of the Navy was one of the users who fought for the use of the Hush-a-Phone. The Navy wanted to have the privacy of the Hush-a-Phone and the ability to record a conversation for documentation purposes. After losing the battle in court, AT&T suggested if a recording device were to be allowed on the network, then a beep should be sounded on the line periodically (every 15 seconds). This beep would alert the user at the far end that the conversation was being recorded. The Bell System suggested if a beep were introduced to the line, then an electrical input was required. You can probably see where this is headed. AT&T was fighting tooth-and-nail for its place as the sole provider of telecommunications services. Bell fought for the right to install the equipment on the line that provided the beep. This was made possible because the Hush-a-Phone decision was based on a nonelectrical input. Therefore, the Bell System was then able to charge the U.S. Department of the Navy for the equipment that introduced the beep and all was settled. AT&T still kept market share by providing all the equipment to access the network or the equipment that allowed other manufacturers' products to interface with its network.

Even though the courts allowed third-party devices to be connected to the network, any device of electrical nature was still prohibited if it wasn't from AT&T (manufactured in its Western Electric Division).

The 1956 Consent Decree

In 1956, the Department of Justice (DOJ) filed an antitrust suit against the Bell System, which had previously been postponed because of World War II. In general, the suit was aimed at getting AT&T to divest itself of Western Electric. This was finally settled in what was known as the **1956 Consent Decree**. The result was this: AT&T could retain ownership of Western

Electric if it only produced products for the Bell-operated companies. Regulators wanted to provide free and fair trade practices, as well as competition, so this decree went on to prevent the Bell System from offering commercial data-processing services, limiting Bell to providing telecommunications services under regulation. This still left the Bell System a regulated monopoly with no competition for equipment and services in its operating areas.

The Carterphone Decision

In 1968, however, the first true case was tested by a company called Carter Electronics of Texas. Carter made a device used to interconnect mobile radios to the telephone network via acoustic couplers (again avoiding an electrical connection as in the Hush-a-Phone). But, despite the lack of direct electrical connection, AT&T vigorously contested the Carter product as dangerous to its network. Eventually, the FCC ruled against AT&T and for Carter. It permitted devices to be connected as long as adequate protective steps were taken. The FCC ruling was paramount in that the direct electrical connection of devices to the network was allowed so long as a protective coupler arrangement was still used. The decision had monumental impact because, prior to the **Carterphone Decision**, manufacturers had a limited outlet for their products. They typically sold their products to the independent operating telephone companies. Now, the floodgates were opened and these manufacturers had a whole new world of opportunity to market their products. Even the foreign manufacturers sped into the equipment market, offering end-user products that had previously been totally controlled by the Bell System. The European and Japanese marketers were quick to enter the PBX and terminal equipment business.

However, the use of a protective device was still an area of frustration with these equipment vendors. Rent for the Bell protective arrangements was a recurring cost that made the purchase of other equipment less attractive. The manufacturers continued to complain about this, and they made a case that AT&T was still protecting its marketplace, leaving no room for competition in the equipment industry.

1975 FCC Registration Program

The competitive complaints resulted in the 1975 FCC registration program for all products that could be attached to the telephone network. As long as a manufacturer could pass the requirements of the FCC registration (Part 68), then its products could be attached to the network without the use of the protective devices. This began what was called the interconnect business. The **interconnect business** refers to companies that connect networks; it can also be stated that companies that provide equipment that allows this interconnection are part of the interconnect business.

The Execunet Decision

Still, additional activity took place. In the 1960s, a small microwave carrier company called Microwave Communications Incorporated (MCI) began constructing a microwave network between Chicago and St. Louis. MCI's initial intent was to provide alternate private-line services called *Execunet* in a high-volume corridor. *Private-line(s) service* is a service for businesses that require a large number of connections to their other office locations. Rather than paying the normal rate to traverse the public network, high-volume users can directly dial branch offices for a fixed monthly fee. These lines, at the time, were part of the public network, but were terminated to preassigned locations (due to programming at the CO switch).

MCI sold its microwave service as an alternative to the AT&T private line service. Initially, MCI only offered the site-to-site, private office connectivity (with the permission of the FCC), but then it directly challenged AT&T by letting users in one town use its microwave link to access local dial tone in the other city and to make local phone calls in the far-end city. MCI took its interconnection request to the courts and won the right to interconnect its network with the telephone company network. At that point, MCI leased lines (in both locations) and allowed customers in St. Louis to dial MCI, and then have the call get local dial tone in Chicago. This new service directly violated FCC regulations. This was illegal, and it was immediately reported to the FCC. The courts ordered that MCI could not provide dial tone, but could provide private line access that terminated on the Bell network. The lengthy legal actions that followed nearly put MCI into bankruptcy (much like the Hush-A-Phone battle), but the little MCI company prevailed and became the "other common carrier" in the industry—one more step toward ending AT&T's monopoly. This was the **Execunet service decision**. In addition, this decision set a precedent, which later allowed the creation of another common carrier, Sprint. Now, three players were in the long-distance market and, slowly, the legislation was chipping away at the stranglehold AT&T had on the communications market.

The Public-Switched Network

Before we go any further with regulations and changes in the industry, let's discuss this network—the Bell System—in more detail, so you can understand its structure and function. The U.S. public-switched network has always been the largest and the best built in the world. Over the years, the network has penetrated to even the most remote locations around the country. Primary call-carrying capacity in the United States is through the PSTN.

The PSTN enables a subscriber to access the end office, connects through the long-distance network, and delivers a call to the end point. This makes the calling cycle complete. The goal of the network design is to complete the call in the least amount of time and over the shortest route possible. The network is dynamic enough, however, to pass the call to longer routes through the hierarchy to complete the call in the first attempt when possible.

The North American Numbering Plan (NANP)

With the network defined, how do consumers use the PSTN? The **North American Numbering Plan (NANP)** is the system used to assign unique ten-digit phone numbers to the PSTN in the U.S., Canada, and the Virgin Islands. The NANP works on a series of ten numbers (Figure 3-2) and enables quick and discrete connection to any phone in the country.

Timing	Area Code	Central Office Code	Station Subscriber Number
Original	N0/1X	NNX	XXXX
Pre-1995	N0/1X	NXX	XXXX
Post-1995	NXX	NXX	XXXX

Figure 3-2 Layout of the North American Numbering Plan (NANP). *N* stands for any digit except 0 or 1, and *X* can be any digit.

The Area Code

When this plan was originally formulated in 1947, the telephone numbers were divided into three sets of digits. The first was a three-digit *area code* or **numbering plan assignment (NPA)**. This started with a digit from 2 to 9 in the first slot of the sequence. Why only numbers 2 to 9? Because the numbers 0 and 1 are utilized in accessing operators or long-distance service. Thus, the exclusion of 0 and 1 in the first digit of the area code facilitated the quicker call setup.

Originally (see the following), the second slot could be the number 0 or 1. This was used by the switching office equipment in a screening mode. As soon as the system sampled the second digit and saw a 0 or a 1, it knew this three-digit sequence was an area code. In the third slot, this could be any digit from 1 to 0. We say 1 to 0 rather than 0 to 9 because 0 represents 10; rotary-dial phones represented the 0 digit with ten pulses.

This worked in combination with local exchange codes (the three numbers immediately following an area code), which could not have a zero or a one in the second digit. What this signaled to the phone switch was that a dialing sequence of **1+n0x** or **1+n1x** (where 1+ meant long distance, *n* meant any number 2 through 9, and *x* meant any number) would be a ten-digit call because only area codes had valid 0 or 1 entries in that position. Any number 2 through 9 in that "second" position indicated an area-code long-distance call because the number being dialed could not be an area code. Back in the early 1960s, we recognized we were running out of area codes, given that only 160 were available. In reality, only 152 area codes were allowed for use by the various states because certain ones were allotted for special services (the N11 area codes, for example, 211, 311, 411, and so forth, were always reserved). With the growth of the system, it was only a matter of time before numbers started running out.

By 1995, the area codes were expanded by allowing any digit in the center slot of the three-digit sequence. This expansion created 640 new area codes for the NANP. The use of these area codes has been so dramatic, there's speculation that even though we got a fourfold increase, these may be depleted by 2010 or sooner!

Our current rate of consumption of telephone numbers is alarming. We are facing a worldwide numbering shortage. Now, the average household in the U.S. has three or more numbers (a second number for a fax, a third one for a modem, a fourth number for teens, a separate number for cell phones, and so forth).

The Exchange Code

A second three-digit sequence called the exchange code follows the area code in a phone number. The **exchange code** is a central office designator that lists the possible number of central office codes available in a region served by a particular area code. The exchange code system automated what had previously been a manual request to an operator to connect to a foreign exchange: a central office serving a different area.

The exchange code (prior to 1960) was set up in the sequence NNX, meaning the first and second numbers used the digits 2 through 9, for the same reasons as in the area code. The digits 1 and 0 were reserved for operator and long-distance access, and the 0/1 exclusion in the exchange code prevented this three-digit number from being confused with an area code. In the third-number slot of the exchange code, any digit could be used. Clearly the greatest limitation in the exchange codes was we would run out. With NNX, we have 640 possible exchange numbers to use ($8 \times 8 \times 10 = 640$), but these were exhausted in a short period of time.

Originally, the offices had names (such as "Main" or "Prospect"). If a user in the Prospect exchange wanted to talk to extension 2800 in the Main exchange, he would ask the operator to be connected to Main 2800. As local exchanges grew, more switching equipment was added to local exchanges, resulting in the reuse of the extension numbers in operator panels at the exchange. So, if you were in operator panel 2, your designation would be Main 2-2800.

As automated dial systems were installed, the names were converted to numbers (by associating each number that began with a 2 with corresponding letters). This led to a transformation where a user would then dial to a remote user by dialing **MA** in **2-2800,** (which was dialed as 622-2800). Over time, the exchange names all but disappeared from use.

In the late 1960s, AT&T began planning the use of an exchange code numbering plan that changed the sequence to NXX, expanding the number of exchange codes in each of the area codes to 800. This added some relief to the numbering plan. When using the NXX sequence, though, the need arose for a forced number 1 in advance of the ten-digit telephone number, so the call screening and number interpretation in a switch wouldn't get confused. This met with some resistance, but ultimately, customers got used to the idea. The first two locations to use this revised numbering plan were Los Angeles and New York City early in 1971.

❓ Line Check 3-1

To check your knowledge of addressing a telephone call in the U.S., answer the following questions:

1. What does NPA mean?

2. What does NXX stand for?

3. What are the final numbers in addressing a call on the Public Switched Telephone Network?   *Station Subscriber Number.*

The Subscriber Extension

The last sequence in the numbering plan is the subscriber extension number. This is a four-digit sequence that can use any digit in all the slots, allotting 10,000 customer telephone numbers in each of the exchange codes. Because the four-digit sequence can be composed of any numbers, the intent is to give every subscriber his or her own unique telephone number when combined with an area code and an exchange code.

This hasn't changed yet, although the possibility that we can still run out of numbers always exists. Therefore, two ideas have been considered: add two, three, or four more digits to the end of the telephone number, or add one or two more digits to the area code or the exchange code.

In either method, users will be asked to dial more digits, an idea that has never been popular, but this might become a necessity. This is far more complicated, however, than just adding a few more digits here and there. The whole world will be impacted by any such decision, and the length of time required to implement such a global change will be extraordinary.

Currently in North America, several new area and exchange codes have been installed where only one existed. This forces users in the area to dial 11 digits (1 plus the 10-digit telephone number) for local as well as long-distance calls. This plan has met quite a bit of resistance because people don't like to dial that many digits and have trouble remembering that many numbers. Regardless of their feelings on the subject, though, there aren't a lot of choices.

The Bell Network Hierarchy (Pre-1984)

Prior to 1984, most of the network was owned by AT&T and its local Bell Operating Companies (BOCs). It was a creation based on growth to provide scalability as newer areas were provided with service. A layered hierarchy of office connections was designed around a five-level architecture (with the offices designated from Class 5 through Class 1). The offices are connected together with wires of various types, called *trunks*. These trunks can be twisted pairs of wire, coaxial cables (like the CATV wire), radio (such as microwave), or fiber optics. The trunks vary in their capacities, but generally high-usage trunks are used to connect between offices. Figure 3-3 shows the hierarchy prior to the divestiture of AT&T, with the five levels evident.

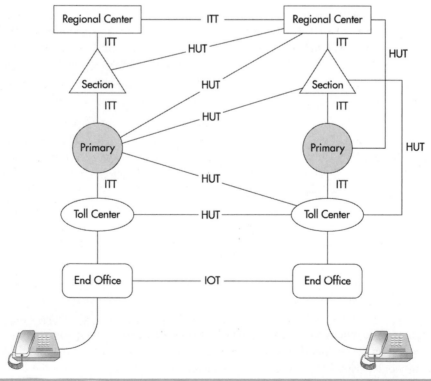

Figure 3-3 The pre-1984 hierarchy as it existed in North America under the Bell System.

The End Office

The Class 5 office is the local exchange or *end office.* It delivers dial tone to the customer. The end office, also called a *branch exchange,* is the closest connection to the end user. Think of a tree: all the activity takes place at the ends of the branches and the customers are the leaves hanging off the branches. Calls between exchanges in a geographical area are connected by direct trunks between two end offices, which are called *interoffice trunks.* Over 19,000 end offices in the United States alone provide basic dial-tone services.*

The Toll Center

The Class 4 office is the *toll center.* A call going between two end offices that aren't connected together is routed to the Class 4 office. The toll center is also used as the connection to the long-distance network for calls where added costs are incurred when a connection is made. This toll center may also be called a *tandem office,* meaning calls have to pass through (or tandem through) this location to get somewhere else on the network. A basic arrangement of a tandem-switching system is shown in Figure 3-3. The tandem office usually doesn't provide dial-tone services to the end user.

However, this is a variable where a single office might provide various functions. The tandem office can also be just a *toll*—a connecting arrangement that's a pass-through from various Class 5 offices to the toll centers. Again, this varies depending on the arrangements made by the telephone providers. The ratio of toll centers that serve local long distance is approximately 9 to 1. Prior to divestiture, approximately 940 toll centers existed.

The Primary Center

The Class 3 office is the *primary center.* Calls destined within the same state area are passed from the local toll office to the primary center for completion. These locations are served with high-usage trunks used strictly for passing calls from one toll center to another. The primary centers never serve dial tones to an end user. The number of primary centers prior to divestiture was approximately 170, spread across the country among the various operating telephone companies (both Bell and independent operating companies).

---

*Prior to the 1984 divestiture, almost 66,000 end offices were in the United States. The equipment is smaller now and it can handle more connections, so the providers consolidated into fewer locations, saving space and money.

The Sectional Center

The Class 2 office is the sectional center. A *sectional center* is typically the main-state switching system used for interstate toll connections designated for the processing of long-distance calls from section to section. Approximately 50 sectional centers existed before the divestiture of the Bell System. These offices didn't serve any end users, but they served among primary centers around the country.

The Regional Center

The *Class 1 office* is the *regional center*, and ten regional centers existed across the country. The task of each center was the final setup of calls on a region-by-region basis. However, the regional centers constituted one of the most sophisticated computer systems in the world. The regional centers continually updated each other regarding the status of every circuit in the network. These centers were required to reroute traffic around trouble spots (for example, failed equipment or circuits) and to keep each other informed at all times. As mentioned, this was all prior to the divestiture of the local BOC by AT&T.

NOTE

The first commercial cellular service was offered on January 1, 1984. This service was offered in Chicago, Illinois, by a company called PrimeCo. Although cellular communications requires a carrier, the network is entirely different from the PSTN. We cover that topic in Chapter 13. Interestingly, many of the cellular companies have either been bought by or merged with AT&T and/or the BOCs.

The Divestiture Agreement

The landscape of telecommunications has changed over the past century, mostly through court actions. Despite the many acts, and regulatory bodies, the players in the industry have largely remained unchanged. AT&T and its other ventures (Western Electric, Bell Labs) still controlled almost the entire marketplace. In 1982, the most monumental decision to be made since the inception of the monopoly in the telecommunications business was reached. In light of all the competitor inquiries and consent decrees taking place, the DOJ was still investigating AT&T, Western Electric, and Bell Labs. This recent action started in early 1974, essentially re-opening the actions that had been started after World War II, and was aimed at the complete breakup of the Bell System. In early 1981, the suit finally made it into the courts but, surprisingly, was brought to a halt on January 8, 1982, when an agreement was reached to drop the suit and submit a modification of the 1956 Consent Decree to the courts. **Judge Harold Greene** of the Federal District Court was presiding when this compromise was reached. This was called the **1982 Divestiture Agreement** or the Modified Final Judgment (MFJ) of 1984.

Incumbent Local Exchange Carriers

The **incumbent local exchange carrier (ILEC)** is the telephone company serving your area and providing you with dial-tone services. The term local exchange carriers (LEC) came into existence after the separation of the Bell System from AT&T. The **Modified Final Judgment (MFJ)** decree specified that the local telephone company, or dial-tone provider, would be kept separate after divestiture. Prior to 1984, the carriers were called the BOCs, and they still are referred to this way. See Figure 3-4 for example of the BOCs. The names of the telephone companies associated with the older Bell System have changed somewhat. Some companies have tried to keep their identity as much as possible. Names that are still used in the industry today, such as Bell South, are examples of this identity. However, the telephone companies were fighting to keep the Bell logo at the same time the parent organization (AT&T) was also trying to keep certain identities. The local carriers won this battle and managed to keep the logo and the Bell name. Surprisingly enough, even though the divestiture of AT&T and the Bell Systems began in 1984, many people still do not separate the two entities. For the public, this is the toughest part of the whole scenario. People still think of the system as one big entity, rather than as organizations that were separated as a result of the court decisions.

3

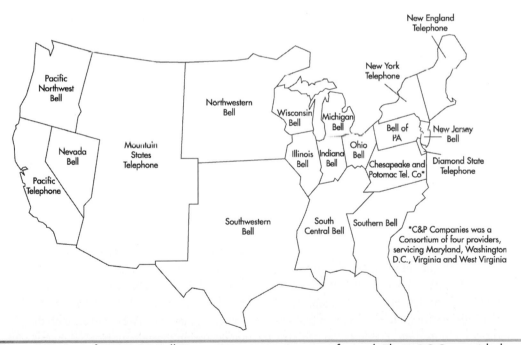

Figure 3-4 Out of AT&T, 23 Bell Operating companies were formed. These BOCs presided over individual states in some instances, but in others, they presided over several states that were more rural.

In early 1999, 15 years after the breakup occurred, a number of users still did not recognize that the change ever occurred, although this number was fewer than ever. Of course, this leads to confusion because the problems that occur on a daily basis are always blamed on the telephone companies, regardless of where the problem resides.

Note that in some areas, some **Independent Telephony Providers (ITP)** *still exist*. These ITPs are local dial-tone providers in areas not served by any of the **Regional Bell Operating Companies (RBOCs)**. Instead, some private individuals bought an exchange switch and provide dial-tone service. It is not profitable for an RBOC to wire these areas because the populations are of limited size and penetration of the market would result in an operating loss. Additionally, these telephone companies (about 1400 exist) were always referred to as independent, so they are also considered ILECs. Although they are not part of the Bell System, these organizations still provide the basic dial tone for many communities. Some of the larger of these independents include GTE Telephone (including their acquisition, ConTEL Telephone Systems), Commonwealth Telephone (which is now part of two different companies: RCN Cable Company and Frontier Communications), Standard Telephone Company, and Centel. The numbers of customers and the areas served by the various independents differ, but their function is the same. These companies provide local dial-tone service as their primary charter.

All these telephone companies were considered ILECs because the term fit better with the service they provided. This service was:

- The dial tone

- The local loop of wire connecting to their equipment and the customer location

- The telephone set to interface to the network

- The interface to the local and long-distance portions of the networks and the access to the long-distance network

- The billing and collection functions for all services

- The installation of all related pieces and components to give the end user access to the network

- The maintenance and repair functions

Because this was a single interface, the customer's only responsibility was to make a single call that did it all. The use of the network led to additional billings, so the only actual responsibility of the customer or user was paying the bill. This all changed in the 1984 divestiture of the network and telephone company interfaces. Consequently, the customer now must decide whom to talk to regarding services and equipment needs. However, with the telecommunications deregulation and privatization occurring throughout North America and other parts of the world, the way we, the consumers, used to do this process is becoming the way we will do it again. What goes around comes around. Soon, the ILECs will be able to compete and offer all the services (and more) that they offered prior to 1984!

Provisions of Divestiture

You will recall that the 1956 Consent Decree was aimed at providing free and fair trade practices in the industry. Despite the small gains made in allowing other providers in the marketplace, further reform was needed to level the playing field. The courts were called on again to break up the monopoly of AT&T and the Bell System. This *divestiture,* or breakup of the Bell system, was called the Modified Final Judgment (MFJ). The main idea was that provisioning of local dial-tone service would remain a monopoly, but all other services would operate in a fair and competitive operating environment. Therefore, the local dial-tone business that would be provided by the LECs would remain regulated. The trade-off was this: AT&T would be allowed to enter other unregulated markets and services (previously off limits because of the 1956 Consent Decree). AT&T was now allowed to operate in long-distance, equipment manufacturing, computer equipment, and sales markets.

3

Out of AT&T, the 23 **Bell Operating Companies (BOCs)** would be split up into several individual entities, each totally independent of the others. AT&T would keep Western Electric manufacturing, Bell Labs, and the Long Lines (Long Distance) division. The 23 Bell Operating Companies were to be consolidated into seven RBOCs. The decision to make seven RBOCs was an effort to provide services to the public without having so many redundant assets. Each company prior to this consolidation had to have duplicate divisions in almost every job function to maintain the network. Note that over time, these were consolidated back into four RBOCs: SBC, Verizon, BellSouth, and Qwest Communications (see Figure 3-5).

Some other important points of the MFJ include the following:

- AT&T had to transfer sufficient personnel, assets, and access to technical information to the new RBOCs, (or whatever new organization was owned by the RBOCs) to enable local exchange services or access to exchange services to be provided without any ties to AT&T.

- All long-distance services, links, personnel, and other facilities had to be relinquished by the BOCs and turned over to AT&T.

- All existing licensing agreements and contracts between AT&T or its subsidiaries and the BOCs had to be terminated.

- Equal access for all interexchange carriers into the RBOCs' switching systems had to be provided. (This broke down the special privilege AT&T enjoyed over its competition.) The equal access for all carriers was to be provided within two years. The only exceptions were electromechanical systems, where it was cost-prohibitive to make changes or for smaller companies serving fewer than 10,000 users.

- After the breakup, the RBOCs could provide, but couldn't manufacture, equipment.

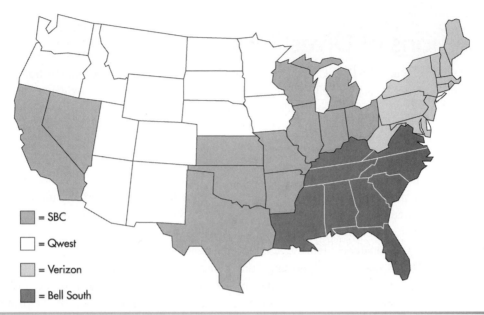

Figure 3-5 Four RBOCs exist today: Qwest, SBC, Verizon, and Bell South. This diagram shows the states where the respective RBOCs provide services. The consolidation of regions was to eliminate inefficiencies and redundant positions.

- After the divestiture, the RBOCs could produce and distribute directories to subscribers.

- Carrying calls between and among offices would be defined as either local-exchange services or interexchange services. The LECs would hand off any interexchange call to an interexchange carrier (IEC/IXC). To define the boundaries of who carried the call and who shared in the revenue, a number of local access and transport areas (LATAs) were created. The calls inside a LATA were the responsibility of the LEC, and connections between LATAs were the responsibility of the IEC.

- Joint ownership or participation in the network between AT&T and the BOCs was prohibited. Although this was a common practice before the breakup, it wasn't supported after the breakup.

The Network Hierarchy (Post-1984)

After divestiture in 1984, the network took a dramatic turn, with the separation of the BOCs from AT&T. The hierarchy of the network shown in Figure 3-6 introduced a new set of terms and connections. The BOCs were classified the same way as independent telephone companies. They are all called LECs and ILECs.

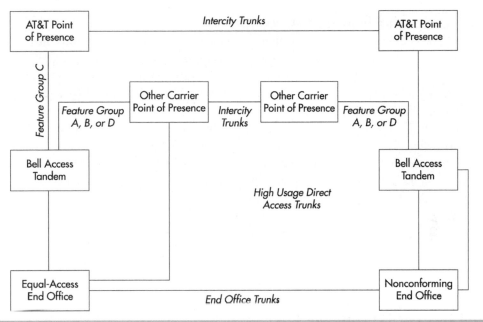

Figure 3-6 Post-1984 hierarchy in the United States. This is much different from the previous hierarchy, but this model now allows individual entities to handle routing within their own organization.

Equal access, or the capability of every IEC or IXC to connect to the BOC for long-distance service, became a reality. Equal access was designed to allow the same access to other long-distance competitors that AT&T had always enjoyed prior to divestiture. Prior to divestiture, a customer attempting to use an alternative long-distance supplier would have to dial a seven- or ten-digit telephone number to get to this supplier's switch. Then, when this connection was completed, a computer would answer the call and place a tone on the line. From there, the caller would have to enter a seven- to eleven-digit authorization code. This code identified the caller by telephone number, caller name and address, and billing arrangements. Only after the computer (switch) verified this information would it then send dial tone to the caller's ear. The caller would then have to dial the ten-digit telephone number of the requested party. This could involve lengthy and frustrating call setup times—especially when the number called was busy.

You can see why users resisted service from other long-distance carriers, the time and the number of digits required, and the frustration of attempts to call busy numbers. That is, unless the organization forced the user to dial across the carriers' networks. The reason for all the digits was simple. The telephone company didn't pass on the caller information to the alternate carrier (MCI, Sprint, ITT, and so forth) that it passed to AT&T. Thus, the choice of many callers was AT&T because the process was simpler. Now, the caller information is passed on in an equal basis, so the access is equal.

Local Access and Transport Areas (LATAs)

LATA was introduced with the divestiture agreement in 1984. One of the problems facing the court system was dealing with the long-distance versus local calling areas. It was a revenue-sharing concern more than anything else. AT&T forced the issue by demanding some form of revenue sharing be put in place, so a single LEC wouldn't have the option of handling all calls and cutting out the IECs/IXCs.

To solve this problem, an agreement was reached that stated the LECs would still maintain a monopoly on local dial tone and local calling. They would be restricted from carrying long-distance traffic, which would fall under the domain of the IECs/IXCs. Many states cover large geographical areas, however, and calling from one end to another would be considered long distance. See Figure 3-7 for examples of LATA arrangements.

The country was broken down into 195 separate bounded areas for local calling (some local tolls are allowed) based on the density of population in each area.*

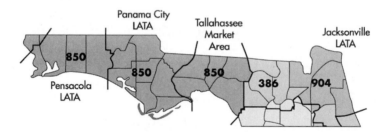

Figure 3-7 LATAs are geographic divisions of service areas, not area codes. A single area code may span several LATAs, and even though the LATAs are within the same area code, the call would be a toll call.

CAUTION

Whenever a call traverses a LATA, a per-minute fee is associated with that call, even though you didn't dial a 1 to reach it. This feature has frustrated many dial-up Internet users trying to access a local number. When you select a number, make sure you find the closest number to avoid a costly surprise on your first bill.

---

*After the Telecommunications Act of 1996 in the United States, this LATA boundary began to erode quickly as a practical matter, even if it technically remained in force. This is because the LECs and the CLECs are extending their reach into local areas; at the same time, IECs/IXCs are offering services intrastate and intra-LATA. Many IECs/IXCs are now registered as CLECs, offering services previously unavailable from a single source.

Again, this was financially motivated. The interconnection between two LATAs would be done by the IECs/IXCs. A completely new set of acronyms emerged because of the divestiture agreement, of which LATA is only one. To complicate things even more, four types of calling are under the LATA concept:

- *Intrastate-Intra-LATA* belongs to the LECs (within the state and within LATA)

- *Intrastate-Inter-LATA* belongs to the IECs/IXCs (within the state outside the LATA)

- *Interstate-Inter-LATA* belongs to the IECs/IXCs (state-to-state outside the LATA)

- *Interstate-Intra-LATA* can be either/or, but was originally given to the LEC (outside the state and within the LATA)

This results in a confused public and, sometimes, confusing tariffs. For example, a call from Philadelphia to Los Angeles can be carried on the IEC network for under $0.10 per minute, yet a call from Philadelphia to Wilmington can cost as much as $0.40 per minute. The difference here is the 3,000-mile call is regulated on the long-distance basis and is under FCC jurisdiction. However, the 29-mile call between Philadelphia and Delaware is regulated by BOC tariff and the Public Utility Commissions. These anomalies will change and are doing so now, but this is the confusion that can crop up when various players are trying to protect their interests.

Tariffs

Simply put, a **tariff** is a description of a service that is offered, the rate of charge for that service, and the rules under which the service is to be provided. A tariff is the basic service agreement between the customer and the provider that must be submitted to the regulators for approval. Before any changes in service can be offered, they must be approved by the regulators. This is a check-and-balance from the MFJ that ensures fair and free competition in the marketplace. In the United States, 50 different regulators are ruling on the tariffs—one for each state.

But who writes the tariff? The RBOCs and AT&T write the tariffs. Although more and more services are being made available quicker than ever before, the universal escape clause is "the tariffs don't allow this service," which is a clear misrepresentation. The BOCs and the AT&T organization write tariffs and submit them to their respective arbitrators, whether it's the FCC for interstate traffic (for AT&T) or the respective Public Utilities Commissions for the RBOCs. An easy way to avoid offering a service or to delay a customer request is to suggest the tariff doesn't allow something.

In the United States, the overseer function has been relegated to the Public Utilities Commission(s) and the FCC. In the rest of the world, rate settings and guidelines differ, depending on the country. Many of the telephone companies are under direct control or ownership of the local government. The telephone service is relegated to the post-office agencies, called Post, Telephone, Telegraph organizations (PTTs). The name stands for the services provided: postal, telephony, and telegraphy. Privatization continues to occur in several parts of the world. Telephone services are being removed from government control and passed on to private organizations. It stands to reason that these organizations may face stiff competition for the services, much the same as what has happened in the United States.

Benefits of Divestiture

Out of all the turmoil, the divestiture of the Bell System allowed advances in the industry that might not have occurred otherwise. AT&T prided itself on quality; however, with such a focus on making the existing network flawless, newer services were rolled out at a snail's pace.

With competition, other suppliers began to enter the new markets and the evolution of the network and service offerings escalated dramatically. The government was right. With increased competition, newer services could be perfected and deployed more quickly. Also, competition tends to drive prices down for the consumer, thus letting more people have access to these emerging technologies.

Digital architectures then rolled out to customers at a furious pace. Why was digital so important? It allowed for higher-quality conversations to be carried over the networks. Digital transmission is not as susceptible to static and noise as are analog transmissions. All signals degrade over distance. This requires periodic amplification or regeneration of the signal. Instead of just pumping up an analog signal on the line with a power booster (and amplifying the noise as well), the digital signal is re-created to a level identical to the original transmission. Digital architectures are responsible for allowing clear long-distance calls, essentially free from static and noise. The result is long-distance conversation that sounds as if you are talking to your neighbor and not someone on the other side of the world. The introduction of digital technologies enabled the carriers to provide multiple conversations on the existing infrastructure (this is covered in Chapter 8), which provided more efficiency and lowered overall costs, while increasing their profits.

When divestiture took place, the monthly costs associated with local dial tone increased by as much as 50 to 60 percent. Wait a minute: if competition is supposed to drive prices down, yet monthly dial-tone service was increased by 50 to 60 percent, how can this be good for consumers?

The previously offered services from AT&T (predivestiture) were bundled services (local and long distance). After divestiture, local costs increased, but long distance costs decreased by 60 percent or more. Here is where it gets complicated. This might sound like a break-even point, but communications follows a different model. In consumer voice services, it is the 20/80 rule. Twenty percent of a customer's actual monthly bill is for the fixed recurring charge (local services), whereas 80 percent of the bill is for the variable usage-sensitive costs associated with long distance.

Basically, an increase of 50 to 60 percent in local services with a reduction of 60 percent in long-distance service means overall communications costs decrease!

The Telecom Act of 1996

In February 1996, the Clinton Administration signed into law the **Telecom Act of 1996**. This act was the culmination of several years of trying to deregulate and provide a competitive marketplace in the telecommunications arena. This law, when enacted, opened the door to an open communications infrastructure. Essentially, what the administration implemented was the concept of an information superhighway.

The Telecom Act of 1996 opened the way for myriad new players to compete for the local dial-tone service. The days of monopolistic control in telecommunications had supposedly ended, allowing competition and choice in all areas of telecommunications. Why did a need exist for competition in local services?

In the United States, dial tone amounted to a $115 billion per year industry, and all the emerging players want a piece of that action. What this means, however, is a group of new players would emerge to provide dial-tone services, while the local telephone companies are unshackled and allowed to penetrate the long-distance arena and data service sectors. In addition, the Telecom Act of 1996 allows the long-distance companies (IECs/ IXC) to enter into new business opportunities. These include dial tone, cable TV services, high-speed Internet access, and two-way video communications capabilities after the infrastructure is in place.

In exchange for losing their monopoly over local service, the ILECs would no longer be barred from providing inter-LATA services, such as long distance and high-speed data connections. The caveat of the Telecom Act of 1996, however, is these ILECs must first prove that an open competitive environment exists at the local loop (meaning the ILECs had to provide local loop services for a fee to anyone who wanted to contract with the phone companies, including requirements that they lease space for competitors' equipment to be installed in their end offices). This was one of the contention points as the newer players emerged and attempted to get into either facilities-based or non-facilities-based dial-tone provisioning.

During the beginning stages of this Telecom Act, elation and overwhelming support for the newly emerging marketplace from all players was the name of the game. As you would expect, however, things did not work as smoothly as intended. We cover more of this in the following CLEC section.

❓ Line Check 3-2

To check your understanding of the most significant recent events in telecommunications, please answer the following questions:

1. What services did the Modified Final Judgment regulate?

2. What services did the 1996 Telecom Act affect?

Interexchange Carriers (IEC/IXC)

The **interexchange carrier (IEC or IXC)** is the long-distance carrier.* In general terms, this carrier connects to the ILEC or CLEC with circuits from its point of presence (POP) to the central office. The major players in this arena are IECs/IXCs, such as Sprint, MCI/WorldCom, and AT&T, as well as Cable & Wireless. The IECs/IXCs can carry long-distance switched and/or private-line service. The major players provide both. Some of the IECs/IXCs, however, primarily provide private-line service, depending on their focus.

Competitive Local Exchange Carriers (CLECs)

The Telecomm Act of 1996 allowed a newcomer to enter the marketplace in direct competition to the RBOCs. These competitive LECs initially offered dial tone as their primary vehicle to attract customers.

With this new marketplace, several new types of companies were formed to offer various services. The newcomers in local services were called **Competitive Local Exchange Carriers (CLECs)**, and they came in two flavors: those who bought their own equipment and created their own networks (called facilities-based providers) and those who simply bought services wholesale, and then sold them at discounted rates (resellers).

In the *facilities-based environment,* the carrier provides its own cables or wireless communications to the door of the business customer. Many of these providers installed fiber straight to the customer's door because of the cheap cost and high flexibility of this medium. Alternately, they may decide to lease the ILEC's local loop to the customer and connect it to the CLEC switch, thereby making it part of their network. At that point, all the communications will be carried right out to the wide area network (WAN), bypassing the local telephone companies. To quickly encourage CLEC deployment, the FCC stated that the ILECs must make room available in their Central Offices (COs) for the CLEC providers.

In a *nonfacilities-based environment,* the new players rent or lease facilities from the local telephone company at a discount from 17 to 28 percent off the local telephone company's tariffs. The telephone companies argue that by having to rent the services to competitors at a discounted rate, they are putting themselves in an unfair position. This practice has been designated as the **Unbundled Network Elements Platform (UNE-P)**. The resellers of dial tone merely turn around and rent UNE-Ps right back to the consumer at a rate less than what the telephone companies charge. The telephone companies contend this is a discount that shouldn't be provided and if competitors want to work in this market, they should build their own capabilities or rent from the telco at the same rates the telco charges other customers. Embroiled in all these battles are the other players, such as the long-distance and cable

---

*IEC was the acronym originally used for interexchange carrier. In time, however, the industry began calling it an IXC. Both are technically correct as they mean the same thing, but IXC seems more commonly used now.

TV providers, who are equally distraught because they also have to pay for access fees to provide services to their consumers. They argue that the telephone companies have been raising the rates for access because of the potential loss of revenue that may occur as a result of the Telecom Act of 1996.

Some CLECs have opened many third- and fourth-tier communities. Because they are the primary competitor or sole provider in the community, users who are willing to take a chance will do so with the new provider. These communities have become a lucrative market for the new CLECs in this area, as opposed to the results achieved by the CLECs in the major metropolitan areas.

As you might expect, many new providers entered the business. In 1999, over 500 CLECs had jumped into the competitive local dial tone business, yet they only achieved 3 to 5 percent penetration into the overall market. Yet, this penetration amounts to (by normal standards) a staggering $4 to $5 billion annually. Each of the competitors entering this market offers some form of discounts on cable services, dial tone, or long-distance access and services to pick up a few market points. One of the early problems these CLECs faced was in the transition of dial tone and the acquiring or *porting* of numbers (literally grabbing them from the existing carrier and adding them to their CO database). Porting was frequently done poorly, leaving the customer with no service. Many customers became disenfranchised when this occurred repeatedly. Often, getting things set up correctly before everything worked took three, four, or more attempts. Many new customers finally gave up on the idea of using a CLEC for their phone service. They decided it was better to pay a few cents more for the reliable service from the RBOCs. Over time, this problem was worked out and porting today is a fairly smooth operation; however, those customers who were burned in the initial days still may have some distrust of CLECs.

NOTE

Because competition in local dial tone service was enabled in 1996, the FCC decided that consumers should be able to take their existing phone numbers with them to the new carrier. This was done to promote local competition because the cost to businesses of changing and re-advertising their numbers would hurt them significantly. This process of taking your phone number with you is called Local Number Portability (LNP). In December 2003, this idea was applied to wireless service as well with Wireless Local Number Portability (WLNP).

These new competitors used loss leaders to attempt to gain a share of the market. As it's used here, *loss leader* describes services that are discounted below operating cost. Through this loss-leader market, the new competitors didn't make any money. Consumers may stand to gain in the short term, but eventually, carriers will have to raise their rates or offer some other value-added services to gain some revenue. Otherwise, they will fail.

In the year 2000, many of these competitors got in trouble financially and faced some serious loss of confidence from their investors. In fact, the companies began to run out of money. This forced a majority of the CLECs to fold; many others either merged with or were acquired by better-funded organizations. The stock prices for these organizations were soaring to heights never seen before, yet they all came tumbling to the ground with the dot.com bust. Between 2003 and 2004, some had emerged from bankruptcy, but they are facing difficult times getting back consumer confidence. Today, only a handful of CLECs remain from the original 500 and we expect that number to consolidate into a few CLECs. Watching how this unfolds in the future will remain interesting, as the industry seems to be shaking down to the original players and a couple of alternatives.

Of course, this also threw the tariff system into some chaos because one of the functions of natural monopolies and tariffs is to manage rates to allow the utility to service customers. The utility then charges different groups the same rate, even though they have different costs for providing the service, because eventually things average out for the monopoly provider. Under a monopoly this can work, but the RBOCs accused the 1996 Telcom Act of allowing CLECs to "cherry pick" all the lucrative accounts with lower provisioning costs and leave the RBOC only with the more expensive, unprofitable accounts and no way to make a profit.

Another class, called Competitive Access Providers (CAP), was also created. These providers bypassed the ILECs and provided alternate access at a large discount to the long-distance carriers or Internet service providers (ISPs). CAPs did not own actual equipment for switching and routing calls—they simply were companies that trenched the roads, installed conduits, and accessed lines to their customers. Yes, many CAPs were a commuter's nightmare; each CAP was responsible for trenching the roads for its own services. In some cases, roads were continually dug up so different CAPs could install their access lines. Most of these companies were acquired by the year 2000 by the major players in the industry (MCI, AT&T, and Sprint) to increase their capacity in rural areas.

☞ Line Check 3-3

To check your knowledge of the types of carriers, please answer the following questions:

1. What are the two types of CLECs?

2. What is provided from the ILECs, by the 1996 Telecom Act, to allow some CLECs to offer services?

3. How many CLECs are left since the 1999 Telecom Act?

Cable TV Companies as CLECs

We have been discussing voice companies so far, but technology over the past century has changed dramatically, especially since the 1970s. Cable TV companies emerged during that time (as well as satellite companies) and put their own connections to the customer's door. Having an access medium to millions of consumers, cable TV companies began to enter into telephony and other forms of the communications business. As the cable companies look at their infrastructure, they already have a high-speed communications channel running either to or by everyone's door. They must recognize, however, that in the past, their primary service was to deliver one-way cable services (TV). To provide high-speed Internet access, enhanced capabilities, and voice communications, these companies were forced to create a two-way communications cable system. This means they either had to add new cables or provide high-speed fiber in the backbone network (to the curb), and then coax to the door. Although this sounds straightforward and easy, it does require significant investments on the part of the cable companies.

3

This alternative proved to be quite effective. By the end of 1999, the cable TV companies had implemented a hybrid fiber/coax network in several cities in the United States and Canada that provided high-speed Internet access, bundled with existing TV services. Moreover, 1999 marked the year when AT&T (the now-streamlined carrier) acquired two of the largest CATV companies: TCI and Media One. Investing over $100 billion to acquire these cable companies gave AT&T access to millions of consumers. Yet in 2003, AT&T, having failed to penetrate the market, sold off its CATV holdings at a significant loss. CATV had managed to draw about 2 percent of the dial-tone business by 2003.

Emerging Areas of Business for the RBOCs

As a result of the Telecommunications Act, the original telephone companies (the RBOCs) broke out into new markets, offering long distance for less and providing cable TV services, Internet access, and videoconferencing capabilities as part of their local infrastructure. Because the local two-wire cable facility (called the *local loop*) was not designed to sustain the high-speed communications, the telcos must continue to update their cable infrastructures. These companies are enamored with technologies that use high-speed, digital subscriber links. Using various techniques, such as asymmetrical digital subscriber link (ADSL) or very high-speed digital subscriber link (VDSL), the telephone companies can provide high-speed communications to the customer's door. In the ADSL marketplace, they envision delivering up to 9 Mbps to a customer's door, whereas outbound from the customer to the network, the service will offer Plain Old Telephone Service (POTS) and up to 384 Kbps data transmission. Two other technologies deviate from this scenario:

1. Rate-adaptive ADSL (RADSL) was introduced, allowing the telco to deliver less than the 9 Mbps downloadable to the door. Instead, they deliver 1.544 Mbps for downloadable and adaptive rates of 256 to 1.024 Mbps uploadable. If the network is busy, then the consumer

gets slower-speed access, but not less than a contracted minimum. If the network is lightly loaded, however, the consumer can benefit from the higher throughputs.

2. The ADSL Forum investigated the need for the previously mentioned speeds. What it determined is the average consumer only needs 1 Mbps downloadable and approximately 160 Kbps uploadable speeds. Therefore, it developed what was termed *ADSL Lite* or *G.lite specification*. Over time, this specification will allow higher-speed access, which, for the short term, is sufficient. In the ADSL marketplace, the telcos deliberately dragged their feet implementing these services. Many reasons exist, but the most common is they don't want to be forced to provide the xDSL service at a discounted rate, as they do the dial tone. In the VDSL marketplace, the telcos envision up to 51 Mbps to the customer's door with a much lower-speed communications channel outbound or a symmetrical 51 Mbps in each direction.

Regardless of the technique used, the telephone companies are in a position to find technologies to support and sustain these speeds on their local, single twisted pair of wires to the customer's door. This is their challenge. Beyond the high-speed communications, the telephone companies can also enter into manufacturing, long distance, and cable TV service.

An interesting event occurred in 1999 when AT&T acquired the local cable TV companies (TCI and Media One) to get access to consumers' doors. Shortly after acquiring these giants, AT&T was challenged to offer the access to competitors at a reduced rate. AT&T immediately balked at that idea and appealed to the FCC because the local utilities commissions were ruling in favor of the competitors. This was, of course, before AT&T sold off its CATV holdings

Creation of the Internet Service Providers (ISPs)

With the passage of the 1996 Telecom Act, we mentioned that the Clinton Administration imagined an information superhighway. What Bill Clinton (or possibly Al Gore and others in the Clinton Administration) was referring to was an increase in competition to provide high-speed links to customers' doors and allow data services, along with voice, to be provided. As already mentioned, the telephone networks (local loops only) were not designed to carry data traffic, so data-centric companies and/or networks needed to be created. These were the first **Internet service providers (ISPs)**. The ISPs' main function was to provide public user access to the Internet (covered in detail in Chapter 9). Originally, access to the Internet was provided over telephone lines through modem communications. Users connected a modem to their computers, plugged in the phone line, and dialed the ISP for access. This is still a primary way for mobile commuters and citizens in rural areas to connect to the Internet today. ISPs also began offering access to DSL service and T1 service (these will be covered in great detail in Chapters 12 and 5, respectively). ISPs serve as the interface between the user and the high-speed Internet backbone. They provide you with an account, e-mail, and sometimes a browser to access the vast information on the Internet in a usable fashion.

What Do You Think?

As a result of the Telecom Act of 1996, do you think that competition in local dial-tone service exists? What has happened since 1996 regarding this competition? Who are the major players left in the industry? What is happening to the companies that are left? Where do you think the telecommunications regulatory scene is heading?

3

The Canadian Marketplace

In 1994, the Canadian Regulatory Telecommunications Committee (CRTC) endeavored to do something similar to what happened in the United States.

The goal was to deregulate or demonopolize the local dial-tone provisioning service. On May 1, 1997, the CRTC provided its interpretation of how it would deregulate and open the market to dial tone to a competitive environment.

One year after the Telecom Act of 1996 in the United States, the CRTC modeled many services and provisions of the law after those accomplished by the FCC. The reason was to provide consistent policies throughout all North America. While the CRTC endeavored to break up the dial-tone monopoly, the cable companies, the long-distance providers, and a rash of emerging facilities-based or non-facilities-based players already filed and petitioned for the right to offer services. Once again, in the Canadian marketplace, the influx of new providers and new opportunities overwhelmed the consumers, even though the implementation is ongoing.

In both the U.S. and Canadian marketplaces, all the dial-tone and long-distance access services have traditionally been available via the local loop. Now, with the cable TV companies trying to get into this business, the dial tone could be provided on either a cable or a local loop. More and more opportunities exist for a wireless connection to the consumer, however, whether residential or business. The wireless dial-tone providers are constantly springing up around the country as they entertain the thought of the Personal Communications Service (PCS). Through a combination of dial tone, the TV services, the high-speed Internet access, and the multimedia communications capabilities to the local door all these activities will come to culmination. No one service alone may warrant all the new emerging players, but as a whole, this marketplace is enormous.

Therefore, as the Telecommunications Act and the CRTC deregulation rolled out in the Canadian marketplace, consumers experienced dramatic changes in the way they do business. Through the convergence of wired and wireless communications, dial tone, and long distance, a variety of other services emerged to create a competitive potential for consumers. One-stop shopping is the wave of the future.

Summary of Events in the Telecommunications Industry

Year	Event
1872	Western Electric was formed. Alexander Graham Bell worked for Western Electric while developing the telephone.
1876	Bell was granted a patent for his invention (March 7, 1876).
1877	Bell offered to sell his invention to Western Union Telegraph for $100,000. Western Union rejected the offer.
1877	The Bell Telephone Company was formed.
1877– 1878	Western Union formed a subsidiary company called the American Speaking Telephone Company to market its own telephone set (the speaker was developed by Tom Edison and the receiver developed by Elisha Gray), the first competitor to the Bell System.
1878	The New England Telephone Company was formed as another of the first competitors to the Bell Telephone Company.
1878	Bell Telephone Company sued the American Speaking Telephone Company for patent infringement.
1879	Bell Telephone Company and New England Telephone Company merged and formed a new entity called National Bell Telephone Co.
1879	The Bell and Western Union case was settled. Western Union agreed to stay out of the telephone business, and Bell agreed to stay out of the telegraph business in areas where Western Union operated.
1880	American Bell Telephone Company became the new name for the Bell System.
1882	American Bell entered into an agreement with Western Electric. WECO was to be the sole manufacturer of Bell equipment.
1884	The first long-distance line was installed between Boston and New York.
1885	AT&T was formed as a subsidiary of American Bell to provide long -distance and telephone service for communities around the country and the world.
1887	The Interstate Commerce Commission (ICC) was formed to regulate interstate carriers.
1893	Bell's first patent expired, opening the door for competition without patent infringements.
1899	AT&T acquired the assets of American Bell.
1910	AT&T aggressively fought the competition by acquiring a controlling interest in Western Union.
1910	The Mann-Elkins Act was added to the Interstate Commerce Act to regulate the activities of the telecommunications industry.
1913	The Department of Justice (DOJ) considered antitrust actions against the Bell System. Woodrow Wilson made this commitment to break up private monopolies.

Figure 3-8 Summary of major telecommunications events from 1872 to 2004. (*Continued*)

Year	Event
1913–1914	AT&T agreed to divest its Western Union stock and stop buying up independent telephone companies, in a commitment by AT&T Vice President Kingsbury in return for dropping an antitrust action.
1918	President Wilson placed the telephone and telegraph systems under control of the Post Office (until 1919).
1921	The Graham-Willis Act established the telephone company as a natural monopoly.
1934	The Federal Communications Commission (FCC) was created to regulate interstate, maritime, and international communications. Congress also established "universal service" as its goal. The FCC investigated Bell System operations, and the DOJ began to formulate a major antitrust action against Bell. However, World War II postponed the action because Bell was considered critical to national defense.
1935	Public Utilities Commissions (PUCs) were formed to regulate intrastate communications and rate setting. Also, the PUCs were instrumental in formulating revenue sharing for calls using more than one carrier.
1956	Consent Decree—Regulators wanted free and fair trade practices in telecom. AT&T could retain ownership of Western Electric if it only produced products for Bell Operating Companies. The Bell System was prevented from offering commercial data-processing services.
1957	Hush-a-Phone decision—Courts ruled Hush-a-Phone was allowed on the public network because it was a nonelectrical device and posed no threat to the Bell Network (AT&T).
1968	Carterphone Decision—FCC ruled that the direct electrical connection of devices to a network was allowed so long as a protective coupler arrangement was used.
1975	FCC Registration Program—FCC ruled as long as a manufacturer could pass the requirements of FCC registration, then its products could be attached to a network without protective devices.
1976	Execunet Decision—Established the "other common carrier" with the allowance of MCI to provide microwave private-line service.
1982	Divestiture Agreement—(Modified Final Judgment) Judge Harold Greene presided over a compromise that broke AT&T and the Bell System into seven Bell operating companies.
1996	Telecom Act of 1996—Deregulated the industry to provide a competitive marketplace in the telecommunications arena.
2003	UNE Ruling challenged—Carriers do not need to provide Unbundled Network Elements (UNE) on high-speed data services.
2004	Court ruling on UNE states the FCC must regulate UNEs, not the presiding states. Leaves the door open to further challenges and evolution in the industry.

Figure 3-8 (cont.) Summary of major telecommunications events from 1872 to 2004.

Just as the industry started to settle down, with all the communications providers vying for a portion of each other's business, another change took place. The CLECs emerged, providing various new opportunities for organizations that weren't already in this business. This includes some of the providers of the CAP services of old. Newer players continue to emerge on the basis of either facilities-based or non-facilities-based provisioning. Resale of dial tone and resale of long distance had all gained a foothold, but a new approach had been added. The power utilities around the United States and Canada that have an infrastructure of fiber in their ground wire (see notes later on the ground wire optics in Chapter 6) now have the opportunity to deliver high-speed, fiber-optic communications right to a pole line near the customer's doorway. Many of the power utility organizations have applied for licensure to provide dial-tone, high-speed WAN communications, video, and TV-type services through the infrastructure under their ground wire. One-stop shopping might become a reality from an electric company that can provide cable, TV, Internet access, and your power—all on a single bill. As a commentary to this industry, most people in the U.S. are apparently enamored of their electric companies.

Most surveys indicate this is a direct contrast to how people feel toward their cable TV and telephone companies. These two providers are all too often looked on with scorn or distaste. If an electric company does offer dial-tone service, you may also expect a significant hit rate in terms of customers signing up to use that utility as the provider for communications services. If the electric companies can provide dial tone and cable TV for less, they will do so across an infrastructure used for their own internal process control systems. This means their cost for providing dial tone across this high-speed fiber backbone, which was put in place over the years, will be marginal.

The Telecom Act of 1996 in the U.S., as well as the events in the Canadian marketplace, is similar to what is happening in most countries around the world. In Europe and in many other places, monopolies that possess a communications bastion on dial-tone services are quickly eroding.

Chapter 3 Review

Chapter Summary

Describe the Initial Formulation of the Carrier Network

- Alexander Graham Bell offered his patent for the telephone to Western Union for $100,000. Western Union rejected the offer, thinking the telephone was a fad.

- Bell got private financial backing, and on July 1, 1877, the Bell Telephone Company was formed.

- Western Union realized its mistake. It employed a telephone from Dr. Gray's receiver and Thomas Edison's transmitter, and formed the American Speaking Telephone Company (ASTC).

- If you subscribed to one of these three individual companies, you couldn't communicate with a neighbor or business connected to the other company's network. Interconnectivity between carriers didn't exist.

- The Bell Telephone Company decided to create a sibling company in 1885 called American Telephone and Telegraph (AT&T) to address this void in long-distance communications. AT&T was responsible for creating and maintaining a long-distance voice and telegraph network.

- In 1899, AT&T had sustained such profitability and grown so large that the fledgling bought the assets of American Bell Company and incorporated the company into its operations.

- With the expiration of this patent, new providers began to spring up everywhere. Within 20 years, over 9,000 local providers existed. This competition was not welcomed by AT&T, which saw its market share being taken by these small upstarts.

- In an effort to ensure its position in the marketplace, AT&T decided it would not allow competitors to connect with its long-distance network.

- Eventually, when these smaller companies began to lose subscribers and became financially stressed from losing money, AT&T swooped in and bought them up. This increased AT&T's overall network.

- AT&T still wasn't satisfied and pushed the envelope even further. It undercut competitors' prices and price-fixed the market. At this point, AT&T was literally forcing out all the competition, leaving customers in many areas with no service as their local companies went out of business.

- As public outrage over AT&T grew, lawmakers got involved, investigating the practices being employed.

List the Major Legal Battles and Regulation, and Their Effects on the Industry

- The Sherman Antitrust Act authorized the federal government to start proceedings against trusts (or companies) to dissolve them in the name of public interest.

- Fearing that Congress would dissolve AT&T (which would have hurt tens of thousands of customers), AT&T decided to change its stance, settle the suit, and make changes. This was known as the Kingsbury Commitment.

- AT&T immediately made the following changes:

1. Relinquished its holdings in Western Union.

2. Stopped the practice of acquiring the independents, unless authorized by the Interstate Commerce Commission (ICC).

3. Allowed the independents to interconnect to the AT&T network.

In 1914, the Sherman Act was supplemented by the Clayton Antitrust Act, which created the Federal Trade Commission (FTC).

- The Graham-Willis Act of 1921 allowed AT&T to be a monopoly on one condition: as long as it promised to cable up the entire country.

- 1927 Radio Act granted federal responsibility of regulation between the Department of Commerce and the Interstate Commerce Commission (ICC).

- In 1934, the Federal Communications Commission (FCC) was created.

- In the 1950s, an innovation known as the Hush-a-Phone, an acoustically coupled device designed to eliminate noise and increase privacy, was tested before the FCC. Even though the courts allowed third-party devices to be connected to the network, any device of electrical nature was still prohibited if it wasn't from AT&T (manufactured in its Western Union Division).

- 1956 Consent Decree—AT&T could retain ownership of Western Electric if it only produced products for the Bell-operated companies.

- Carterphone decision—The FCC ruling was paramount in that direct electrical connection of devices to the network was allowed, so long as a protective coupler arrangement was still used.

- As long as a manufacturer could pass the requirements of the FCC registration (Part 68), then its products could be attached to the network without the use of the protective devices. This began what was called interconnect business.

- Execunet decision—MCI's initial intent was to provide alternate **private line services** (which it called *Execunet*) in a high-volume corridor. MCI took its interconnection request to the courts and won the capability to interconnect its network with the telephone company network. This established another common carrier (Sprint).

What Is the PSTN and What Are Its Addressing Mechanisms?

- Primary call-carrying capacity in the United States is through the Public Switched Telephone Network (PSTN).

- Through the North American Numbering Plan (NANP), we enable quick and discrete connection to any phone in the country.

Define RBOCs and Their Formulation

- This divestiture, or breakup of the Bell System, was called the Modified Final Judgment (MFJ).

- The 23 Bell Operating Companies were to be consolidated into 7 Regional Bell Operating Companies (RBOCs).* (Note, these seven RBOCs are now consolidated to four.)

List the Main Points of the Telecomm Act of 1996

- The Telecom Act of 1996 was the culmination of several years of trying to deregulate and provide a competitive marketplace in the telecommunications arena.

- This act allows the long-distance companies (IECs/IXC) to enter into new business opportunities. These include dial tone, cable TV services, high-speed Internet access, and two-way video communications capabilities after the infrastructure is in place.

- Likewise, the RBOCs could enter service areas formerly reserved for the IECs/EXCs. The caveat of the Telecom Act of 1996, however, is these companies must first prove that an open competitive environment exists at the local loop.

- The newcomers in local services were called Competitive Local Exchange Carriers (CLECs).

- With the passage of the 1996 Telecom Act, the Clinton Administration imagined an information superhighway. This allowed for the creation of the first Internet service providers (ISPs).

Define the Various Types of Carriers and the Services They Provide

- The RBOCs still provide local service, and since the 1996 Telecom Act, they are entering the long-distance and DSL arenas.

- The incumbent local exchange carrier (ILEC) is any company that has provided service in a locale. ILECs are sometimes ITPs; other times, ILECS are the RBOCs.

- Competitive Local Exchange Carriers (CLECs) provide dial tone, local, long-distance, and in some cases ISP access.

- IEC/IXC provide long-distance service.

- ISPs provide high-speed or dial-up Internet access.

---

*Be aware that this arena is constantly changing, as you pursue your career in the telecom field. Stay current on the regulations and how they affect the industry.

Key Terms for Chapter 3

1914 Clayton Antitrust Act *(78)*
1921 Graham-Willis Act *(79)*
1927 Radio Act *(79)*
1956 Consent Decree *(82)*
1982 Divestiture Agreement *(90)*
Bell Operating Companies (BOC) *(93)*
Carterphone Decision *(83)*
Competitive Local Exchange Carrier (CLEC) *()100*
Exchange Code *(86)*
Execunet Service Decision *(84)*
Federal Communications Commission (FCC) *(79)*
Hush-a-Phone *(81)*
Incumbent Local Exchange Carrier (ILEC) *(91)*
Independent Telephony Providers (ITP) *(92)*
Interconnectivity *(76)*
Interconnect Business *(83)*
Interexchange Carrier (IEC/IXC) *(100)*
Internet Service Provider (ISP) *(104)*
Judge Harold Greene *(90)*
Kingsbury Commitment *(78)*
Modified Final Judgment (MFJ) *(91)*
North American Numbering Plan (NANP) *(85)*
Numbering Plan Assignment (NPA) *(85)*
Private Line Services *(110)*
Public Switched Telephone Network (PSTN) *(74)*
Regional Bell Operating Companies (RBOC) *(92)*
Tariff *(97)*
Telecom Act of 1996 *(99)*
Unbundled Network Elements Platform (UNE-P) *(100)*

Key Term Quiz

1. _____ is the term for local dial-tone providers that are not one of the RBOCs.

2. The _____ was AT&T's first response to the threat of a breakup by the government.

3. The _____ is the phone network we utilize in America today.

4. The _____ was the government's first attempt to legislate the telecom arena. The powers of the _____ led to the Clayton Antitrust Act.

5. The _____ is the presiding governmental body with jurisdiction over the telecommunications arena. The FCC was created by the _____.

6. The _____ opened competition in all areas of telecom.

7. The _____ allowed AT&T to be a natural monopoly, as long as it promised to cable up the entire country.

8. _____ are the lines provided to the upstart telecommunication companies at wholesale prices. These lines are then resold to the public at discounted rates (over normal lines from RBOCs).

9. A _____ is a description of a service that is offered, the rate of charge for that service, and the rules under which the service is to be provided.

10. _____ was the presiding federal judge over the Modified Final Judgment. This judgment broke up the Bell System.

Multiple-Choice Quiz

1. How many levels were originally used in the network hierarchy?

    a. Two

    b. Three

    c. Four

    d. Five

2. What portions of the network remained with the Bell Operating Companies after the breakup of the telephone network?

    a. Long lines

    b. Long distance

    c. Local dial tone

    d. All of the above

3. How many regional offices were used across North America in the beginning?

    a. One

    b. Ten

    c. One hundred

    d. None of the above

4. What is the name given to the companies that were spun off from the AT&T organization?

    a. BOC

    b. RBHC

    c. ITP

    d. CLEC

5. What was the name given to the parent companies of the Bell Telephone Companies after the divestiture agreement?

    a. CAP

    b. RBHC

    c. RBOC

    d. CLEC

6. What is the name of the wiring that the telco brings to the consumer's door?

    a. Local loop

    b. Wire

    c. DSL

    d. Single mode fiber optics

7. Ten digits were used in the North American Numbering Plan (NANP). The first three digits are referred to as NPA assignments. The second three digits are referred to as:

    a. NANP

    b. NNX

    c. NXX

    d. NPA

8. When are we expected to run out of phone numbers?

    a. 2004

    b. 2010

    c. 2020

    d. 2030

9. The name given to the local telephone companies after the breakup of 1984 is _BOC_.

10. What do we call the telephone companies that used to be part of AT&T?

   a. ILEC

   b. CAP

   c. DLEC

   d. CLEC

11. How many independent LECs are there?

   a. 140,000

   b. 122,000

   c. 50,000

   d. 1,400

12. What is the term used for the new providers of dial tone? *1996*

   a. ILEC   *Incumbent local exchange – provider local service*

   b. LEC

   c. DLEC

   d. CLEC   *– competes with the already established local telephone companies*

13. What is the responsibility of the IEC/IXC?

   a. Dial tone

   b. Long distance

   c. Equipment

   d. None of the above

14. What are the newer data suppliers called? _CLEC_

15. When the independent telephone companies provide a service to their local community, they are called a(n) _____ILEC_____.

   a. CLEC   *– competitive local exchange*

   b. DLEC

   c. ILEC

   d. ITP

Essay Quiz

1. What practices did the Bell Telephone Company employ that resisted competition?

2. Regulation in the telecommunications arena was needed to provide fair business practices. What was the effect of declaring telecommunications a natural monopoly?

3. What are the benefits of divestiture?

4. What are the limitations of service provided by tariffs?

5. What is the intent of the 1996 Telecom Act?

Demonstration

The class should visit a Central Office or data center in the community and view the phone-switching system/data switches and connections involved. Contact your local representatives of the carrier to schedule a tour. Notice the complexity and sophistication of the PSTN environment today, and then answer the following questions.

1. Who is the manufacturer of the switch?

2. What is the model number?

3. How many lines does it provide?

4. What are the types of connections offered?

5. Note the basics of interconnection with an IEC/IXC provider(s) and the trunking involved. What are they?

6. What types of systems are in place to ensure the system remains on in case of emergency? Do they have fire suppression systems? HVAC? Battery back-up devices?

7. Is the actual facility specially engineered to resist natural disasters?

8. What is the average uptime in a percent? What does this translate to in days and hours of downtime? Does this figure surprise you?

If a CO is unavailable, an ISP would serve as an alternate. To schedule a tour, contact your local provider.

Lab Projects

In this activity, you need a computer with Internet access. If you do not have one, most local libraries now have Internet access and computers you can use.

1. Launch the computer's Internet web browser by double-clicking it. Or launch it from the Start menu.

2. Visit the FCC web site. Type this web address into the browser's Subject line: www.fcc.gov.

3. On the menu on the left side of the page, under the heading Strategic Goals, click the segment titled Competition.

4. Read the passages and focus on the 1998 rules—the three entry points for local competition. Have these goals been met?

5. Under the Objectives paragraph, how would you respond to the following topics?

- Foster sustainable competition across the entire telecommunications sector.
- Promote and advance universal service.
- Ensure that consumers have choices among communication services and are protected from anti-competitive behavior in the increasingly competitive telecommunications landscape.

Have these goals been met successfully since the 1996 Telecom Act?

1. Next, visit the site www.savecompetition.com and read the articles related to Unbundled Network Elements Platform (UNE-P) located on the left side toolbar.

2. Look at the article titled "Congressman John Conyers, Jr. from Michigan and Congresswoman Zoe Lofgren from California letter to U.S. Attorney General John Ashcroft requesting the Department of Justice investigate Bell companies' non-compete practices"(from Dec 18, 2002).

3. Read the other articles on the page from that timeframe. Have your views of competition and the achievement of the goals been supported or have your views been changed?

4. Write a summary of your findings. How have the RBOCs responded to competition? Compare this practice with the practices of AT&T in the late 1890s and early 1900s. Record your observations.

Chapter 4

Signaling System 7, Intelligent Networks, and Number Portability

LEARNING OBJECTIVES:

Once you complete this chapter, you will be able to:

Describe the signaling systems.

Understand what role signaling plays in a network.

Discuss the benefits of out-of-band signaling.

Learn why signaling is so important to the carriers.

Understand the basic call flow through the network using the signaling systems.

Dissect the pieces of the network from an Advanced Intelligent Network perspective.

Describe the components of an intelligent network.

Discuss the architecture of the entire network signaling, intelligence, and number portability issues.

Describe the application of signaling systems to enact intelligent features in the network.

The ability of a caller to go off hook anywhere in the world today, dial a string of digits, wait a mere few seconds, and then miraculously talk to someone continues to be a mystery to many. The telephony network's capability to establish the connection almost instantly and tear it down just as fast is what really creates the mystique. How can the network figure out where to send the call so quickly, get the connection, and ring the telephone on the other end? All this happens in under a second when dialing domestically (and only a few seconds when dialing internationally), and the user is oblivious to the intricacies of what occurs. What happens behind the scenes constitutes the backbone of the signaling systems. The networks are now dependent on the capability to handle subsecond call setup and teardown. Yet, at the same time, end users are expecting the networks to become more intelligent. Combining Intelligent Peripheral (IP) equipment and the signaling systems adds a new dimension to the industry and to the network as a whole. Moreover, now that you can take your number with you when you move within a town, the network is friendlier by far than ever before. Look at the combination of Local Number Portability (LNP), Signaling System 7, and the advanced intelligence in the network and you have a dynamic infrastructure to handle your every calling need.

Evolution of Signaling Systems

Several signaling systems have been introduced into telecommunications networks. This is referred to as Common Channel Interoffice Signaling System 7 (CCS7 for short). This mode of signaling, where the information is carried separately from the speech channels, is known as Common Channel Signaling (CCS). *CCS* can also result in the allocation of a single, dedicated resource to signaling and allow it to be responsible for the control of large numbers of individual voice circuits. The current one in use is called **Signaling System 7 (SS7)** in North America. *SS7* is simply a highly sophisticated and powerful form of CCS that uses a single high-speed channel to carry the signaling information for multiple speech channels.

Although the names are different, the functions and the purposes of the two systems are the same. As with many telecommunications systems, the North Americans do things somewhat differently than the rest of the world. Any signaling system is responsible for many chores in its set of core requirements, but one of the most significant reasons the carriers employ these systems is to save time and money on the network. Besides that, the carriers also want to introduce new features and functions of an intelligent network. The best signaling systems are designed to facilitate this intelligence in the network nodes designated as signaling devices, separate and distinct from the switching systems that carry the conversations.

Pre-SS7

Prior to the implementation of common channel SS7, Per-Trunk Signaling (PTS) was used exclusively in the networks. The *PTS* method was used for setting up calls between the telephone companies' exchanges. PTS carries the signaling information for an individual channel inside the same speech path we speak on, so the signaling is done on a trunk-by-trunk basis. This method continues to be used in some parts of the world where SS7 has not yet been implemented. Admittedly, the number of exchanges using the PTS method is declining and SS7 is gaining in its deployment worldwide. The network is always in a state of change, though, and this is no exception. PTS sends DTMF tones (touch-tones) or rotary pulses to identify the digits of the called party. The trunk also provides all the intelligence for monitoring and supervision (call seizure, hang up, answer back) of the call. Telephone systems at the customer's location (PBXs) that are not SS7-compatible use the PTS method.

When call setup is necessary on a long-distance call, each leg of the call repeats the call-setup procedure until the last exchange in the loop is reached. In essence, the call is being built by the signaling as progress is occurring on a link-by-link basis. As each link is added to the connection, the network is building the entire circuit across town or across the country. Each leg of the call setup takes approximately 2 to 4 seconds, using the configuration shown in Figure 4-1, with a total call setup taking approximately 6 to 12 seconds (at a minimum) to as much as 43 seconds from end-to-end.

Let's start back at the beginning. From there, we can build on the pieces as we proceed through the systems and the linkage. Most people take the process of making a call for granted. We just assume that dial tone will be there whenever we pick up the handset to make a call. We expect to get our calls through in a matter of seconds. The connections that must exist, anywhere in the country or the world, always have to be ready and available on a moment's notice. Yet, think of the process in slightly more definitive terms, and this timing and sequencing all makes sense. Years ago, this was considered a treat when the telephone companies introduced dial-up capabilities. However, it isn't that old!

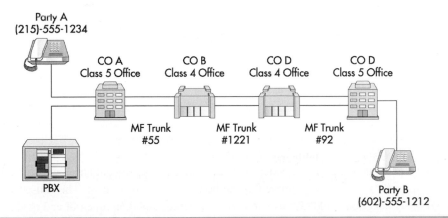

Figure 4-1 The call process in action shows the way a connection was built from a source to a destination. This process was quite slow in the beginning.

Call Processing

Assume this: to place a call, the user must first pick up the handset of the phone and obtain a dial tone. After receiving a dial tone, the user then dials the digits desired. For this example, the user on telephone number 215-555-0123:

1. Dials 1-602-555-1234.

2. As the digits are sent, Central Office (CO) *A* (the calling party's CO) performs routing analysis and seizes/out pulses 602-555-1234 on Trunk #55 connected to CO *B* (the calling party's tandem office). Notice the lead digit 1 is dropped.

3. From there, CO *B* receives the incoming trunk seizure and performs routing analysis.

4. It seizes (grabs the circuit)/out pulses the digits 602-555-1234 on Trunk #1221.

5. Next, CO *C* performs routing analysis and seizes/out pulses 555-1234 on Trunk #92 heading to CO *D*. Notice that the area code (602) is dropped.

6. CO *D* performs routing analysis and seizes the line connected to station 1234 and applies ringing voltage, causing the phone to ring.

7. Finally, the called party answers and conversation can flow between the parties.

Answer supervision and disconnect supervision are repeated onward through all switches and trunks in this process. What was not obvious during this entire process is the amount of time that was consumed from the beginning to the point where the call is answered. In the old days of telephony, this process may have taken as much as 43 seconds.

SPECIAL NOTE

The connection was "built" on a link-by-link basis. Any processing time at each switch (CO) was cumulatively added as each new link was included in the connection. That is 43 seconds of nonbillable time!

This is an inefficient use of the circuitry when a call is successful, and even more inefficient if the call fails because the carrier ties up the network and never completes the call. Hence, no revenue is generated. This inefficiency costs the carriers a significant amount of money, so something had to be done to improve this method of call establishment. The call-establishment part of the connection could take as much as 24 seconds, and then time out and never get to its final destination. However, the carrier tied up parts of the network without establishing a connection. Although this is inconsequential for a single call, a network carries hundreds of millions of calls per day, so this accumulated lost time is expensive.

Introduction to SS7

The ITU-TS developed a digital-signaling standard in the mid-1960s called Signaling System 6 (SS6), which would revolutionize the industry. Based on a proprietary, high-speed data-communications network, SS6 later evolved to SS7.

The success of the signaling standards lies in the message structure of the protocol and the network topologies. The protocol uses messages to request services from other entities on the network. The messages travel from one network element to another, independent of the actual voice and data they pertain to, in an envelope called a packet. A *packet* contains a small amount of data used on the network. A packet is like an envelope containing a single-page letter. The packet (envelope) also contains the addresses of the sender and the receiver and a stamp. The first development of the SS6 in North America was used in the United States on a 2,400-bps data link. Later, these links were upgraded to 4,800 bps. Messages in the form of data packets were used to request connections on voice trunks between COs. Placing 12 signal units (of 28 bits each) assembled packets into a data block. This is similar to the methods used today in SS7 architectures. SS6 used a fixed-length signal unit (28-bit signal units), but SS7 uses variable-length signal units. The most recent version of SS7 uses a 56-Kbps data link throughout North America, whereas in the rest of the world SS7 runs at 64 Kbps. The difference between 56 and 64 Kbps is that the local exchange carriers have not yet fully deployed the use of B8ZS[1] on the digital circuits. Consequently, the 56 Kbps is an anomaly in the SS7 networks. Further, the North American carriers were still installing SS6 through the mid-1980s (even though it was invented in the 1960s), while SS7 deployment began in 1983, leaving two separate signaling systems in use throughout North America. SS6 networks are slow, whereas SS7 is much faster. The use of a full DS-1 (1.544-Mbps) data link is still being considered in the North American marketplace.

4

SPECIAL NOTE

The SS6 network was installed in the mid-1960s right up through the mid-1980s, whereas the telephone companies began installing SS7 in 1983.

Purpose of the SS7 Network

The two primary uses of the SS7 network are call setup and transaction processing. Because SS7 is a network-signaling protocol, the information carried by SS7 is used to work with a variety of access signaling methods, such as Integrated Services Digital Network (ISDN) and Analog Display Services Interface (ADSI).

---

[1]The reference to bipolar 8 zero substitution (B8ZS) is covered in detail in Chapter 5

The primary purpose of SS7 was to access remote databases to look up and translate information from 800[2] and 900 number calls. The 800 number, also called a *global title,* is a fictitious address that needs to be translated using a Global Title Translation (GTT) into an SS7 network address. The 800 number address is converted to a ten-digit telephone number that represents a local telephone number (commonly called the POTS[3] number) in some part of the network. You can assume that if you dial 1-800-call-bud, the network will have to do some form of translation to determine where to route this call. Unlike other area codes that are geographically assigned—602 is in Arizona, 202 is in Washington, D.C., and so forth—800 codes may be used at any location. For example, one number may be used in Alaska, another in Hawaii, and still another in Florida. When a switch needs a translation, it identifies the type of translation needed (for example, 800 number to regular telephone number) and sends the request to a node whose routing table tells it where such translations can be performed. A single location in the routing table of the switch may serve to provide 800 number translations, 900 number translations, calling card validation, pre-paid validations, and so forth. Several benefits exist to using this lookup process. Carriers do not need to maintain a full database at each switching node. The SS7 protocol carries critical information that enables residential and business services to work harmoniously across the network. Both residential services (for example, automatic callback and calling number delivery) and business services [for example, network message service and network automatic call distribution (NACD)] depend on SS7 to work beyond the limits of a single switch. The second purpose of the SS7 network and protocols is to marry the various stored program controlled systems throughout the network. This allows quick and efficient call setup and teardown across the network in one second or less. Moreover, this integration provides for better supervision, monitoring, and billing systems integration. An additional benefit of the SS7 network is the replacement of the SS6 network.

Also important is to recognize how SS7 allows telephone companies to implement regulatory changes that open the industry to local competition. For example, the Telecommunications Act of 1996, discussed in Chapter 2, requires **Local Number Portability (LNP)** to ensure fair local competition. Without an SS7 infrastructure and SS7 interconnection between network providers, LNP cannot be implemented to any meaningful degree.

SS7 networks allow the introduction of additional features and capabilities into the network, such as call forwarding and caller ID display. This makes SS7 attractive to the carriers, so they can generate new revenues from the added features. SS7 also allows the full use of the channel for the talk path because the signaling is done out of band on its own separate channel. This is more efficient in the call setup and teardown process.

---

[2]800 service in this reference is to all toll-free calling plans, including 800, 888, 877, 866, and so forth.
[3]POTS is the acronym for Plain Old Telephone Service

Check what you have learned:

1. SS6 uses 12 different packets and they consist of _____ bits of information.

2. SS7 uses _____ length packets and has many various messages.

3. SS6 is slow, operating at less than 9,600 bps, whereas SS7 operates at _____ kbps.

4. The conversion of an 800 number to a POTS number is called a _____.

What Is Out-of-Band Signaling?

Out-of-band signaling is signaling that does not take place in the same path as the conversation. For *in-band signaling,* the dial tone, dial digits, and ringing occur over the same channel on the same pair of wires. After the connection has been established, our conversations are sent over the same path used for the signaling. Traditional telephony used to work this way. The signals to set up a call between one switch and another always took place over the same trunk that carried the call.

In early days, out-of-band signaling was used in the 4-kHz voice-grade channel. In Figure 4-2, you can see the 4-kHz channel. The telephone companies used band pass filters on their wiring to contain the voice conversation within the 4-kHz channel. The band pass filters were placed at 300 Hz (the low pass) and at 3300 Hz (the high pass). A portion of the range of frequencies above the 3300-Hz filter was used to carry these signals. The signals were sent

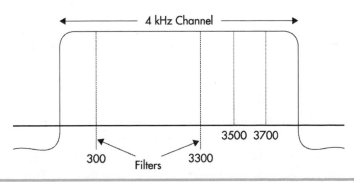

Figure 4-2 The standard 4-kHz channel was selected by the Bell System in the beginning. This channel is band-limited to 3 kHz through the band pass filters.

across the 3500- and 3700-Hz frequencies. Although these out-of-band frequencies worked, the number of tones that could be sent was limited, as were the number of states that could be represented by the tones.

Out-of-band signaling evolved to a separate digital channel for the exchange of signaling information. This channel is called a signaling link. *Signaling links* carry all the necessary signaling messages between nodes on a separate channel. Thus, when a call is placed, the dialed digits, trunk selected, and other relevant information are sent between switches using signaling links, rather than the trunks, which carried the conversation.

Note that while SS7 is only used for signaling between network elements, the ISDN D channel extends the concept of out-of-band signaling to the interface between the subscriber and the CO switch. With ISDN service, signaling that must be conveyed between the user station and the local switch is carried on a separate digital channel, called the D channel. The voice or data that constitute the call are carried on the B channel. In reality, the out-of-band signaling results in a virtual circuit because the signaling information is running on the same path as the B channels. Time slots on the same physical paths separate the signaling and the conversational data flows. Therefore, the signaling is virtually out of band, while it is physically in the same bandwidth.

Why Out-of-Band Signaling?

Out-of-band signaling has several advantages that make it more desirable than traditional in-band signaling:

- It allows for the transport of more data at higher speeds [56 Kbps can carry data much faster than Dual Tone Multiple Frequency (DTMF) out pulsing].

- It allows for signaling at any time in the entire duration of the call, not only at the beginning.

- It enables signaling to network elements to which there is no direct trunk connection.

The SS7 Network Architecture

If signaling is to be carried on a different path than the voice and data traffic it supports, then what should that path look like? The simplest design would be to allocate one of the paths between each interconnected pair of switches as the signaling link. Subject to capacity constraints, all signaling traffic between the two switches could traverse this link. This type of signaling is known as *associated signaling*.

Instead of using the talk path for signaling information, the new architecture includes the connection from the Signal Switching Point (SSP), which integrates with the Telco CO switches, to a device called the **Signal Transfer Point (STP)**. The SSP is nothing more than the CO switching system that will forward the SS7 traffic between SSPs and the **Signal Control Point (SCP)**. The STP is a packet-switching system that forwards the signaling information through the network. It is then the responsibility of the STP to provide the necessary signaling information through the network to effect the call setup.

When necessary, the STP sends information to the SCP for translation or database information on the routing of the call. The SCP is a database location where information about the network and users is maintained. The pieces combined to form the architecture of the SS7 network are described in Table 4-1 and shown in Figure 4-3 with the connection of the overall components.

Component	Function
Signal Switching Points (SSP)	*SSPs* are the telephone switches (end offices and tandems) equipped with SS7-capable software and terminating signaling links. They generally originate, terminate, or switch calls.
Signal Transfer Points (STP)	*STPs* are the packet switches of the SS7 network. They receive and route incoming signaling messages toward the proper destination. They also perform specialized routing functions.
Signal Control Points (SCP)	*SCPs* are the databases that provide information necessary for advanced call-processing capabilities.

Table 4-1 Components of the SS7 Networks Are Shown in This Table.

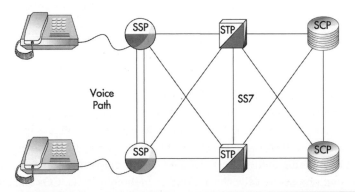

Figure 4-3 A typical interconnection of an SS7 network shows the links that all interconnect. This network is designed to be redundant to prevent catastrophic outages.

Several points should be noted:

- Paired STPs perform identical functions. They are redundant. Each SSP has two links (or sets of links), one to each STP of a mated pair. All SS7 signaling to the rest of the world is sent out over these links. Because the STPs are redundant, messages sent over either link (to either STP) will be treated equivalently.

- Four links (or sets of links) interconnect two mated pairs of STPs. These links are referred to as a *quad.*

- SCPs are usually (though not always) deployed in pairs. As with STPs, the SCPs of a pair are intended to function identically. Pairs of SCPs are also referred to as mated pairs of SCPs. Note that a pair of links does not directly join them.

- Signaling architectures such as this, which provide indirect signaling paths between network elements, are referred to as providing *quasi-associated signaling.*

SPECIAL NOTE

To achieve the carrier grade services with SS7, mated pairs of equipment and links were used. This is an expensive but necessary solution.

 ## What Do You Think?

In 1983, the telephone companies considering the installation of SS7 networks. During this initial period the design only called for the connection to a single STP and SCP from a CO. The links to and from the CO and all the components were set as simplex (meaning there was only a single link). In 1991, C&P Telephone Company (later Bell Atlantic and then Verizon) used STPs that had a single connection to the network. As the telephone companies were rolling out SS7, they signed major contracts with some smaller companies to provide their services and equipment. These agreements allowed them to separate from the original AT&T Western Electric organization.

C&P Telephone Company had major contracts with a company called DSC that manufactured SS7 switching equipment. In an effort to produce the extra switches and peripheral equipment, DSC escalated production and had little time to test the equipment before shipping it.

Then, in June 1991, a software glitch caused the entire SS7 Bell network to fail. The systems were functioning until, all of a sudden, the SS7 network components signaled all their peers to stop processing calls. As a result, even though all the COs and circuits were functioning properly, it took the network up to eight hours to process a local call. Calls to the LD network were fine because they used different routes and equipment pairs.

When the local CO receives the call from a telephone set, it captures the automatic number identification (ANI) information (this is the calling telephone number) and captures the dialed number information service (DNIS) or the called telephone number. Using these two pieces of information, the CO creates a data packet and sends it to the STP for call setup and look-ahead routing purposes. Because the STPs were no longer communicating across the separate SS7 network, they could not find or reserve the routing from one CO to the next. This happened even though the COs and the trunks connecting them were ready to process calls. Without a SS7 message, there is no communications.

The same problem occurred in the Los Angeles on the same day at the same time for the same duration. This, of course, was extremely troublesome.

The long-distance network was not immune to this problem. AT&T was doing some upgrades in its network that same year and had a similar problem, where it could not process a long-distance call for an entire day. Forty million long-distance calls offered to the AT&T network could not be sent. Even though the actual communications network was operating, the signaling network was malfunctioning.

Because of this and other outages, the FCC and the International Standards Committees decided to make the network fully redundant. This requires great expense to install two of everything (STP and SCP), as well as all the redundant links. However, we depend on the telephone networks for life-support services that must be available 24 hours a day.

Do you think we should skimp on costs or beef these networks up even more?

Take into account that the networks only work when the equipment and the links are all working together.

Basic Functions of the SS7 Network

The basic functions of the SS7 network include some of the following pieces of information:

- The exchange of circuit-related information between the switching points along the network.

- The exchange of non-circuit-related information between the databases and the control points within the network.

- The facilitation of features and functions by marrying the stored program control systems together throughout the network into a homogeneous network environment.

Further, the SS7 network allows these features to be put into place without unduly burdening the actual network call-path arrangements.

- It handles the rerouting of network traffic in the event of circuit failures by using automatic-protection switching services.

- Because it is a packet-switching concept, the SS7 network prevents misrouted calls, duplication of call requests, and lost packets (requests for service).

- It allows the full use of out-of-band signaling, using the international signaling protocol arrangements for call setup and teardown.

- It allows growth, so that new features and functions can be introduced to the network without major disruptions.

Signaling Links

SS7 signaling links are characterized according to their use in the signaling network. Virtually all links are identical in that they are 56-Kbps (or 64-Kbps) bidirectional data links that support the same lower layers of the protocol. What is different is their use within a signaling network. The bidirectional nature of these links allows traffic to pass in both directions between signaling points. Three basic forms of signaling links exist, although they are physically the same. They all use the 56-Kbps DS0A in North America and 64-Kbps DS0C data facilities in nearly every other portion of the world (except Japan, where they still use a 4.8-Kbps link). The three forms of signaling links are:

- **Associated signaling links**. The simplest form of signaling link is referred to as the associated signaling link, as shown in Figure 4-4. In *associated signaling,* the link is directly parallel from the end office with the voice path for which it is providing the signaling information. This is not an ideal situation because it would require a signaling link from the end office to every other end office in the network. Some associated modes of signaling are in use, but they are rare.

- Where you will most often find associated signaling deployed is at an end-user location using a single T1 and common channel signaling.

- In some cases, it may be better to directly connect two SSPs together via a single link. All related SS7 messages to circuits connecting the two exchanges are sent through this link. A connection is still provided to the home STP using other links to support all other SS7 traffic.

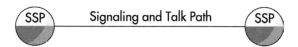

Figure 4-4 Associated signaling is the simplest form to use.

- **Nonassociated signaling links**. In the nonassociated signaling link arrangement, there is a separate logical path from the actual voice path, as shown in Figure 4-5. Multiple nodes arc usually involved to reach the end destination, while the voice may have a direct path to reach the final destination. Nonassociated signaling is a common occurrence in many SS7 networks.

● The primary problem with this form of signaling is the number of signaling nodes the call must use to progress through the network. The more nodes used, the more processing and delay that can occur. Nonassociated signaling involves the use of STPs to reach the remote exchange. To establish a trunk connection between the two exchanges, a signaling message will be sent via SS7 and STPs to the adjacent exchange.

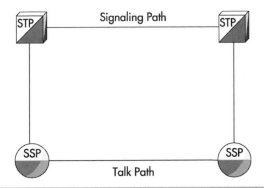

Figure 4-5 Nonassociated signaling separates the talk path from the signaling path.

● **Quasi-associated signaling links**. In quasi-associated signaling, both nodes are connected to the same STP. In quasi-associated signaling, a minimum number of nodes are used to process the call to the final destination, as shown in Figure 4-6. This is the preferred method of setting up and using an SS7 backbone because each node introduces additional delay in signaling delivery. By eliminating some of the processors on the setup, the delay can be minimized.

● SS7 networks favor the use of quasi-associated signaling. The signaling path is still through the STP to the adjacent SSP.

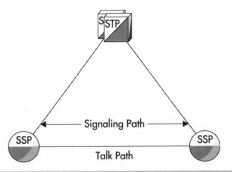

Figure 4-6 In quasi-associated signaling, the number of nodes involved in signaling is minimized.

The Link Architecture

Signaling **links** are logically organized by link type (*A* through *F*), according to their use in the SS7 signaling network. These are shown in Figure 4-7 with the full linkage in place.

A Link. An *access* (*A*) *link* connects a signaling end point (SCP or SSP) to an STP. Only messages originating from or destined to the signaling end point are transmitted on an *A* link.

B Link. A *bridge* (*B*) *link* connects one STP to another STP. Typically, a quad of *B* links interconnect peer (or primary) STPs (the STPs from one network to the STPs of another network). The distinction between a *B* link and a *D* link is rather arbitrary. For this reason, such links may be referred to as *B/D links*.

C Link. A *cross* (*C*) *link* connects STPs performing identical functions into a mated pair. A *C* link is used only when an STP has no other route available to a destination signaling point because of link failure. Note, SCPs may also be deployed in pairs to improve reliability. Unlike STPs, however, signaling links do not interconnect mated SCPs.

D Link. A *diagonal* (*D*) *link* connects a secondary (local or regional) STP pair to a primary (internetwork gateway) STP pair in a quad-link configuration. Secondary STPs within the same network are connected via a quad of *D* links. The distinction between a *B* link and a *D* link is rather arbitrary. For this reason, such links may be referred to as *B/D links*.

E Link. An *extended* (*E*) *link* connects an SSP to an alternate STP. *E* links provide an alternate signaling path if an SSP's home STP cannot be reached via an *A* link. *E* links are not usually provisioned unless the benefit of a marginally higher degree of reliability justifies the added expense.

F Link. A fully associated (*F*) *link* connects two signaling end points (SSPs and SCPs). *F* links are not usually used in networks with STPs. In networks without STPs, *F* links directly connect signaling points.

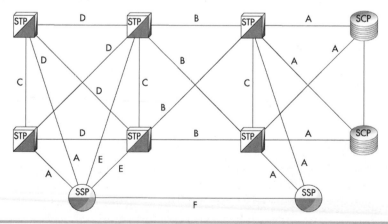

Figure 4-7 The various forms of links shown in an SS7 network.

Links and Linksets

A **linkset** is a grouping of links joining the same two nodes. A minimum of 1 link to a maximum of 16 links can make up the linkset. SSPs usually have one or two links connecting to their STPs, based on normal capacity and traffic requirements. This constitutes a one- or two-link linkset. SCPs have many more links in their linksets to handle the large amount of messaging for 800 and 900 numbers, calling cards, and Advanced Intelligent Networks (AIN) services.

Combined Linksets

Combined linkset is a term used to define routing from an SSP or SCP toward the related STP, where two linksets are used to share the traffic outward to the STP and beyond. The requirement is not that all linksets be the same size, but the normal practice is to have equally sized groupings of linksets connecting the same end node. Using a linkset arrangement, the normal number of links associated with a linkset is shown in Table 4-2.

4

Type of Link	Number of Links
A Links	Maximum of 16 links
B/D Links	Installed in quads up to a maximum of 8 links
C Links	Installed individually up to a maximum of 8 links

Table 4-2 The Configuration of Linksets.

Linksets are defined as a grouping of links between two points on the SS7 network. All links in a linkset must have the same adjacent node to be classified as part of a linkset. The switches in the network will alternate traffic across the various links to make certain the links are always available. This load spreading (or balancing) serves many functions. Some of these functions are:

- To indicate when a link fails.

- To recognize when congestion is occurring in the network.

- To use the links when traffic is not critical and to be aware when a link is down before it becomes critical.

Routes and Routesets

The term **routeset** refers to the routing capability of addressing a node within the SS7 network. Every node within the network has a unique address. This address is referred to as a *point code*. The addressing scheme or point code is the major routing characteristic of the CCS7 (SS7) network. The terms "routeset" and "point code" are synonymous.

The point code is made up of nine digits, broken down into three three-digit sequences. An example of this is 245-100-000. Reading the point code from left to right, we find that:

- The first three digits refer to the *network identifier* (245).

- The next three digits refer to the *cluster number* (100).

- The final three digits refer to the *member number* (000).

In any given network, there can be 256 clusters and each cluster can have 256 members. The network number in this case is for Stentor Communications in Canada.

The routing of SS7 messages to a destination point code can take different paths or routes. From the SSP perspective, there are only two ways out from the node: one toward each of its mated STPs. From that point on, the STPs decide what routes are appropriate, based on time, resources, and status of the network. From the SSP, various originating and terminating (destination) addressing scenarios are defined as follows:

- If the route chosen is a direct path using a directly connected link (SSP1-STPA), then the route is classified as an *associated route*.

- If the route is not directly connected via links (SSP1-SSP2), the route is classified as a *quasi-route*.

- All routing is controlled by nodal translations, providing flexible and network-specific routing arrangements. Figure 4-8 shows this.

SS7 Protocol Stack

The SS7 uses a four-layer protocol stack that equates to the seven-layer OSI model. These protocols provide different services, depending on the use of the signaling network. The layers constitute two-part functionality: the bottom three layers are considered the communications transmission of the messages, whereas the upper portion of the stack performs the data-processing function. Refer to Figure 4-9 for the protocols.

The stack shows that the bottom three layers make up the **message transfer part (MTP)**, similar to the X.25[4] network function. The *MTP* is the combination of the three bottom layers of the SS7 protocol stack (physical, data link, and network). At one time, SS7 messages were all carried on X.25. Now, newer implementations use SS7 protocols, whereas in older networks or third-world countries, X.25 may still be the transmission system in use. Some recent implementations have begun using SS7 over TCP/IP, but that is covered in the section "Signaling Control Transport Protocol (SCTP)."

---

[4]X.25 was an older packet data-networking protocol that was used for data transmission during the period of 1974 to about 1996, when the Internet protocols replaced X.25. For more details on X.25, see Chapter 7.

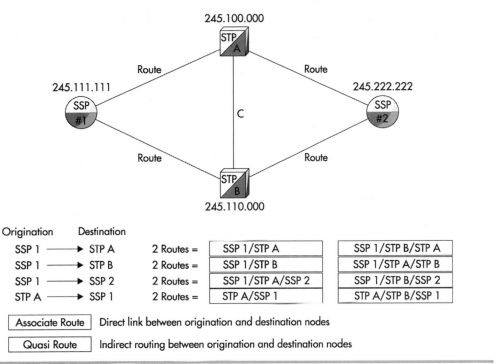

Origination	Destination			
SSP 1 ⟶ STP A		2 Routes =	SSP 1/STP A	SSP 1/STP B/STP A
SSP 1 ⟶ STP B		2 Routes =	SSP 1/STP B	SSP 1/STP A/STP B
SSP 1 ⟶ SSP 2		2 Routes =	SSP 1/STP A/SSP 2	SSP 1/STP B/SSP 2
STP A ⟶ SSP 1		2 Routes =	STP A/SSP 1	STP A/STP B/SSP 1

Associate Route	Direct link between origination and destination nodes
Quasi Route	Indirect routing between origination and destination nodes

Figure 4-8 Routes and routesets define the various choices connecting the signaling points.

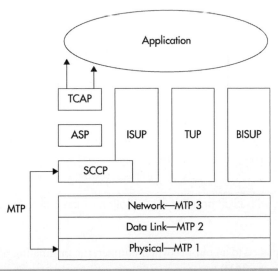

Figure 4-9 The SS7 protocol is specifically designed for the reliable delivery of the messages.

When necessary, the SCCP is used as part of the MTP to support access into a database and, occasionally, for the **ISDN User Part**. This extra link is the equivalent of the transport layer of the OSI model supporting the Transaction Capabilities Application Part (TCAP).

The *SS7 network* is an interconnected set of network elements used to exchange messages in support of telecommunications functions. The *SS7 protocol* is designed both to facilitate these functions and to maintain the network over which they are provided. Like most modern protocols, the SS7 protocol is layered. Functionally, the SS7 protocol stack can be compared to the Open Systems Interconnection (OSI) reference model. OSI is a seven-layer stack designed to model several communications and transparent functions. The SS7 protocol stack serves a similar purpose.

Like any other stack, the *SS7 protocol stack* is specifically designed for reliable data transfer between different signaling elements on the network. Guaranteed delivery and the prevention of duplication or lost packets are crucial to network operations. To satisfy differing functions, the stack uses various upper-layer protocols, but consistently uses the same lower layers.

Basic Call Setup with ISUP

The important part of the protocols is the call setup and teardown. The ISUP or ISDN user part is responsible for the protocols for call setup and teardown. This next example is shown in Figure 4-10.

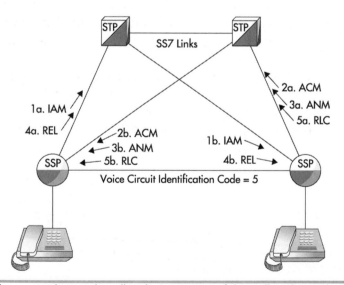

Figure 4-10 Call setup with ISUP handles the initiation of the call to the end point.

When a call is placed to an out-of-switch number, the originating SSP transmits an ISUP **initial address message (IAM)** to reserve an idle trunk circuit from the originating switch to the destination switch (1a). The IAM includes the originating point code, the destination point code, the circuit-identification code dialed digits, and, optionally, the calling party numbers and name. In this example, the IAM is routed via the home STP of the originating switch to the destination switch (1b). Note that the same signaling links are used for the duration of the call, unless a link failure condition forces a switch to use an alternate signaling link. The destination switch examines the dialed number and determines that it serves the called party, and that the line is available for ringing. The destination switch transmits an ISUP address complete message (ACM) to the originating switch (2a) via its home STP to indicate that the remote end of the trunk circuit has been reserved. The destination switch rings the called party's line and sends a ringing tone over the trunk to the originating switch. The STP routes the ACM to the originating switch (2b), which connects the calling party's line to the trunk to complete the voice circuit from the calling party to the called party. The calling party hears the ringing tone on the voice trunk.

In this example, the originating and destination switches are directly connected with trunks. If the originating and destination switches are not directly connected with trunks, the originating switch transmits an IAM to reserve a trunk circuit to an intermediate switch. The intermediate switch sends an ACM to acknowledge the circuit reservation request, and then transmits an IAM to reserve a trunk circuit to another switch. This process continues until all trunks required to complete the connection from the originating switch to the destination switch are reserved.

When the called party picks up the phone, the destination switch terminates the ringing tone and transmits an ISUP answer message (ANM) to the originating switch, via its home STP (3a). The STP routes the ANM to the originating switch (3b), which verifies that the calling party's line is connected to the reserved trunk and, if so, initiates billing.

If the calling party hangs up first, the originating switch sends an ISUP release message (REL) to release the trunk circuit between the switches (4a). The STP routes the REL to the destination switch (4b). If the called party hangs up first or if the line is busy, the destination switch sends an REL to the originating switch, indicating the release cause (for example, normal release or busy).

On receiving the REL, the destination switch disconnects the trunk from the called party's line. It next sets the trunk's state to idle, and then transmits an ISUP release complete message (RLC) to the originating switch (5a) to acknowledge the release of the remote end of the trunk circuit. When the originating switch receives (or generates) the RLC (5b), it terminates the billing cycle and sets the trunk state to idle in preparation for the next call.

ISUP messages may also be transmitted during the connection phase of the call (that is, between the ISUP ANM and REL messages).

SS7 Applications

At this point, we switch gears and look at some of the applications that are possible because of SS7 implementations. The use of AIN features, ISDN features, and wireless capabilities became a reality because of the functions of SS7 integration. Some of the features are listed here. Remember, they are formulated and possible because of SS7, although they may be part of other systems or concepts. These include:

- 800/900 services

- Enhancements in 800 services within call centers

- 911 enhancements

- CLASS[5] features

- Calling card toll-fraud prevention

- Credit card approval and authentication

- Software/virtual-defined private networks

- Call tracing

- Call blocking

All these features and functions are possible with the SS7 protocols and signaling systems. Many of the features are possible through the stored-program CO switches. However, when you activate features that work across the network (or the world), SS7 facilitates the delivery mechanism. Other systems will be introduced in the future to implement more intelligence in the networks, such as the AINs, but they will require the infrastructure of the signaling systems to enact and carry their messages.

What Do You Think?

Can you imagine what it would be like if we still had the old signaling systems and "dumb" telephone switches? Features like call forwarding, voice mail, and calling number display would all be nonexistent. Can you imagine what it would be like trying to make a call to a traveling person? The phone might ring off the hook and never get answered. You would not know if the person was around, traveling, or even alive!

Intelligence in the network is important. Think about all the different ways the use of this network intelligence and signaling affects your life. Discuss it among your peers and see if you can come up with a list of the various ways these improvements impact your daily life.

---

[5]CLASS is the acronym for Custom Local Access Signaling Systems, which add features to a telephone line and a Centrex line. These are designer features, and the user usually gets to pick and choose the ones desired from a large list of 400+ features.

Intelligent Networks (INs)

Intelligent Networks (INs) consist of intelligent nodes (computer peripherals), each capable of processing and communicating with one another over low- to mid-speed data communications links. All nodes in the intelligent SS7 network are called signaling points that work with packet transmissions. A signaling point has the capability to do the following:

- Read the packet address

- Determine if the packet is for that node

- Route the packet to another signaling point

Signaling points provide access to the SS7 network and the various databases on the network. They also act as transfer points.

The switching network contains Service Switching Points (SSP) and provides the basic infrastructure needed to process calls and other related information.

- The SSP provides the local access because it emerged as the CO. The SSP can also be other tandem points on the network or an ISDN interface for the Signal Transfer Point (STP).

- The STP provides packet switching for message-based signaling protocols for use in the IN and for the SCP.

- The SCP provides access to the IN database. The SCP is connected to a Service Management System (SMS).

- SMS provides a human interface to the database, as well as the capability to update the database when needed.

- IPs provide resource management of devices, such as voice announcers. IPs are accessed by SCP when appropriate.

The IN enables customers to tailor their specific service requirements within hours instead of days. Full IN implementation is expected to continue evolving. Some of the features available include the following:

- Find-me service

- Follow-me service

- Single (personal) number plans

- Call routing service

- Computer control service

- Call pickup service

Advanced Intelligent Networks (AIN)

AIN is a collection of components performing together to deliver complex call-switching and handling services. The SSP is the CO that provides robust call-switching capabilities. When switching decisions require complex call processing, the SSP relies on the SCP, a subscriber database, and it executes service logic. The SSP uses SS7 signaling, specifically TCAP messages, requesting the SCP to determine the best way to handle the call. The process supports telephony features, including 800 and 900 calling, credit/debit card calling, call forwarding, and virtual private networks (VPNs). AIN has promised an architecture that is amenable to rapid development and deployment of new services. How to maintain the stringent performance requirement of a CO service within this rapidly changing environment is a major challenge in the advancement of AIN.

IPs and Service Nodes (SN) are elements of the AIN; they must be reliable to be deployed and used in the CO. IPs work in cooperation with SCP to provide media services in support of call control. Service nodes combine the functions of the SCP and the IP. When viewed as point nodes in the network, these elements (IP and SN) are subject to failure and require redundant components and multiple communication paths. Software and procedures in support of CO reliability are also required.

When switching decisions require complex voice processing services, the SCP cannot always provide all the required services to the SSP. The SCP cannot provide termination of voice circuits and play recorded messages, collect touch-tone input, or perform other voice-processing services. The call must be redirected to an IP.[6] The IP provides the voice processing services unavailable from the SCP.

AIN provides more features and functions that are not provided by INs. AIN does not specify the features and services, but it does specify how end users use them. An essential component in AIN is the Service Creation Element (SCE). Today, telco personnel at end offices handle service configuration and changes. The SCE specifies the software used to program end-office switches. Over time, the SCE will reside at the users' organization, allowing customers to tailor their services on an as-needed basis, without telephone company assistance.

Some of these enhanced features available include the following items:

- Calling name delivery

- Call rejection

---

[6]The use of the Intelligent Peripheral (IP) should not be confused with the acronym for the Internet Protocol (IP). Unfortunately, many acronyms are the same, but they have different meanings.

- Call screening (visual or audio)

- Call trace

- Call trap

- Personal identification numbers (PINs)

- Selective call acceptance

- Selective call forwarding

- Spoken caller identification

Some of these features are already available at certain COs, but they are not yet ubiquitous. Limitations to these services are based on the capabilities of end-office switching equipment—service offerings and tariffs will not be consistent throughout telephone companies.

Information Network Architecture

Information Network Architecture (INA) is still in development and is viewed by many as the successor to AIN. Others, however, believe that two separate systems will eventually develop. AIN is designed to facilitate the voice network, whereas INA will manage the broadband network. The common belief is that INA will provide better utilities for managing new broadband services offered by telephone companies.

Intelligent networking delivers computer and telephone-integration capabilities inside the network. Two major market forces and architectural frameworks are merging to create the most explosive network services opportunities. Enterprise **Computer Telephony Integration (CTI)** applications and AIN services are being integrated to provide an array of advanced

 Try This

Look in the front of your local telephone company's phone book to see how many of the previous features are available where you live. Make a list of which ones are available.

If the phone book does not carry this information:

Call your local provider and ask what features are available, and then ask for some of the specific ones previously listed. See how many features the local provider offers in your area.

carrier-delivered services. *CTI* is the use of computers to perform telephony applications. Some of the features that will be available to consumers include:

- Virtual call centers

- Consumer interactive applications

- Centrex productivity enhancements

- Formal and informal call centers

- Virtual ACDs

Combining AIN and CTI Services

The evolution of AIN and CTI services underpins the marriage of these two architectural frameworks. AIN has its roots in the Local Exchange Carriers' (both ILEC and CLEC) and Inter Exchange Carriers' (IEC) desire for vendor- and switch-independent network architectures.

Improving the speed of service provisioning and delivering advanced network services are crucial to maintain a competitive posture. As early as 1986, Ameritech (now SBC) began proposing a concept called Feature Node Service Interface (FNSI). Through successive industry efforts, AIN emerged as a network standard in the early '90s. Figure 4-11 shows the basic framework of the AIN architecture.

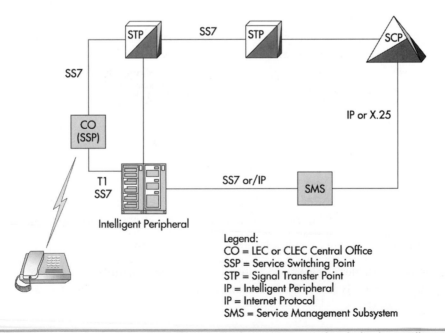

Figure 4-11 AIN architecture framework is a simple architecture that links the intelligence within the network.

What Do You Think?

Virtual means "not quite" or "almost." Is a computer to telephone integration scheme that creates a virtual call center full of people or "not quite" people? What do you call an "almost" person?

Carriers and manufacturers alike keep coming up with silly ways of naming services without consideration for the dictionary. Or do they?

Advanced Intelligent Network (AIN) Architecture

The arrival of the AIN has little effect on network architecture. The reason is this: the purpose of the AIN is neither the creation of new services nor the redesign of the SS7 network. Instead, the AIN is an attempt to standardize and define the best ways in which new services might be developed and deployed.

One node that appeared in the IN assumes a greater role in the AIN. This is the SMS that provides a human/database interface. Currently employed in the IN, the SMS utilizes a man-machine interface and command-line language for building services. AIN approaches to service building will increase the importance of the SMS to the network. The following drawing illustrates AIN architecture. This node is seen in Figure 4-12.

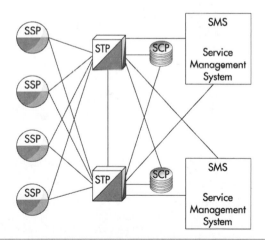

Figure 4-12 The SMS in an IN links the human to a machine (database).

CTI is a complement to AIN proposed by the PBX manufacturers. The end users want:

- Advanced applications
- Faster feature delivery
- Control and customization of applications

Using an external processor, custom applications are configured to enhance the functionality of a PBX, especially in an Automatic Call Distribution (ACD) environment. Figure 4-13 shows the basic connections in a CTI application.

Both CTI and AIN use an external processor to deliver advanced complementary services to the switch. The *switch* controls call-processing access to the external processor via an open interface. Both provide a graphical user interface (GUI)-based Service Creation Environment (SCE) for rapid service and application configuration. IPs provide additional context information for call treatment. Integrated voice-response units are the most widely deployed IPs. Reporting, billing interfaces, and real-time monitoring tools are available in both.

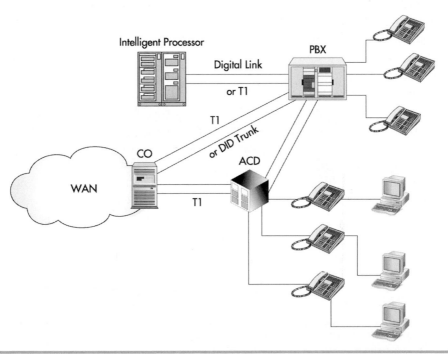

Figure 4-13 Basic CTI application uses the IP to perform the functions necessary to service the end user.

With the introduction of the IN, these two technologies were brought together by necessity. Services rich in voice-processing content and requiring an abundance of digitized voice storage could no longer be created solely with the innate capabilities of the switch. The variety of service offerings, their complexity, and, in many cases, the requirement for multilanguage support quickly outpaced the voice-processing capabilities and capacities of the switch. Voice-processing systems were integrated with switching systems to support these new services.

The Intelligent Peripheral

The SCP software programming (usually referred to as the Application or the Process) allows it to deal with the requests contained in the messages sent to it through the SS7 network. These messages may be in the form of a query sent from a switch. The SCP is capable of interpreting the request, extracting the required data from a database, and returning it in a form understood by the switch software.

The same functionality allows the SCP to access and make available services of another kind at a different type of signaling point in the network. Sometimes, this entails invoking features for which the switch is not equipped. At other times, it entails utilizing an IP. The IP is home to a process that can deal with the requests from the SCP by providing the services of a variety of devices.

A caller may dial a frequently called number by saying the name of the party desired. Many of the cell phones have this feature built in. Commercials have been shown using this feature, whereby the caller speaks into the telephone and says something like, "Call home." The call gets placed correctly because the word "home" is an entry in a database that can be easily retrieved. The database provides the normal telephone number, which is then returned to the switch where the caller is connected. The switch can now route the call exactly as it would have if the caller had dialed the home phone number.

Providing a voice-translation peripheral at every local CO would be cost-prohibitive. The cost of the service, therefore, would be beyond the reach of normal users. Worse yet, when someone came up with an improvement in the service, every switch in the world would have to be reprogrammed before the improvement became universally available.

For these reasons, it makes much more sense to keep the equipment (and the software necessary to make it work) at a limited number of locations around the network. Thus, the local switch only needs to know where to send the message to obtain a phone number translation of the verbal request.

The IP provides these features. The caller can make a verbal request, press buttons on the phone keypad, or use a computer keyboard or another input device for services from another system. Future telephones and cell phones will all have a limited version of the computer keyboard. The devices available at the IP will be able to receive and translate all of these different ways of making a service request.

On receiving the request sent to it by the SCP, the IP will respond by returning data to the switch or terminal, or by sending a voice announcement to the telephone of the caller.

Some of the services provided by the IP may be services provided directly to the switch rather than to a telephone subscriber. In this way, even older, less-capable switching equipment may be able to respond to and/or send signaling it was not designed to understand. And, the switch would be able to respond to requests for services offered by new technologies simply by subscribing to the services of an IP where those technologies can be found.

Service requests are sent through the SS7; therefore, the IP requires links to the SS7. On the other hand, the services provided (various signaling types, and so forth) are related to a switch and must be delivered in the voice network. This means the IP must also have trunk connections into the PSTN.

The IP must provide voice-circuit support and some mechanism for obtaining information about an incoming call. Several mechanisms are available for capturing call information, including the following items:

● ISUP signaling

● ISDN signaling

● In-band DTMF signaling (as previously described)

● DTMF (the touch-tones from the phone as previously described)

BellCore[7] developed transaction protocols to handle the call processing, using an 1129-protocol specification. The 1129 transaction is triggered when a call comes in and is initiated with the delivery of a message from the IP to the SCP. Thereafter, the transaction continues with queries issued by the SCP and synchronous responses to these queries returned by the IP, reporting results of the requested action.

The BellCore recommendations call for multiple IPs within the network. Each is capable of working with multiple independent-service control points via communication across multiple data paths. Each IP operates as though it is distributed across multiple host platforms interconnected by multiple LANs. Introducing IP into an AIN environment is a major expense, requiring significant investment in hardware, networking, and supporting software.

The BellCore philosophy is to provide redundant components and data paths, eliminating single points of failure wherever possible. However, many situations exist whereby an IP or SN provides a service, yet the service does not warrant redundant infrastructure. Therefore, a solution is required for the IP or SN to provide suitable reliability inherently.

---

[7]BellCore is now called Telcordia Technologies Inc.

Intelligent Peripheral Services   The IP must be capable of establishing and maintaining communication with multiple SCPs. Furthermore, it handles the following functions:

- Encoding and decoding complex messages

- Interpreting these messages

- Performing the requested service

It must also be capable of switching functions, including the following:

- Call setup

- Transfer

- Call teardown

- Detect call presentation and abandonment.

- Process requests requiring service logic

- Access databases

Finally, beyond the capabilities described in the 1129 interface specification, the IP needs support services, such as logging, administration, alarm processing, statistics gathering and reporting, and database and network access. The IP falls into two categories of service: application processing and resource processing.

The application processor supports the call-processing logic and access to the databases and data networks. It initiates transactions, receives instructions, and reports success or failure of the action. The application processors also require connections to communication networks and hosts. An IP needs multiple data paths because it must be able to contact multiple hosts and survive the loss of a single communication pathway. It needs to communicate with SCPs to receive instructions and communicate with switching facilities to terminate circuits. It also needs to communicate with other network elements, such as the SMS (for provisioning), and with internal and external databases. This requires multiple data paths and alternate routing.

The resource processor manages the switching, voice-channel facilities, and media-processing resources. The media processing normally requires multiple processors and disk storage to handle the media streams. It may also require switching, such as a time-division multiplexer or external switches.

These two elements are different from each other. They perform different functions; consequently, they require different hardware and software-processing elements.

The architecture for AIN with the SSP, SCP, and IP in place on the stack is shown in Figure 4-14.

4

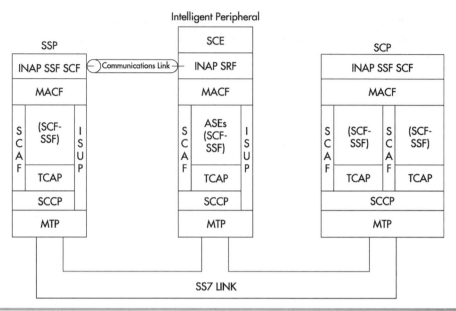

Figure 4-14 The AIN protocol stack uses an IMS to perform many of the service functions.

Software Architecture: Client, Router, Server The objective is to build an IP in which application processors drive multiple resource processors. This requires software on the application processor capable of supporting the physical structure. A client-router-server scheme is used.

The client includes the application, media-processing logic, and the controls; it also manages the resources and drives a state machine. The IP, driven by the 1129 message set, operates as a state machine. This state machine is driven by messages from the SCP and by trigger events from the network.

The router handles message routing and session management functions. It makes decisions about how to route traffic and load balance.

The servers support both local and remote devices. The local devices include local file systems, databases, and locally attached devices, such as encryption boxes. The remote devices are networks and hosts. The remote servers must be able to support multiple processors

The Application

The application must be capable of supporting real-time, online updates, which must be done without any disruption of service. The system administrator must be able to introduce new instructions and commands/responses without affecting service. On the fly changes to parameters, such as timers and retry limits, are necessary. The state machine itself must remain operational without call loss while the application logic is being changed.

Possible Outcomes for AIN

Building IPs in support of an AIN is possible. These peripheral devices must be economical and reliable enough to operate in a CO environment. Multiple hardware elements are required. Communication paths must be redundant.

Estimates are that by 2007, telephone-industry spending will be about $27 billion. The prediction is that products and expenses supporting AIN will expand exponentially. Approximately $5 billion was spent on AIN products and services in 1998. Telephone industry spending on AIN will include STP, SCP, SSP, IPs, Service Creation Environments, and various hybrid products.

Recent studies indicate that the demand for AIN features and functions will be driven by the following factors:

- Demand for more customer control and services:

  Businesses are placing more strategic reliance on telecommunications. They need features and functions tailored to their specific needs. The number of functions and services required will be dictated by the lifestyle and competitive environment of the end user. AIN is the only way to support such requirements. Services will have to be user-friendly and somewhat network-centric to meet the demands of the future user.

- Greater geographical distribution and newer technologies:

  Future niche markets will probably emerge. They need to be widely accessible by the suppliers (LEC and IEC) to be effective and acceptable. AIN services must also become technologically stable to support multiple-vendor products and service on multiple-switching systems. AIN-based services must find a way to work across carrier boundaries.

- Mobility and mobile applications in a changing world:

  Business and personal uses of cellular phones, voice mail, pagers, and e-mail are growing exponentially. The need to support a mobile user is now equally important. AIN-based services must use cross-vendor products and billing mechanisms to be effective. Wireless networks are among the fastest growing applications and services in the industry. The growth rate in this area shows little sign of slowing. Personal Communications Services (PCS) networks are growing as rapidly and demanding more services. Soon, an AIN will need to allow calls to a user via a single number, regardless of where that user resides. We now have more than 1 billion wireless users in the world.

4

- Internet, broadband, and multimedia:

  A CIR[8] report notes that most of the services AIN is currently concerned with are narrowband and voice-oriented. However, the CIR report predicts that many of the services currently identified with AIN will migrate to the Internet. In addition, AIN concepts will increasingly be required for multimedia and broadband services.

Focus

SS7 is an essential technology supporting and developing ISDN, IN, mobile (cellular) telephony, PCS and information systems, personal communications, and many other applications. Currently, this technology is being pursued by the telecommunication industry, including carriers, large private networks, switch manufacturers, and an increasing number of software developers. The traditional methods of in-band signaling and other common channel-signaling methods in the telecommunication networks have given way to an overlay network using a more capable, layered SS7 protocol.

Although the primary function of SS7 is to handle call control-signaling requirements for voice and data transmission services, it can provide a number of advanced services by use of network databases. These include toll-free and alternate billing, rerouting, virtual networks, and other highly sophisticated telecommunications services denoted by IN services.

Additionally, the **transaction capability** of the SS7 protocol makes it applicable to a broad range of new services dealing with remote operations. In cellular telephony, SS7 is used for mobility management and handover functions.

IN describes architecture designed to facilitate the implementation of highly sophisticated telecommunications services, including:

- Features and functions

- Multivendor interworking

- Differing priority services offered by fixed networks, mobile networks, and PCS

This millennium will hold several benefits and service advantages unavailable in the past. These advantages will all be geared toward satisfying the changing needs and demands of the consuming public. As IN and AIN evolve, newer services will be introduced. The various new providers, such as the CLECs and the CATV companies, will compete to meet the one-stop shopping demands of the customer. AIN will be one of the deciding factors steering consumers to the various providers. Providers who implement AIN features first will have an edge in acquiring a customer base.

---

[8]Communications Industry Reports is a research firm specializing in market research and analysis of the telecommunications industry.

For now, the edge goes to the incumbent LECs because they own the infrastructure. However, changes may occur that could allow others to capture their share of the market.

SS7 and Internet Protocol (IP)[9]

Much of the growth in SS7 networks requires that the carriers add dedicated 56-Kbps or 64-Kbps circuits between and among the nodes. As already discussed, most carriers add these circuits in redundant pairs to provide reliability. The voluminous growth of database dips and SS7 queries, because of network expansion, AIN, LNP, and **Wireless LNP (WLNP)**, means that more dedicated circuits must be installed. Network operators can no longer accurately predict the volume or growth rates of their SS7 circuits and networks. The amount of additional traffic required in the wireless networks, that is, **Global System for Mobile (GSM)** networks with General Packet Radio Service (GPRS) and SMS service, is approaching explosive proportions. To accommodate this growth, carriers have been over-provisioning to ensure that network blockage will not occur.

4

WATCH OUT!

Earlier, we described IP as an Intelligent Peripheral. Now we are describing it as the **Internet Protocol**.

The use of three-letter acronyms (TLAs) is running amok in the industry. Sooner or later, we will have acronym overload. Can you imagine what it would be like to show up for class and have an IP and NPA (instructor present and no preset agenda)?

As more SS7 links are being installed in the SS7 network, devices such as STPs, SCPs, home location registers (HLR), and visitor location registers (VLR)[10] are increasing in size and complexity. HLR and VLRs are databases. The *HLR* is the one that owns a user's account (the telephone number and all related information). The *VLR* is a temporary database used to determine your location when you roam from one place to another. Moreover, these databases require faster processors to handle the loads being generated. High-speed database engines and processing units are expensive. Because the systems are installed in redundant architectures, they become less efficient because operators must connect myriad devices in the network. Each time a new STP or HLR/VLR is added to the network, a reconfiguration of the entire network is necessary, resulting in additional network-management costs.

---

[9]This use of acronyms becomes complicated whenever the acronyms are the same for different terms, such as Intelligent Peripheral and Internet Protocol

[10]The use of the HLR and VLR in a wireless network is the same as the SCP in the wireline network.

Network planners are anxious to find alternatives that can reduce their STP or HLR port consumption and delay major unit replacements. Today's SS7 network planners face the following obstacles:

- Their SS7 networks are growing exponentially.

- Dedicated 56- to 64-Kbps SS7-link solutions are expensive when we contrast that to the shared resources of other networks.

- Ports on the nodes (that is, STP, HLR/VLR) are being rapidly consumed.

- New technology may be required; replacing existing STPs is expensive.

HELP! I'VE FALLEN AND I CAN'T GET UP!

When we use SS7 and fixed communications at a specific location, it is easy to deliver the caller ID when dialing 911. What happens when you are running around with a cell phone? If you call on a cell phone and get connected to a 911 dispatch center, the ability to track you is much more complex. You might not get rescued in time.

Now, let's add to the complexity by calling from a mobile phone and use the IP. How on Earth do you think the emergency teams will ever find you?

This is why so much money is spent on the networks today, to ensure that "after you have fallen, someone will help you get up."

The carriers began to look for other solutions. The following questions were initially considered:

1. With all the emphasis on moving to "shared packet networks," would it be possible to reliably transport SS7 messages on an IP network?

2. Can the cost advantages be maximized through a shared IP network?

3. Is there a way to ensure the reliability of an IP datagram if it is carrying SS7 traffic?

4. Can other solutions be used to minimize the load on the existing nodes in the SS7 network?

The availability of cost-effective hardware and the growing global knowledge of IP networking have led many of the carriers to reconsider the way they deploy the SS7 networks. Advancements in reliable IP communication (using various tools such as MPLS, QoS,[11] RSVP,[12] and others) and the market successes of **Voice over IP (VoIP)** allow the carriers to

---

[11]Quality of Service, a networking term that specifies a guaranteed throughput level.
[12]Multiprotocol Label Switching (MPLS), Quality of Service (QoS), and Resource Reservation Protocols (RSVP) are all protocols developed to improve quality of service and reliability of data delivery on an IP network.

consider the next logical step—the convergence of SS7 and IP networks. For the network planners, any means or device for off-loading SS7 traffic must be:

- Capable of handling carrier-grade traffic loads

- PSTN/SS7 network transparent—there must be no additional point codes and no network reconfiguration requirements

- As reliable for message transfers as the current PSTN

- Remotely manageable with support for existing operations standards such as Simple Network Management Protocol (SNMP)

The industry response to this dilemma is the development of a new standard protocol for routing SS7 messages over IP, called SCTP. This Internet Engineering Task Force (IETF) standard ensures the reliable transmission of SS7 messages routed over IP networks.

4

Signaling Control Transport Protocol (SCTP)

Signaling Control Transport Protocol (SCTP) is an IP transport protocol developed by the Signal Transport (SIGTRAN) working group of the IETF. The basic structure of the SCTP stack is shown in Figure 4-15 with its sublayers defined. *SCTP* is used to replace the User Datagram Protocol (UDP) and Transmission Control Protocol (TCP) transports for performance and security critical applications, such as voice signaling where protocols such as SS7 and ISDN are carried over IP. To place it on an equivalent level of the SS7 protocol, it is more related to the MTP-2 layer, as shown in Figure 4-16.

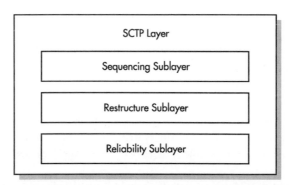

Figure 4-15 The SCTP sublayers are shown in relation to the OSI model.

In SCTP, data transfer is packet-based and delivery is guaranteed. This makes SCTP more suitable for handling transaction-based applications (specifically, signaling protocols) than TCP, where an application is forced to deal with the complexity of an undelineated data stream (UDP) where an application needs to implement its own retransmission algorithms.

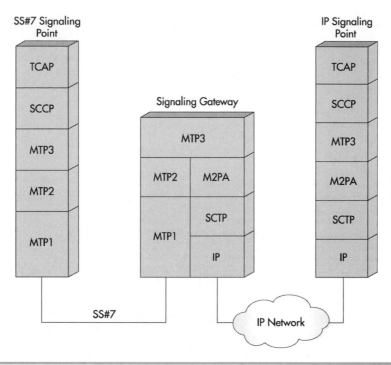

Figure 4-16 The SCTP, as it relates to MTP-2 of the SS7 protocol stack.

SCTP is designed to handle congestion and packet loss better than existing standards. Each SCTP association (an SCTP association is similar to a TCP connection, except that it can support multiple IP addresses at either or both ends) is divided into a number of logical streams. Data is delivered in order for each stream. Much like TCP, SCTP uses a message acknowledgment and retransmission scheme that ensures message delivery to the remote end. However, SCTP provides multiple message streams to minimize the head-of-the-line blocking effect that can be a disadvantage with TCP. A key advantage of SCTP is its capability to support multiple network interface controllers that allow applications to dynamically determine the fastest and most reliable IP network for message transmission.

Voice over IP (VoIP) Impacts

What this all means is that the convergence of voice and data networks is rapidly being accepted. The need to merge these services is also a direct result of the integration of VoIP. With VoIP, the use of **session initiation protocols (SIP)** and session advertising protocols (SAP) takes advantage of the call setup and the service notifications. This involves the transparent transport of SS7 signaling information between circuit-switched networks that are connected over an IP network. The goal is to provide voice telephony subscribers the same ubiquitous access and features, regardless of whether the backhaul for the call is over a circuit-switched network or a VoIP network. Additionally, infrastructure to provide transport of SS7 over IP has the potential to be significantly less costly than traditional SS7 infrastructure equipment.

VoIP Telephony Signaling

Telephony signaling functions include the following:

- **Call Processing:** Performs the state machine processing for call establishment, call maintenance, and call teardown. This also includes address translation and parsing, which determine when a complete number has been dialed and make the dialed number available for address translation.

- **Network Signaling:** Performs signaling functions for establishment, maintenance, and termination of calls over the IP network. Two widely used standards are H.323 and Simple Gateway Control Protocol (SGCP)/Multimedia Gateway Control Protocol (MGCP).

- **H.323 Protocols:** This ITU standard describes how multimedia communications occur between or among user terminals, network equipment, and assorted services on local and wide area IP networks. The following H.323 standards are used in VoIP gateways:

  - **H.225:** Call Signaling Protocol. Performs signaling for establishment and termination of call connections based on Q.931.

  - **H.245:** Control Protocol. Provides capability negotiation between the two end points, such as voice compression algorithm to use, conferencing requests, and so forth.

  - **RAS:** Registration, Admission, and Status Protocol. Used to convey the registration, admissions, bandwidth change, and status messages between IP telephone devices and servers called *Gatekeepers,* which provide address translation and access control to devices.

  - **RTCP:** Real-Time Transport Control Protocol. Provides statistical information for monitoring the quality of service of the voice call.

  - **SGCP/MGCP Protocols:** SGCP is a standard that describes a master/slave protocol for establishing VoIP calls. The slave side or client resides in the gateway (IP telephone), and the master side resides in an entity referred to as a Call Agent. SGCP has been adopted by the cable modem industry as part of its standard use of VoIP. SGCP is evolving to the MGCP.

SS7 and Wireless Intelligent Networks (WIN)

The Wireless Intelligent Network (WIN) mirrors the wireline intelligent network model. The distinction between the wireless and the wireline network is that many of the wireless call activities are associated with the end user's movement, not just the actual phone call.

In the WIN, more call-associated pieces of information are communicated between the

Mobile Switching Center (MSC), which is the equivalent of a CO switching system, and the SCP or HLR. The WIN moves service control away from the MSC and up to a higher element in the network, usually the SCP.

MSC as Service Switching Point (SSP): In the intelligent network, the *SSP* is the switching function portion of the network. The MSC provides this function in the wireless intelligent network.

Service Control Point (SCP): This device provides a centralized element in the network that controls service delivery to subscribers. High-level services can be moved away from the MSC and controlled at this higher level in the network. It is cost-effective because the MSC becomes more efficient: it does not waste time processing new services, and it simplifies new service development.

Intelligent Peripheral (IP): The IP gets information directly from the subscriber. This can be in the form of calling card or credit card information, a PIN number, or voice-activated information. The peripheral receives information and converts the DTMF digits or spoken word into data and hands it off to another element in the network—such as the SCP—for analysis and control.

Signal Transfer Point (STP): The *STP* is a packet switch in the signaling network that handles distribution of control signals between different elements in the network, such as MSCs and HLRs, or MSCs and SCPs. The advantage of an STP is that it concentrates link traffic for the network. An STP can also provide advanced address capabilities such as global title translation and gateway screening, as previously explained.

Location registers: The *location registers* are used to supplement MSCs with information about the subscriber. The number of subscribers supported by a switch changes as roamers move in and subscribers move to other switches. The database of active subscribers changes dynamically. Each MSC cannot have the database for all potential users of that switch. Location registers help get around that problem.

Home location register (HLR): Each MSC carries a list of the assigned users to that MSC in their "home" location, their default location. The *HLR* is where the telephone account information is stored when the user is first set up.

Visitor location register (VLR): Within an MSC, a VLR maintains the subscriber information for visitors or roamers to that MSC. Every MSC or group of MSCs has a VLR.

GSM Network Connection to SS7 Networks

The MSC is the central switching function of the GSM network. The MSC is connected to a SS7 network for the purpose of signaling and performing database queries. The SS7 network uses a network node called the STP, which is a packet-switching node (this can be SS7, IP, or X.25). Using a 64-Kbps channel connection between STPs, the network can process its signaling information.

Next in a SS7 network is the use of the SCP, which houses the databases congruent to the network. In many cases, these databases interact with the HLR, VLR, EIR, AuC, and PSTN nodes. The SCP is used whenever a GTT is required that converts numbers (800-322-2202 equates to 480-706-0912) and whenever the Mobile Application Part (MAP) is used. These services link across an SS7 interface. The GSM architecture using the SS7 protocol is shown in Figure 4-17.

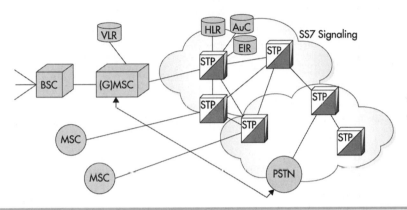

Figure 4-17 GSM architecture and SS7 lend themselves to performing the functions for a wireless user.

The Signaling Protocol Stack for GSM

The normal SS7 network uses the bottom three layers of the OSI model in what is called the MTP1-3. These parts provide the routing and data-link functions across the physical link. The Signaling Connection Control Part (SCCP) is used when database queries are required, and when providing both connection and connectionless access to the SS7 networks. The combination of the MTP1-3 and SCCP creates what is called the actual MTP.

When looking at the upper layers of the OSI model comparison, the SS7 protocols support the use of the following protocols, shown in Figures 4-18 and 4-19:

- Telephone User Part (TUP) for a voice circuit-switched call across the PSTN (Figure 4-18).

- ISDN User Part is a newer implementation and replaces the TUP (Figure 4-18).

- Transaction Capabilities Application Part (TCAP) is an application layer that supports the features and functions of a network (Figure 4-18).

- Mobile Application Part (MAP) sits on top of the TCAP as a means of supporting the difference application service entities for mobile users (Figure 4-18).

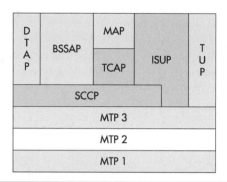

Figure 4-18 The protocols for GSM and SS7 networks are shown as the interconnecting solutions for connectivity.

- Base Station Systems Application Part (BSSAP) is a combination of the BSSMAP and DTAP (Figure 4-19).

- Base Station Systems Mobile Application Part (BSSMAP) transmits messages that the BSC must process. This applies generally to all messages to and from the MSC where the MSC participates in RR management (Figure 4-19).

- Direct Transfer Application Part (DTAP) transports messages between the mobile and the MSC, where the BSC is just a relay function, transparent for the messages. These messages deal with MM and CM (Figure 4-19).

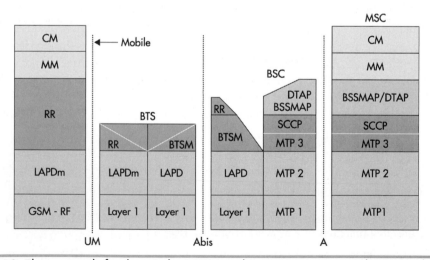

Figure 4-19 The protocols for the wireless GSM architecture compare and contrast the wireline networks.

Number Portability

In 1984, when the breakup of AT&T began, the FCC and others had a vision that PCS would become a reality. The Telecommunications Act of 1996 took this one step closer to the expectations of the regulators. The ultimate goal was to provide seamless and transparent communications for the consumer, with a choice of providers.

An essential stipulation of the Telecommunications Act of 1996 requires that customers must be able to change local carriers while maintaining the same telephone number. The capability to make numbers *portable* across service providers drives significant investment in the network infrastructure for both wireline and wireless carriers. Although the carriers were not required to reroute calls from their networks to ported numbers until June 1999, the advent of wireline number porting also had an immediate and significant financial impact. Porting is the process of carrying the number from one port of a telephone system to a port on another telephone system. When porting, the telephone systems may or may not belong to the same company. A port is nothing more than an interface on a computerized system—like the printer port on a PC. This also has an impact on the capability to complete outgoing calls between wireline and wireless numbers.

LNP is the process of keeping the same telephone number when you change locations or when you change telephone companies. All calls to entire NPA-NXX (refer to Chapter 3 for the NPA discussion) blocks require LNP processing to determine if the specific number has been ported. Consequently, the demand on the network resources will be increased because there will be a technical necessity to use the number portability (NP) databases to complete wireless-to-wireline calls. The providers involved need to address both the cost and the service issues.

Several other issues are in play here at the same time. LNP is only one of the major impacting changes. The wireless and wireline carriers are dealing with other regulatory issues, such as the right-of-way, physical interconnection problems, the needs of integrating operational support systems, and settlements between the carriers for access and cocarrier charges.

The Three Phases of LNP

As previously stated, the ultimate goal of the Telecommunications Act of 1996 includes the capability of the end users (customers) to take their numbers anywhere. This constitutes full-location transportability.

Consumers do not understand many of the LNP issues. They do not comprehend what it means to the carriers. Polls of end users reveal that 80 percent of residential customers would not be willing to change service providers if they had to change their telephone numbers. Moreover, 90 percent of business subscribers would be unwilling to change service providers if it involved changing telephone numbers. To foster competition, the concept of LNP was created and offered to the public.

Consequently, look at the three steps of LNP to get to an end. The three steps include:

- *Service provider portability*. The first step in LNP permits subscribers to keep their current telephone numbers when they change service providers. Changes in service providers can mean between and among the ILEC, CLEC, wireless cellular, wireless PCS, wireless SMR, and cable TV providers, to name the most common. Applying initially to the wireline providers, service provider portability will eventually extend to the wireless networks. This initially started in 1998 for wireline carriers and finally moved to the wireless carriers in November 2003.

- *Service portability*. When a subscriber wants services unavailable through the local end office, service portability allows the customer to secure these services from another switching system without changing telephone numbers. This lets the customer change the mix of services available for use.

- *Location portability*. The final step in LNP enables customers to keep their telephone numbers when they move away from a service area covered by the current CO. The farther away the customer moves, the more the technological challenge posed by LNP. For example, consider the problem encountered if Bud moves from Phoenix to Boston and wants to keep his number (602) 555-XXXX. The ramifications of this example impact the entire numbering plan and the geographic boundary of the service providers.

LNP for Cellular and PCS Suppliers

Few carriers reveal their final plans in advance. They will indicate that they plan to meet the mandates of the law, but they do not explain exactly how they will do so. However, let's look at the technological and financial impacts on their systems.

PCS and SMR Providers   These carriers seem to be the ones seeking a niche in the market. As they offer services to their customers, they view themselves as an alternative to the ILEC wireline services and, at the same time, as complementary. The providers offer the same features and functions as the wireline service providers, including:

- Call forwarding (busy or don't answer)
- Voice messaging
- Three-way calling
- Caller ID
- Call transfer
- Internet access

The PCS providers using LNP in their potpourri of offerings are now marketing to their customers to eliminate their wired home telephones. Why pay for two different lines and service offerings when you can do it all on one telephone (and number)? This has gained in popularity especially since the implementation of the Wireless LNP.

The LNP deadline for Wireless LNP implementation in the top 100 Metropolitan Statistical Areas (MSA) was November 2003. The implication is that the wireless carrier implementations would be fully **Interim Standard 41 (IS-41)**[13] compliant, using an LNP trigger mechanism. In addition, wireline LECs, all cellular, broadband PCS, and certain specialized mobile radio (SMR) carriers (like NexTel) must be able to deliver calls from their networks to ported numbers anywhere in the nation. Furthermore, those carriers must offer LNP throughout their networks, including the capability to support roaming transparently.

LNP Differences

Wireless providers handle their customers differently than do the wireline operators. In general, major differences arise in the way they handle customer care. Some are good at managing the customer interface; others never see the customer and rarely get involved with solving problems. With over-the-air provisioning, many customers add or delete features and functions via a telephone call to the wireless provider.

The way the infrastructure is established is also a potential problem. The wireless providers have completely different overlays in the network for rating calls. The wireline operators have geographically bounded rate centers, whereas the wireless providers have different boundaries. It is normal for a wireless provider to backhaul a call several miles (or more) to process out of its MSC. The calling area for a wireless provider is set up in an entirely different manner than the wireline operator.

The wireless operators' billing systems are also different. In the wireline networks, customers do not pay to receive calls (with the exception of a collect or an 800 number call), whereas in the wireless network, airtime is billed for every minute of usage. Moreover, in the wireline network, the caller gets unlimited outbound local calls, whereas in the wireless networks, airtime is billed for all local calls. The wireless providers have been attempting to minimize the visibility by offering packages of X minutes for Y dollars per month. However, in revenue generation, the wireless providers have the advantage because they pre-bill for the service whether the customer uses it or not. Only a few operators deviate from this scenario.[14] Now, with LNP, they must know where the call is going and how it is terminated to capture the usage. Most important, they need the originating and terminating minutes to bill when the customer exceeds the allotted time in the package.

---

[13]IS41—the interim standard from ANSI for the interoperation between wireless suppliers. In effect, IS-41 was a proprietary version of SS7 standards between cellular providers.

[14]Cingular, a wireless operator, offers to carry over customers' unused minutes to the next month, and so forth. McLeod, a different operator, offers the option to pay only for the minutes used, although the rates vary from the packaged deals. A few providers offer all-you-want local minutes (and now, unlimited in-network minutes), opening the door to all new competitive pricing plans.

Somehow, the interface between the wireless and the wireline carriers must come together to make this all transparent. Further, the wireless carriers need an interface to the Number Portability Administration Center (NPAC), which requires more updates and more SS7 links to facilitate the LNP operation.

What Is It All About, Anyway?

LNP is a far-reaching mandate. Because of the Telecommunications Act of 1996 competition in the long-distance market has grown and prospered. Therefore, the FCC mandated LNP as a requirement for new entrants into the business of local access and to foster the competitive spirit.

The deadline was further pushed to November 2004 so that broadband PCS suppliers could build their basic infrastructure. Regulators felt that if the LNP issue was to be addressed while these carriers were still building their infrastructure, it would have a negative impact in their market segment. Implementation occurred in November 2004, with many delays and a good amount of confusion for the carriers and the end users alike.

The wireless providers must now make the wireline LNP systems work within the wireless system. There are still many unanswered questions about how the systems will work for the wireless networks and providers. These include:

- How will the wireless carriers transfer the line information to the NPACs?

- What happens to the roaming possibilities?

- How will over-the-air provisioning be handled now that LNP has been added?

- What will become of the mutual compensation billing systems they use?

- When "calling party pays" becomes a reality, who gets billed when the wireless carriers don't have LNP information telling them where the call was terminated?

Where's the Money?

One of the big issues in complying with the LNP mandates is the fact that there has to be a return on investment for the carriers. The cost implications of building out the network to accommodate the LNP requirements are significant. The FCC recognized this issue when mandating that LNP be implemented among the local providers (ILECs), the CLECs, and the wireless providers.

Several mechanisms will help the carriers recoup their costs. These include the capability of the carriers to bill back to the consumer. The consumer will pay for the overall implementation. A federally approved monthly charge was enacted, to last no more than five years. The wireless providers have considered the option of just paying the ILECs for the LNP services, but this can be too expensive for them. As a result, the interoperation of the SS7 and IS-41 systems is critical. To enact true number portability, the use of database "dips" (queries submitted to the database) will require more robust access to SS7 databases between and among the providers. This interaction has proliferated more use of SS7.

There is more, though, and not only about recouping costs, but also about gaining revenue. After the initial implementation of WLNP, the turnover between and among these service providers (referred to as *churn*) was active. Lead times of two to three weeks were normal to "port" a number from one wireless provider to another. This was especially frustrating for consumers who were told that such a change could be handled in a matter of hours. The real impact will come when people can transfer their wired telephone number to a wireless phone, or their wireless number to a wireline provider.

Basic LNP Networks

The components of LNP are not that much different from the original SS7 networks. The pieces serve different functions. Looking at the components in Figure 4-20, we see:

- The switching service point (SSP) is the local CO or tandem.

- The Signal Transfer Point (STP) is a packet-mode handler that routes data queries through the signaling network.

- The Signal Control Point (SCP) is the database for features, routing, and GTT.

- The local service management system (LSMS) and the Service Order Administration (SOA) can be provisioned separately, but when combined, they are referred to as the NPAC connectivity.

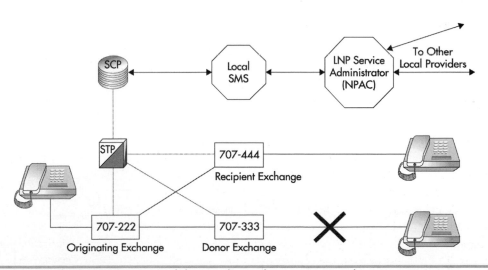

Figure 4-20 The basic LNP network layout shows the components that are now interconnected to swap information.

For wireless providers, the LNP capabilities depend on the MSA served. Even if a wireless network does not support LNP, the wireless provider's methods and procedures should be updated to support troubleshooting for calls placed to ported wireline numbers, so they can determine where the call terminates.

Location Routing Number (LRN)

The **Location Routing Number (LRN)** is a ten-digit number to uniquely identify a switch that has ported numbers. *LRN* depends on IN or AIN capabilities deployed by the wireline carriers' networks. The LRN for a particular switch must be a native NPA-NXX assigned to the service provider for that switch. The NPA-NXX was discussed in Chapter 3.

LRN assigns a unique ten-digit telephone number to each switch in a defined geographic area. The LRN now serves as the network address. Carriers routing telephone calls to end users that have changed from one carrier to another (and kept the same number) perform a database dip to obtain the LRN corresponding to the dialed telephone number. This is the functional equivalent of call-forwarding to the new location. The database dip is performed for all calls where the NPA-NXX has been flagged in the switch as a portable number. The carrier then routes the call to the new provider based on the LRN.

Figure 4-21 shows the flow of LRN information, which is the same for both a wireline and a wireless provider.

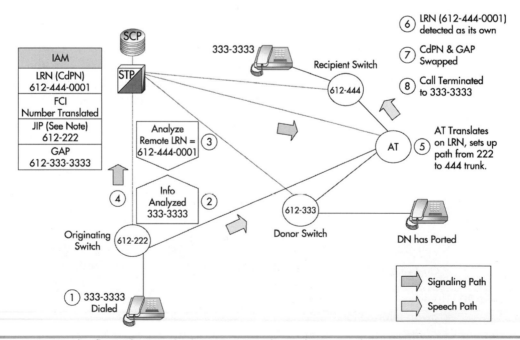

Figure 4-21 The flow of a LRN lookup is a complicated process, but a necessary one.

To clarify the previous explanation, consider the following example. When the caller dials the number (333-3333, in this case), the originating switch (612-222) sends its signaling information (info dialed 333-3333) through the STP to the SCP, which analyzes the route and returns the LRN (612-444-0001). Next, an IAM is forwarded from 612-222 through the STP to the access tandem. The Access Tandem (AT) translates the LRN and sets up a speech path (trunk) from 222 to 444. Switch 612-444 detects the LRN (612-444-0001) as its address; therefore, the called number and the generic address parameter are swapped. From there, the call is connected (terminated) at 333-3333. Throughout the process, the donor switch is not involved

LNP Impact on Routing and Rating

Changes are required for the wireline and the wireless providers. Both have different billing and rating measures to satisfy their network demands. ILECs were tied to the regulatory boundaries of the local utility commissions and the FCC, whereas the wireless carriers were not.

Both providers must change the way calls are routed, rated for access, and rated for end-user billing to include the use of the LRN in the future. The wireless providers will have to include the LRN differently than they did in the past. The simplest way of doing this is to use the standard V&H[15] coordinates, and then apply from-and-to billing and access ratings to the call.

Demand for LNP

Original predictions of LNP were that 90 percent of wireless users would choose a different carrier if they could keep the same number. The wireless carriers are fraught with fear over that prediction. This demand and churn rate did not occur, but 30 percent did churn during the first few months of WLNP in November 2004. After the initial high churn, things have settled down to a modest 4 percent.

Churn hurts these suppliers in light of the packages that are being offered. The possibility of getting free minutes and/or free local calling from a new supplier is enough to make the wireless carriers' customers change providers. The concept of using long-term contracts to keep customers is now outdated, but it was a way to hold the customer for at least some extended period. Future offerings to hold the customer are not finalized, but one can expect several new packaging options.

---

[15]For years, the telephone companies have used a database with the vertical and horizontal coordinates of all their COs and used distances between the V&H coordinates to render the bills. Now, they typically use a flat rate service, but link the database as the reference points between two COs.

Location NP is becoming a bigger issue and demand is becoming a hotter topic for the carriers and customers alike. However, location portability raises many other issues that have not been fully fleshed out, such as:

- Added database dips because of the number of ILECs and IECs that can be involved in a call process.

- E-911 emergency-response call handling will become more complicated.

- Rating and billing issues. How do you process a call? Who pays?

- Loss of the NANP geographical significance. In the old days, we knew where a caller was by the telephone number.

- Customer Premises Equipment (CPE) impacts the capability to process local versus long-distance calls from a database, which must be kept updated. This also puts more burdens on the CPE (PBX, key systems, and so forth).

New local calling plans will be needed, but separate from the rate center plans in place and regulated today. Possibly, rate-center consolidation will be an alternative for number portability from a centralized location and a better way of handling local versus long-distance calling. Toll alerts may be needed in the signaling network. When a number has been flagged as ported to a new LRN, the network will intercept and advise the calling party that it will be a toll call. This involves more database dips and more equipment to interface in the network. Who pays for this?

Scenarios

These scenarios look at the different choices that may appear in the implementation of LNP by the wireline or wireless carriers. The first, as shown in Figure 4-22, is a non-LNP intermediate office using MF trunks between suppliers.

1. Call is placed to ported subscriber.

2. Originating switch performs LNP query.

3. SCP replies.

4. LNP IAM packet is sent to non-LNP tandem.

5. Non-LNP tandem dials over MF trunk, only LRN is sent (in the called-party ID parameter), dialed number is lost, and call fails.

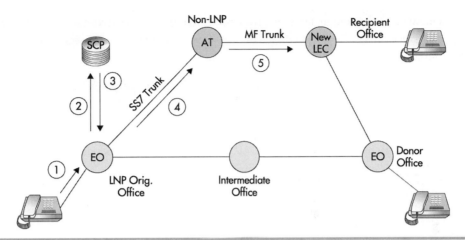

Figure 4-22 The non-LNP office is connected in a different way, creating a different lookup procedure.

The next scenario, shown in Figure 4-23, deals with a dialed number pulsed to a non-LNP tandem via MF signaling.

1. Call is placed to a ported subscriber from a donor switch.

2. Donor switch performs the LNP query.

3. SCP replies with the LRN.

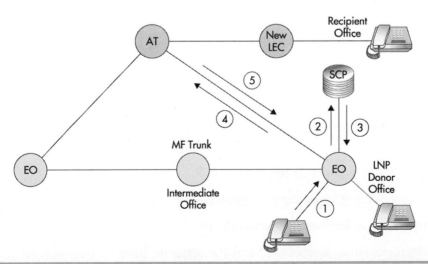

Figure 4-23 Scenario with non-LNP tandems using a dial-up multifrequency translation.

4. Donor switch sends the dialed digits over an SS7 trunk to a non-LNP tandem (if the donor is provisioned to send only the dialed digits to non-LNP switches, the signal ported number option).

5. The non-LNP tandem sends the call based on the dialed number back to the donor switch. The call will keep going through Steps 2 to 5 until the network management system ends the call. (This is *message looping,* a possible big problem in a wireless network.)

In the third scenario, shown in Figure 4-24, we see the operator services involved in a dial 0 call.

1. The subscriber (708-232-1111) dials 0 and is connected to the Telephone Operator Position Services (TOPS) operator.

2. The operator receives a request to connect to 708-828-2222 and bill to the originator's station.

3. TOPS determines that the requested number has been ported and sends the LNP query to the SCP.

4. The LNP SCP sends back the response with the LRN (312-225-0000) of the recipient switch.

5. TOPS routes the call to the recipient switch.

6. The recipient switch terminates the call to the ported number, 708-828-2222.

Occasionally, a database file must be accessed. Using a Line Information Database (LIDB), this scenario follows the flow into and out of the database to determine the location of the called party.

1. Subscriber A (708-232-111) dials 0-708-828-2222, and the call is routed to TOPS.

2. TOPS sends a "bong" to the subscriber, requesting the calling card number.

3. TOPS routes the calling card number to LNP SCP to obtain the correct LIDB point code address.

4. LNP SCP returns the LIDB point code to STP.

5. STP queries LIDB for calling card validation.

6. LIDB returns calling card validation to TOPS.

7. TOPS routes billing number to LNP SCP to obtain the correct calling party service provider (LRN).

8. LNP SCP returns LRN of the billing number and the TOPS-populated appropriate AMA module.

9. TOPS routes called party number (708-828-2222) to LNP SCP for LRN.

10. LNP SCP returns LRN of the recipient switch.

11. TOPS routes the call.

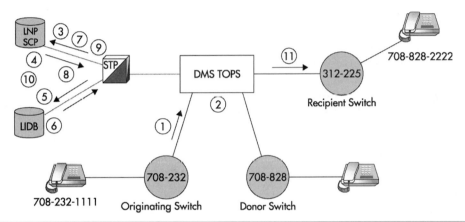

Figure 4-24 Scenario with the operator model and how the LNP process works with the use of the TOPS.

Wireless and Wireline E-911

When you think about LNP in a wireline environment, the process is straightforward. The caller places an emergency call from a fixed location, which is easily identifiable. Routing of the E-911 call is to the proper public safety answering point (PSAP) based on a known prearranged location from each telephone. ANI is mapped one-to-one for all wireline calls using the appropriate callback number and a location from an automatic location information (ALI) database. This is shown in Figure 4-25.

911 calling and routing is built on the limited capability of the CAMA[16] trunks (trunks that were originally used for cost accounting and messaging call information), and the CAMA will remain in use for some time to come. This does cause some difficulty for the wireless companies, because the need to send more information for wireless 911 calls cannot be met the same way as in wireline calls. Figure 4-26 shows the wireless 911 process using LNP.

---

[16]CAMA is an acronym that stands for cost and message accounting.

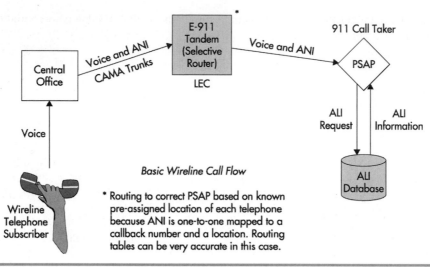

Basic Wireline Call Flow

* Routing to correct PSAP based on known
pre-assigned location of each telephone
because ANI is one-to-one mapped to a
callback number and a location. Routing
tables can be very accurate in this case.

Figure 4-25 Wireline E-911 can deal more easily with the issues when using an ALI database.

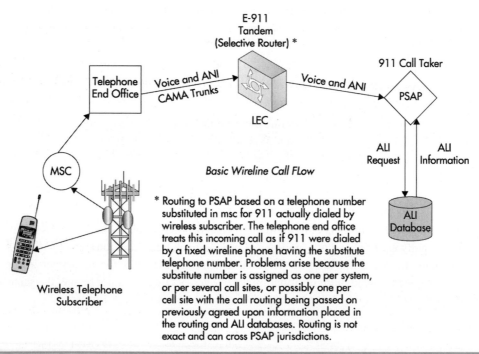

Basic Wireline Call FLow

* Routing to PSAP based on a telephone number
substituted in msc for 911 actually dialed by
wireless subscriber. The telephone end office
treats this incoming call as if 911 were dialed
by a fixed wireline phone having the substitute
telephone number. Problems arise because the
substitute number is assigned as one per system,
or per several call sites, or possibly one per
cell site with the call routing being passed on
previously agreed upon information placed in
the routing and ALI databases. Routing is not
exact and can cross PSAP jurisdictions.

Figure 4-26 Wireless E-911 is more difficult with LNP.

Is 911 important? Nearly 25 percent of all the calls (over 100,000) per day are from wireless subscribers. This poses significant technical and managerial challenges for the network operators.

The Planned Goal

The goal is to have a fully transparent network that can handle the wireless 911 calls and quickly respond to the caller. Upgrades across the network require that a satellite Global Positioning System (GPS) installed at the wireless network interface will help in locating the caller and will route to the appropriate PSAP every time. Using the GPS, the feeling is that the caller can be located 67 percent of the time within 125 meters (410 feet), because the call will be routed to the PSAP with the appropriate x, y locator coordinates. The ALI will be updated to support both ANI and x, y lookup. The call to the PSAP will arrive with a mapping system showing the x, y coordinates of the calling party.

4

Benefits of Using LNP and Roaming Capabilities

The benefits of making and receiving calls in a wireless network or a wireline network are the epitome of revenue generation. When a user on the wireless network is receiving a call today from the wired world (or vice versa), the network uses its own appropriate databases. In this case, the wireless networks rely heavily on their own SCPs, which house the database information of their callers.

HLRs keep track of all network suppliers' users, based on their own network ID. The HLR database has all the appropriate information to recognize the caller by user **electronic serial number (ESN)** and mobile telephone number. The *ESN* is made up of 32 bits of information. The database controls the features and functions the user has subscribed to. When a call comes into the network today, the called number is sent to the HLR responsible for the number dialed. These are SS7 messages. The HLR then looks into its database and determines where the caller is located, or if the user is on the air.

If the user is located somewhere else, a VLR entry exists at a remote MSC. This entry has been updated by the remote end when the user activated the telephone (powered it on and registered) or when an already powered device rolled into range of a cell site from the new location. Then an SS7 message is sent out to the HLR that the called party is now in someone else's database. See Figure 4-27 for the registration process.

If a call is coming in from the network, the SS7 inquiry comes into the HLR, which then sends a redirect message to the remote MSC (the VLR) serving the end user.

Using this roaming capability, database dips are occurring much more frequently. Many of the wireless networks are already taxing their databases. They are trying to move more information out to the STP or the local switches, rather than constantly overloading the SCP.

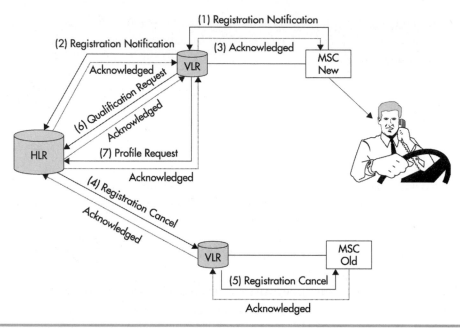

Figure 4-27 Mobile registration keeps tabs on the users at the VLR and another database called the ALI.

Incoming Calls to an Idle Mobile

Using the IS-41 and SS7 linkage, when a call comes in to a mobile number, the immediate link is to the HLR. The HLR then sends out a query to the VLR indicating that a call is coming in for the mobile. See Figure 4-28 for the process of incoming to idle sets.

The VLR verifies the information and sends back confirmation to the HLR, indicating that the call should be steered to the temporary local directory number (TLDN), which is effectively a call-forwarding arrangement. The call is then forwarded to the end-user device, using the dynamically assigned DN.

Once the call is received at the remote MSC, the call is logged into the appropriate billing and accounting system for reciprocal payment and processing. At the end of the month, the billing systems are polled and processed by a service bureau for peering arrangements.

Calls to a Busy Set or a Set That Doesn't Answer

Assume this: after the TLDN has been assigned by the VLR and the call has been redirected to the set, the set is busy or does not answer. Now the VLR sends an SS7 message back to the HLR and requests additional information, such as "What do I do now?"

The VLR then sends out a page to the mobile unit. If there is no response, then the SS7 message to release the call is sent back to the HLR.

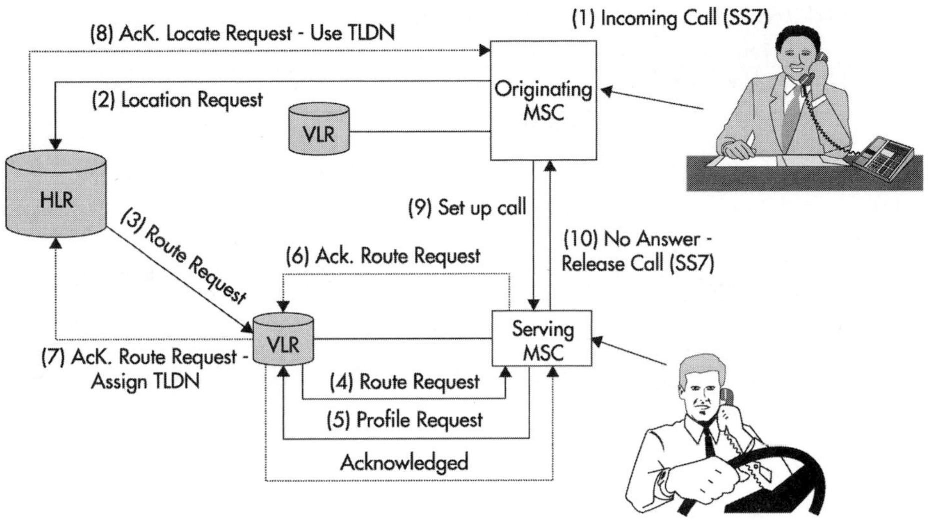

Figure 4-28 An incoming call placed to an idle mobile set will ring through as normal.

No Answer with Call Forwarding

Assume that the VLR assigned a TLDN to process the call to the called telephone user, and then sends out the page, but the caller does not answer. This time, the VLR goes back to the HLR for a clarification on the next step. The HLR does a database dip and finds that the called party has call-forwarding to another number, such as a business wireline number or a voice-mail system. This information is then fed back to the VLR for processing. The VLR next sends the message back to process the call to the forwarding number, as shown in Figure 4-29. The VLR is completed, and the HLR has provided all the information necessary. The SS7 network now sends the incoming call request to the wireline end office, alerting it that a call is coming in for the forwarded number, and the process continues.

Calls to a Busy Set with Message Waiting

Assume that the call is coming in for a wireless user, but the wireless user is on the phone. Now the VLR goes into react mode and assigns a second TLDN back to the HLR, indicating to forward the call to the new number. The call is then sent to the serving MSC on a separate telephone number reserved for this call. Then a message is sent through the airwaves to the air interface, indicating that a new call is coming (in the form of a beep). The caller can then choose to answer the call or ignore it. This same process is used to give priority to outbound wireless calls, with some inbound wireless calls going directly to voice mail when a wireless channel is not allocated to the cellular user end point.

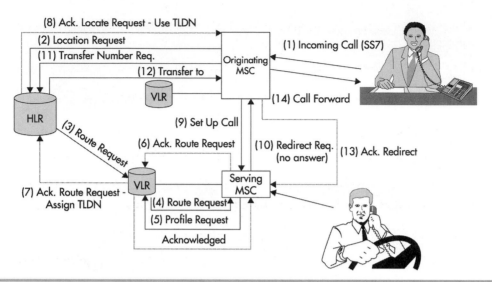

Figure 4-29 Call forwarding to a mobile set can also be accomplished.

Chapter 4 Review

Chapter Summary

In this chapter, you have learned that the networks are continually evolving.

- Early signaling systems were discussed initially. These were replaced with the newer SS7 architectures that use a form of packet switching to send the messages.

  As we become more dependent on communications networks, risk must be avoided.

- To help avert the risk, the networks deployed redundancy to prevent the disasters of the early 1980s.

- This was expensive, however, and the carriers expect to recover the cost of their investments by charging for added features and functions.

- Many such features are now available.

  Later, the industry demanded more intelligence be enacted inside the core of the network. No longer did we get a plain telephone with a rotary dial pad.

- Instead, we now have a feature-rich network that continually adds more functionality.

- But with every new feature comes more dependency on active database access in the network.

- This potentially could bog down the network; thus IPs are used to offload some of the work of the network resources.

- The IP can add more functions and create virtual network services.

Later, we saw the need to align the Internet with signaling systems.

- This introduced a different approach to the capture and reformat of data packets.

- We hope this integration of SS7 with Internet protocols will be more efficient.

As additional features become available, users realize they can personalize their systems. They demand that changes be tied to the number and not the carrier.

- Thus, LNP became a reality to meet the demand for this personalization.

- Ultimately, this use of a single number and portability creates new associations between wired and the wireless networks.

- Over the past 20 years, the networks have become transparent because of the sophisticated signaling, intelligent networks, and portability across various platforms.

Key Terms for Chapter 4

Advanced Intelligent Networks (AIN) *(140)*
Computer Telephony Integration (CTI) *(141)*
Electronic Serial Number (ESN) *(171)*
Global System for Mobile (GSM) *(151)*
Home Location Register (HLR) *(156)*
Initial Address Message (IAM) *(136)*
Intelligent Peripheral (IP) *(140)*
Interim Standard 41 (IS-41) *(161)*
Internet Protocol (IP) *(151)*
ISDN User Part (ISUP) *(136)*
Links (A, B, C, D, E, F) *(132)*
Linkset *(133)*
Local Number Portability (LNP) *(124)*
Location Routing Number (LRN) *(164)*
Message Transfer Part (MTP) *(134)*
Mobile Switching Center (MSC) *(156)*
Routesets *(133)*
Session Initiation Protocol (SIP) *(154)*
Signal Control Point (SCP) *(127)*
Signaling System 7 (SS7) *(120)*
Signal Transfer Point (STP) *(127)*

4

REVIEW

Transaction Capability *(150)*
Visitor Location Register (VLR) *(156)*
Voice over IP (VoIP) *(152)*
Wireless LNP (WLNP) *(151)*

Key Term Quiz

1. The current signaling system in use throughout the world is called ___SS7___ .

2. The ___MTP___ addresses the bottom three layers of the OSI model for transferring messages in the SS7 network.

3. The ___IPs work in cooperation with SCP___ provides media services in support of call control in the AIN.

4. Keeping your telephone number when you move from location to location is called ___roaming___ .

5. Changing from carrier to carrier in the wireless networks and keeping the same number is called ___porting___ .

6. The database that holds the information about the wireless subscriber is the ___SCP___ .

7. When roaming, a user's information is placed in a temporary database called the ___VLR___ .

8. The _____ is now being used in conjunction with _____ to make signaling more _____ .

9. ___LRN___ is a ten-digit number to uniquely identify a switch that has ported numbers.

10. The ___SSP___ is a packet-switching hardware component that routes the SS7 messages.

Multiple-Choice Quiz

1. SS7 was first deployed in the industry in what year?

    a. 1980

    b. 1982

    c. 1983

    d. 1989

2. The preferred form of associated signaling is_____.

    a. Nonassociated

    b. Associated

    c. Fully associated

    d. Quasi-associated

3. The telephone carriers were still installing SS6 through_____.

    a. 1983

    b. 1985

    c. 1980

    d. 1973

4. The Central Office (CO) is now called the_____.

    a. STP

    b. SSP

    c. SCP

    d. TCAP

5. SS7 uses a _____-layer protocol stack.

    a. 7

    b. 4

    c. 3

    d. 5

    e. 6

6. Originally, the carriers used frequencies that carried signaling information using_____.

    a. 300–3300 Hz

    b. 100–400 Hz

    c. 3600–3900 Hz

    d. 3500–3700 Hz

7. The location where the databases are kept in an SS7 network is called the_____.

    a. STP

    b. Database engines

    c. SCP

    d. SSP

4

REVIEW

8. The SS7 protocols used to carry the message are called:

   a. X.25

   b. IP

   c. TCP

   d. MTP

9. The original SS6 used _____ different signaling units.

   a. 12

   b. 28

   c. 256

   d. 128

10. The signaling units used in the SS6 networks were made up of _____ bits.

   a. 256

   b. 128

   c. 12

   d. 28

11. SS7 circuits run on links that operate at_____ in North America:

   a. 1.544 Mbps

   b. 56 Kbps

   c. 66 Kbps

   d. 4.8 Kbps

12. The routeset and the _____ are synonymous.

   a. Route

   b. Linkset

   c. Point code

   d. Database

13. STPs are usually installed in _____.

   a. The middle of the network

   b. Mated pairs

    c. Stand-alone mode

    d. Half-duplex

14 The three types of LNP are:

    a. Location, service, and cost

    b. Location, provider, and number

    c. Service, number, and provider

    d. Wireless, wireline, and provider

15. The mandate for wireless number portability was set for _____.

    a. November 2003

    b. November 2001

    c. November 2006

    d. November 2002

16. LRN is a _____ number to uniquely identify a switch that has ported numbers.

    a. Ten-digit

    b. Seven-digit

    c. Three-digit

    d. Five-digit

17. All calls to entire NPA-NXX blocks will require LNP processing to determine if the specific number has been_____.

    a. Changed

    b. Charged

    c. Routed

    d. Ported

18. Who will ultimately pay for the services and features of LNP?

    a. ILECs

    b. IECs

    c. Consumers

    d. Vendors

Essay Quiz

1. The signaling systems of today add new dimensions to the telephone networks. Explain how the network and features can help you do your daily activities, paying particular attention to the issues of call setup and teardown.

2. Describe the overall network architecture of the signaling system on a hierarchical basis.

3. Using the Intelligent Network, what do you think could be a new service that the telephone companies could introduce to support the consumer?

4. If you had the option to port a telephone number across the country, what implications do you think might come into play? Describe what current network numbering plans and other issues you think could arise.

5. Describe the main reasons you, as a customer, might use LNP or WLNP today (try to think of at least five reasons).

Lab Projects

1. Label the following drawing with the appropriate pieces:

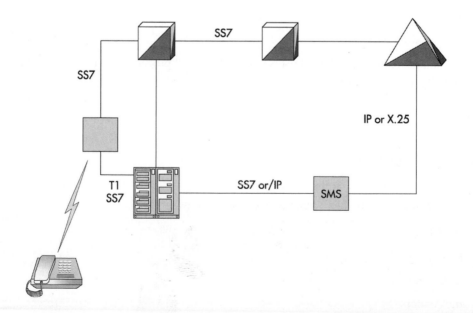

2. Place a call to your local telephone company. Explain that you are a student taking an introductory class on telecommunications and ask if the company has the following services available:

a. Local Number Portability. If the answer is yes, how long does it take to transfer a wireline number from one location to another? If the answer is no, why doesn't the company have it? How long would it take if you wanted to order Local Number Portability right now?

b. Now ask them if they can port your home number from their CO to a wireless carrier (select one of the big players, such as Cingular, Verizon, or Sprint). If so, how long will it take? If not, when can such a move take place?

c. Now call your local wireless supplier (assuming you have one) and go through the same scenario, this time asking if you can port your number from their network to another wireless provider. If so, how long will this take? If not, why not? How long would it take if you wanted to order this service right now?

d. Next, ask if you can take the wireless number and port it to your wireline carrier. If the answer is yes, how long will this take? If the answer is no, why not? How long would it take if you wanted to order this service right now?

e. Discuss the results you achieved with your instructor and your class.

Chapter 5

Digital Versus Analog Communications

LEARNING OBJECTIVES:

Once you complete this chapter, you will be able to:

Explain what analog communications means.

Discuss the differences between analog and digital communications.

Describe the process of carrying the analog signal.

Explain impairments in the analog signal transmission.

Converse fluently about the use of digital transmission systems in the telephone hierarchy.

Describe the way we regenerate the digital signal on the link.

Explain the implementation of the T-carrier system.

Discuss the differences between the analog and digital systems to carry voice and data.

Describe the framing and formatting of a T1.

Explain why there are differences in the digital transmission protocols.

In the data and voice communications field, one of the most common points of confusion is between the words "analog" and "digital." Most people recognize that the term **digital** refers to the expression of information in terms of 1's and 0's. Each value in a digital signal is discrete. The system measures and represents the values in whole numbers. For example, the difference between two points is a value of 1, so the next value up is 2, and then 3, and so forth. This discreteness eliminates the variable values found in an analog wave, where an infinite number of values exist between 1 and 2 (for example, 1.1, 1.25, 1.33, 1.5, and so forth).

But few can easily make the mental connection between this fact and the real-world requirements of moving voice signals expressed in a 1's-and-0's format. In dealing with the term "analog," everyone merely refers to voice communications. This chapter can help you make and understand the connection between these two terms. Not that you will become an electrical engineer, but you will be able to converse with the best of them! If one single element must be understood, it is this: analog and digital formats are means used to move information across any medium. Some media typically deal with analog, others deal with digital, and the rest deal with both. Thus, this discussion can help you understand the reasons why the different transmission systems are used.

Analog Transmission Systems

As mentioned earlier, the network was originally developed solely to provide voice communications services. Initially, the communications circuits AT&T built through the Bell Systems and its own communications capabilities used strictly analog technology. Yes, it changed into a digital world, but it was built around analog communications for voice. What does this mean?

In an **analog** communications system, the initial signal (in this case, the spoken word) is directly translated into an electrical signal. Chapter 2 describes how the telephone set accomplishes this task in more detail. The characteristics of an analog signal deal with two constantly changing variables: the amplitude and the frequency of the signal. The strength (amplitude) of the electrical signal varies with the loudness of the voice, while the frequency of the electrical signal varies with the pitch or tone of the voice. Both variables (amplitude and frequency) change proportionately with the original sound waves.

If the signal were to be monitored with an oscilloscope, the displayed pattern would visibly and recognizably change as the sound changed. This is shown in Figure 5-1, where the signal characteristics can be seen on an oscilloscope. For a more graphic example, think of the visual displays in some discos, where the music is fed into a light display that varies as the music changes. In fact, if you had two oscilloscopes and could watch the sound waves on one scope and the electrical signals generated by the microphone on a second scope, the two images would be identical for all practical purposes.

Figure 5-1 Using an oscilloscope, you can see the characteristics of an analog signal.

In an analog telephone communications system, the electrical signal, not light, changes. In Figure 5-2, an analogy to this concept using a musical beat is shown. The lights of the disc jockey's equipment will change and flash with the beat of the music. In this case, the lights are changing based on the electrical characteristics of the signal. What is actually happening? In telecommunications terms, you could say that the actual **sound** is produced by banging

Figure 5-2 The music creates analog light patterns on the DJ's equipment based on the beat, which are really the electrical characteristics of the sound.

airwaves together. This banging of airwaves is really the movement of the air molecules. Technically, this is called compression and rarefaction. But who wants to get technical?

The human voice is an interesting phenomenon. As you speak, you generate sound. You bang the air waves together quite a few times in a relatively short period. This was discussed in Chapter 2, but to stick with this thought, you create an analogous sinusoidal wave. This wave is then converted into its electrical equivalent. Quite simply, if you were to take the sounds created by the voice and modify them based on the pitch and the strength of the sound, you could produce this sinusoidal wave (see Figure 5-3). The wave is what would happen electrically if you were to use a magnetic field to change the sound into electricity. Working around a baseline of zero electrical voltage, you then would have a 360-degree rotation of electrical current. This 360-degree wave around the zero line is called a *hertz,* named after the electrical engineer who documented this concept. The wave starts at the zero line and rises as the amount of energy increases. This ultimately peaks at some point, and then it begins its descent. The electrical energy will then proceed from the height on a downward slope to the zero line. From there, it will continue on its slope below the zero line to a peak (this is called the negative side of the wave). Continuing to a peak voltage on this side of the line, the energy will hit its peak value, and then begin an upward slope back to the zero line. The wave has made a complete 360-degree cycle. One complete cycle constitutes one hertz (1 Hz), used in a reference against one second in time. A 1-Hz signal produces one complete revolution in one second, whereas a 100-Hz signal completes 100 revolutions in one second.

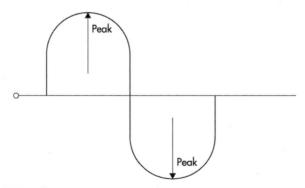

Figure 5-3 The sinusoidal wave rotates 360 degrees around a magnetic force. This one wave or revolution is called a hertz (Hz).

The human vocal chords can bang the airwaves together between 100 and 5,000 times per second. Simply stated, then, the voice is producing up to 5,000 cycles of information per second. When this is converted into its electrical equivalent, there are up to 5,000 hertz. We do not like to state such big numbers, so let's abbreviate this to 5 kilo (meaning thousand) hertz—5 kHz, for short. From this electrical equivalent, you now have an analogy or a look-alike to your sound waves. This is a constantly changing variable of electrical energy. Both the amplitude and the frequency will change from 100 to 5,000 times per second. This is something the telephone companies learned to deal with from the beginning of our communications industry. Over time, however, they found that the human voice generates usable and understandable information from 300 to 3,300 cycle changes per second or 3 kHz of electrical cycles as a norm, as seen in Figure 5-4. As with any communications channel capacity, the telephone company did not want to give users any more than they needed to carry on a voice conversation. Over the years, as the network expanded, the telephone companies limited the bandwidth of a telephone call to a 3-kHz channel capacity. This was a money issue.

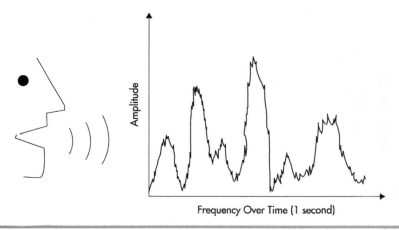

Figure 5-4 The human voice generates usable and understandable information from 300 to 3300 Hz as a normal speech pattern.

QUESTION

Given a limited amount of bandwidth, how can we allow a human conversation to take place across the network and produce reasonable representations of the original voice? And how can we do it cheaply?

The range of frequencies generated goes from 300 to 3300 Hz (see Figure 5-5). The telephone company, therefore, limits our use of the channel to just that amount. In the radio frequency (RF) and electromagnetic spectrum, the telephone companies divided all their capacities into 4-kHz slices. On each of these 4-kHz slices (wires or radio channels), they installed frequency bandpass filters at 300 and at 3300 Hz. Anything that falls in the middle of this allocation of RF spectrum will be allowed to pass. Anything that falls outside of this range will be filtered out (thrown away). This is called a *band-limited channel*. Because the voice can normally go as high as 5 kHz, there will be cases where you hit the higher range of frequencies with your conversation (such as words with the *S* and the *F* sounds) and it will be flattened out through the filters. This might sound unreasonable, but what it produces is a little fuzziness on the line.

Neither the human ear nor the telephone equipment is sensitive enough to recognize any significant problems. Once the electrical equivalent of the sound is created (through the telephone set or another device), the electricity is sent down the wires.

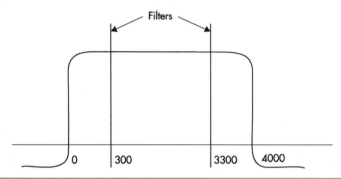

Figure 5-5 The range of frequencies allowed on the circuit is 300 to 3300 Hz using bandpass filters to allow speech more cost-effectively.

When a call is proceeding down the wires, resistance in the wires to the electrical signal immediately begins to diminish its amplitude. The signal gets weaker and weaker. This weakening of the energy will eventually lead to the total absorption of the electrical energy or the loss of the signal beyond recognition. This is called *attenuation of the electrical signal.* The signal can only travel so far before it runs out of strength and disappears. An analogy to this is a relay race runner who is trained to run around a quarter-mile track as fast as he or she can. By the time the runner gets to the end of the quarter mile run, all strength and energy are expended. The runner is out of steam, as shown in Figure 5-6. If the runner did not have someone to pass the baton

Figure 5-6 If we use the analogy of a runner being out of steam (energy) after running around the track as fast as he or she can, the same is true with the electrical energy we place on the wire.

off to, but had to go around the track again, the second lap would take forever. That is, if the runner made it around the track at all before passing out and falling flat on the ground.

To keep the signals moving along the wires, amplifiers are used to boost the signal strength, as shown in Figure 5-7. These amplifiers are usually spaced about 15,000 to 18,000 feet apart. Typically, we only need one amplifier between the customer location and the telephone company Central Office (CO)—two, at most. The CO is usually located close to the customer, within five to seven miles on average. Only in remote locations will it be farther away. This may not be the case where the telephone companies have closed the CO. The consolidation of COs across the United States specifically has led to greater distances from the CO to the customer.

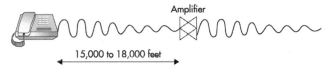

Figure 5-7 Amplifiers are used to boost the signal every 15,000 to 18,000 feet.

Noise is a second activity that occurs on these wires concurrent with the transmission. *Noise* (introduced line loss, frayed wires, lightning, electrical inductance, heat, and so forth) is always present in the form of white noise or hiss. It also begins to cause a deterioration of the signal. Noise is always on the line, but because noise is a natural property of transmitting on a wire, noise increases with distance and from cabling problems, creating a second energy on the wire that competes with the desired signal. This means that as the signal strength is decreasing with distance, the noise is becoming stronger. Amplifiers cannot discern the noise from the actual conversation. Thus, the amplifier not only boosts the signal, it also boosts the noise. This creates a stronger, but noisier, signal that leads to some extremely noisy circuits, represented in Figure 5-8. The results of amplification are cumulative over distance. The more amplifiers that must be used, the worse the overall signal gets. This is a function of the equipment, the electrical characteristics, and the finances combined.

Note that if analog technology were still in wide use, some of the latest advances in digital signal processing (DSP) could now be used to clean up an amplified voice transmission somewhat. However, a better approach to producing clean signals was developed many years ago.

Analog-to-Digital Conversion

Because the analog version of the network was a problem for the network suppliers and the telcos alike, both turned to a digital form of communication. To convert the voice conversation from analog to digital, a device called an analog-to-digital (A/D) converter employs a sampling technique. **Sampling** refers to the process of measuring representative portions of a signal over time.

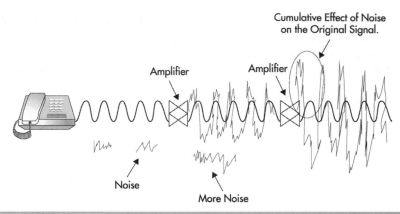

Figure 5-8 Amplifying both signal and noise leads to an additive value of the noise, creating a noisy circuit.

We assume that chronologically adjacent portions will differ only slightly. If the samples are taken frequently enough and played back faithfully at the other end, the ear will be unable to differentiate the playback from the original. A different sampling technique is used in movies and other video applications. When a movie is made, there is no truly continuous record of the images; instead, a series of still images, sampling the reality at 30 samples (or "frames") per second, is recorded and later presented to the viewer. Normally, the viewer cannot distinguish between the playback of the samples and the real thing.

As mentioned earlier, the bandwidth of the audio signal we want to transmit is 3000 Hz (3,300 minus 300). Based on the Nyquist Theorem, the minimum sampling rate would be 6600 Hz

Try This

To get a better view of the range and the waves in a human speech pattern, try to use your PC or notebook computer to record speech, and then play it back.

Start by hooking up a microphone to the PC.

Press Start—Programs—Accessories— Entertainment—Sound Recorder.

Record a sound file using the Red record button.

Play the file back and observe the way the playback looks in the sinusoidal waves being shown. The file will show several starts and pauses in the speech pattern, as well as the signal values in a sinusoidal wave.

If you have a more sophisticated program, you can edit this file and show it in far more detail by setting the values to show more detail. This part will depend on your equipment.

(2 * 3300 Hz). In fact, a somewhat higher rate of 8000 Hz (samples per second) is used as shown in Figure 5-9. This addresses the need for guard bands. *Guard bands* account for the fact that filters are not perfect and some signals beyond the bandpass filter limits still propagate on the wire (this is why the audio channel in telephones is 4000 Hz wide to carry signals that max out at 3300 Hz).

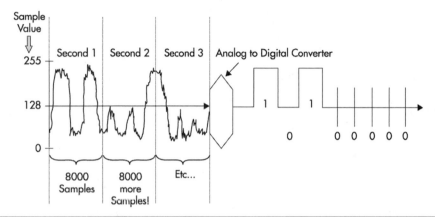

Figure 5-9 To address the higher range of frequencies, the sampling rate is increased to 8,000 per second.

Each sample measures the amplitude level of the voice signal at a particular point in time. One sample comprises 8 bits, where a bit represents a 1 or a 0. An 8-bit byte can represent any decimal number from 0 to 255 (00000000 is zero, 00000001 is one, 00000010 is two, 00000011 is three, 0000100 is four, 0000101 is five, and so on up to 11111111, which equals 255). Therefore, a total of 256 possible levels exist, sufficient to re-create the analog signal faithfully at the receiving end. More samples would produce a higher-quality replication, but 256 values is an adequate compromise between audio quality and bandwidth conservation.

Eight-thousand samples per second (which conforms to the Nyquist Theorem) with each sample requiring 8 bits generate a digital stream of data at a rate of 64,000 bits per second. We know this as the digital signal zero (DS0).*

The square waves travel down the same pair of wires you are accustomed to, but to handle the digital signal, the amplifiers are removed. Additional equipment (such as loading coils) is

---

*The digital signal zero is the digitized equivalent of one voice channel. The bits are each in the form of a square wave, in contrast to the familiar sinusoidal wave typically seen on an oscilloscope. The DS0 is also one speech channel capable of carrying 64,000 bits of digital information (voice or data).

Try This

The mathematics using binary sequences is all about the exponents of 2. Let's try some examples of how this works. Represent a value of 37 in binary using an 8-bit sequence:

Here is how you do that: First, you can set up a template using the values of 2 as follows:

$2^7 = 128$	$2^6 = 64$	$2^5 = 32$	$2^4 = 16$	$2^3 = 8$	$2^2 = 4$	$2^1 = 2$	$2^0 = 1$

Now, you fill in a value of 1 for on and a value of 0 for off to create the binary value of your number, which as you recall is decimal 37.

0	0	1	0	0	1	0	1

The result is $32 + 4 + 1 = 37$, and that is represented as 0010 0101.

Now, try this for the number 163!

128	64	32	16	8	4	2	1

Record your answer here: _____

also removed. In short, the entire circuit is reengineered from end-to-end. In place of the removed equipment, digital regenerators (or repeaters) are used. A repeater does not amplify the signal. Instead, a **repeater** listens to the input waves, interprets each digital one or zero that was sent, and then creates a new, clean signal as its output. In this way, the noise is never retransmitted, and each repeater regenerates a digital signal that is an exact replica of the original signal with no degradation over distance. The strength of the digital signal is based on a 3-volt pulse of a short duration. Therefore, the repeaters must be placed closer together, typically every mile, as shown in Figure 5-10. This requires more equipment, which is an expense to the telcos and network suppliers alike. Nevertheless, when the samples are played back at the far end, customers receive the transmitted signal in a form indistinguishable from that sent from the original A/D converter at the sending location.

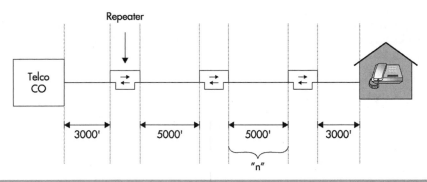

Figure 5-10 Repeaters are placed approximately one mile apart.

Digital Signaling

As mentioned earlier, digital signals consist of 1's and 0's. But even this statement can be a bit confusing. How do you insert a 1 or a 0 onto a wire? Unlike the varying levels used in analog transmission, signaling on a digital circuit can be as simple as sending one voltage level to represent 1's (+3 V), while no voltage represents a 0. This is called a unipolar signal. The receiving equipment measures the voltage level once each bit time. **Unipolar** is defined as using only one value of the voltage (a 1 is represented by a positive voltage: +3 V).

A *bit time* is the length of time it takes to transmit 1 bit. For example, at 9,600 bits per second, 1 bit time equals 1/9600 of a second (about 104 microseconds). The measurement is taken in the middle of the bit time, when the likelihood of getting a precise level is maximized, as shown in Figure 5-11.

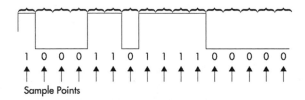

Figure 5-11 Measurements of the pulse are taken in the middle of the bit time to get a precise level of the reading.

Many types of digital signaling exist. The previous description presents the type of signaling used for Morse code. A slightly more sophisticated scheme, called either alternate mark inversion (AMI) or bipolar signaling, is used for wide-area digital transmissions. We can say that **alternate mark inversion** means this: when you present a 1 on the circuit, alternating 1's

5

will be inverted in their polarity. This **bipolar** (a 1 is a +3 V or a −3 V) signal uses both positive and negative polarity, hence, bipolar. Because voice is inherently analog (it varies continuously, rather than occurring in a discrete, numerically related pattern), an analog-to-digital (A/D) conversion must be performed if you want to transmit voice digitally. The section "Digital Data in an Analog World" covers how to change an analog signal into a digital format. But, first, you must answer the important question, "Why bother to convert to digital?" One reason is quality. Another reason is overall cost. When voice is converted to data, it allows the telco to better utilize circuits.

Analog signal paths must use amplifiers if the paths cover any significant distance. Because amplifiers retain and even strengthen noise in a conversation, the more amplifiers used in a transmission path, the noisier the background. So, when you use an analog circuit to call your grandfather in the old country to wish him a happy birthday, you will be most fortunate if either of you can understand the other over the background noise. To compensate for this problem of a noisy overseas (or long-distance) call, we use an age-old technique: Yell!

By yelling into the phone to overcome the noise, you do little to help the situation. When you raise your voice to new heights, you increase the amplitude. This makes the signal strong (stronger than what the telephone companies expect). The telephone companies have, however, installed equipment on the line that will limit the maximum signal strength. These *pads,* as they are called, sense that the amplitude is much higher than normal, so they introduce loss to compensate and bring the amplitude down. This serves to compound the problem, because the loss in decibels (dB) will steal away the amplitude, but it will do nothing for the noise. So, you have gained nothing, as you can see in Figure 5-12.

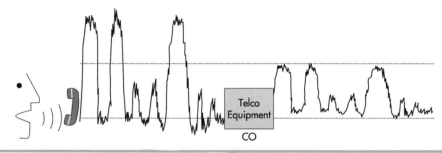

Figure 5-12 Yelling to increase the signal strength adds nothing to the conversation. In fact, yelling may hurt more than it helps because the higher amplitude is filtered off the line.

The digital equivalent of an amplifier is a repeater. It is a replacement technique. Why? Well, we'll explain.

As the digital pulse is placed onto the wires, only the 1's (3 V) need to be of any concern. But, as the pulse is placed onto the wire, it immediately begins to propagate down the wires. The wire will immediately begin to act on this pulse by diminishing its strength. The result will be a constantly decaying pulse of electricity. (See Figure 5-13 for a representation of what might be happening.) Because this decaying process begins immediately, the likelihood of the pulse falling into obscurity is high. So, this regenerator (a la the replacement technique) is placed on the link at approximately every 5,000 to 6,000 feet. As the pulse declines in strength, it must be kept at sufficient strength to be recognized as a pulse and not as noise. This distance is used to keep the signal above what is called the pulse detection threshold level. If the strength of the pulse falls below this detection threshold, the pulse will be mistaken for noise and ignored.

Figure 5-13 The digital signal decays quickly, requiring that something be done to ensure the pulse will make it to the end of the wires.

When the pulse arrives at the repeater, the repeater will replace it. It will literally absorb the signal—and make it disappear. The repeater has done its job. However, the other side of this repeater has a reverse function. Therefore, it will basically put a brand-new pulse on the line in the original's place. Thus, a brand new 3-V pulse will be introduced. The signal begins to propagate immediately down the next leg of the circuit. And the process starts all over again.

But whereas an amplifier simply strengthens the input signal, a repeater detects the 1's and 0's of the original signal and retransmits them out the other side, as good as new. In particular, any noise introduced into the signal between the source and the repeater is completely ignored as long as it stays below a certain tolerance level. Amplitude decreases will still occur between repeaters and noise will be introduced, but so long as a repeater can recognize the original pulses (1's), those are the only parts of the received signal that will be used to build the new output signal. Thus, if a communications path is built with digital technology, it is entirely possible to deliver a signal identical to that sent from the first digital transmitter in the path to the ultimate receiver, as shown in Figure 5-14. Because the pulse is short in duration and a

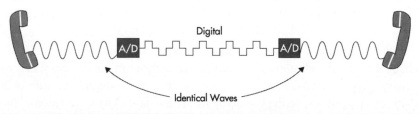

Figure 5-14 If you design the circuit properly, you should be able to deliver a signal identical to the one originally created by the first transmitter in the path.

discrete value of energy rather than a constantly varying voltage level, more repeaters are required on the link. Telcos must use three to four times as much equipment on the same distance of wire with digital communications at the local loop.

Note the last part of the earlier statement ". . . from the first digital transmitter in the path." Because voice is analog, a conversion will occur at some point. From the voice source to that first conversion point, noise can be introduced that will remain in the signal. Obviously, the closer to the voice source that the A/D conversion takes place, the better.

Say you have a conversation with someone in another state or another country, and that conversation is as clear as if the person to whom you are speaking were right in front of you. You can be sure that most, if not all, of the technology involved is digital rather than analog. Such quality results in happier customers, cleaner transmission, improved data communications, and happier carriers. This is why all the excitement exists in the industry about the benefits of digital transmission.

There is another benefit to using digital rather than analog transmission, although it directly benefits the service providers more than their customers. Digital technology facilitates combining and manipulation of signals, providing a carrier with more flexibility in how it moves the signal from source to destination.

Digital Data in an Analog World

We have been focusing on voice transmission, a communications technology that starts and ends with an analog signal—a voice. But what about data communications? Because it starts out as digital, doesn't that simplify things? The answer is no, not so you'd notice.

Until the last few decades, digital service was unavailable to users. Because of this, an entire technology came into being that provided methods for carrying digital signals across the analog voice network. The critical component in this technology is the modem. The word "modem" is a contraction of the terms modulator and demodulator. In a nutshell, the function of a *modem* is to provide digital-to-analog (D/A) conversion (and, of course, the reverse) for a digital device that needs to communicate with a remote digital device across the analog telephone network. Figure 5-15 shows this multiple conversion process.

Recall earlier we stated that the phone system takes voice and performs A/D conversion for transmission. This is a contrast we should explain. When voice is being transmitted across the network, it typically enters the network as analog voice. At the initial point of digitization (typically at the first CO), the voice is then converted into digital signals. These digital signals are then multiplexed onto a carrier (such as a T1) and moved from CO to CO.

Data, on the other hand, starts as a digital signal in the terminal device. When you prepare to transmit data, you must use a device (modem) to convert the digital data into analog signals, so the data can be presented to the line in the standard format. The modulation of the data into analog signals occurs at the modem. Conversely, the receiving end demodulates the analog signal and converts it back to a digital signal.

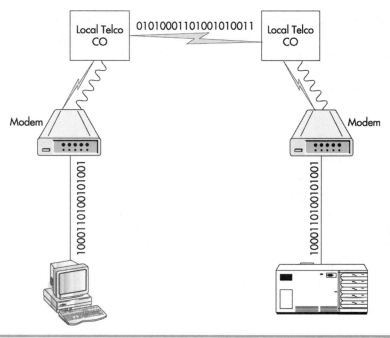

Figure 5-15 Multiple conversions take place on the end-to-end communications circuits today.

However, as you can imagine, the data are originally created in digital form, converted into analog form (modulated), and carried out to the telco. From there, the data are reconverted into a different digital format and carried across the network. Several steps of conversion occur throughout the network. Finally, at the receiving end, it is demodulated back into its original form.

Because, in fact, telephone companies' backbones are now mostly digital (with the local-loop signals that originate as analog transmissions being digitized at the CO), a communications path using modems includes not one or even two but as many as four D/A or A/D conversions—and that's only one way! This is a result of the legacy compatibility requirements of local phone systems.

The local loop (sometimes called the "last mile") has been held back because of the vast installed base of end-user equipment (analog telephones, fax and answering machines, and so forth) and the telco equipment (literally hundreds of millions of load coils, amplifiers, and analog line cards). However, even this last bastion of analog transmission is under assault.

The future of the telecommunications networks will be all digital. While in the past, the cost of digital devices exceeded that of analog equivalents, the price curve for the analog devices has long since flattened—whereas the cost of digital components has steadily dropped and continues to do so. Until the local loop is fully digitized, we will operate in a world of mixed analog and digital components. But, except for that local loop, expect virtually every other communications medium to employ digital technology.

❓ Line Check 5-1

1. The signals are using small amount of voltages on the line. Therefore, to get the benefit from the digital circuitry, how far apart are repeaters placed?

2. What is another major consideration in upgrading to digital local loops?

3. What are the two values of the one pulse in the AMI signal?

T1 and the T-Carrier

In the early 1960s, the existing carrier and cabling systems were rapidly becoming strained for capacity. In addition, the demand for newer and higher-speed communications facilities was building among customers, as well as within the systems themselves. As a result, the Bell System introduced T1 service, a new digital technology.

When this digital technology was being introduced, it was deployed in the public network as a means of increasing the traffic capacity within the telephone company on the existing wire-pair cable facilities as interoffice trunks (IOT). The older systems, including the **N-carrier** system, used a two- or four-wire connection through an analog multiplexing device to deliver either 12 or 24 analog channels. This was still an inefficient use of the line capacity, and the analog service was noisy and required expensive line-treatment equipment. Therefore, the telephone company introduced its newer technology to overcome the limitations of the existing plant and transmission services.

Some of the problems with the analog systems were also related to the circuit quality. Anyone who can remember the older analog network knows that a call placed across the country from the East Coast to the West Coast was significantly different from such a call made today. The static and noise on the line made the call sound more like it went to the moon and back. Because that's all that was available, that's what the user became accustomed to. Because of the quality issues related to distance, long-distance calls rarely took alternate paths around congested switch centers—even if it was the only option for completing the call—because of the severe impact on voice quality.

But with the introduction of digital transmission over T-carriers, the use of older analog systems was ending within the telephone company networks. The telcos had to find a way of improving the utilization of the cable plant on an interoffice basis to overcome problems with underutilized pairs of wires. In addition, the continued installation of inefficient systems was expensive and bulky. The average length of the wires between the telco's offices was approximately 6.5 miles. As calling requirements continued to grow, the telcos needed to increase the traffic-handling capacity on these interoffice routes. The telcos were in a quandary, however. First, they didn't want to continue running bulky cables between offices because there simply wasn't enough space. Second, costs for maintaining the cable plant were escalating. Something had to be done quickly. Figure 5-16 shows the use of wires between the telco offices. These wires provide the interoffice communications from telco to telco. The end user or customer was kept on the old analog twisted pairs of wire. From a user's perspective, the changes were invisible, except that some improvement in call quality was evident because of the transition in the telco infrastructure to digital. Recall that, earlier, you learned that the use of digital repeaters eliminated much of the noise.

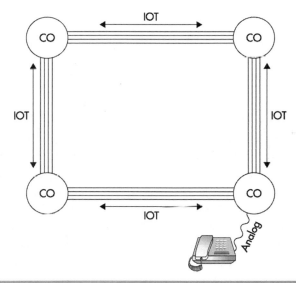

Figure 5-16 The telco offices used a tremendous amount of wire between them.

Analog Transmission Basics

Before going much further, you should have a brief refresher on the dial-up telephone network to help you understand the need for the digital architecture that was introduced through the use of the T-carrier system. The telephone system was designed around providing analog dial-up voice telephony. Everything was based on voice communications services on a switched (nondedicated) basis. A user could connect his or her telephone to that of another user on the network through either an operator-connected or a dial-up (a later evolution) addressing scheme. The *T-carrier* transmits digital signals over twisted-pair circuit. The telephone companies use an alpha designator (an alphabetic character) for each of their carriers (*N*-carrier was used to describe their analog system, whereas the *O*-carrier was their over-air microwave carrier and *L*-carrier was their coaxial carrier).

Because voice is the primary service provided, the telephone set, as seen in Figure 5-17, was designed as a device that takes the sound wave from the human vocal cords and converts that sound into an electrical current, represented by its analog equivalent.

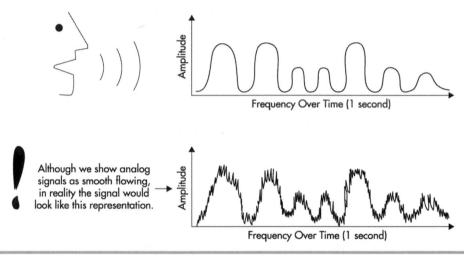

Figure 5-17 The telephone set was used to convert the analog speech into an electrical signal.

The Evolution to Digital

The telcos were looking to enhance the quality of calls and better utilize the cable facilities. The T-carrier system allowed them to increase the call-carrying capacity, while taking advantage of the unused transmission capacity of their existing wire pair facilities, and to improve the quality of transmission by migrating away from the older analog techniques. The evolution to **T-carrier** was important for a number of reasons:

- The T-carrier was the first successful system designed to utilize digitized voice transmission.

● The T-carrier identified many of the standards that are employed today for digital switching and digital transmission, including a modulation technique.

● The transmission rate was established at 1,544,000 bits per second.

● The T-carrier technology defined many of the rules—or protocols—and constraints in use today for other types of communications.

In many cases, the telephone companies used a single pair of twisted wires to carry a phone call. This meant that as uses of the interoffice facilities grew, the cable plant grew exponentially. As more COs (or end offices) were added, the need for meshing these together grew. Interconnecting each office with enough pairs of wire to service user demands was becoming a nightmare. Figure 5-18 depicts the need for cabling or interoffice trunking to support the growing demand for services. As each new end office was added, the wiring systems had to grow to serve customer demands.

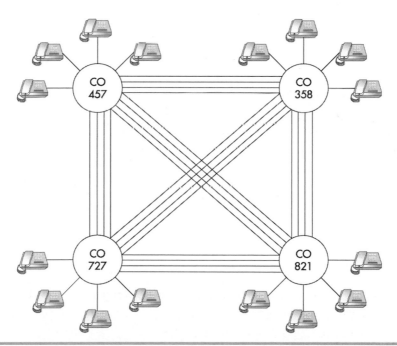

Figure 5-18 The need for intercommunications between and among COs was exponential, and it created a wiring nightmare for the telcos.

Remember, the telephone companies saw this carrier system as a telco service only. Even as the end-user population grew, the telcos still held back on deploying this digital capability to the end user. The telcos used the higher efficiencies to support the end user digitally, from end office to end office or through the network. The user was still relegated to a single conversation on a twisted pair using analog transmission. Thus, this system operated in an analog format on the local loop, but digitally on the IOTs. In metropolitan areas, the telcos were reaping the benefits of the T-carrier system. Figure 5-19 is a representation of the telephone company deployment of analog/digital transmission capacities.

Some immediate benefits were achieved: the quality of transmission improved dramatically, and the utilization of existing wire facilities increased. A single four-wire facility on twisted wires could now carry 24 simultaneous conversations digitally at an aggregated rate of 1.544 Mbps.

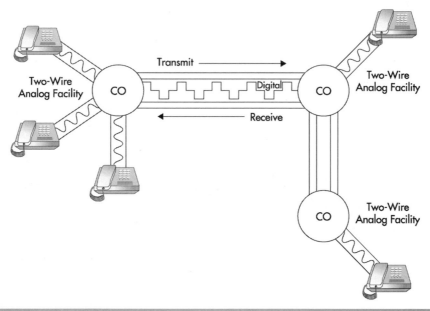

Figure 5-19 The telephone companies deployed analog and digital facilities between the transmission paths.

As digital switching systems were introduced into the dial-telephone network, they were designed around the same techniques employed in the T-carrier system. The digital-switching matrices of the #4 and #5 electronic switching systems (ESS) developed by Western Electric (now called Avaya) and the DMS systems (10, 100, 250) developed by Northern Telecom, Inc. (now called Nortel Networks), utilize **pulse code modulation (PCM)** internally, so digital carrier systems and channels can be interfaced directly into the digital switching systems. By adhering to the standards set forth, the operating telcos and the long-haul carriers could build integrated digital switching and digital transmission systems that did the following:

● Eliminated the need to terminate the digital channels or equipment to provide analog interfaces to digital-switching architectures.

● Avoided the addition of quantizing noise that would be introduced by another D/A conversion process. Whenever a conversion of the signal from A/D or from D/A is necessary, the risk of errors and noise increases.

These techniques were used to provide lower-cost, better-quality, dial-up telephone services. However, this same technology underlies the idea of full end-to-end digital networking services that is the basis of Integrated Services Digital Networks (ISDN), the future and the higher-end broadband services that are emerging.

❓ Line Check 5-2

5

Test Your Skills

The evolution to T-carrier was important for a number of reasons:

1. It was the _____ successful system designed to utilize digitized voice transmission.

2. It identified many of the _____ that are employed today for digital switching and digital transmission, including a modulation technique.

3. The transmission rate was established at _____ bits per second.

4. The _____ technology defined many of the rules, or protocols, and constraints in use today for other types of communications.

❓

Analog-to-Digital Conversion

The sample now had to be created into a bit stream of 1's and 0's, as already stated. To represent the true tone and inflection of the human voice, enough bits need to be used to create a digital word. Using an 8-bit word creates enough different points on a wave to do just that. The wave is divided into 256 possible amplitude combinations at the moment of the sample itself. Figure 5-20 shows how the sampling is accomplished using two states and 8 bits to create 2^8 or 256 points on the analog wave. As each sample is taken, the amplitude of the wave is sampled. There are two sampling standards—*A-law* and *Mu-law*—but they perform the same function: assigning a numeric value at a sampling instance. A-law is used with most of the international coding techniques, whereas Mu-law is used in North America.

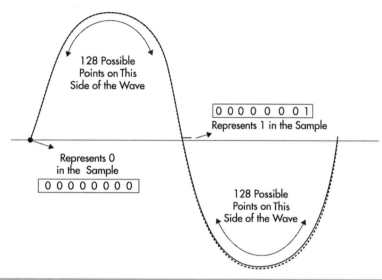

Figure 5-20 The wave is divided into 256 possible amplitude values, so digital transmission can be accomplished.

Once the sample has been taken and the digital equivalent created into an 8-bit word, the digital (or square) waves representing that word can be transmitted. The 1 represents the presence of a voltage and the 0 represents the absence of a voltage, as shown in Figure 5-21.

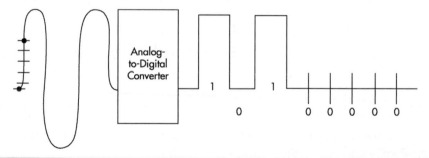

Figure 5-21 The values are now prepared to be sent; a 1 is equal to the presence of voltage, and a 0 is shown as no voltage.

This conversion uses PCM to create the sample. Using PCM and the rules established, the transmission of the digital equivalent of the analog wave results in 8,000 samples per second * 8 bits per sample = 64,000 bits per second as the basis for a voice transmission in PCM mode (see Figure 5-22).

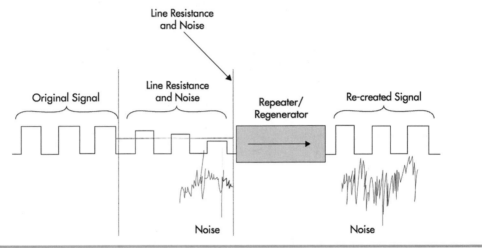

Figure 5-22 The signal is re-created rather than amplified to regenerate it in its original, error-free state.

✎ Line Check 5-3

Nyquist's Theorem included a three-step process to create the PCM signal. The steps are:

1. Sample the data at twice the highest frequency (S = $2f_h$), which is 8,000 samples/sec.

2. Quantize the information by using an 8-bit sample (2^8 = 256 quantizing values), which also produces the 8,000 samples * 8 bits/sample = 64,000 bps channel.

3. Digitally encode the data using the ±3 V pulses (a digital 1 is ±3 V and a digital 0 is 0 V).

The Movement to End Users

To deliver this digital capability to the customer, a special assembly or individual-case-basis (ICB) tariff arrangement was initially used. This emergence didn't occur until the mid-1970s. At first, this was done with some reluctance, but as the movement caught on, the deployment was both quick and dynamic. The telcos had to modify the outside plant to accommodate the end-user needs. To do this, they first had to engineer the circuit. Next, they had to remove all the analog transmission equipment from the line. Then, any splices, taps, bridges, and other problems that caused loss and noise, and thereby impaired transmission on the circuit, had to be removed or cleaned up. Repeaters were next added to the line.

The first deployment of this service was for voice, but data quickly became the dominant rider of the new digital transmission. Also note that as T1 became more readily available, the primary use (75 percent) was to consolidate multiple analog lines onto a single digital trunk for WATS service and Private Branch Exchanges (PBXs). This digital transmission capability was designed around the voice dial-up network, so the service was a natural fit.

T1 Basics

T1 is characterized by the following operating characteristics.

1. A Four-Wire Circuit

Because this technology evolved from the old twisted-pair environment, four wires were used. Two wires are used to transmit, and two wires are used to receive. Other facilities can be used, but for now, think of it this way.

2. Full Duplex

Because four wires are used, transmission and reception can take place simultaneously. Many customers derive other uses, such as one-way only for remote printing, file transfer, and so on, or two-way communications for alternate service, such as voice communications.

3. Digital

This is an all-digital service. Data, analog facsimile, analog voice, and the like are all converted to digital pulses (1's and 0's) for transmission on the line.

4. Time-Division Multiplexing

The digital stream is capable of carrying a standard 64-Kbps channel; 24 channels are multiplexed to create an aggregate of 1.536 Mbps. Time division allows a channel to use a slot 1/24 of the time. These are fixed time slots made available to the channel.

5. Pulse-Code Modulation

Using the example, the analog voice or other signal is sampled 8,000 times per second. An 8-bit word is used to represent each sample, thus yielding the 64-Kbps channel capacity.

6. Framed Format

As the pulse-code modulation scheme is used, the 24 channels are time-division multiplexed into a frame to be carried along the line. Each frame represents one sample of 8 bits from each of the 24 channels. Added to this is a framing bit. The net is a frame of 193 bits, as shown in a frame in the following illustration. There are 8,000 frames per second; therefore, a frame is 125 microseconds long. Framing accounts for 8 Kbps overhead (1 bit * 8,000 frames). Adding this 8 Kbps to the 1.536 Mbps (discussed in the paragraph on time-division multiplexing) yields an aggregate of 1.544 Mbps.

F	1	2	3	4	5	6	7	8	9	10	11	12	13	14	15	16	17	18	19	20	21	22	23	24

The frame consists of 24 samples, each 8 bits long, plus 1 bit of framing overhead. 8,000 frames per second will be generated.

7. Bipolar Format

T1 uses electrical voltage across the line to represent the pulses (1's). The bipolar format serves two purposes. It cuts the required bandwidth in half from 1.544 MHz to 772 kHz, which increases repeater spacing. And the signal voltage averages out to zero, reducing crosstalk and allowing direct current (DC) power to be simplexed on the line to power intermediate regenerators. Think of this as an alternating current (AC) version of a DC line. Every other pulse will be represented by the negative equivalent of the pulse. For example, the first pulse will be represented by a positive 3 V (+3 V), the next pulse will be represented by a negative 3 V (−3 V), and so on. This effectively yields a 0 voltage on the line, because the ± equalizes the current. This bipolar format is also called AMI. A mark is a digital 1, and a space is a digital 0. Alternate marks (ones) are inverted in their polarity.

8. Byte-Synchronous Transmission

Each sample is made up of 8 bits sampled from each channel. Timing for the channels is derived from the pulses that appear within the samples. This timing keeps everything in proper sequence. If the devices on both ends of the line do not see any pulses, they lose synchronization. This means the T1 will be synchronous unto itself, using its own internal timing, rather than an external timing source. When using the T1 as the basis of other higher multiplexing schemes, this is important to remember. The timing is derived from the pulses on the specific link, so the link is timed to itself. If you need to multiplex into higher-speed services, additional stuffing bits may have to be added to get the individual T1s timed to a common timing arrangement.

9. Channelized or Nonchannelized

The basic T1 circuit is made up of 24 individual channels. Each channel has a 64-Kbps capacity. In addition 8 Kbps of capacity is added to manage the circuit. This is why T1 is called a *channelized service*. However, the newer multiplexing equipment can be used to configure a T1 circuit in a number of different ways. For example, the T1 circuit can be used as a single channel of 1.536 Mbps for a router connection to the WAN or as two high-speed data channels at 384 Kbps each, plus a separate video channel of 768 Kbps. The point is this: the service does not have to be configured in 24 channels, but it can be reconfigured into any usable data stream needed (equipment allowing, of course).

In addition to twisted pair, other suitable media (fiber, digital microwave, coax, and so forth) can also be used. The T1 is still treated as a four-wire circuit. As a four-wire circuit, the telco will normally terminate the four wires into a demarcation point (DEMARC) or network interface unit (NIU). Individual circuits can be terminated into a recommended jack—RJ-48 (sometimes called *dumb jacks*) or RJ-68 (called *smart jacks*). These jacks serve as the interface to the four wires. In a larger environment or where multiple circuits are involved, other methods of termination can be used.

From the RJ-48, a cable using one of a number of possible connectors) will be extended to the customer premises equipment (CPE). Usually, the CPE is a **channel service unit (CSU)** or equivalent. Figure 5-23 is a representation of the connection from the CO to the CPE.

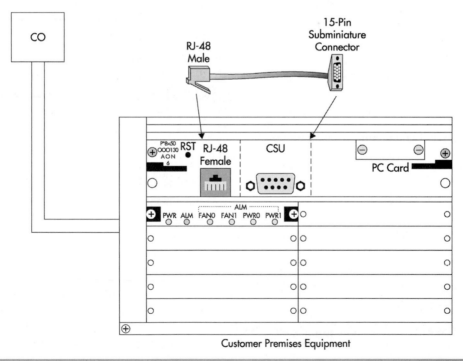

Figure 5-23 The connection is run from the CO to the CPE.

The CPE uses time-division multiplexing to carry the multiple voice and data conversations across the line. Time-division multiplexing is somewhat efficient in that it allows time slots to be dedicated to each of the conversations to be carried on the line. Using fixed time slots, conversations will be in the same relative slot (or bucket) for each sample.

The time slot is always present, and if no traffic is being generated between points across the line, the time slot goes unused. The slot is empty. For this reason, time-division multiplexing still has inherent inefficiencies. Attempts to get the full 1.536 Mbps of service from a T1 would be thwarted because of the fixed time-slot problem. Figure 5-24 is a representation of this time-division multiplexing (TDM or MUX) scheme.

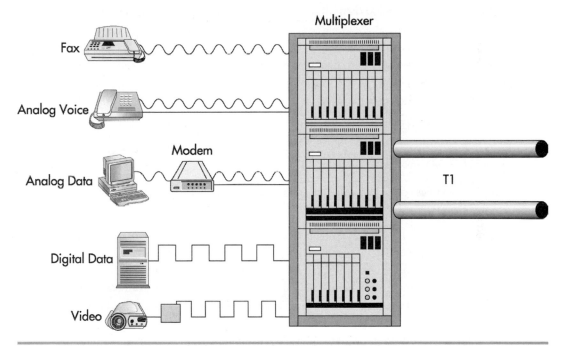

Figure 5-24 Time-division multiplexing uses the 24 channels in their own time slots.

The framing bit can be equated to a pointer or an address. Because the line is moving bits of information at 1,544,000 per second, it would be easy to skew left or right and get information out of sequence. Therefore, the extra 8,000 bits of information (1 bit per frame, 8,000 frames per second) create a locator for the equipment to lock in on. This pointer allows the devices to read a pattern of bits to know which frame is being received or transmitted and the location of each channel thereafter.

Framing has undergone several evolutions over the years. The first use of T1 service was for voice, so the information was easier to use. When you convert voice or data to digital pulses, it all looks the same. Data is unique because if you insert any pulses, this can affect the data, whereas it would be unnoticeable with voice. The evolution of framing followed a sequence as outlined in Table 5-1.

Framing	Use	Pattern/Use
D1	Voice or analog data	Alternating 1's & 0's
D2	Voice or analog data	12-frame sequence Superframe
D1D	Voice or analog data	Upgrade compatibility for D1
D3	Voice or analog data	Superframe format and sequence bits
D4	Voice & data (digital)	Superframe
D5*	Voice & data (digital)	Superframe
ESF	Voice & data, plus maintenance	Extended superframe (ESF)

*D5 doesn't really exist as a standard. However, in the electronic switching systems, this framing was termed a software version of the D4 format.

Table 5-1 The Evolution of the Framing Used the Sequence Shown Here.

The D4 superframe uses a framing pattern for voice and data. The framing pattern in the D4 superframe is a repeating 12-bit sequence (1000 1101 1100) that allows signaling bits to be "robbed" in the 6th and 12th frames of the superframe. The 8th bit from each sample in Frames 6 and 12 is used to provide signaling. This pattern of the framing format is shown in Figure 5-25.

Table 5-2 shows the actual framing of a data stream in the D4 framing format. The framing bit pattern repeats every 12 frames. Twelve frames make up a superframe (SF). Once again, this requires each of the 24 channels to be robbed of the least significant bit (LSB) in the 6th and 12th frames. This has an impact on the data capacity that always limits the user to 56 Kbps of effective throughput (resulting in a net overhead of 192 Kbps given up to provide signaling).

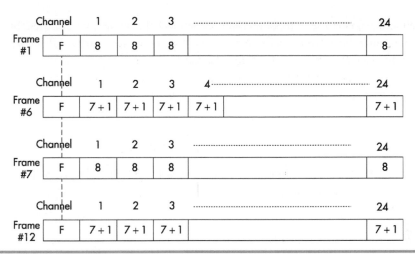

Figure 5-25 The framing pattern used in a D4 framing on a T1 circuit.

		Framing Bits		Bit Use in Each Time Slot		Signaling Bit Use Options	
Frame	Bit	Terminal Frame F1	Signaling Frame F1	Traffic (All Channels)	Signaling	Transparent	Signaling Channel
1	0	1	—	1–8	—		
2	193		0	1–8	—		
3	386	0	—	1–8	—		
4	579	—	0	1–8	—		
5	772	1	—	1–8	—		
6	965	—	1	1–7	8	—	A
7	1158	0	—	1–8	—		
8	1351	—	1	1–8	—		
9	1544	1	—	1–8	—		
10	1737	—	1	1–8	—		
11	1930	0	—	1–8	—		
12	2123	—	0	1–7	8	—	B

Table 5-2 Superframe Format. The 6th and 12th Frames Are Used to Denote the Presence of Signaling Bits.

In Figure 5-26 the use of bipolar communications helps to prevent electrical buildup and aids in the detection of errors. Because the signal uses both the upper and the lower segment of the wave, the signal only uses half of the bandwidth.

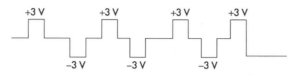

Figure 5-26 Bipolar is used to prevent any problems with voltage buildup, detect errors, and use only half the bandwidth.

Byte Synchronous

When transmitting on the T1, timing and synchronization come from the bits transmitted. Because each sample is made up of 8 bits, a byte is formed. The transmitters and receivers synchronize on the basis of the pulses in the byte format. If a string of 0's is transmitted in several frames, then synchronization is lost; the devices get amnesia as to where they were. Consequently, conventions on the transmission of the byte were established. These conventions are called the *1's density rule*. What this means is that to maintain synchronization, a certain amount of 1's must be present.

For voice communication, this doesn't pose a problem because the voice generates a continuous change in amplitude voltages which, when encoded into an 8-bit word (byte), displays the presence of voltage (1's). However, in data transmission, strings of 0's are possible (even probable) when refreshing or painting screens of information. Hence, the 1's density rule comes into play.

Simply put, the 1's density rule states this: in every 24 bits of information to be transmitted, there must be at least three pulses (1's), and no more than 15 0's can be transmitted consecutively. A more stringent requirement set by AT&T in the implementation of its digital transmission is that, in every 8 bits of information, at least 1 pulse must be present. This basically equates to 12.5 percent of the pulses must be a 1.

Think of how this affects data transmission. If your data must have at least one pulse per byte, you have to change the way you deliver data to the line. A technique known as *pulse stuffing* is used to meet these conventions: the 8th bit in every byte was stuffed with a 1. This limited the data transmission rate to 56 Kbps because 7 usable bits, plus a stuff bit, had to be transmitted. The end-receiving equipment will receive 00000001 and be unable to tell if we sent 00000001 or if we sent 00000000, and the last bit was forced to a 1 for timing purposes. Because of this rule, we cannot trust the 8th bit, so we relegate ourselves to using 7 bits for data and the 8th bit for timing, all the time. Figure 5-27 is a representation of the 1's density rule and pulse stuffing.

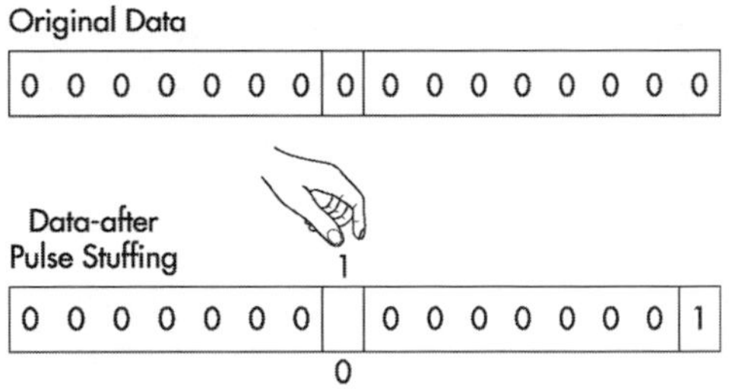

Original Data

0 0 0 0 0 0 0	0	0 0 0 0 0 0 0 0

Data-after
Pulse Stuffing   1

0 0 0 0 0 0 0		0 0 0 0 0 0 0	1

0

Figure 5-27 The 1's density rule employs pulse stuffing to prevent long strings of zeros.

To overcome this bit stuffing and yet meet the 1's density requirement, a technique known as **Bipolar 8 Zero Substitution (B8ZS)** was developed. At the customer location, B8ZS is implemented in the CSU. As data bits are delivered to the CSU for transmission across the line, the CSU (a microprocessor-controlled device) reads the 8-bit format. The CSU immediately recognizes that a string of 8/16/24 zeros will cause the following problems,

- It strips off the 8-bit byte and substitutes a fictitious byte.

- It strips eight 0's off the data stream and discards them.

- It then inserts a substitute word (byte) of 00011011.

To let the receiving end know this is a substitute word and not real data, however, two violations to the bipolar or AMI convention are created. Remember, the bipolar convention states that alternating voltages will be used for the pulses.

In the fourth and seventh positions, violations will be created that act as flags to the receiver that something is wrong. See Figure 5-28 for a graphic representation of this substitution.

Channelized Versus Nonchannelized

Up to now, discussions have focused on using the T1 for 24-channel capacity at 64 Kbps per channel. For the average user, this was the norm. However, as newer uses for the T1 service became evident, it became possible to configure the capacity to meet the need:

- A single channel of 1.536 Mbps is possible for point-to-point video conferencing.

- High-speed data on a channel of 512 Kbps, plus 16 channels of lower-speed data and voice at 64 Kbps each, are possible needs. Any other mix of services might be required.

To accommodate the mix of needs, the end user (CPE) equipment can be superrate or subrate multiplexed. This is fine, except you must ensure that the provider (LEC, CLEC, and

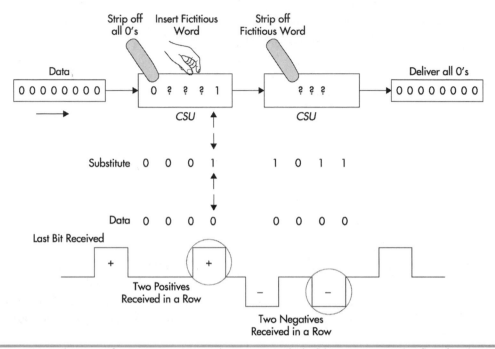

Figure 5-28 The use of B8ZS (pronounced "Bates," only kidding!) creates the flag for the equipment to recognize this is a substituted pattern.

IEC) knows you are using the service for something other than the conventional 24 channels at 64 Kbps.

If confusion exists, the carrier or provider could do some reconfiguring in the network (at its end) that could literally disrupt service for the throughput being used. Consider what would happen if a 512-Kbps data channel were somehow rerouted through a telco office, and then brought back and forced into a single 64-Kbps channel. This obviously would not work. Hence, all parties should know what uses are being made of the transmission capacity.

Line Check 5-4

Although T1 can be used for many different applications, its physical and logical characteristics are the same. Summarizing the T1 characteristics, it is:

- Generic version uses a four-wire circuit, but other media are allowed

- Full-duplex

- Digital

- Time-division multiplexed (TDM)

- PCM is used to convert analog to digital

- Framed format (D4 or ESF)

- Bipolar

- Byte synchronous

- Channelized (normally) or nonchannelized

Digital Capacities

One of the by-products of the T-carrier system was that the transmission rate employed became the standard building block for a multiplexing hierarchy. In high-speed digital transmission systems, a carrier combines many lower-speed signals into an aggregate signal for transport. To simplify this process and to hold the line on the costs of equipment, standard rates were defined.

Each of the transmission rates was assigned a number that identified the rate and configuration for the signal. Each time a higher speed is created, the lower speeds are combined and extra bits (bit stuffing) are added to come up to the signaling rate. These extra bits allow the equipment (multiplexers) to compensate for distances, clocking, and so forth, which cause transmission delay cycles.

The designations for the digital transmission are called *digital signal level-X*. Many times, people will transpose or intersperse these designators. For example, a T1 is often referred to as a DS1 in the industry. To clarify this point, *T1* is the first level of the T-carrier system. It has physical components, such as the wires, plugs and jacks, repeaters, and so forth. These physical devices combine to create the T1. DS1 is the multiplexed-digital signal, first level, carried inside the T-carrier. The *DS1* is the electrical signal (the pulses) running on the T1.

The digital hierarchy for North America includes the following.

DS0

Although originally not a formally defined rate, the **DS0** is a 64-Kbps signal that makes up the basis for the DS1. A combined 24 DS0s produce the DS1. The standard 64-Kbps pulse-coded modulation (PCM) signal is the basis for all the future networks employing digital signaling. Included in this is the ISDN.

DS1

The digital signal level 1 (DS1) is a TDM, pulse-code modulation aggregate of 1.544 Mbps, regardless of the medium used to carry the signal. The use of the channel is to get the 1.544 Mbps, but currently, the carriers may use a different service called HDSL type I or type II, or SDSL to deliver the T1 service to the customer premises. These HDSL and SDSL designations are used to describe a digital subscriber line (DSL), which we cover in Chapter 12. The physical side of this capacity is called the T1. T-1 service is distance-sensitive for the cost. Comparative costing for a T1 between the East and West Coasts is approximately $12,000 to $20,000 per month, while T-1 service between two endpoints on the same CO switch can cost around $100 per link.

DS1C

DS1C is a digital signal equivalent to two DS1s, with extra (stuff) bits to conform to a signaling standard of 3.152 Mbps. Few (if any) of these circuit capacities are still in use today. In the early days of digital and data transmission, the 3-Mbps data rate was used to link mainframes together. The physical side of this circuit is called T1C.

DS2

DS2 is a composite of four DS1s multiplexed together, yielding an aggregate rate of 6.312 Mbps. The Bell System used a DS2 capability to deliver subscriber loop carrier (SLC-96) to customers. A total of 96 DS0s could be carried across the DS2. This service was used more by the LECs in their outside plant world. However, the 6 Mbps data rate is now becoming repopularized with the promise of ADSL technologies in the local loop. If you can get 6- to 8-Mbps downloads from the Internet on our local wires, the carriers (ILEC and CLEC) stand to gain from not having to replace their infrastructure. DS2 is the highest data rate sent on normal local loop copper wire pairs. This is also called a T2 by the LECs.

DS3

The *DS3* is a 44.736-Mbps aggregate-multiplexed signal, equivalent to 28 DS1s or 672 DS0s. The T3 service is typically used by high-end data and voice customers who can afford the cost of this channel capacity. A price used for comparative purposes is from the East Coast to the West Coast, for which the T3 costs approximately $60,000 to $103,000 per month. You can see where smaller companies could not financially justify the use of the T3. T3 service is provisioned on coaxial cable or, alternately, carried on fiber-optic cable.

DS4/NA

The *DS4/NA* is a 139.264-Mbps aggregate-multiplexed signal, equivalent to 3 DS3s or 2016 DS0s. The high-end and long-haul telecommunications carriers use this size of channel capacity. It is unlikely that a DS4 would ever be installed at a customer location.

DS4

The *DS4* is a 274.176-Mbps aggregate-multiplexed signal, equivalent to 6 DS3s or 4032 DS0s. See Table 5-3 for a summary of these bandwidths. These rates are based on the ANSI T1.107 guidelines. From an international perspective, the ITU has set a hierarchy of rates (G.702) that differs from the North American standard. A comparison of these rates is shown in Table 5-4. As you can see, differences exist between the North American standards and the international standards.

Designator	Capacity (Kbps)	Equivalent DS-1	Equivalent DS-0	Stuff Bits
DS0	64	—	1	
DS1	1,544	1	24	8,000
DS1C	3,152	2	48	64,000
DS2	6,312	4	96	136,000
DS3	44,736	28	672	1,504,000
DS4/NA	139,264	84	2016	5,056,000
DS4	274,176	168	4032	14,784,000

Table 5-3 The Summary of the ANSI T1.107 Rates.

Designator	Capacity (Kbps)	Equivalent DS1	Equivalent DS0
E1	2,048	1	32
E2	8,448	4	128
E3	34,368	16	512
E4	139,264	64	2048
DS0	64	—	1
DS1	1,544	1	24
DS2	6,312	4	96
DS3	44,736	28	672
DS4	139,264	84	2016

Table 5-4 A Comparison of the ITU G.702 and ANSI Bandwidth and Rates of Speed.

However, other rates are evolving for transmission capacities. The standard 64 Kbps is derived from using pulse-code modulation. In several vendor products, 64 Kbps for the transmission of voice and/or analog data is considered too much bandwidth to carry traditional voice or analog data. Therefore, lower-speed capacities are derived at 32 Kbps.

In Table 5-4, the rates can be expanded to show a global designation. The North American digital rates are used within three main countries (the U.S., Canada, and Japan). However, in the rest of the world, a European standard designated as the E-x series is used. An *E-1* is the international equivalent of the T1, but different at the same time. For example, an E-1 is 2.048 Mbps and carries 32 channels.

❓ Line Check 5-5

Summarizing the levels of digital transmission speeds and capacities, you can see the family includes the following:

DS0—operates at 64 Kbps

DS1—operates at 1.544 Mbps

DS1C—operates at 3.152 Mbps

DS2—operates at 6.312 Mbps

DS3—operates at 44.736 Mbps

DS4/NA—operates at 139.264 Mbps

DS4—operates at 274.176 Mbps

Memorizing these numbers is unnecessary, but it can help you to understand the approximate rates obtained through these multiplexing schemes.

Signaling

Signaling comes into play when dealing with voice and dial-up data services. Traditionally, signaling is provided on a dial-up telephone line, across the talk path. This is referred to as *in-band signaling.* You might recall that the need to find bits to send between transmitter and receiver was accomplished in the 6th and 12th frames. *Bit robbing,* or stealing the 8th bit in each of the channels (1–24) in these two frames, allows for enough bits to signal between the transmit and receive ends. These ends can be Customer Premises Equipment (CPE) to the CO for switched services, or CPE to CPE for PBX-PBX connections, and so on.

The most common form of signaling on a T1 line is four-wire E&M signaling of type I, II, or III. The easiest implementation, acceptable to all vendors and carriers alike, is four-wire E&M type I.

Signaling is used to tell the receiver where the call or route is destined. The signal is sent through switches along the route to a distant end. The common types of signals are:

- On hook
- Off hook
- Dial tone
- Dialed digits
- Ringing cycle
- Busy tone

Four-wire E&M is used for tie lines between switches. Occasionally, other services are bundled onto a T1 circuit. These could include:

- Direct inward dialing (DID)
- Direct outward dialing (DOD)
- Two-way circuit
- Off-premises extension (OPX)
- Foreign exchange service (FX)

With these other services, the type of signaling might differ. DID/DOD on a PBX might use ground-start trunks, which requires a ground to be placed on the individual circuit to alert the CO that service is requested or some other change is on the line. Regardless of the type of signaling or the services used, signaling requires bits of information. The way to overcome the robbed-bit signaling limits data to 56 Kbps. Common Channel Signaling (CCS) is a method to get the clear-channel capability back.

Remember, constant demands occur on the use of T1 for clear channel capacity. The use of bit stuffing to conform to the 1's density rule for timing was overcome by using B8ZS. Now, to overcome bit robbing for signaling, CCS can apply.

If the 24th channel in the digital signal is dedicated, 23 clear channels can pass 64,000 bits of information. The choice is how much to give up. Table 5-5 is a decision table to help decide this process.

This CCS technique is also called the *transparent mode for signaling*. A single 64-Kbps channel (#24) is given up, rather than 8 Kbps per channel [*] 24 (192 Kbps) for the robbed bit. Carriers now use CCS7 (or SS7 as it is called in the United States) in their newer digital dial-up services under the auspices of Intelligent Networks and ISDN. In the T1 world, this means the Primary Rate Interface (PRI) at 23BD—simply stated, 23 bearer (B) channels at 64 Kbps clear

5

If (switched)	Then	Overhead (Kbps)
Voice only	Robbed bit	192
Voice and analog data	Robbed bit	192
Voice, analog data, and 56-Kbps digital data	Robbed bit	192
Digital voice or digital data @ 64 Kbps	CCS	64
Digital data @ 64 Kbps or greater	CCS	64

Table 5-5   The Decision Matrix to Use Robbed Bit or Common Channel Signaling.

channel, plus a data channel for signaling at 64 Kbps (D). The choices are not always obvious, but understanding the requirements helps steer the decision better.

Clocking (Network Synchronization)

Any digital network synchronization between the sender and the receiver must be maintained. As the DS1 (the digital signal level 1 of 1.544 Mbps) is delivered to the network, it is likely to be multiplexed with other digital streams from many other users. All these signals will then be transported as a single signal over high-capacity digital links (DS3 and above). Further, if the line is directly interfaced to a digital switching device, then synchronization must be maintained between the customer's transmitter and the switch.

Synchronization is imperative in a digital transmission system. If the timing of arrival or transmission is off, then the information will be distorted. Regardless of whether voice, data, video, or image traffic is present, the presentation of a digital stream of 1's and 0's is contingent on a timed arrival between the two ends.

Potential Synchronization Problems

When a digital system is scheduled to receive a bit, it expects to do just that. However, clocking or timing differences between the transmitter and receiver can exist. Therefore, while the receiver is expecting a bit that the transmitter hasn't sent, a slip occurs. Most likely, slips will be present because of multiple factors in any network. These can result from the two clocks at the ends being off or from problems that can occur along the link.

Along the link, problems can be accommodated. The use of pulse stuffing helps, but other methods also can help. Each device along the link has a buffer capability. This buffer creates a simple means of maintaining synchronization. Pulse stuffing is done independently for each multiplexer along the way, enhancing the overall reliability of the network. However, pulse stuffing also has its negatives. The overhead at each multiplexer is basically a penalty.

Telecom Careers

Working in This Field:

A well-trained technician working for a local telephone company or a long-distance company can do well in this job field. Troubles will occur on a network and, most definitely, on a digital circuit. With approximately 6 to 12 months of exposure to testing and troubleshooting T1 circuits, a technician can earn upwards of $65,000 annually.

A lot of larger companies have hired their own internal staff, many from the carrier community, to aid in keeping their mission-critical voice and data networks fine-tuned and running smoothly. These companies have been paying between $55,000 and $75,000 per year for pcoplc with thcsc skills.

If this area interests you, you can get more information from http://www.telecommjobs.net.

Further, at both ends, the location and timing of each stuff bit must be determined, and then signaled to the receiver to enable it to locate and remove the stuff bits. When destuffing occurs, a timing problem known as *jitter* can cause degradation of the signal. When passing through multiple switching sites, the signal must be de-stuffed from a received signal, and then restuffed to a newly transmitted signal. This is expensive in both equipment and overhead.

Obviously, when slippage occurs or if a problem exists in the network buffers, the retransmission of a frame or frames of information will be required. For voice, this isn't too bad, but for data transmission, it can result in errors that can render the data unusable.

Chapter 5 Review

Chapter Summary

In this chapter we started by looking at the way the analog signal is created and carried across the circuit. As we progressed, it became obvious that the analog signal was exposed to noise, loss, and other forms of interference.

- To solve the analog problems, the idea of a digital transmission was introduced. Digital changes the sinusoidal wave form from a constant variable of amplitude and frequency to a discrete value of 1 or 0.

- As the digital signal traverses the medium (wires), it immediately begins to corrupt. Losses induced by the link and noise introduced by other methods couple to diminish the signal strength of the digital pulse. Therefore, a digital repeater (or regenerator) is used to re-create the signal as it moves down the link. Regenerators are typically spaced about 5,000 feet apart.

- Using a digital signal as a baseline, the concept of the T1 was introduced. A T1 is a digital circuit that is carried on the four copper wires. To preserve the T1 signal, a framing and formatting method places the bits in a special pattern.

- Clocking (timing) is critically important to the preservation of the original signal and to the overall performance of the network.

- A family of digital transmission speeds was developed for the benefit of the telcos, but later evolutions led to the use of the T-carrier by the end user.

Key Terms for Chapter 5

Alternate Mark Inversion (AMI) *(193)*
Analog *(184)*
Bipolar *(194)*
Bipolar 8 Zero Substitution (B8ZS) *(213)*
Channel Service Unit *(208)*
Digital *(184)*
DS0 (Digital Signal Zero) *(215)*
N-carrier *(198)*
Pulse Code Modulation (PCM) *(202)*
Repeater *(192)*
Sampling *(189)*
Sound *(185)*
T-carrier *(200)*
Unipolar *(193)*

Key Term Quiz

1. Most people recognize that the term ___digital___ refers to the expression of information in terms of 1's and 0's.

2. The ___DS0___ represents a 64-Kbps channel.

3. Human speech creates ___sound___ by banging the airwaves together.

4. A ___repeater___ re-creates the original signal and resubmits it to the circuit.

5. If you use a _____ rate of 8,000 times per second, you can create enough possible combinations to re-create the signal in good faith.

6. Using a technique called _____, you can overcome the problem of long strings of zeros in your data

7. When you present an electrical pulse on a digital circuit, you use _____ signaling to prevent killer voltages from building up on the line.

8. Normal digital signals used in computer systems and other services use a _____ electrical pulse.

9. In 1960, the Bell System rolled out the _____ as its first means of providing a digital circuit.

10. The old analog networks were represented using the N-carrier _____ carrier.

11. Nyquist proved a theorem that became the basis for _____.

Multiple-Choice Quiz

1. When did the Bell System begin to install T1 in the U.S.?

   a. 1955

   b. 1934

   c. 1982

   d. 1960

2. What was the name of the inventor of the PCM technique?

   a. Alexander Bell

   b. Heinrich Hertz

   c. Harry Nyquist

   d. Dr. Watson

3. A T1 carries how many DS0 channels of voice or data?

   a. 24

   b. 48

   c. 12

   d. 96

4. To create the 64-Kbps transmission, you apply the following steps:

    a. Sample the channel at 2× the highest frequency

    b. Quantize the information

    c. Digitally encode the signal

    d. All of the above

5. T1s are called _____synchronous

    a. Bit

    b. Byte

    c. Frame

    d. CSU

    e. DSU

6. AMI stands for

    a. Alternating Marked Information

    b. Available Mark Inverted

    c. Alternate Mark Inversion

    d. Any Mark Incident

7. The AT&T 1's-density rule states that in every 8 bits, there will be at least _____ pulse(s) and there may be no more than _____ consecutive zeros.

    a. 1 and 24

    b. 3 and 24

    c. 3 and 8

    d. 1 and 8

    e. 1 and 15

8. How many T1s are used to create a T3?

    a. 3

    b. 28

    c. 24

    d. 2

    e. None of the above

9. The analog channel that the telephone company uses is how wide?

    a. 4,000 Hz

    b. 3,000 Hz

    c. 300 Hz

    d. 3,300 Hz

10. What is the term for losing the strength of the signal?

    a. Amplification

    b. Regeneration

    c. Attenuation

    d. Gain

11. The typical distance from a CO to a consumer is _____ miles.

    a. Three

    b. Five

    c. One

    d. Two

12. How far is the spacing between a regenerator?

    a. 3,000 feet

    b. 18,000 feet

    c. 5,000 feet

    d. 15,000 feet

13. What is the time you use to represent a one or a zero?

    a. 1 nanosecond

    b. 200 microseconds

    c. 50 milliseconds

    d. 104 microseconds

14. How many possible combinations of values do you get with the digital representation in PCM?

    a. 256

    b. 3

5

    c. 128

    d. 2

Essay Quiz

1. Why would you want to use a digital transmission network over an analog network?

2. What is meant by the last mile?

3. How does the sampling in a digital transmission work under PCM?

4. Why does the telephone company use a bipolar signaling system?

Lab Projects

1. Contact your local telephone company (or the school's telecomm department) and ask for a tour of its switching center. Make sure to tell them you are a student and working on a lab. While there, ask them to show you the following T1 termination points:

    ● The DEMARC point (the smart jack)

    ● The T1 CSU and the plugs used for that connection

    ● The multiplexor (MUX)

    ● Additional equipment they may be using on the link, as appropriate

2. After seeing this demonstration, draw a graphical representation of what you saw. Bring it to class and be prepared to share your findings with your classmates and instructor.

3. While you are visiting this department, ask about whether they use pulse stuffing or B8Zs. Ask them to show you what they have and ask why they chose to use one over the other. Prepare a report for your instructor and be prepared to discuss this finding with your class.

Chapter 6

Integrated Services Digital Network and SONET

LEARNING OBJECTIVES:

Once you complete this chapter, you will be able to:

Describe ISDN.

Discuss what ISDN really means to the telecommunications industry.

Understand why ISDN was initially developed.

Discuss why ISDN is more widespread internationally than in the U.S.

Describe the various services available in ISDN networking.

Understand reasons for the limited deployment of ISDN.

Discuss the benefits of fiber standards.

List the speeds of SONET and SDH.

Explain the differences between WDM and DWDM.

Understand the SONET link architecture.

Explain the basic components of the SONET model.

In Chapter 5, we discussed digital and analog transmission, as well as the operation of digital carrier systems such as T1 technologies and related services. The use of the digital services for dial-up communications was not discussed. To provide circuit-switched digital communications for both voice and data, the carriers developed a service called **Integrated Services Digital Network (ISDN)**. *ISDN* is designed to support a perceived need for data transmission. Also, ISDN is a mechanism that allows on-demand digital transport of voice and other services on a call-by-call basis. ISDN was conceived in the 1970s and was made available to the public in the early 1980s as the next-generation telephone network. This network would overcome the limited data-transmission capabilities of existing voice networks. Networks prior to ISDN required the use of modems to transmit data at rates between 4,800 and 9,600 bps.* This type of transmission was less than reliable in many cases.

To summarize, ISDN is based on all-digital transmission, using state-of-the-art technology to allow access to the raw bandwidth that the carrier believes is needed by the customer. Figure 6-1 displays ISDN as the combination of present and future services.

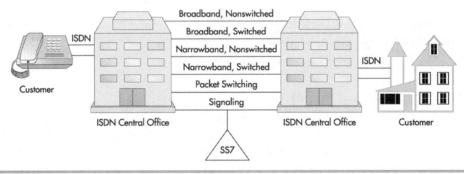

Figure 6-1 Present and future services of ISDN.

ISDN Defined

ISDN, as defined by the International Telecommunications Union-Telecommunications Standardization Sector (ITU-TSS), is a network service evolving from the telephony networks that provides end-to-end digital connectivity to support a wide range of services, including voice and non-voice, that users will have access to through a limited set of standard multipurpose interfaces.

---

*In the 1980s, data rates were limited to 9,600 bps or less. Later, the speeds were increased to 33.6 Kbps and 56 Kbps because of advances in digital technologies.

Proponents of ISDN state that the services include the capability to:

1. Transmit the name and number of the calling party to your telephone before you answer the call. This would be of some interest to the residential user as a means of screening calls. Today, these features are provided without ISDN because of enhancements made to the Central Office (CO) switching systems. Features and functions that were earmarked for ISDN are now delivered on the Plain Old Telephone Service (POTS) networks. Think of the benefits to any telephone-intensive business as an incoming call delivers the customer's information (phone number, contact person, account status, and so forth) as the agent answers the call.

2. Allow access to multipoint and dial-up voice and data conference calls from the desktop. The use of voice and data calls through digital technology will be at a rate of 64 Kbps or multiples thereof. For example, an agent can get a customer on the phone, access a database, and display customer marketing information on his or her terminal, PC, or other device all at the same time.

3. Pick and choose the services to be provided on a line-by-line basis, with access to various services as needed. The use of voice, data, and video conferencing can be allowed on a call-by-call basis.

4. Use the same line to transmit telemetry information without interfering with the ongoing voice and data calls in progress.

You can imagine the impact these features would have on the industry as a whole if the need for the scarce resources were to be reduced further by technology. Therefore, ISDN is a series of products and services designed by the carriers—for the users—to increase the productivity and contain the costs associated with doing business. Not quite!

No doubt, these enhancements offer a variety of applications that will only be limited by the user's imagination. Conceptually, ISDN is a vehicle that delivers digital data (voice and data services). ISDN is *not* a product and is *not* a package of hardware offerings from the suppliers.

How do users perceive the usefulness of a network topology and the ensuing benefits that can be derived? For many, the offerings of ISDN match what can be done today without ISDN. For example, the caller ID display, which equates to automatic number identification (ANI), can be accomplished today by using the CO digital switching technology that's already there. Another example is the use of ISDN for telemetry purposes; by using a dial-up modem and some mechanical interfaces, the same function can be accomplished by other technologies.

So why all the hype? If everything can be done using existing technology, why do you even need ISDN? Once you look at the possibilities of using the same lines and interfaces that you have today, integrated across the network on a call-by-call basis, you can eliminate the need for special lines dedicated to specific applications.

NOTE

ISDN is a transport system that delivers digital data (this includes voice and data). ISDN is not a product or a hardware solution. Most people mistake what ISDN is all about.

Who Made the Rules?

The ITU is the responsible body for the development of ISDN standards on a global basis. The name *ITU-T* came about because of the privatization trend separating telephone service from the post office and the general elimination of telegraph service. Because its members were no longer Post, Telephone, and Telegraph (PTT) Companies, the organization couldn't properly be called the CCITT (translated as the Consultative Committee for International Telephony and Telegraph). The CCITT was always a consulting committee to the International Telecommunications Union. So, the ITU-TSS is the Telecommunications Standard subsection of the ITU. The CCITT was composed of study groups (SG). Each SG has its own area of expertise. Some of the better known ones related to ISDN are:

SG VII	Public data network (X.25) X series standards
SG VIII	Terminal equipment for telematic services
SG XI	ISDN and telephone-network switching and signaling
SG XII	Transmission performance of telephone networks and terminals
SG XV	Transmission systems
SG XVII	Data transmission over public telephone networks
SG XVIII	Digital networks, including ISDN

Although they are called standards, the ITU-T technically publishes *recommendations*.

The ITU created an ISDN reference model or a picture of what an ISDN should look like. This model identifies a series of functional groupings of equipment and reference points where the critical functions must be performed to ensure communication between the groupings. Don't think of the groupings and functions as different pieces of equipment. Instead, they are functions that must be performed. These recommendations were contained in the findings, known as the red book, that came out in 1984. Subsequent work has been done on the definition and implementation of ISDN services. The additional information is contained in the blue book, dated 1988. Figure 6-2 is a representation of the ISDN reference model.

ITU's emphasis was to ensure that ISDN will be just as ubiquitous as the present-day Public Switched Telephone Network (PSTN) when fully deployed. Because ISDN is an enhancement to the PSTN, this should pose no great threat. However, the ITU has also expressed the need for portability in the deployment of ISDN in its universal state. This means an ISDN terminal

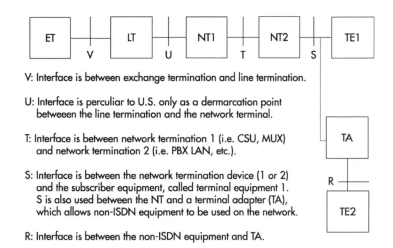

V: Interface is between exchange termination and line termination.

U: Interface is perculiar to U.S. only as a dermarcation point betweeen the line termination and the network terminal.

T: Interface is between network termination 1 (i.e. CSU, MUX) and network termination 2 (i.e. PBX LAN, etc.).

S: Interface is between the network termination device (1 or 2) and the subscriber equipment, called terminal equipment 1. S is also used between the NT and a terminal adapter (TA), which allows non-ISDN equipment to be used on the network.

R: Interface is between the non-ISDN equipment and TA.

Figure 6-2 The ISDN reference model is shown as a means of identifying the components.

should be capable of being plugged into an ISDN anywhere in the world, and still provide full features and functions. This creates a dilemma for the ITU because the PSTN hasn't achieved the same portability on a global basis. The interfaces are different, the line terminating impedances aren't the same, and the signaling is different. Thus, plugging into any point around the world cannot be accomplished because of the architectural differences among the carriers.

Line Check 6-1

1. The CCITT name has been changed to more adequately reflect its actual function. What is its new name?

2. ITU's position was to make ISDN as commonplace as what other form of network?

Why Do We Need ISDN?

The carriers and manufacturers alike would like to convince us to use ISDN more now than ever, and that the only way we can successfully use the all-digital end-to-end capabilities of the telephony network is through the implementation of ISDN. These providers might be correct, but like any other sales-based organizations, they also have a tendency to oversell the capabilities and possibilities. The most overused and abused term these days is the concept of ISDN. Everyone wants us to believe that the system and network are there today for our unmitigated use of all the features and capabilities. Unfortunately, goals and expectations usually exceed implementations and budget restrictions. To implement a digital network at the local loop level, substantial investment by the local exchange carriers is still required. Many carriers have never moved toward ISDN architecture.

As the need for higher-speed transport increases, the limits of the available analog interface to the LEC and the IEC are quickly surpassed. More and more users are demanding added call-carrying capacity to move information around the world. The primary areas that consume bandwidth are additional speed for data communications; transfer of files from host to host, host to server, local area network (LAN) to LAN, and LAN to wide area network (WAN); and access to the Internet with its streaming protocols for video and voice. The bulk of the ISDN services being installed are data applications to surf the Web and carry voice over IP (VoIP) on the Internet.

Another need is the demand to transfer graphic information. As desktop applications communicating complex documents from workstation to workstation are enhanced, even greater carrying capacities of bandwidth are necessary to move these files. The typical multipage, text-based document will be fine, but the complex document that incorporates the use of graphics and annotation with voice, data, text, video, and any other format will require the transmission of files between 100 and 500 megabytes. Thus, a requirement for megabit speeds is necessary.

As more complex information entered into the systems and the demand for bandwidth increased, the use of ISDN clear-channel capacity was expected to increase productivity and reduce costs. The advantage originally envisioned by carriers was its capability to reduce call durations on data transfers because of the higher throughput when compared to analog modem transmission of data on dial-up lines. The shorter the call is, the less expensive it will be from the standpoint of the carrier (both the LEC and the IEC). This would aid in providing services to a greater number of users without adding circuit capacity and overbuilding the network.

Therefore, the carriers also stand to improve efficiency in the use of their networks, which reduces their operating costs. This all sounds too good to be true: both the supplier and the user will have lower costs! In theory, it should work; the reality remains to be seen. In fact, ISDN usage has increased call durations as users increased their volume of data moving on the network by using ISDN to connect to Internet service providers (ISPs) and surfing the Internet. Understand also that ISDN was implemented more in Europe than in North America. In Europe, the carriers had little to offer their customers, whereas in North America, several options existed when the time came to implement ISDN, as you will see in subsequent chapters.

Now you can probably appreciate the original motivation for the implementation, acceptance, and standardization of the ground rules for this capability. Other benefits of ISDN include:

- More flexibility for the user on a call-by-call basis (moving data or voice to multiple destinations selected by the called party phone number)

- Better control over the network by the carriers

- All-digital transmission is more reliable and less expensive than analog

- Quicker setup time on calls

- Additional services from the carriers, which equates to more revenue

- Fewer new cable facilities needed in the office and the residence, because multiple simultaneous services can be used over a single two-wire connection at the local loop

- Analog to digital/digital to analog conversions become the customer's responsibility

- Signaling out of band becomes the customer's responsibility

- Carriers can provide improved network management and maintenance control

- High-speed facsimile, dial-up video, slow-scan video, Internet access, and packet switching will become more cost-advantageous, thereby encouraging more use of these services

The Overall ISDN Concept

The concept of ISDN was originally introduced in 1979: the evolution of telephony applications that provide digital end-to-end connectivity to support a wide range of services, including voice and nonvoice, through a set of limited multipurpose user interfaces. The reason for this concept was the obsolescence and cost-prohibitive nature of the older analog technology. Since the days when a dial-up voice connection was riddled with crackling and popping on the line, users have been clamoring for the local and long-haul carriers to improve service. The evolution of analog-to-digital transmission techniques significantly improved the transmission of voice and facilitated the ultimate introduction of higher-speed data communications. Summarizing some of the telecommunications requirements placed on the networks and carriers would be appropriate here. The following are the candidates for integrated digital communications through the evolved networking techniques.

6

Telegraph

The telegraph was the first electrical communications system to be introduced. It used direct-current pulse signals on single-wire earth-return lines and, later, on two-wire lines. Detecting signals over long distances was made possible by the use of sensitized galvanometers. Transatlantic cables were in use in the mid-1800s. Pulse codes, such as Morse code, were devised and highly skilled operators could achieve speeds of 30 words per minute. The use of the telegraph and the ensuing delays over the transmission path distorted the actual human side of communications. Unnecessary words were eliminated to expedite data transmission. The telegraph introduced the first forms of digital coding and used a protocol to ensure accuracy and the reception of messages. Although many North American students in telecommunications will never see a telegraph device (unless they visit the Smithsonian Institute), these are still quite common in other parts of the world where telecommunications is somewhat backward. For the sake of seeing something and relating to how it looks, a picture of a telegraph device is shown in Figure 6-3.

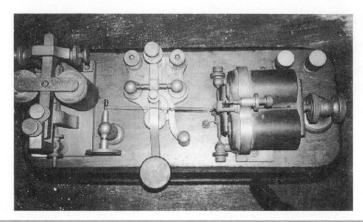

Figure 6-3 Although obsolete in North America, the telegraph is still found in other parts of the world.

Telephone

Users can now communicate directly with each other without the need for a protocol or the intervention of a skilled operator to interpret the message. After the operators were removed from the picture, telephone communications needed improvements to allow a novice caller to use the system comfortably over great distances. Automatic switching, an invention necessitated in the network, increased the ease of use and the ability of unskilled callers to access other telephones without human operators. The intelligence of the switching systems further led the network providers to seek an all-digital solution for noise-free calling, feature-rich enhancements, and intuitive call setup and teardown. Today, it is easy for most people to place a call anywhere in the world because of the enhancements to the telephone network. Touch-tone dialing, digital transmission, and inexpensive cost-per-minute all contribute to the services expected on an ISDN network.

Telex

At about the same time Alexander Graham Bell was promoting the telephone, the typewriter (invented in 1867 by Christopher Sholes) was finding its way into the office. Minor adaptations to an electric typewriter permitted transmission of telegraph code for each letter and number on the keyboard. Not until the 1930s, however, did interconnection using the Telex expand without the need for a skilled telegraph operator. One of the reasons this process was slow to be accepted was the protocol needed for the machines to call and answer back with a discrete identity. Telex machines that used a punched tape constituted the first attempt to introduce direct machine-to-machine communications without the intervention of the operator. Many people in the industry now think this technology is dead, especially because of the proliferation of facsimile and other data terminals—however, Telex is still alive and strong on an international spectrum. For the sake of seeing something historical to our network, a photograph of a teletype is shown in Figure 6-4.

Figure 6-4 The teletype was once a popular means of communicating. Now, it is primarily an international device.

Data Communications

Telex and telegraph are the original data networks introduced into the industry. The term "data communications" became more commonplace after the introduction of digital computers, which encouraged the concept of time-sharing tasks requested by many terminals and devices. Today, the use of data communications over the PTSN is continually on the rise.*

Because bandwidth standards of the PSTN were set for the support of voice communication, not data communication, carriers limit the speed of information flow between communications devices (up to 56 Kbps on dial-up analog lines if you are lucky enough to have a circuit that will support this speed).

Packet Switching

Using a dedicated circuit or a switched circuit to communicate information has been one of the primary means of communicating data. Public packet-switching techniques were introduced as

---

*For many of us in North America, dial-up data is considered passé because we have high-speed connections (cable, T1, xDSL, and so forth), whereas in many parts of the world, dial-up data communications using a modem is still the *only* viable offering from the local supplier.

an evolution of these facilities. Public *packet-switched networks* were modeled to support the bursty nature of data communications and the concept that all data calls do not necessarily need simultaneous two-way communications. Data is broken into small packets (pieces) and sent out along the network. Several users' packets might be traversing the network on the same virtual link without any degradation of the response or loss of data integrity. Each packet would be individually routed from a particular source to its own particular destination, automatically selecting the best route to the destination from the available circuits. This method allows the carriers to gain greater use of their facilities and enables users to communicate at decent rates of speed, without the use of dedicated or private lines. A common packet-switching technique is called *X.25* (still used throughout the world by banks, finance companies, insurance companies, and carriers), which is shown in Figure 6-5.

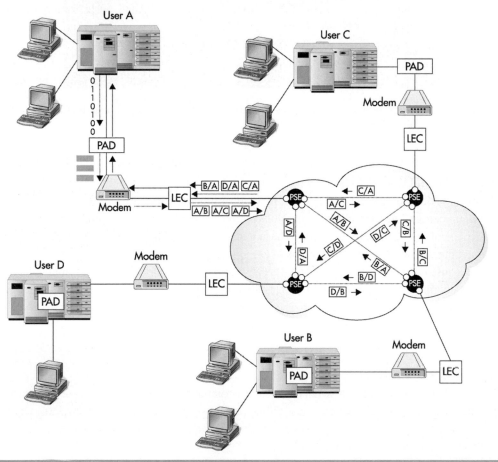

Figure 6-5 An X.25 packet-switching network is shown in this graphic. Packet switching is still very much alive in the world today.

Integration

The existence and use of separate networks to provide voice, data, telegraph, and other services has, in some ways, been an advantage in tailoring the network to the service being provided. However, using separate lines and access methods to these services has also been a disadvantage. To gain access to the various services, the user had to subscribe to that network. The user was presented with an overhead and management problem in administering the effective use of each of the facilities provided. Moreover, in periods of peak loading, some facilities may be overburdened, while others sit idle. To eliminate this problem, users and suppliers alike began to explore and demand an integrated plan. This plan calls for access, through gateways or other methods, to any service by any user through a common set of lines. The existence of integrated networks will allow for user management of the entire telecommunications function through the single thread to the outside world. This is what the overall objective of the ISDN is: to provide the user with easy access to multiple services over a single connection to the network. The least important element of the title ISDN is the word "digital," even though it is the digital network that allows for this universal and simple access to the wide range of services to be provided. To meet this objective, the comparisons shown in Table 6-1 must be implemented.

Locally	Publicly
At the user's handset, the following features and functions are required.	Within the network, the carriers must implement changes that are transparent to the end user, yet provide the functionality necessary to enable the service.
Duplex operation of simultaneous voice, data, telemetry, and signaling on a single link must exist.	Capacity must exist to switch voice, data, telemetry, and signaling information independently from a subscriber location over a single line.
Transparency must exist on the message content used in the various services.	The capability must be put in place to extract the message address information, check information for validity, and transmit the message information to the desired address.
Operation must take place over the two-wire connection (twisted pair) within the distance limitations and other characteristics of the copper wire.	The ability to access specialized networks (packet switching, for example) and pass message information to and from these networks in a protocol-transparent way must be provided.
Extended areas must be serviced through the use of digital regenerators. The old analog amplification equipment must be replaced.	Charge and billing information must be identified and billed across the various services between the providers.

Table 6-1 Comparing Services on ISDN. (*Continued*)

6

Locally	Publicly
Rapid access and setup times must be made available. Power consumption across the line (span power) must be kept at a minimum during idle stages. Setup times must be provided end-to-end within 2 seconds, replacing older methods of call setup requiring 6 to 30 seconds.	The capability to address or subaddress the customer premises equipment (CPE) and ensure proper operation when addressing and connection take place must be provided.
Transmission and timing systems to detect framing and bit timing must be provided in both directions.	Some form of local power to the CPE from the network switching exchange must be provided. This must be able to switch on local power to "power up/power on" the customer's equipment.
Good error-free performance (a typical error rate of 10^{-7} is expected) must exist. A rate of one error in every 10 million bits transmitted produces a 10^{-7} error rate.	
Compatibility in interfaces to other forms of digital transmission media, such as radio, fiber optics, cellular, and coax, must exist.	
Protection must be provided against power cross-connect faults, lightning, and so on.	
Remote equipment must be suitable for mounting independently on premises for integration with customer-provided terminal equipment.	

Table 6-1 Comparing Services on ISDN.

These are not simple tasks. The concept is complex to define and even more difficult to perform. This is particularly true in the regulatory environment here in the United States, where clear lines of demarcation have been established with the divestiture of AT&T from the telephone company subsidiaries.

❓ Line Check 6-2

1. The original intent of ISDN was to provide what features?

    a.

    b.

    c.

      d.

      e.

      f.

2. Why do you think ISDN is so popular in other parts of the world?

The ISDN Architecture

ISDN is based on the Open Systems Interconnection (OSI) layered communications model adopted by the ITU. The architecture generalizes the OSI model and applies it to information and signaling transfer and system management. The inclusion of the transmission media in the model highlights the need to evolve ISDN from today's metallic environment in the local loop plant to a fiber-optic environment and on-premises wiring to higher grades of twisted pairs or fiber optics, while the system management reflects the market's need for the customer-controllable and easily maintainable systems and services.

Physical View

Two ITU-T ISDN user network interfaces are used for connection to end-user devices. They are the **Basic Rate Interface (BRI)**, 2B + D, and the **Primary Rate Interface (PRI)**, 23B + D/30B + D. The basic operation of the bearer service (B) is the 64-Kbps channel capacity that carries the payload (that is, voice, data, and so forth). The *D channel* is a data channel used for out of band signaling. These are covered below. However, see Figure 6-6 for the basic rate concept

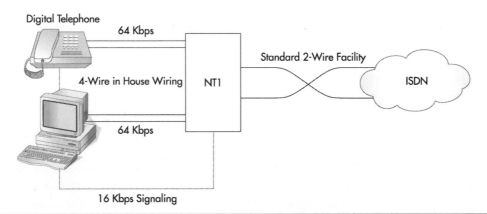

Figure 6-6 The Basic Rate Interface (BRI) includes 2B plus 1D.

and Figure 6-7 for the primary rate concept. While the most common PRI configuration is a single *D* channel per physical facility, multiple links (up to 20) can share a single *D* channel. This will lead to increased information-carrying capacity for the interface. The *D* channel on one 23B + D can be used to control a number of 24B PRI connections.

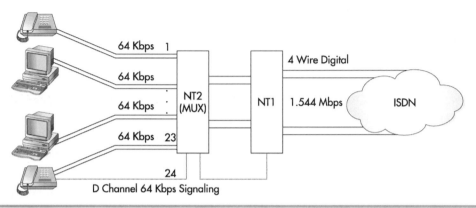

Figure 6-7 The Primary Rate Interface (PRI) is a 23B plus 1D in North America.

The ISDN circuit is provisioned from the provider as a single two-wire loop; the two *B* channels and the single *D* channel are time-division multiplexed onto the circuit. At the customer premises, the NT-1 terminates the telco signal and breaks the two *B* channels into an internal four-wire circuit. (This device is customer-provided in North America but telco-provided in the European system.)

The CO-to-NT-1 circuit is commonly referred to as the *U loop,* with the NT-1 connector facing the U loop known as the *U interface.* The four-wire internal circuit between an NT-1 and an NT-2 is known as the *T loop,* and the circuit between the NT-2 and the terminal device (known as a Terminal Equipment, Type 1, or TE-1) is the *S loop.* NT-2 multiplexer units are rarely seen, however, so the connection between the NT-1 and the terminal devices has come to be known as the *S/T loop* and the interfaces as *S/T interfaces.*

Because of the difference in provisioning between North American and European standards, you need to know what signal you are receiving at the demarc. Both S/T and *U* interface devices are readily available, and it's important to get the correct match to the loop type to which you will connect.

Additionally, because users want to connect analog devices such as fax machines and so forth to the ISDN circuit, these TE-2 devices must be connected through a terminal adapter (TA), which converts the analog signal to digital. (On a practical level, most hardware today contains multiple devices, with customers usually seeing only a telco interface facing the demarc and Ethernet data ports and/or analog phone jacks externally available to the end user.)

The *PRI* offers an economical alternative for connecting digital PBXs, LANs, host computers, and other devices to the network. The *BRI* brings customers integrated voice and data, as well as advanced voice features. The BRI is a standard interface and offers the user the benefit of multivendor compatibility.

? Line Check 6-3

1. In North America, ISDN comes in two versions. What are they called and what are the capacities?

a.

b.

2. The rest of the world uses a European standard. What are the European versions called and what are the capacities?

a.

b.

?   6

To maximize terminal portability and ensure easy change from one network to another, the same BRI and PRI interfaces are used for interconnecting terminals, hosts, digital PBX, and other devices in the premises network. The ISDN architecture includes premises application processors that provide information movement and management and end customer-control features. Examples of some of these features are:

- Voice messaging
- Text messaging
- Message center attendants
- Message detail recording
- Electronic directory
- Traffic data
- Customer station rearrangement

At the network ISDN node, the integrated channelized access is separated into components (either physically or logically, depending on the implementation) and diverted to the appropriate functions. The network ISDN node also provides interconnections to four types of networks:

- Channel-switched networks
- Circuit-switched networks
- Packet-switched networks
- Common channel-signaling networks

Logical View

Two different views of ISDN service have been defined. They include both logical and physical views. *Logical view* defines what is functionally connected (how things interoperate), whereas *physical view* includes how things plug into each other (as an example) and how they provide the services.

Circuit Mode Services

The 1984 CCITT red book defines, in Q.931 (I.451), messages and procedures for basic call setup and disconnect, and includes a potential framework for supplementary voice services. Carriers use **Link Access Procedure for Data (LAP-D)** as the link layer protocol and the extended Q.931 as the network layer protocol for the *D* channel. *LAP-D* is a framing and formatting protocol for ISDN.

The extension furnishes signaling for implementing all of today's Centrex and advanced PBX features in ISDN. New functional messages are added, as well as messages conveying activation and deactivation of feature buttons and dial feature/access codes. The extended version of Q.931 protocol is being expanded to include functional messages for advanced signaling in the premises network and for features unique to ISDN. For an overview of the message format, see Figure 6-8. This is the High-Level Data Link Control (HDLC) frame format for LAP-D messages that will traverse the data channel. ISDN provides transparent circuit mode services for the transfer of information. Protocols for layers 2 to 7 are supplied by end-user devices.

The out-of-band signaling infrastructure for the premises network is provided by the *D* channel in the BRI and PRI. It can also be provided by the public Common Channel Signaling (CCS) network that transports the user-to-user signaling transparently from one premises switch to another. This extends the benefit of today's CCS network to premises network users and facilitates the interconnection of geographically scattered premises switches.

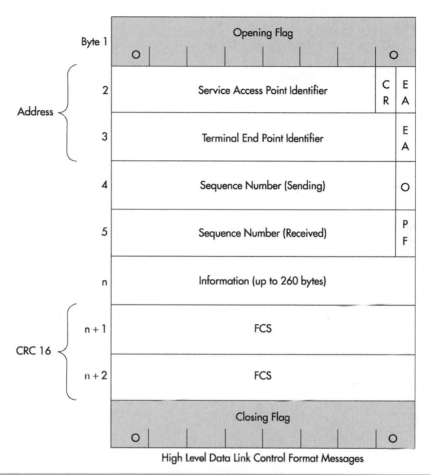

Figure 6-8 The message format uses a basic HDLC protocol.

In the public network, the **ISDN user part (ISUP)** and the Signaling Connection Control Part (SCCP) of the CCITT Signaling System 7 (SS7) support end-to-end ISDN features, while the transaction capability supports communications between the network switches and network application nodes. Recall these pieces from Chapter 4 discussing the use of SS7.

Packet Mode Services

The ISDN architecture supports packet-switched data services on the 16-Kbps *D* channel and the 64-Kbps *B* channel, using X.25, X.31, and the LAP-D-based packet-mode protocol.

X.31 extends X.25 to provide dial-up packet-switched services in an ISDN. It uses Q.931 signaling to establish the physical channel connection to the packet handler, after which the conventional X.25 in-band call control is used to establish the logical connection.

The LAP-D-based packet-mode protocol is the next step toward integrated signaling. It uses Q.931 signaling to establish the physical and logical connections. The LAP-D-based packet-mode protocol also decomposes bearer capabilities into building blocks to allow the freedom to distribute functions between the network and the premises system. This allows tailoring of individual services to application needs.

LAP-D layer 2 supports multiple logical links on a single physical link. The minimum-functionality packet switched service uses a portion of LAP-D consisting of:

- Multiplexing
- Error detection
- Frame delimiting

Other LAP-D functions such as error retransmission, packet sequencing, and acknowledgment can be performed on an end-to-end basis by end-user devices. The LAP-D-based packet-mode protocol initially supports X.25-like services. Unlike an X.25 service, full X.25 is terminated only by the end-user devices; the intermediate switch provides the minimum-functionality packet switching. Consequently, the X.25 services supported by the LAP-D-based packet-mode protocol have lower transnetwork delay and higher throughput. The LAP-D-based packet-mode protocol, together with its Q.931 signaling procedure, provides a mechanism for the customer to request services on the basis of application needs on a call-by-call basis. This means a user can use the signaling channel to establish a voice call on the link at 64 Kbps as an independent action (Figure 6-9). The call can proceed as normal until the two parties agree to conclude the conversation and mutually hang up, ending the connection between them.

❓ Line Check 6-4

LAP-D layer 2 of the OSI model supports multiple logical links on a single physical link.

1. What are the minimum-functionality packet-switched services that use a portion of LAP-D?

   a.

   b.

   c.

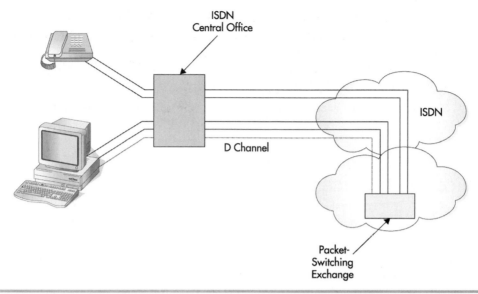

Figure 6-9 The *D* channel can be used to set up an independent 64-Kbps call using the LAP-*D* protocols.

Immediately following this call, the user can now use the signaling system to link the two *B* channels together and form a 128-Kbps data connection to a remote host (Figure 6-10) to conduct a file transfer to the host system. Note that the host system is using 128 Kbps whereas the telephone is idle. This is called **bonding** the two channels together.

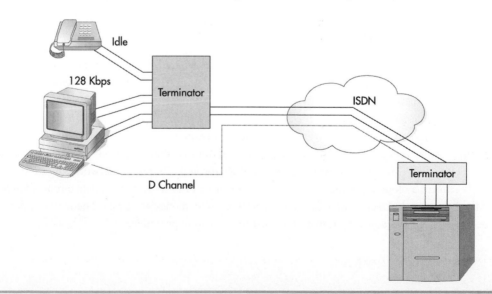

Figure 6-10 Two B channels can be bonded together to handle a data file transfer at 128 Kbps.

❓ Line Check 6-5

1. Bonding is the process of linking two or more bearers (channels) together to get a higher data rate. How many channels do you think can be bonded together on a BRI?

2. If you have a PRI, what is the maximum number of channels that can be bonded together?

Application Services

The marriage of the terminal and the telephone expands the horizon of services that the network must provide. More and more required functions go beyond information movement into information management and its applications. Voice messages are left on recording systems that can be controlled by the end user for playback and editing. Electronic directory services can request that the switch dial a number directly when a button on the phone is pushed. These applications require the higher-layer protocols available in ISDN. ITU's recommendations for the various layers are:

- X.224 as the transport layer protocol

- X.225 as the session layer protocol

- X.226 as the presentation layer protocol

These are shown in the context of a comparison with the OSI model in Figure 6-11.

The Exchange Carrier Networks

The key element in realizing the ISDN exchange carrier networks is the local switch. As long as the carrier (LEC) has a switch that offers the basic interfaces to ISDN, the switch acts as the ISDN node. The switch (typically the end office) will provide simultaneous voice and data services to Centrex and local dial-tone users over a basic rate interface. This switch will support the full range of Centrex voice features using the extended version of Q.931, as well as circuit-switched and packet-switched data. In addition, the switch will more than likely support modem pooling for internetworking with non-ISDN data terminals through the public network. Figure 6-12 shows this in a modem pooling arrangement. This moves the services (a la data circuit switched) onto the network. Users will access these services on an as-needed basis. The network now becomes the service provider, instead of just the dial-tone provider.

Application	
Presentation	X.226
Session	X.225
Transport	X.224
Network	Q.931
Data Link	Q.921
Physical	Twisted Pair

Figure 6-11 The protocols used in ISDN compared to the OSI protocol stack

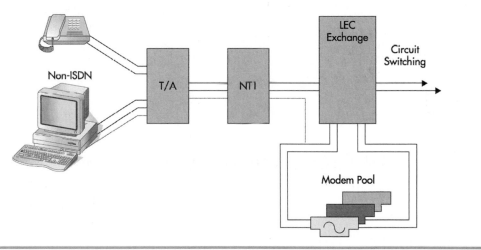

Figure 6-12 A modem pool can be used to link non-ISDN terminals to ISDN terminals.

The switch will also support the end-user applications processor environment. This application processor will provide message services, electronic directory, message detail recording, and traffic data statistics. Using SS7 Transaction Capability Application Part (TCAP) and switching services point (SSP), the switch will interact with network databases to process calls (Figure 6-13). This will allow the exchange carrier to implement intelligent network architecture and offer such services as virtual private networks, enhanced services, and centralized network control as part of the ISDN capabilities. The use of the primary rate interface connected to the switch will allow the transparent end-to-end transport of user-to-user information for applications such as caller name, security check, and feature transparency.

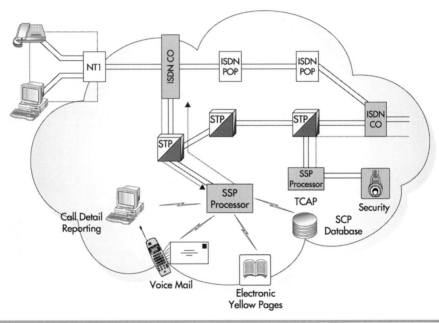

Figure 6-13 SS7 TCAP and SSPs interact with databases to handle the call processing.

NOTE

SS7 was discussed in Chapter 4. The TCAP provides the added features and functions. The SSP is the CO that processes the request.

Additional flexibility can be derived through the use of remote switching modules (RSMs) and **digital loop carrier (DLC)** carrier systems, shown in Figure 6-14. The *subscriber loop carrier* is a remote link that may be run on copper or fiber, placing a concentrator near the customer. A DLC system is a part of the copper-wire, local-loop telephone system. A *DLC system* aggregates the subscriber calls within a neighborhood, office building, or industrial park, and multiplexes the calls over a single line (T1/E1 or fiber), back to the telephone company CO, where all the switching equipment is located. This device allows connections in a remote switching function. Using these devices, ISDN services can be provided to remote locations. On the network side (IEC), using signaling system 7 (SS7) in conjunction with the ISDN user part, access can be provided. The combination of channel, circuit switching, X.25 packet switching, and common-channel signaling is derived through a series of ISDN gateways for the inter-/intra-LATA services.

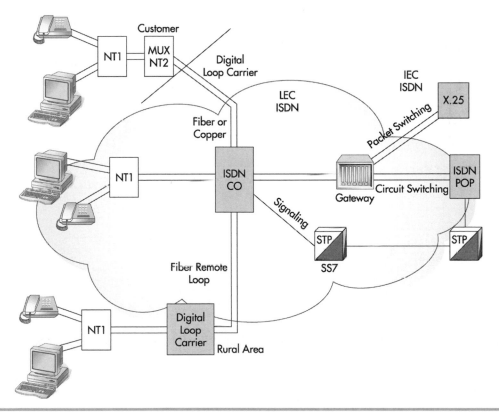

Figure 6-14 Using remote switching modules and digital-loop carrier equipment, ISDN can be provided at remote locations.

CAUTION

DLC assists in an ISDN connection remotely, but is an impediment to the expansion of DSL (Digital Subscriber Line) services because the DLC is run on fiber. When installing DSL services, the arrangement is that the circuit is run on copper, not fiber. If a DLC is used, it circumvents the capability of the copper facility.

The Interexchange Network

The interexchange-carrier network services can be accessed through a major ISDN node either by switched services through the local exchange carrier or directly using private line services. The same four supporting transit components are accessible through the IXC network services. Service functions can be attained through a digital cross-connect system (DCS) supporting circuit mode service speeds of 64, 384, and 1,536 Kbps, as shown in Figure 6-15. The use of a packet-switching system (IPSS) supports the X.25 packet data network. DCS-based private-line services and customer-controlled reconfiguration (CCR) are provided as well. ISDN services also add capabilities through network applications processors that operate off the common-channel signaling network to provide advanced 800/888/877/866 services, software-defined networks, and so on.

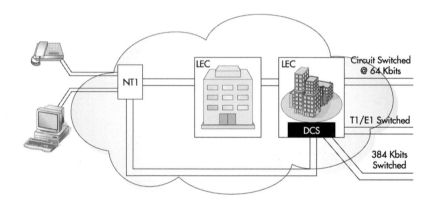

Figure 6-15 ISDN supports different services and capacities when operated at the digital cross-connect systems.

The Premises Network

The premises line of services and products is designed around the full integration of voice and nonvoice applications, as shown in Figure 6-16. Intelligence is also provided through a network gateway or node in an ISDN environment. ISDN-capable PBXs, acting as the gateways to the exchange carrier public network, are accessed through the PRI. Using this arrangement, a variety of transport services and facilities can be accessed, taking full advantage of the call-by-call service selection capability of Q.931. Add-on capabilities, such as the following, will be available through these ISDN-capable PBXs:

- Message center services

- Voice messaging (voice mail)

- Office telecommunications services (OTS)

- Electronic mail (E-mail)

- Centralized management systems

- Least-cost routing (LCR)

- Address translations

- Security

- Feature transparency

- Station message detail recording (SMDR)

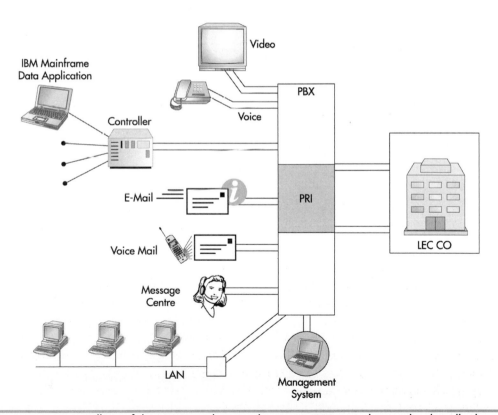

Figure 6-16 Regardless of the voice or data applications, ISDN can be used to handle the transport of a range of services.

Basic Operating Characteristics

The basic structure for ISDN operating characteristics is digitally encoded data using a standard of 64 Kbps as the basic rate and 1,536 Kbps as the primary rate. This is a derived channel using pulse-code modulation techniques, the North American standard for digital transmission.

North American T1 differs from the international or European standard of 30 channels at 64 Kbps, plus overhead of 1 channel at 64 Kbps, yielding a digital stream of 2.048 Mbps—the E1. Other differences exist in the encoding and *companding* (how the systems encode and decode the voice signals) techniques that require translation from North American to European standards and vice versa.

Other rates of bandwidth are used in the ISDN concept. They use fractional portions of the DS1/E1 for speeds higher than the 64-Kbps rate. This is also referred to as *multirate ISDN*. See Figure 6-17 for a representation of this.

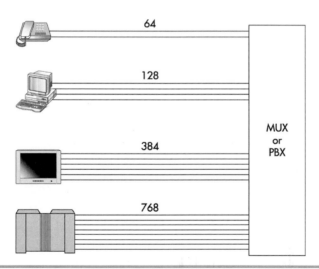

Figure 6-17 Multirate ISDN is a concept of using fractionalized pieces of the T1/E1 to achieve speeds above 64 Kbps.

NOTE

Multirate ISDN can operate at 64,384 or 1,536 Kbps. The services are arranged through a digital cross-connect system.

Bearer Services

ISDN works on the principle of transport services known as **bearer services**. The *bearer service* offers the capability to transport digital voice or nonvoice services using this standard. Packet services can also be transported across the bearer service at higher rates of speed (up to 64 Kbps). Bearer services, as previously mentioned, are divided into two categories. The first is the BRI, which uses two bearer services at 64 Kbps and one data channel operating at 16 Kbps, with an additional 48 Kbps of overhead, yielding a 192-Kbps data stream over the typical two twisted wires (Figure 6-18) from the business or residence to the local exchange. The second category is the PRI, which uses 23 bearer services and one data channel, all at the 64-Kbps per channel speed, yielding a 1.536-Mbps data stream from the business to the local exchange. As mentioned before, this is the North American standard (used in the United States, Canada, and Japan), whereas the international standard uses 30 bearer services, plus one data service, all at the 64-Kbps rate, yielding a 2.048-Mbps data stream. These framing formats are shown in Figure 6-19.

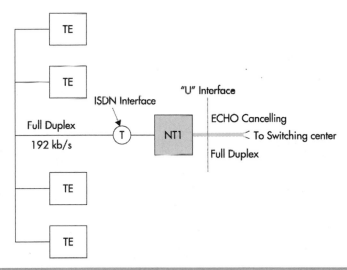

Figure 6-18 ISDN yields a total of 192 Kbps multiplexed on a two-wire circuit, of which the user only sees 144 Kbps, and can usually use 128 Kbps for communication.

The primary rate under either the North American or the international standard uses existing T1/E1 technology and is the main emphasis for the business world. Applications are based on the use of WATS. In WATS (800/888/877), FX, tie lines and data lines all combine

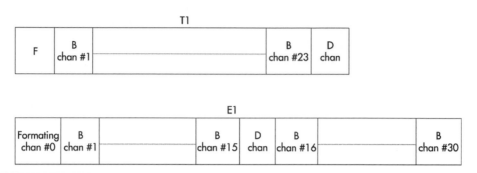

Figure 6-19 Internationally, ISDN on an E1 achieves 30 bearers in a framed format.

into a single primary rate. Because T1/E1 technology has proliferated so much in the United States and the rest of the world over the past few years because of the economics involved, the evolution to a PRI is relatively simple. The connection through a digital PBX, multiplexer, network node, DCS, or other T1/E1-compatible equipment requires little change in the network and simple card changes in the customer premises network.

Fiber-Based Networks

Digital transmission speeds were initially carried on the existing wired and wireless systems in place at the telephone company and interexchange carrier levels. These systems included microwave, coaxial, and twisted-pair copper wires. As newer fiber-optic systems were introduced, a new **Synchronous Digital Hierarchy (SDH)** evolved. Throughout the world, SDH was accepted, yet in the United States, the term **synchronous optical network (SONET)** was adopted. Although the international and United States versions of SDH/SONET are similar, they are not identical.

SONET provides for increased throughput and bandwidth via a set of multiplexing parameters. These roles provide certain advantages to the industry, such as:

- Reduced equipment requirements in the carrier's network.

- Enhanced network reliability and availability.

- Conditions to define the overhead necessary to facilitate managing the network better.

- Definitions of the multiplexing functions and formats to carry the lower-level digital signals (such as DS-1, DS-2, and DS-3).

- Generic standards encouraging interoperability between different vendors' products.

- A flexible means of addressing current, as well as future, applications and bandwidth usage.

SONET defines the **Optical Carrier (OC)** levels defined as OC-level-N where N is the numerical value used (such as level-1, -3, and so forth.) and the electrical equivalent rates in the synchronous transport signals (STS) for the fiber-based transmission hierarchy.

Background Leading to SONET Development

Prior to the development of SONET, the initial fiber-based systems used in the PSTN were all highly proprietary. The proprietary nature of the products included the following:

1. Equipment

2. Line coding

3. Maintenance

4. Provisioning

5. Multiplexing

6. Administration

The local and long-distance providers were frustrated with the proprietary products because of interoperability problems, sole-source vendor solutions (which held these providers hostage to one vendor), and cost issues. These carriers approached the standards committees and demanded that a set of operational standards be developed that would allow them to mix and match products from various vendors. In 1984, a task force was established to develop such a standard. The resultant standard became SONET.

NOTE

SONET is the acronym for Synchronous Optical Networks. It is primarily used in North America.

The SONET Line Rates

SONET defines a technique to carry many signals from different sources and at different capacities through a synchronous optical hierarchy. The flexibility and robustness of SONET are some of its strongest selling points. Additionally, in the past, many of the high-speed multiplexing arrangements (DS-2 and DS-3) used bit interleaving to multiplex the data streams through the multiplexers. SONET uses a byte-interleaved multiplexing format. *Byte interleaving* simplifies the process and provides better end-to-end management by providing consistency throughout the network, making it easier to perform diagnostics and troubleshooting.

The basic SONET signal is called the Synchronous Transport Signal level-1 (STS-1) operating at 51.84 Mbps. *STS* represents the electrical pulses that will be converted to optical pulses on the network. The first step in using the SONET architecture is to create the STS-1. SONET specifies a synchronous transport signal (level 1) of 51.84 Mbps, which is a DS3 with extra overhead. The overhead allows for diagnostic and maintenance capabilities on each synchronous transport signal (STS). The fiber equivalent of the STS-1 is an optical carrier level 1 (OC-1). The *OC-1* is the light-based equivalent of the electrical signal. This is the basic building block for chunks of bandwidth as they are multiplexed together to form much higher capacities. At level 1, we start with a transmission rate of 51.84 Mbps. Increments of SONET include the capacities shown in Table 6-2. These transport systems and carrier levels work from the base of a T3 plus overhead, creating an STS-1.

The SONET Hierarchy

Electrical Signal	Optical Value	Speed	Capacity
STS-1	OC-1	51.84 Mbps	28 DS-1 or 1 DS-3
STS-3	OC-3	155.520 Mbps	84 DS-1 or 3 DS-3
STS-12	OC-12	622.08 Mbps	336 DS-1 or 12 DS-3
STS-24	OC-24	1.244 Gbps	672 DS-1 or 24 DS-3
STS-48	OC-48	2.488 Gbps	1344 DS-1 or 48 DS-3
STS-192	OC-192	9.953 Gbps	5376 DS-1 or 192 DS-3
STS-768*	OC-768	40 Gbps	21,504 DS-1 or 768 DS-3

*The OC-768 rate and STS-768 rate are newly defined. As the capacities are increased, the rates will follow.

Table 6-2 SONET Rates Shown at Their Best and Most Popularly Implemented Operations.

NOTE

SONET supports rates from 51.84 Mbps to 40 Gbps.

SONET goes further than just defining the multiplexed values of speed. It breaks the architecture of the link into three separate steps for purposes of defining the interfaces and defining responsibility. These layers include (a fourth is added here to describe the layer-by-layer responsibilities):

- *The Photonic layer*. Deals with the transport of bits and the conversion from an STS electrical pulse into an OC signal in light pulses.

- *The Section layer*. Deals with the transport of the **STS-N** frame across a physical link. The functions of the section layer include scrambling, framing, and error monitoring.

- *The Line layer*. Deals with the reliable transport path of overhead and payload information across a physical system.

- *The Path layer*. Deals with the transport of network services such as DS1 and DS3 between path-terminating equipment.

SONET incorporates each of these into architecture such that overhead and responsibilities are clearly defined. This layered architecture is shown in Figure 6-20. Note that the four layers are shown in this graphic. The photonic and section layers are one, but have been subdivided for clarity in showing the structure. The photonic and section layers deal with the physical medium or the OSI layer 1 protocols.

The SONET architecture consists of three parts:

- The *section* is defined as the transport between two repeating functions or between line-terminating equipment and a repeater.

- The *line* is defined as the transport of the payload between two pieces of line-terminating equipment.

- The *path* is defined as the transport of the payload between two pieces of path-terminating equipment (multiplexers and so forth) or the end-to-end circuit.

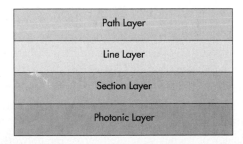

Figure 6-20 The SONET protocol stack deals with the physical medium and physical layer protocols.

This is shown in Figure 6-21, where the pieces are laid out on a plane. The graphic shows how the pieces all work together in a fiber link. The fiber specification is what was originally used in SONET (and SDH internationally). Newer microwave and satellite termination equipment is being introduced, however, to provide the same capacities and formats. SONET defines the responsibility of the carriers in multiplexing the signal onto the physical medium, as well as the points of demarcation for the various carriers involved with the circuit.

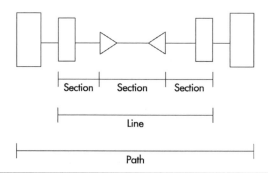

Figure 6-21 The link architecture of SONET is shown in three pieces comprising the section, the line, and the path.

Line Check 6-6

Describe the three components of SONET.

SONET Frame Format

In each of the layers listed, overhead is added to the data being transported to assure that everything is kept in order and errors can be detected. This overhead allows for testing and diagnostics along the entire route between the functions specified in the SONET layers. A new frame size is also used in the SONET architecture. The older M13 asynchronous format (used on a T3) was insufficient. To get the network back to a synchronous timing element, a frame is created that consists of 90 octets (8-bit bytes) across and 9 rows (810 bytes) down. This is the OC-1 frame, or the equivalent of the DS3 frame, plus the extra overhead. With the change in size, however, the frequency of frames generated across the network is now brought back to 8,000 per second. The 125-μsecond clocking and timing for the digital network can be reestablished. The frame shown in Figure 6-22 is 90 bytes (columns) wide and 9 rows high, yielding the 810-byte frame format. This frame is for the OC-1 or 51.84 Mbps capacity.

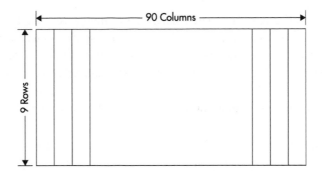

Figure 6-22 The SONET frame is quite large to start, but overhead accounts for some of the formatting. The 810-byte format is sufficient to handle the overhead (framing and formatting), as well as a high-speed payload, such as a DS-3.

Of the 90 columns, the first 3 (3 * 9 = 27 bytes) are allocated for transport overhead. The transport overhead is divided into two pieces. 9 bytes (3 columns, 3 rows) for section overhead and the remaining 18 bytes (3 columns by 6 rows) for line overhead. This is for maintenance and diagnostics on the circuit.

The 783 remaining octets (87 columns, 9 rows) are called the synchronous payload envelope (SPE). From the SPE, an additional 9 bytes (1 column, 9 rows) are set aside for path overhead. The *path overhead* accommodates the maintenance and diagnostics at each end of the circuit—typically, the customer equipment. Thus, the leftover 774 bytes are reserved for the actual data transport.

$$Payload = (774 \text{ bytes} * 8 \text{ bits/byte}) * 8,000 \text{ frames/sec}$$

$$Payload = 49.536 \text{ Mbps}$$

Of this 49.536 Mbps payload, the OC-1 can transport (carry) a DS-3 or 28 DS-1s.

Line Check 6-7

1. How many total bytes are formulated in an OC-1?

2. How many frames per second are carried on the OC-1?

Asynchronous transfer mode (ATM) was designed to run on SONET. ATM is a 53-byte cell format that uses the STS payload for the transport of information. This mapping of ATM cells into the payload allows for the fluid and dynamic allocation of the bandwidth available. As it is advertised, ATM starts at 50 and 155 Mbps, and then works its way up to 622 Mbps. To achieve the 155-Mbps rate, three OC-1s are *concatenated* (kept together as a single data stream) to produce an OC-3C. This works out rather nicely. ATM is discussed in greater detail in Chapter 11.

While using the SONET specification for carrying data, cells are mapped horizontally into the SONET frame, shown in Figure 6-23. However, newer things have occurred since the initial SONET standards were developed. Today, SONET operates at speeds of up to the OC-192, which is the equivalent of 192 T3s. OC-192 is 9.958 Gbps of throughput. However, using a **dense wave-division multiplexing (DWDM)** concept (sending different colors of light onto the fiber), you can achieve approximately 32 OC-192s on a single piece of fiber, or 320 Gbps. Moreover, the manufacturers are rapidly pursuing data rates at 1.6 terabits per second (Tbps) and more on a single fiber. With these speeds being generated on the fiber, nearly unlimited bandwidth will be available in the future. This, of course, allows for voice, data, and video on a single access link using ATM and SONET at a fraction of the original costs.

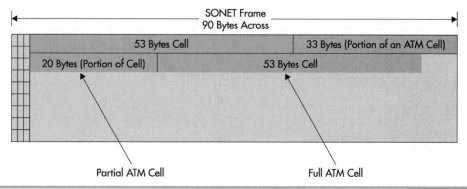

Figure 6-23 ATM cells can be easily mapped on a SONET frame.

Consumers have been pushing the carriers and manufacturers alike to provide higher transmission rates. Vendors, of course, have been responding in kind.

The use of the higher-speed communications methods also leads to newer transmission rates. Many vendors have announced that they will use SONET OC-192, which will deliver 10-Gbps Ethernet speeds across the WANs. This becomes a battleground for the various suppliers: the telcos want to deliver gigabit speeds over their ATM backbone, whereas the newer carriers (such as Global Crossing, Qwest Communications, and Level 3 Communications) want to deliver gigabit speeds across SONET backbones and do not care what form is provided here.

? Line Check 6-8

1. What does ATM stand for?

2. ATM is designed to be carried on what transmission system?

SONET Topologies

Several different topologies can be used in a SONET network using the various multiplexers. These include the normal topologies most networks have had around for years. They include the following:

- Point-to-point

- Point-to-multipoint

- Hub and spoke

- Ring

The variations allow the flexibility of SONET in the WANs built by the carriers, but now they are becoming the method of choice at many large organizations. In each of the topologies, larger organizations are finding the benefits of installing highly reliable interoperable equipment at the private network interfaces and access to the public networks.

Point-to-Point

The SONET multiplexer, the entry-level PTE for an organization (or the equipment installed by the LEC at the customer's premises to access the network), acts as a concentrator device for the multiple lower-speed communications channels, such as DS-1 and DS-3. In its simplest form, two devices are connected with an optical fiber (with any repeaters as necessary) as a point-to-point circuit. As the entry-level point into SONET architecture, the inputs and outputs are identical. In this environment, the network can act as a stand-alone environment and not have to interface with the public switched networks. See Figure 6-24 for the point-to-point multiplexing arrangement.

Point-to-Multipoint

The next step is to consider the point-to-multipoint arrangement. This will use a form of add-drop multiplexing to drop circuits off along the way. In a large corporate network spanning the

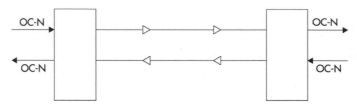

Figure 6-24 Point-to-point service with SONET is one of the basic forms of connecting locations.

country (or any subset), a single high-speed link may be employed. The SONET **add-drop multiplexer (ADM)** is used for the task, dropping circuits out and adding new ones in without demultiplexing the entire high-speed signal. In Figure 6-25, the ADM is installed between two far-end locations, so signals can be added or dropped off as necessary. This is a better solution than renting three different circuits between points A-B, A-C, and B-C, which adds to the complexity and cost. By using a circuit from A-B-C with ADMs, the service can usually be more efficiently accommodated.

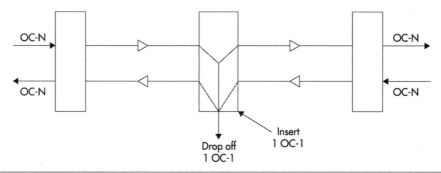

Figure 6-25 ADMs installed along the way let you add or drop traffic streams without demultiplexing the entire data stream. This is more efficient than terminating and demultiplexing along the way.

Hub and Spoke

The hub-and-spoke method (sometimes referred to the *star network*) allows some added flexibility in the event of unpredicted growth or constant changes in the architecture of the network. SONET multiplexers can be hubbed into a digital cross-connect (DCC), where it is concentrated, and then forwarded on to the next node. Hubbed is an industry accepted term.

Most of the SONET and fiber based manufacturers refer to their hubbed networks. This is used in many larger organizations where district or branch offices are tied into regional offices on the network through the hub. Flexibility in the network architecture can accommodate changes that might be necessary in the event of major changes in the organization. Hubs will act as the cross-connect points to link the various echelons in the network together. These may be developed in a blocking or nonblocking manner. Typically, some blocking may be allowed. The hub-and-spoke arrangement is shown in Figure 6-26.

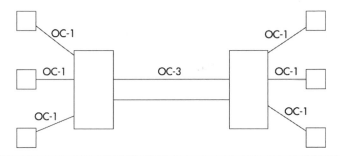

Figure 6-26 Hub and spoke in a SONET multiplexer network is shown as another layout possibility. The hub and spoke is also referred to as a star topology.

Ring

Next is the real glory of SONET! In a ring architecture employing SONET **automatic protection switching (APS)**, the best of all worlds comes to fruition. In automatic protection-ring topologies, ADMs are used throughout the network and a series of point-to-point links are installed between adjoining neighbors. The bidirectional capability places the most robustness into the network; however, unidirectional services can also be installed. The primary advantage of the ring architecture is survivability in the event of a failure in a cable or network node. The multiplexers have sufficient intelligence to reroute or reverse direction in the event of a failure. If more than one fiber link is installed, the systems could use alternate paths, but they must recover in milliseconds (which APS on SONET is designed to do). Figure 6-27 shows the ring topology with dual fibers run (bidirectional service) between the ADMs.

While the ANSI committees were working on SONET, another movement was underway. In Europe, the standards committees were also wrestling with the logical replacement to the **Plesiochronous** (pronounced *plee-zee-ock-ron-us*) **Digital Hierarchy (PDH)**, which is an asynchronous multiplexing plan to create high-speed communications channels. The Europeans came up with a separate multiplexing hierarchy (SDH) in support of the SONET standards.

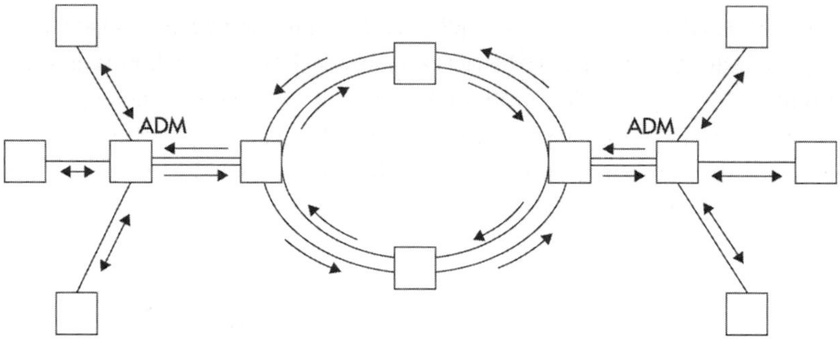

Figure 6-27 The ring architecture of SONET multiplexers is what SONET was created to provide. The ring offers resilient networking.

Line Check 6-9

1. What are the four topologies you use with SONET?
2. In the event of a cable or node failure, SONET uses what mechanism to keep the network running?

Synchronous Digital Hierarchy (SDH)

Ever since the standards bodies approved the recommendations for the SDH (and SONET), the services have been effectively used to improve and revolutionize the industry. Significant cost efficiencies and performance improvements have been shown. SDH provides a means for the rest of the world to use the capabilities of fiber-based transport systems and multiplexing architectures to improve on the older PDH, which was inefficient and expensive. The PDH—this means it is asynchronous or almost synchronous—evolved in response to the demand for POTS, and was not ideally suited to deliver the efficient use of bandwidth and high-speed services.

Digital networks continue to expand in complexity and penetration within the carriers' networks, now moving closer to the consumer's door. High-speed communications prior to the formulation of SDH in 1990 operated at speeds of up to 139.364 Mbps. However, the carriers implemented coaxial and radio-based systems operating at 140 Mbps to 565 Mbps. The networks were severely constrained because of the high cost of the transmission medium (coaxial cable especially). The multiplexing rates used plesiochronous rates, which led to the European PDH. After the development of fiber and the enhancements of integrated circuitry, the newer transmission speeds and complex networking architectures became realistic. In Europe, the evolution and deployment of ISDN also led to the proliferation of the B-ISDN standards, which allow a simple multiplexing technique. Broadband ISDN is another means of describing ATM to carry much higher-speed connections.

Synchronous Communications

What does the term "synchronous" mean anyway? *Synchronous* means within time. Why is this so important to the telecommunications industry? The easiest way to describe the need for synchronization is this: the "bits" from one telephone call are always in the same location inside a digital transmission frame, such as a DS1. In the United States, telephone calls using digital transmission systems create a DS-0. The DS-0s are multiplexed 24 per DS-1 channel. DS-1 lines are synchronously timed and mapped; therefore, it is easy to remove or insert a call. Finding the location creates an easy add-drop multiplexing arrangement. Timing is crucial on a telecommunications network because a timing relationship occurs between when something is sent and when it is received. To keep the network operating in an orderly fashion, this relationship becomes more critical.

Plesiochronous

Plesiochronous means almost synchronous. Variations occur in the timing of the line, so bits are stuffed into the frames as padding (filler). The digital bits (1's and 0's) vary slightly in their specific location within the frame, creating jitter. This occurs on a frame-to-frame basis, which disrupts the timing and requires other actions, such as resynchronization, padding, or restarting the framing to reestablish timing. If any of these actions are necessary, data will be stopped until the systems can recover the timing between them.

We describe our data transfer in four ways:

- Asynchronous—meaning *without* timing

- Synchronous—meaning *within* time

- Plesiochronous—meaning *almost* synchronous

- Isochronous (pronounced *eye-sock-ron-us*)—meaning *self-timing*

SDH Frame

The SDH forms a multiplexing rate based on the STM-N frame format (STM is the acronym for Synchronous Transmission Mode). The STM-N general frame format works as follows. Similar to the SONET OC-1 (albeit larger), the basic STM-1 frame consists of:

$$270 \text{ columns} \times 9 \text{ rows} = 2{,}430 \text{ octets}$$

$$9 \text{ columns} \times 9 \text{ rows} = 81 \text{ octets section overhead}$$

The remaining 2,349 octets create the payload. Higher-rate frames are derived from multiples of STM-1 according to value of N. The standard STM-1 frame is shown in Figure 6-28. This is similar to, but different from, the frame in an OC-3 at the same time. SONET also has a frame format that includes a data rate of 155.52 Mbps, but the formatting is slightly different from that of the SDH.

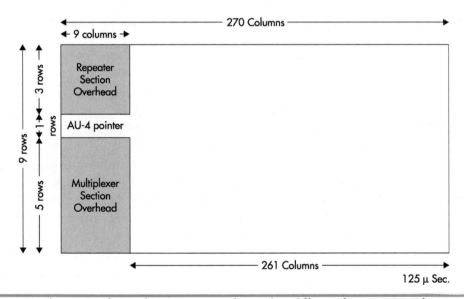

Figure 6-28 The STM-1 frame formats are similar to, but different from, SONET frames.

❔ Line Check 6-10

1. What is the size of the STM-1 frame?

2. What equivalent Optical Carrier (OC-x) is the size of the STM-1?

The typical rates of speed and the appropriate STS and STM rates are shown in Table 6-3.

Electrical Rate	Optical Rate	Speed
STS-1	STM-0	51.84 Mbps
STS-3	STM-1	155.52 Mbps
STS-9	STM-3	466.56 Mbps
STS-12	STM-4	622.08 Mbps
STS-18	STM-6	933.12 Mbps
STS-24	STM-8	1.244 Gbps
STS-36	STM-12	1.866 Gbps
STS-48	STM-16	2.488 Gbps
STS-192	STM-64	9.953 Gbps

Table 6-3 Comparing the STS and STM Rates. The Common Rates Are STM 1, 4, 16, and 64.

Only four of the hierarchical levels are defined in the standard and are commercially available. These are the STM-1, STM-4, STM-16, and STM-64. Today, typical installations are limited to multiplexing STM-16s onto a high-speed fiber channel.

As the data are prepared to place in the frame, several different modes of transport are available. At the input, the data flows into a container with a size designation. For example, the C11 is the equivalent of a T1 transport mechanism at 1.544 Mbps. The C12 will carry the E1 transport mechanism at 2.048 Mbps. Another transport is the C2, which is the equivalent of a DS2 operating at 6.312 Mbps. Each of these levels of container is then input into a **Virtual Container** (VC level *N*). SDH defines a number of **containers**. A *container* describes a corresponding plesiochronous rate, such as an E-1 at 2.048 Mbps. The information from a PDH signal is mapped into the relevant container. This is done similarly to the bit-stuffing procedure used in conventional PDH multiplexers.

Next, the VCs are mapped and multiplexed within the frame into a tributary unit level *N*. This completes the input from a container to a virtual container to a tributary unit. The levels are pretty much the same designation, as shown in Table 6-4. The T1, E1, and T2 lines can be mapped and multiplexed into the VCs that convert the format needed within SDH. The containers are then aligned with the timing of the system to create a Tributary Unit (TU).

Using a SONET multiplexing arrangement to produce the Administrative Unit 3 (which by all stretches of the imagination is the T3, or the seven T2s) follows the TU. Here, the Administrative Unit Group is the equivalent of three Administrative Unit 3s. You can now derive the fact that the three administrative units creating the administrative unit group *s* are

6

an OC-3 operating at 155.52 Mbps. Finally, comparing the multiplexed rates into these Administrative Unit Groups in both SDH and SONET, the outcome is the STM-N. You can add the services as necessary to get to the STM-4, which is the 622.08-Mbps transport, or the STM-16, which is our 2.488-Gbps transport system. You can see the two systems are closely aligned to each other; just different multiplexing and formatting arrangements are used in defining the overall platforms.

Equivalent	Rate	Input	Mapping	Aligning
DS-1	1.544 Mbps	C11	VC-11	TU-11
E-1	2.048 Mbps	C12	VC-12	TU-12
DS-2	6.312 Mbps	C2	VC-2	TU-2
E-3/T-3	34.368/44.736 Mbps	C3	VC-3	TU-3
E-3/T3	34.368/44.736 Mbps	C3	VC-3	AU-3
E4	139.264 Mbps	C4	VC-4	AU-4

Table 6-4 Levels of Input as They Map into the Tributary Units.

SDH brings harmony to the overall multiplexing of the various signals and transport rates. It also acts as the gateway between SONET and SDH structure. Over a decade has passed since the actual ratification of the standards, and now more than ever, the benefits are visible. Transcontinental links are now in heavy use across the world on fiber-based architectures.

Working in the Field:

Recently an optical architect position was advertised on the www.Telecomcareers.net web site that included a specialization in the area of installing and operating the optical networks for a carrier. When you choose a career in the telecommunications industry, many areas of specialization will become available. If this topic is one of interest, then we recommend you consider positions as optical networking specialists. An optical specialist will be responsible for the layout of the equipment, compliance monitoring, and project management of the installations. These careers can be quite lucrative depending on the company and the opportunity.

Waves of Light on the Fiber

Ten years ago, the implementation of the OC-48 SONET specification had the industry believing that limitless bandwidth was available. You can imagine that a mere decade ago the 2.5 ± Gbps capacities of the optical fiber networks were innovative and exceeded your wildest imagination about how we would ever fill these communications channels. Yet, the industry began to recognize the changes in consumption patterns. The demand for multimedia communications and video WAN started to erode even the highest transmission capacities available. To solve this problem, researchers began to experiment with the use of more than one light beam on the same cable. By using different radio frequencies on a cable TV system, the carriers were able to expand the number of TV channels available to them on the same coaxial systems. The same can be done with various channels or frequencies of light. Using different frequencies of light (various shades of red and blue, for example), several different channels can be present on the fiber simultaneously, each with independent bandwidth.

Wave-division multiplexing (WDM) can carry multiple data-bit rates, allowing multiple channels to be carried on a single fiber. The technique, quite literally, uses different colors of light down the same fiber to carry different channels of information, which are then separated out at the distant end by a diffraction grating that identifies each color. All optical networks employing WDM with add-drop multiplexers and cross-connects permit this. DWDM systems multiplex up to 160 or more wavelengths in the narrow beam window, increase capacity on existing fiber, and are data-rate transparent.

WDM was first developed to increase the distance signals could be transported in long-distance networks, from 35 to 50 km to as much as 970 km or more with optical amplifiers. Subsequently companies discovered that DWDM would work in metropolitan networks just as well. These DWDM ring systems can be connected with ATM switches and Internet Protocol (IP) routers. ATM networks are expected to use SONET/SDH physical layer interfaces with OC-12 add-drop multiplexers.

Where normal digital transmission systems use time-division multiplexing (TDM), cable TV analog technologies use frequency-division multiplexing (FDM). Wave-division multiplexing (WDM) is a combination of the two schemes combined. The use of a TDM multiplexer breaks the bandwidth down to specific timeslots, such as found in SONET-based networks. However, by using the combination of frequency (different wavelengths) and time (timeslots), the fiber can be used to carry orders of magnitude more than traditional fiber-based systems. Furthermore, several different wavelengths and colors of light can be used to produce far more capacity.

6

The Benefits of a Combined Network

By combining the benefits of low error rate and high-speed fiber networks with the strengths and survivability of SONET/SDH and placing the multiple bands of light on a single fiber, you can achieve bandwidth beyond your wildest imagination. In the future, you will likely see a designer's networking strategy where designer bandwidth can be customized on a user-by-user level. This is being highly touted by the RBOC companies with their emphasis on fiber to the premises (FTTP) or at a minimum FTTN/ FTTC (fiber to the node/curb). My next-door neighbor may want a connection from the telco on fiber at 1 Gbps, whereas I may want a higher-speed communications channel at 10 Gbps. Custom-built or demand-activated services designed to support our needs for the next decade will become commonplace.

Chapter 6 Review

Chapter Summary

In this chapter, you learned about the reasons for the development of ISDN. Clearly, the carriers were the motivated players in this development. They were looking to improve their services, reduce their costs, and entice the customers to use more services. What you learned is as follows:

- ISDN is a digital network that enables you to use the circuit-switched network for on-demand dial-up connections.

- Users in North America were slow to adopt ISDN because of the price and because a dial-up modem at 56 Kbps can achieve close to the 64-Kbps digital speeds of ISDN.

- However, in the rest of the world and, specifically, in Europe, ISDN is the norm for the dial tone that is delivered. The carriers in Europe and many other countries introduced ISDN as their basic service offering.

- ISDN also supports nonvoice communications for dial-up data and packet-switched data.

- To use the digital services, the BRI and the PRI were developed.

- With either service, a channel capacity up to the maximum of the link itself can be bonded. BRI allows us a total of 144 Kbps, whereas the PRI will deliver a 1.536-Mbps rate.

- Fiber-optic networks use SONET in North America and SDH in the European communities.

- Speeds starting at 51.84 Mbps to 9.953 Gbps are the rates specified for SONET and SDH alike. The packaging is what differs.

- Dense wave-division multiplexing (DWDM) is fast becoming the norm in the industry. DWDM uses both frequency and time-division multiplexing to attain high-data transfer rates.

- The SONET link architecture includes the three components of the section, the line, and the path.

- The differences between SONET and SDH are subtle, but they still leave room for incompatibilities.

- SONET and SDH both deliver a set of multiplexing schemes to reap high-speed communications across the network.

Key Terms for Chapter 6

Add-Drop Multiplexer (ADM) *(262)*
Asynchronous transfer mode (ATM) *(260)*
Automatic Protection Switching (APS) *(263)*
Basic Rate Interface (BRI) *(239)*
Bearer Services *(253)*
Bonding *(245)*
Containers *(267)*
Dense Wave-Division Multiplexing (DWDM) *(260)*
Digital Loop Carrier (DLC) *(248)*
Integrated Services Digital Network (ISDN) *(228)*
ISDN User Part (ISUP) *(243)*
Link Access Procedure for Data (LAP-D) *(242)*
Optical Carrier Level *n* (OC-*n*) *(255)*
Plesiochronous Digital Hierarchy (PDH) *(263)*
Primary Rate Interface (PRI) *(239)*
Synchronous Digital Hierarchy (SDH) *(254)*
Synchronous Optical Network (SONET) *(254)*
STS-N (Synchronous Transport Signal level *N*) *(257)*
Virtual Container (VC) *(267)*

Key Term Quiz

1. The use of _____ enables the user to simultaneously transmit voice and data services across a single line.

2. When large customers want to use ISDN, they will normally order a _____, which gives them the equivalent of a T1 service.

3. If a user wants to surf the Web at greater speeds, the process of _____ will enable the user to link two channels together and transmit at a rate of 128 Kbps.

4. The call-carrying capacity of the _____ channel is called the bearer services.

5. The North American use of a fiber-based network has been categorized in what is called the _____ standard.

6. When using SONET, the standard form of capacity is designated as the _____, which operates at 51.84 Mbps.

7. Internationally, the standards committees created _____ as a similar, but different, service to SONET.

8. _____ uses a 53-byte cell and was designed to run on SONET.

9. If you combine frequency and time-division multiplexing on a fiber network, the result is _____.

10. Carriers deploy a ring topology in fiber-based networks to provide _____, in case a system component or a cable fails.

Multiple-Choice Quiz

1. What does ISDN stand for?

   a. International Systems for Digital Networks

   b. Innovative Switching Digital Networks

   c. Integrated Services Digital Networks

   d. Integrated Switching and Digital Networking

2. The intent of installing the ISDN networks was to use the services for:

   a. Voice and non-voice services

   b. Dedicated point-to-point data circuits

   c. Digital Telex

   d. Analog data

3. The beneficiaries of ISDN were supposed to be (include all that apply):

   a. Customers

   b. ILECs

   c. IECs

   d. CLECs

4. ISDN offers two services known as:

   a. PRI and B8ZS

   b. BRI and E1

   c. T1 and E1

   d. BRI and PRI

5. The protocol used at layer 2 OSI model for the signaling is called:

   a. LAP-B

   b. LAP-D

   c. LAP-P

   d. LAP-M

6. The capacity to link multiple channels together is called _____.

   a. Binding

   b. Linking

   c. Superrating

   d. Bonding

7. The signaling portion of the ISDN network is designed to use the standards of _____.

   a. SS6

   b. X.25

   c. DSS

   d. SS7

8. PRI services come in two versions for the U.S. and for the rest of the world, described as:

   a. 2B + D and 23B + D

   b. 23B + D and 30B + D

   c. 24B + 31B + D

   d. 23D + B and 30D + B

9. The most common user interface is the:

   a. PRI

   b. Multirate service

    c. Local loop

    d. BRI

10. The BRI supports a total subscriber data transmission rate of_____.

    a. 128 Kbps

    b. 129 Kbps

    c. 144 Kbps

    d. 256 Kbps

11. When the carriers introduced the ISDN networks, they expected data transmission calls to be:

    a. More expensive

    b. Shorter per call

    c. Longer per call

    d. ISDN doesn't support data connections

12. The responsible standards committee for ISDN is _____:

    a. AT&T

    b. International Standards Organization (ISO)

    c. International Telecommunications Union-TSS

    d. Open Systems Interconnect

13. What does the acronym SONET stand for?

    a. Synchronous opportunity networks

    b. Synchronous optical networks

    c. Standards-based optical networks

    d. Standard optional networking

14. The SONET link architecture by ITU-T standard is broken into ____ pieces.

    a. 1

    b. 2

    c. 3

    d. 4

15. The point between two different repeaters is called the _____.

   a. Line

   b. Path

   c. Photonic

   d. Section

16. The end-to-end communications is called the _____.

   a. Link

   b. Line

   c. Photonic

   d. Path

17. The basic SONET rate called the OC-1 operates at _~~51.84 mbs~~___.

   a. 34 Mbps

   b. 49.76 Mbps

   c. 51.22 Mbps

   d. 51.84 Mbps

18. The basic rate for SDH is called the _____. *OC-1*

   a. STM-1

   b. STS-1

   c. STM-4

   d. OC-1

19. The STM-1 is the equivalent to an _____. *OC-3*

   a. OC-1

   b. OC-3

   c. STS-1

   d. STS-4

20. PDH stands for _____:

   a. Plesiochronous Data Header

   b. Plesiochronous Data Hierarchy

    c. Plesiochronous Digital Hierarchy

    d. Plesiochronous Data Header

21. What is the payload of an OC-1?

    a. 34.11 Mbps

    b. 49.53 Mbps

    c. 50 Mbps

    d. 51.84 Mbps

22. Wave-division multiplexing combines the _____ and _____ division multiplexing schemes.

    a. Time and space

    b. Frequency and statistical

    c. Frequency and space

    d. Frequency and time

23. The ability to multiplex as much as 128 or more wavelengths on a piece of fiber is called _____.

    a. Wave-division multiplexing

    b. SONET

    c. Add-drop multiplexing

    d. Dense wave-division multiplexing

24. SONET and SDH use a ring topology when _____ is required.

    a. A loop

    b. Add-drop multiplexing

    c. Survivability

    d. Duplex operation

Essay Quiz

1. Why do you think that ISDN never caught on in North America, yet is far more widely deployed in Europe?

2. If a common carrier, such as AT&T, wants to run a network service to support an organization's mission-critical data, what form of network topology might work best?

3. Why did the standards bodies feel they needed to upgrade our dial-up telephone networks to a digital network as specified in ISDN?

4. The industry has always been split in two factions: the North American way and the rest of the world (typically designed by the Europeans). This chapter highlights this problem, especially with the use of ISDN and SONET/SDH. Do you think more should be done to standardize the use of our technologies? Should the industry force a more global single implementation of these services? Why?

Lab Projects

1. Log on to http://www.fiber-optics.info/fiber-history.htm and read the history of fiber optics. After you complete the readings, discuss the contents and concepts shown in the web site with your fellow students. Can you understand the need for the cladding around the center core? Why do you think that bending is such a concern for installers? Be prepared to discuss with your instructor the differences and capacities of the three common diameters of fiber. Do you know the three most common ones?

2. Log on to http://www.ralphb.net/ISDN/proto_l2.html and view the tutorial on ISDN. When you finish, work together with your fellow students and fill in the frame format for the frame format of a 2B + D at the following U interface by listing the number of bits in each category. This is shown on the web site listed.

Sync	$12 * (B_1 + B_2 + D)$	Maintenance

With this frame, how many bits are carried in each frame? How long does each frame last?

Chapter 7

Data Standards in Use

LEARNING OBJECTIVES:

Once you complete this chapter, you will be able to:

Discuss how the computing model went from a mainframe environment to a distributed environment.

Explain problems that are encountered when using multiple vendors and converters.

Define types of standards and which organizations are responsible for making them.

Describe the OSI model and the seven-layer structure.

Compare the differences between the OSI and other models, such as TCP/IP, IBM's SNA, and DEC's DNA.

This book already has covered voice communications. In the mid-1940s the invention of the computer changed the landscape of the world forever. Originally, computers performed simple mathematical functions. Eventually, software was developed so computers could perform other functions, such as creating shipping orders, doing product billing, and keeping track of product inventories. The computer has simplified our lives in many ways, but it has also added complexity. For example, computers are now used to send data over networks that were initially designed to send only voice communications. This has created a new set of challenges for designers of communications networks.

The Need for Computing

One of the first electronic computers was developed by John William Mauchly and J. Presper Eckert, Jr. It was called the **Electronic Numerical Integrator and Computer (ENIAC)**, and it was completed in 1945. The ENIAC was a huge machine that filled an entire room and weighed somewhere around 30 tons. It performed mathematical calculations and also provided temporary storage. To function, programmers had to alter and "plug" in wiring connections to a series of over three thousand switches physically. This process was tedious, but it still saved time because advanced computations done by hand took almost a day to complete. The ENIAC reduced this process to under a minute.

In the early days of computing, a large computer was centrally located in an office. All input and output was generated within this computer room, with all operators kept to one location. This was known as a **mainframe environment**.*

As long as the data-processing function was localized to the mainframe and all transactions were performed in the computer room, no problem existed. IBM, the giant in mainframe computing, was responsible for almost all business applications in the early days of computing.

Like all things, however, this industry evolved. Soon the movement was from the computer room to the desktop, where users wanted connectivity to the mainframe. This was accomplished through the use of specialized wiring systems. Nothing is new here, other than these special wires were expensive. The wires had to carry the data from the terminal to the computer and data back from the computer to the terminal. This was accomplished with the use of traditional communications techniques—by converting the data into electrical energy and carrying it

---

*Mainframes used to be the dominant device for all computing. Over 90 percent of all applications resided on mainframes until the early 1990s, when servers began replacing them. Technology has allowed microprocessors to shrink computing power to a fraction of the size of former machines. In fact, today's desktop is much more powerful than an entire room of computers from 20 years ago. Mainframes are slowly being phased out because of cheaper, more flexible technologies such as servers.

down the wire—and the data was represented in digital form without notice where the electricity was converted back to data.

Shortly thereafter, further changes occurred. Not only did we need connectivity from the desktop to the computer room, now we also needed it from a desktop across town or across the country. These demands required a dramatic change to occur in the industry. We were now expected to transfer data over long distances. That process was going to change the way we conducted business. The data communications industry became the next battleground.

The data-processing people all thought that data processing and data communications should be similar enough so they could control the deployment. (The telephony people felt this computer stuff was a pain anyway, so they were content to let it reside in the data processing arena.) Some problems existed with this whole situation, however. To send the data across town or across the entire country, it would be necessary to use a device called a modem. A *modem* is a modulator/demodulator. In layman's terms, a modem is a device that takes our computer signal and converts it to a signal that can be carried on a voice telephony network to another modem on the far end, and then forward it to the computer at the far end. (We will discuss modems in detail in Chapter 8.) As long as the data looked like voice, the data folks wanted to send it back to the telephony department, especially when they didn't understand or care to understand how this analog (phone) network functioned.

Thus, the marriage of the three techniques (computing, voice, and data) began back in the late 1950s and into the 1960s. This transition was slow because the telephone monopoly controlled the delivery of the transport system.

Distributed Computing

Data processors began looking for a way to make the network digital to avoid the digital-to-analog and the analog-to-digital conversions. This process seemed too lengthy, and as each step was taken, a risk occurred of introducing errors into the data stream.

7

The data-processing evolution kept going from the mainframe environment to one leaning toward distributed computing. **Distributed computing** means sharing computer resources among devices. Having multiple computers, printers, and scanners all attached to a network is an example of distributed computing. The mainframe environment has now been largely replaced with servers, forming client-server networks. Client-server networks use a computer called a *server* to host data and programs and management functions, and provide access to other peripheral devices (other devices that lie on the network).

NOTE

Client-server is a form of distributed computing; the terms are interchangeable.

Smaller-scale computers that handled specific functions were introduced to off-load processes from the mainframe. However, many of the mainframe computers in use at the time were incompatible with the mid-range computers, such as those made by the manufacturers Digital Equipment Corporation (DEC) and Data General. This led to a new set of problems that had to be dealt with.

As the smaller computer companies were competing with the mainframe world, two major players were doing battle: IBM and DEC. Each had its own hardware and software platforms. Now, organizations began to move computers from different manufacturers into their buildings. No problem: these were specific application processors, so there was no conflict. That was true, but a user who needed access to the mainframe and the specialty machine now required two separate sets of wires run to the desk and two different terminals on top of the desk. This is reminiscent of the situation portrayed in the historical section of this book (see Chapter 2), where the interconnection of various telephone companies would not work and users needed two or three phones on their desks to intercommunicate. The battle was being fought over compatibility, rather than technology. The problems were just starting.

Problems with Multiple Vendors

Compatibility has always been an issue in computing. That is why AT&T had always had its network protected (only AT&T equipment could be connected to the network until the 1970s)—to ensure all equipment would function properly and not damage other components of the network. To understand the compatibility problem that existed in computer networking, let's look at the environment managers had.

In early days of computing, all mainframes came from "*the* computer manufacturer," IBM. IBM developed the architecture as a hierarchy, in which devices were placed on different levels of importance. Depending on the level and the importance of the user, information flowed in certain directions.

Figure 7-1 shows the transfer of information among users. This system worked pretty well because IBM had everything in place. IBM delivered the hardware, the software, the connections, and the talent to make everything work together. This was all based on a proprietary and closed architecture called **Systems Network Architecture (SNA)**. Figure 7-2 shows the architecture in its stack. The SNA is a seven-layered architecture that IBM created to make everything work in harmony. Using this structure, IBM would fix any portion that did not work—for a fee, of course.

Later, machines appeared from competing vendors that used a different approach and couldn't connect with the IBM system. These offshoot companies, such as DEC, were often

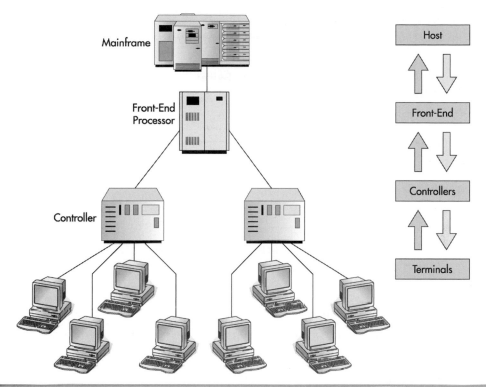

Figure 7-1 In a mainframe computing environment, information flows between devices.

founded by ex-IBM employees upset with the strategy and direction that IBM used. They
wanted to offer the customer lower-end machines at more reasonable prices and in a more
open environment. Let's face it, though: when an engineer or manager leaves one place of
employment, it's tough to leave behind all learned information, so the cross-pollination of
ideas and goals took root. In the design and rollout of its products, DEC introduced its own
closed and proprietary architecture (shown in Figure 7-3), called **Digital Network Architecture
(DNA)**, that just happened to have seven layers.

These seven layers were based on DEC hardware, software, connections, and talent to
make everything work in harmony. Sounds familiar, doesn't it?

Users who employed a multivendor approach to meet their computing needs were faced
with two separate architectures. Most companies needed users to be connected to both
systems. Moreover, many of the specialty applications the users wanted required the data that
was stored in the mainframe. This meant the users were rekeying the data from printed reports

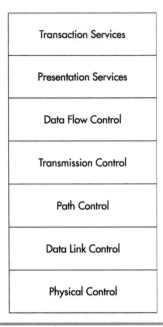

Figure 7-2 The IBM proprietary SNA stack operates in a seven-layered architecture.

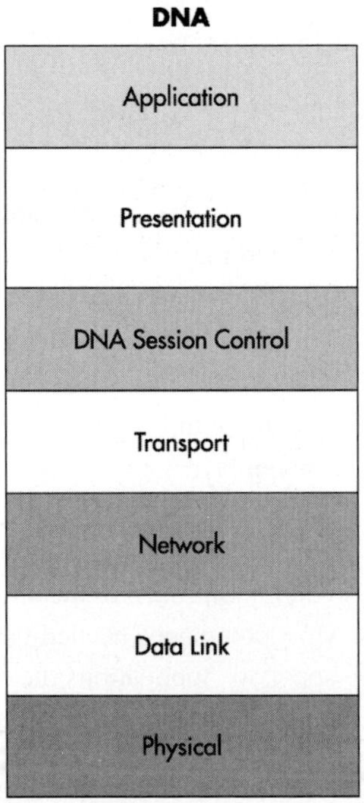

Figure 7-3 DEC's DNA stack.

that came from the mainframe into the second computer system. This created a new set of problems:

● The timeliness of the data was suspect. Because of the time it took to rekey the data, it could be obsolete before it was ever entered.

● The accuracy of the information was questionable because data-entry errors are not uncommon when one is rekeying the data.

● The cost of the information was now more expensive because the input was done at least twice.

● Data synchronization became an issue because new data entered in one database was not yet entered in the second database. (This is why changing your address at a bank and so forth might not change all records.)

This scenario was critically flawed. To visualize how this played out, you need to imagine what it took to deploy in a customer's office. An office would have a mainframe from one vendor and a mid-range computer (a smaller computer with less processing power) from another vendor (to run different applications). The user experience was confusing because users had to log on to both devices to gain access.

The problem being faced was like the difference between moving material with a tractor-trailer and moving the same material with a pickup truck. Cargo moved in a tractor-trailer might be packaged into boxes too big for the pickup and, therefore, need to be repackaged into smaller containers. Conversely, tractor-trailer drivers are harder to find. They demand higher salaries and require specialized operator's licenses, whereas you could use almost any normal driver and place him or her behind the wheel of a pickup.

When management contacted the mainframe vendor, they explained their mid-range computer users wanted to connect to the mainframe to manipulate data. Also, to modify the data, management wanted users to move data from the mainframe to the mid-range computer. Once finished, users wanted to move the altered data back to the mainframe. In addition, the users wanted the same keystrokes to be utilized on both systems for ease of use.

The response from the mainframe vendor was simple—take out the mid-range computer and install mainframe terminal hosts. (Remember that because of proprietary software and hardware, the same keystrokes would not work across systems.)

When the business contacted the mid-range computer vendor and explained the situation, a similar answer was given. The suggested solution was to remove the other equipment and equip all users with the same hardware.

This solution was not practical in any case. To tear out all the proprietary cabling and hardware, buy and install new hardware, and then re-cable an office would be disruptive to business and incur significant costs. So, what was a company to do? How could it give all users access to data, as well as the ability to save and manipulate the data wherever they wanted?

Fortunately, others had already gone through this problem and a new supplier had emerged: the third-party manufacturers of black boxes.* **Black box** is a generic term used to describe third-party protocol converters. In reality, the box was not black at all; the name referred to the fact that no one really knew what the box did. Users only knew that when they typed commands on their terminals, the data came out on the other side in a usable format on the other hardware. This process worked both ways, so the systems now worked with each other and user satisfaction increased.

These protocol converters were not inexpensive, but they were certainly a more attractive option than the other choices management had. With a connection to each machine, the converter sat in the middle. This is shown in Figure 7-4, where the two hosts are connected to the converter. This solution sounds simple enough, but it brought a whole new list of problems with its use.

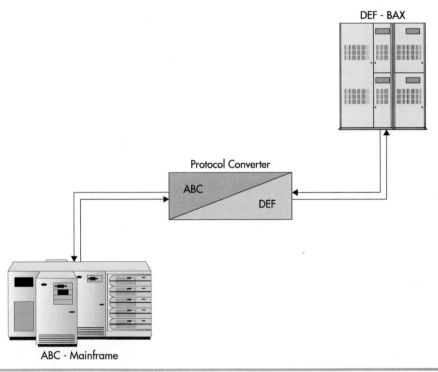

Figure 7-4 The layout of where within the network a black box or protocol converter would lie and the function it performs.

---

*Black box was the name given to any device when we did not really know what was going on inside. The device just did what it was supposed to do. The reference to "black box" is not to the Black Box Company in Pittsburgh, PA, which offers several excellent products and services.

Problems with Converters

After the installation, things worked fairly well. That is, until things stopped working smoothly. When the IT department investigated, the mainframe users had not done anything different; neither had the mid-range computer users. The IT manager thought the problem must be the converter. When the converter company was contacted, it responded that the converter wasn't altered, so it must be the internal users. Too often, what had happened was this: one of the two competing systems that the protocol converters were connecting had changed something in its communication systems, and now the protocol converter would have to be upgraded to match this proprietary change.

This reminds us of the problem with the divestiture of AT&T. Each party placed blame on the other, and no one accepted responsibility for the problem. This finger pointing runs rampant in the industry, even today. In using multiple vendors and multiple hardware devices, initial trouble reports all too often are referred to the other company.

What Is a Standard?

When we begin talking about standards, several players are involved. But first, let's describe a standard.

A **standard** is simply a definition or a description of a technology and how it will be used. The purpose of developing standards is to help vendors build components that will function together or facilitate use by providing continuity with other products. This section discusses what standards are, why they exist, and some of the ways they could affect you.

Two kinds of standards exist: de facto and de jure. **De facto** means "in fact." If more than one vendor "builds to" or complies with a particular technology, one can reasonably refer to that technology as a standard. An excellent example of such a standard in data communications is IBM's Systems Network Architecture (SNA).*

No independent standards organization has ever "blessed" SNA as an official, or **de jure**, standard. But dozens, if not hundreds, of other vendors have built products that successfully interact with devices and networks.

Moreover, some technologies become standards because the creating vendors intend them to become standards (such as Ethernet, which you learn about in Chapter 10). Others become standards despite the creating vendors (such as Lotus 1-2-3 menu structure).

7

---

*Note that de facto standards rarely become standards overnight. SNA was available for some time before vendors other than IBM could or would provide products that supported it.

One reason vendors often build to de facto standards is that the standards-making process is lengthy. For a new or revised standard to become agreed on takes a minimum of 4 to 12 years. With product cycles now being deployed in under one year in some areas of the communications industry, waiting for the finalization of a standard before introducing a product could result in corporate suicide. The networking protocol called Ethernet, which connects devices on a local area network, is a good example of a standard that started as a de facto standard. Intel, Xerox, and DEC introduced Ethernet with the intent of making it a de jure standard. But that process took years, and the final result was slightly different from the technology originally created by the three vendors. Nonetheless, many networks were created based on Ethernet before the 802.3 de jure standard was finalized, bringing profit to its creators and operating environments to their customers. Generally, de facto standards are controlled by the vendors that introduced them. For example, Microsoft Windows is a de facto standard. Many vendors provide programs that comply with and operate in this environment. But if Microsoft decides to change the way a new version of Windows works, in theory, it can make all of those programs obsolete.

In practice, Microsoft is most unlikely to do this—at least intentionally—because much of its market power stems from the fact that all those other products are built to its standard. Were Microsoft to make such a change, it is likely that those other software providers would look elsewhere for a target operating system. Microsoft's stock would drop precipitously, to say the least! Or, as we saw, the Department of Justice or foreign trade unions would alter the way Microsoft does business.

"De jure" means in law, although standards do not generally have the force of law. In some parts of the world, when a standard is set, it, in fact, becomes law. If a user or vendor violates the rules, the penalties can be quite severe. A user who installs a nonstandard piece of equipment on the links could be subject to steep fines and up to one year in prison. These countries take their standards seriously. In the United States, no such penalties exist; we are more relaxed in this area. But a standard is a de jure standard if an independent standards body (that is, one not solely sponsored by vendors) successfully carries it through a more or less public standards-making procedure and announces that it is now a standard.

In the real world, the standards-making bodies rely in large part on vendors to develop the details of new and revised standards. In fact, most standards bodies have vendor representatives as full participants. This is a fascinating political process with much pushing and pulling to gain advantage in the market. The vendors participate for several reasons, not the least of which is to get the jump on competitors that are not as close to the process. Another reason includes the ability to state (in marketing materials) that the vendors contributed to, or were involved in, the testing of a new standard. Yet another reason is the opportunity to influence the actual details of a standard to favor technology with which the vendors are most familiar.

To be fair, it should be stated that the primary goal of most of those involved in the standards process is to define a good and useful standard. But when the process produces a dual standard, as in the case of the Ethernet and Token Ring (local area network standards), you can presume that the "best" was compromised somewhat in favor of what everyone could agree on.

Even de jure standards (usually identifiable by virtue of their unintelligible alphanumeric designations, such as X.25, V.35, V.42 bis, and so on) change in ways that significantly affect the market and you. One set of standards that affects thousands of users is the set of modem standards, which is discussed in Chapter 8. But beware a vendor that trumpets compliance with a new standard! The vendor's claim might be legitimate, but if no other vendors have products available in the same space, the company might simply be hyping its own product, hoping it eventually will become a standard. Or there might be a standard under development, but not yet approved. In the latter case, if that standard changes before final approval, the vendor's current products will instantly become nonstandard without changing in any way. Another example of this was video recorders of the 1980s. Two types were introduced: VHS and Betamax. Although Betamax had more heads than the original VHS did and, therefore, had a higher-quality picture, VHS was chosen by the purchasing public as the standard. After a few years, Betamax could not compete and suppliers stopped providing this technology.

 ## What Do You Think?

Without the application of standards, how would our world be different? What do standards do to the industry as a whole? Discuss with your fellow classmates what the industry would be like if there were no standards.

7

Standards Bodies Within the U.S.

Because we have already mentioned that standards are a "definition or description of a technology," who is involved in creating them?

Standards are developed by collaboration among various groups, forums, committees, and other regulating agencies. In the United States, many standards bodies exist, but there are eight major players in the communications world. These are as follows:

- International Organization for Standardization (ISO)

- International Telecommunications Union-Telecommunication Standards Sector (ITU-T)

- American National Standards Institute (ANSI)

- Institute of Electrical and Electronics Engineers (IEEE)

- Electronic Industries Association (EIA)
- Telcordia
- Internet Engineering Task Force (IETF)
- The forums

We will look a little more deeply at these organizations and their primary function, as well as their place within the market.

ISO

The **International Organization for Standardization (ISO)** is a conglomerate of multinational members that focus on standards creation committees from various government agencies worldwide. It has participation from over 148 countries and government agencies. The ISO combines collaborative cooperation in scientific, technological, and business activities. The main goal of the *ISO* is to ensure quality, productivity, and competitive practices through a business modeling program. The ISO is responsible for the creation of data networking standards, which we cover in the section of this chapter titled "OSI Introduced." One of the most widely accepted data networking standards is called the **Open Systems Interconnection (OSI)** reference model.

ITU-T

The International Telecommunication Union (ITU) is an organization with roots in the United Nations. A subdivision within the ITU, specializing in the **Telecommunications Standards Sector (ITU-T)**, is what we will focus on. The ITU-T is further divided into smaller groups, each relating to a specialized aspect of the industry. Groups come to an agreement and ratify a proposal, which then becomes part of the ITU-T standard. Changes to this standard are incorporated every four years to provide a gradual transition to newer standards, without being too disruptive to business practices. The ITU is best known for contributions defining standards occurring over phone lines, as well as transmission over public digital networks (the *V* series and the *X* series, respectively).*

ANSI

The **American National Standards Institute (ANSI)** is a private, nonprofit organization that serves as the coordinating body and administrator of U.S. standards. Note that ANSI serves as

---

*The *V* series refers to V.32, V.33, V.42, and the *X* series refers to X.25, X.35, ISDN, and so forth.

a voluntary standardization and conformity assessment organization. The primary goal of ANSI is to ensure and enhance U.S. business and competitiveness in the global arena. Its participation is on a voluntary level, through nearly 1,000 companies, government agencies, and other institutions and international members.

ANSI provides the means for the U.S. to influence global standardization activities and the development of international standards. It is the dues-paying member and sole U.S. representative of the two major non-treaty international standards organizations, the International Organization for Standardization (ISO) and the International Electrotechnical Commission (IEC), via the U.S. National Committee (USNC).

ANSI submits proposals to the ITU-T and is the U.S. voting member in the ISO. Its European counterparts are European Telecommunications Standards Institute (ETSI) and Committee of European Post, Telegraph, and Telephone (CEPT).

The 1990s brought standardization into the limelight as a source of strategic and competitive advantage in the ever-expanding global economy. Never before had the importance of standardization been greater. Companies view standards not only as key to impacting product development, quality, or environmental compliance, but also as an imperative in competing successfully in the global marketplace. The effective use of strategic standardization in achieving competitiveness, quality, product certification, and conformity assessment became a critical issue facing the business and the standardization communities in this decade.

In late 2000, the first-ever U.S. National Standards Strategy (NSS) was approved. Developed over a two-year period by a diverse group of interested parties, the *NSS* is a roadmap to developing reliable, market-driven standards in all sectors. It reaffirms that the U.S. is committed to a sector-based approach to voluntary standardization activities, both domestically and globally. It provides an outline of key principles necessary for the development of standards to meet societal and market needs, and a strategic vision for implementing these principles nationally and internationally.

During the first years of the twenty-first century, those involved in standards-setting activities clearly recognized a growing need for globally relevant standards and related conformity assessment mechanisms. Market forces such as global trade and competition; societal issues such as health, safety, and the environment; an enhanced focus on consumer needs and involvement; and increasing interaction between public-sector and private-sector interests were significantly impacting standardization and conformity-assessment programs. Standards themselves had expanded well beyond documents identifying product specifications to focus, instead, on performance issues and also to include processes, systems, and personnel.

The U.S. voluntary standardization system is highly regarded and recognized as one of the most effective and efficient standards systems in the world today. The past 85 years have brought many changes and improvements to the institute and the voluntary standards system, many of which are not mentioned here in this brief overview. But ANSI continues to serve the role for which the American Engineering Standards Committee was created—to coordinate

7

U.S. standards activities. As the U.S. economy changes, so must the institute continue to evolve to meet the challenges of a global marketplace and the demands of its constituents. It will continue to be an organization committed to serving the U.S. voluntary standards system and its members, the backbone of a system that is first among equals.

IEEE

The **Institute of Electrical and Electronics Engineers (IEEE)** is the world's largest professional society of engineers. The mission of the *IEEE* is to provide creativity and quality control in the fields of electronics, electrical engineering, and other related fields. It also helps oversee the creation of international standards in communication and computer technologies. The IEEE had a special focus group in networking standards for local area networks (LANs), which are designated by the 802.*x* family. These are the 802.3, 802.4, 802.5, and 802.11*x* series. We cover these LAN standards in detail in Chapter 10.

EIA

The **Electronic Industries Association (EIA)** is also a nonprofit organization that deals with the production aspect of electronics. The *EIA* is an educating body that informs the public about standards development and adoption. Its greatest contributions in standards development are the interfaces that devices utilize (such as Category 5 UTP cable and RJ-11 and RJ-45 cable jacks). These connectors allow different manufacturers' devices to interface with each other through a common standard. Prior to the EIA's participation, connectors were proprietary, and only their connectors worked on their products.

Telcordia

Telcordia Technologies Inc. was formerly called Bellcore. Obviously, its contribution to the communications industry is unparalleled. Since divestiture, Telcordia has maintained a role in developing standards for the PSTN in the United States. In addition, the company collaborates with leading academic, industrial, and government institutions that provide access to a multitude of unique laboratories and research facilities across the country. Telcordia provides integration with talent pools in various aspects in the industry.

IETF

The **Internet Engineering Task Force (IETF)** is a standards body that presides over the Internet. Because the Internet was relieved of oversight by the National Science Foundation (NSF) in 1996, a civilian organization was created to oversee the Internet. The *IETF* is unique in that it publishes standards for the Internet, but also allows standards developed outside its scope to be implemented (on occasion). The IETF ensures that protocols put on the Internet will not cause catastrophic failure of the network when a newer technology is introduced. The IETF is composed of representatives of the major hardware manufacturers and carriers alike.

The Forums

Forums are newer groups that have emerged in creating standards. *Forums* are generally composed of all the hardware manufacturers in an alliance whose purpose is to advance deployments of newer technologies. Examples of forums would be the MPLS frame-relay forum. They are designed to ensure interoperability of networks, applications, and services. Forums encourage developments through standards bodies and create agreements on internetworking products, as well as educational programs to instruct people on the newer technologies. These forums publish their works and findings in documents called white papers. These papers are used in evaluating the effectiveness of changes suggested to the standard before they become accepted by the standards bodies. Forums provide a place where the manufacturers can brainstorm and share their ideas to allow their products to enter the marketplace.

✆ Line Check 7-1

1. With so many standards bodies, which ones are the ultimate final decision makers for the industry?

2. If there are other groups with some presiding interests, what is the purpose of forums?

3. What exactly is a white paper and who can access that information? How does publishing these documents and making them available benefit the standards process?

7

Data Standards in Use

Now that we have identified the standards bodies influencing the industry, let's look at some of the standards most widely used today.

We mentioned that standards allow different manufactures of devices/software to work independently of each other. It is important to realize protocols are a set of rules describing how a technology will be used, but protocols are not always standards.

The idea of having a standard to allow data networking is fundamental to interoperation. ISO created a networking standard called the Open Systems Interconnection reference model (OSI). The OSI model defines the rules for different systems to connect without requiring extensive changes to the hardware or software.

CAUTION

Although the OSI model is a framework to allow different systems to interconnect without extensive changes to hardware or software, in some cases, third-party software or hardware is needed for this conversion.

The model is a layered framework for network system design and communication across all types of systems. Seven layers are in the OSI model that individually defines how transportation occurs across each segment of the network. These seven layers are:

- The Application layer   (layer 7)
- The Presentation layer   (layer 6)
- The Session layer   (layer 5)
- The Transport layer   (layer 4)
- The Network layer   (layer 3)
- The Data Link layer   (layer 2)
- The Physical layer   (layer 1)

As we send information from one place to another, it will follow these seven segments.

Line Check 7-2

Explain the effect (value) of using a layered model in regard to the following ideas:

- Complexity
- Interfaces
- Interoperability
- Evolution of technology (advancement)
- Ease of learning/teaching

OSI Introduced

In 1978, the ISO was asked to come up with a solution that would allow transparent communications and data transfer between and among systems, regardless of manufacturer.

This was originally thought of as the task of the data communications devices. Thus, a new committee was formed to evaluate how this might happen.

Everyone in the industry held his or her breath. What form of solution would be achieved? Because this was a committee made up of users, vendors, and manufacturers of the systems, as well as standards members, what could be expected? The result was to come several years later, with what we now have come to know as the ISO/OSI reference model. No, they did not just reverse the letters of the organization: ISO/OSI is the acronym for the International Organization for Standardization Open Systems Interconnect reference model. The ISO/OSI is a seven-layer architecture, just like the other two architectures that already existed (SNA and DNA)—two of the member companies of the committee were IBM and DEC. This seven-layered architecture is shown in Figure 7-5. The seven layers are covered in more detail later in this chapter but are listed here:

- The *application layer* sits at the top of the model. This is the direct interface with the application used when requesting a service. The application layer provides communications services to the end user.

- The *presentation layer* sits below the application layer and provides a service to the application layer. The presentation layer is where formatting, code conversions, data representation, compression, and encryption are handled for the application.

- The *session layer*, located under the presentation layer, is responsible for the establishment and maintenance of connections between client and server processes. The control of the direction of data transfer is handled in the session layer.

- The *transport layer* is right below the session layer. The transport layer controls the connection for error recovery and flow control. It is responsible for assuring error-free data delivery end-to-end in a cost-efficient manner.

The next three layers deal with the network-specific issues of the communications process. Whereas the upper four layers deal with the end-to-end communications and data transfer, the bottom three layers are concerned with the node-to-node connection. This portion of the network may be provided by a single entity (such as a carrier, PTT, or third-party communications company).

- The *network layer* sits just under the transport layer and is responsible for the switching and routing of the connection. Also, this layer is responsible for taking the data that is to be shipped from node-to-node, not end user-to-end user. Congestion control, alternate routing, and other such connectivity services are handled here. The network layer provides the transfer of data in a connectionless service. This layer is also responsible for logical addressing.

7

- The *data link layer* is responsible for the delivery of the information to the medium. It creates frames of information, if required, and sends the frames along to the wires. Additionally, the data-link layer is responsible for the reliability of the information and error checking on a node-to-node basis. This layer provides the physical addressing.

- The *physical layer,* which sits below the data link layer, is the actual electrical or mechanical interface to the physical medium. This layer has the physical pieces and the necessary components based on the dependency of the medium. The physical layer is responsible for transmitting the bits onto the guided medium (wires). It specifies various physical portions, such as the voltage levels, the pins to use in placing the voltage onto the link, and whether the signal will be electrical or photonic (fiber) or modulated onto a nonguided (radio)-based service. You see how all these pieces tie together later in this chapter.

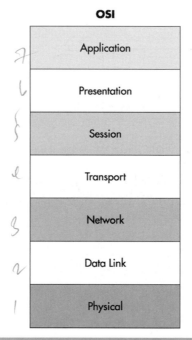

Figure 7-5 The seven-layered architecture of the OSI model

Even with all the effort placed on creating this set of protocols and the entire architecture, many industry and end-user groups were somewhat frustrated. They wanted a single solution to provide the transparent communications between systems of different manufacturers, although what they got was yet another seven-layer architecture. Most were shocked that the standards committees would ratify such an approach. In reality, this was the best way to provide the solutions, but this approach wasn't totally understood at the time. The seven layers are independent of each other. Even though they provide services to the upper layer and rely on the lower layer, some freedom still exists. This is important because in the event that any protocol suite in one of the seven layers needs to be changed, the rest of the architecture will remain intact. This methodology makes the stack more effective, only requiring the suspect layer to be converted, and then processed. A single software solution would not have done that.

Figure 7-6 compares the three seven-layer architectures—the OSI as a base, the SNA, and the DNA—to see how they line up against each other. In fairness to both DEC and IBM, their architectures were in place before the OSI model was created, so they cannot be expected to be the same.

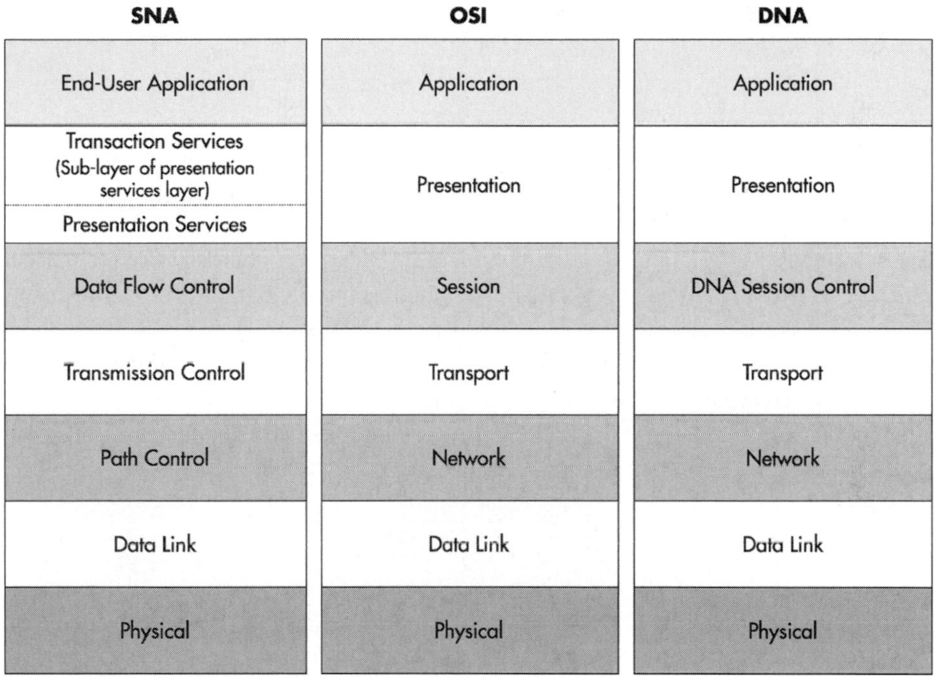

SNA	OSI	DNA
End-User Application	Application	Application
Transaction Services (Sub-layer of presentation services layer) / Presentation Services	Presentation	Presentation
Data Flow Control	Session	DNA Session Control
Transmission Control	Transport	Transport
Path Control	Network	Network
Data Link	Data Link	Data Link
Physical	Physical	Physical

Figure 7-6 Comparison of the OSI model to IBM's SNA and DEC's DNA

Over the years, DEC changed the architecture of its DECNet protocols to be more consistent with the OSI, but IBM has basically done nothing over the past 27 years to change. IBM has always felt that it already had the single largest and most widely accepted architecture installed at all of the Fortune 1,000 companies, so there was no need to change what already worked. Even though the OSI architecture was begun around 1978, it was not totally accepted until 1984 and there have been few implementations of it. In 1988, the OSI architecture was finally ratified as a true standard. More implementations were seen overseas than in North America.

Part of the reason was the cost of moving over to a new architecture. The U.S. government wanted a standard applied to all its purchases in the past. In an effort to initiate OSI acceptance and implementation, the Government Service Administration (GSA) specified a modified version of the OSI reference model. If you wanted to sell something of a computing or data communications nature to the government, you had to comply with its modified version. This was called the Government Open Systems Interconnect Profile (GOSIP). Yes, you could say the U.S. government was responsible for starting GOSIP.

This model has been the reference on which many of the changes of the past 20 years were based. Although few manufacturers have attained fully open systems, they have attempted to use the OSI as a model for their future compliance.

NOTE

Remember, little incentive existed for any manufacturer to comply fully with the OSI model because the openness could potentially jeopardize future revenue streams.

Now, back to this complex model. The seven layers always confused even those with a rigorous background in the data-processing or data-communications industry. How can we show you in one chapter of text how this works and keep it simple?

We assume you are likely a novice or getting into some new portion of the industry, and this is your reference manual. So, let's try it with our usual method: a story. Figure 7-7 shows two neighbors, Bud and Marcus, who think they can develop their own communication system, rather than use the local phone company. Simple, right?

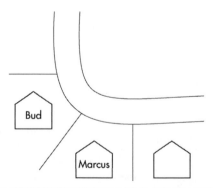

Figure 7-7 Here are two people moving into a neighborhood.

So, they consider their options and come up with the choices shown in Table 7-1. The option is shown in the first column, and the pros and cons are in the other two columns. These are not all-inclusive. We limited our list to a few options.

Option	Benefits	Deterrents
Use a megaphone and yell out the window from one house to the other	• Easy to install over relatively short distances • Can be implemented immediately	• What if one person isn't home? • What if Bud wants to talk to Marcus at 2 A.M.? • Loss of transmission because of distances. • Noisy for other neighbors in the area. • Total lack of privacy.
Throw pebbles at the window. When the receiver hears the pebbles on the window, open the window and yell out	• Pebbles are readily available • The method of signaling each other is straightforward	• Given the distance, the throw will take some effort. This can cause damage. • In inclement weather, this can be awkward and inconvenient.
Use a flashlight and send the signals in Morse code	• Easy to use • Quick communications	• Marcus doesn't know Morse code. • During daylight hours, the sun may diminish the light. • Batteries can fail.
Go next door and visit. Have conversations during the visit.	• Easy to accommodate • Doesn't cost anything	• Weather may make this difficult. • What about those 2 A.M. conversations?

Table 7-1 Summary of Communication Options.

7

In the figures that show the table results, benefits and losses are associated with the communications options. Therefore, the two owners decide to model their communications device after the service they wanted—the telephone. The two neighbors aren't going to go out and build a Central Office (CO). After all, they just want the convenience of speaking with each other. So, they decide to build on a model. Let's use the OSI model and make sure this all ties in while we provide transparent communications.

Bud comes up with the idea that he and Marcus need to send their information across a medium. The earlier options used the airwaves as the medium, but weather conditions and other factors limited this. Therefore, both neighbors agree to use a physical medium.

They decide to install a piece of everyday common household string between their houses. This is shown in Figure 7-8, where the string is run in a direct line of sight between both parties. The string is laid out, and the two parties are connected with the medium.

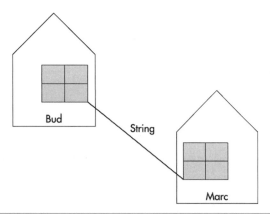

Figure 7-8 The physical link is a string connecting both parties.

Given that the physical string is now attached, it is obvious that something is still missing. Therefore, the neighbors decide they have to use the model to handle their next step. One neighbor comes up with the idea that they need to address the physical medium with some electrical or mechanical interface (layer 1 of the OSI). All they need is a mechanical interface. The neighbor suggests each neighbor attach a tin can on his end of the link to build this interface. Using everyday household tin cans on both ends of the string, they have now addressed the bottom layer of the OSI model (see Figure 7-9.)

Figure 7-9 The physical layer. Here are the string and the two cans connected to it.

To make this all work properly, both neighbors must build the connection in the same way. Bud has attached the string through the side of the can, while Marcus has attached the string to the bottom of the can. Although this might work, when you pull the string tight, the can at one of the ends is in an awkward position.

The agreement is this: they both will take an empty can, punch a hole through the bottom, and then attach the string from the outside of the can, through the hole in the bottom, and knot it off inside the can. Then they will pull the string tight to get a good connection. Now the bottom layer of the OSI is handled.

The strings are now attached the same way, so can the parties communicate now? Well, maybe! They decide to test it. So, one of them picks up the tin can on his end and starts to talk to the other. One of the users might be preoccupied with the television set and will not hear that the communications system is being used. The whole conversation is wasted thus far. So, the parties need a means of using the link. They build a protocol that will solve this problem. First, the two parties agree they should have an alerting mechanism to let the other party know a conversation is requested. They decide that when one party wants to talk to the other, the originating party will grab the can on his end and yank on it three times. This will cause the can on the other end to rattle around. When the called party sees the can bouncing around, he will know the party on the other end wants to talk. To use the data link (layer 2), both users establish a protocol called the *yank and rattle*. One end yanks the string, causing the can on the other end to rattle. Now they have overcome the obstacle.

We can skip the details of layer 3 for now because they do not apply here. Look at Figure 7-10 and it should become fairly clear why. The strings are attached to both parties directly. The connection is a point-to-point private line. No switching or routing decisions need to be made because the connection always goes to the same location. Therefore, the network layer doesn't apply per se, so it will be transparent. Now the neighbors have the necessary connection and the alerting mechanism, so they should be able to communicate without much ado, correct? Maybe not, but see what happens.

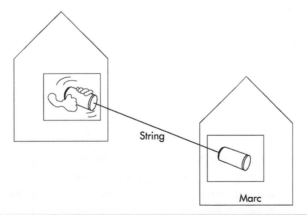

Figure 7-10 To use the data link and understand when one party wants to communicate, the yank and rattle protocol is used. If your can rattles, someone who wants to speak with you is on the other end.

Bud now decides he wants to talk to Marcus. Bud picks up the can and yanks it three times. This causes Marcus's can to bounce around on the other end, which alerts Marcus that Bud wants to talk to him. Kind of like a ringing phone, isn't it? Marcus jumps up and grabs the can, picks it up, places it to his mouth, and says, "Hello." At the same time, Bud is yelling into the can on the other end of this connection for Marcus to pick up: "Hello, Marcus, are you there?"

Are these two parties communicating? No, they are not. Both have the cans to their mouths and no one is listening. If both parties are talking and no one is listening, then no information is transferred. So, a new set of protocols is required. Let's introduce the transport layer in the OSI model now.

Because this whole idea is Bud's, the neighbors agree that whenever someone wants to initiate a communication, he will begin by speaking into the can. The person receiving the communication alert will begin by listening through the can. Now, the problems already encountered are handled. So, we should be able to communicate without any further complications, right? Here is the transmission process as it has been defined.

Bud: (Yanks the string.)

Marcus: (Picks up the can on his end and places it to his ear because that's the rule.)

Bud: "Hi, Marcus! Can I borrow your lawn mower today?"

Marcus: (Takes the can from his ear, places it to his mouth, and begins responding.) "No way; you told me last week that you were going to finally buy your own."

Bud: (At the same time Marcus is responding.) "I know I told you last week that I was going to buy my own, but I haven't had a chance to get to the store yet."

Now both parties are talking at the same time. After a given amount of time, they will probably both be listening at the same time. The communications flow is not working properly. So, they have to add a new set of protocols to allow the orderly transfer of the information. The problem stems from the half-duplex nature of the link. Only one transmitter/receiver is on each end. Two possible solutions exist. These are as follows.

First, a second string could be run between both parties. On this new string, Marcus and Bud will attach two new cans, just as they did for the first connection. Each can will be labeled T or R. The T can on Marcus's end will be connected to the R can at Bud's end, and vice versa. Now, when an alert comes in, each party will pick up the two cans at his end. The T can will be placed in front of each party's mouth, and the R can will be placed in front of each party's ear (see Figure 7-11). Now they have two separate transmission paths: one for transmitting and one for receiving. This is probably the best option, but Bud and Marcus are reluctant to do this because it adds the complexity of maintaining two strings between their houses and requires twice as many cans on each end. This will take up too much space in their homes.

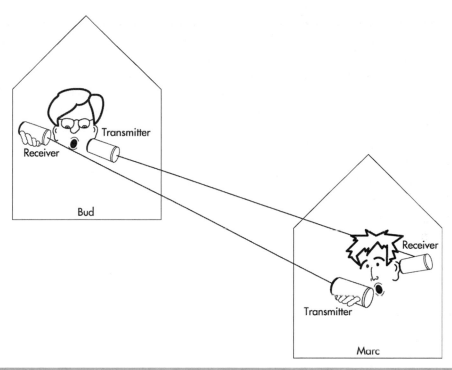

Figure 7-11 To establish rules regarding transmission, one can must be labeled for transmit and one for receive. This is necessary to prevent both parties from listening to the same pair of cans (in which case no information would be shared).

The other alternative is a set of rules (protocols) that will define the session layer (the control of the data transfer between the two ends, that is, call setup, maintaining a connection, reestablishing a lost connection, and call teardown). The session layer will work like this. Because this is Bud's idea, whenever Bud or Marcus yanks on the string, Marcus always listens first and Bud always talks first. The problem occurs when the transmitting end is done sending and wants to await the reply: the two parties need to know how to time this out properly. So, Bud will talk first (have you noticed that Bud talks a lot?). When Bud finishes his statement, he will use an "over" protocol. When Marcus hears the word "over," he will take the can from his ear and place it to his mouth. At the same time, Bud will take the can from his mouth and place it to his ear. Then Marcus finally gets a chance to talk. When Marcus finishes, he will say "over," and the process will revert back to the beginning, and so on.

At last, the two parties have the ability to communicate with each other. Essentially, they can send their information back and forth, as they had planned. Now that this whole scenario is established, you have probably noticed that a couple of layers were missed in the OSI model. These would be handled transparently by Marcus and Bud because they are working with the same communications protocols. However, let's go back and look at these layers to see how they will play out under our example.

The three layers we have yet to address are the network, presentation, and application layers. So, let's complicate the issue by introducing the following add-on needs. Just as Marcus and Bud get the communications working by the rules established, a new neighbor, Jen, moves in next door to Marcus. This is going to happen all around the neighborhood, and we should be prepared. Jen is neighborly and decides she might have a need to speak to Marcus and Bud occasionally. The rules already in place can be used to provide the connectivity among all three parties—Figure 7-12 shows this.

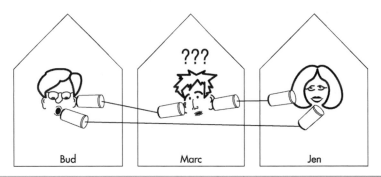

Figure 7-12 Connectivity.

To set up communications between Jen and Marcus, a string can be run between the two houses with cans attached to the string. The rule will be as follows:

Because Marcus was here first, Marcus will always speak first and Jen will listen, regardless of who rattles the can. The "over" protocol can also be used to provide the session layer, and so on. Now, Helen also needs to talk to Bud, but, as the figure shows, for this to happen, they need to run the string from Jen to Bud. This is not a problem for Jen or Bud. As a matter of fact, we can even color-code the cans (red for Marcus, blue for Bud). But this scenario is a problem for Marcus. For Bud and Jen to connect the string to each location, the string must go in one side of Marcus's house, pass through, and exit the other side to connect to Bud. So, Marcus will have to leave his windows open on both sides of his house at all times for this to work. Marcus doesn't like this idea. He offers to become a network-layer relay point. The process, as shown in Figure 7-13, will work this way.

When Bud wants to speak to Jen, he will pick up the one can associated with this communications system. He will then yank the can, causing Marcus to pick up and immediately listen. Bud will then say, "Marcus, this is a call for Jen." On hearing this, Marcus, who has two cans and strings, will grab the other can that is connected to the string to Jen's. Marcus will yank the can, causing Jen to pick up the can and listen. Marcus speaks first on this connection, so this is fine. He has a can to his ear from Bud and the other can to his mouth leading out to Jen.

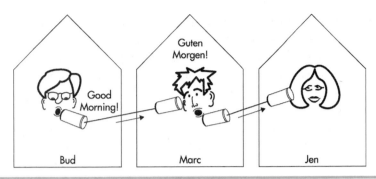

Figure 7-13 In this figure, Bud is trying to speak to Jen.

Marcus also found out that if he puts the cans to and from Bud directly against the send and receive cans from Jen, Bud's voice will travel through to Jen. This could emulate a layer-three routing situation.

A problem exists with this whole scenario that isn't as obvious. Jen only speaks German. Bud only speaks English. Now the problem: If Bud speaks English into the can connected to Marcus, how do we make the format or language conversion into something that is usable and understandable to Jen? Luckily, when Marcus was in school, he took German 101. He didn't excel, but he has a working knowledge of the language. Now, when Marcus hears Bud say, "Good morning, Jen," in English, Marcus will relay the information out through the other can in German as "Guten Tag!" When Bud finishes and says "over," the process switches. Bud takes the can from his mouth and moves it to his ear. Marcus takes the can connected to Bud and moves it from his ear to his mouth. At the same time, he takes the can connected to Jen and moves that one from his mouth to his ear.

Jen, in turn, moves the can from her ear to her mouth and begins to speak or respond. When Helen responds with "Morgen, wie geht's?" Marcus hears it and converts it to Bud as "Morning. How are you?" And so it goes. The presentation layer has just been addressed to accommodate the format or protocol (language) conversion, so transparent communications can take place. The only layer that has not been addressed in this case is the applications layer. What is the application in this regard? Chitchat: "I just called to say hello!"

By now, you should have an understanding from this simplistic comparison of how the process works through the OSI model. Furthermore, the importance of this all taking place transparently should be obvious. If the rules had to be negotiated between the parties every time communication would take place, this would be far too cumbersome. What's needed is a protocol, so the next time a connection to another neighbor is needed, the same rules can be applied.

We already have a simplistic network here, so let's draw it to a conclusion by introducing a couple of other players. Mary moves in behind Bud. There will be a need for Mary to communicate with Bud, Marcus, and Jen. Rather than trying to run strings all around the neighborhood, we'll just use our relays and rules already in place. So, Mary connects a string to Bud. Communication to Bud is simple. To reach Marcus, the call will go through Bud to Marcus. To reach Jen, the call will go through Bud and Marcus, ultimately, to get to Jen. One added complication is Mary only speaks French. Therefore, when Mary says "Bonjour" to Bud, he repeats the information to Marcus as "Good morning." Marcus then finally sends it to Jen as "Guten Morgen."

Now, Roy moves in behind Marcus. The neighbors run a connection between Marcus and Roy—no problem. Roy only speaks pig latin, but that's okay because Marcus can deal with it. Now, when Mary wants to speak to Roy, she calls through Bud in French, which Bud converts to English, and sends on to Marcus. Marcus receives the message in English and converts it to pig latin for Roy. The connection is sent through and routed/switched depending on the intended target location. Jen, as you recognize, is left out of this conversation, but she has no need to be connected. The result is shown in Figure 7-14.

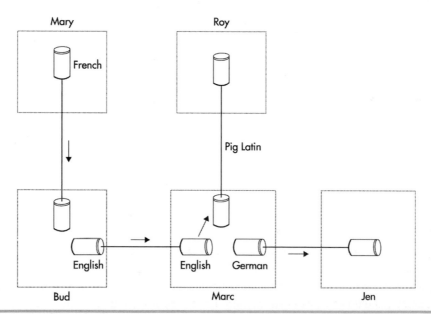

Figure 7-14 The flow of information is from Mary to Bud (in French). Bud translates the information to English (which Marcus understands) and sends it over his outbound connection. Marcus makes the conversion of the conversation to Roy in the language he understands (pig latin) and routes it over the appropriate connection.

The connection is routed and switched transparently between and among the neighbors. Marcus has also become similar to a central switching system and service provider. Now, for voice or data, the telecommunications network is built to handle communication from any user to any other, regardless of the language (format and protocol) or origin of creation (manufacturer).

This is what the OSI model was designed to do for us. Is it here? Partially. Work continues on the standards, especially in how this can all be achieved. Many manufacturers are implementing OSI compatibility in different ways, which still results in vendor–proprietary standards issues. That description is probably more than most of us need to know about this. However, we should at least be aware of what the reference was meant to do for the industry as a whole. If we substitute our players in the previous example, then we can have an organization using a computer platform manufactured by Company Bud. This is connected to or through a computer manufactured by Company Marcus, ultimately sharing and swapping information with a computer manufactured by Company Jen, and so on. The communications network might well be used as a point-to-point, point-to-multipoint, or switched dial-up service. Protocols and services such as ISDN, X.25, switched 64 Kbps, and leased-line T1 have been applied, so the connectivity arrangements mimic those of the tin cans and string.

As long as the same rules apply for electrically and mechanically attaching to the string (wires, light beams, and radio waves), this should all work.

Other Network Architectures

Using the OSI as the reference is fine. It will be the basis of all future development. Other architectures were in existence or sprung up during the wait for the ubiquitous implementation of OSI. We might never complete adoption of the OSI model, but most technologies that don't adhere to the model are in decline or in conversion, such as:

- SNA, which is now over 30 years old and has undergone few modifications from the original implementation. Many large organizations still use SNA in their legacy mainframe environment, but the movement for the future will be to migrate to a more vendor-neutral solution.

- DECNet is 28 years old, but has gone through several revisions in an attempt to create openness. DEC was acquired by Compaq Computer, and then Compaq was acquired by HP. Thus, DEC and its DECNet ceased to operate. Legacy systems are still in place using DECNet, but new installations are no longer available.

- TCP/IP, a set of protocols that works on a four-layer architecture, was developed back in the late 1960s and deployed more in the early 1970s for the government. Now, TCP/IP is the protocol for the Internet and the primary set of protocols that LAN, metropolitan area network (MAN), and wide area network (WAN) users are implementing for openness and robustness in their networking needs. It has been updated to support OSI-compliant communication. Version 4, which was introduced in 1983 to 1984, is the most commonly used, but the current version is version 6 (IPv6). Full deployment of IPv6 will likely start occurring after 2008.

SNA

Systems Network Architecture was previously discussed in this chapter, so the continued discussion will concentrate on the subtleties of the SNA to OSI comparison. In 1974, IBM introduced its SNA architecture. *SNA* defines a structure and all the protocols required to implement a network in which a wide variety of computers, software, and terminal devices can interact and provide a high degree of network efficiency.

SNA Components

Each device in an SNA network—from the individual dumb terminal to the host computer—functions with a certain level of control, depending on its position in the hierarchy. It will then operate under the control of the device at the next level up. Terminals, for example, function under the control of the cluster controller. The controller functions under control of the front-end processor, and the front-end functions under control of the host. This is the true hierarchical concept IBM introduced.

The network addressable unit (NAU) is any segment or code that emphasizes the device to a network, program, or device. Basically, three different types of NAUs exist, as follows:

- The systems services control part (SSCP)

- The physical unit (PU)

- The logical unit (LU)

The SSCP   The **systems services control part (SSCP)** functionally resides in the communications access method of a mainframe computer or the control program in a mid-range computer. Figure 7-15 shows a representation of this control part. This function controls the addressing and routing tables, the name service to address translation services, the routing tables for the network, and all instruction sets that deal with these entities. The SSCP establishes the communications connection between nodes in the network, provides the informational flow control and queuing services for network efficiency, and selects the route for the nodes to communicate with each other.

The Physical Unit   IBM defines the **physical unit (PU)** as a single device on the network. Figure 7-16 is a representation of the PU. In a host computer and a front-end communications processor, this is implemented in software. In a terminal device (less intelligence applied in these), the PU is implemented in firmware.

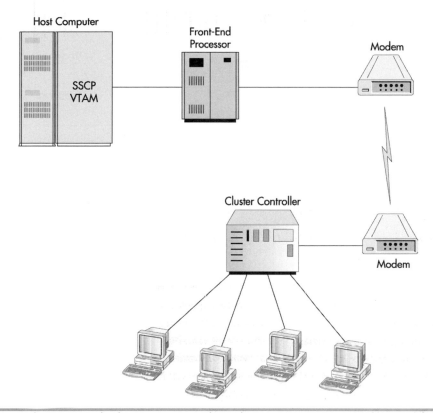

Figure 7-15 The SSCP is the host computer where the main processing and control functions are located. It establishes the link between devices on the network and allows the devices to communicate with each other.

IBM defines the PUs as follows:

- Type 1 is a dumb terminal or a printer.

- Type 2 is a cluster controller (3274) for the terminals or a batch terminal.

- Type 3 is under study.

- Type 4 is a communications controller, such as the front-end processor (37X5).

- Type 5 is a host computer with an SSCP.

In SNA, the SSCP controls the physical unit. Each PU is treated as a physical entry point on the network between the network and one or more logical units.

The Logical Unit   The **logical unit (LU)** is the basic communications entity in SNA. The *LU* is a port where end users access the SNA network. Figure 7-17 shows this access method. Two

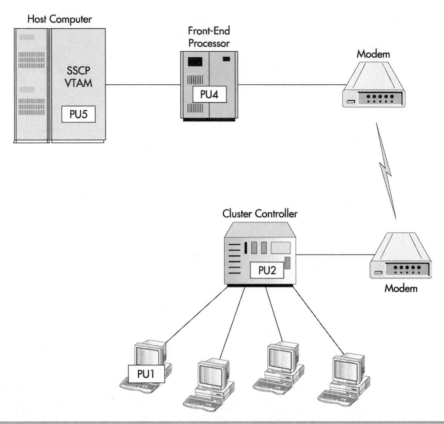

Figure 7-16 The PU is any device on the network. It might be a host computer, a front-end processor, a cluster controller, or a printer. The number associated with each device lets the network know what each device is.

LUs communicate through what is called an *LU-LU session,* a temporary connection where data can be exchanged on the basis of some mutually agreed on protocols. The layers of SNA, shown a little differently in Figure 7-18 than in previous versions of the architecture (not to change but to clarify the architecture), build on each other from the bottom up. Every SNA node contains the bottom two layers shown in this figure. These two layers—the Data Link Control (DLC) and the path control (PC)—combine as what is called the *path control subnetwork.* This process saves time and improves efficiency in the network by not having to read the entire stack of protocols only to forward information onward.

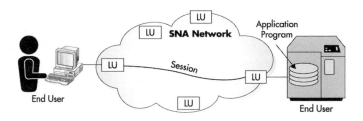

Figure 7-17 The LU is a port where end users access the SNA network.

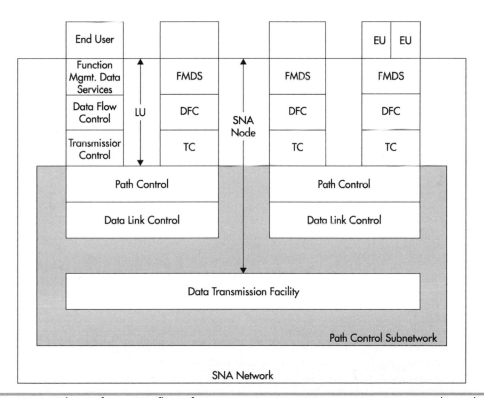

Figure 7-18 When information flows from point *A* to point *B*, sometimes it passes through intermediate nodes (LU), where only the final address is read and the information is passed on.

This is the basic method for the movement of information from a source to a destination node. Sometimes, this can involve passing through intermediate nodes. The LU, which resides in the SNA nodes, consists of the upper three layers in Figure 7-18 and uses the data-transport capability of the path control subnetwork. The different types of LU are:

- *LU0* are sessions for special applications where IBM or the end user defines the parameters.

- *LU1* is a session between a host application and a remote batch terminal.

- *LU2* is a session between the host application and a 3270 display terminal.

- *LU3* is a session between a host application and a printer in the 3270 display family.

- *LU4* is a session between a host application and a word processor or between two terminals.

- *LU5* is under study.

- *LU6* is an intersystem communication—a session between two or more different applications, usually in two or more different systems. The more common type of this LU is Advanced Program-to-Program Communications (APPC), a session between an application program in a host and an application program residing in an intelligent workstation or terminal. This is also called the LU6.2.

The first SNA networks were simple tree networks, using the hierarchy shown. All terminals and controllers were attached to a single host computer. LUs in the terminal and controller communicated only with LUs in the host, but never with each other. All these arrangements were purely hierarchical. Later versions of SNA allowed multiple hosts to reside on an SNA network and communicate as peers on the network. However, LUs in the terminals and controllers still only communicated with host LUs, never with each other. The difference was they could communicate with LUs in multiple hosts, instead of a single host.

Later advances in very-large-scale integration (VLSI) changed the computer networking strategies. Dumb terminals became intelligent workstations. Personal computers and mid-range computers were introduced that changed the complexion of the network. Because these devices contained their own processing and storage capability, a natural evolution was to allow for distributed processing. SNA evolved with the market and adopted more of a peer-to-peer processing capability and the advanced peer-to-peer networking strategy.

Digital Network Architecture (DNA)

Digital Network Architecture (DNA), by Digital Equipment Corporation (acquired by Compaq Computer Corporation, later acquired by Hewlett-Packard), is the model and architecture for the functions of DECNet. *DECNet* is a system of communications software and hardware that enables DEC's operating systems and components to function in a network with other DEC systems. It is open enough to communicate with systems manufactured by others. DECNet is a group of computers with equivalent DEC software and communications hardware that connect with physical channels or lines. Each computer implemented in a network with DECNet software is called a *system*.

DNA defines standard protocols, interfaces, and functions that allow DECNet systems to share data and access various resources, programs, and functions. DNA currently has two separate stacks of protocols: one supports proprietary protocols and interfaces on a DEC environment, while the other supports the protocols defined in an open systems environment (OSI model). Using a layered approach, DNA is functionally grouped into services and functions based on the layers associated with DECNet. Functionally, DNA is broken down into the following:

- User functions

- Network functions

- Communications functions

Using a slightly different view of DECNet compared to the OSI model that was shown earlier, DNA is shown in Figure 7-19. Two separate stacks are shown here: The first is DEC's version. Next to that version is the function served by this layer. The labeling on DNA is different from that on the OSI, indicating that DECNet is not 100 percent compatible with the OSI reference.

The DNA model was demonstrated when DEC introduced its DECNet Phase V. It met with only moderate interest and limited implementation in the industry. DEC has introduced a family of products and services over the years to allow access to and from DEC computing platforms and other manufacturers' platforms.

❓ Line Check 7-3

1. What are the differences among the OSI reference model, SNA, and DNA, considering they each contain the same seven layers?

2. If SNA was the most popular architecture, why didn't the DNA people use the same model and software in making DNA?

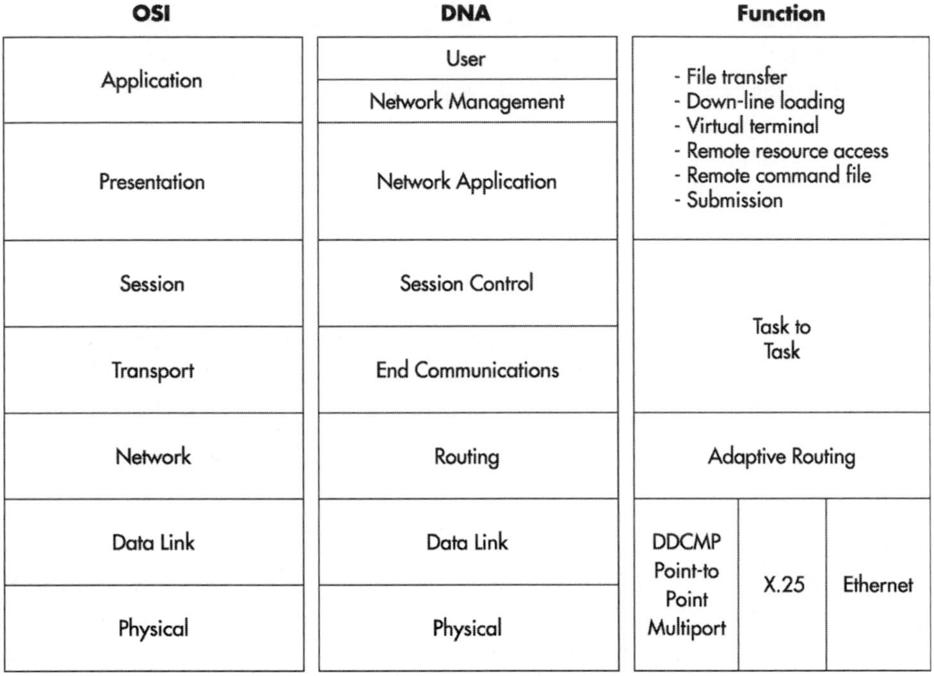

OSI	DNA	Function			
Application	User	- File transfer			
	Network Management	- Down-line loading			
Presentation	Network Application	- Virtual terminal - Remote resource access - Remote command file - Submission			
Session	Session Control	Task to Task			
Transport	End Communications				
Network	Routing	Adaptive Routing			
Data Link	Data Link	DDCMP Point-to Point Multiport	X.25	Ethernet	
Physical	Physical				

Figure 7-19 The DNA model compared to the OSI model: the names are different, but the ultimate function is the same. Functions and applications of the layers are shown in the far right.

Internet Protocols (TCP/IP)

While the industry and standards bodies wrestled with openness in the communications and computing arenas, another evolving set of protocols emerged. Transmission Control Protocol with Internet Protocol (TCP/IP) is also a layered architecture composed essentially of four layers. The TCP layer is more commonly called the Transport layer, and the IP layer is more commonly called the Internet or Network layer. A result of a government contract to look at the internetworking of computers in the event of a national disaster, the protocols emerged from the original Advanced Research Projects Agency Network (ARPANET). Developed by Bolt, Beraneck, and Newman of Cambridge, this simple, but robust, set of protocols was geared toward linking systems in an open architecture. The TCP/IP continued its evolution from the original ARPANET to what we know as the Internet. The TCP/IP architecture is shown in Figure 7-20. This is a four-layer stack that deals with the equivalent seven-layer architecture of OSI, SNA, and DNA.

Figure 7-20 The TCP/IP protocol stack is a four-layer protocol that accomplishes the same steps as the OSI model. The switching and routing functions are performed by the TCP/IP protocols themselves.

The TCP/IP is the most widely accepted set of protocols in the industry. Included in all forms of the UNIX operating systems, and now the protocol of choice in many LAN-to-WAN environments, the TCP/IP is the "middleware" for interconnectivity. The two most prevalent features of this protocol stack are its capability to work with nearly any environment because it can use application program interfaces to emulate most services on other architectures and its capability to "packetize" the data and send it out.

IP

Internet Protocol (IP) performs logical addressing and routing of packets (**datagrams**) across networks. Packets using IP can traverse many intermediate networks in a journey from a source network to a destination network.

7

CAUTION

Confusion can result from terms used in networking. The term "packet switching" refers to any type of packetized data (data sent in discrete units, rather than a continuous stream of data). Within the OSI model, more specific terms are used, with segments referring to units at layer 4, packets describing units at layer 3, and frames describing units at layer 2. The term datagram is interchangeable with the term packet in layer 3 of the OSI model.

The routing and switching of this data is handled at the IP (network) layer. To be somewhat simple in our analogy, IP is also a dumb protocol. When a packet is prepared for transmission across the medium, IP does not route the information across a specific channel. Rather, it just puts the header on the packet and lets the network deal with it. Therefore, the outward-bound packets can take various routes to get from point *A* to point *B*. This means the packets are not sequentially numbered. IP makes its best attempt to deliver the datagrams to the destination network interface, but it makes no assurances that

- The data will arrive.

- The data will be error-free.

- The nodes along the way will concern themselves with the accuracy of the data and sequencing, or come back and alert the originator that something is wrong in the delivery mechanism.

This might sound strange in a networking environment, but it allows robustness to be achieved. The nodes along the network merely read the header information and route the packet to the next logical downstream neighbor. If anything gets corrupted on the network, the node will not know where to send the packet, so it will throw it away. The network may not send a message back to the originator to let it know the packet did not get delivered. Another possibility is the nodes along the network can send the packet out on the basis of the best route (based on some costing algorithm or the number of points to pass through). Yet, in the transfer of the packets, if one of these routes is busy or broken, the packets will be rerouted around the problem to another node.

A packet could possibly be sent along the network in a loop (see Figure 7-21), causing it to re-circulate on the network like a spinning top. If this were a frequent occurrence, the network could get quite bogged down with recirculating packets. Therefore, IP has a field in its header that allows a certain number of "hops." The field contains a **Time to Live (TTL)** on the network. Rather than let an undeliverable packet route around and around the network, the TTL value is decremented every time the packet passes through a network node. The counter starts at 255 hops or less. The default value is typically 128, but can be changed by a network administrator. Once it counts down to 0, the node will discard the packet.

IP does not guarantee packet delivery, so some packets in a conversation may be delivered, while others might be lost. IP does not have a mechanism to know this has happened, and it has no numbering sequence to put everything back in order. Why would anyone favor such a dumb protocol? Because this robustness to deliver the datagrams across the network and throw away bad or undeliverable datagrams helps improve the efficiency of network utilization. It's not that error detection doesn't occur; it happens at other layers in the OSI model. To see where, look no further than TCP.

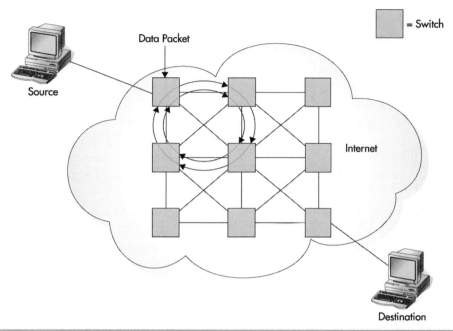

Figure 7-21 A packet caught in a loop between multiple routers can cause congestion on the network and slow other datagrams.

TCP

No network manager or administrator would accept not knowing whether data gets delivered across the network. Therefore, working together with IP is the **Transmission Control Protocol (TCP)**. *TCP* provides the smarts to overcome the limitations of IP. Here, the controls will be put in place to ensure the reliable data stream is sent and delivered. At the sending end, TCP breaks data streams into datagrams for packaging into IP and puts a byte-count header and datagram-sequence number on the information that will be delivered to the IP protocol layer. This is encapsulated as part of the data in the IP datagram.

The receiving end—when it gets the datagrams—is responsible for putting the data back into its proper sequence and ensuring its accuracy. If things are not correct, the byte count acknowledgment (ACK) or **non-acknowledgment (NAK)** message is sent back to the sending end. The sending end receiving a NAK will resend the bytes necessary to fill in the blanks. Furthermore, TCP holds all datagrams of a given communication in a queue, so if datagrams are received out of sequence, they can be reassembled into their original order before being

7

transmitted up to higher OSI layers. Thus, it buffers the data at the receiving end. This makes data reception and accuracy the responsibility of the sender and receiver, not the network's responsibility.

This process prevents the network from getting bogged down. If errors or loops are occurring in the network, and the network is responsible for the guarantees of delivery and sequencing (as seen in the X.25 section), then the network will be overloaded with administrative functions. The network is, after all, a transport system, not a computer-processing function.

Once the datagrams have been formed by TCP and given source and destination addresses by IP, the network is ready to receive them at layers 2 and 1 to effect the transport across the network.

Before TCP can start sending segments, it must first establish a connection with the remote end via a three-step handshake. IP host *A* starts the TCP session by sending a synchronize (SYN) message to a specific port address on host *B*. Host *B* responds with an **acknowledgment**, and host *A* acknowledges the acknowledgment; hence, three steps. Often, you will hear this explained as SYN, ACK, and ACK, which means:

- Host *A*: Synchronize (SYN)
- Host *B*: Acknowledge the synchronize (SYN ACK)
- Host *A*: Acknowledge the acknowledge (ACK)

The SYN and SYN ACK messages contain a window size, which is the amount of bytes that each host may send to the other before it must stop and wait for an acknowledgment from the receiving host.

In addition to the window size, there is also a congestion window, which controls TCP's behavior during congestion. This behavior begins immediately following the three-step handshake. The sending host (host *A,* in this case) sends only one packet and awaits an acknowledgment. The sending host then sends two segments, and waits for an acknowledgment. If this is successful, the sending host sends four segments, and waits for an acknowledgment. The sending host then sends 8, 16, 32, 64, and so forth. The limiting factor that kicks in long before the sending host sends multiple back-to-back packets is the window size, which must be less than 64 KB (kilobytes).

Assume that host *B* is connected to Ethernet, so the Maximum Transmission Unit (MTU) size is 1,500 because 64 KB divided by 1,500 approximately equals 43. This means TCP normally cannot have more than 43 segments in the pipeline before receiving an acknowledgment. The reader should be aware that this example is based on a 1,500-byte MTU. The use of larger or smaller MTUs will affect the amount of unacknowledged segments that may be in the pipe before an acknowledgment is required.

Chapter 7 Review

Chapter Summary

Discuss How the Computing Model Went from a Mainframe Environment to a Distributed Environment

- In the early days of computing, a large computer was centrally located in a datacenter. This was known as a mainframe environment.

- The data-processing evolution led to one of distributed computing. Distributed computing means we are sharing computer resources between devices.

- The client-server architecture is a form of distributed computing,

Explain Problems That Are Encountered When Using Multiple Vendors and Converters

- IBM developed the architecture as a hierarchy, in which devices were placed on different levels of importance.

- If a multivendor approach in meeting computing needs is employed, there will be multiple separate architectures to work with.

- Many of the specialty applications the users wanted required the data stored in the mainframe. This left a new set of problems:

  1. The timeliness of the data was suspect.

  2. The accuracy of the information was questionable.

  3. The cost of the information was now more expensive because the input was done at least twice.

  4. The frequency of the input was becoming exponential.

Define Types of Standards and Tell Which Organizations Are Responsible for Making Them

- A standard is simply a definition or description of a technology and how it will be used.

- Standards are developed by collaboration among various groups, forums, committees, and other regulating agencies.

- In the United States, many standards bodies exist, but eight major players are in the communications world.

Describe the OSI Model and the Seven-Layer Structure

- ISO created a networking standard called the Open Systems Interconnection (OSI) reference model.

- Model (OSI) in 1974.

- The OSI model has seven layers that individually define how transport occurs across each segment of the network.

    The seven layers are:

The Application layer	(layer 7)
The Presentation layer	(layer 6)
The Session layer	(layer 5)
The Transport layer	(layer 4)
The Network layer	(layer 3)
The Data Link layer	(layer 2)
The Physical layer	(layer 1)

Compare the Differences between the OSI and Other Models, such as TCP/IP, IBM's SNA, and DEC's DNA

- SNA defines a structure and all the protocols required to implement a network.

- Each device in an SNA network, from the individual dumb terminal to the host computer, functions with a certain level of control, depending on its position in the hierarchy.

- The network addressable unit (NAU) is any segment or code that emphasizes the device to a network, program, or device. Basically, three different types of NAUs exist, as follows:

1. The systems services control part (SSCP)

   This function controls the addressing and routing tables, the name service to address translation services, the routing tables for the network, and all instruction sets that deal with these entities.

2. The physical unit (PU)

   IBM defines the physical unit (PU) as a single device on the network.

3. The logical unit (LU)

   The logical unit (LU) is the basic communications entity in SNA. The LU is a port where end users access the SNA network.

- The TCP/IP architecture is a four-layer stack that deals with the equivalent seven-layer architecture of OSI, SNA, and DNA.

- IP is responsible for the **packetization** of the data. Then a header is placed on the datagram for delivery to the data link. The routing and switching of this data is handled at the IP (network) layer.

- IP makes its best attempt to deliver packets to the destination network interface; however, it makes no guarantees.

- TCP, on the other hand, is an Intelligent Protocol that provides the smarts to overcome the limitations of IP. Controls are in place to ensure the reliable data stream is sent and delivered.

Key Terms for Chapter 7

Acknowledgment (ACK) *(318)*
American National Standards Institute (ANSI) *(290)*
Black Box *(286)*
Datagrams *(315)*
De facto *(287)*
De jure *(287)*
Digital Network Architecture (DNA) *(283)*
Distributed computing *(281)*
Electronic Industries Association (EIA) *(292)*
Electronic Numerical Integrator and Computer (ENIAC) *(280)*
Institute of Electrical and Electronics Engineers (IEEE) *(292)*
Internet Engineering Task Force (IETF) *(292)*
International Organization for Standardization (ISO) *(290)*
International Telecommunications Standards Sector (ITU-T) *(290)*
Internet Protocol (IP) *(315)*
Logical Unit (LU) *(310)*
Mainframe environment *(280)*
Non-Acknowledgment (NAK) *(317)*
Open Systems Interconnection Model (OSI) *(290)*
Packetization *(321)*
Physical Unit (PU) *(308)*
SSCP *(308)*
Standard *(287)*
Systems Network Architecture (SNA) *(282)*
TCP *(317)*
Telcordia *(292)*
TTL *(316)*

7

REVIEW

Key Term Quiz

1. A _____ is simply a definition or description of a technology and how it will be used.

2. A _____ standard means "in law," although standards do not generally have the force of law.

3. The term _____ refers to any third-party device on the network that is responsible for protocol conversions.

4. In the early days of computing, a large computer was centrally located in an office. All input and output was generated within this computer room, with all operators kept to one location. This type of computing model is called a _____.

5. The _____ standards body is the presiding body that ratified the OSI model.

6. The term that means we are sharing a computer's resources between devices is _____.

7. IBM had already created a proprietary layered model for devices to share information. This model is called _____.

8. _____ makes its best attempt to deliver the datagrams to the destination network interface; however, it makes no assurances that the data will arrive, the data will be error free, or the nodes along the way will concern themselves with the accuracy of the data and sequencing, or come back and alert the originator that something is wrong in the delivery mechanism.

9. The _____ ensures data will be delivered in a reliable fashion.

10. When a large file is sent down the protocol stack, the IP function is responsible for the segmentation of this data. This process creates a segment or packet of data called a _____.

Multiple-Choice Quiz

1. What does OSI mean?

   a. Open Systems Interface

   b. Only System Interface

c. Open Systems Interference

d. Open Systems Interconnect

2. What organization is responsible for creating the OSI?

a. ITU

b. ISO

c. IBM

d. IEEE

3. What year was the model ratified?

a. 1974

b. 1978

c. 1983

d. 1988

4. When the OSI model was being developed, it was intended to solve some of the problems experienced between:

a. IBM and DEC

b. Sun and HP

c. IBM and Data General

d. DEC and Data General

5. The OSI model has how many layers?

a. Four

b. Six

c. Seven

d. Eleven

6. IBM's SNA has how many layers?

a. Four

b. Five

c. Six

d. Seven

7. When DEC created its architecture, what was it called?

   a. DECnet

   b. DNI

   c. DNA

   d. Digital Networking Standards

8. What layer did we eliminate when a point-to-point leased line was used?

   a. Application

   b. Transport

   c. Network

   d. Data Link

9. What OSI layer is responsible for the electrical and mechanical interface?

   a. 1

   b. 2

   c. 3

   d. 4

10. What OSI layer performs the transparent transmission of information between the two ends?

   a. 4

   b. 5

   c. 6

   d. 7

11. What OSI layer is responsible for translation and protocol conversion?

   a. Application

   b. Presentation

   c. Network

   d. Transport

12. What was the public response to the OSI model in the U.S. when it was introduced?

    a. It was widely accepted.

    b. Few people implemented it without some modifications.

    c. The U.S. government made everyone abide by it.

    d. North Americans began to replace their IBM systems.

13. What is the protocol suite that the U.S. government and the rest of the world now use to form the Internet?

    a. DNA

    b. TCP/IP

    c. SNA

    d. GOSIP

14. How many layers does the TCP/IP protocol model have?

    a. Four

    b. Five

    c. Six

    d. Seven

Essay Quiz

1. What factors in the workplace led to the migration from mainframe environments toward a distributed computing model?

2. What is the difference between a de facto standard and a de jure standard?

3. What is the purpose of the seven-layer architecture of the OSI reference model?

4. Compare and contrast the function of the TCP/IP protocols.

Lab Projects

1. In the following section, we have stacks with empty labels. Fill in the labels in the appropriate slots in these models.

OSI Model

TCP Model

2. Log on to the LAN and conduct the following exercises:

   a. Check your IP address by clicking on "**Start**," | "**Run**" Type in "**Command**." When the command prompt appears, type in "**ipconfig/all**." This will deliver the IP address assigned to your machine and the subnet mask used, along with the default gateway, and DHCP and DNS servers' addresses.

   b. Now type in **ipconfig/release** and wait. You should now get a released IP, and the address will be all 0's.

   c. Finally, type **ipconfig/renew** and wait. This time you will get the renewed address (this is probably going to be the IP address you had earlier) with all the other pieces previously listed.

Chapter 8

Data Communications

LEARNING OBJECTIVES:

Once you complete this chapter, you will be able to:

Define data communications.

Describe where data is created.

Describe the steps in communications of data devices.

Discuss the ways data are formatted.

Define the components of a data transmission system.

Assess the differences between asynchronous and synchronous data.

Describe the different modes of switched data transmission.

Understand the use of multiplexing techniques.

Describe the circuit usage that serves data best.

Everyone who has ever had to deal with data communications has shuddered at least once. Telecommunications engineers, data-processing personnel, and vendors alike all throw data communication terms and acronyms around as though they were going out of style. The interesting point is that many of them don't understand what they are saying. Many people think, "If I learn the buzzwords, everyone will think I know what I'm talking about." Nothing could be further from the truth; these folks make complete fools of themselves in front of knowledgeable professionals. However, no mystique is associated with the use of data communications. Although some complexities do exist in this technology, the basics are fairly straightforward. To understand data communications, you must have an understanding of the telephone channel and its uses. We hope the preceding seven chapters have given you some idea of the network, the signaling formats, the differences between digital and analog transmission, and the protocols/standards used. If you can surmount the initial hurdle of setting up a data transmission, the rest can be fairly well assimilated.

In 1997, for the first time in the history of the telecommunications industry, an equal amount of data was carried across the networks as voice traffic. This shows the heavy emphasis on the growth of data communications. Currently, the growth of voice on the networks is averaging between 3 and 4 percent per year, at best. However, data is growing at a rate of 30 percent per year. It will take 12 years to double the amount of voice carried on the network today at the current growth rate, whereas the amount of data is doubling approximately every 90 days.

Understanding that the data world grew out of the voice world is important. This is why the coverage of the voice network spanned so much of this book so far. Voice traditionally paid for the data transmissions on the network, and today, 90 percent of all the revenues generated across the wide area networks (WANs) are the result of voice usage. But that continues to change quickly as more emphasis is placed on data communications. Make no mistake about this: the data communications architecture started with the use of the analog dial-up network.

? Line Check 8-1

At what rate are data and voice growing per year? Why is that significant?

To communicate from a terminal, a computer, or another piece of equipment, you merely put the pieces together in the proper order. The sequence in simple terms is as follows:

1. Select and deal with the transmission medium.

2. Use communicating devices that will present the proper signal to the line. This communicating device is called the Data Circuit-Terminating Equipment (DCE).

3. Add a device called the Data Terminal Equipment (DTE) that will send the origination signal to the DCE device.

4. Set up or abide by accepted rules (protocols).

5. Use a preestablished alphabet that the devices understand.

6. Ensure the integrity of information before, during, and after transmission.

7. Deliver the information to the receiving device.

This chapter presents some history and descriptions of our current data transmission systems and the elements involved in all data communications processes. Later chapters focus on specific technologies, such as packet, frame, and cell switching, using the concepts and terminology introduced here.

❓ Line Check 8-2

Match the steps taken to communicate via data services

____   Set up or abide by accepted rules (protocols).

____   Ensure the integrity of information before, during, and after transmission.

____   Add a device called the Data Terminal Equipment (DTE).

____   Select and deal with the transmission medium.

____   Deliver the information to the receiving device.

____   Use communicating devices that will present the proper signal to the line (the communicating device is called the DCE).

____   Use a preestablished alphabet that the devices understand.

8

❓

Data Concepts

Similar to learning computer programming, learning data communications technology is a nonlinear process. That is, whatever starting point you choose, you almost have to use terms that will be defined elsewhere. The usual solution to this problem is iterative teaching: teach a basic set of concepts, and then go back, use, and expand on those concepts, refining them along the way. (I prefer to think it works like this: I am going to tell you what I am going to tell you. I am going to tell you. Then, I am going to tell you what I told you!) Our basic set begins with a discussion of some important concepts that permeate the world of data communications. Those concepts include:

- Standards
- Architectures
- Protocols
- Error Detection
- Plexes
- Multiplexing
- Compression
- Modems

Standards

A **standard** is a definition or description of a technology. The purpose of developing standards is to help vendors build components that will function together or facilitate use by providing consistency with other products. Recall Chapter 7, where the Open Systems Interconnection (OSI) reference model was described.

Rather than go into great detail about the standards covered in the previous chapter, it may be more appropriate to think in terms of what the standards do for you in the industry.

Without a standard, the use of data communications would be sheer pandemonium! Each vendor would build equipment to whatever specification desired, most of which would be non-conforming to other manufacturers' equipment. An end user attempting to communicate would be at risk of trying to get data transferred that is:

a. Reliable

b. Consistent

c. Understandable

d. Usable

As a result, we look to our committees, described in Chapter 7, to assist in formulating sets of rules that all can adopt. These committees do not produce solutions. Instead, they produce guidelines on how things should work and interoperate. Then, it is up to the manufacturers to produce products that conform to these guidelines.

Architectures

As with constructing a building, an overall design is needed when planning a communications environment. For a building, that design is described by architectural drawings. *Communications architecture* is a coordinated set of design guidelines that, together, constitute a complete description of one approach to building a communications environment.

Several communications architectures have been developed. Some of the best known include IBM's SNA and DEC's DNA. Architectures were covered in Chapter 7, along with the OSI model. For those already familiar with the Open Systems Interconnection (OSI) reference model, most of this chapter (excluding codes, which reside at the presentation layer) addresses the physical and data-link layers. The newest architecture to run away with the industry and the fancy of all developers is the Internet architecture using TCP and IP protocols. Every day, new applications and protocols are being developed to run on the Internet architecture. This includes voice, data, streaming audio and video, and multimedia applications. The future will bring IP-enabled TV.

The circuit-switched data-communications architectures were modeled after the voice architectures. This is understandable, because data networks arc merely a logical extension of the dial-up voice network. Devices are, therefore, constructed to fit into the overall voice network operation. Data equipment is designed and built to mimic the characteristics of a human speech pattern. Now, however, we see that voice is data and data are, too! This paradigm shift marks the true convergence of voice and data onto a single architecture. The world appears ready to embrace the technologies that will fall out from this convergence.

What Is Data Communications?

Data communications is the process of transmitting information in binary form between two or more points. Often, we refer to data communications as computer communications because much of the information is exchanged between computers and the peripheral devices. Regardless of where the information comes from, data may be as simple as binary ones and zeros, or it may include complex information, such as digital audio or video. What is also important is that data involves most of what we do on a daily basis, such as control and signaling systems (traffic lights, bridges, and so forth) and financial systems (bank by phone, funds transfer, and so forth). Without data, most of our commercial systems will cease to function.

How Data Is Created and Stored

Before going into how data is created and stored, it is probably appropriate to define data communications. Simply stated, data communications is the process of communicating information:

1. Across a medium

2. From a sender to a receiver

3. Over a distance

4. In a usable and understandable format

Most people refer to data communications as computer communications, because the bulk of information being transmitted is from computer-to-computer or computer- to-terminal device. Computers are used to generate information between human and machine. By using some form of input device, such as a keyboard, a human can transform information in an electrical form and store it on magnetic or optical media.

Two such storage devices on a computer would be a hard drive and a floppy disk. Newer devices, such as memory sticks, CD-RW, and DVD-RW devices, provide an array of storage media to the user.

To create the information three processes are used:

1. First, the transmitter is where the information originates.

2. Next, a medium is used to carry the information from the transmitter to the receiving device.

3. Last, the receiver subsystem is used to accept the information.

If you take these pieces apart one at a time, the pieces are fairly straightforward and simple to understand.

The Transmitter

The **transmitter** is the device that sends the information to be distributed. The information can also originate at the transmitter (as in keyboard entry) or it could have been moved to the transmitter through some other means. Information can be input via scanners, bar code readers, card readers, and so forth. While the information is being input, the user merely enters the information and the computer does the rest. Normally, the concern is not *how* the data is being created, but knowing that it is. What they all have in common is that the information can't be shared unless it is transmitted. Some transmitter devices are shown in the following illustration.

A myriad of devices can be used as transmitters or input devices.

The Medium

For localized data communications, the process of moving the data is from the input device (the transmitter) across some medium, usually electrical wires, optical cables, or along the airwaves. As a standard, we use a **medium**, such as a cable, to electrically move the information from the keyboard to whatever storage device is attached to the computing system. In the case of a personal computer (PC), the information is moved across a data bus inside the computer from the keyboard to the hard disk, the simplest form of communications in the PC technology world.

However, if the data must be moved from the PC to a disk storage system that is not internal, then a different cable is used to connect the intelligence of the PC to a hard-disk controller located somewhere else. Moreover, the medium could be in the form of radio waves, light beams, or any other form of communications channel. No single restriction or preferred method moves the information from the terminal device to the receiving device. Any choice will be taken into consideration, based on the distance or the cost of transmitting the information. The medium, however, must be economical and support the necessary throughput.

The medium may be an optical fiber in which light signals are changed in accordance with certain conventions to represent the user data.

The Receiver

The **receiver** may be a user computer, a receiving modem, or a receiving multiplexer. Or the receiver can be a computer system, a disk subsystem, or an output device, such as a printer or a plotter. A variety of these devices are shown in the following illustration. If the many parts

8

of data communications systems were examined, they would fit into one of those three basic components.

Regardless of the component used, the issue is the same: the movement of information from the sender across the medium to the receiver. This is called *data communications*.

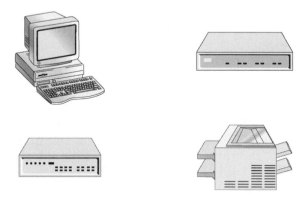

These devices may well represent the receiving device, including (clockwise from the upper left) the PC, the modem, the printer, and the multiplexer.

Protocols

Protocols are key components of communications architectures. **Architectures** are guidelines on how environments connecting two or more devices can be constructed, so most components of a given architecture in a network will be found on each communicating computer in that network. Protocols are the rules for communications between counterpart components on different devices. However, one aspect of protocols also applies to hardware: whether they are synchronous or asynchronous.

Transmission Protocols (Synchronous vs. Asynchronous)

All lower-level data communications protocols fall into one of the two following categories: synchronous and asynchronous. The words themselves are based on Greek roots, indicating they either are "in" or "with" time (synchronous) or "out of" or "separated from" time (asynchronous). The underlying meanings are quite accurate, as long as you understand to what they must be applied.

All data communications depend on precise timing or clocking. The discussion of analog versus digital transmission in Chapter 5 covers how voltage levels are sampled in the middle of a bit time to maximize the odds that the sample value will be clearly distinguishable as a 1 or a 0. But how does the equipment determine precisely when the middle of a bit time occurs? The answer is clocking: equipment at both ends of a circuit must be synchronized during transmission, so the receiver and the sender agree regarding beginnings, middles, and ends of bits during transmissions. There are two fundamentally different ways to do this clocking: asynchronously and synchronously.

Simply put, **asynchronous transmissions** are clocked (or synchronized) one byte at a time. **Synchronous transmissions** are clocked in groups of bytes. But the differences in how these two approaches work go beyond the differences between individual bytes and groups of bytes.

Asynchronous communications is also called start/stop communications and has the following characteristics.

Every byte has added to it one bit signaling the beginning of the byte (the *start bit*) and at least one bit (possibly two) added at the end of the byte (the *stop bits*). Bytes with 7 data bits typically also include a *parity bit* (this is an error-checking bit), whereas 8-data-bit bytes usually do not. Thus, generally speaking, 10 or 11 total bits are transmitted for every asynchronous byte. To get 7 usable data bits, you must transmit approximately 10 to 11; strictly speaking, you use a 30 to 35 percent overhead. Figure 8-1 shows the layout of a data byte in an asynchronous form. This was a special concern when data communications was initially used in the late 1950s and early 1960s. Back then, the cost per minute of a dial-up line was much more expensive than today's costs. Thirty cents of every dollar was spent just to provide the timing for the line.

```
S               S  S
T               T  T
A  1 000 001  P O  O
R               P  P
T
```

Figure 8-1 The layout of the byte is set up with 1 start bit, 7 data bits, 1 parity bit, and 2 stop bits, creating an 11-bit byte to be sent. Only seven of these bits constitute the data to be sent.

The data movement between devices requires some intelligence. The terminal is dumb to the proper sequencing of information. Regardless of its capability (mainframe, mini, PC), the Data Terminal Equipment (DTE) uses the intelligence of Data Circuit-Terminating Equipment (DCE) to move the data between devices. From a minicomputer, an asynchronous (not timed, random data generation) controller port passes the data to a DCE. The DCE then sends information serially to the remote end. The **DTE** is the workstation or computer. The **DCE** is the data communications device, such as the modem on a dial-up connection. Figure 8-2 is a representation of the normal progression of the data communications process. The figure shows that data are created in the minicomputer or PC as parallel data. Inside the computer, a byte of data called the *character* is created and moved from the terminal device to the modem device. The modem accepts the data in the parallel form and converts it to the line code of serial data.

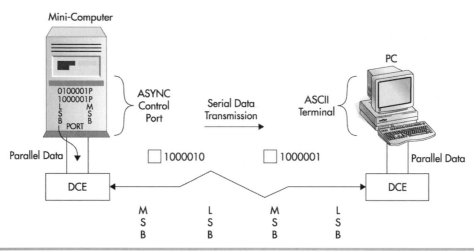

Figure 8-2 As the data are presented from the terminal to the modem, they are converted for the capability of the line.

Parallel means that inside the bus of the computer, 8 bits at a time are moved using a separate channel for each bit. However, to get the data on the telephone line, you must convert it to serial data. One bit at a time is sequentially (serially) sent out on the transmit wire to the far end.

     This also makes nominal speed calculations for such connections easy: dividing the rated speed of the circuit (for example, 9,600 bits per second) by 10 bits per byte gives a transmission speed in characters per second (for example, 960 cps). As a rule, you divide the bits per second by 10 to get the nominal speed of an asynchronous circuit. (*Nominal* here means best-case. In the real world, circuits rarely deliver 100 percent of their nominal capacity, but it's a starting point for capacity calculations.)

     In asynchronous communication, the bytes are sent without regard to the timing of previous and succeeding bytes. This means none of the components in a circuit ever assumes that just because 1 byte just went by, another will follow in any particular period of time. Think of a person banging away on a keyboard. The speed and number of characters sent in a given period do not indicate in any way how many or how quickly characters can be sent in the succeeding similar period.

     Clocking is controlled by DTE, which can be one of many devices, such as a PC, a terminal, a mainframe computer, a printer, point-of-sale equipment, and so forth. For example, when a personal computer is used to dial up a connection, clocking on bytes going toward the DCE is generated by the sending PC, as shown in Figure 8-3. That first start bit reaching the modem begins the sequence, with all succeeding bits in the same byte arriving in lockstep at the agreed-on rate until the stop bit is received. Then, clocking stops until the beginning of the next byte arrives. Any intervening devices (especially modems) between the communicating DTEs take the clocking from the data sent by the originating DTE for any given byte.

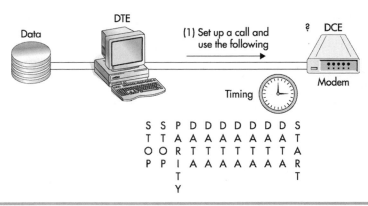

Figure 8-3 The DTE sends the clocking information to the DCE. The DCE does not know when to expect the data, so the DTE starts the sequence by using a start bit.

Most PC and minicomputer terminal communications employ asynchronous techniques. The default communications ports on PCs (the "serial" or COM ports) only support asynchronous communications. To use synchronous communications on a PC, a special circuit board is required.

Synchronous Communication

Synchronous communications have the following characteristics:

- Blocks of data, rather than individual bytes (characters), are transmitted.

- Individual bytes do not have any additional bits (parity) added to them on a byte-by-byte basis.

- Data blocks include some error-detection or error-correction methodology to alert to timing failures or other data corruption, except for parity.

Bytes are sent and clocked in contiguous groups of one or more bytes. Each group is immediately (with no intervening time) preceded by a minimum of two consecutive synchronization (SYN) bytes that begin the clocking (*SYN* is a special character defined by the specific synchronous protocol, of which there are many). All succeeding bits in the group are sent in lockstep until the last bit of the last byte is sent, followed (still in lockstep) by an end-of-block byte. This layout of the SYN is shown in Figure 8-4. Clocking is controlled by data communications equipment (DCE). Specifically, on any given circuit, one specific DCE component is optioned (that is, configured) at installation time as the master device. When the circuit is otherwise idle, the master generates the same synchronization character previously

8

mentioned on a periodic basis to all other DCE devices, so all DCE clocks on the circuit are maintained in continuous synchronization.

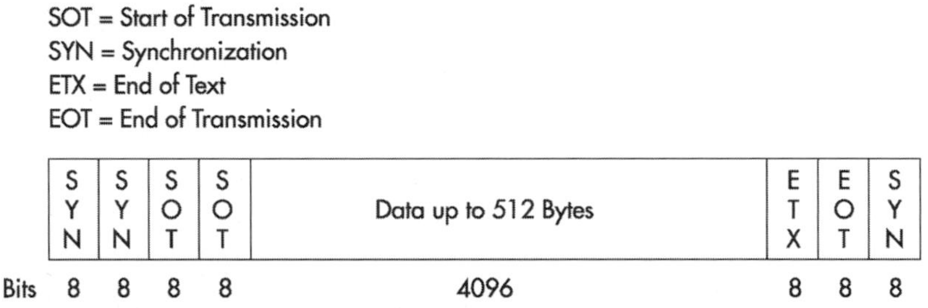

SOT = Start of Transmission
SYN = Synchronization
ETX = End of Text
EOT = End of Transmission

S Y N	S Y N	S O T	S O T	Data up to 512 Bytes	E T X	E O T	S Y N
Bits 8	8	8	8	4096	8	8	8

Figure 8-4 The block of data sent in a synchronous transmission holds much larger quantities of data. In this case, 512 bytes can be sent per block. The data are sent as the 8-bit bytes, without start and stop bits in between.

Except in cases where smaller numbers of bytes (fewer than about 20) are sent at a time, synchronous communications makes more efficient use of a circuit, as you can see in Table 8-1

Data Bytes	Asynchronous Bits	Synchronous Bits*	Synchronous Savings
1	10 (1 start bit + 7 data bits + 1 parity bit + 1 stop bit) = 10 bits	32 (8 bits SOT + 8 bits EOT + 8 bits ETX) + 8 bits of data = 32 bits minimum (SYN not counted)	−220 percent (32 − 10)/32 = 2.2
5	50 (10 bits * 5)	64	−28 percent
10	100 (10 bits *10)	104	−4 percent
20	200 (10 bits * 20)	184	8 percent
30	300 (10 bits * 30)	264	12 percent
100	1000 (10 bits * 100)	824	18 percent
1,000	10,000 (10 bits * 1,000)	8,024	20 percent
10,000	100,000 (10 bits * 10,000)	80,024	20 percent

*includes overhead bits

Table 8-1 Comparing the Savings of Synchronous Versus Asynchronous Transmission.

Generally speaking, all circuits running at greater than 2,400 bits per second operate in synchronous mode over the wire. This is simply because building modems to reliably operate asynchronously at higher speeds over analog circuits is much more difficult than taking this approach. Asynchronous modems that run faster than 2,400 bits per second incorporate asynchronous-to-synchronous converters. They communicate asynchronously to their respective DTEs, but they communicate synchronously between the modems, as shown in Figure 8-5. The start and stop bits are stripped off while in the buffer, and the data are prepared to go across the link synchronously. This doesn't normally impact performance: when smaller groups of characters are sent, there is time to include the additional overhead for synchronous transmission. When larger groups are sent, the reduced overhead of synchronous transmission comes into play. In practice, these higher-speed modems communicate with other modems at even higher than their rated speeds. The extra bandwidth is used for overhead functions between the modems.

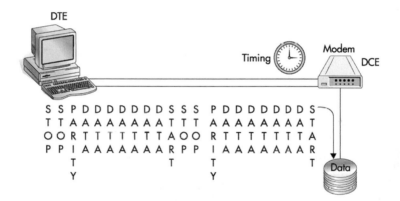

Figure 8-5 The DTE communicates to the modem asynchronously. The modem then stores (buffers) the data and sends it out synchronously. Overhead is stripped off as necessary.

? Line Check 8-3

Describe what a protocol is.

What is the difference between asynchronous and synchronous transmission?

Error Detection

At the beginning of the chapter, we mentioned that ensuring the integrity of the information was one of the key responsibilities of a data communications environment. We must somehow guarantee with an extremely high degree of certainty that the information is received in exactly the same form as it was sent.

More precisely, two tasks are required: detecting when transmission errors occur and triggering retransmissions in the case an error is detected. The responsibility of protocols is to trigger and manage retransmissions.

All code sets used in data communications are designed to use all their bits to represent characters (letters, numbers, and other special characters). A not-so-obvious implication of this fact is this: every byte (eight bits) received in such a code set is by definition a valid code. How can you detect whether the received code is the code that was sent?

The solution is, somehow, to send some additional information, some data about the data (sometimes described as *metadata*), along with the primary data. All error-checking approaches depend on this approach. The additional data is created during the communications process, used to check the underlying data when it is received, and then discarded before the information is passed to its final destination.

In order of increasing reliability, the major methods used to detect data communications errors include:

- Parity bit, or vertical, redundancy checking (VRC)

- Longitudinal redundancy checking (LRC)

- Cyclic redundancy checking (CRC)

Suppose you are a rich aunt or uncle of mine, and I am living in a foreign country and have run out of money. I called you to request that you electronically transfer some money into my account at the foreign bank. Being extremely generous, you have decided to send me $1000.00. If the network used is not perfectly reliable and appropriate error-detection methods are not applied by the transmitting financial service, a change in a single character—for example, changing the decimal point—could result in your sending me considerably more money than you intended: a total of $1000000.

Parity-bit checking would attempt to detect this error by checking the parity of each byte sent against a standard for the error detection.

What are the chances of my getting my inheritance early in this way? Not very high, given the odds that only the decimal point would change, and only to a 0 (out of either 126 [when using a seven-bit ASCII code] or 254 [when using an eight-bit code]). But consider the probability of detecting the error, assuming it occurred. Using parity bits in what we call vertical redundancy checking (VRC), the likelihood of detecting this kind of error (which requires several bits to be wrong at one time to change an entire character) is about 65 percent. **VRC** is a process of stacking the character vertically (one bit on top of the other) and adding one more bit called a parity bit. If *even parity* is used, then the total of all bits sent, including the parity bit, should be even. Odd parity, conversely, should always create an odd value.

A somewhat better method, longitudinal redundancy checking (LRC), increases the odds of detection to about 85 percent. **LRC** occurs when the data are stored in the buffer. Blocks of data are stored by stacking the bits vertically and creating a full buffer (for example, 8 bytes might be stored). Next the DCE adds a bit across (longitudinally) each row of the stored data. A combination of VRC and LRC is used when storing the data in a buffer. First, the VRC can be calculated on each individual byte. Then, the LRC can be calculated by working across the string and creating a whole new byte.

Cyclic redundancy checking (CRC) is a bit different. The **CRC** method improves the odds of detecting and correcting such a multibit error to 99.99995 percent or even higher. Here, the DCE stores the data in the buffer and then calculates a mathematical summation of all the data bits. Then, it divides this value by a prime number polynomial. The result leaves you with a remainder (value). This remainder is appended to the data and sent across the line. The following shows more detail.

Because the networks used to send monetary amounts generally use CRC techniques, it doesn't look as though I'm going to get rich because of their errors. But let's examine these methods in a bit more detail anyway.

Parity Bit/Vertical Redundancy Checking (VRC)

The parity-bit approach to error detection simply adds a single parity bit to every character (or byte) sent. Calculations are performed by the sending device to determine if the parity bit is set to 0 or 1 (the only two possibilities, of course) and recalculated by the receiving device. If the calculations match, the associated character is considered good. Otherwise, an error is detected.

This is much simpler than it sounds. Two approaches are typically used: even and odd parity. Other forms of parity exist, such as mark and space parity. It makes no difference which is used. The only requirement is that the sending and receiving devices use the same approach. To illustrate even parity, consider the ASCII-bit sequence representing a lowercase letter *a*: 1100001. Because we are using even parity, we require that the total number of 1 bits transmitted to the receiver to send this *a*, including the eighth-parity bit, be equal to an even number. Their position in the underlying byte is irrelevant. If you count the 1's in the 7-bit pattern, you get 3, an odd number. Therefore, we set the parity bit to 1, resulting in 11100001, an 8-bit pattern with an even number of (that is, four) 1's. (The parity bit is sent last. In the illustrations, the bits farthest to the right are sent first, so we show the parity bit being added at the left.) Figure 8-6 shows an ASCII illustration of the word "hello," complete with even parity bits.

8

As you can see from the figure, the bytes are represented as vertical sets of numbers, thus vertical redundancy checking: if we orient the digits vertically, we add a vertical bit that is redundant to help check the correctness of the underlying byte. The vertical orientation is arbitrary, of course. However, when we illustrate longitudinal redundancy checking, you will see a reason for this display approach.

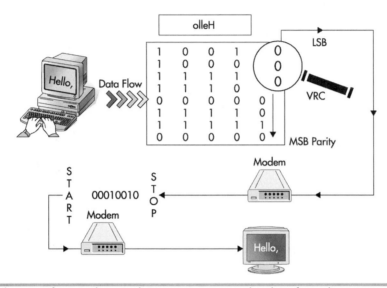

Figure 8-6 The use of vertical parity bits as we transmit the data from the terminal. Note that the additional bits are added vertically in the most significant bit slot (MSB).

Having gone to the trouble of describing parity bits, we must confess they are of limited use in data communications. Parity checking will catch 100 percent of errors where the number of bits in error is odd (1, 3, 5, and so forth) and none of the errors where the number of bits in error is even. Put another way, if an error occurs (and communications errors rarely affect only a single bit), only about a 65 percent chance exists that parity checking will detect it. (The probability is better than 50 percent because there are somewhat more single-bit errors than any one type of multibit error, whether the numbers of the latter are odd or even.)

Parity checking is used extensively inside computers. There it makes sense because it is entirely plausible that errors would occur one at a time (if they occur at all). Parity checking does well in this environment. Also, some networks still have users set their communications software to use parity checking. But even their equipment uses a more sophisticated protocol for file transfers. Some more sophisticated error-detection protocols are described in the following paragraphs.

Longitudinal Redundancy Checking (LRC)

The concept of LRC follows directly from VRC, taking VRC a step further. This example uses 8-bit, rather than 7-bit, bytes. But LRC checking needs to operate on a group of bytes, rather than on 1 byte at a time. For this example, it doesn't matter what the bits represent, so let us create a set of eight 8-bit bytes. As you will see, although the bit patterns do not matter for the example, the number of bytes used does (see Table 8-2).

1	0	1	0	1	0	1	0
0	0	1	0	0	0	1	0
1	1	1	0	1	1	1	0
1	0	1	0	0	0	1	0
0	1	1	0	0	1	1	0
1	1	1	0	1	1	1	0
0	1	1	0	0	1	1	0

Table 8-2 Setting up the Data for a VRC Checking Pattern. The 7-Bit Bytes Are Stacked Vertically, Leaving a Slot at the Bottom of Each Row for the Parity Bit.

If we only use VRC (odd parity), as previously described, we could produce the pattern shown in Table 8-3. But, of course, we said that VRC only catches about 65 percent of errors, hardly acceptable.

Using Odd Parity

1	0	1	0	1	0	1	0
0	0	1	0	0	0	1	0
1	1	1	0	1	1	1	0
1	0	1	0	0	0	1	0
0	1	1	0	0	1	1	0
1	1	1	0	1	1	1	0
0	1	1	0	0	1	1	0
1	1	0	1	0	1	0	1

Table 8-3 The VRC bit is inserted, but the odds are still low on catching the errors. For example, if two bits change, the errors may get through.

But what if we apply odd parity checking across the bytes in addition to vertically? In that case, the completely filled-in Table 8-4 would be generated. Adding both the horizontal and vertical checking, together referred to as LRC, improves the odds of detecting errors to about 85 percent. Not bad, although we wouldn't want to trust our money to such a transmission. But there is another disadvantage to LRC. Using 8-bit bytes for every eight data bytes, an additional two LRC bytes must be transmitted. That works out to 20 percent added overhead for error checking (2 LRC bytes divided by the 10 total bytes transmitted in the set), not counting any degradation due to the time required to compute the check bytes. This is not an efficient error-checking mechanism. In fact, considering that error checking is only one of several sources of transmission overhead, it is abysmal.

Using Odd Parity Both Vertically (VRC) and Horizontally (LRC)

1	0	1	0	1	0	1	0	1
0	0	1	0	0	0	1	0	1
1	1	1	0	1	1	1	0	1
1	0	1	0	0	0	1	0	0
0	1	1	0	0	1	1	0	1
1	1	1	0	1	1	1	0	1
0	1	1	0	0	1	1	0	1
1	1	0	1	0	1	0	1	0

Table 8-4 The Vertical and Longitudinal Redundancy Checks Inserted. This Creates a New Column on the Right Side and a Single Bit Across the Bottom.

LRC does have one advantage over CRC, the approach discussed next. Far fewer computational resources are required for calculating the LRC bytes than for calculating a CRC (unless the CRC is implemented with hardware). In fact, until recent generations of PCs became available, with their vastly more powerful CPUs, CRC checking for asynchronous data communications in the PC environment was impractical because of its computationally intensive nature. Now, however, it is routinely used. Read on to see why.

? Line Check 8-4

You try the math. Following are a couple of examples using the Vertical and Longitudinal Redundancy Checks. Try your hand at doing them and see how well you do.

Vertical Redundancy Using Even Parity

1	0	0	0	1	1	1	0
1	0	1	1	0	0	1	1
0	1	0	0	1	0	1	0
0	1	0	0	0	1	0	0
0	1	0	1	1	1	1	0
1	0	1	0	0	0	1	1
1	1	0	1	1	0	0	1

Vertical Redundancy Using Odd Parity

1	0	0	0	0	1	1	0
0	0	1	1	0	0	1	0
0	1	0	1	1	0	0	0
1	1	0	0	0	1	0	0
0	1	0	1	1	1	1	0
0	0	1	0	0	0	0	0
1	0	1	1	0	0	0	1

Vertical and Longitudinal Redundancy Using Even Parity

1	1	1	0	0	1	1	1	
1	0	1	1	0	0	1	1	
0	0	1	0	0	0	0	0	
1	1	1	0	0	0	0	0	
0	1	1	1	1	1	1	1	
0	0	1	0	0	1	0	1	
1	0	0	0	0	0	0	0	

8

Cyclic Redundancy Checking (CRC)

Although no practical error-checking algorithm can guarantee detection of every possible error pattern, CRC comes close. A complete explanation with examples of how CRC works (as shown in several data communications textbooks) requires several pages of somewhat hairy binary algebra. Rather than put you through that, we'll describe some of the method's key characteristics and indicate how this method is used.

Like the previously described approaches to error detection, CRC relies on on-the-fly calculation of an additional bit pattern, called a frame check sequence (FCS), that is sent immediately after the original block of data bits. The *frame check sequence* is the appended data that represents the *modulus*, or remainder, of a mathematical division operation. The length of the FCS is chosen in advance by a software or hardware designer on the basis of how high a confidence level is required in the error-detection capability of the given transmission. All *burst errors*, or groups of bits randomized by transmission problems, with a length less than that of the FCS will be detected. Frequently used FCS lengths include 12, 16, and 32 bits. Obviously, the longer the FCS, the more errors will be detected.

The FCS is computed by first taking the original data-block bit pattern (treated as a single huge binary number) and adding to its end (after the low-order bits) some additional binary 0's. The exact number of added 0's will be the same as the number of bits in the desired FCS. (The FCS, once calculated, will overlay those 0's.) Then, the resulting binary number, including the trailing 0's, is divided by a special previously selected divisor (often referred to in descriptions of the algorithm as *P*).

P has certain required characteristics:

- *P* is always 1 bit longer than the desired FCS.

- P's first and last bits are always 1.

- *P* is chosen to be "relatively prime" to the FCS; that is, *P* divided by the FCS would always give a non-0 remainder. In practice, that means *P* is normally a prime number.

- The division uses binary division, a much quicker and simpler process than decimal division. The remainder of the division becomes the FCS.

Specific implementations of CRC use specific divisors; thus, the CRC-32 error-checking protocol on one system should be able to cooperate with the CRC-32 protocol on another system. Likewise, the CRC-ITU protocol (which uses a 17-bit pattern, generating a 16-bit FCS) should talk to other implementations of CRC-ITU. Selection of a specific *P* can be tuned to the types of errors most likely to occur in a specific environment. But unless you are planning on engineering a new protocol, you need not worry about the selection process. This already has been done for you by the designers of your hardware or your communications software. Figure 8-7 illustrates the CRC creation process.

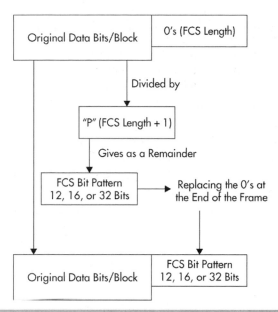

Figure 8-7 The process of calculating the CRC is complex, and it takes processor time and overhead in the data stream. However, the benefit is that the integrity checks on the data produce much better results.

CRC is typically used on blocks or frames of data, rather than on individual bytes. Depending on the protocol being used, the size of the blocks can be as high as several thousand bytes. Thus, in terms of bits of error-checking information required for a given number of bytes of data, CRC requires far less transmission overhead (for example, CRC-32 sends four 8-bit bytes' worth of error-checking bits to check thousands of data bytes) than any of the parity-based approaches.

Although binary division is efficient, having to perform such a calculation on every block transmitted does have the potential to add significantly to transmission times. Fortunately, CPUs developed in the last few years are up to the challenge. Also, unlike most other check-digit types of error correction, the receiving device or software does not have to recalculate the FCS to check for an error. Instead, the original data, plus the FCS, are concatenated together to form a longer pattern, and then divided by the same P used as a divisor during the FCS creation process. If no remainder occurs from this last division, then the CRC algorithm assumes no errors exist. And 99.99995 percent of the time, there are no errors.

8

Let's try to clarify that:

When we calculate the math of a CRC-16, for example, we use a modulo 2 summation. Then, we divide by the prime number polynomial, which produces the remainder. The remainder is appended to the data and sent across the medium.

At the receiving end, the modem receives the data into its buffer, where it performs the same math. It uses the modulo 2 summation (a binary addition with no carries) and divides by the polynomial. The remainder should be the same as the appended remainder. If it is, you can assume no errors have occurred. If the remainders do not agree, then you know at least one (but possibly many) data error has occurred during transmission. Therefore, the modem asks the sending end for a retransmission of the same data. This is called a NAK (a nonacknowledgment).

Plexes—Communications Channel Directions

The next area of discussion is the directional nature of your communications channel. Three basic forms of communications channels exist: simplex, half-duplex, and full-duplex.

One-Way (Simplex)

Simplex is a service that is one way and *only* one way. You can use it either to transmit or to receive, but not both. This is not a common channel for telephony (voice) because there are few occasions where one person always speaks and everyone else listens. Feedback, one of the capabilities that we prize in our communications, would be eliminated in a one-way conversation. Broadcast television is an example of simplex communications. The picture is sent to your receiver. However, the receiver never sends back any information because it is a receive-only system.

Designing an efficient data-communications application using a simplex channel can require quite a bit of ingenuity. A good example is stock ticker-tape radio signals. Remember, in a true simplex system (such as this one), absolutely no feedback is possible from the receiver to the transmitter. How then does someone using such a signal get useful, timely information? After all, unless you are simply gawking at the symbols as they go by, it is not practical to wait for, on average, half of the symbols to pass to find out if the particular stock in which you are interested just went up or down.

The answer is a combination of communications and computer technology. The applications that implement this technique memorize locally (on a PC) the entire repeating communications stream once, and then accept each new symbol/price combination received as an update to the local "database." The user inquires against that local database, getting what appears to be instant information, even though it might have been received several minutes ago. Naturally, the computer must be set to continually receive; otherwise, the user will have no assurance that the data is even remotely current.

Another approach requires the user to specify in advance to the software a set of symbols to collect. As that stock information goes by, the program snags only the specified information for retention and local inquiry. This is not any faster than the previous approach, but it does require less local-storage capability.

Two-Way Alternating (Half-Duplex)

The normal use in conversations involves a **half-duplex** operation on the link. In half-duplex, the channel is used two-way, but only one way at a time. We speak to a listener, and then we listen while someone else speaks. The telephone conversations we engage in are normally half-duplex under accepted human protocols, but in practice, they may be full-duplex (both parties can speak at the same time). Although the line or medium (air, in this case) is capable of handling a transmission in each direction, most human brains cannot deal well with simultaneous transmission and reception.

Many computer and communications configurations use half-duplex technology. Until a few years ago, most leased-line multidrop modems were half-duplex. Of course, some still exist in other parts of the world, but they are slowly being replaced. One of the key differentiators among such modems was their turnaround time, that is, how quickly a pair of such modems could reverse the channel direction. This was measured in milliseconds—the fewer, the better. Entire communications protocols were built around this technology, for example, IBM's Bisynchronous Communications (BSC). All block-mode (for example, IBM 3270s) terminals still operate in half-duplex mode only, even if other facilities are available. This simply means that at any given time, the terminal is either sending to its associated computer or receiving from it, but not both at once. This does not cause a problem because the entire system is designed around this behavior, and it works quite well. Of course, almost half of any given circuit's raw capacity (if the capacities of the two directions are added together) is wasted.

With some technologies, half-duplex can be used so effectively, the one-way-at-a-time characteristic of the circuit is invisible. It appears to be full-duplex (see the following). An excellent example of such an approach is local area network (LAN) communications. Many actual LAN technologies, including both Ethernet and Token Ring, natively use half-duplex on the wire. But the information moves so quickly and the responses are so fast, the path appears to an observer to be full-duplex. There are full-duplex LANs, but this varies depending on the installation and the date and type of the equipment used. All newer Ethernet switches can operate in full-duplex mode, yet they are autosensing to determine if the terminal has a card that can also communicate in the same manner. The chipsets on the NIC cards make the determination of which mode to use.

8

Try This

Using an Ethernet switch, plug in a desktop PC, and observe which lights illuminate. The choices are 10/100, FDX, and Traffic.

Now, plug in an older PC or a laptop with a half-duplex card, and see how the autosensing occurs.

What lights are now illuminated?

Two-Way Simultaneous (Duplex) or Full-Duplex

True full-**duplex** communications make maximum use of a circuit's capacity—if the nature of the communications on that circuit takes advantage of it. In data communications, a circuit is implemented and used in full-duplex mode if a device can send to a computer and receive from the computer at the same time. Although we mentioned that human conversation is typically half-duplex, in reality it can be, and often is, full-duplex. People can speak over the other party in a conversation.

One point that confuses some people is this: the terms "simplex," "half-duplex," and "full-duplex" can refer to varying levels of communications architecture. If the three levels are considered to be three points on an increasing scale of capability, you can say that a given level of communications architecture must rely on lower levels, with at least the capability of that given level, as presented in Table 8-5.

This Capability Level	Requires All Lower Levels to Have at Least the Following Capability	But Can Also Function Without Impairment on Top of Levels with the Following Capabilities
Simplex	Simplex	Half- or full-duplex
Half-duplex	Half-duplex	Full-duplex
Full-duplex	Full-duplex	(no higher levels)

Table 8-5 The Comparison Is Shown with the Capability and Directionality of the Circuit.

What does this table mean? It means that a wide-area analog-data circuit built to handle full-duplex communications (requiring the telephone company to support simultaneous communications in both directions and the use of full-duplex modems) can fully support half-duplex or simplex communications. But if a similar circuit is implemented with half-duplex modems, then full-duplex communications on that circuit will not work, although simplex will work.

Air is a full-duplex channel. But a simplex signal, such as the output from a stereo speaker system, has no trouble traversing this full-duplex channel.

❓ Line Check 8-5

What is the one form of plexes that handles all choices?

❓

Compression

Compression is a method used to get more data across a busy circuit. Most data are repetitive, meaning they have repeating patterns. Think of the example used in describing the transfer of funds into the foreign bank account. The number used was $1,000.00. What is common is the number of zeros in this data transmission. Moreover, when systems send continuous data, the amount of repetition is extremely high (for example, how many $1,000.00 checks are being processed by banks at any given time?). We can compress the amount of repetitious data bytes either by suppressing them or by representing them with less data.

Think of compression differently. Let's use an analogy. Assume data are like oranges. We want to ship oranges across the country so, at the receiving orange plant, the oranges can be squeezed and the juice can be extracted for sale. Although this is done regularly, a different approach can be used. Instead of shipping the oranges, which are heavy and bulky when packed in crates, we squeeze them on the originating end. Then, we flash freeze dry the orange pulp and juice, making an orange concentrate. We have eliminated much of the excess before shipping, saving valuable space and weight on the transport. At the receiving end, the packaging plant now adds water to reconstitute the orange juice and package it in cartons for sale. The compression enabled us to ship much more orange concentrate in fewer vehicles, yet the resultant product is the same after we reconstitute it.

The *presentation layer* of the OSI model performs certain requested functions often enough to warrant finding a general solution for them, rather than letting each user solve the problem individually. Unlike all the lower layers, which are just interested in moving bits reliably from here to there, the presentation layer is concerned with the syntax and semantics of the information transmitted.

A typical example of a presentation service is encoding data in a standard, agreed on manner. Most user programs do not exchange random binary-bit strings. They can exchange people's names, dates, amounts of money, and invoices. These items are represented as character strings, integers, floating-point numbers, and data structures composed of several

8

simpler items. Different computers have different codes for representing character strings, integers, and so on. To make communication possible for computers with different representation, the data structures to be exchanged can be defined in an abstract way, along with a standard encoding to be used "on the wire." The presentation layer handles the job of managing these abstract data structures and converting from the representation used inside the computer to the network standard representation.

The presentation layer is also concerned with other aspects of information representation. In this case, data compression can be used to reduce the number of bits to be transmitted for better utilization of the data circuits or application data handling.

Compression can take on many forms in software at the presentation layer or in the hardware levels of the lower layers (data-link layer) of the OSI model.

Although compression is not exactly a modulation technique, it does (usually) produce faster transmissions. To understand how compression works, consider first how human beings communicate. Most human communication is inherently redundant. This does not imply waste; rather, human beings use that redundancy as a continual cross-check on what information is being sent and meant. For example, in face-to-face conversation, much more information is being sent than just the words. Facial expressions, tones of voice, limb positions and movement, overall carriage of the body, and other less obvious cues all contribute to the information stream flowing between two people having a conversation. But much of the information is duplicated. For example, anger can be communicated by the words themselves, but it can also be conveyed by tone of voice, facial expression, involuntary changes in the color of one's complexion, the stress in the voice, arm movement, and other cues. If some of these items were removed, the message received might be just as clear, but the total amount of raw information might be reduced.

NOTE

Data compression operates at the presentation layer (layer 6) of the OSI model. Yet some line-compression techniques can be handled at the data-link layer (layer 2) as well. If you perform data compression at the presentation layer, you are doing software compression, whereas if you perform the compression at layer 2, you are doing more hardware compression.

In data communications, compression is a technique applied either in advance to information to be transmitted or dynamically to an information stream being transmitted. The underlying technology is essentially the same in both cases: removal of redundant information. A detailed discussion of compression techniques is beyond the scope of this book. But in this section, we describe basic approaches to explain the fundamentals of the technology. The simplest form of compression is the identification and encoding of repeating characters into fewer characters. For example, consider the transmission of printed output across a network to a printer. A typical report contains a high number of blank characters, often occurring consecutively. Suppose every such string of four or more consecutive blanks is detected and replaced with a 3-byte, special-character sequence, encoded as follows:

- The first character is a special nonprinting character that marks the beginning of the sequence.

- The second character is the character that is to be repeated, in this case, a blank.

- The third character is a 1-byte binary number indicating how many times the character is to be repeated. With 1 byte (using binary format), we can count up to 255, high enough to get some real savings!

How much can we save? Look at Table 8-6. We'll assume that on average, blanks occur in 10-byte consecutive streams, a pessimistic assumption.

Total Characters in Print Stream Before Compression	Blanks in Print Before Compression	Total Characters in Print Stream After Compression	Percentage Savings
1,000	10	993	1
1,000	100	930	7
1,000	500	650	35
50,000	2,000	48,600	3
50,000	5,000	46,500	7
50,000	20,000	36,000	28

Table 8-6 Comparison of the Compression Technique and Resultant Savings

As can be seen from the table, the savings depends on the number of occurrences of the character to be repeated. In practice, this is a reasonably powerful technique. In the example, we addressed only blanks; any character except the special character would be fair game.

But what if we want to send that special character? After all, unlike print jobs, many transmissions must be able to handle every possible code. There are none left over that are "special." No problem—we add the following rules:

- We'll never try to compress multiple occurrences of the special character.

- Every time we encounter the special character as input during the encoding process, we'll simply send it twice. If the receiving hardware sees this character twice, it drops one of the occurrences.

8

With this approach, we only have to select a special character that is unlikely to occur frequently. Then, if it does occur frequently in a particular transmission, our compression algorithm doesn't break; it will just be inefficient for that one transmission.

Note how the overall redundancy is squeezed out of a transmission using this approach. But, just as in human communications, eliminating redundancy increases the risk that some information will be misinterpreted. In human communication, if the reddening of an angry person's face and other visual cues were not visible (for example, if the conversation were on the telephone) and the speaker was otherwise self-controlled, the listener might misinterpret angry words as being a joke. After all, many subcultures routinely use affectionate insults without anger. Unrecognized anger is a serious loss of information. In data communications without compression, omission of a single space in a series of spaces might cause a slight misalignment on a report, but will most likely not seriously distort its meaning. If compression is used and the binary count field is damaged—that is, changed to another binary digit—dozens or even hundreds of spaces or other repetitive characters might be either deleted or added to the report, seriously compromising its appearance and, perhaps, distorting its meaning. Consider the havoc that could be wrought on a horizontal bar chart! The error-checking techniques discussed earlier become much more important in a system that uses compression!

Compression-Bit Mapping

Bit mapping is used in a number of applications besides data communications. It is often used on data that exhibits a large number of specific character types, such as zeros or blanks. A simple implementation of bit mapping uses 1 byte and describes either the presence or absence of the character type. Bit mapping will allow blanks or empty characters to be compressed. If a large string of uncompressed data appears at the presentation layer, it can then be compressed using a bit-mapping technique. In this particular case, a leading byte will be generated indicating which of the following bytes of the specific character have been compressed. The binary 1's show the position of data, and the binary 0's show the position of blanks.

This system only compresses one particular character. If the data stream contains a high incidence of more than one character, other variations of bit mapping can be used that employ more than 1 byte in the control format. An example of bit mapping is shown in Figure 8-8.

Bit Mapping Half-Byte

Another form of data compression can take place when a repetitive string of information appears consistently. Using this example, six characters of information may be generated with the first 4 bits in each character appearing the same. In this case, using **half-byte** compression, a control character can be generated representing the constant string of data, with the result being only the last 4 bits of each byte being transmitted. This method can compress the data by as much as 30 to 40 percent. Figure 8-9 shows an example of half-byte bit mapping.

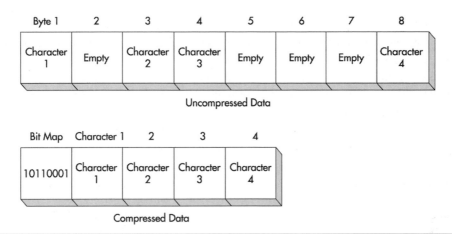

Figure 8-8 In bit mapping, the data compression is done on a byte-by-byte arrangement.

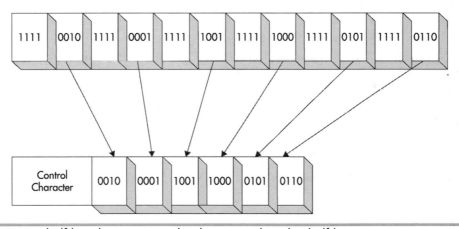

Figure 8-9 In half-byte bit mapping, the data is combined in half-byte sequences.

8

Run-Length Encoding

Run-length encoding is a variation of character suppression, requiring three characters to convey this information. This technique is often employed in data streams where the same characters appear constantly and frequently. It is most effective when transmitting graphics images or screen dumps, but it is not effective when short strings of repetitive characters are in the data. Figure 8-10 shows an example of the format using run-length encoding.

Control Character Indicates Compression Follows	Repetitive Character	Counter

Figure 8-10 Run-length encoding is useful in repetitive data, such as video screens and long strings of repetitious data.

The repeated characters are compressed using a simple process:

1. The first character transmitted indicates the next two characters are compressed data.

2. The second character is the actual code used for the repeating character.

3. The third character is the counter field that describes how many times the character appears in the data string.

Kermit protocols use the run-length encoding technique. **Kermit** is an extensible file-transfer protocol developed at Columbia University in 1981 for transferring text and binary files without errors between diverse systems over error-prone communication links. It is a suite of communications software programs. Most other protocols are designed to work only on certain kinds or qualities of connections and/or between certain kinds of computers, so they work poorly on other systems and links. They offer few, if any, methods to adapt to unplanned-for situations. Kermit, on the other hand, enables you to achieve successful file transfer and the highest possible performance on any given connection.

The Kermit technique uses three characters slightly differently:

1. The first character is the control character.

2. The second character is the counter.

3. The third is the actual code for the repeated character.

Other Forms of Compression

Another more sophisticated method of compression requires pattern recognition analysis of the raw data, rather than just detection of repeating characters. Again, some special character must be designated, but now it precedes a special short code that represents some repetitive pattern detected during the analysis. For example, in graphics displays capable of showing 64K (65,536) colors, every screen pixel has associated with it two 8-bit bytes (which together can represent 65K different values) indicating the color assigned to that pixel. If someone sets the screen to display white on a blue background, the 2-byte code for blue is going to appear thousands of times in the data stream associated with that display. The repeating 1-byte compression algorithm described earlier will not detect anything to compress. But if analysis shows that a 2-byte pattern occurs many times in succession, a more sophisticated approach might assign a specific character (preceded by the special character) to represent precisely 20 (or some other specific number of) consecutive occurrences of that 2-byte sequence. The savings can be considerable, but again, they depend on the characteristics of the data being transmitted.

A third, computationally intensive approach to compression has been designed, especially for live transmission of digitized video signals. Unlike most other compression methods, this approach does not involve movement of representations of the entire digitized data stream from one point to another. Video signals consist of a number of still frames composed each second (visualize 30 photographs per second in the highest-quality case). Although the first picture must, of course, be sent in its entirety, special equipment and algorithms must then continuously examine succeeding video frames to be transmitted, identifying which pixels have changed since the last "picture" was taken. Then, information addressing only the changed pixels is sent to the receiver, rather than the entire new frame. The receiving equipment uses this change information combined with its "memory" of the previous frame to continuously, locally build new versions of the picture for display. This approach is particularly fruitful for pictures that, in large part, remain static, for example, video conferencing. In video conferencing, usually the only moving features of the picture are the human beings. The table(s), walls, and other room fixtures stay still, therefore requiring transmission only once. Frequently, only the lips move for long periods of time.

One other compression-related concept is worth mentioning: lossy vs. lossless compression. "What?" I hear you ask. Does lossy mean what it sounds like? Would we ever tolerate transmission that loses information? The answer, for some applications, is yes.

Lossy is a term describing a data-compression algorithm that reduces the amount of information in the data, rather than just the number of bits used to represent that information. The lost information is usually removed because it is subjectively less important to the quality of the data (usually an image or sound) or because it can be recovered reasonably by interpolation from the remaining data. MPEG and JPEG are examples of lossy compression techniques.

Moreover, you have probably settled for information loss when working daily with computers, and it caused you no hardship at all. If you use a personal computer with a video graphics adapter (VGA) screen, but display any type of graphic that inherently has Super VGA (SVGA)-level resolution, your VGA screen loses the additional definition in the image that is visible only when an SVGA controller card and monitor are used. And, in fact, this example, while not involving compression as such, demonstrates precisely the type of situation where lossy compression would be tolerated: transmission of video images.

Lossless is a term describing a data-compression algorithm that retains all the information in the data, allowing it to be recovered perfectly by decompression.

8

⍰ Line Check 8-6

1. What is the main purpose of compression?

2. What is the difference between lossy and lossless compression?

⍰

Multiplexing

The paths available for moving electronic information vary considerably in their respective capacities, or *bandwidth*. If a company requires many paths over the same route (for example, many terminals, each requiring a connection to one distant computer), it often makes sense to configure one large-capacity circuit and bundle all the smaller requirements into that one big path. The process of combining two or more communications paths into one path is referred to as multiplexing. **Multiplexing** is a means of getting better usage of an underutilized channel. There are three fundamental types of multiplexing, all of which have significant variations. These main types are:

- Space-division multiplexing (SDM)

- Frequency-division multiplexing (FDM)

- Time-division multiplexing (TDM)

Although many of the actual multiplexing functions take place at the lower levels of the OSI model, the transport layer is also responsible to maintain and understand any multiplexing needs between computing devices.

Using the transport layer to establish the multiplexing routines between the two end computing devices on a peer-to-peer level, the various forms of multiplexing can be achieved across the lower layers.

Space-Division Multiplexing (SDM)

Space-division multiplexing (SDM) is the easiest multiplexing technology to understand. In fact, it is so simple, it would hardly rate its own special term, except that **SDM** is the primary method by which literally millions of telephone signals reach private homes. With SDM, signals are placed on physically different media. Then those media are combined into larger groups and connected to the desired end points.

For example, telephone wire pairs—each of which can carry either a voice conversation or other data—are aggregated into cables with hundreds or even thousands of pairs, as seen in Figure 8-11. The latter are run as units from telco COs out to wiring center locations, from there splitting out to individual customer buildings.

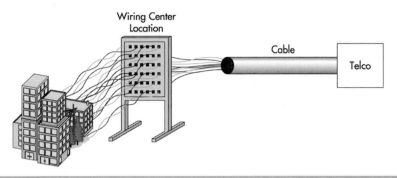

Figure 8-11 Space-division multiplexing uses the separation of the media in physical examples, as shown here.

The biggest advantage of SDM is also its biggest disadvantage: the physical separation of the media carrying each signal. This is an advantage because of the simplicity of managing the bandwidth. you must only label each end point of the medium appropriately. No failures (other than a break in the medium) can affect the bandwidth allocation scheme. But because a direct physical correlation exists between the physical link and the individual communications channel, a provider has some difficulty in electronically manipulating the path to achieve efficiencies of technology or scale. For example, probably the largest single factor blocking the conversion of the overall telephone network to all-digital technology is the embedded base of copper wire (and analog amplifiers) supplying telephone service to millions of homes and businesses.

Frequency-Division Multiplexing (FDM)

Frequency-division multiplexing (FDM) is inherently an analog technology. **FDM** achieves the combining of several digital signals onto (or into) one medium by sending signals in several distinct frequency ranges over that medium.

One of FDM's most common applications is cable television. Only one cable reaches a customer's home, but the service provider can, nevertheless, send multiple television channels or signals simultaneously over that cable to all subscribers. Receivers must tune to the appropriate frequency (channel) to access the desired signal. Figure 8-12 demonstrates the combining of signals on a cable television coaxial cable.

Certain modems have built-in FDM capabilities. Users can control the portion of the bandwidth to be allocated to each user or application on the modem.

Time-Division Multiplexing (TDM)

Time-division multiplexing (TDM) is a digital technology. **TDM** involves sequencing groups of a few bits or bytes from each individual input stream, one after the other, and in such a way

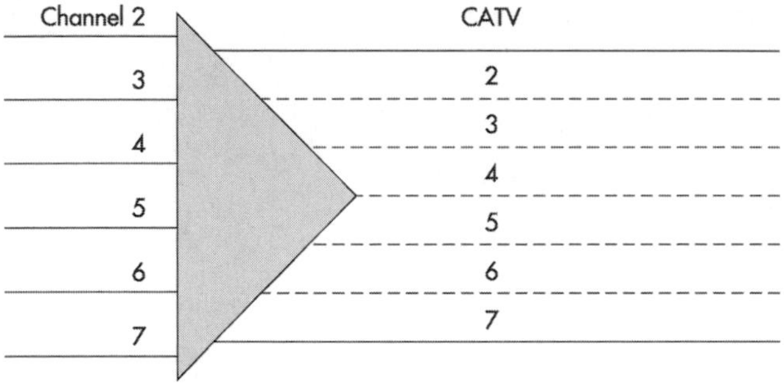

Figure 8-12 FDM allocates portions of the bandwidth (channels) to each user. Each user gets a small piece of the bandwidth 100 percent of the time.

that they can be associated with the appropriate receiver. If done sufficiently and quickly, the receiving devices will not detect that some of the circuit time was used to serve another logical communication path. All high-speed communications technologies discussed use some form of TDM without exception, so it is worthwhile to try to understand it.

Consider an application requiring four terminals at an airport to reach a central computer. Each terminal communicates at 2,400 bps, so rather than acquire four individual circuits to carry such a low-speed transmission, the airline has installed a pair of multiplexers. A pair of 9,600-bps modems and one dedicated analog communications circuit from the airport ticket desk back to the airline data center are also installed. Recall the discussion of T1 multiplexers (which are TDM) from Chapter 5.

The time-division multiplexers (called MUXes) work together to merge the data streams onto the 9,600-bps circuit in such a way that each terminal appears to have a dedicated 2,400-bps circuit. The multiplexer has enough buffer (or storage) space, so any clerk can press a key. The keystroke is stored locally until the timeslot assigned to that clerk's terminal comes along. A *timeslot* is a moment in time when the entire channel is allocated to an individual user. The user gets the entire channel for a short period of time. Because the channel is shared among four users, each user receives the entire channel every fourth timeslot and, therefore, gets approximately one-fourth of the channel capacity.

Today, most organizations would use even higher-speed communications channels, such as a T1. This gives the organization 1.544-Mbps transmission capability using high-speed digital transmission on a single four-wire circuit. A TDM is shown in Figure 8-13.

Were the multiplexer configured for only two clerks' terminals, the information from the computer could appear much more quickly. This, in effect, is what a variation on a TDM called a statistical time-division multiplexer (STDM), does. The sending STDM analyzes the

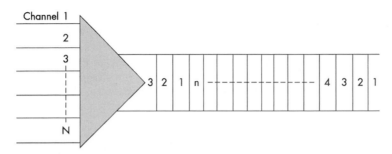

Figure 8-13 In TDM, the user gets 100 percent of the channel (bandwidth) for a small portion of the time. The more users allotted to the channel, the more timeslots.

data stream on the fly to determine which ports or "tail circuits" are active—that is, how much service they require. If they are inactive, or less active (slow typists?), they are provided fewer of the time slots (or bandwidth). This allocation changes dynamically, depending on the traffic pattern.

If ten terminals are connected to a 9600 circuit via an STDM, each terminal can be set to 2,400 bits per second. As long as all terminals are not busy at full speed at every moment, the STDM can make it look as though each terminal has its own 2,400-bit-per-second circuit, even though the aggregate bandwidth required to support these settings without using an STDM would be 24,000 bits per second!

Paradoxically, STDM techniques are used more at lower speeds than on the really fast multimegabit circuits. At very high speeds, the equipment is so busy just performing TDM functions that too much extra computer power would be required to do the on-the-fly analysis for STDM. Packet-switching networks, on the other hand, use a de facto form of STDM by placing packets on the network based on the amount of data generated by each station on the network.

At this point, you might think that TDM is a perfect solution. Yet when using TDM and assigning a timeslot to a user for the duration of the transmission, what happens when that user has nothing to send? The timeslot is passed with no data in it. The TDM is wasteful when the channel is not in use. On application, using a single timeslot may be starving for added capacity, while another application is not using the capacity available to it.

A solution to this problem is to use an inverted MUX (IMUX) function. **IMUX** allocates the slots to the application as necessary. This is similar to statistical TDM. The IMUX function is used in many packet-conceptual models to allocate bandwidth to applications when needed, and then to free up the capacity for others when not needed.

8

❓ Line Check 8-7

1. Which method of multiplexing do you think is working on a CATV system?

2. Which multiplexing method is used for a T1 or T3 network?

3. What is the main purpose of multiplexing?

Codes

The concept of a *bit*—an electronic expression of a 1 or a 0—should now be clear. However, how do you get from 1's and 0's to transmitting your résumé over wires?

Digital alphabets have been designed for electronic communications. They use 1's and 0's to represent human sensible characters. Specifically, each set of codes is a standardized set of patterns of 1's and 0's used to represent letters, numbers, and other symbols that are transmitted and received electronically.

The alphabets most frequently used are either American Standard Code for Information Interchange (ASCII), which is fairly universal, and Extended Binary Coded Decimal Interchange Code (EBCDIC), which is an IBM alphabet. These two code sets are used to convert a series of 1's and 0's into an alphabetic or numeric character.

American Standard Code for Information Interchange (ASCII)

One character (also known as a byte or octet) must be represented as a consistent bit pattern by both sender and receiver. As you use a keyboard, you create a stream of combinations of letters, numbers, and symbols.

ASCII (usually pronounced *as-key* with a mild accent on the first syllable) is strictly a 7-bit code, meaning it uses the bit patterns representable with seven binary digits to represent character information. At the time ASCII was introduced, many computers dealt with 8-bit groups as the smallest unit of information. The eighth bit was commonly used as a parity bit for error checking on communication lines. When ASCII was originally defined for use by the United States government, the bit pattern was defined to be seven data bits long. With 7 bits, it is possible to differentiate 128 different patterns, as shown in Figure 8-14. So, to re-create these typed characters with 1's and 0's, you can use a combination of up to 128 possible ASCII characters. Using the combinations in this table, you should be able to transmit just about everything you presently understand in your vocabulary. And in fact, for many years, the 7-bit ASCII was used for most non-IBM mainframe communications. But two factors caused this form of ASCII to become less popular.

Bit 4	Bit 3	Bit 2	Bit 1	Bit 7 Bit 6 Bit 5 Col Row	0 0 0 0	0 0 1 1	0 1 0 2	0 1 1 3	1 0 0 4	1 0 1 5	1 1 0 6	1 1 1 7
0	0	0	0	0	NUL	DLE	SP	0	@	P		P
0	0	0	1	1	SOH	DC1	!	1	A	Q	a	q
0	0	1	0	2	STX	DC2	"	2	B	R	b	r
0	0	1	1	3	ETX	DC3	#	3	C	S	c	s
0	1	0	0	4	EOT	DC4	$	4	D	T	d	t
0	1	0	1	5	ENQ	NAK	%	5	E	U	e	u
0	1	1	0	6	ACK	SYN	&	6	F	V	f	v
0	1	1	1	7	BEL	ETB	'	7	G	W	g	w
1	0	0	0	8	BS	CAN	(	8	H	X	h	x
1	0	0	1	9	HT	EM	)	9	I	Y	i	y
1	0	1	0	A	LF	SUB	*	:	J	Z	j	z
1	0	1	1	B	VT	ESC	+	;	K	[	k	{
1	1	0	0	C	FF	FS	,	<	L	\	l		
1	1	0	1	D	CR	GS	-	=	M	]	m	}
1	1	1	0	E	SO	RS	.	>	N	^	n	~
1	1	1	1	F	SI	US	/	?	O	_	o	DEL

Figure 8-14 The ASCII code set is the most common code set for terminals. It uses a 7-bit code to produce the characters discussed earlier in the compression section.

First, most computers handle data in 8-bit chunks (rather than 7) to represent characters. The terms "byte" and "octet" almost always refer to 8-bit, not 7-bit, patterns.

Second, while 7-bit ASCII can, indeed, represent all the English letters and numbers, with some symbols left over for special characters and control information, many other characters are used in written communication that cannot easily be expressed in a 128-character code set. Accented characters in the Romance languages, character graphic-drawing symbols, and typographical indications in word processors (bolding, underlining, and so forth) are just a few examples of symbols difficult to handle with standard ASCII.

Extended ASCII

Extended ASCII is a superset of ASCII. *Extended ASCII* is the code used inside virtually all non-IBM computers, including personal computers. It is an 8-bit code set, doubling the possible distinguishable characters to 256. The 7-bit ASCII codes are present in extended ASCII in their original form with a 0 prefixed to the base 7 bits. Another 128 characters are also available with the same base 7 bits as the original ASCII, but with a 1 prefixed instead.

But, whereas ASCII is a standard, extended ASCII is, well, not quite standard. While the original 128 characters communicate well from vendor-to-vendor, even in extended ASCII, every application defines its own use of the additional 128 characters. For example, you can easily write out ASCII text from most word-processing programs, with the result being readable by most other word processors. But if you attempt to read a document created by a word processor in its native form with another, different word processor, you will only be successful if the latter specifically contains a translation module for material created by the first.

Extended Binary Coded Decimal Interchange Code (EBCDIC)

IBM created an entirely different code set before the ASCII code was invented, and its code uses twice as many combinations as the ASCII code set. IBM's 8-bit, 256-character code set, used on all of its computers except personal computers, is called **Extended Binary Coded Decimal Interchange Code (EBCDIC)**. (Most people pronounce this *eb-suh-dick* with a mild accent on the first syllable.)

As with ASCII, certain of the characters are consistent wherever EBCDIC is used. But other characters vary, depending on the specific communicating devices. In Figure 8-15, the white space can be used differently, depending on the EBCDIC dialect in use.

Bits 4		0	0	0	0	0	0	0	0	1	1	1	1	1	1	1	1
Bits 3		0	0	0	0	1	1	1	1	0	0	0	0	1	1	1	1
2		0	0	1	1	0	0	1	1	0	0	1	1	0	0	1	1
1		0	1	0	1	0	1	0	1	0	1	0	1	0	1	0	1
8 7 6 5																	
0 0 0 0		NUL	SOH	STX	ETX	PF	HT	LC	DEL			SMM	VT	FF	CR	SO	SI
0 0 0 1		DLE	DC$_1$	DC$_2$	DC$_3$	RES	N;	BS	IL	CAN	EM	CC		IFS	IGS	IRS	IUS
0 0 1 0		DS	SOS	FS		BYP	LF	EOB	PRE			SM			ENQ	ACK	BEL
0 0 1 1				SYN		PN	RS	UC	EOT					DC$_4$	NAK		SUB
0 1 0 0		SP										¢	.	<	(	+	|
0 1 0 1		&										!	$	*	)	;	¬
0 1 1 0		-	/									,	%	_	>	?	
0 1 1 1												:	#	@	,	=	"
1 0 0 0			a	b	c	d	e	f	g	h	i						
1 0 0 1			j	k	l	m	n	o	p	q	r						
1 0 1 0				s	t	u	v	w	x	y	z						
1 0 1 1																	
1 1 0 0			A	B	C	D	E	F	G	H	I						
1 1 0 1			J	K	L	M	N	O	P	Q	R						
1 1 1 0				S	T	U	V	W	X	Y	Z						
1 1 1 1		0	1	2	3	4	5	6	7	8	9						

Figure 8-15 EBCDIC is IBM's version of a code set. It uses 8 bits to represent the alphabetic, numeric, and special characters

Unicode

Two hundred fifty-six codes might seem all anyone would need. But consider the requirements of Chinese, which has thousands of characters. Or the Cyrillic alphabet, which, although it does not have a terribly large number of characters, does not overlap with any of those defined in ASCII or EBCDIC. Another code set, called Unicode, is now being implemented in some products. Unlike the 8-bit extended ASCII and EBCDIC code sets, *Unicode* uses 16 bits, or 2 bytes, per character. While only 1's and 0's are used, this allows up to 65,536 (2 to the 16th power) separate character definitions. Of course, each character takes up as much storage and transmission time as two 8-bit characters. Unicode is a truly international code set, allowing all peoples to use their own alphabets if they choose.

Line Check 8-8

Name the four code sets typically used for data communications.

Modulation

How does the transmission process work? How does the data get onto the voice dial-up telephone line? You use a device to change the data. This device, known as a modem, changes the data from something a computer understands (digital bits of information) into something the telephone network understands (analog sine waves, or sound). Because you need to send the information beyond the local bounds of the CO, you need to change the data pulses from one form to another that can be transmitted across telephone lines. Traditionally, the telephone network (and especially the local loop) is optimized to transmit analog signals in the voice band. Therefore, you need to make the data look like voice. A **modem** generates a continuous tone, or carrier, and then modifies or modulates it in ways that will be recognized by its partner modem at the other end of the telephone circuit. The modems available to do this come in variations, each one creating a change in a different way. Remember, the word "modem" is a contraction for modulation and demodulation. **Modulation** is a change. We change the channel by applying the data to it in the form of an analog signal. The signal may vary, depending on the type of modulation you use. For the communications process to work, you need the same types of modems at each end of the line, operating at the same speeds. These modems can use the following types of modulation schemes (or change methods):

Amplitude Modulation (AM)

Amplitude modulation (AM) represents the bits of information (the 1's and 0's) by changing a continuous carrier tone. Figure 8-16 illustrates amplitude modulation. Because there are only two stages of the data, 1 and 0, you can let the continuous carrier tone represent the 0 and the modulated tone represent the 1. This type of modem changes the amplitude (think of amplitude as the height of the sine wave or the loudness of the signal). Each change represents a 1 or a 0.

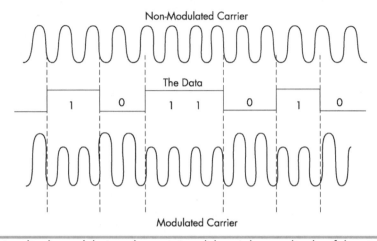

Figure 8-16   Amplitude modulation changes (modulates) the amplitude of the signal. The high amplitude value represents a digital 0, and the low amplitude value represents a 1. The amplitude is changed, but the frequency remains constant.

Because this is a 3-kHz analog dial-up telephone line, the maximum amount of changes that can be represented and still be discrete enough to be recognizable to the line and the equipment is about 2,400 per second. This cycle of 2,400 changes per second is called the *baud rate*. Therefore, the maximum amount of data bits that can be transmitted across the telephone line with AM modulation is 2,400 bits per second. Most amplitude modulation modems were designed to transmit 300 to 1,200 bits per second, although others have been made to go faster.

As we look at the different ways to change the 1's and 0's generated by the computer into their analog equivalents, we have another choice in the process. Voice communications (or human speech itself) is the continuous variation of amplitude and frequencies, so you could choose to use a modem that modulates the frequency instead of the amplitude.

Frequency Modulation (FM)

Frequency modulation (FM) is provided by an FM modem. This modem represents the 1's and 0's as changes in the frequency of a continuous carrier tone (think of frequency as the pitch on the line). Because there are only two states to deal with, we can represent the normal frequency as being a 0 and slow down the continuous carrier frequency when we want to represent a 1 to the telephone line, as shown in Figure 8-17. We can also do this just the opposite way (a low frequency represents the 0 and a higher frequency represents the 1; as long as both modems work the same way, the process will work). The modem uses the same baud rate on the telephone line as the amplitude modulation technique, that being 2,400 baud or discrete changes per second. These modems modulate 1 bit of information per cycle change per second, or a maximum of 2,400 bits per second. Note that the baud rate and the bits per second rate are somewhat symmetrical.

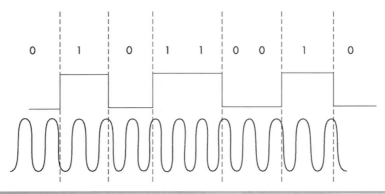

Figure 8-17 FM modems modulate the signal by leaving the amplitude constant and changing the frequency (number of cycles per time period).

Historically, computer users and application designers have demanded higher transmission speeds. Throughput was expensive under the old dial-up telephone network, so we asked for additional speed to get more throughput at a lower cost. The engineers came up with a new process that modulates on the basis of phases.

Phase Modulation

If we can change the phase of the sine wave as it is introduced to the line—at positions of 0, 90, 180, and 270 degrees—we can encode the data with more than 1 bit of information at a time. A phase modulation technique enables us to transmit a di-bit of information per signaling-state change. A **di-bit** is a 2-bit combination. Using two states (0 or 1) and 2 bits at a time, we get four combinations. This gives us 4,800 bits per second of throughput.

The di-bit represents the information shown in Table 8-7

As you can see, two bits of information on a 2,400-baud channel produce the 4,800 bits per second. This was a step in the right direction. But we wanted more, so a combination of phase modulation and amplitude modulation was developed.

8

The Four Phases in Phase Modulation Cause a 90° Shift When a Di-Bit Is Received.

Bits	Phase
00	0
01	90
10	180
11	270

Table 8-7 The Di-Bit Represents the Two-Bit Combinations Modulated onto the Carrier.

QAM

Called **Quadrature with Amplitude Modulation (QAM)**, this combination enables us to use up to 16 possible steps of phase and amplitude modulation. QAM is mostly used with 4 bits of information per baud rate, thereby producing 9,600 bits per second of throughput across an analog telephone line. Theoretically, the system should be able to produce 38,400 bits per second of information (four phases at 4 bits per phase at 2,400 baud = 38,400 bits per second).

However, in practice, line rates can rarely support sustained throughput across the telephone network at this speed. Also, the telco limits the bandwidth to 3 kHz, and we use 2,400 baud. If we try to send more data at a higher baud rate, the band limitation (bandpass filters) will strip the frequencies that go beyond the filters. This is a function of the telco equipment on the line at the CO. Thus, we usually have to settle for analog data transmission at slower speeds.

The driving force behind improving modulation techniques has always been to increase the speed possible over an analog circuit. Why? In addition to the obvious reason (that is, accomplishing the task more quickly improves productivity), the cost of communications over dial circuits is directly proportional to the amount of time those circuits are in use. Going faster saves money. But when the absolute best available modulation technology is in use, you have not yet necessarily squeezed the absolute best transmission volumes out of a circuit. You can push it even further by using compression.

NOTE

Early modems changed one of the two characteristics of the analog wave, either amplitude or frequency. These modems operated at lower speeds ranging from 300 to 2,400 bps.

Later modems began using multiple changes and multibit modulations, such as phase and phase-plus amplitude modulation. These modems produce data rates up to 33.6 Kbps.

V.90 and V.92 Modems

Practically all new PCs and laptop computers sold today have a new modem integral to them. The use of modem technology has become commonplace. Today, the new modem technology is asymmetrical in that it transmits at one speed and receives data at a different rate. The world was looking for better ways of moving data, but it had to deal with the limits of the wires in the local loop. Over the decades, the cost of modems has dropped, while the ability to move the data was going in an upward fashion. Something had to be done because the amount of data we were moving was rapidly escalating. Enter the 56-Kbps modem (V.90 standard), which operates at a 33.6-Kbps transmit rate and a 56-Kbps receive rate.

Technically, the rated speeds have not been attainable in North America. The FCC and the Canadian CRTC limit the speeds on copper communications links to no greater than 53 Kbps. The rate was selected years ago when we were still trying to drive modem communications at 9.6 Kbps. The FCC's concern was that any speeds above the 53-Kbps set would cause the wires to overheat and cause significant noise on adjacent pairs of copper wire. So, the decision was something that no one ever thought would occur. Alas, here we are with a modem that can achieve 56 Kbps and the regulators have capped it. Moreover, the asymmetrical rate of speed facilitates access to one of the most commonly used networks today—the Internet. The 56-Kbps modem works well because the user has little data to send (typing <www.tcic.com>, for example, requires little data) but lots to receive (a web page can be millions of bytes in size). Note: large downloads can take hours using a 56K-modem, so it could be said that 56K-modems do not work well. Plus, line conditioning often limits speeds to much less than 56K, which means even with a 56K-modem, it may take a while to download a web page that contains lots of graphics. So the different speeds allow for dial-up communications on a telephone company circuit (a voice channel) in one direction and a digital-access method for the return path at a much higher rate of speed.

Typically, however, when users access the network with these modems, they will transmit at between 28.8 and 33.6 Kbps upstream and receive approximately between 38 and 45 Kbps downstream. You can get a slightly better response from the 56-Kbps modem, but there are still circuit limitations, such as noisy cable, errors, and other restrictions imposed by the FCC that must be dealt with.

Here's a note that puts this all in perspective, though—in the early 1980s, we were transmitting data at between 4,800 and 7,200 bps, and the modems were expensive (hundreds to thousands of dollars at the time). We have achieved quantum leaps in technological advancements and have seen the cost drop to a few dollars. Most of the new PCs being configured and sold today have an internal modem built in as a matter of standard equipment. In the past, we had to buy the modem separately. What we can expect is faster and better, but cheaper.

V.92 Technology Overview

The newest data standard in modem technology is called V.92. **V.92** helps to narrow the gap between dial-up and broadband services by delivering an improved Internet experience to analog modem users. Organizations such as ISPs and long-distance carriers are now offering V.92 to customers. Moreover, newer PCs come equipped with the V.92 standard as a norm. People who use and support V.92 technology benefit by:

- Becoming more competitive by enabling their network to offer the latest technology to their subscribers and exceeding the service offerings of other ISPs.

- Generating more revenue and decreasing customer churn by offering subscribers tiers of services or by charging more for V.92 features such as Modem on Hold.

- Utilizing Quick Connect and V.44 compression to decrease usage costs and improve the subscriber experience.

V.92 presents key enhancements to the V.90 56K technology, including Modem on Hold, V.44, Quick Connect, and PCM Upstream. These terms are all explained in detail in the next sections. Each of these enhancements represents a push forward to a more user-friendly dial-up experience.

Modem on Hold

Modem on Hold enables end users to suspend their data connection either to initiate or to receive a voice call. If the phone conversation is completed within the allotted timeframe, the user may resume the data connection without redialing.

Under previous standards, analog modems were not compatible with the call-waiting service offered by the telephone companies. When the phone line was engaged in a data session, call waiting was either disabled (caller gets a busy signal) or the modem disconnected when interrupted by the call-waiting tone. However, V.92 modems use the call-waiting beep to trigger the on-hold feature. To receive calls while online, users must subscribe to a call-waiting service, and for initiating calls, a three-way calling service.

When a call comes through a phone line tied up by a data connection, the call-waiting beep prompts the client modem to alert the user to an incoming call. With software added to the client's PC, the alert message is displayed in a pop-up dialog box. For users who subscribe to a caller ID service, the incoming call's number is also displayed.

On dialing in, the Network Access Server (NAS) queries the RADIUS server for Modem on Hold information. That information is stored by the NAS until the end user opts to use Modem on Hold.

If the user decides to pause surfing and take the call, the client modem requests the server modem to go on hold. The two modems then negotiate and determine the maximum time allowed before the server modem terminates the connection. The client modem flashes the line and connects the user to the voice call.

If the user exceeds the allotted Modem on Hold time set by the server, the NAS disconnects from the client modem and sends a disconnect reason type to the RADIUS server. Although V.92 technology allows a maximum on-hold time of 16 minutes, due to pre-set timeouts in higher protocol stacks, the client might not be able to take full advantage of the on-hold time without causing interruption of the data application. However, Modem on Hold allows enough time for the user to decide either to drop the data connection or to communicate to the calling party about terminating the call. It also may include software to warn the user when the predetermined timeout approaches.

For users who use their primary telephone line for Internet access, Modem on Hold eliminates the risk of missing important phone calls while online. For some households, it saves the cost of buying a second phone line for Internet connections. The ability to seamlessly switch between voice and data services eliminates the time and cost of reconnecting, which also allows fuller line utilization.

V.44

V.44 may improve data compression up to 6:1 compared to the 4:1 maximum with the existing V.42 compression standard. Compression is done at layer 2 of the OSI when using the modem. Older compression techniques used a 2:1 or 4:1 compression technique. These were called **V.42 and V.42bis standards**.

Note that software modems will be able to take advantage of V.44 compression, but most serial ports limit maximum transfer rate to 115.2 Kbps. With a 48-Kbps connection and 6:1 compression, a data rate of 288 Kbpsz could be achieved.

Quick Connect

The **Quick Connect** feature of V.92 shortens the modem connection time up to 50 percent where the connection is recognized by the modem. This reduction in modem start-up time is accomplished by storing the calling-line parameters in the user's modem, which enables a faster handshake between the modem and the server. A handshake is the negotiation stage when a user dials a connection. First, the modems agree to communicate at a set speed at which they both can communicate. Then, the handshake continues between the modems where the systems will agree to the amount of data, any parity and compression being used, and so forth. On these recognized connections, V.92 may shorten the connection time from the typical 25 to 30 seconds to about 15 seconds.

8

Initial implementations have improved connect times by more than 10 percent, and future modem implementations should produce further reductions. With V.90, modems assume each call is made on a different line to a different destination. The following sequence takes place:

1. The client modem calls the server modem.

2. The two modems perform a negotiation of their settings

3. The link-layer connection, including error control and data compression, is established.

4. Point-to-point protocol (PPP) negotiation and authentication (challenge/response) take place.

With V.92, the client modem learns and remembers the line characteristics of the previous call. During call setup, the client modem probes the line to compare its characteristics with those stored in memory. If a match occurs, the negotiation of settings starts at the previously negotiated rate and bypasses the full training probe. If it does not recognize the line characteristics, a normal V.90 negotiation begins.

PCM Upstream

PCM Upstream increases the upstream data rate from the current V.34 speed (33.6 Kbps) to as high as 48 Kbps. PCM Upstream redesigns the upstream modulation process to minimize signal loss during the analog-to-digital conversion. A higher upstream data rate is accomplished by manipulating the client modem settings, so the analog signal it transmits can be reconstructed to a more precise digital signal on the CO PCM Codec. V.90 and V.92 modems only achieve rates above 33.6 Kbps when the far end of the communication is a digital connection all the way to the network. Said another way, there can be only one digital-to-analog conversion in the circuit to achieve rates higher than 33.6 Kbps.

A filter is inserted into the client analog-modem transmitter. The server modem determines the channel characteristics and designs coefficients for the client filter to use, so line impairments are mitigated.

The most obvious benefit to PCM Upstream is faster uploading of files, including ftp uploads or e-mails with large image file attachments. As an example, digital camera users who frequently upload photos for printing or sharing with family and friends can accomplish this task much more quickly.

NOTE:

Increasing the upstream rate decreases the downstream rate to a maximum 48 Kbps. By increasing the upstream bandwidth, PCM Upstream introduces more symmetry to the dial-up connection. This improves the quality of applications that require symmetric data flow, such as Voice over IP (VoIP) calls and multiplayer online gaming. For users who pay local or long-distance toll charges, faster upload speeds their sessions, which saves them money.

Chapter 8 Review

Chapter Summary

In this chapter, you learned about many of the operational characteristics of data communications.

First, you learned that data is compiled and created in devices that span terminals, PCs, ATM machines, fax, printers, and so forth. These devices are known as your DTE. To communicate the data to another location, you add another device called a modem, which is a change agent. The modulators and demodulators add or extract the data from the medium. The modems are also known as DCE.

Second, you learned you use various methods of communicating using protocols and architectures. The standards-based network architectures are called de jure standards, and proprietary standards are called de facto. The standard protocols you use for transmission include the rules for transmitting synchronously or asynchronously.

Third, you learned you must be aware of errors that will occur on the medium as you send your data. To prevent the errors from becoming problematic, you use error-checking sequences, including VRC and LRC. To improve these techniques, you can use CRC and detect as much as 99.9995 percent of all data errors.

Fourth, to get the most bang for your communications dollars, you can multiplex your data onto the channel by using multiple inputs on a single output. This provides better use on an underutilized circuit. You have the choice of using SDM, FDM, TDM, or STDM. But to improve the data even more, you may also choose to compress your data by using either bit-mapping or half-byte bit mapping. Another choice is to use run-length encoding. Compression enables you to get more data on an overutilized circuit.

Fifth, no transmission can take place unless you have selected an alphabet that works between the devices (sender and receiver). Thus, several code sets are available, including ASCII, Extended ASCII, EBCDIC, and Unicode. The ASCII code set is the most popular in use today.

Sixth, to send the data using modem protocols, you need to use one of the standard modulation techniques, such as AM, FM, Phase, or QAM. Each of these gives you different speeds and throughputs. The newer modems using V.90 and V.92 standards will deliver the 56 Kbps and other features.

Key Terms for Chapter 8

American Standard Code for Information Interchange (ASCII) *(362)*
Amplitude Modulation (AM) *(365)*
Architectures *(334)*
Asynchronous Transmission *(335)*
Bit Mapping *(354)*

Compression *(351)*
Cyclic Redundancy Check (CRC) *(341)*
Data Circuit-Terminating Equipment (DCE) *(335)*
Data Communications *(331)*
Data Terminal Equipment (DTE) *(335)*
Di-bit *(367)*
Duplex *(350)*
Extended Binary Coded Decimal Interchange Code (EBCDIC) *(364)*
Frequency-Division Multiplexing (FDM) *(359)*
Half-Byte *(354)*
Half-Duplex *(349)*
IMUX *(361)*
Kermit *(356)*
Longitudinal Redundancy Check (LRC) *(341)*
Lossless *(357)*
Lossy *(357)*
Medium *(333)*
Modem *(365)*
Modem on Hold *(370)*
Modulation *(365)*
Multiplexing *(358)*
PCM Upstream *(372)*
Protocols *(334)*
Quadrature with Amplitude Modulation (QAM) *(368)*
Quick Connect *(371)*
Receiver *(333)*
Run-Length Encoding *(355)*
Simplex *(348)*
Space-Division Multiplexing (SDM) *(358)*
Standard *(330)*
Synchronous Transmission *(335)*
Time-Division Multiplexing (TDM) *(359)*
Transmitter *(332)*
V.42 and V.42bis standards *(371)*
V.44 *(371)*
V.92 *(370)*
Vertical Redundancy Check (VRC) *(341)*

Key Term Quiz

1. In data communications, the modem is the _____.

2. The _____ is a method used to catch 99.99 percent of the errors.

3. Most telephone conversations include politeness and use a _____ transmission.

4. The use of _____ allows more efficient use of an overused transmission facility.

5. When transmitting graphics (like JPEG and MPEG files), we can use _____ compression techniques.

6. The use of _____ allows more efficient use of an underutilized circuit.

7. Digital circuits such as T1 and T3 use _____.

8. The _____ code set uses 7 bits (byte) to represent its characters.

9. _____ occurs when the data are being applied to the circuit.

10. The use of _____ allows for multiple bits per modulation event.

Multiple-Choice Quiz

1. The use of data communications is growing at what percentage per year?

   a. 5 percent

   b. 4 percent

   c. 30 percent

   d. 10 percent

   e. 25 percent

2. Voice communications amounts to approximately _____ of the revenue to the carriers?

   a. 3 percent

   b. 4 percent

   c. 30 percent

   d. 90 percent

3. List the seven steps required to start the communications process.

   1.

   2.

   3.

   4.

   5.

   6.

   7.

4. Data transmissions that involve timing are called:

   a. Transmit and receive

   b. Synchronous and asynchronous

   c. STDM

   d. Timing the data sequence

5. Data compression techniques include _____ and lossless.

   a. Asynchronous

   b. Synchronous

   c. No-loss

   d. Lossy

6. The two most common encoding schemes used today for data transmission are:

   a. Unicode and hex

   b. IBM and EBCDIC

   c. EBCDIC and Unicode

   d. ASCII and EBCDIC

7. Using the ASCII code set, you can get _____ combinations of 1's and 0's.

   a. 228

   b. 128

   c. 65,635

   d. 64

8. How many combinations will you get with the IBM code set?

   a. 65,535

   b. 16,125

   c. 128

   d. 256

[handwritten: pp 373 TDM, FDM SDM, STDM, QAM]

9. List the acronyms for the four main forms of multiplexing: _____

10. A modem is

   a. TDM Time-Division Multiplexing

   b. DTE Data Terminal Equipment

   c. DCE Data Communications Equipment *[circled]*

   d. None of these

11. How many bits does it take to create a byte?

   a. 7

   b. 8 *[circled]*

   c. 5

   d. Alphabet (codeset)-dependent

12. What is the baud rate of a 33,600 bps modem?

   a. 33,600

   b. 56,000

   c. 24,000

   d. 2,400 *[circled]*

13. FM modems typically transmit data at _____ bps.

   a. 2,400 *[circled]*

   b. 1,200

   c. 56,000

   d. 33,600

14. _____ allow more data per unit time to be transmitted on a circuit.

   a. Compression and code sets

   b. Multiplexing and demultiplexing

   c. Compression and rarefaction

   d. Compression and multiplexing *[circled]*

15. Data transmitted at speeds greater than 2,400 bps are sent _____.

   a. Asynchronously

   b. Statistically

   c. Compressed

   d. Synchronously

16. Computers, printers, and cash registers are examples of _____.

   a. Data Communications Equipment

   b. Multiplexors

   c. MUX

   d. Data Terminal Equipment

   e. Code sets

Essay Quiz

Several people in the industry have stated that dial-up communications are dead. They believe that high-speed connections through xDSL, CATV, satellite, leased lines, and other methods have made dial-up communications obsolete. Do you believe that is true? Prepare a one-paragraph response defending your answer.

Lab Projects

1. (Students may be teamed up to do this.) Using a dial-up modem, connect to another modem and send data between the two systems. This can be done at a public library if you do not have a possible connection.

2. Logging on to the Internet with either a high-speed or a dial-up connection, perform a Google or Yahoo! search on modem technologies. In particular, there are several modem tutorials and "how things work" articles that might be of interest. After reviewing one or more tutorials, search for web pages to view the various offerings from vendors. Make a list of some of the more popular models, and then compare and contrast the speeds, protocols, and compression techniques used.

Chapter 9

The Internet

LEARNING OBJECTIVES:

Once you complete this chapter, you will be able to:

Discuss the history of the Internet, describing factors that influenced its formulation and progression.

Explain the technologies that led to the development of Mosaic.

Define the HTTP protocol and the World Wide Web.

Describe the function of an ISP point of presence.

Explain what applications are shaping the Internet traffic of tomorrow.

In the twentieth century, the communications world changed forever through the birth of a revolutionary new network. Advances in computers and communications allowed a pairing of the technologies, providing a means of sharing the vast amounts of information compiled all over the world by providing it to almost anyone, with the simple click of a mouse. This network is known as the **Internet**. The Internet achieved worldwide acceptance in the late 1980s, was commercialized in 1995, and today has over a billion users.

The Internet is a social, as well as a technological, phenomenon. A huge number of people otherwise unfamiliar with data processing have either bought or leased computers, modems, cable modems or xDSL technologies, and related paraphernalia. They have been able to successfully use this resource, even though they are unfamiliar with the technologies on which it is based.

With some qualifications, the Internet ultimately may be one of the few innovations that justifies the hype associated with it. Often described as a "network of networks" or the "information superhighway," the Internet provides a path to incredible amounts of information, much of it free for the taking (free if you don't count the basic network access costs). This chapter attempts to provide you with a basic understanding of exactly what the Internet is, why you should be interested in it, its capabilities, how to acquire and use those capabilities, and its future.

A Brief History of the Internet

The history of the 1950s and 1960s invokes images of the Cold War. Today, many young people can't totally appreciate the battle between the axes of good and evil. The truth of the situation is that the U.S. government and the former Soviet Union were engaged in a strategic battle across the world. The threat of war was real, and life evolved around this struggle.

In 1957, an organization of the U.S. government called the **Defense Advanced Research Projects Agency (DARPA)** was created in response to advances in the Soviet Union's launch of a space satellite. DARPA's specific goals were to "direct and perform advance projects in the field of research, designated by individual project or category."

DARPA realized that to gain superiority in the technology arena, information from key government research laboratories and a few universities under contract to the government for various research projects needed to be shared from these geographically diverse locations. In addition to information, advances in computers also allowed raw computing power to be shared. The idea of creating a network to accomplish this goal was conceived, and the idea of the DARPAnet was born. The Department of Defense funded this idea with a $20,000 grant.

NOTE

DARPA is the central research and development agency within the Department of Defense. DARPA has had a change of its name four times in the last century. Originally named ARPA, and then changed to DARPA in 1972, it was redesignated to ARPA in 1993, and then changed to DARPA yet again in 1996. For continuity and research purposes, we call it DARPA throughout this book because this reflects the current name of the organization.

DARPA is still active in the pursuit of technological innovation on advanced research and technologies. You can view some of these initiatives by visiting the DARPA web site located at www.darpa.mil.

At approximately the same time, the U.S. Air Force was contracting researchers to make the nation's telecommunications infrastructure capable of surviving a nuclear attack. One researcher in particular, Paul Bryan from the RAND Corporation, theorized a distributed telecommunications network where information could flow to the proper destination, even if some links in the network were incapacitated or removed. This idea created what is now known as packet switching. In its simplest form, **packet switching** involves breaking up information into smaller, more manageable, pieces, and then routing them to a destination. In Chapter 7, you learned about the TCP/IP protocols that make the Internet work. Further discussion of these protocols will be given in depth in Chapter 11 of this book.

In 1965, this technology was initially tested. MIT's Lincoln Lab connected its computers with DARPA's facilities using a 1,200-bps connection. Within four years, sites in Stanford Research Institute; University of California, Santa Barbara; University of California, Los Angeles; and University of Utah were connected, forming the DARPAnet. The predecessor of the Internet as we know it today was online.

Universities

With universities receiving government grants for research, it was only logical that they were added to the DARPAnet. The researchers could now share their results with other research groups working on similar advances in technology. Over time, additional universities, companies dealing with the government (see Figure 9-1), and even some overseas institutions were added, making this an international network.

The bandwidth connecting all these institutions was continuously increased to support all kinds of communications. In reality, the Internet (as we now know it) started out as a 56-Kbps data communications network used to connect these sites together. Although this was an enabling speed, bandwidth was utilized quickly, so multiple 56-Kbps lines were used. Over the years, telecommunication technology advanced and costs came down, which made it feasible

9

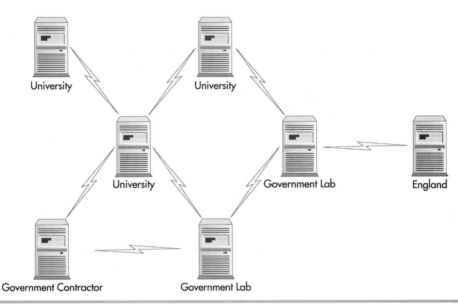

Figure 9-1 The Internet began growing as universities, contractors, and overseas locations were added.

to lease T1 lines to connect locations. Not only did this provide more bandwidth to the sites, the quality of transmission over these dedicated facilities made the communication more reliable.

With the increased speeds, demand rose from the private sector to connect to this network. To meet the need for the private sector's entry to the Internet, DARPA turned over the network to the National Science Foundation (NSF) in 1988. In 1991, the Internet was opened to commercial use and the NSF began transitioning the DARPAnet into the Internet. With more users on the network, further demand began putting stress on these T1 connections, so the NSF began converting the backbone of the network to T3 lines running at 45 Mbps. This was fine for the government network, but as the private sector gained access, it would be too slow and become unusable. Therefore, the backbone network was upgraded again to a newer, faster technology called the asynchronous transfer mode (ATM), which you learn about in Chapter 11.

Growth exploded on the Internet during the 1990s, with most users connecting to the backbone with dial-up 56K connections. The dot.com businesses began springing up, and the Internet quickly became crowded. This was to the lament of the universities and research facilities that had always been connected to a network that was designed for *them.* The academic groups began complaining to the government that their network was too slow to support their applications, and they wanted something done about it. Since the 1996 Telecom Act, the Internet was to be an unregulated environment, so the government had no authority: administration was already in the private sector. This didn't make the universities happy, so they pressured the government to do more.

Internet 2

The government had a solution to get by the congestion on the Internet, and in typical government form suggested a separate network for universities and research institutions which would be called **I2 (Internet 2)** or the **Abilene network**. This is amazing because the universities never invested in and paid for the original Internet; it was a government-sponsored project that provided them access. Why should the universities get a free private network, when they benefit most from research that turns into commercial projects? After all, most of the software and hardware that made the Internet work more efficiently came from private businesses (that usually provide their technology at a reduced price to educational institutions).

No one is quite sure, but many believe legislators did not want to oppose any legislation that would "benefit" education. In any event, the I2 was created to allow universities to have a less-congested network to run their applications faster. In 2000, work began on planning this I2 for educational facilities. As of June 2004, over 240 universities, and a partnership with 70 companies and 40 organizations (including the government), are connected. Feel free to research more about the I2 at http://www.internet2.edu.

The one advantage the I2 has is the capability to try out newer technologies, beta test them on a private network, and work out some of the initial issues without crippling the Internet. After all, who could work with the Internet crippled because of a new product rollout? The I2 is currently testing the newer version of IP (Internet Protocol IPv6).

CAUTION

Although the universities now have the I2, they still have free access to the public Internet. Their users have the ability to use both systems. In reality, academia has been given the best of both worlds by having a dual-network system to use. Again, all this is financed by the government and your tax dollars. Although the I2 claims it has newer capabilities, such as quality of service (QoS), which will be covered in the section "Protocols Needed for Successful Implementations of VoIP," QoS can be available on the public Internet (if proper bandwidth and software are employed).

Private Wide Area Networks (WANs)

Many businesses and organizations had set up their own private networks connecting their different sites even before the Internet was in widespread use. As the IP protocol became popular, carriers began deploying **private IP-enabled networks** to transmit data. These networks are not the public Internet but rather private data networks running IP protocols. Many of these networks provide access to the public Internet, but they have controlled inward access to protect the privacy of the internal network. This connection to the Internet is what allows e-mail to flow between companies and organizations. Private networks have been deployed worldwide by the large carriers and can offer guaranteed response time on their

9

networks (<60 ms is common). Private Internets will continue to grow in popularity as Voice over the Internet Protocol (VoIP) becomes more accepted.

CAUTION

"Internet" is a term that refers to the public Internet. There are also private versions of Internets called intranets and extranets. An *intranet* is a private company's web pages and databases available only to internal users, while an *extranet* provides access to a company's channel partners and, sometimes, to its customers. Intranets are often accessible both onsite and through remote connections, known as virtual private networks (VPNs), while extranets are vital in the business-to-business (B2B) supply model.

Early Internet Services

Protocols

Let's get a little technical for a moment. TCP/IP was previously defined. TCP/IP is a protocol suite, not just a single protocol. The base protocols described by the letters TCP/IP refer to the lower three or four layers of the OSI model. Application-layer protocols ride on top of TCP/IP. Among these are Telnet, File Transfer Protocol (FTP), Simple Mail Transfer Protocol (SMTP), and Simple Network Management Protocol (SNMP). After all, the Internet was created for the express purpose of swapping files (FTP) and sending e-mail back and forth (SMTP). The other incidental, yet necessary, protocols were added to make sure things worked properly.

FTP

When you use a browser to access a list of files or updates to programs on a web site, and you click on an icon or link to retrieve that file, there's a better than even chance that the file is being retrieved using **File Transfer Protocol (FTP)**. FTP is not the protocol used for routine browser operations, but the major browsers do incorporate the capability of moving files around using FTP. FTP existed long before the World Wide Web. Most operating systems come with software that enables you to use FTP directly without using a browser. However, FTP typically has a command-line interface in such an environment. If you are comfortable with the C:> prompt, then you might want to use FTP in cases where you have problems getting the browser to work properly. A few graphical user interface (GUI)-based FTP implementations are also stand-alones rather than integrated into a browser. This could be useful in cases where you are going to spend some time doing nothing but retrieving files, for example, from a vendor's support site.

SMTP

The service that was, and still is, used most on the Internet is electronic mail (e-mail). Originally, it was much less sophisticated than the capabilities used today. In fact, most implementations of that time sent only the text of a message, the address of the recipient, and a text subject string with no attachments of any kind, no separate names of the addressees (versus just their addresses), and no copy-to's. This rudimentary form of e-mail enabled strictly the exchange of ASCII text to one person at a time.

Nevertheless, this mail capability was based on the same underlying protocol used for most mail on the Internet today: the **Simple Mail Transfer Protocol (SMTP)**. Describing SMTP in terms of the OSI model, it is a layer 7 protocol. SMTP rides on top of TCP/IP, as do other protocols mentioned in the section "Protocols Needed for Successful Implementations of VoIP" (see Figure 9-2).

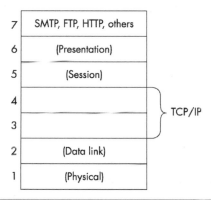

Figure 9-2 The protocols used for the application sit on top of TCP.

SMTP is pretty simple. This has caused some problems because it does not, in and of itself, incorporate ways to send attachments, particularly not binary or program-type attachments. However, a number of vendors have come together, built software, and established conventions that allow these capabilities.

Although it's among the least sophisticated mail environments in the world, SMTP mail is sort of taking over the world. Why? SMTP is built into nearly all systems that use the Internet, so it is used to allow the mail servers to connect and transfer e-mail back and forth to each other. This is the kind of mail you get when you sign up with an **Internet service provider (ISP)**.

The form of an SMTP or Internet mail address is **name@domain.name**. For example, the Internet mail address of one of the authors of this book is **bud@tcic.com**. The SMTP mail protocol was developed around an ASCII text transmission system. This poses an interesting situation when a user wants to transmit information to a colleague.

But how "standard" is this standard? Say you spend the whole day preparing a report. Great pains are taken to build a table with four columns of text. Background shading is applied in your word processor to highlight certain fields in the file. The headers on each of the columns are bolded and italicized in the word-processing formatting service. And, last, you lay this all out with reverse text for emphasis (white text on a black background for important fields, black text on white background for normal text). Eureka!

You have finally finished your document. Now you want to e-mail it to your colleague for review and discussion. A few compliments are expected for the fruits of your labor. So, you type up an e-mail message announcing your accomplishment, paste the document to the mail message, and let it fly through the Net. Soon you call your colleague and ask what he or she thinks about it. Alas, you are told it is garbage! No, the text is not garbage, but the format of the document that arrives is garbage. The formatting has all disappeared.

No longer are the table and column format intact. The bolding and shading have also disappeared. Moreover, the text is all over the place, indented where it shouldn't be, and so forth. You are crushed! What happened? After all that work, the other end thinks the document is trash. Well, let's analyze what happened.

Today, word-processing systems use an extended ASCII code set. That means an 8-bit code set is used to format the document in current packages. The Net, on the other hand, was built on a true ASCII code set (7-bit ASCII). As a result, when you transmit the document, the receiving device is looking at the 7 bits (not 8) and interpreting the information using a different language. The result is what shows up. To solve this problem, other protocols such as file attachments (MIME and binary) are used in the mail programs on the market today. Relief at last!

One of the major successes in the area of intervendor cooperation was the creation of a couple of standards for including attachments with e-mail. The preferred one of these is called **Multipurpose Internet Mail Extensions (MIME)**. A MIME attachment can include nearly anything that can be represented in digital form. Moreover, most of the more sophisticated e-mail software packages can automatically create MIME inclusions without users having to go through several steps. MIME extends the format of the Internet mail to allow non-U.S.-ASCII textual messages, nontextual messages, multipart message bodies, and non-U.S.-ASCII information in message headers.

E-Mail Protocols (POP and IMAP)

The SMTP protocol is used to send e-mail between and among different users. But the **Post Office Protocol version 3 (POP3)** is an application-layer Internet standard protocol used to store e-mail for later retrieval from a remote server to a local client over a TCP/IP connection. Nearly all individual ISP e-mail accounts are accessed via POP3. When you check for e-mail, you normally use POP3.

Earlier versions of the POP protocol (POP1 and POP2) have been made obsolete by POP3. Today, when you refer to POP, you almost always mean POP3 in the context of e-mail protocols.

POP3 and its predecessors are designed to allow end users with intermittent connections, such as dial-up connections, to retrieve e-mail when connected, and then to view and manipulate the retrieved messages without the need to stay connected. Although most clients have an option to leave the mail on the server, e-mail clients using POP3 generally connect, retrieve all messages, store them on the user's PC as new messages, delete them from the server, and then disconnect.

The newer and more capable **Internet Message Access Protocol (IMAP)** is an application-layer Internet protocol used for accessing e-mail on a remote server from a local client. IMAP e-mail retrieval protocol supports both connected and disconnected modes of operation. E-mail clients using IMAP generally leave messages on the server until the user explicitly deletes them. This and other facets of IMAP operation allow multiple clients to access the same mailbox.

Most e-mail clients can be configured to use either POP3 or IMAP to retrieve messages, but ISP support for IMAP is not as common. IMAP and POP3 are the two most common Internet standard protocols for e-mail retrieval. Both are supported by virtually all modern e-mail clients and servers, although in some cases, they are used in addition to vendor-specific, typically proprietary, interfaces.

Unique ID Listing (UIDL) is a POP3 command typically used in the implementation of a client leave mail on server option. POP3 commands identify specific messages by their ordinal numbers on the mail server. This creates a problem for a client intending to leave messages on the server because these message numbers may change from one connection to the server to another. For example, if there were five messages when last connected and message #3 is deleted by a different client, when next connecting, the last two messages' numbers decrement by one! Luckily, the POP3 RFC specifies a method of avoiding numbering issues. Basically, the server assigns an arbitrary and unique string of characters in the range 0x21 to 0x7E to the message. This ID is never reused for any message. When a POP3-compatible e-mail client connects to the server, it can use the UIDL command to get the current mapping from these message IDs to the ordinal message numbers. Using this mapping, the client can then determine which messages it has yet to download, which saves time when downloading.

Whether using POP3 or IMAP to retrieve messages, clients use the SMTP protocol to send messages. E-mail clients are sometimes referred to as either POP or IMAP clients, but, in both cases, SMTP is also used.

E-mail attachments and non-ASCII text are nearly universally conveyed in e-mail in accordance with MIME formatting rules. Neither POP3 nor SMTP requires e-mail to be MIME formatted, but because essentially all Internet e-mail is MIME formatted, POP clients by default must also understand and use MIME. IMAP is designed to assume e-mail is MIME formatted.

9

TELNET

Telnet (not Telenet) is a means to sign on to a remote system network directly as a user of that system (see Figure 9-3). This is not the same as using the World Wide Web, although it uses the same Internet connections. When you use a browser to access a web page, every time you click on a link, you send a request for a specific set of information to a specific web site. That web site, if it can, sends back just the information you requested. Generally speaking, it then completely forgets it had anything to do with you. No "conversation" takes place: Each exchange is a stand-alone transaction.

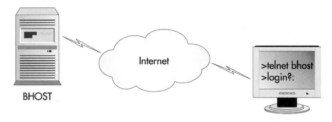

Figure 9-3 Telnet enables remote users to sign on to a system as if they were present locally.

In the case of Telnet, however, you sign on to a remote machine. To do this, you have to have an account on that machine, although some machines, notably in university environments, may let you sign on anonymously or even create your own account. So, Telnet is also a means of signing on to a mainframe: when this service is initiated, the application is executed from your PC, but it runs on the mainframe.

Usually, if you are trying to sign on to a system anonymously, you use the user ID "anonymous" and a password consisting of your complete e-mail address. The software normally does not check the latter. Rather, it's just a courtesy and a convention that you comply with to get the free service you're about to use. With the popularity of the Web, Telnet is not used as commonly today as it was in earlier years, but it is still used for accessing and configuring network devices. To use Telnet, go to the prompt on your operating system (OS) and type **Telnet** [space] and the name of the system you want to access. Or you can Telnet a specific IP address of the form nnn.nnn.nnn.nnn. FTP can also be used to access a remote system in the same way, with the same address and convention.

Moreover, using Telnet, remote execution of programs is accommodated. The program runs on the remote computer to which you connect. It offers a means of accessing mainframe applications from a PC.

SNMP

Simple Network Management Protocol (SNMP) is integral to the management of the Internet. Most users will never be involved with SNMP because it is used by people operating the Internet, rather than by end users. This protocol was an extra that was thrown in to manage the remote sessions and terminal connections. Initially, SNMP was a means of gaining access to the Internet trouble-reporting function. Mention of SNMP is made here because four initial programs (and protocols) were built into the Internet and the TCP/IP protocol suite. This is one of them.

Introduction to Mosaic and the World Wide Web

Early Internet services required a certain user familiarity with the protocols previously mentioned. This turned off many prospective users, who found the commands clumsy and difficult to execute. A "friendlier" interface was needed to gain widespread acceptance and greater participation on the Internet. With the evolution in personal computing from DOS to Windows and the Mac platform, some inventors realized if a GUI could be applied to the Internet, it would overcome these frustrations. These developments led to the development of Mosaic and the World Wide Web.

WWW

Many non-technical users were intimidated by the previously mentioned protocols. They did not feel comfortable with using SNMP or Telnet. Even FTP and SMTP were somewhat taboo for many of the non-Internet-savvy people attempting to use the Internet. Something needed to be done.

The **World Wide Web (WWW)** (or, as it's most often called, *the Web*) is a virtual structure running on top of the basic Internet itself. All the things that were there before the World Wide Web are still there, but the vast majority of Internet users are not aware of them because the Web itself is so much easier to use. Browsers (and, therefore, the Web, which consists of browsers and web sites talking back and forth) use a protocol called **Hypertext Transfer Protocol (HTTP)**. One of its key characteristics was mentioned earlier, but this bears repeating: Exchanges (or transactions) based on HTTP are "stateless." This means that unless special measures are taken, web sites do not maintain true "conversations" with users of those web sites. Instead, when a call is made to a web site using HTTP, the TCP protocol provides for a connection as long as the page is required and loaded. Then it stops until a new page is called for.

Every time you access a web site—that is, every time you get a page from a web site—the web site recognizes the request from you, responds to it, and then forgets about it. You may be

9

thinking, "But many web sites I interact with seem to keep track of what's going on from one screen to the next."

You are correct; the developers have figured out ways to do this, but those ways don't use the basic HTTP capability. They use some additional capabilities that are built into browsers. The developers of the major browsers realized this was a problem that had to be solved. What happens is this: when a web site wants to retain some contacts to an exchange, it causes the browser to create something called a cookie on the user's local disk drive, somewhere on a directory below the browser. Cookies can be line entries in a file of cookies or they can be one per file; Netscape maintains a file of cookies.

A **cookie** is just a sequence of information that the web site places on the local disk to retain some information. It may have the user's name and ID, and possibly some information that the user filled in on a form on the web site. One common use of a cookie is to retain an ID and password that is granted to the user as part of the exchange with the web site to allow the user to get into the web site in the future without having to go through an elaborate sign-on procedure. Thus, cookies can be beneficial to efficiency and user satisfaction. However, there has been a fair amount of concern that cookies can also be used to compromise the privacy of individuals. Some people do not want a web site to retain information about them, especially without telling them about it. Discussions are under way to address this concern. By the time you read this, enhancements may be made to browsers that enable them to tell the user when information from a cookie is about to be used. In practice, we don't believe users will make heavy use of this capability because it will slow down access to web site services.

The three developments that made the Web useful were browsers, hypertext, and hyperlinks. **Hypertext** was a way of encoding formatting information, including fonts, in a document while using plain ASCII characters. **Hyperlinks** were essentially addresses embedded in the hypertext web page. By selecting the hyperlink, you were taken directly to a new page.

Browsers

Browsers basically automated the searching on keyword function we had done via menus using Gopher.* Browsers today are large and complex programs. Marc Andreesen was instrumental in creating one of the first browsers, called Mosaic. *Mosaic* became the foundation of Netscape's Navigator. Netscape's success can be attributed to the fact that it followed the AOL model of giving away free the browser software. Netscape even gave away the source code to its browser on the theory that, eventually, it would result in a better product. This same philosophy made Linux such a strong operating system for PC platforms. AOL later acquired Netscape, so what goes around comes around.

---

*Gopher is a text-based ancestor of the Web; a Gopher client, like a Web browser, jumps from Gopher site (server) to site retrieving text-based information at the command of its user. Gopher was replaced with the proliferation of the Web browsers which utilize graphics, animation, and other multimedia content in addition to text information.

Browsers are also part of the client-server world. The money lies in getting the service providers to buy your suite of server software that provides the data to the browsers. This suite of software may also provide many other features and capabilities such as calendar, proxy, LDAP, and mail servers.

Hypertext

In the UNIX world (where this entire Internet started), there were only two kinds of files:

1. ASCII text-based files that were all the documentation, source code, and configuration files.

2. Binary files that were the executable program files.

Unfortunately, no one considered fancy formatting, multiple fonts, graphics, and tables. ASCII text was boring in the modern world of animated color. The question became, How can we add this capability?

Individual vendors' products, such as Word (registered trademark of Microsoft), utilize proprietary code sets in which the font and size (for example) are embedded. Other products, such as WordPerfect (registered trademark of Corel), chose to embed special tag characters, indicating the beginning and end of special font and size groups of characters. Unfortunately, with special (non-ASCII) characters embedded in the text, these were no longer text documents, but binary documents that could only be operated on by proprietary vendor-specific programs, which were not universally available or free.

How then could we keep the documents on the Internet open, free, standardized, and composed strictly of ASCII characters, so anyone could read them? How could we extend the capability without making the previous version obsolete? A major problem with a specific vendor's product was this: when the new one came out, the older versions couldn't read the newer version's formats. This was a major inconvenience, and software updates were required to fix the problem.

The solution was to go with the tag approach. Rather than using special characters as tags, we simply used a sequence of ASCII characters, which meant something specific to the browser and did not impair the ability of a dumb ASCII terminal to read them. For example the tag <title>Important Subject</title> will cause the browser to display that line as a title. For the curious, you may view the source of a web page and see all these tags. All you have to do is go to the View menu and select Source. You are then presented with all the original ASCII information. Although it's a little difficult to read because of all the tags, all the text is there, as are all the references to other web pages (HREF) and all the font and formatting information. While we are on the subject, you might try converting one of your text documents to Rich Text Format (RTF). Here, the formatting stuff is all in the beginning of the document, just another (standardized) way of sending formatting information in plain ASCII-text format.

9

If you are using an older browser, it simply can't properly display the text within the new tag, but the text is still there and you can read it. Fortunately, new versions of the browser are readily available and free for the downloading.

Hypertext then allows the standard ASCII text characters to define special formatting, which the browser can display.

Hyperlink

A *hyperlink* is the complete address to launch one specified web page from within another web page. The link visible on the browser-presented web page might say something innocuous like "more info." If you viewed the source and searched for the HREF or more info, following the <href> will be the actual path to that page. Selecting the hyperlink caused a lot of background processing. The browser took the Universal Resource Locator and fabricated a query to that location, just as though you had filled in that value manually in your browser window. It then set up a connection, downloaded the desired page, and terminated the connection.

URL

The **Uniform Resource Locator (URL)** was simply the Internet address of the web page. URLs were displayed in this form: `www.tcic.com`. This URL took you to TCIC's main web page. Selecting a hyperlink from that page took you to a **Universal Resource Identifier (URI)**, which pointed to the files in the directory tree of the host server. Each slash (/) in the name identified a directory level on the server. In some cases, where a document management system was employed to build and provide web pages, these slashes were logical divisions within the resource and had nothing to do with actual directories. Today, the trend is to use dynamically built web pages. They can be better customized (see the discussion on cookies) to the user's needs, you don't have to store thousands of different web pages, and the processors are fast enough to create them quickly.

DNS

One of the most interesting and important parts of the Internet is the **Domain Name Service (DNS)**. In short, the DNS system permits human-readable names to be quickly translated into IP addresses that are needed to route the packets across the network.

As described in the addressing section for IP (in Chapter 11), the IP address is structured by network and then by host. It is read from left-to-right by the router in trying to find the proper destination network.

The human-readable addresses are hierarchical from right-to-left. For example, take the address `Bud@TCIC.com`. First, we know it is somewhere in the .com domain. If I am `George@biguniversity.edu`, I need to find Bud's address. The university probably has no idea of what the address might be, so the local e-mail system makes a query of the unnamed "." domain. Several of these servers are around the Internet and they are updated daily by the ICANN as names are registered.

To register a domain name, you (or your ISP) must contact a registrar company and pay an annual fee. The registrar will then contact ICANN and submit your domain name request (if available) to the domain name servers. Prior to the commercialization of the Internet, Stanford Research Institute (SRI) performed this function. Proposals exist to open other domains (for example, .biz .store, and so forth) and to let other entities administer the names within that domain.

Each country has its own top-level domain and administers these domain names itself. All public entities such as cities, counties, and states are under the .us domain. Some of the country domains are .uk for United Kingdom, .cz for Czech Republic, .de for Germany, .au for Australia, and so forth.

Each domain then has its own DNS server, so when George is trying to send e-mail to Bud, his e-mail server asks the "." domain for Bud's address. The "." domain replies that it can only provide the address of the .com DNS. We then ask the .com DNS, which replies with the DNS address of TCIC. Because TCIC is under an ISP, what we get is the address of the DNS server at that ISP. Finally, we get Bud's real address. Now, this address is put into the e-mail packets and they are sent on their way. In addition, we, the users, never knew about all the fooling around that went into finding the address in the first place.

⑦ Line Check 9-1

1. What enabling mechanism allows your web browser to be directed to the proper web server through the use of a URL?

2. Who controls the Domain Name Service of this domain name registry?

JAVA

The early Internet was strictly ASCII text-based. Initially, when the Web first came into being, one created web pages by using a text editor where pages were defined in hypertext markup language (HTML). Then came the inclusion of Graphical Interchange Format (GIF) files. These were simply references in the hypertext document to a location that contained the graphic file displayed. Next, came the desire to automate or animate web pages.

Sun Microsystems invented a clever (and, to some, controversial) language called **Java**, which is a registered trademark of Sun Microsystems.

The basic problem was that to animate a page, the local machine had to execute some software. This opened the door to viruses. Sun's clever idea was to have the browser execute the program, rather than the host hardware. The good part was you were somewhat protected from malicious programs. The bad part was the browser was interpreting the Java language on the fly and this interpretation was slow. (Faster machines help a lot here.) The original idea was the browser could prevent the Java script from doing any damage (like wiping out the hard drive). Unfortunately, the more powerful we needed the Java to become, the more capability it needed on our host machine. Microsoft, naturally, has its own approach to page automation called **Active-X**. The good part is that Active-X runs as machine code. The bad part is that Active-X runs as machine code and can, therefore, contain viruses. The user is given the opportunity to download or not download the Active-X code. If you trust the source, go ahead and run it. If you are not sure, cancel the download and do without the animations.

Standards

Within the Internet, standards are created and managed on a voluntary basis. The IETF makes recommendations to the IAB for inclusion as standards. Remember, the whole Internet started as a volunteer-based network, each standards group building on what was done before. Anyone who determines a new feature is needed or a problem needs fixing creates a solution. That solution is implemented on the person or group's own network, and when ready, it can be submitted to the IETF as a Request for Comments (RFC). It is then published on the relevant newsgroups for others to try it and comment. After it has survived this torture test, it is ready for formal adoption. Because the whole Internet is voluntary, it is up to the network administrator to decide whether or not to use that RFC. Failure to implement it, however, may mean compatibility problems with other networks.

This process is practical and different from that used by the formal international standards organizations, such as the International Standards Organization (ISO) and the International Telecommunications Union (ITU). These organizations have a formal membership, a proposal submission system, and a review procedure that is designed to form a consensus.

Commercial Opportunity?

Where do you shop? Chances are that most of your shopping is done at physical storefronts or malls within a few miles of your home. Perhaps you also shop from catalogs that reach you by *snail mail* (that is, the post office).

What chance does a small vendor located thousands of miles away from you have of marketing products to you? Until the Internet became available, the vendor had little chance. That vendor could publish nice color catalogs and mail them out. Many small companies have done just that and have become large companies by doing so. A good example of this is L.L. Bean.

This is an expensive route to take, though, because the production of a good catalog is costly, and postage is expensive if you want to distribute a large number of pieces. The point here is that even the cost of trying is high.

Enter the Internet. Literally tens of millions of people either have or will have access soon, and, with minimal investment (a few thousand dollars), a vendor can in theory reach all of them. A nice potential market, wouldn't you say? Many think the answer to this question is a resounding yes! However, there are a few flies in the ointment, depending on your point of view.

Currently, you can attempt to reach potential customers via the Internet in several ways:

- Send out a large number of electronic messages (the electronic equivalent of junk mail, referred to as "spam" by those who would prefer not to receive such transmissions).

- Place advertising for products and services on others' web sites.

- Utilize software to track viewers' habits (adware) and send them targeted e-mail based on their web-browsing statistics.

- Create a web site (see the following) to describe products and services, and perhaps to take orders for those same products and services.

Web Advertising

One of the distinguishing characteristics of computers is that, if programmed correctly, they can aid in focusing transmission of commercial messages (that is, advertising) to only those people most likely to be receptive to those messages. The Internet embodies a number of ways to advertise to its users. One, just mentioned, is spam. But spam is a sledgehammer approach; by definition, it is not focused. Other, much more subtle approaches are available. One approach is using **banner ads**—colorful, sometimes animated rectangles on web pages, similar to magazine ads but with a significant difference: when clicked on, they normally change the user's current web page to one on the advertiser's web site. This is referred to as a **link**. Banner ads are usually placed (for a fee, of course) on sites with a lot of traffic, so they are the Net equivalent of putting up a poster for some kind of product or service in the window of a supermarket.

Spam

What is your definition of junk mail? Do you like to receive it? Do you often purchase products as a result of receiving it? We didn't think so. Although people who receive small amounts of postal mail might like receiving anything at all in their mailbox, most would prefer it to be a bit more person-specific than typical junk mail. **Spam** is the name of unsolicited e-mail on the Internet. Although new users of the Internet may initially be excited by messages in their electronic inboxes with titles like ****!!!!*Make big money stuffing envelopes!!!!****, after the

9

fifth, tenth, or hundredth such message, this quickly becomes tedious. The risk that something worthwhile is buried among the garbage is always present. Although the DELETE key is always there, it takes some time to filter out the spam, and time is usually in short supply.

The good news is this: with a small expenditure of money and a little applied intelligence, you can greatly reduce the amount of spam you see. Products, both for regular e-mail and for newsgroups, are available that are capable of filtering out many unwanted messages (see Figure 9-4). In addition, many of these products provide filters to sort mail by sender and subject matter, so it is easy to retrieve specific messages. For example, Qualcomm's Eudora Pro e-mail program can select e-mail and delete it before reading it on the basis of an unlimited set of user-specified character sequences, whether those sequences appear in a message's subject, in the main body of text, or as part of the sender's name.

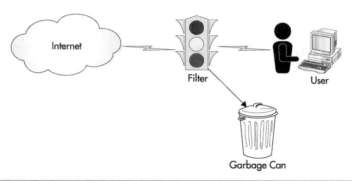

Figure 9-4 Today's e-mail products offer filters for sorting out your regular mail from unsolicited messages.

If you never want to see a message containing the word "toner" in the subject (many scam artists try to sell copier and printer toner via the Net—we have no idea why), you don't have to. Anawave's Gravity, a sophisticated newsgroup reader program, has similar filtering capabilities. On the other hand, as P. T. Barnum said, "there's a sucker born every minute," and the law of large numbers says that if you send out thousands of such messages, at least a few suckers are going to read them and respond. Because the cost of sending out spam is so much smaller than the costs associated with paper mail, it is likely that people will continue to send it out.

That isn't to say efforts haven't been made to curb spam. In 2003, the CAN-SPAM Act was passed in the U.S. In reality, the CAN-SPAM Act didn't cure SPAM because it allows businesses to bombard you with marketing, provided they offer you some way to opt out from further mailings and they don't hide behind anonymous headers and misleading subject lines. Enforcement of this bill is difficult because of the sheer volume of complaints and unwanted messages. A few cases have been prosecuted from the CAN-SPAM Act, and the providers have had financial judgments imposed against them. These providers either have ceased and desisted or have been put out of business altogether.

In 2003, 35 percent of the e-mail sent could be classified as SPAM, and because of the bill's implementation (with no punishment for businesses that provide opt-outs) the amount of spam has increased. Verisign found 80 percent of all e-mail traffic sent in 2004 was classified as SPAM.* According to the ITU, SPAM and anti-spam products cost users $25 billion in 2003.

The alarming growth of spam is mind-boggling; some expect e-mail to melt down unless spam is controlled. With over 10 billion messages being sent every day, in a year that number is expected to triple. Something needs to be done to protect inboxes everywhere and free up the valuable bandwidth on the NET today.

The U.N. has gotten involved and is trying to pass legislation from 60 countries to curb worldwide spam (7/2004).

If you regard Internet mail as a faster alternative to the post office, then spam can be considered unavoidable. At least in the case of the electronic version, methods are available to automatically handle a portion of it: no recycling is required.

Adware and Spyware

In 2002, few people understood the difference between a banner ad and adware.**

In a sense, these are two different approaches to the same thing: getting an advertising link in front of consumers. **Adware** differs from banner ads in the means by which it is presented to the user. Instead of being part of a web site, adware causes a new browser to open with an ad on it.

By 2006, if you are an Internet user, you have definitely experienced this annoying feature. Adware has been criticized because it sometimes includes other software that tracks your personal information and passes it on to third parties, without your knowledge or permission. This practice has been dubbed **spyware**, and it has prompted an outcry from computer security and privacy advocate groups.

Several commercially available products and many free software packages can remove these threats, but with the abundance of programs, some are not detected by every package. Both adware and spyware are extremely difficult to eliminate without these tools. In many cases, you can delete a program, only to find it restored the next time you power up your system.

How pervasive is spyware? In one study, the ISP Earthlink revealed that half a million spyware monitors and Trojan horses were discovered in a million and a half scans that year. Each infected computer had an average of 27 spyware programs on it.

9

---

*Source www.itfacts.biz, November 16, 2004.

Other research firms have estimated the percent of spam to be 77 percent (MX Logic), December 30, 2004.

**AdWare is also a registered trademark that belongs to AdWare Systems, Inc. AdWare Systems builds accounting and media buying systems for the advertising industry and has no connection to pop-up advertising, spyware, or other invasive forms of online advertising.

This widespread threat of information theft and privacy implications has led Congress to pursue the Cyber Trespass Act (2004). It requires "anyone who is not the owner or authorized user of a computer to provide an opt-in screen prior to transmitting or enabling any information collection program, which can collect personally identifiable information or information about web sites visited." Consumers also must be informed of the type of information the software collects or sends, or the purpose for which the information is collected or sent. The bill also requires that spyware the consumer consents to download must be easily uninstalled "without undue effort or knowledge" on the part of the computer user.

The legislation is pending approval from the Senate and approval by the president before it becomes law, but congressional forces have stepped in to prevent widespread theft and fraud from these malicious programs.

Line Check 9-2

What is the difference between a banner ad and adware?

What is the difference between adware and spyware?

Which is more detrimental to a system's performance?

Web Site

Another way you can advertise your wares on the network is to create a web site. Creating a web site is more than just a way to advertise (see Figure 9-5). A **web site** puts your corporate or personal image up close and personal in front of any web user who wants to access it. Unlike spam, however, the creation of a web site ranges from outright cheap to expensive, depending on the features involved. On a per-user basis, a web site may not be expensive compared to print advertising, but the skills, as well as the resources involved in creating a web site, are completely different.

What does it take to create a web site? Here are just some of the requirements. First, you need a computer. An ISP may provide one for you if that's the way you'd like to go. An ISP can provide either a dedicated computer—one that is going to be your own web site—or a shared (sometimes referred to as a virtual web site) computer, in which case your web pages share the computer, the disk space, and so on, of a number of other web sites. Two categories of computers, or rather operating systems (OSs), tend to be used for web sites: UNIX-type computers and Windows computers.

```
Welcome to

        Widgets Inc.


- Product Catalog

- Locations

- Technical Support

- Links to Related Sites


Comments? Email webmaster@widgetsinc.com
```

Figure 9-5 A web site provides more than advertising. It allows for online sales, product support, and a place where customers can find out further product information.

In practice, any computer that runs a UNIX variant, such as a Sun, an IBM RS 6000, or any other computer capable of running some variant of UNIX, can be used. Windows 2000/2003 computers and LINUX OS are increasingly popular because they are somewhat easier to manage. The size of the web site you can create tends to be larger with a UNIX computer, though. Now the implementation of Linux-based systems is becoming the norm because of the simplicity and the cost of the software. In addition, the movement against Microsoft—the NT platform—is now greeted with mixed results. Linux seems to be a movement all its own now. At least it seems easier to create larger sites with a UNIX/Linux computer than with a Windows-based machine.

You need much more than just a computer, however. To create a web site, you need connections to the Internet that require an ISP (discussed in the section "Using the ISP") and a way to create the pages. Markup languages have been around for quite some time. They are distinguished from What You See Is What You Get (WYSIWYG) systems because they are text. Markup languages use what are called tags. A *tag* is a word surrounded by angle brackets <tag-goes-here> that tells the system processing the markup language what to do with text that immediately precedes or follows the tag. Markup languages are particularly useful for manipulating large amounts of text in a consistent way. If you are going to use a WYSIWYG system, then everybody working on a project must have an entire series of standards defined in excruciating detail. For example, normal paragraphs have to be a certain point size, headers have to be a certain point size, and so on. All users must know how those work and set their WYSIWYG editors accordingly. With a markup language, instead of saying exact point size

9

for heading, you would say heading 1. Programs exist today that simplify the process, including Flash MX™ and Shockwave MX™, along with Dreamweaver MX™ from Macromedia.* Other programs are available from myriad vendors to do the same things.

A major additional element is here. For example, it is easy to create a basic newsletter document, but a good newsletter requires skills far beyond just the use of a word processor, no matter how sophisticated that word processor is. Page layout skills, an understanding of design elements, and, of course, an understanding of the subject matter are all required. In the case of a web page or site, a significantly larger number of factors must be taken into account. For example, there is always a temptation with modern tools to create strikingly beautiful web pages with all kinds of wonderful graphics. However, graphics of any size require a considerable amount of bandwidth or network capacity to be moved out to the people who are going to view them. Most people still access the network via dial-up lines (2003 figures indicate 75 percent). For the most part, those lines at the moment max out at 33.6 Kbps (upload). Some faster speeds are available, but it is a mistake to design a web page for popular use, and then not take into account the vast majority of people who do not have fast connections to the Web. The 56-Kbps modems discussed earlier do not produce fast enough connections for busy web sites or dense graphic images. Large files only frustrate visitors to a web site and chase them away forever. This problem is sometimes aggravated by the fact that companies typically have dedicated, higher-speed connections to the Internet and the Web. By higher speed, in this case, we mean as fast as a T1 circuit, or 1.544 million bits per second. Very large companies have T3s, or 45 million bits per second. Connect these to a local area network (LAN) in a developer's area and the people who are doing the testing on the web site will see all those lovely pictures positively snap onto their screens. Those same graphics, however, will take a long time to reach a typical dial-in user's screen. The Web is not referred to as "World Wide Wait" for nothing. Of course, now that cable modems and digital subscriber line (DSL) services are reasonably priced, users will see a ramp-up in the ability to download files and web sites much faster. Remember, however, that only 15 to 20 percent of the U.S. population (home users) is on these higher-speed connections.**

The cost of a web site varies radically. At the low end, it is possible to get an account on America Online and create a web site for no extra cost. We are talking about $20 per month or so. But for this price, the amount of storage you get is minimal—two or three megabytes—and you do all the work yourself. This may be enough to host a large amount of web pages, depending on the graphics and the format of the site. All you have is a facility.

---

*Flash, Shockwave, and Dreamweaver are registered trademarks of Macromedia Inc.

**Sources: Federal Communications Commission and Leichtman Research Group, Inc. As of the third quarter of 2004. The statistic is 15 to 20 percent, depending on whether your sample is the total population of U.S. citizens or the total number of households with Internet access.

Many other companies have gone into business to service this market differently—notably many ISPs. The real cost of setting up a web site is not the network—it's the computers themselves, which for high-capacity machines could easily cost in the tens of thousands of dollars, possibly even the low hundreds of thousands for a single high-capability server. Some of the more frequently accessed sites are hit (accessed) literally millions of times per day. You don't want to use a low-end PC to handle something like that. The second major cost is people time.

We mentioned previously that the skills aren't all that rarefied, but they are still rare. Because of that, people who know how to do a good job on a web site still command premium rates. A typical high-end web site can cost as much as $50,000 to $100,000 up front; it can easily cost several times that. Also, there are continuing maintenance costs. One of the most common phenomena seen on the Web today is that a company, possibly well funded, spends the bucks to create a web site, puts it online, and gets buried by the number of accesses coming in initially. Those accesses will taper off unless at least two things happen:

1. The web site is kept up to date. That doesn't mean just current information; it means the web site undergoes a perceptible change, whether in its content or in its layout, on a continuing basis. People won't come back frequently if, when they do come back, they don't see anything new.

2. Enough bandwidth is ensured for the site to handle the actual number of users accessing it. In this context, bandwidth is not just the network access, it's also the capability of the server. As with many other environments, everyone typically blames the network itself when access is slow. More often than not, it turns out that the slowness of the access is because of the undersizing of the server's capabilities.

Advertising, of course, is not the only reason to create a web site. Many companies, like Amazon.com, for example, have created a web site that is an entire enterprise. Of course, the site has advertising, but it also has a great deal of content regarding products or services for sale. In the most complete cases, products and services are for sale directly via the Web. Some sites only offer the ability to request information, while others give you choices to order and pay immediately while online. You have to focus on what is out there in the WAN.

Billions of people now routinely access the Web on a daily basis. However, people are, in some cases, still reluctant to put the necessary information on the network to make real purchases. Both of the major vendors of web browsers—Netscape and Microsoft—have addressed this concern by incorporating something called a **secure sockets layer (SSL)** into their browsers, as have the people who created web sites that sell products and services (see Figure 9-6). SSL has now been renamed **transport layer services (TLS)**, but it still functions the same way. TLS (and SSL in its earlier form) is pretty good because few people understand that the encryption is present.

9

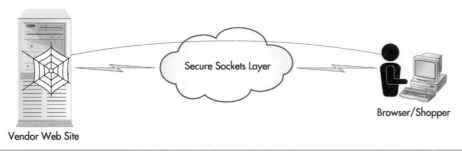

Figure 9-6 TLS (SSL) provides encryption for online sales to protect personal information during transmission.

You should be aware that the Web is almost a dynamic environment. One of the characteristics is that things change rapidly. Web pages come and go, companies appear and disappear, and the features of individual web pages, as previously mentioned, change rapidly. There are some ways to try to keep on top of this. One is to use searchers. A few services or web sites specialize in helping other users find web sites. Paradoxically, these services or searchers are free. How do they do it? They accept a great deal of advertising, and this advertising is focused in a way that occurs in no other medium. The web sites that provide searchers pay attention to what individuals search for, and, based on what those individuals request, different advertising appears along with the responses to the searches.

Major web services that provide searching are AltaVista (http://www.altavista.com), Yahoo! (http://www.yahoo.com), Google (http://www.google.com), Microsoft Network (http://www.msn.com), and Excite (http://www.excite.com). The technology used by these companies is amazing.

Enormous databases are kept current on a continuing basis via automated searchers that go out themselves and collect information from everywhere on the Net. Those databases are then indexed and used for searches for users. The searches are amazingly fast. Of course, to an individual who does not realize what's going on behind the scenes, the searches may not be so amazing. A typical search may return 100,000 results. That would be daunting, but at least in Excite's case, the results are sorted in a descending order, according to the likelihood of satisfying the request.

Getting Started with the Internet

It is reasonable to describe the Internet as a *peer-to-peer network,* which means that as long as things are set up properly, any computer on the Net can communicate directly with any other computer. What do we mean by *any computer*? Any computer in the world with a connection to the Internet and a properly configured suite of TCP/IP software can participate fully in any service for which it and its users have authorized access. Of course, in practice, performance considerations may limit what you can do with any particular computer. Essentially, by buying computer equipment costing under $1,000, ordering a dial-up telephone line (the extra line can cost as much as $30 a month), and signing up with a local ISP for about $9.95 per month, an individual or an organization can gain full access to the Internet. The ISPs and computer manufacturers have teamed together and now offer free computers (not really powerful, but they do the job) if you subscribe to the ISP for three years. Specific providers such as Microsoft Network and America Online (AOL) are the larger providers of this service.

And, it's not only for access to information. In addition to pulling information from the network, individuals can publish information to the network. To do this effectively, you must have access to a computer that is connected to the network full-time (that is, 24 hours per day). However, many network providers (ISPs and others) are more than happy to provide shared access to such full-time-connected computers for a nominal fee (as little as $10 per month, specifically for this publishing capability) or, in some cases, as part of a basic Internet access fee (see Figure 9-7).

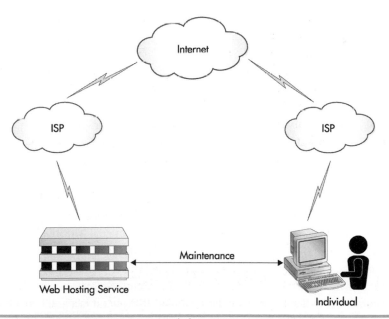

9

Figure 9-7 Web hosting using a remote Web hosting service and Internet access.

Using the ISP

Obviously, the Internet backbone is critical, but it's just a start. The vast majority of Internet users (both companies and individuals) are not part of the backbone. Moreover, the backbone providers are generally not in the business of providing end-user (or end-business) connections, other than to their own personnel and customers. Instead, a group of intermediary companies called ISPs has sprung into being. The commercialization of the Internet by the Clinton and Gore administration in the U.S. created this new ISP business. In 1992, the decision was made to commercialize the Internet as the Information Superhighway. Soon thereafter (1994–1995), the emergence of the ISPs exploded. It is your friendly local ISP that you go to get a connection to the Internet. ISPs themselves connect to the backbone directly, usually for a fee (which is recouped, month by month, from customers like you).

To gain access to the Internet, you need an Internet service provider (ISP). ISPs come in two flavors: regional and national. You might also want to consider an international category. National and international carriers tend to be well-known companies. Such organizations as AT&T, MCI, and MSN fall into this category. They have access points, or points of presence (POPs), all over the world. If you travel, it would be worth your while to check into the dial-in services for these services before choosing an ISP. This is a major factor. All have 800 number access, but it tends not to work terribly well over long distances because you are going through the dial-up network, and, as has been mentioned elsewhere, the dial-up network was not designed for data.

Regional ISPs tend to have slightly lower access charges than the international ones. This is probably because of the additional cost of those international circuits. Another possible advantage of a regional ISP is that, in the region it focuses on, it probably has more dial-in points than the national carriers. So, if one of the dial-in points (or numbers) has a problem, you can use an alternative one in your area. The national and international ISPs are gunning for your business. In most cases, they have brought their prices down close to those of the regional carriers. Moreover, they have the advantage of providing dial-in points across the country and even around the world.

Another factor in selecting an ISP is less obvious than the number of dial-in points. This factor is the ISP's connection to the backbone of the Internet itself. The number of simultaneous users an ISP can effectively handle is directly related to the speed of its connection into the Internet. We discuss high-speed circuits in Chapter 5. An ISP that has only a T1 connection to the Internet does not have enough capacity to handle significant numbers of people. This is not usually a problem with the national and international ISPs, but it is a real consideration when selecting among regional carriers, of which several are often available in any given region. Normally, you probably want to use an ISP that has at least a T3 (a big pipe) connection and perhaps several T3 connections to the Internet. This ISP connection to the Internet factor is particularly important if you are selecting an ISP on behalf of a medium to large company, as opposed to just an individual. A company with hundreds or thousands of individuals connecting to the Internet simultaneously can put a big load on an ISP. It may increase the ISP's total traffic by a double-digit percentage if it's only a regional ISP. The moral of the story: do your homework. Another consideration in selecting an ISP is the variety of connection alternatives for the user to the ISP. Obviously, dial-up will be supported, but at press time, straight dial-up only reaches speeds of 33.6 Kbps upline to the Net and as much as 53 Kbps downline from the Net.

That's a lot faster than speeds in the past, but it isn't nearly as fast as some available alternatives. Another alternative available now is xDSL (sometimes referred to simply as DSL), which represents a variety of technologies that, as a class, deliver megabit-per second speeds to homeowners. We thoroughly cover xDSL in Chapter 12. However, an ISP has to have a special connection to your local telephone company for you to access the ISP using xDSL.

As a practical matter, xDSL is still limited in availability now and for the next few years. It may not dominate the landscape if other services become generally available (like broadband or fixed wireless), but xDSL could always take off because it provides higher bandwidth than just about any other service to individual homes at a fraction of the cost of equivalent services.

Much discussion and effort (by the carriers) is now being placed on bringing fiber to the curb (FTTC) or fiber to the premises (FTTP). Here again, this is going to be a slow evolution and will have a higher per-user cost to deliver. Verizon and SBC (the largest RBOCs) are suggesting a slightly different approach because of the cost. Verizon wants to bring FTTP, and SBC is content with FTTC, connected to xDSL services to the door.

Other means of connecting to ISPs involve dedicated circuits, cable, switched 56, and even frame relay. You have to decide what you need and what you are willing to pay for, but you also have to check with the ISP to find out what it is willing to accept.

If you are selecting an ISP for a business, two ISPs may be better than one (see Figure 9-8).

Over the past couple years, several ISPs have had total failures for hours at a time. If you are going to purchase a service like this for your business users, then, as with any other service, you need to consider what happens if the provider fails. One way to handle this is to purchase service from two different ISPs. Another way is to use an ISP that can provide redundant dedicated connections to your business. Don't forget to arrange for diverse routing from your location to the ISPs as well. This may involve, for example, getting circuits to two different central offices (COs), something that the telephone companies tend to resist, but it is still a good idea if you can swing it.

Some of the other miscellaneous things to think about when selecting an ISP include factors that you might consider when selecting any vendor.

9

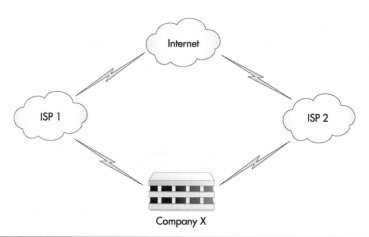

Figure 9-8 By having two ISPs, redundancy is achieved. If a problem happens in the local loop on one circuit, the other circuit is still functional.

Among these are optional services, prices for those services, what support and coaching are available for setting up the use of the ISP, and a hidden gotcha that you should know. The key question is, Will the ISP still be in business a few months from now? It doesn't take much equipment to set up an ISP, and many individuals have taken advantage of this fact. We are not recommending that you automatically discriminate against a small ISP; in fact, some of the best ones out there are small organizations. Nonetheless, you may not be comfortable dealing with a small company, if only because you may have concerns about its capability to handle growth. Again, do your homework.

The Function of the ISP's Point of Presence

As previously mentioned, the **point of presence (POP)** is an ISP's physical location with a connection to the backbone of the Internet. The backbone of the Internet spans the country and passes through three main concentration points, where it is broken down into further networks by the various carriers. These Network Access Points (NAPs) are located in New York, Chicago, and San Francisco. The Internet backbone has continually been upgraded since its inception. Originally, the backbone was T3 service, but it has been upgraded to multiple paths of OC-192 capacity.

Colocation

Computers are sensitive to environmental conditions and need certain requirements to operate optimally. When a company is running a web server or business applications, having the system up translates directly into dollars and cents. Therefore, the goal is to ensure uptime of its systems. Because over 90 percent of problems in communication happen within the local loop, having a direct connection to the Internet backbone minimizes local loop problems. Because a POP connects directly to the Internet backbone, locating equipment within the POP nearly eliminates local loop problems.

CAUTION!

POPs are located in many major cities across the United States, but not all POPs provide colocation services. Colocation is usually available at a data center. If no space is available, it is a generic POP.

Within an ISP's POPs, there is space for customers to place their web-hosting servers or an alternate place for data backup. When an ISP lets you physically locate your equipment in its POP, this is called **colocation service**. There are several benefits for utilizing colocation services, including the following:

- Physical security-locking cabinets and a secure data center
- Fully redundant power (AC and DC systems)
- Backup generators
- HVAC system to ensure proper air quality
- Controlled environment (temperature, humidity)
- Fire-threat detection and suppression systems
- Flexible bandwidth options that are easily scalable from megabit service up to gigabit services, and optical networking
- 24 × 7 × 365 on-site support and remote hands available

If a company decides to host a web server on its own physical premises, it needs to meet the previously mentioned requirements. This proves to be quite costly, and in most cases, it is financially beneficial to locate servers at a POP or data center. By sharing the redundant systems within the center with other users, it costs companies less than employing their own individual systems. Within a data center, there are cages separating customers, so physical security still exists.

9

NOTE

Colocation service has dropped in price and runs less than $1,000 a month for a class I facility. Remember, customers are responsible for providing their own equipment and content. For $1,000, customers are provided 100 Mb/s connectivity and their own rack space.

Access

Access from the POP to the customer is provided in various forms, depending on the technology utilized. Access to the backbone within the data center is provided in increments, from megabit speeds right up to the hundreds of megabits, depending on user requirements. A further advantage of being directly connected to a POP comes when a user needs more bandwidth.

In the outside world, ordering a circuit or more bandwidth often requires provisioning a new line. This provisioning process takes an average of 30 days (when it's readily available), or up to months (when new high-capacity circuits are needed). By being directly connected to the backbone, more bandwidth can be provisioned within days, as this only requires pulling a line within the POP.

Connections from the customer site to the POP vary, and these access methods are technologies covered in other chapters in this book. Access methods to the POP include ISDN, T1, T3, frame relay, ATM, GigE, SONET, and fiber optics in various increments (OC3, OC12, OC48).

The Future of the Internet

Many people are concerned that the Internet will experience spontaneous self-destruction because of its rate of growth. We mentioned earlier that change happens rapidly on the Internet. In fact, a concept called "Internet time" is in common use. It is difficult to quantify *Internet time,* but it means that things you would expect in other environments to take years take only months, or even days, on the Internet.

However, we were talking about the growth of the Internet. The two major concerns regarding the growth of the Internet are:

1. The traffic levels will grow to the point where things will bog down completely.

2. The number of nodes or computers on the network will exceed the number that can be handled by the addressing scheme.

In many respects, portions of the Internet have already run out of gas as far as performance is concerned. All the major backbone providers are adding capacity at a rapid clip. It remains to be seen whether they can keep up with demand. After all, the growth eventually has to taper off a little bit because it is unlikely that more than one computer can be used by every man, woman, and child. Once everybody has a computer, we're limited to the growth of the population. Moreover, the population has not been growing nearly as quickly as the Internet has. Of course, that point may not be reached for a while, so in the meantime, we may experience a fair amount of pain. We can't predict whether the Net will self-destruct. We suspect it will go through phases of slowing and speeding as new capacity comes online and new facilities become available on the network, bringing in new users and increasing use by existing users. Many of the manufacturers are now hyping the Optical Internet, meaning that the capacity of fiber optics will enhance the Internet for the foreseeable future.

That is, of course, if some of the ISPs buy it!

As far as the network address availability is concerned, we're happy to report that the powers that be on the Internet have defined a new standard—IPv6, which will not have any problems with the number of nodes it can address any time in the next decade. Not only that, but the designers have done a good job of stripping out unnecessary overhead to make this protocol inherently slightly faster than the existing IPv4 protocol now in use on the network. The main question is not whether IPv6 can handle the number of addresses that it will have to handle but, rather, how quickly it can be brought online. Naturally, migration issues arise because millions of people are running software that does not support IPv6 at this time. A certain amount of backward compatibility is built into the new protocol, but we suspect that the people operating the network will have to dance quickly to get from where they are now to where they want to be in a smooth fashion. IPv6 migration, from the older version IPv4, will take place within the next ten years. The exact date of this complete migration is uncertain because of the high cost of replacing every router in a network. Few organizations have implemented IPv6 at press time.

Voice over Internet Protocol (VoIP)

Lately, all the rage in the industry is the convergence of the voice and data transmission systems. This is nothing new. We have been trying to integrate voice and data for years, but a subtle difference exists with today's convergence scenarios:

- In the beginning, the convergence operation mandated that data be formatted like voice, and then it could be transmitted on the same circuitry. Circuit-switched voice and data used the age-old techniques of a network founded in voice techniques.

- Now the convergence states that voice be formatted or packetized into data, so the two can reside on the same networks and circuitry.

Circuit-switching technologies are making way for packet-switching technologies. These changes take advantage of the idle space in voice conversations, where it has been determined that during a conversation, only about 10 to 25 percent of the circuit time is utilized to carry the voice. The rest of the time, we are in idle condition by:

1. Listening to the other end

2. Thinking of a response to a question

3. Catching a quick breath between our words

In this idle capacity, the compression of voice can facilitate less circuit use and encourage the use of a packetized form of voice. Data networking is more efficient because we have been using data packeting for years through packets, frames, or cells.

The use of a packet-switching transmission system enables us to interleave voice and data packets (and video) where idle space occurs. As long as a mechanism exists to capture the information and reassemble it on the receiving end, it can use bandwidth more efficiently. This bandwidth utilization and effective-saving expectations have driven the world into a frenzy over packetizing voice and interleaving it on a data network, especially the Internet. When voice communications are packetized and routed over a packet-switched network, they are sent to their destination using the IP header as an addressing mechanism. This is called **Voice over Internet Protocol (VoIP)**.

Carriers have been told that by packetizing voice, they can get an elevenfold increase of traffic (and subsequent revenues) on the existing wires they have today. Can you imagine any carrier turning this down?

It is relatively simple for anyone to set up a computer to put voice (and even streaming video) over the Internet. This may be accomplished utilizing software like Microsoft's Net meeting, using go2call, or even using one of the many Instant messenger programs out there today. The problem exists that your packetized voice or video packet will make its best effort to get to the terminating party in a timely manner. Because of the congestion of the Internet, anyone who has used that software will tell you that it isn't the same quality as a regular voice call. Echos, delay, and unintelligible speech often result because of the inherent problems with the Internet. VoIP, however, is a better solution.

Packet data networking has matured over the same period of time that the voice technologies were maturing. The old basic voice and basic data networks have been replaced with highly reliable networks that carry voice, data, video, and multimedia transmissions. Proprietary solutions manufactured by various providers have fallen to the side, opening the industry to a more open and standards-based environment. In 1996, there was as much data traffic running on the networks as voice traffic. Admittedly, industry pundits are all still saying that 90 percent of the revenue in this industry is generated by voice applications. This may be an accounting problem because on average, 57 percent of all international calls originating in North America going to Europe and Asia are carrying fax, not voice. Yet they are considered dial-up voice-communications transmissions because of the methodology used. Moreover, the voice market is growing at approximately 3 to 4 percent per year, whereas data is growing at approximately 30 percent per year. Because data traffic is growing much faster than telephone traffic, there has been considerable interest in transporting voice over data networks (as opposed to the more traditional data over voice networks). Support for voice communications using the IP, usually just called VoIP, has become especially attractive given the low-cost, flat-rate pricing of the public Internet. In fact, toll-quality telephony over IP has become one of the important steps leading to the convergence of the voice, video, and data communications industries.

Delivering high-quality commercial products, establishing public services, and convincing users to buy into the vision are all still in their infancy. The evolution of all networks begins this way, so there is no mystique in it. IP telephony will also have to change somewhat. We will expect it to deliver interpersonal communications that end users are already accustomed to using. These added capabilities will include (but not be limited to):

- Calling line ID (CLID)

- Three-way calling

- Call transfer

- Voice mail

- Voice-to-text conversions

Users are comfortable with the services and capabilities delivered by the telephone companies on the standard dial-up telephone set using the touch-tone pad. IP telephony must match these services and ease-of-use functions to be successful.

IP telephony will not replace the circuit-switched telephone networks overnight. They will coexist for the near future. Analysts expected that in 2005, the amount of IP telephony would account for 20 percent of all voice traffic domestically, and approximately 10 to 15 percent of international traffic. This amounts to 50 billion minutes of traffic, so it is consequential.

We must be prepared for both alternatives to carrying voice in the next decade. Thus, the differences between the two opposing network strategies will be ironed out and the world may shift into a packet-switched voice network over the next decade. As of summer 2004, several local governments and many Fortune 500 companies had begun to make the migration to VoIP strategies. These migrations will be phased in over the next seven years, with more companies joining the mix.

Protocols Needed for Successful Implementations of VoIP

One of the arguments against IP-based telephony today is the lack of **quality of service (QoS)**. The manufacturers and developers are working to overcome the objections by producing transmission systems that assure a QoS for lifeline voice communications. Mission-critical applications in the corporate world will also demand the capability to have a specified grade of service available. The Computer Telephony Integrated (CTI) applications with call centers that are web-enabled and interactive voice recognition, response, and other speech-activated technologies will demand a quality of service to facilitate the use of these systems. Each will demand the grade and quality of service expected in the telephone industry.

9

Another critical application for IP telephony will be the results of quality of voice transmission. Noisy lines, delays in voice delivery, and clicking and chipping all tend to frustrate users on a voice network. Packet data networks carrying voice services today may produce the same results. Therefore, overcoming these pitfalls is essential to the success and acceptance of VoIP telephony applications. Merely installing more capacity (bandwidth) is not a solution to the problem; it is a temporary fix. Instead, developers must concentrate on delivering several solution sets to the industry, such as those shown in Table 9-1.

Strategy	Description
Integrated Services Architectures (Int-Serv)	Int-Serv includes the specifications to reserve network resources in support of a specific application. Using the RSVP protocol, the application or user can request and allocate sufficient bandwidth to support the short- or long-term connection. This is a partial solution because Int-Serv does not scale well because each networking device (routers and switches) must maintain and manage the information for each flow established across their path.
Differentiated Services (Diff-Serv)	Easier to use than Int-Serv, Diff-Serv uses a different mechanism to handle the flow across the network. Instead of trying to manage individual flows and per-flow signaling needs, Diff-Serv uses DS bits in the header to recognize the flow and the need for QoS on a particular datagram-by-datagram basis. This is more scalable than Int-Serv and does not rely solely on RSVP to control flows.
802.1p Prioritization	The IEEE standard specifies a priority scheme for the layer 2 switching in a switched LAN. When a packet leaves a subnetwork or a domain, the 802.1p priority can be mapped to Diff-Serv to satisfy the layer 2 switching.

Table 9-1 Different Approaches to QoS.

The QoS requirements for IP telephony can, therefore, be summarized as shown in Table 9-2, which considers the layered approach that vendors will be aggressively pursuing. IP telephony packets entering the network will be treated with a priority to deliver the QoS expected by the end user. The routers and switches in the network will assign a high-priority marking on each datagram carrying voice and treat these packets specially. Queues throughout the network will be established with variable treatments to prioritize voice packets over data packets.

Layer Addressed	Technique	Variable
1	Physical port	Variations of port definitions, or the prioritization of port interfaces based on application
2	IEEE 802.1p bits	Dedicated paths or ports for high-bandwidth applications, but very expensive to maintain
3	IP addressing	RSVP protocol (Int-Serv) DS bits in the IP header (Diff-Serv)

Table 9-2 QoS Requirements for IP Telephony.

Chapter 9 Review

Chapter Summary

Discuss the History of the Internet, Describing Factors That Influenced Its Formulation and Progression

- In 1957, an organization of the U.S. government called the Defense Advanced Research Projects Agency (DARPA) was created in response to advances in the Soviet Union's launch of a space satellite.

- In 1965, MIT's Lincoln Lab connected with DARPA's facilities on a 1,200-bps connection. Four years later, sites at Stanford Research Institute, UCSB, UCLA, and University of Utah went online, and the DARPAnet went online. The predecessor of the Internet as we know it today was born.

- In 1991, the Internet was opened to commercial use and the National Science Foundation began transitioning the DARPAnet into the Internet.

Explain the Development of Mosaic

- The World Wide Web (WWW) has essentially replaced all of these older search-engine capabilities.

- The three developments that made the WWW useful were browsers, hypertext, and hyperlinks.

- Hypertext was a way of encoding formatting information, including fonts, in a document while using plain ASCII characters.

- Hyperlinks were essentially addresses embedded in the hypertext web page. By selecting the hyperlink, you were taken directly to a new page.

- The early WWW often resorted to Archie, Veronica, Gopher, or WAIS to do the transfer.

- Browsers (and therefore, the Web, which consists of browsers and web sites talking back and forth) use a protocol called Hypertext Transfer Protocol (HTTP).

- Netscape's success can be attributed to the fact that it followed the AOL model of giving away the browser software free.

- Netscape even gave away the source code to its browser on the theory that thousands of heads are better that a few, and eventually this will result in a better product.

Define the HTTP Protocol and the World Wide Web

- In the UNIX world (where this entire Internet started), there were only two kinds of files: ASCII text-based files and binary files.

- Unfortunately, no one considered fancy formatting, multiple fonts, graphics, and tables. ASCII text was boring in the modern world of animated color.

- The solution was to go with the tag approach. Rather than using special characters as tags, we simply used a sequence of ASCII characters, which meant something specific to the browser and did not impair the capability of a dumb ASCII terminal to read them.

- Hypertext then allows the standard ASCII text characters to define special formatting that the browser can display.

- Initially, when the Web first came into being, one created web pages by using a text editor where pages were defined in **Hypertext Markup Language (HTML)**.

- The World Wide Web is just a virtual structure running on top of the basic Internet.

Explain How ISPs Function

- ISPs themselves connect to the backbone directly, usually for a fee (which is recouped, month by month, from customers like you).

- ISPs operate in tiers, with backbone providers being Tier 1 providers with direct backbone access, and downlevel providers buying service from a Tier 1 provider and reselling it to their downlevel customers. This is especially true of regional providers. It can be graphically displayed by performing a tracer from a local PC to a remote site and observing the names of different provider routers in the output.

- ISPs construct rooms full of routers, modems, DSUs, and so forth. They use their local telco to connect both among their own locations and to the Internet backbone itself or to other backbone providers in the case of the central organizations.

- ISPs provide access to their customers through dial-up modems or high-speed links leased through the phone company, cable provider, wireless connection, or other means.

- Other means of connecting to ISPs from a telco provider involve dedicated circuits, switched 56, and even frame relay.

Explain What Applications Are Shaping the Internet Traffic of Tomorrow

- Lately, the hype in the industry is the convergence of the voice and data transmission systems.

- Circuit-switched voice and data is using the age-old techniques of a network founded in voice techniques.

- Now the convergence states that voice will look like data and the two can reside in packetized form on the same networks and circuitry.

- The cost of data transmission has been touted as being free on the Internet, the only cost being the access fees. However, the cost of data networking has been rapidly declining on private line intranets, drawing attention from both a public and a private networking focus.

- Because data traffic is growing much faster than telephone traffic, there has been considerable interest in transporting voice over data networks (as opposed to the more traditional data over voice networks).

- Another critical application for IP telephony will be the results of quality of voice transmission.

- Support for voice communications using the Internet Protocol (IP) has become especially attractive given the low-cost, flat-rate pricing of the public Internet.

- Toll-quality telephony over IP has now become one of the important steps leading to the convergence of the voice, video, and data communications industries.

Key Terms for Chapter 9

Abilene Network *(383)*
Active-X *(394)*
Adware *(397)*
Banner Ad *(395)*
Browsers *(390)*
Colocation Service *(407)*
Cookies *(390)*
Defense Advanced Research Projects Agency (DARPA) *(380)*
Domain Name Service (DNS) *(392)*

FTP *(384)*
Hypertext Markup Language (HTML) *(414)*
Hyperlink *(390)*
Hypertext *(390)*
Hypertext Transfer Protocol (HTTP) *(389)*
Internet *(380)*
Internet 2 (I2) *(383)*
Internet Message Access Protocol (IMAP) *(387)*
ISP *(385)*
Java *(393)*
Link *(395)*
Multipurpose Internet Mail Extensions (MIME) *(386)*
Packet Switching *(381)*
Points of Presence (POPs) *(406)*
Post Office Protocol version 3 (POP3) *(386)*
Private IP-Enabled networks *(383)*
Quality of Service (QoS) *(411)*
Secure Sockets Layer (SSL) *(401)*
Simple Mail Transfer Protocol (SMTP) *(385)*
Simple Network Management Protocol (SNMP) *(389)*
Spam *(395)*
Spyware *(397)*
Telnet *(388)*
Transport Layer Services (TLS) *(401)*
Unique ID Listing (UIDL) *(387)*
Uniform Resource Locator (URL) *(392)*
Universal Resource Identifier (URI) *(392)*
Voice over Internet Protocol (VoIP) *(410)*
Web Site *(398)*
World Wide Web (WWW) *(389)*

Key Term Quiz

1. The Internet used exclusively by educational institutions for testing newer technologies and sharing applications is called ___Internet2 /Abilene___

2. If you need to transfer a large file over the Internet and you can't send it by e-mail, you could use ___FTP___.

3. The ___QoS /VoIP___ protocol is imperative for ensuring network quality with VoIP.

4. The device that converts understandable web site names into IP addresses is called ___DNS___.

5. The name for a web site is a _____, which is represented as _____.

6. The name for a company that provides access to the Internet is an _____.

7. An encoded set of information that the web server asks your browser to keep for it when you visit a web site is called a _____.

8. The government organization _D_____ is responsible for creating the Internet.

9. _____ is the term to describe unsolicited "junk mail" on the Internet.

10. A _____ is a location where an ISP connects to the Internet.

Multiple-Choice Quiz

1. What is the Internet?

   a. A government network

   b. A network of networks

   c. The geeks' network

   d. A U.S.-based network

2. Who really invented the Internet?

   a. Al Gore

   b. The U.S. government

   c. DARPA

   d. Telephone companies

3. When you use the Internet, the core protocols are TCP and IP.

   a. True

   b. False

4. The Internet was developed initially for the transfer of what types of information?

   a. Video and multimedia

   b. Voice and streaming audio

   c. E-mail and small file transfers

   d. Virtual terminal and Telnet

5. Currently, what is the most commonly used version of the Internet Protocol (IP)?

   a. IPv4

   b. IPv5

   d. IPv6

   d. IPv8

6. What does DNS stand for?

   a. Domain Network Service

   b. Domain Name Convention

   c. Domain Name Service

   d. Digital Naming Systems

7. When we refer to the Web, what are we talking about?

   a. A spider web

   b. The World Wide Web

   c. Web-based mail services

   d. Web naming

8. IP stands for:

   a. Internetwork Packets

   b. Internet Payloads

   c. Internet Protocol

   d. Interworking Protocols

9. By the year end of 2005, it is expected that the Internet will be carrying _____ of the voice traffic.

   a. 3 percent

   b. 10 percent

   c. 20 percent

   d. 50 percent

10. Which of the following protocols is preferred for transferring a large data file?

   a. MIME

   b. SMTP

    c. SIP

    d. FTP

11. How can people get access to the Internet?

    a. Through the local computer hardware stores

    b. Through the local banks

    c. From an ISO provider

    d. Through the local or regional ISP

12. If a user wants to get access at high speed, what inexpensive telco option is available today?

    a. DSL

    b. Dial-up modems

    c. B-ISDN

    d. T3

13. Normally, a home or small business user will use _____ ISPs.

    a. Three

    b. Two

    c. One

    d. Four

14. What companies are now competing with the local telco for providing access to the ISP?

    a. Long-distance dial-up

    b. Cable TV

    c. Gas and electric companies

    d. All of the above

Essay Quiz

1. Why was the Internet so frustrating to early users?

2. What is the difference between an online service provider and an ISP?

3. What is the implication of VoIP on the Internet?

Lab Projects

Lab 9.1 Making an Internet Phone Call

For this lab students will need computers equipped with an internet connection (preferably high speed access) and microphone headsets. Several inexpensive headsets are available at your local electronics store.

NOTE:

Students will have to download a softphone application from the web. For purposes of this lab we have selected X-Lite from XTEN. Several other providers can be found on the Internet. Refer to the specific instructions on their site if you use a different application from X-Lite.

First the students will have to download the X-Lite soft phone from www.xten.com and install the software. After the software is installed you should have the icon as seen below on the desktop of in the tray at the bottom of your screen.

1. Click the X-Lite Icon.

2. Click on the menu button. It is a strange icon located between the **CLEAR** button and the green phone icon

3. Double-click **System Settings.**

4. Click **SIP Proxy.**

5. Double-click **{Default}.**

6. Configure the Soft Phone as follows:

> **6.1** Choose **Yes** from the **Enabled** drop-down menu.
>
> **6.2** In the Display Name field, type your name.
>
> **6.3** In the User Name field, type the value that is associated with your PC.
>
> **6.4** Leave the Authorization User field blank.
>
> **6.5** Leave the Password field blank.
>
> **6.6** In the Domain/Realm field, follow the instructions from the Xten web site.
>
> **6.7** In the SIP Proxy field, follow the instructions from the Xten web site configuration.
>
> **6.8** Leave the Outbound Proxy field blank.
>
> **6.9** Choose **Never** from the **Use Outbound Proxy** drop-down menu.
>
> **6.10** Choose **Always** from the **Send Internal IP** drop-down menu.
>
> **6.11** Choose **Default** from the **Register** drop-down menu.

7. Click **Back** and ignore the rest of the fields.

8. Click **Advanced System Settings.**

9. Click **SIP Settings.**

> **9.1** In the Register Proxy field, type **60.**

10. Click **Back.**

11. Click **Audio Settings.**

> **11.1** In the Hold In Jitter Buffer (ms) field, type **40.**

12. Close the Menu window.

Your Soft Phone has three lines. Use any line to call any phone in the classroom, either PC or Soft Phone. Note the quality of the call.

Chapter 10

Local Area Networks (LANs)

What Is a LAN?

In the early 1980s, IBM introduced the PC, a system that was functionally a terminal device with its own intelligence that eventually had a hard disk. The disk operating system (OS) was stored on the hard disk, so the machine could operate independently. Prior to that, most devices were dumb terminals that were connected to a mainframe or midrange computer. Although other manufacturers had created their own versions of the PC (Apple, Tandy, and others), the PC was the first desktop device to use a hard disk.

A new sharing of resources was needed to allow the installation of PCs with hard disks at the user desktop. The resultant innovation was called a local area network (LAN). The first LANs were resource-sharing capabilities. Because the LAN was hard-disk sharing, it was typically set up in one department and was localized.

Later, the introduction of the laser printer led to a new problem. One specific user in the department might have a laser, while others had an older dot-matrix printer. In the early 1980s, this dot-matrix output was nothing to write (or print) home about. Therefore, everyone wanted a personal laser printer rather than a dot matrix. Clearly, management did not want to spend $5,000 for every employee to have his or her own laser printer. The LAN was the resource-sharing service, so the printer moved onto the network.

What is a LAN? Originally, the industry defined **local area networks** as data communications facilities with the following key elements:

- High speed

- Very low error rate

- Geographic boundaries

- A single cable system or medium for multiple attached devices

- A sharing of resources, such as printers, modems, files, disks, and applications

High Speed

At the time (the early 1980s), use of communications speeds above 1 Mbps on either a wide or local area basis was exceedingly rare, other than on terminals locally connected to a mainframe. Therefore, high-speed communications meant transfer rates of megabits per second.

Nevertheless, why not simply use the existing wide area network (WAN) protocols for LANs? The reason, in a word, is overhead. One major source of overhead in WAN protocols is their routing capabilities. These range from relatively simple (for example, IBM's SNA, which traditionally requires much human intervention to establish or change routes for network traffic) to extremely complex (for example, Digital's DECNet, which can generally figure out where to send something without any assistance at all). But regardless of their sophistication, they add overhead not required in a LAN. Thus, LAN protocols eliminate routing overhead by functioning as though all nodes are physically adjacent.

Most LAN technologies currently in use provide maximum communications speeds well above 1 Mbps (see Table 10-1). This table is a summary of the typical speeds available from the various approaches. AppleTalk is the only true LAN in the table that falls below 1 Mbps. It is, nonetheless, popular because of its excellent ease of configuration.

LAN Name	Typical Speeds	Current Status
AppleTalk	256 Kbps	Obsolete
AT&T StarLAN	1 Mbps	Obsolete
Arcnet	2.5 Mbps	Obsolete
Wireless LANs (original)	1–2 Mbps	Obsolete
Token Ring (original)	4 Mbps	Obsolete
Ethernet (original)	10 Mbps	Current
Wireless LANs (updated)	11 Mbps	Current
Token Ring (updated)	16 Mbps	Outdated
Fast Ethernet (updated)	100 Mbps	Current
Gig-Ethernet (updated)	1,000 Mbps	Current/emerging
Wireless LANs (updated)	54 Mbps	Current
Wireless LANs (updated)	100–500 Mbps	Future/emerging
10Gig-Ethernet (updated)	10,000 Mbps	Future/emerging

Table 10-1 A Comparison of Various Architectures and Speeds for LANs, Both Current and Future.

Very Low Error Rate

An **error rate** is the typical percentage of bits that can be corrupted on a regular basis during routine transmissions. As mentioned in the discussion of data communications, error checking ensures that such damaged bits are retransmitted, so applications never see the errors. But the data-link protocols in use for WANs must contend with much higher error rates than would normally be experienced using LAN technologies.

Wide-area analog communications typically experience one error in somewhere between 10^3 and 10^4 bits transmitted. A very low error rate is at least two orders of magnitude better than this, or one error in 10^{6-8} transmitted bits. Several technologies meet this challenge.

In a typical WAN protocol stack, error checking takes place at multiple stack levels. At each level, that error checking requires both additional bits in the transmitted frames and additional processing time at both ends. If some of that error-checking overhead can be eliminated because of fewer errors to catch, higher speeds can more easily be achieved—which, not coincidentally, is another of the prime characteristics of a LAN.

The physical elements of a LAN do not depend on the vagaries of the telephone companies' facilities. Those LAN elements are digital and are designed specifically to deliver high-speed communications with very low error rates. Thus, the higher levels of the protocols can be relied on to handle the few errors that do creep in.

Geographic Boundaries

A LAN is bounded by some geographic limitation. (Otherwise, by definition, it would not be local.) Engineering considerations and physics impose this limitation; vendors did not impose it by fiat. The technologies employed to meet the other requirements (especially the requirement for high speed at a low error rate) tend to preclude more wide-area transmission capabilities.

The geographic limitations of the various LAN technologies are expressed in different ways. There is usually a maximum distance from one node (or connected, network-addressable computer) to the next, expressed in tens or perhaps hundreds of meters. And there is usually a maximum distance from one node to any other network node.

Network technologies that only reach up to the bounds of a single *campus*, or group of colocated buildings, satisfy these specific limitations. We may also state that the LAN connects a department, a workgroup, or a division. It may connect a whole company, depending on the size and geographic dispersion of the organization. However, as you will see, a number of new technologies and connectivity options have worked together to mitigate the distance limitations significantly, which applies to LANs as they were originally defined and designed.

Single Cable System or Medium for Multiple Attached Devices

One of the less obvious but, nonetheless, essential characteristics of a LAN is that all devices on it are viewed and, to all intents and purposes, function as being adjacent. This implies that no special routing capabilities are required for communications traffic from one device to another: just put the information on the LAN, and it will reach its destination. To put this into the ISO context, no routing functions should be required for a LAN to operate. Consequently, a LAN works at layer 2 of the OSI model (data-link layer) and below.

To accomplish this feat, all the devices must reside or appear to reside (from the point of view of an attached device) on a single cable system. Thus, each end-node-to-end-node link is also functionally a point-to-point link. No routing choices need be made if every machine you can talk to is right next door. All signals from all devices propagate throughout that cable system. In reality, the LAN is a broadcast multipoint circuit on which all devices have equal access.

Different types of LANs accomplish this function in different ways. Some of those ways are covered on Ethernet and TR signaling.

NOTE

To summarize, we can say that a LAN is:

A resource-sharing capability

High speed

Low data errors

Single cable system

Geographically bounded

No common control (the system uses distributed resources)

What Do Users of LANs See When They Use the Network?

Configurations vary widely. However, when a user turns on his or her workstation, it normally runs a number of programs automatically until the user is prompted to enter identification (that is, user ID) and a password. This is called logging in. If you ask the user (with, of course, precise grammar), "Into what are you logging?" he or she will answer, "I'm logging in to the network, of course!"

Logging in to a bunch of wires? Well, not exactly. Because security and access to services are typically (although certainly not always) provided for a given user from a single file server, users often perceive and refer to that server as "the network" or "the LAN." For single-server shops, this causes no problems.

However, referring to a server as a LAN can cause quite a bit of confusion. Consider the case of having multiple servers on a single wiring facility. This is certainly a reasonable thing to do, particularly if the servers provide different types of services. Is each a LAN? Are they all, collectively, "the LAN"? If someone logs in to one of these servers from a different cable plant, on which LAN is that person?

Why Use a LAN?

For many, the answer to "Why use a LAN?" is "How could we work without them?" Nevertheless, businesses operated for centuries without LANs and automated data processing functioned successfully for more than a decade without them. What changed?

Performance

One major change was the increasing popularity of minicomputers back in the 1970s. Mainframe communications architectures had been optimized for the use of large numbers of terminals. In fact, a special category of communications hardware (front-end processors) was developed to off-load the additional work necessary to manage such terminals. Refer to the discussion of IBM SNA in Chapter 7.

If the communicated information from the terminals could be presented to the minicomputers more efficiently (that is, in groups without generating one interrupt per keystroke), the minicomputers could serve far more terminal users. A new input/output method was needed.

Wiring

Another issue, again in the minicomputer environment, was the snarl of wiring that communications was generating in computer rooms throughout the world, as well as in buildings containing those terminal users. Before LAN, almost every logical (non-wide area) connection from a terminal to a computer required a separate set of physical wires from the terminal to the computer. Even if not every terminal needed access to every computer, wiring such as this was common. Figure 10-1 shows the spider web of wires that would be required to link the various devices together. This is expensive to install, difficult to manage, and inefficient in the use of ports and facilities.

What if a network device could be used to consolidate the terminal wiring? Terminal servers (a different technology than Microsoft's Windows Terminal Services) are LAN

Terminals

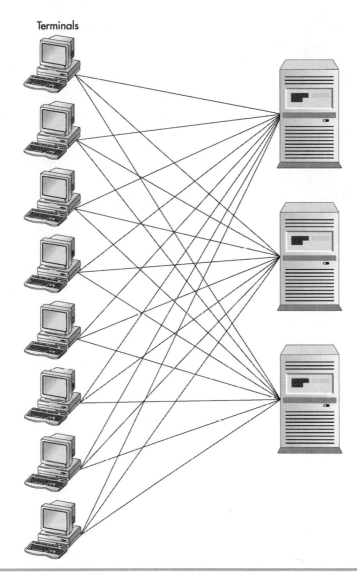

Figure 10-1 When using a direct connection to the mini or mainframe, a spider web of wires became the problem.

devices that can perform such a function, as shown in Figure 10-2. This might not look all that much better than the previous figure. Nevertheless, terminal servers can be located near the terminals, with one long cable back to the main computer system instead of one per terminal.

Not only did these terminals generate wiring snarls, but also sites with multiple minicomputers were common. Suppose you had six computers, each with a need to reach all the others on

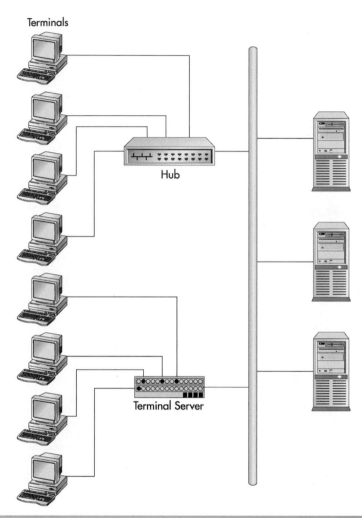

Terminals

Hub

Terminal Server

Figure 10-2 The terminal server helps the connection and wiring problem, but this can still be problematic for the overall operation.

occasion. You could easily end up with a network wiring diagram like the one shown in Figure 10-3.

Imagine what a mess this would be if there were 8, 10, or 20 computers to connect! But if you used a common cable system instead, you might get something similar to the setup depicted in Figure 10-4. Clearly, this is an improvement, but the real question is: Is it easier to manage? You bet! In addition, the number of components required and, therefore, the cost decrease geometrically.

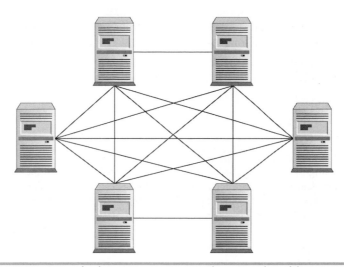

Figure 10-3   The wiring to multiple computers created an equal problem trying to connect the minicomputers together. Wiring snarls were common in that day.

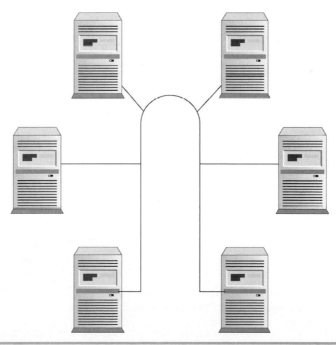

Figure 10-4   A solution to the problem eliminates the excessive wiring problem with a single cable system connecting all the minicomputers together with a high-speed link.

Initially, LANs were developed to address these problems. Other issues, such as the sharing of printers, were initially not of concern—that issue came later. Connection of terminals to the minicomputers provided access to the printers on those computers, as well as WAN communications resources on those computers.

NOTE

The wiring in a LAN is designed to reduce the snarl or spider web that we were accustomed to seeing in a building. Many organizations have joked that if they ever had to remove the mess of wires from their building, the building would collapse. The wires may be all that is holding the building together. Although this is said in jest, you do have to understand that once wires are placed in a building, rarely are they ever removed. The wires get so wrapped up and entwined with each other that it becomes physically impossible or risky to attempt the removal of individual wires.

Shared Resources

Much of this progress occurred before personal computers (PCs) were generally available. With the advent of PCs, additional requirements surfaced. A general need appeared for resource sharing where the resources were not connected to a central computer. One of the two primary-resource categories that were first shared was a printer. High-quality printers were initially quite expensive. Management was understandably reluctant to provide one laser printer for each user of a personal computer.

Printers could be connected in three general ways:

- To a central server, perhaps providing file services as well as print services

- To a user's computer, allowing others the use of that computer at the same time the user was using it

- Directly to the LAN by themselves, if the specific printer had LAN capability

The other major resource first shared was file services. *File services* provide a PC user the ability to reference files on another machine (the server) as though those files were actually located on the user's PC. Why not have them on the user's PC? There are several reasons.

- Initially, large disks were also expensive. It wasn't too long ago that a 100MB drive cost over $1,000.00, whereas today a 300GB drive is under $200.

- The larger drives were also much faster. Network managers in some cases could provide better disk input/output performance across the network.

- Users do not back up data. If information is stored centrally, then it can be backed up under management control, rather than relying on users to protect their data.

Shared data could be accessed by multiple users on a server without having to give each user his or her own copy of the files on the user's PC. The observant reader might ask at this point, "Why not just use a mainframe or minicomputer as before?" This is a good question. Perhaps the answer is that the applications becoming available on PCs were so much more functional and attractive (remember "user-friendly") than those applications users had access to on larger computers.

Distributed Systems

The term "distributed processing" predates LANs. However, LANs make it much easier to implement. What is distributed processing? It is not simply spreading functions out among multiple computers, although many people believe that is all there is to it. **Distributed processing** has a few basic premises:

- Do the work close to where the results are required (minimizing communications costs, a key objective of distributed processing).

- Dedicate processor(s) configured appropriately to their specific functions.

- Use cheaper MIPS (a raw unit of processing power that is generally less expensive when purchased in smaller units).

For robustness—the capability to continue key functions in the presence of failures—provide a certain degree of redundancy. Do not have just one processor in any given function category.

Of course, distributed processing is also designed into WANs, but allowing computers to communicate at high speeds among themselves is much easier to accomplish in a LAN environment.

Client-Server Architecture

The basic premise of **client-server** design is similar to that of distributed processing: dedicate processor(s) configured appropriately to their specific functions. But in this case, a certain amount of predefinition is applied. Specifically, it is usually assumed that, for a given application, precisely two processors will be involved: a desktop PC used by a human being (the client) and one other machine (the server). The division of labor between these two can be assigned in many ways. Many books have been written on the subject, so we don't pursue it here. However, we mention the general approach because, in most cases, a critical characteristic of client-server design is high-speed communications between clients and servers, speed that can only be easily accomplished via LAN technologies.

10

Scalability

A key benefit often provided by both distributed systems and client-server architectures is scalability. Roughly speaking, scalability is the capability to increase the power and/or number of users in an environment smoothly without major redesigns or swapping out of equipment and software. The key difference is that with smaller machines, each upgrade is less expensive, and the added capacity is readily available. With mainframes, each upgrade is a big bite, and it takes a while to exhaust the new capacity once you have it.

Scalability is more an argument in favor of many small processors, rather than specifically for LANs. However, the easiest way to connect those processors is with a LAN.

How They Work

A LAN environment includes—at a minimum—nodes and wiring. First, let's cover what makes up a node.

Node Configuration Elements

A LAN node is a computer that has a unique network address. That address consists of a sequence of letters and numbers (or, possibly, just numbers) that, just like your postal address, identifies the node. so messages sent to it can be delivered to the correct device. LAN nodes have certain basic elements. The key components of the LAN include:

- Processor (computer, possibly, but not necessarily, including keyboard and monitor, and so forth)

- Software

- LAN network interface card (NIC)

- Medium

The processor can be just about any computer currently available. The software and NIC, however, deserve more discussion.

LAN Software for LAN Nodes

Every LAN node requires a complete, functional implementation of the International Standards Organization's (ISO's) Open Systems Interconnect (OSI) model. This does not mean the specific software is the ISO standard software; rather, it simply means all the functions described in the OSI model must be addressed, one way or another. With the exception of part of layer 1 (the physical layer), all the OSI functions are accomplished in software, so it should be no surprise that most LAN software involves not one, but several, software modules that collectively allow a node to communicate.

At the bottom layer of the protocol stack (of these software modules) is certain software that is built into the NIC (in read-only memory, or ROM) as part of the physical layer. This is generally invisible to the user—or even to the installer—but it is critical. It also limits the network card to one layer 2 protocol. When installed, the onboard NIC software executes in the same "address space" or protocol family: Ethernet cards can only talk in Ethernet because the ROM software is not reprogrammable. This might be handled directly by the node's OS, or it might have to be addressed directly by the installer. In the early days of the PC, the configuration of this address space was difficult. This has improved with newer PCs and OSs.

The next layer of software is the network driver. This software is the go-between or interface between the rest of the software on the node and the NIC. It is the responsibility of the NIC manufacturers to provide such drivers with their interface cards. Providing such standard software is much more difficult than you might assume. As with all the other software on a node, the NIC interface software runs under the OS supporting that node. Computers, especially personal computers, can run many different OSs. A different driver implementing a given interface standard is required for each OS.

Above the level of the driver software is the province of Network Operating Systems (NOS). Because the driver standards insulate these environments from the hardware, these NOS can support several different types of LANs. The NOS software on a node provides two major functions:

- It provides all the communications functions specified in the OSI model above layer 2.

- It intercepts and satisfies resource requests on the node for resources that would normally appear on the node but, instead, are to be provided via the LAN (for example, file access, communications access, and so forth). This is sometimes called the *network redirector*.

These resource requests can originate directly from the keyboard (for example, a user types a file from a server disk to the screen) or from a program (for example, a word processor program retrieves a document from a remote server). Such requests are normally satisfied so transparently, the user or requesting program is completely oblivious to the fact that a LAN function occurred.

LAN Network Interface Cards (NICs)

NICs typically fit into an expansion slot on a computer. In newer machines, however, the network interface is often integrated into the computer in the factory. The latter approach usually results in a lower overall cost, but it can reduce or eliminate the opportunity to change or upgrade the network interface later.

Functions performed by a NIC include the following:

- Providing a unique LAN address for the node that is built in by the manufacturer. This is called the Medium Access Control (MAC) address.

● Performing the link-level functions with other nodes appropriate to the physical connection and protocol used on the particular LAN.

● Accepting protocol frames of information at full LAN speed, buffering (storing) them on the card until the computer is ready to process them.

● Recognizing, examining the address information of, and ignoring received protocol frames that are not addressed to the node in which the NIC is installed.

● Responding to certain management signals on the network. These might be inquiries as to the status of the card, recent communications loads imposed on it, or commands to stop communication on the network.

All NOS node software functions in parallel with other software on a node. For example, the computer does not stop doing word processing when LAN communications occur. Thus, the node can, on occasion, get quite busy, perhaps so busy that information arriving across the network might not always be dealt with promptly. However, this information (data) continues to arrive at the NIC at the rated speed of the LAN. What happens if the bits pile up in the NIC? If the buffer on the NIC fills and more bits continue to arrive, some bits will be lost ("dropped on the floor," in the vernacular). Obviously, the more buffer on the NIC, the less likely this is to happen.

The part of the NIC doing local communications might or might not be as fast as the node receiving the information. If it is not that fast, then the NIC is a communications bottleneck. If overall performance is not satisfactory, this is one possible cause.

The type of bus in the node can also have a major effect on the local NIC speed. We are not speaking here of the LAN "bus," described in the following section, but, rather, the internal architecture of the node, as in the motherboard bus speed of a PC.

❓ Line Check 10-1

What are the typical components of the LAN?

Topologies

The word "topology" is used in at least two different ways when discussing LANs. Unfortunately, speakers rarely identify which of the two meanings they are using. Even worse, they often muddle the two meanings together. We try to distinguish the two meanings by qualifying the term into physical topology and logical topology.

Physical topology constitutes the way one lays out the wires in a building. The major physical topologies include:

- Bus

- Ring

- Star

- Combinations of these (for example, tree, double ring)

Logical topology describes the way signals travel on the wires. Unfortunately, logical topologies share much the same terminology as physical topologies. Signals can travel in the following fashions:

- Bus

- Ring

- Star (or switched)

So, is there any difference between physical and logical topologies? Emphatically, yes! As you will see, most of the logical topologies can be used on most of the physical topologies.

Physical Topologies

The bus physical topology has the following key characteristics:

- All locations on the communications medium are directly electronically accessible to all other points.

- Any signal placed on a bus becomes immediately available to all other nodes on the bus, without requiring any form of retransmission.

Physical bus topologies are usually drawn as a line with nodes attached, as shown in Figure 10-5. Note that the bus is a single high-speed cable with all devices connected to it. But as you will see when we cover media, some buses do not require any wires at all.

The ring physical topology has the following key characteristics:

- Each node is connected to only two other nodes.

- Transmissions from one node to another pass via all intervening nodes in the ring.

Complete failure of a node, together with its NIC, can (in theory) cause the entire network to fail. We say "in theory" because, in practice, ring NICs are designed to fail "open"; traffic continues to pass.

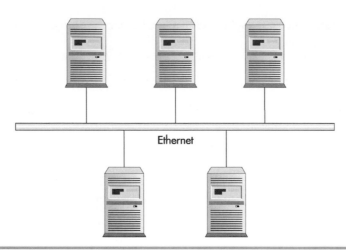

Figure 10-5 The physical bus is a single straight cable (medium) to which all nodes are attached.

Although ring topologies are composed of a number of machine-to-machine individual segments, they are typically drawn as shown in Figure 10-6. Some types of rings have additional active devices to construct the ring itself. This architecture is not a perfect circle as we think of it, but it is still a ring.

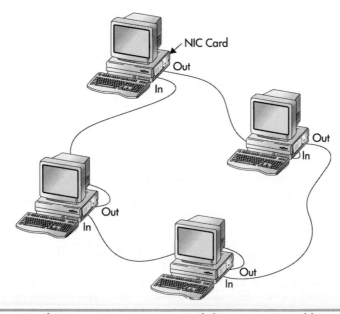

Figure 10-6 A ring topology connects upstream and downstream neighbors with a cable (medium). A node is only concerned with its next-door neighbors.

The star physical topology has the following key characteristics:

- Each node connects to a central device with its own wire or set of wires.

- The central device is responsible for ensuring that traffic for a given node reaches it.

- Data might or might not pass through multiple nodes on the way to its destination, depending on the specific capabilities of the central device.

Star topologies often are drawn something like the one shown in Figure 10-7.

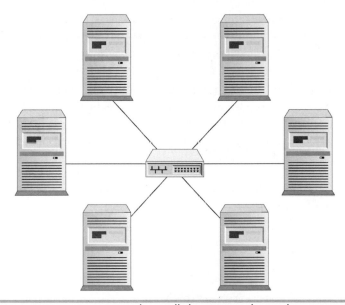

Figure 10-7 The star is a concentrator where all devices are homed into a single control box. Occasionally, star diagrams do not show it.

NOTE

What are the three most prominent physical topologies?

Logical Topologies

As mentioned earlier, logical topologies include bus, ring, and star (or switched). A logical bus operates with each transmission visible to every other node on the LAN. The easiest way to do this, of course, is with a physical bus. All devices connect to the same wire.

But consider the user of a star physical topology. If the central device instantly retransmits every frame it receives from one wire out to every other wire, how can the individual devices detect whether they are on a physical bus or physical star? Do they care? The answer to both

10

questions is a qualified no. A certain amount of engineering goes into building such devices. However, Ethernet, for example, was originally designed to function on a physical bus. Nowadays, almost all Ethernet installations consist of physical stars.

Bus topologies require a method of handling collisions—times when two or more nodes attempt to transmit at the same time or overlapping times. Different methods are used with different protocols.

A logical ring consists of a network where any given transmission passes from one device to another in a fixed sequence until it reaches its destination. This is naturally most obvious on a physical ring. However, it also can be implemented on a physical bus or a physical star. In the case of a physical bus, although all devices see all transmissions, each transmits on the common medium in a fixed sequence, sending packets only "downstream." An advantage of this tightly disciplined line protocol is there can never be a collision. All devices know their turn and follow it. On the other hand, there can be quite a wait until someone's turn arrives.

A **logical star** cannot be built on a physical ring or bus. It requires a central device to make intelligent choices as to the disposition of each frame, sending the frame only to the correct destination. Ethernet switches, a relatively recent development, operate in this fashion. Collisions cannot happen in this environment, although buffer overruns in the central device can occur if it is not quick enough to keep ahead of the frame arrival rate.

NOTE

LANs come in two different topologies: physical and logical.

Physical is how the wires are run.

Logical is how the devices communicate with each other.

Ethernet

Ethernet was the first commercial approach to using a LAN on a bus topology. Ethernet is the most commonly used LAN technology today, accounting for more than 80 percent of the installations worldwide. Although certain recently developed technologies are faster, Ethernet still enjoys continued popularity and growth for a number of reasons:

● For its speed, Ethernet is by far the least expensive networking approach. Its various standards supporting a wide variety of media are sufficiently well defined that products from multiple vendors can be mixed and matched with a reasonable expectation that they will work well together.

- Ethernet equipment exists to allow virtually any intelligent device to connect to an Ethernet.

- A variety of interfaces still exist for dumb terminal interconnection through terminal servers.

- Ethernet is fast enough for the vast majority of applications in use today, despite what we hear in the press or from the vendor community.

- The Ethernet standards continue to evolve to keep pace with other LAN techniques.

The Ethernet standard(s) define an approach to building a contention-based LAN on a bus topology. As originally defined and implemented by Xerox, Intel, and Digital Equipment Corporation (the DIX design), the bus appears to be a single straight-cable system to all connected devices. The cable is available to multiple users at the same time, even though only one user at a time can send data if a shared bus is installed.

NOTE

The Institute of Electrical and Electronic Engineers (IEEE) is responsible for the standards setting and administration for LANs. The committees associated with setting these standards are called the 802 committees. Technically, the LAN protocol implemented most widely and still referred to as Ethernet is defined in the 802.3 standard, and it is not precisely the same as either of the two "Ethernet" standards (I or II) defined by the Xerox-Intel-DEC triumvirate.

Concepts

Every LAN using a bus (that is, a shared medium) design must incorporate a contention management or arbitration mechanism that results in only one signal being present at a time. No matter how many devices share the medium, they have to wait their turn. Otherwise, signals on the cable would conflict. Ethernet uses a contention-management approach called carrier sense, multiple access with collision detection (CSMA/CD) to ensure that devices "speak" politely, one at a time. **CSMA/CD** is designed to provide equal use of the network for all attached devices. CSMA/CD breaks down into three meaningful two-word terms:

Carrier Sense—All stations listen to the cable continuously. Many non-Ethernet signaling approaches send a single unvarying signal (a carrier) and impose variations on it, based on the desired information to be transmitted, whether data, voice, or music. Ethernet is different in that nodes do not send out any signal unless they have something to say. Therefore, when stations monitor the cable, they are listening for the presence of a carrier signal, whether modulated or not. If a device that wants to transmit detects a carrier on the cable, then it knows that another device either is preparing to send, is sending, or has just finished sending information onto the cable. In any case, the waiting device will hold back until the carrier signal vanishes.

Multiple Access—If no one is using the cable, any of the network devices attached to the Ethernet can transmit data onto the network at will. No central control exists, and there is no need for one. Networks degrade (or experience reduced performance) in different ways, depending on their design. One factor that does not in and of itself degrade an Ethernet is the attachment of literally hundreds of devices (the theoretical limit of the number of addressable stations on the network is 1,024). Because the wire is truly idle, unless a device is transmitting, only active devices impose any load on the network. Thus, a myriad of devices can be connected, so long as most of them are not transmitting at any one time.

NOTE

If all those attached devices need to transmit lots of data, great congestion will ensue. However, that might be acceptable for some networks—not the congestion, but the threat of it.

Collision Detection—In the event that two devices attempt to transmit at the same time or even during overlapping time intervals, a collision will occur.

On an Ethernet, if a collision occurs, the data is lost and each system must retransmit. To retransmit immediately, however, will only cause exactly the same result—a new collision. The first device that detects the problem will stop the regular transmission and send out a special jamming signal, which tells all attached devices that a collision occurred. Every device will hear the jam signal because all devices continue to listen to the network, even if they are transmitting.

Any device that was attempting to transmit at the time the jam signal arrives will assume a collision occurred. It will, therefore, calculate and wait a semirandom amount of time. What is semirandom? Each device uses a preprogrammed back-off algorithm to wait a certain period of time before retransmitting. So, the individual devices will wait different amounts of time. The calculation (algorithm) is an attempt to generate a random number, but the (guaranteed unique) address of each device is a part of the calculation. Thus, the amount of time waited in such circumstances will always be different for each involved device, ensuring the next attempt by the device that waits the shortest time will succeed. Well, almost.

The problem is this: the only devices that apply the waiting algorithm are those that experienced the collision. Any other device that has occasion to transmit will only follow the standard Ethernet approach (listen and then transmit). If a new participant "decides" it is time to transmit, it could do so just as the "fastest waiter" in the previous group finishes its wait and goes ahead with its second try. If this happens, another collision will occur.

You might well ask, "How does anything ever make it through an Ethernet?" Remember, unless devices attempt to transmit at almost exactly the same time, collisions will not happen. The second device waits its turn and then transmits.

Nonetheless, if you understand how the collision detection and avoidance mechanism works, it should be no surprise that as the number of communicating devices attached to an Ethernet increases, the number of collisions also increases. In practice, close management is indicated when steady traffic on an Ethernet exceeds about 30 to 40 percent of the capacity of the network because of the ever-rising possibility of collisions. Also, because of the "listen, wait, transmit" nature of Ethernet, combined with an inevitable percentage of collisions and back offs, users on it will yield an effective throughput of approximately 3.3 to 4 Mbps, based on a standard 10-Mbps Ethernet.

Half-Duplex

If you have ever seen a fast typist using a terminal connected to a minicomputer via Ethernet, you might have concluded that Ethernet is a full-duplex protocol. However, Ethernet is a half-duplex protocol. Ethernet is so fast, though, that it is functionally full-duplex. Although no more than one frame can occupy the wire at a time—and in the case of a typist, it is possible that each 64-byte frame might literally include only 1 byte of data in each direction—the frames are moved back and forth so quickly, it looks to a human being as if the typing and the receiving of characters are simultaneous.

If two files were copied, one from node A to node B and the other from node B to node A, at exactly the same time, the flow of frames in both directions would so intermingle that, again, it would appear that the transmission was going in both ways simultaneously. Nevertheless, because at any one instant only one frame can occupy the wire at a time, the medium is only half-duplex, and the file copies would be faster with Ethernet operating in full-duplex mode than in the "native" half-duplex mode because both machines could be sending and receiving simultaneously through different virtual circuits.

Newer Ethernet standards have been developed to allow a full-duplex operation. This is done through the use of a switch, whereas if a straight bus is used in a traditional Ethernet, then it will operate at half-duplex. Figure 10-8 shows this comparison.

Bandwidth

Ethernet was created in the beginning to operate at 10 Mbps. An advantage exists to making all implementations run at the same speed: no significant speed matching is required when connecting multiple Ethernet segments, even those built using different media.

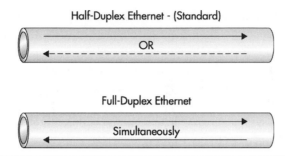

Figure 10-8 The Ethernet protocols allow for either half-duplex or full-duplex services today.

As with all protocols, not all of the bandwidth on Ethernet is available for carrying application-related data. Some bits are required for overhead functions. Ethernet supports a variable-length frame: the minimum frame length is 64 bytes; the maximum frame size is 1,518 bytes. A **frame** is a layer 2 format using what is called the MAC frame. This is a protocol that sets the data into specific functions and fields. The variation results from changing the amount of data transmitted. In the Ethernet (802.3) protocol, 18 bytes in each frame are dedicated to overhead, as shown in Table 10-2.

Function	Bytes	Description
Destination address	6	Ethernet address of the node to which the frame is addressed.
Source address	6	Ethernet address of the sending node
Length/Type	2	This field indicates the number of MAC-client data bytes that are contained in the data field of the frame.
		If the Length/Type field value is greater than 1,536, the frame is an optional type frame, and the Length/Type field value identifies the particular type of frame being sent or received. Indicates the layer 3 protocol that delivered the data to Ethernet at the sending station.
Data	46–1,500	The "payload"—the actual data being transmitted.
CRC	4	Cyclic redundancy error detection bytes

Table 10-2 The Format of the Information Contained in an Ethernet Frame.

Destination Address

Both the destination and the source addresses are 6-byte fields, usually represented in hexadecimal format, for example, 08-00-46-CE-88-05. Ethernet interfaces (NIC cards) on a LAN receive and process all frames transmitted on the LAN. The main job of the receiving interface is to compare the destination address in each received packet with its own address. If the addresses match, the frame is delivered to higher protocol layers at the node (computer) for further processing and eventual handoff to an application. If the addresses do not match, the frame is discarded.

Source Address

As previously mentioned, every Ethernet node contains an interface device; today these are mostly built in or installed at the factory, and other times they are provided as part of an add-on printed circuit board that implements the interface. Every single one of those devices worldwide contains (or should contain) a unique 48-bit Ethernet address, usually stored in programmable read-only memory (PROM). Every company that wants to manufacture such Ethernet devices applies to the IEEE (in the past, Xerox performed this function) for a unique 3-byte code. As the company manufactures the interfaces, it "burns in" its 3-byte code into the first 3 bytes of the 6-byte address of that device. The other 3 bytes of the address are normally assigned sequentially, 1 byte per device, but they can be assigned in whatever way the manufacturer wants. The only requirement is that every device have a different 6-byte address. If properly followed, this system guarantees that every manufactured Ethernet device will have its own unique 6-byte physical address.

Type (or Length)

The Type field in Ethernet was originally designated the Length field. This field was recast as the Type field in the standardization transition from proprietary Ethernet to standardized 802.3. The function of the Type field is to carry a record of which layer 3 protocol (IP, IPX, Appletalk, and so forth) delivered the packet to the Ethernet layer 2.

This was especially important when networks used multiple layer 3 protocols. Each layer 3 protocol would have its own definition of valid and invalid packets, Without some knowledge of which protocol originated this packet, Ethernet would have to deliver its payload to all layer 3 protocols operating on the receiving machine (even if the protocol was not operating on the sending machine). To better control this process and the resultant errors it created (every time you send to three layer 3 protocols, the packet will be a mismatch and an error at two of the three protocols), a protocol called Logical Link Control (802.2, LLC) uses the Type field to ensure delivery only to the correct layer 3 protocol.

That is not to say, however, that the original idea of recording length was without merit. Valid lengths for Ethernet frames are from 64 to 1,518 bytes inclusive. The length field in the frame indicates only the number of payload bytes, and that value can range from 46 to 1,500 bytes inclusive. Notice that a frame cannot contain fewer than 46 bytes of data. What happens if the sending device provides fewer bytes to be transmitted? The controller will add pad bytes to bring the overall frame size up to the minimum length of 64 bytes. The undersized frames are called runts. If a runt gets onto the cable, the interface cards will accept the frame and determine that it is too short, thus discarding it immediately.

Why is there a minimum length? An interaction occurs between minimum frame length and the ability to detect collisions. Each medium supported by the Ethernet standard has a defined maximum length for any one segment. One factor that goes into determining that length is the need to ensure that a device transmitting a frame onto the segment will still be listening if a collision occurs—and it will recognize that the collision happened to its own transmitted frame. Devices stop listening for their own collisions a short time after they finish transmitting. Therefore, once a device begins transmitting, it must continue to do so long enough for the most distant device to receive at least the beginning of the frame, plus the time required to receive a jam signal from that distant device if such an event occurs.

If the minimum frame size were smaller, then the defined maximum segment sizes would also have to be shorter. To allow longer-than-specified segment lengths, the minimum frame size would have to be increased, requiring additional pad characters and reducing the efficiency of the Ethernet protocol. The 64-byte minimum cannot be claimed to be "ideal." Instead, it is an engineering judgment call by the original designers of the Ethernet protocol. If installers adhere to the rules regarding segment lengths, no undetected collisions can occur.

Data

Data is the frame's payload, the reason the frame is being transmitted in the first place. The data can be up to 1,500 bytes, although it does not have to be arranged in 8-bit octets (bytes); it can be any pattern of up to 12,000 bits (that is, 8 * 1,500). In most cases, the actual number of application-related bytes carried will be smaller than this, because some of the 1,500 bytes will be used by higher-level protocols for their overhead bytes. Sometimes many more bytes are used per frame than are required by Ethernet itself. The average-size Ethernet frame is judged as between 300 and 350 bytes. If a frame exceeds the maximum length of 1,518 bytes (1,500 payload and 18 overhead), the frame is considered a giant. Giants will also be discarded by the receiving interfaces.

CRC

The cyclic redundancy check (CRC) digits allow the receiving node's Ethernet interface to determine whether or not a frame was received intact. If not, the frame is discarded. If the interface is one of the more expensive available, it might also keep track of the number of frames discarded to facilitate management and detection of network faults. Error checking was covered earlier in this book.

10BASE5

This discussion of Ethernet makes multiple references throughout **10BASE5**, **10BASE2**, **10BASE-T**, and 10BASE-products to a three-segment, two-repeater rule. Generally, in 10BASE-x products this is taught as the *5-4-3 rule*, with no more then five segments joined by four active repeaters, with stations restricted to three of the five segments. This is a good time to explain the naming standard used for the various Ethernet substandards. Bearing in mind that these were defined by committees, here goes. Each term is made up of three parts: the first part (here, 10) indicates the network runs at 10 Mbps. The second part (BASE) indicates the network is a baseband network. **Baseband** means the data is not modulated (which, in practice, is what permits only one conversation on the medium at a time). The last part (in this case, 5) indicates some physical component of the cabling system. In the case of 10BASE5, it indicates one segment can reach up to 500 meters (1,640 feet) in length.

Ethernet was originally defined to operate over a particularly heavy type of coaxial cable, one thicker than most individuals' thumbs. People in the industry often referred to it as orange hose—an apt name because of its usual color. A more conventional term for the 10BASE5 medium is ThickNet, a truncation of thick-wire Ethernet.

ThickNet is the only Ethernet medium that must be configured as a physical bus. Each device that is attached to the cable uses a separate transceiver device. Initially, these devices were tapped into the cable, so a good copper-to-copper connection (electrical) is made. As previously mentioned, thick wire can be configured in segments up to 500 meters long. Up to three segments can be connected in series using two Ethernet repeaters. If more segments are so connected, the (small) delays unavoidably introduced by the repeaters might foul up the collision detection part of the protocol.

Up to 100 direct physical attachments can be made to one segment, although there are ways to attach far more network devices than that. Up to 1,024 network addresses can reside on a segment or set of segments connected by repeaters. As with the other rules, violators of this configuration rule might be punished by undetected collisions.

Barrel connectors are small, passive devices used to connect two pieces of coaxial cable to make a longer one. Barrel connectors are not defined parts of the Ethernet standard. They can be used, but the rules for segment lengths simply apply to the aggregate length built up of smaller wire pieces; that is, a 500-meter length can include one or more barrel connectors, but it still is limited to 500 meters.

Terminators are also small, passive devices. But, unlike barrel connectors, terminators are defined Ethernet components and are essential to proper operation of a 10BASE5 Ethernet. Every 10BASE5 segment must have precisely two terminators installed, one on either end. One and only one of those terminators must be properly grounded. We used to tell students this was required to ensure that the bits do not "fall out of the wire." But in a matter of speaking, terminators are intended to ensure that the bits do "fall out of the wire." Improperly terminated coaxial cable ends can reflect transmissions back onto the wire, interfering with themselves and/or later transmissions and generating unnecessary collisions. Examples of the terminator are shown in Figure 10-9.

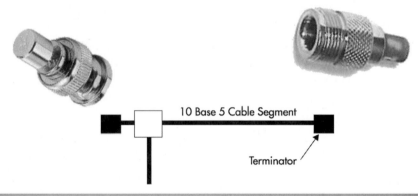

Figure 10-9 Terminators are used at the ends of the cable to absorb the energy from the wire. If a terminator were not present, the cable system would not work properly.

10BASE2

10BASE5 wiring is extremely difficult to work with and costly on a per-foot basis. With improving technology, companies determined that by applying some engineering smarts, they could design a new Ethernet standard (still 802.3) for use on a much lighter, flexible, and less-expensive type of coaxial cable. 10BASE2, also often referred to as thin wire (also ThinNet), is specified to run on RG-58A coaxial cable. However, there are quite a number of differences between the configurations of 10BASE5 and 10BASE2.

NOTE

RG-58A cable is almost identical to cable that you probably have running into your home for cable television. Please do not use TV cable for a network because you may cause damage to the network components or your computers.

The minimum distance between connectors is 0.5 meter (1.6 feet). One 10BASE2 segment can be up to 185 meters (607 feet) long, much shorter than a 10BASE5 segment.

As with 10BASE5, every segment must end with a terminator, in this case, one designed for 10BASE2. As you can see in the next section, there are differences in how the coax is terminated and in how it is laid out when compared with 10BASE5. The 10BASE2 cabling uses a T-connector to link various devices together. This is shown in Figure 10-10.

Figure 10-10 When using a 10BASE2 cable, the T-connector provides the pass-through and termination as necessary. The distances are limited to 185 meters.

10BASE-T

10BASE-T defines a standard for running Ethernet over unshielded twisted-pair (UTP) wiring. The prospect of using existing, in-place (but unused) telephone wiring provided much of the impetus for the development of this standard. Many organizations had already been using some of the existing wiring in their buildings after the breakup of the Bell System in 1984. What happened was that Bell came along and told users that the in-house (station) wiring was theirs. Bell would no longer be in the in-house wiring business and would not maintain the wires as it had in the past. Realizing that the number of wires in the building just for the telephone systems was extraordinary, and that installing new wiring was expensive, many organizations saw the opportunity to use the existing spare telephone wires to run their higher-speed LAN connections. However, in practice, little of the wiring that was in place (when the standard came out) could meet Ethernet performance requirements. Even if these wires could meet the standards, the vendors required they be certified. This meant the vendor would send in a team of wiring experts who would test and certify each cable run. Reality revealed that it was more expensive to certify the existing wiring than to install all new wires. This proved to be a catch-22 for the end user.

Nonetheless, the much lower wiring cost of 10BASE-T (primarily because of the lower cost of telephone wiring as opposed to coaxial cable), as well as the availability of people who know how to work with UTP wiring, has made this cabling approach extremely popular. New installations today use 10BASE-T for horizontal (that is, to the desktop) wiring.

10BASE-T PIECE PARTS

10BASE-T NICs are functionally similar to 10BASE2 NICs. That is, there is no separate transceiver as is required with 10BASE5 architecture. The connections are quite different, however. Ethernet UTP wire is terminated at each end with an eight-pin modular RJ-45 jack (only four pins are used). The modular jack plugs directly into the NIC; no T-connector is required. Each cable supports only one Ethernet node, as with the pure star ThinNet approach. See Figure 10-11 for a representation of the 10BASE-T environment. At least category 3 wire must be used. Its length must not exceed 100 meters (328 feet).

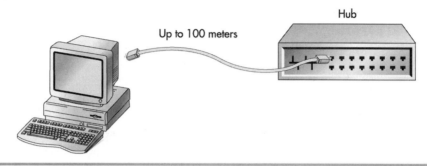

Figure 10-11 A 10BASE-T arrangement uses standard telephone wires and an RJ-45 jack. In this case, the hub is a concentrator where all wires hub back to a closet location. This LAN has a physical star and a logical bus in it.

A 10BASE-T hub is usually required. This is another version of the LAN in a box. The box or hub is the backbone network, whereas the horizontal run to the desktop is the drop. The only exception is if only two devices are to be connected: two 10BASE-T devices can be linked via a crossover 10BASE-T cable. A crossover cable flips the pairs from the sending end to the receiving end. 10BASE-T hubs are functionally identical to multiport repeaters, although some vendors provide sufficiently fast central hubs that the two-repeater rule can be slightly relaxed.

10BASE-T hubs come in two broad categories:

- Work group hubs, sometimes referred to as *stackable hubs*
- Backplane chassis, sometimes referred to as *concentrators*

Work group hubs are relatively inexpensive (some for less than $50) devices that typically support 12 or 16 connections. If they incorporate Simple Network Management Protocol (SNMP) management agents, the cost increases by several hundred dollars. Work group hubs, by definition, have few options in their configurations. Nevertheless, their low cost and simple environmental requirements (they can be mounted in a rack or simply placed on a table or on the floor) make them extremely popular.

Chassis-based concentrators offer great modular flexibility. Such devices consist of a power supply, some control logic, and several slots into which interface boards can be inserted.

Each interface board can support several 10BASE-T cables, often 12 to 24. Depending on the manufacturer, other boards might be available to support different types of networks out of the same chassis.

10BASE-F (Fiber)

Newer uses of various cabling systems have always been explored. The fiber-optic medium has caught everyone's attention because of the declining costs of the glass and the electrical characteristics (that is, the freedom from electrical and radio frequency interference and the isolation from electrical components being nonissues) of the fiber. When users discovered the fiber could be used inexpensively in the backbone network, they were thrilled. They could use a high-speed medium that was impervious to the electrical, mechanical, and radio frequency interference. This high-speed medium also had greater run-length standards, so the network could be stretched to areas that were previously unavailable. Furthermore, none of the grounding and bonding issues that come with copper cable were issues on the fiber network. When the Ethernet standard ramped up to higher speeds (100-Mbps Ethernet, for example), the fiber would support these higher speeds with ease. Thus, the backbone saw more implementations with the **10BASE-F** installed.

The 10-Mbps standard was still used in the backbone network, but UTP wiring was still the least expensive proposition for wiring to the desktop. Therefore, a medium changer is required. In the closets where the LAN will run from floor to floor, or from closet to closet, fiber is used. At the hub, ports exist for the connection from hub-to-hub via the fiber backbone. Inside the hub, the electronics are present to convert the fiber backbone to a copper station drop or, in more precise terms, from the light to the electrical pulses needed for the copper. A typical configuration of the 10BASE-F environment is shown in Figure 10-12. This could be extended to the desktop, but, as already stated, the cost of putting fiber cards acting as transceivers in a PC or workstation is too steep for the average user. Therefore, this is done in a mixed environment.

10Broad36

Some networks have been built based on a broadband coaxial cable in the backbone. This might be more prevalent in a campus area (such as a college, a corporate park, or a hospital) where multiple buildings are interlinked. The use of the broadband cable was an expedient to support the needs of the organization's voice, data, and video needs because all of these components were analog transmissions that were connected between buildings. Therefore, the broadband backbone cable (such as a CATV cable) was used when the Ethernet was introduced. Hence, **10Broad36** is a 10-Mbps Ethernet on a broadband cable, limited to 3,600 meters. Customers who needed to link multiple buildings together were constrained by the 500-meter

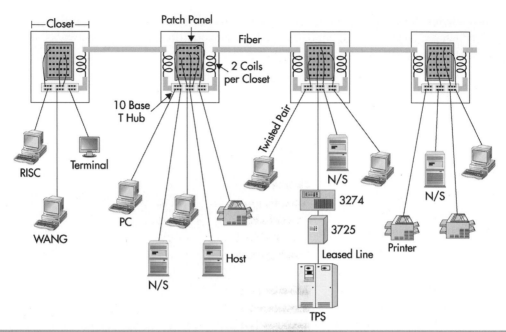

Figure 10-12 A 10BASE-F uses fiber in the backbone. Fiber extends the distances and still interfaces to the copper-based cables that run to the desktop.

distance limitations of the Ethernet baseband coax. Even with the two-repeater rule, the most that the cable could be extended was 1,500 meters—just under a mile. Although this might sound like enough cable to reach just about anywhere, that one mile of cable gets used quickly when it needs to be snaked through ceilings, up and down from the ceiling heights, and so on.

Recall earlier the notion of the 5-4-3 rule. If three segments are used for nodes, two additional connections (segments) can be used with half-repeaters on each end. In this case, the two segments connected with half-repeaters may not have any active nodes on them.

Therefore, the existing broadband cable offered a significant distance increase to Ethernet users who had to exceed the distance allowances. Using a 10-Mbps transmission speed on a broadband cable, the distance limitations were increased to 3,600 meters. This is a sevenfold increase in the distances over which the cable could be run. So, the vendors came up with a solution to the distance and medium needs for the end user. Broadband cable inherently is an analog transmission system. Special devices called frequency agile modems (FAMs) were attached to the cable to modulate the electrical signal onto the carrier. The cable is normally broken down into various channels of 6 MHz each. Using a bridging arrangement, two channels could be connected together as a 12-MHz channel and used to transmit 10-Mbps Ethernet on this coax. This allowed more flexibility in overall networking capability because the Ethernet, as stated at the beginning of this chapter, has been implemented in a variety of media.

This has also been accepted as a connection under the IEEE standards committee. See Figure 10-13 for a cable using the broadband Ethernet connection.

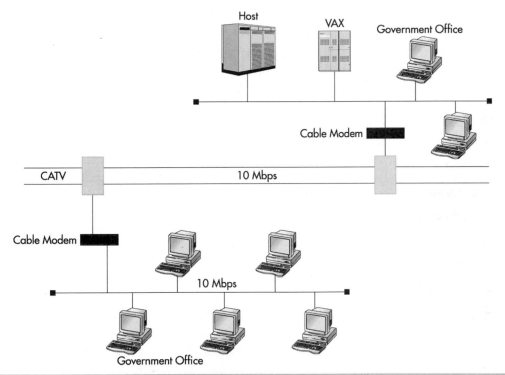

Figure 10-13 The CATV companies offer 10-Mbps Ethernet connections through the use of their cable modems. The FAMs shown on the cable convert the digital signals to analog and vice versa.

Fast Ethernet

As previously described, the uses of LANs have changed over the years. While in the past, the primary use was for movement of files and access to data by applications, a frequent use of LANs now is to load applications from servers. Also, the character of those applications has changed. The executables themselves have moved into the multiple megabyte range, and in some cases, graphic files are also now in the millions of bits. What all this means is that faster networks are needed. Another factor driving the need for speed is larger, higher-resolution monitors. A modern 1024 × 768 monitor displays slightly over 1 million bits for one screen's worth of information. That would require, ideally, slightly more than $1/10$ of a second to traverse an Ethernet. In practice, it would take considerably longer. One-tenth of a second may not sound like a great deal, but on a small network of ten users, a whole second might be eaten up just by the one screen to each user. In practice, it would be worse because contention would slow things down.

Some applications are considerably worse than this. Large, high-resolution graphics files make some environments entirely unsupportable by a standard Ethernet. For example, the size of a single digitized magazine cover can approach 70 megabytes. Bottom line: we need more speed. Many organizations ship files back and forth in their offices, such as computer aided design (CAD) files. At one time, a CAD file may have been 30 MB, but today, they range from 100 to 500 MB and larger. These files would eat up the network.

The culture of the workforce has also changed considerably. The days of simply typing ASCII text characters on a screen have gone. With Internet and intranet access, the user now does more information processing. Moreover, that information is represented through a GUI, in which the graphics interfaces are denser. The amount of data traveling across our networks is rapidly becoming exponential. The 10-Mbps Ethernet was pushed aside in favor of the 100-Mbps Fast Ethernet. **Fast Ethernet** is nothing more than the same framing and formatting, just an order of magnitude faster. Some organizations have moved to a 10-Mbps switched Ethernet as a means of forestalling the change of all the NIC cards in the PCs. This made sense, but it only begs for the actual upgrade later. Now newer switches and hubs are autodetecting, where a mix of 10- and 100-Mbps Ethernet NIC cards can be used on the same network. Autodetection is the capability to sense the speed of the NIC card connected to the switch or hub and set the speed accordingly. This is effective when a mixed environment is in use. This complicates the issue slightly, but it also gains time for the inevitable changes.

Most computer manufacturers now install 10/100-Mbps Ethernet cards directly in the PCs when they are made. This saves the LAN administrator from having to buy the cards separately. A minor issue is associated with the manufacturers installing these cards. Not all NIC cards are created equal. Many are made with special features and functions not available in others. Therefore, some conflict could occur on the LAN when these mixed variations are all on the same network. The other problem is the computer manufacturers that install the NICs usually require special drivers for their machines. Thus, a user must be aware that differences will arise and the price we pay for free LAN cards is the added burden of keeping on top of the myriad protocols and drivers required. The best advice we have heard is to allow autodetect for the clients but to be cautious with it on servers.

As the convergence of voice and data caught on in the industry during the late 1990s, the move was to incorporate voice, data, and streaming video at the desktop on the LAN. Given the limits of the 10-Mbps Ethernet with the specifications previously discussed, the movement to 100 Mbps escalated.

The term "Fast Ethernet" is primarily used today to refer to a technology technically described as **100Base-T**. In 1996, when the technology was introduced, Fast Ethernet referred to any of several technologies. There is some confusion here. One of the technologies was switched Ethernet. Fast Ethernet no longer refers to switched 10-Mbps Ethernet. Likewise, full-duplex Ethernet, at least the full-duplex variation of 10BASE-T, is no longer referred to as Fast Ethernet. Just as with 1,200-bps modems, which once were described as "high-speed," the advent of better technologies has resulted in changing the terminology used to describe the older technologies.

Two technologies deserve the name Fast Ethernet. Of the two, the vast majority of analysts have declared 100Base-T the winner, as discussed in the next section. The other is 100VGAnyLAN, which is discussed in the section titled with its name. Make no mistake though; 100VGAnyLAN is dead.

100BASE-T

When developers were trying to determine what the successor to Ethernet should be, they had two basic choices: try to stick to the basic technology as closely as possible, just increasing its speed, or try to make fundamental improvements to solve flaws that had become more obvious over time. Two camps developed, one taking each approach. The winning camp is the one that took the first approach. Their product: 100Base-T. The good news about 100Base-T is this: the frame size and characteristics are identical to those in standard Ethernet. The actual definition is **802.3u** standard. It uses CSMA/CD and, in general, can be understood and managed by network administrators and software in the same way that 100Base-T could be managed. The bad news is collisions still occur, and the product still taps out at considerably less than the nominal 100 Mbps that it is supposed to be able to handle. You might describe it as "Ethernet on steroids." The actual throughput on a 100Base-T is about 33 to 40 Mbps, if using a hub, and about 60 Mbps, if using an Ethernet switch.

NOTE

The Fast Ethernet standards have pretty much been relegated to the term "100BASE-T." The good news is 100BASE-T uses the same framing, formatting, and contention systems as 10BASE-T. The standard defined in IEEE is 802.3u.

Fast Ethernet is, however, the most popular replacement for standard Ethernet by far. In large part this is because of good marketing, but there is definitely something to be said for not having to do major retraining of your network administrators and technicians. In 1998, 50 percent of all new LANs installed were at the 100-Mbps rate. In 1999, that number jumped to almost 67 percent. Today, more than 90 percent of all NICs are 10/100. This varied between the shared bus concept in a hub and the switched version using a switch.

Like the original Ethernet, 100Base-T supports several media. Notably absent from this list is coaxial cable. Both standard copper wiring and fiber are supported. As with all high-speed technologies, the copper implementation has severe distance limitations. Most of the high-speed technologies do not support end devices more than 100 meters away from their central electronics locations. Fast Ethernet is no exception.

Fast Ethernet can be handled on copper wire running on category 5 UTP (unshielded twisted pair). In the case of category 5, Fast Ethernet can operate in either half- or full-duplex on two pairs of wire. Operating on two pairs, Fast Ethernet is referred to as 100Base-TX. This is by far the most popular implementation of Fast Ethernet.

The variation supported on copper for Fast Ethernet is shielded twisted pair (STP). Generally speaking, STP should only be installed in special cases where the potential interference either to or from the network is an issue. STP is much more difficult to install, with more demanding grounding requirements than UTP. It neither increases speed nor improves usage of the pairs in the cable. As far as network performance is concerned, it works the same as on UTP.

In addition to copper wiring, 100Base-T is supported on fiber; as with category 5, fiber supports both half- and full-duplex operations. Why might you use fiber? It doesn't improve the speed. In the case of Fast Ethernet, the main reason to use fiber would be to extend the available distances. Fast Ethernet over copper, as previously mentioned, only reaches 100 meters to the desktop. A more severe limitation is that distances between copper-connected Fast Ethernet hubs and switches must not exceed five meters, as shown in Figure 10-14. The use of fiber considerably relaxes these limitations.

Fast Ethernet Hub

If copper
5 meters maximum

Fast Ethernet Hub

Figure 10-14 The fast Ethernet hubs must be within five meters of each other when linking them with copper. Fiber helps to overcome these limitations.

As with standard Ethernet, there are variations on the way the wiring can be used. Buyers must select among shared, switched, and/or full-duplex use of the media and obtain the right electronics to install at both ends of the cable. The default is shared half-duplex. One should be aware that, just as in standard Ethernet, the contention experienced with a shared half-duplex configuration means that in no case except a two-user network will you be able to count on getting anywhere near the 100-Mbps nominal performance of a Fast Ethernet. However, this should not usually be a major problem. Just as with standard Ethernet, medium or even large work groups can be set up that still get a significant performance improvement over standard Ethernet by using shared half-duplex Fast Ethernet.

If you are building a backbone, you probably want to use switched, full-duplex Fast Ethernet. This will deliver close to the rated 100-Mbit performance to each node, and it costs considerably less than the available alternatives. Note, for anything but shared half-duplex, you must use either category 5 UTP or fiber cabling. Naturally, the cost of the electronics involved to deliver switched or full-duplex is more than that for shared half-duplex—in fact, it's two to three times the cost of the less-expensive approach.

Because all Fast Ethernet implementations are based on either copper or fiber, the cabling is done in a star or a radial configuration; no physical bus topologies need apply. This means, in theory and in practice, each node can be upgraded individually. The manufacturers build the central electronics (hubs, switches, and so forth) with the capability, in most cases, to handle either 10- or 100-Mbps Ethernet on a port-by-port basis. This means better electronics can be swapped at the central location, the network can be brought back up, and one-by-one individual users' machines can be upgraded, as shown in Figure 10-15, where the hubs/switches can operate on a port-by-port basis.

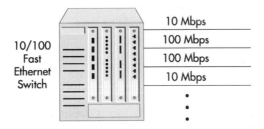

Figure 10-15 A hub or switch can support the 10- or 100-Mbps speeds and connections on a port-by-port basis. This lets the user upgrade as needed without forced migrations.

Several manufacturers make NICs that operate at both 10 and 100 Mbps. These are described as 10/100 cards. But any given computer can run at only one speed at a time—why do we need the dual speed? Most environments upgrade individual computers in groups.

Certainly, it is rare to replace all the computers in an environment at one time. Computers are often replaced one at a time, as users' needs change. With 10/100 cards, a company can make a long-term decision to move toward 100Base-T without having to upgrade all the central hubs. The company can upgrade the desktops and then upgrade the hubs as it makes sense to do so. In most cases, the 10/100 cards automatically sense the speed of the connected wire (that is, of the central electronics port) at the time the PC is booted.

NOTE

The ports will sense the speed at the time of network connectivity. Try unplugging the wire and plugging in a different speed network cable. You never have to reboot, unless you are on a legacy OS.

A changeover plan could be developed in one of two ways. One plan would be to replace all the NICs in desktops over time with 10/100 cards. These cards are not significantly more expensive than standard Ethernet cards. Once all the cards are replaced, then replace the central electronics with 100Base-T switches and hubs, reboot all the desktops, and you are done. The second approach would be to replace the central electronics with switches and hubs with units that have 10/100 ports. These are more costly, but they give a degree of flexibility that isn't in the first scenario. Not all desktops have to be upgraded—ever. Once all the central electronics are upgraded, you can begin upgrading the desktops. In a pinch, some desktops can be upgraded in parallel, although this complicates the management efforts.

100VGAnyLAN

Back before 100Base-T had established its market share, a group of technically oriented companies, including Hewlett-Packard, felt the second approach to upgrading Ethernet—improving its flaws as opposed to just increasing its speed—was the better approach. The result of their efforts was 100VGAnyLAN. This technology, like the Betamax VCR, is clearly superior to its competitor (100Base-T). Unfortunately, as with the Betamax, it didn't win over the market. You can still buy 100VGAnyLAN products, but the system is regarded by most as an also-ran.

100VGAnyLAN had much to recommend it. Its designers chose to eliminate the CSMA/CD method of allocating capacity. Instead, 100VGAnyLAN uses what is called a demand-priority allocation scheme, where each NIC notifies its corresponding hub that it has something to send. The hub pays attention to these notifications and solicits the input once notified. It also is possible to designate high-priority traffic, such as video, enabling a better pattern of performance for such traffic in this technology.

100VGAnyLAN also had the capability to support either Ethernet or Token Ring traffic. This traffic cannot be on the same hub, but you can use the same kind of hubs for both, significantly reducing the complexity of a LAN-implementation environment. The rules for cascading 100VG hubs are no more restrictive than those for standard Ethernet, and they are considerably more flexible than those for 100Base-T. As with 100Base-T, the cable running out to the workstations can be 100 meters long. The distance between hubs, however, can also be 100 meters, 20 times the limitation of 100Base-T.

There are some disadvantages to 100VGAnyLAN, partially explaining its failure in the marketplace. For one thing, its initial specification required four pairs of unshielded twisted-pair wiring, no matter which category is being used. Another disadvantage is more political than technological. Since the beginning, Ethernet has used CSMA/CD as its media allocation scheme; 100VGAnyLAN does not. It uses demand priority. This is an advantage, but purists in the Ethernet camp have attacked 100VGAnyLAN on this basis. Few vendors subscribed to the 100VGAnyLAN technological specification. At this point, it is only enthusiastically supported by Hewlett-Packard—and even HP has moved on to support 100Base-T.

Gigabit Ethernet

While we do not know of anyone who alleges that full-duplex switched 100Base-T is insufficient to handle any likely desktop requirement, if you put together enough high-speed desktop LANs, the backbone to serve them needs to be a better technology than that desktop LAN technology, whatever it is. Moreover, if the use of voice, data, video, and multimedia finally becomes a reality on a single architecture, then the need for more than 100 Mbps to the desk may become a reality. Gigabit Ethernet (1,000 Mbps), also called **GigE**, was developed with the goal of providing these applications to the individual user in the future. The IEEE standards committee defined GigE as the **802.3z** standard.

Like 100Base-T, GigE comes in half- and full-duplex variations.

In its half-duplex implementation, GigE has some severe limitations regarding delivery of actual capacity. There is an interaction in all Ethernets between minimum packet size and size in terms of the radius of the actual maximum network configuration. The smaller the minimum frame size, the smaller the maximum radius of the network. This relationship is compounded in a bad way by increasing the speed of the network transmission. Because the goal in upgrading to a faster variety of Ethernet is to keep the same frame size limitations, the radius of the GigE without using a special technique is limited to about 20 meters—obviously impractical. What the designers have done is implement a special technique that involves transmission of a special signal in any case where a frame smaller than 512 bytes is transmitted on a GigE. This means, for large frames (for example, those associated with large file transfers), GigE might deliver close to its full speed. However, many networks being used by human beings, as opposed to machines, generate large numbers of small frames averaging only 300 to 350 bytes. In the worst case, such a network, even if implemented on GigE, would experience performance little better than that delivered by 100Base-T in its full-duplex incarnation. The technique also allows for a 200-meter network diameter by allowing multiple frames to be sent consecutively without the traditional "Ethernet wait" up to a limit of 4,096 bytes. This development, plus the wide-scale use of full-duplex GigE, frees the network engineer from worrying about what kind of traffic is going to be carried by that network relative to its performance in GigE transmission lines.

In half-duplex mode, CSMA/CD is used as the access control method in combination with this special carrier timing like other forms of Ethernet.

GigE provided no quality of service (QoS) guarantees, although the proponents of GigE decided to provide QoS-like services. This means that even though its nominal speed is high, it still is not an ideal technology for satisfying isochronous-type traffic (for example, video). The new standard—the **802.3q**—is designed to handle QoS features for GigE.

REMINDER

The GigE is defined using the 802.3z standard. The quality of service (QoS) mechanism is defined in the 802.3q standard.

If one implements full-duplex GigE, the issue regarding distance pretty much disappears. GigE requires the use of fiber.

There are two kinds of fiber: multimode and single mode. **Multimode fiber** should be able to reach up to about 550 meters, whereas **single-mode fiber** should be able to reach distances approaching 3 kilometers (Km) in conventional implementations and more than 80 Km when using Long- Range Ethernet (LRE).

To mix the services together between clients and servers, the standard can use a hub or switch using 10 Mbps and 100 Mbps to the client, and 1,000 Mbps in the backbone (uplink to the server). This is shown in Figure 10-16.

Virtual LANs

In a traditional shared-media network, traffic generated by a station is propagated to all other stations on the local segment. For a given station on shared Ethernet, the local segment is the collision domain because traffic on the segment has the potential to cause an Ethernet collision. The local segment is also the "broadcast domain" because any broadcast is sent to all stations on the local segment.

VLANs provide the capability to define broadcast domains without the constraint of physical location. For example, instead of making all the users on the third floor part of the same broadcast domain, you might use VLANs to make all the users in the HR department

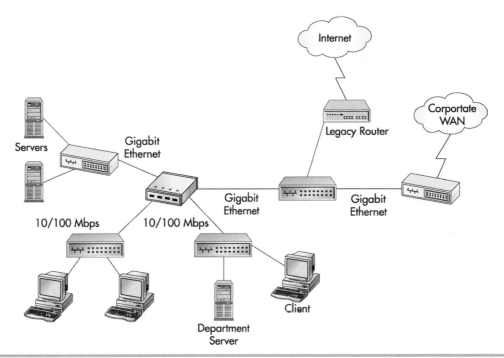

Figure 10-16 A combination of regular Ethernet plus Fast Ethernet and GigE can be had in a single switch. This allows for the migration in the workplace over time as bandwidth needs dictate.

part of the same broadcast domain. The benefits of doing this are many. First, these users might be spread throughout different floors on a building, so a VLAN would enable you to make all these users part of the same broadcast domain. To that end, this can also be viewed as a security feature: because all HR users are part of the same broadcast domain, you could later use policies, such as access lists, to control which areas of the network these users have access to or which users have access to the HR broadcast domain. Furthermore, if the HR department's server is placed on the same VLAN, HR users will be able to access their server without the need for traffic to cross routers and potentially impact other parts of the network.

A broadcast frame is one that is sent to all devices on a network. Because it will be sent to all devices, the network could become flooded with these frames.

Normal LAN traffic is sent to a unicast device. A frame is sent from one PC to another by **MAC address**. This unicast address is also used for a response.

Sometimes you need to send a multicast frame to several selected users on a network. An example might be using a streaming video conference, where the frames are sent to ten users at different locations who participate in the conference. Multicast messages are sent to specific addresses (IP) of users who signed up for the conference, without being sent to every address on the LAN or VLAN. By tagging the specific frames for VLAN recipients, the same effect occurs. Instead of sending all HR traffic to all devices on all floors, you can send only to the tagged address pool in the VLAN and minimize the traffic that is not required by others.

Ethernet bridges and switches divide a network into smaller "collision domains," but they do not affect the broadcast domain. In simple terms, a virtual local area network (VLAN) can be thought of as a mechanism to fine-tune broadcast domains.

A **VLAN** is a collection of switch ports that make up a single broadcast domain. A VLAN can be defined for a single switch or can span multiple switches. VLANs are logical entities created in the software configuration to control traffic flow. Membership in workgroup segments can be determined logically, instead of by user location. Moves, adds, and changes can be easily configured as the network evolves. A VLAN allows a single switch and a single wiring infrastructure to support multiple logical separate networks, as if each VLAN were its own system of switches and cables.

IEEE 802.11 Wireless LANs

Many people misnomer this as wireless Ethernet. Although it is not Ethernet, it normally connects to an Ethernet backbone. So, IEEE **802.11** must be discussed in the context of our 802.3 LANs. The IEEE 802.11 standard defines the physical layer and the MAC layer for a wireless LAN. The standard defines three different physical layers for the 802.11 wireless LAN, each operating in a different frequency range and at rates of 1 Mbps and 2 Mbps. In this section, we focus on the architecture of 802.11 LANs and their media access protocols. You'll see that although IEEE 802.11 belongs to the same standard family as Ethernet, it has a significantly different architecture and media access protocol. The IEEE 802.11 represents the first standard for wireless LAN products from an internationally recognized, independent organization. The IEEE manages most of the standards for wired LANs. The wireless LAN standard (802.11) represents an important milestone in WLAN systems because customers can now have multiple sources for the components of their WLAN systems. There are still applications where the existing proprietary data communications are a good fit because they may optimize some aspect of the network performance. However, 802.11-compliant products expand the users' options.

802.11 LAN Architecture

The principal components of the 802.11 wireless LAN architecture are shown in any architectural drawing. The fundamental building block of the 802.11 architecture is the cell, known as the Basic Service Set (BSS) in 802.11 parlance. A **BSS** typically contains one or more wireless stations and a central base station, known as an access point (AP) in 802.11 terminologies. The stations, either fixed or mobile, and the central base station communicate among themselves using the IEEE 802.11 wireless MAC protocol. Multiple APs may be connected together (using a wired Ethernet or another wireless channel) to form a so-called distribution system (DS). The DS appears to upper-level protocols (for example, IP) as a single 802 network, in much the same way that a bridged, wired 802.3 Ethernet network appears as a single 802 network to the upper-layer protocols. In fact, many of the wireless devices are bridges.

How It Will Be Used in End Applications

The IEEE 802.11 standard defines the protocol for two types of networks: ad-hoc and infrastructure (AP) networks.

- An **ad-hoc network** is a simple network where communications are established among multiple stations in a given coverage area without the use of an AP or server. The standard specifies the etiquette that each station must observe, so they all have fair access to the wireless media. The IEEE 802.11 standard also provides methods for arbitrating requests to use the media to ensure that throughput is maximized for all the users in the base service set. IEEE 802.11 stations can also group themselves together to form an ad-hoc network—a network with no central control and with no connections to the "outside world." Here, the network is formed on the fly, simply because mobile devices happen to be in proximity to each other, have a need to communication, and, either by configuration or through the lack of APs, find no preexisting network infrastructure (for example, a preexisting 802.11 BSS with an AP) in the location. An ad-hoc network might be formed, for example, when people with laptops meet together (for example, in a conference room, a train, or a car) and want to exchange data in the absence of a centralized access point. There has been a tremendous recent increase in interest in ad-hoc networking, as communicating portable devices continue to proliferate. This is shown in Figure 10-17.

10

Figure 10-17 The ad-hoc network is a useful way for groups to collaborate the work effort without wiring everyone together.

● The infrastructure network uses an AP that controls the allocation of transmit time for all stations and allows mobile stations to roam from cell-to-cell. The AP is used to handle traffic from the mobile radio to the wired or wireless backbone of the client-server network. This arrangement allows for point coordination of all the stations in the basic service area and ensures proper handling of the data traffic. The AP routes data between the stations and other wireless stations, or to and from the network server. Typically, WLANs controlled by a central AP will provide better throughput performance. This is shown in Figure 10-18.

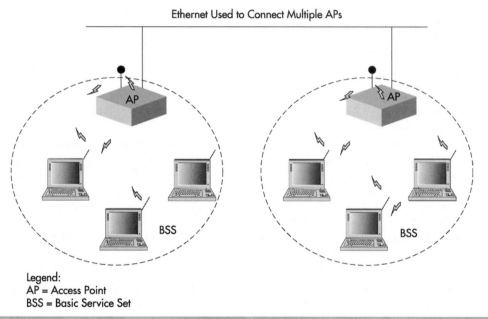

Figure 10-18 An infrastructure approach can also be used with the wireless LAN.

Physical Layer Implementation Choices

The physical layer in any network defines the modulation and signaling characteristics for the transmission of data. At the physical layer, two RF transmission methods and one infrared are defined. Operation of the WLAN in unlicensed RF bands requires the use of spread-spectrum modulation to meet the requirements for operation in most countries. The RF transmission standards are **Frequency Hopping Spread Spectrum (FHSS)** and **Direct Sequence Spread Spectrum (DSSS)**. Both architectures are defined for operation in the 2.4-GHz frequency band, typically occupying the 83 MHz of bandwidth from 2.400 GHz to 2.483 GHz.

1. Differential BPSK (DBPSK) and DQPSK are the modulation for the direct sequence.

2. Frequency hopping uses two to four levels of Gaussian (white noise) FSK as the modulation signaling method.

Different frequency ranges, with some overlapping frequencies, have been approved for use in Japan, the United States, and Europe, and any WLAN product must meet the requirements for the country where it is sold. The physical-layer data rate for FHSS in the original 802.11 system is 1 Mbps. For DSSS, both 1-Mbps and 2-Mbps data rates are supported. The revised standards of 802.11b (up to 11 Mbps) and 802.11a and 802.11g (up to 54 Mbps), only use DSSS. So, at this point, FHSS is almost a forgotten technology.

Infrared Physical Layer

One infrared standard is supported that operates in the 850- to 950-nM (nanometer) band with peak power of 2 W. The modulation for infrared is accomplished using either 4- or 16-level pulse-positioning modulation. The physical layer supports two data rates: 1 and 2 Mbps.

Direct Sequence Spread Spectrum (DSSS) Physical Layer

The DSSS physical layer uses an 11-bit Barker Sequence to spread the data before it is transmitted. Each bit transmitted is modulated by the 11-bit sequence. This process spreads the RF energy across a wider bandwidth than would be required to transmit the raw data. The receiver reverses the RF input to recover the original data. The advantage is reduced effects of narrowband sources of interference.

The IEEE 802.11 protocol also has the option to use a short Request To Send (RTS) control frame and a short Clear To Send (CTS) frame to reserve access to the channel, which can resolve some problems in certain wireless networks (at the expense of additional overhead). When a sender wants to send a frame, it can first send a RTS frame to the receiver, indicating the duration of the data packet and the ACK packet. A receiver that receives an RTS frame responds with a CTS frame, giving the sender explicit permission to send. All other stations hearing the RTS or CTS then know about the pending data transmission and can avoid interfering with those transmissions. An IEEE 802.11 sender can operate using the RTS/CTS control frames or can simply send its data without first using the RTS control frame. The RTS sequence is shown in Figure 10-19. The RTS and CTS protocols were used in our wired data networks in the past, but they have been reduced considerably in today's applications.

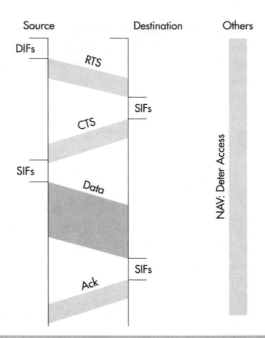

Figure 10-19 In an effort to prevent the collisions, the CTS and RTS techniques are used. This is an older technique that was used in the early days of data transmission.

The use of the RTS and CTS frames helps avoid collisions in three important ways:

1. Because the receiver's transmitted CTS frame will be heard by all stations within the receiver's vicinity, the CTS frame helps avoid both the hidden station problem and the fading problem.

2. Because the RTS and CTS frames are short, a collision involving an RTS or CTS frame will only last for the duration of the whole RTS or CTS frame.

3. When the RTS and CTS frames are correctly transmitted, there should be no collisions involving the subsequent DATA and ACK frames.

Frequency Hopping Spread Spectrum (FHSS) Physical Layer

The FHSS physical layer has 22 hop patterns to choose from. The FHSS physical layer is required to hop across the 2.4-GHz ISM band covering 79 channels. Each channel occupies 1 Mhz of bandwidth and must hop at the minimum rate specified by the regulatory bodies of the intended country. A minimum hop rate of 2.5 hops per second is specified for the United States.

Each of the physical layers uses its own unique header to synchronize the receiver and to determine signal modulation format and data packet length. The physical layer headers are always transmitted at 1 Mbps. Predefined fields in the headers provide the option to increase the data rate to 2 Mbps for the actual data packet.

The MAC Layer

Unlike the 802.3 Ethernet protocol, the wireless 802.11 MAC protocol does not implement collision detection. There are a couple of reasons for this:

1. The ability to detect collisions requires the ability to both send (your own signal) and receive (to determine if another station's transmissions are interfering with your own transmission) at the same time. This can be costly.

2. More important, even if you had collision detection and sensed no collision when sending, a collision could still occur at the receiver. This situation results from the particular characteristics of the wireless channel.

Given the difficulties of detecting collisions at a wireless receiver, the designers of IEEE 802.11 developed an access protocol that aimed to avoid collisions, hence the name carrier-sense, multiple access, with collision avoidance (**CSMA/CA**), rather than to detect and recover from collisions (CSMA/CD).

First, the IEEE 802.11 frame contains a duration field in which the sending station explicitly indicates the length of time that its frame will be transmitting on the channel. This value allows other stations to determine the minimum amount of time—network allocation vector (NAV)—for which they should defer their access.

The MAC-layer specification for 802.11 has similarities to the 802.3 Ethernet wired line standard. The 802.11 protocols use CSMA/CA to avoid collisions, instead of detecting a collision like the algorithm used in 802.3. Detecting collisions in an RF transmission network is difficult, and for this reason, collision avoidance is used. The MAC layer operates together with the physical layer by sampling the energy over the medium transmitting data. The physical layer uses a clear channel assessment (CCA) algorithm to determine if the channel is clear. This is accomplished by measuring the RF energy at the antenna and determining the strength of the received signal. The best method to use depends on the levels of interference in the operating environment. The CSMA/CA protocol allows for options that can minimize collisions by using Request To Send (RTS), Clear To Send (CTS), data, and acknowledge (ACK) transmission frames in a sequential fashion. The solution to this problem in 802.11 involves changing the carrier-detect time for stations, depending on their state: long, if looking for an empty channel; medium, if trying to complete a transmission; and short, if sending a collision or other housekeeping message.

10

Communication is established when one of the wireless nodes sends a short message RTS frame. The RTS frame includes the destination and the length of message. The message duration is known as the network allocation vector (NAV). The NAV alerts all others in the medium to back off for the duration of the transmission. The receiving station issues a CTS frame, which echoes the sender's address and the NAV. If the CTS frame is not received, it is assumed that a collision occurred and the RTS process starts over. After the data frame is received, an ACK frame is sent back, verifying a successful data transmission.

A common limitation with wireless LAN systems is the "hidden node" problem. This can disrupt 40 percent or more of the communications in a highly loaded LAN environment. It occurs when a station cannot hear the transmission of another station when the media are busy. The hidden node is shown in Figure 10-20.

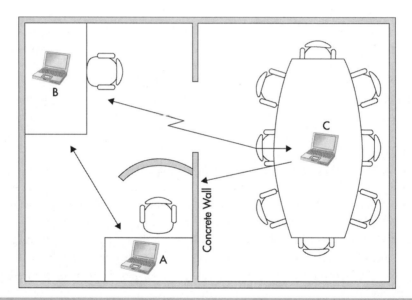

Figure 10-20 The hidden node problem is not addressed by the 802.11 committees, but it can be problematic with a widespread network where devices are shielded from each other.

In the diagram, station *B* is able to communicate with both stations *A* and *C*, but communication between stations *A* and *C* is obstructed (by thick walls, radio interference, distance, and so forth). Unless station *B* is acting as a Base Station and relaying messages between stations *A* and *C*, then stations *A* and *C* are unable to communicate with each other.

In addition, stations *A* and *C* are unable to sense when the other (hidden) station is using the wireless link, and they could both transmit at the same time, thus causing collisions and subsequent retransmission. The IEEE 802.11b protocol standard uses an RTS/CTS mechanism to decrease the effect of the hidden node problem, but studies have shown that when more than 10 percent of stations are hidden from other stations, a standard 802.11 network will experience lower performance because of packet retransmission.

With the emphasis now on Voice over IP (VoIP) telephone applications, the 802.11 standard allows the interconnection of the traditional PBX and LANs, as shown in Figure 10-21.

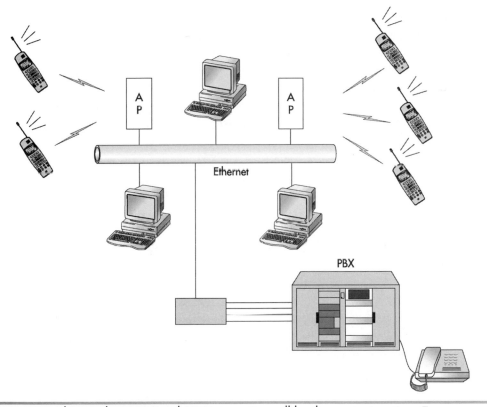

Figure 10-21 The wireless LAN and PBX integration will be the next migration. Everyone wants to run VoIP over WLAN today.

Distribution System (DS)

For the APs in an **Extended Service Set (ESS)** to communicate, they use an abstract medium called the **Distribution System (DS)**. The DS is what connects the BSS together, and it may consist of both wired and wireless LAN segments. Each AP determines if communications received from the BSS should be relayed to a destination within the local BSS, forwarded across the DS to a different AP, or forwarded into the wired LAN infrastructure for delivery. Networking equipment outside the ESS views the ESS and all its stations as a single MAC-layer network, where all the stations appear to be physically stationary. This misdirection by the ESS allows networking protocols that have no concept of mobility to work correctly with the mobile stations of the WLAN.

Assuming a good mix of security and technology, organizations seriously consider the continued use of this service for short- and long-term needs. Now that the Regional Bell Operating Companies (RBOCs), as well as hotels, airports, other public buildings, and other third parties, have service offerings with Wireless APs (called hot spots), a company has the opportunity to rapidly experiment and deploy the use of WLANs. We see this as a high-priority opportunity for the company because of the return on investment that comes with this form of connectivity.

The industry is rife with several new technologies and frequencies that attempt to satisfy the requirements for the future. These include *802.11*, **802.11a**, and **802.11b** Wireless LAN (WLAN) and, now, the **802.11g** standard services. Each of these series offers a different speed of connectivity, as seen in Table 10-3. The 802.11g standards are an attempt to provide forward and backward compatibility between the older 802.11, 802.11b, and the newer 802.11a. The access methods and speeds are shown in Table 10-3.

Technology	Speed	Frequency	Access Method
802.11	1 and 2 Mbps	2.4 GHz	DSSS, FHSS, IR
802.11b	1, 2, 5.5, and 11 Mbps	2.4 GHz	DSSS
802.11a	All speeds up to 54 Mbps	5.3, 5.5, and 5.7 GHz	OFDM
802.11g	All speeds up to 54 Mbps and backward compatible with 802.11b	2.4 GHz	OFDM, DSSS

Table 10-3 Summary of the Speeds, Frequencies, and Access Methods Used for Wireless LANs Today.

❓ Line Check 10-2

Is the wireless LAN the same as wireless Ethernet?

Ease of Setup

To install a wireless LAN, you must install and configure APs and PC Cards. The most important part of this effort is proper placement of the APs. Access-point placement is what ensures the coverage and performance required by the network design, while also ensuring coverage does not extend into unwanted locations (such as parking lots and so forth). Several features provide assistance in the installation process:

Site Survey

For complete wireless LANs employing a cellular architecture, proper placement of APs is best determined by performing a site survey, in which the person installing the WLAN can place APs and record signal strength and quality information, while moving about the intended coverage area. While most vendors provide a site survey tool, these utilities vary in the amount and quality of information they provide, as well as in their logging and reporting capabilities.

Power over Ethernet.

Some vendors ship APs that can be powered over the Ethernet cable that connects the access point to the wired network. This is usually implemented by a piece of equipment in the wiring closet that takes in AC power and the data connection from the wired switch, and then outputs DC power over unused wire pairs in the networking cable that runs between the module and the AP. This feature eliminates the need to run an AC power cable to the AP (usually located on the wall or ceiling), making installation quicker and more affordable.

The **802.3af** standard specifies "Power-over-Ethernet (PoE)" or "Active Ethernet" that eliminates the need to run 110/220 VAC power to wireless APs and other devices on a wired LAN. Using PoE, system installers need to run only a single CAT5 Ethernet cable that carries both power and data to each device. This allows greater flexibility in the locating of APs and network devices, and it significantly decreases installation costs in many cases.

PoE begins with a CAT5 Injector that inserts a DC voltage onto the CAT5 cable. The Injector is typically installed in the wiring closet near the Ethernet switch or hub.

Some Wireless APs and other networks accept the injected DC power directly from the CAT5 cable through their RJ45 jack. These devices are considered "PoE-Compatible" or Active Ethernet-Compatible.

Devices that are not PoE-Compatible can be converted to PoE by way of a DC Picker or tap. These are sometimes called Active Ethernet Splitters. This device picks off the DC voltage injected into the CAT5 cable by the Injector and makes it available to the equipment through the regular DC power jack.

Easy-to-Use NIC and AP Configuration Tools

Once the APs are installed, both APs and NICs must be configured for use. As with any technical product, the quality of the user interface determines the amount of time required to configure the network for operation. In addition, some vendors supply tools for bulk configuration of APs on the same network, greatly easing network setup. Finally, having a variety of methods to access the AP is helpful to ensure simple setup. Configuration options include Telnet-, web-based, or SNMP-based over the Ethernet cable, from a wireless station, or via a serial port built into the access point.

Ease of Management

Because an 802.11 wireless LAN differs from standard 802.3 and 802.5 wired LANs only at OSI layers 1 and 2, we should expect at least the same level of manageability from these products as we find for wired networking products. At a minimum, the products should come with SNMP 2 support, so they can be automatically discovered and managed using the same tools employed for wired LAN equipment. And we should assess carefully what can be controlled via the SNMP MIB. Some products measure and control a number of Ethernet and radio variables in the access point, while others provide only a basic Ethernet MIB.

802.11 Improved: 802.11a/g Orthogonal Frequency Division Multiplexing

The 802.11 **Orthogonal Frequency Division Multiplexing (OFDM)** physical layer delivers up to 54 Mbps data rates in the 5-GHz band. The OFDM physical layer, commonly referred to as 802.11a, will be one of the high-speed wireless LANs products for the future. However, you will see that some of the problems with the 5-GHz band are the noninteroperability between the 2.4-GHz band and the 5-GHz bands, so the 802.11g standard was created using OFDM as the backward-compatible solution.

Orthogonal Frequency Division Multiplexing (OFDM) Carriers

OFDM divides the data signal across 48 separate subcarriers to provide transmissions of 6, 9, 12, 18, 24, 36, 48, and 54 Mbps, of which 6, 12, and 24 Mbps are mandatory for all products. For each of the subcarriers, OFDM uses phase-shift keying (PSK) or quadrature amplitude modulation (QAM) to modulate the digital signal, depending on the selected data rate of transmission. In addition, four pilot subcarriers provide a reference to minimize frequency and phase shifts of the signal during transmission. This form of transmission enables OFDM to operate extremely efficiently, which leads to the higher data rates and minimizes the effects of multipath fade (where signals bouncing off different objects are received out of phase with each other and work to cancel out the intended signal).

OFDM is a physical-layer encoding technology for transmitting signals through the RF. This method breaks one high-speed data carrier into several lower-speed carriers. These, in turn, are transmitted in parallel across that particular RF spectrum. The 802.11a subcommittee has elected to use the transmission technique for its standard in the 5.5-GHz Unlicensed National Information Infrastructure (UNII) bands, and also in the 2.4-GHz ISM band as the physical layer standard for the 802.11g subcommittee.

OFDM is a multicarrier transmission technique that divides the available spectrum into many carriers, each one being modulated by a low-rate data stream. OFDM is similar to FDMA in that the multiple-user access is achieved by subdividing the available bandwidth into multiple channels, which are then allocated to users. However, OFDM uses the spectrum much more efficiently by spacing the channels closer together. This is achieved by making all the carriers orthogonal to one another, preventing interference between the closely spaced carriers.

Coded Orthogonal Frequency Division Multiplexing (COFDM) is the same as OFDM, except forward error correction is applied to the signal before transmission. This is to overcome errors in the transmission because of lost carriers from frequency selective fading, channel noise, and other propagation effects. The acronyms OFDM and COFDM are used interchangeably, but it is assumed that any practical system will use forward error correction and, thus, would be COFDM.

Orthogonal FDM's (OFDM) spread-spectrum technique distributes the data over a large number of carriers that are spaced apart at precise frequencies. This spacing provides the "orthogonality" in this technique, which prevents the demodulators from seeing frequencies other than their own. The benefits of OFDM are high-spectral efficiency, resiliency to RF interference, and lower multipath distortion. This is useful because multipath channels are in a typical terrestrial-broadcasting scenario (that is, the transmitted signal arrives at the receiver using various paths of different length). Because multiple versions of the signal interfere with each other—intersymbol interference (ISI)   it becomes hard to extract the original information.

OFDM splits the available bandwidth into many narrow band channels. The carriers for each channel are made orthogonal to one another, allowing them to be spaced close together with no overhead, as in the FDMA example. Because of this, no great need occurs for users to be time multiplex as in TDMA, so no overhead is associated with switching between users. This is shown in Figure 10-22.

The orthogonality of the carriers means each carrier has an integer number of cycles over a symbol period. Because of this, the spectrum of each carrier has a null at the center frequency of each of the other carriers in the system. This results in no interference between the carriers, allowing them to be spaced as close as theoretically possible. This overcomes the problem of overhead carrier spacing required in FDMA.

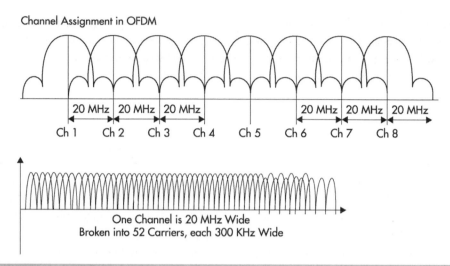

Figure 10-22 The 20-MHz channels are divided into 52 subcarriers of 300 kHz each to handle the orthogonal frequency division multiplexing. The data is spread across 48 of these subchannels.

The Future Speeds for Wireless LANs

Hardly a day goes by when you do not hear of some latest and greatest technique to implement faster, better, and cheaper wireless LANs. The standards committees are constantly looking for newer methods to speed the WLAN to comparable speeds to the wired LAN. In this light, a new protocol summary called the **802.11n** is designed to support speeds of 100+ Mbps. Although not yet ratified at press time, the 100-Mbps standard is quickly making headlines.

One caution that is always at the forefront is the risk of noncompatibility or non-compliance with the newer standards. Every vendor is busy producing products that will use the faster specifications (100 Mbps), but no standard has been adopted. This means a user may implement a vendor-specific solution that may not be suitable in the future. If the standards are ratified with a different speed or approach to the solution, then the vendor may have to modify the technology to comply. At what cost to the end user? The old adage "buyer beware" comes into play during this cycle.

Still another technique in use is the double speeds (many vendors are offering products that will operate at twice the 802.11a or 802.11g rates) up to 108 Mbps. This is a streaming sequence they use—by taking two separate channels, the vendor splits the data and sends it across the air as two individual data streams. At the receiving end, a suitable and compatible piece of equipment must receive the data, extract it from the carrier, and then multiplex it back together as a single stream to the DS. This proprietary solution requires that all devices be made by the same manufacturer or else it will not work. Moreover, by using two channels to get this speed, the end user (albeit the manufacturer) is jamming the signals on other channels and causing interference to others who are trying to use these same channels. This is not a good working solution, so you need to be aware of the risks and pitfalls of these different choices.

Token Rings

Another access method that can be used in a LAN is the token-passing concept. This concept was never as popular as Ethernet and has dropped from popularity in local networks at the workstation level, but it can still be found in large data centers where mainframe computers are used. Many of the largest corporations in the world still use this method in the data center because the architecture (IBM mainframes and look-alike) requires it.

The token-passing concept is an access method that was initially developed to work on a physical and a logical ring. Remember, LANs are used in both physical and logical topologies. A **topology** is the layout of the physical wiring plan to provide a single shared cabling system. If you think about some of the constraints and limitations of the bus topology covered in the previous chapter, the issue is the collisions that can occur on a network. The issue that seems to arise in the discussion of the topology of the physical Ethernet is that the signal (information) has to propagate (travel) down to the ends of the cabling system. At the ends of the system are terminators that absorb, or remove, the electrical pulses from the cable. To send information and be assured that the information reaches its destination, the transmitting device can only use 50 percent of the time to generate the information onto the wire. The other 50 percent of the time allotted to this device is devoted to listening to the cable to make sure the signal makes it all the way to the end without colliding with some other device's data. This would appear to be somewhat wasteful, because only a 50 percent duty cycle is allowed. To overcome this situation, the use of a ring topology was introduced. Along with the topology, a collision-avoidance scheme was also introduced. If a device wants to transmit, it must have a "permission slip" to do so. This permission slip is in the form of an electrical signal, called a **token**, which travels around the network constantly. Only one user will be on the network at a time. Only one token is needed.

The IBM Token Concept

In 1984, IBM announced plans to produce a set of network interfaces that adhered to the IEEE 802.5 token-passing concept. This access method was IBM's defense against the use of Ethernets. Users were in one of two camps, either supporting or criticizing peer implementations of the LAN topologies. Many of the IBM systems would not work on an Ethernet, so immediately, a new connectivity solution was introduced to support the big iron and the in-between hardware.

10

IBM's version and the standardized IEEE version of tokens included the use of a deterministic system. A **deterministic system** is one with an outcome that can be predicted because all its causes are either known or the same as those of a previous event. In other words, the system uses a preset of timing and token passing, so you know how long the token will take to circulate around the ring and know that no contention system will impede that flow.

By using a single token, the network allows only one device at a time to transmit. Therefore, the risks and problems associated with the CSMA/CD LANs are eliminated. Each device gets its fair share of use on the network. To do this, the devices are allowed a time to use the token as it arrives.

REMEMBER

The IEEE specification for a Token Ring network is the 802.5.

Initial Layout

In the early days of the Token Ring, the cables were installed as a physical ring. In Figure 10-23, the actual layout of the cabling is shown. In this initial layout, each device installed on the ring is connected to the physical and closed ring of wires. Wires run to an inbound slot on a device—to the network interface card (NIC), which is now called a token interface card (TIC)—and then out to an outbound side of the device. What this means is that every device

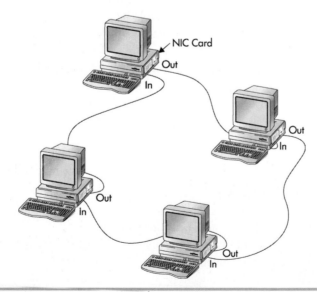

Figure 10-23 IBM's Token Ring uses a closed wire system to pass the data around the circuit.

has a wire in/wire out connection. This is done on a four-wire cable. As the devices are attached to the network, they are wired from the upstream neighbor and to the downstream neighbor. This continues around the LAN until the circle is closed.

The LAN in a Box Solution

Using a version of a star network, the multistation access unit (MAU) was introduced. In Figure 10-24, a MAU was installed in a star configuration in a telephone closet. The ring now is a physical star and a logical ring.

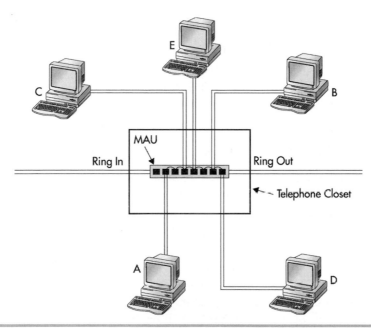

Figure 10-24 The MAU is a concentrator and acts just like a hub. The hub prevents a single-cable disconnect from bringing down the entire network.

The original Token Ring topology was delivered at 4 Mbps. Distances of wires run from device-to-device could not exceed a total length of 1,600 feet. Newer rings operated at 16 Mbps, but the distance was cut in half for a total cable run of 800 feet. To solve this problem, IBM included a repeater function in the MAU, so each port on the MAU would regenerate the signal and overcome the risk of signal loss. The MAU typically had only eight ports, as shown in the figure, plus a ring-in and a ring-out port. This allows multiple MAUs to be hooked together in a ring fashion and allows for more than eight devices to be clustered into a single logical ring.

10

Speeds

The deterministic nature of the ring using a token-passing access control does not have the same problems as an Ethernet. There will be no collisions, because only a single token exists and only one device can transmit when it controls the token. Consequently, the ring can be more effectively used. The effective throughput of a 4-Mbps token-passing ring is approximately 3.3 Mbps. This parallels the performance of the Ethernet even though the raw speeds are different. Further, IBM's second version of the Token Ring card introduced a higher rate of speed. Operating at 16 Mbps, the faster speed using a deterministic access control method yields approximately 12 Mbps.

Media Access Control Layer

The data-link layer is subdivided into two parts: the MAC and the logical link control (LLC) functions. A Token Ring, therefore, can be shown (Figure 10-25) as it is compared to the layers of the OSI model. This comparison shows that the following apply:

- The physical link deals with the physical structure of the cabling system and the access method used at the physical layer. This is labeled layer 1 in the figure.

- The data-link sublayer—the MAC layer—shows the access control in support of the IEEE and the International Telecommunication Union (ITU) model for access control.

- The LLC brings the various topologies together in a common format. The LLC represents the upper portion of layer 2 of the OSI model.

The Frame

The **Token Ring** uses three different types of frames in its ongoing operation. These three frames are determined by the service they provide on the network. They are:

- The token
- The frame
- The abort message

The Token

The token is made up of 24 bits of information (three octets). The three octets define the start-and-stop sequence within this frame. A token will traverse the network constantly, even if no traffic exists. Refer to Figure 10-26 for the frame format of the token. The first octet in the token is the start delimiter (SD).

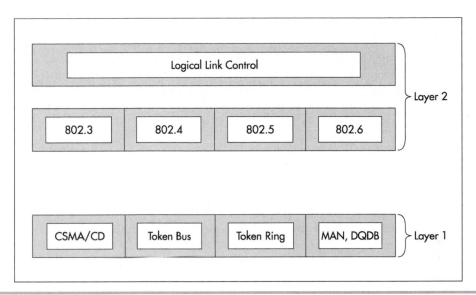

Figure 10-25 The 802.5 Token Ring is a layer 2 protocol operating at the MAC layer of the OSI.

Skipping to the third octet in the token is the end delimiter (ED). Much like the SD, the ED is used as a specific sequence to signal the end of a token.

Now, back to the middle octet in the token. This octet is called the access control (AC) byte, which equates to the working portion of the token. The 8 bits are made up of a series of working bits that define what is happening inside the token, as shown in Figure 10-27. Bits 1 through 3 in the access control byte are marked as priority (P) bits. Each device on the network

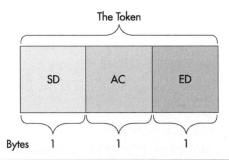

Figure 10-26 The token is composed of three octets when it traverses the network in idle state.

has an assigned priority. Eight priorities can be used on the network. In order of succession, 000 will be the lowest-priority device and 111 will be the highest-priority device. For a node to transmit information on the network, it must have the token (of course, the token must be free). The device must have equal or greater priority than the token to use it. This will allow certain devices to have a higher priority to send information than others.

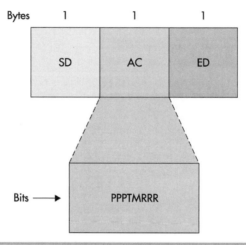

Figure 10-27 The bit sequencing inside the token lets the devices know the status of the token.

The fourth bit is called the token (T) bit; it signals what is present, a token (T = 0) or a frame of data (T = 1). Two possibilities exist as the token comes around: it is either a free token or a busy token containing user information.

Bit number 5 is used as a monitor (M) bit for network token control. A device on the network is assigned the responsibility of monitoring what happens on the network. The transmitting station (sender) sets the M bit in the token to a 0. As the token goes by the active monitor, it sets the M bit to a 1. If the monitor station receives an incoming priority token or a frame with the M = 1 set, it knows the transmitting station did not take the information off the network after a round trip. The monitor station then takes the token off and cleans it up. Then it issues a new token to be used on the network. There is still only one token on the network at this point. To prevent any major problems on such a network, the monitor station is set up to handle the problems with tokens on the network.

Bits 6, 7, and 8 of the AC byte are allocated as reservation (R) bits. Remember the priority levels? Well, if a server or any other device has information to send across the network and it has a high priority, it can reserve the token for its use on the next pass around the network.

The Abort Sequence

Figure 10-28 shows the abort sequence used in the Token Ring network. In the event that problems exist on the network, the nodes are designed to recognize the problem and discard the token. The abort sequence includes the capability to read the start delimiter and the end delimiter, to place them together, and to issue this to the network by the detecting node. This alerts all nodes on the network that the problem exists. Things that can go wrong will go wrong. This can include such problems as data corruption, lost tokens, time-outs, address problems, and so on.

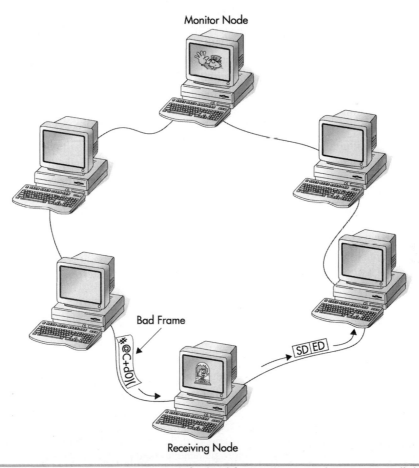

Figure 10-28 The abort sequence is used if a bad frame is received. Dropping all the data, the processor on the NIC places the SD and ED bytes together, and it sends them out to all nodes.

The Frame

Above and beyond the token format, the ring carries a frame of information known as the data frame, which is shown in Figure 10-29. The **data frame** has a variable length based on the data inside. This is composed of the following pieces:

- The SD in the token frame

- Access control (AC)

- These constitute the first 2 bytes of the data frame

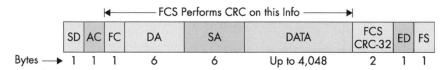

Figure 10-29 The token is now called a frame when data is appended to the sequence. The description of each byte in the frame is similar to that of the Ethernet.

Following these two bytes come:

- The frame control (FC) byte, which indicates the type of data in the frame.

- The destination address (DA) of the token, a definition of where the frame is being sent. The destination address is 6 bytes (48 bits) long.

- The source address (SA), the indicator of where the frame came from or who sent it. This address is also 6 bytes long.

- The data. In this field, the actual information being sent is provided. It can be just information, or it can also contain such information as MAC or LLC information or routing information. This allows all physical and data link overhead to be contained inside the data packet transparently. The data field is a variable amount of information that can be up to 4,048 bytes on a 4-Mbps network and up to 16,192 bytes on a 16-Mbps network.

NOTE

This is much larger than a typical Ethernet frame, and, therefore, less overhead is associated with each frame. The result is more potential throughput than Ethernet.

- The frame check sequence (FCS), which is a CRC-32 error-detection pattern that checks the validity of the information in the FC, DA, SA, data, and FCS bytes. Using a 32-bit CRC, the error-detection capability is better than 99.99995 percent. If a single bit error occurs in the transmission of the frame, the frame will be tossed out. This is fairly stringent, but must be used to ensure the integrity of the data on the network.

- The end delimiter (ED) from the original token. This is a single byte of information.

- The frame status (FS) byte, which indicates the status of the actual frame. In this byte control, mechanisms are used to determine what has happened since the data was initially sent by the transmitting station.

REMEMBER

The Token Ring network is deterministic. The network uses 1 bit time per station attached. This helps to plan the network performance. The frame and token combination allow for integrity checking and acknowledgment of receipt.

In Figure 10-30, the various bits used in the FS byte are shown. There are reasons for this technique. First, the figure shows the byte is composed of a sequence that mimics ACxxACxx where:

- The *A* bits are used by the receiving device to indicate the destination address was recognized.

- The *C* bits are used by the receiving device to indicate the information (data) was copied.

- The *x* bits are not used and, therefore, are ignored.

- The *A* and *C* bits inside the FS byte are important for the overall control of the network.

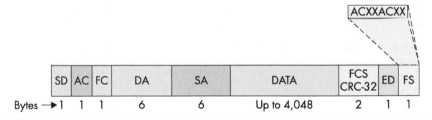

Figure 10-30 The frame check sequence is the means of verifying that the data is received correctly. If it is not, a retransmission will be requested.

Other Protocols Used on a LAN

As much as a LAN is a physical medium used to move data in a localized area, other protocols are used to help in making them work. These other protocols are mainly used for the operation and administration of the LAN. The protocols simplify the network administrator's job of assigning addresses, managing less intelligent devices on a LAN, and handling other addressing issues. The following protocols are part of the LAN and, at the same time, tightly integrated with the layer 3 protocols (like IP) used on a LAN.

Address Resolution Protocol (ARP)/Reverse ARP

On some media (such as IEEE 802 LANs), media addresses, and IP addresses are dynamically discovered with two other members of the Internet protocol suite:

- **Address Resolution Protocol (ARP)**
- **Reverse Address Resolution Protocol (RARP)**

On a single physical network, individual hosts are known on the network by their physical hardware address. Higher-level protocols address destination hosts in the form of a symbolic address (IP address in this case). When such a protocol wants to send a datagram to destination IP address w.x.y.z, the device driver does not understand this address.

Therefore, a module ARP is provided that will associate the IP address to the physical address of the destination host. It uses a lookup table (sometimes referred to as the ARP cache) to perform this translation.

When the address is not found in the ARP cache, a broadcast is sent out on the network, with a special format called the ARP request. If one of the machines on the network recognizes its own IP address in the request, it will send an ARP reply back to the requesting host. The reply will contain the physical hardware address of the host and source route information. Both this address and the source route information are stored in the ARP cache of the requesting host. All subsequent datagrams to this destination IP address can now be translated to a physical address, which is used by the device driver to send out the datagram on the network. Figure 10-31 is a representation of the ARP request being sent out across the LAN to resolve the MAC address of a device.

ARP uses broadcast messages to determine the hardware MAC-layer address corresponding to a particular internetwork address. ARP is sufficiently generic to allow use of IP with virtually any type of underlying media-access mechanism. When the MAC address is unknown, ARP will generate a message across the LAN. The message will be that the sender has an IP address to send, but it does not know the MAC address. This broadcast asks for the MAC layer address to use. All devices on the network will hear the broadcast, but only the device with the IP address will respond. It will send back a message to use the following MAC address, as shown in Figure 10-32. ARP was designed to be used on networks that support hardware broadcast. This means, for example, that ARP will not work on an X.25 network.

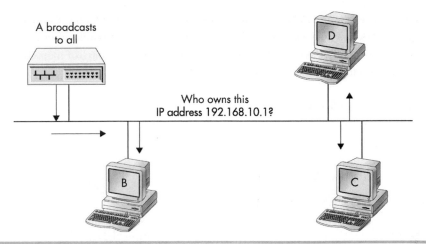

Figure 10-31 The ARP request is broadcast across the network looking for a device to recognize its IP in the request.

Reverse Address Resolution Protocol (RARP)

The RARP protocol is a network-specific standard protocol. It is described in RFC 903. Some network hosts, such as diskless workstations, do not know their own IP address when they are booted. To determine their own IP address, they use a mechanism similar to ARP, but now the

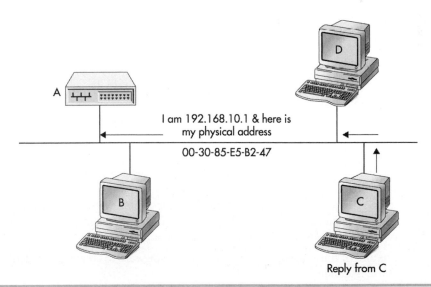

Figure 10-32 The ARP reply is sent back to the original device with a MAC address appended to the request.

hardware address of the host is the known parameter, and the IP address the queried parameter. See Figure 10-33 for the RARP query. It differs more fundamentally from ARP because a RARP server must exist on the network that maintains that a database of mappings from hardware address to protocol address must be preconfigured.

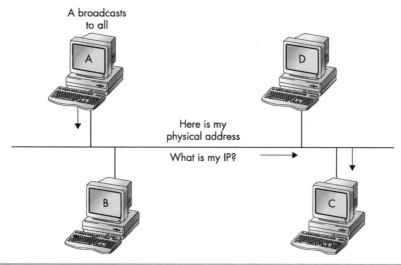

A broadcasts
to all

Here is my
physical address

What is my IP?

Figure 10-33 RARP is the opposite of ARP, where the station device knows its MAC and is looking for its IP address.

RARP Concept

The reverse address resolution is performed the same way as the ARP address resolution. The same query format is used as for ARP. Some differences arise from the concept of RARP itself:

- ARP assumes every host knows the mapping between its own hardware address and its protocol address. RARP requires one or more server hosts on the network to maintain a database of mappings between hardware addresses and protocol addresses, so they will be able to reply to requests from client hosts.

- Because of the size this database can take, part of the server function is usually implemented outside the adapter's microcode with a small cache optionally in the microcode. The microcode part is then only responsible for reception and transmission of the RARP frames. The RARP mapping itself is being taken care of by server software, running as a normal process in the host machine.

- The nature of this database also requires some software to create and update the database manually.

- In case multiple RARP servers are on the network, the RARP requester only uses the first RARP reply received on its broadcast RARP request and discards the others.

RARP uses broadcast messages to determine the Internet address associated with a particular hardware address. RARP is particularly important to diskless nodes, which may not know their internetwork address when they boot. See Figure 10-34 for the response from the RARP server.

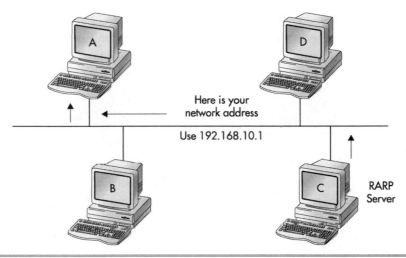

Here is your
network address

Use 192.168.10.1

RARP
Server

Figure 10-34 The RARP reply issues the IP address to the host that provided its MAC address.

❓ Line Check 10-3

The protocol used for a diskless workstation to determine its IP address is called _____.

The protocol used to resolve an IP to a MAC address is called _____.

Bootstrap Protocol (BOOTP)

The **Bootstrap Protocol (BOOTP)** can be seen as an extension of RARP, enabling a client workstation to initialize with a minimal IP stack and request its IP address, a gateway address, and the address of a name server from a BOOTP server. If BOOTP is to be used in your network, then the server and client are usually on the same physical LAN segment. BOOTP can only be used across bridged segments when source-routing bridges are being used, or across subnets, if you have a router capable of BOOTP forwarding.

The BOOTP specifications can be found in RFC 951—Bootstrap Protocol. Updates to BOOTP, some relating to interoperability with DHCP, are also described in RFC 1542—Clarifications and Extensions for the Bootstrap Protocol, which updates RFC 951 and RFC 2132—DHCP Options and BOOTP Vendor Extensions. The updates to BOOTP are draft standards with a status of elective and recommended, respectively.

The BOOTP protocol was originally developed as a mechanism to enable diskless hosts to be remotely booted over a network as workstations, routers, terminal concentrators, and so on. It allows a minimum IP protocol stack with no configuration information to obtain enough information to begin the process of downloading the necessary boot code.

Dynamic Host Configuration Protocol (DHCP)

The current specifications can be found in RFC 2131—Dynamic Host Configuration Protocol (DHCP) and RFC 2132—DHCP Options and BOOTP Vendor Extensions.

The **DHCP** provides a framework for passing configuration information to hosts on a TCP/IP network. DHCP is based on the BOOTP protocol, adding the capability of automatic allocation of reusable network addresses and additional configuration options.

DHCP consists of two components:

1. A protocol that delivers host-specific configuration parameters from a DHCP server to a host.

2. A mechanism for the allocation of temporary or permanent network addresses to hosts.

IP requires the setting of many parameters within the protocol implementation software. Because IP can be used on many dissimilar kinds of network hardware, values for those parameters cannot be guessed at or assumed to have correct defaults. The use of a distributed-address allocation scheme based on a polling/defense mechanism, for discovery of network addresses already in use, cannot guarantee unique network addresses because hosts may not always be able to defend their network addresses.

DHCP supports three mechanisms for IP address allocation:

1. Automatic allocation—DHCP assigns a permanent IP address to the host.

2. Dynamic allocation—DHCP assigns an IP address for a limited period of time. Such a network address is called a *lease*. This is the only mechanism that allows automatic reuse of addresses that are no longer needed by the host to which it was assigned. The lease is a short-term assignment of the address used in DHCP.

3. Manual allocation—The host's address is assigned by a network administrator.

NOTE

Responses from the DHCP server to the DHCP client may be broadcast or unicast, depending on whether the client is able to receive a unicast message before the TCP/IP stack is fully configured. This varies between implementations. The DHCP protocol issues an address with a lease for configurable intervals.

Internetworking

Internetworking refers to the connecting of two or more networks—LANs, WANs, or a mixture of the two.

The creators of LANs designed them to be truly "local." This was not an arbitrarily imposed design restriction. By not requiring a LAN to be capable of wide area communications, the engineers could take advantage of a much more controlled environment. That control allowed the use of techniques that, while not practical over a wide area, could deliver far higher communications performance than WAN communications of the day, as well as reliability orders of magnitude faster than those same WAN communications.

But, people being what they are, a demand soon materialized for the capability to provide LAN-type communications (that is, fast, having a lower error rate, and using typical LAN protocols) over areas wider than those originally envisioned as being supportable by LANs. And engineers, being what they are, came up with not one but several ways of accomplishing this. All involve the use of additional devices that, in varying ways, take a LAN signal and send it farther than the original LAN specification allows.

Terminology is important here. We cover four types of devices that provide such extended LAN connectivity. The first type (repeaters) is considered to extend the reach of a given LAN. As such, using repeaters is not technically "internetworking," although we describe it in this section because it nonetheless involves extending the reach of LAN technology in a given environment. All three of the other technologies (bridges, routers, and gateways) are considered to provide connections among or between different LANs, thus providing true internetworking capabilities. The reason for this division between repeaters and the rest should become apparent as we cover the devices in more detail. We begin with the simplest of the devices and then go on to more sophisticated products.

Repeaters

Repeaters are relatively unintelligent connections between two LAN segments of the same type (Ethernet, Token Ring, and so forth). A repeater is sensitive to the traffic's content only at the OSI layer 1 (physical) layer. An Ethernet repeater will transmit any traffic that can be sent on Ethernet, a Token Ring repeater will send on all Token Ring traffic, and so on, without

10

having any knowledge of the frame or data being passed. This is because a repeater only looks at each signal on the wire for the individual bit it represents. Repeaters satisfy only three key functions:

- Distance
- Electrical isolation
- Media conversion

Repeaters, as layer 1 devices, perform their role by listening to an incoming signal on the medium, interpreting its digital value, and then creating a new signal of the same value. In that way, they clean up the signal received because the repeater does not merely amplify an incoming signal, but interprets it as a 0 or 1 and creates a new signal. This is the fundamental advantage of sending digital information over sending analog information—the capability of the repeater to create a clean new signal as opposed to an amplifier. An amplifier would boost the incoming signal, but it would also amplify the noise that had accumulated during the transmission.

Bridges

Bridges are intelligent connections between two LANs of the same type. They operate at layer 2 of the OSI reference model (data link). Bridges provide filtering and forwarding services across the link. A filter is used if an addressable device is on the network sending the frame (this is done so a frame of information does not get sent across the wires to another segment or network that has no need to see the frame). Forwarding takes place when the bridge sees a frame addressed to a node on the other side of the link. In this way, bridges differ from repeaters in that they recognize and manage frames, not bits. Repeaters can have one input and one output, and they can be used to connect two physical LAN segments or they can have multiple ports. A multiport repeater is usually referred to as a hub.

Routers

Routers are devices that connect LANs to other LANs (often through WAN connections). Routers connect local networks to the Internet and allow networks to connect to networks through the Internet, through dedicated T-1 lines, or through other means. Working at layer 3 of the OSI model (routing, or network layer), the router will be responsible for finding a path from the source to its destination. Routers support layer 3 protocols, such as AppleTalk, IPX, and TCP/IP, the protocol that enables the Internet.

There are several considerations about this process because the router is more sophisticated; therefore, it is more complex to manage. However, this added complexity brings significant gains to the users who are looking to internetwork their LANs, in speed, resiliency, and flexibility. Routers can evaluate which is the best path to take when multiple paths are available and can switch paths as network conditions change. Routers also can make the distinction between local traffic, which can stay within the LAN, and remote traffic, which needs to leave the LAN for an external destination network, which lowers the bandwidth requirements on the WAN links. Many large organizations now use routers in their backbone network to connect segments (departments, floors on a building, and so forth) together with alternative paths to get from one LAN segment to another. The feeling is the resiliency is worth the added complexity.

Gateways

Gateways connect two networks of different types (that is, a LAN to an X.25 network). They operate at higher levels of the OSI model; ISO levels 4 to 7 (transport, session, presentation, and application). In effect, the gateway handles everything above the network layer in the OSI model. The controlling portion of a session, the format and protocol conversion to make all things common, and the actual application interface reside in the gateway's domain for interconnectivity.

Benefits of using gateways include an initial cost savings, high performance, and high flexibility and scalability.

REMEMBER

Repeaters operate at the physical layer (1).

Bridges operate at the data-link layer (2) and below.

Routers operate at the network layer (3) and below.

Gateways operate at the application layer (7) and below.

LAN Switching versus Nonswitched

When discussing driving habits, some people say, "Speed kills." That may be true, but in the case of networks, lack of speed can kill. You can design networks in many ways, but one of the most popular and straightforward is to design a backbone whereby a high-speed path exists for high-speed requirements at a central point (topologically speaking) and all subsidiary networks connect to that backbone, as shown in Figure 10-35. This model has several assumptions. One is this: a need exists for connections between the subnetworks or from each of the subnetworks to that central backbone, possibly for server or application access. These assumptions are not necessarily valid. For example, if the business primarily uses LANs to provide office-automation capabilities, there may be a whole series of islands of automation where it doesn't matter that they are islands. We certainly don't want to be loading applications across the wide area, and if all you are doing is loading applications and storing such data as word-processing or spreadsheet information, then you don't need a backbone to connect with disparate networks.

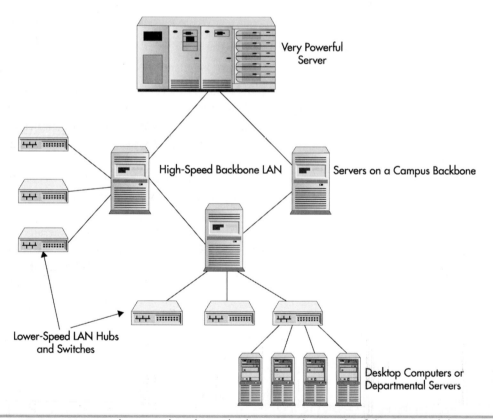

Figure 10-35 LANs can be mixed and matched to serve the needs of the user and the speed required to meet the demand. Lower speeds may be used at the desktop, whereas higher-speed network services can also be introduced.

Many cases occur, however, where backbones are required, so speed is important. The technologies suitable for high-speed networks are described later in this chapter. Here, we are talking about a way to deliver somewhat higher speed to desktops or for small backbones.

The typical office-automation network designer has to make a choice about where various components reside. The major components are data and applications. Ideally, we believe that data ought to be stored centrally, whereas applications ought to be executed from the desktop. Why? It's a matter of performance. The internal bus speeds of even medium-speed desktop computers far exceed the capabilities of cost-effective LANs. Loading applications takes a long time, relatively speaking. When you have a lot of people doing this at the same time, it can bury a network. You can pay the money to upgrade in the way we're going to describe here, but an easier approach is simply to distribute the applications to the desktop. But, you say, that is a maintenance nightmare! In the past, it was. Applications are available today that will distribute software to the desktop in a cost-effective and efficient manner. It is not necessary to touch every desktop to install or update applications if you have LAN connectivity to those desktops from a distribution server.

We realize, however, that not every company has installed such software distribution capabilities or is convinced this is the way to go. So, what do they do when the performance penalty of loading applications from servers to all the desktops begins to bury their networks? Wouldn't it be nice if they could simply change the central equipment in the network and get a speed kicker? They can, in fact, do exactly that!

With older technology, such as coaxial Ethernet, this wouldn't work. But the technology we're going to discuss—switching—does allow for a speed boost, a real capacity boost, without necessarily touching the desktops in any way.

The key fact to remember here is that most LANs employ shared media. Generally, when we refer to shared media, we mean Ethernet hub-based LANs and Token Rings. Even though both topologies in modern networks are wired with star-type wiring, the equipment at the center, as previously discussed, causes every node in a ring or Ethernet segment to see all the traffic generated by all the other nodes. They are designed this way, and it is a good way to design a network for many reasons. However, when the traffic starts increasing, everybody sees all the increases. That's a problem. How do we address it? We replace the central piece of equipment—an Ethernet hub or a Token Ring MAU—with a corresponding switch.

The job of a switch is twofold:

- A switch has to make the traffic on the wires to the devices to which the switch is connected look exactly as it did before, from the point of view of the connected devices, because we are not planning on changing the electronics in those devices.

- A switch examines every packet coming in on every wire and, on a packet-by-packet basis, forwards those packets outbound to only the port or circuit where the packet has to go.

10

This may sound like routing, but it happens at a much lower (and, therefore, faster) level of the architecture than that at which routing takes place. Routing is done at OSI layer 3 on protocols such as IPX or TCP/IP, and it involves rebuilding packets as they transfer from network-to-network. Switching is done down at layer 2, the MAC layer, and doesn't rebuild any frames. Switching merely controls where they can travel and where they shouldn't, on the basis of the hardware addresses of the connected network devices, so it's fast. But the speed alone is not what creates the major benefit here. The major benefit is the only traffic put on a wire going to a device is traffic destined for that device (plus broadcast traffic, unfortunately). So, that wire only sees traffic to and from that device. In effect, what this means is the wire now has the full-rated bandwidth of the network dedicated to only that device and the connections it's talking to. That bandwidth is no longer shared. Whereas before you might have had an Ethernet running at 10 Mbps and 30 devices sharing that bandwidth, now each device sees 10 Mbps coming to its doorstep and no other traffic to degrade that. This is a major performance upgrade.

REMEMBER
Switching is done at layer 2 of the OSI model. LANs operate at the MAC layer.

Some limitations do exist, however. For one thing, this is not necessarily a good way to upgrade server connectivity. If you think about it, you will realize the connection going into the server is still 10 Mbps, or 16 Mbps in the case of Token Ring. Traffic on wires going to workstations without a switch would have lots of traffic that wasn't designated for those workstations when using either Ethernet or Token Ring. But in a typical small network, all of the traffic is going to or from the server if there is only one server. So, giving it a switched connection doesn't help much because all the traffic is still going to have to appear on that circuit. Now you've upgraded both the workstations and the server connection, and you have an overall increase that means you're less likely to have bottlenecks.

The beauty of this approach (switching to improve connectivity capacity to workstations) is you only have to change the central hub. The electronics in the workstations remain the same, as does the wiring. Even if the hubs cost two or three times per port what a nonswitching hub would cost, it is still cost-effective when you consider the alternatives.

In addition to a simple lowering of the traffic levels, collisions are usually avoided in this approach because there aren't other devices on any particular segment that are trying to get in at the same time. Put another way, the segment becomes a single wire connecting, or virtually connecting, two devices talking back and forth through the hub without any interfering traffic to get in the way. It all becomes a matter of need and preference on how this is implemented.

Chapter 10 Review

Chapter Summary

When the 1980s rolled around, the PC was invented and began to find its place in the office. This device was expensive, so a resource-sharing need emerged. To solve this problem, the LAN was created. A LAN is a resource-sharing arrangement that is localized to a department, floor, or division. It allows for a high-speed communications medium with low error rates and offers these services without common control. This means no one device controls the network, as was the case with mainframe and mid-range computer platforms.

As the LANs are deployed, we structure them with both a physical and a logical connectivity solution. The three main forms of physical topology are the bus, ring, and star. Hybrids of the three topologies exist when we structure the logical connection, such as a physical star and a logical bus connection.

Ethernet is the predominant LAN technology used across the world. As a shared medium and half-duplex service, it was introduced to deliver 10 Mbps. Later evolutions include full-duplex, switched, and higher speeds operating at 100, 1,000, and now 10,000 Mbps. A hub used in a closet accommodates the hybrid of a star and bus combination. To arrange for migrations paths, the NIC can be an autosensing 10/100-Mbps card that will operate at the highest speed available.

IBM developed the Token Ring as a competitive solution to Ethernet. However, at 4 Mbps, people were not impressed. Also, the proprietary nature of the IBM systems discouraged many from endorsing this system. Later, the Token Ring was adjusted to run at 16 Mbps, but it still found little acceptance. Today, Token Ring is all but obsolete.

Wireless LANs are based on infrared or radio frequency. They operate at 1–2–5.5–11 and now 54 Mbps. The wireless LANs today are one of the fastest deployed services that companies and residential users are installing. The standards are similar to, but different from, Ethernet. WLANs are IEEE 802.11*x*, whereas Ethernet is an IEEE 802.3.

When a device does not know its MAC address but does know its IP address, the ARP protocol is used to resolve the two addresses. Conversely, when a diskless workstation knows its MAC but does not know its IP, then RARP is used. BOOTP is used to assign the IP to a diskless workstation from a pool of IP addresses that are stored.

DHCP is another way to assign addresses to devices (hosts, terminals, diskless workstations) as IP addresses. The DHCP server assigns an IP on a lease for short term. This can be renewed on a periodic basis.

Key Terms for Chapter 10

100Base-T *(455)*
10BASE2 *(447)*
10BASE5 *(447)*
10BASE-F *(451)*
10BASE-T *(447)*
10Broad 36 *(451)*
802.3af *(471)*
802.3q *(460)*
802.3u *(455)*
802.3z *(459)*
802.11 *(462)*
802.11a *(470)*
802.11b *(470)*
802.11g *(470)*
802.11n *(474)*
Address Resolution Protocol (ARP) *(484)*
Ad-Hoc Network *(463)*
Baseband *(447)*
Basic Service Set (BSS) *(462)*
Bootstrap Protocol (BOOTP) *(487)*
Bridges *(490)*
Client-Server *(433)*
CSMA/CA *(467)*
CSMA/CD *(441)*
Data *(446)*
Data Frame *(482)*
Deterministic System *(476)*
Direct Sequence Spread Spectrum (DSSS) *(465)*
Distributed Processing *(433)*
Distribution System (DS) *(469)*
Dynamic Host Configuration Protocol (DHCP) *(488)*
Ethernet *(440)*
Error Rate *(425)*
Extended Service Set (ESS) *(469)*
Fast Ethernet *(454)*
Frame *(444)*
Frequency Hopping Spread Spectrum (FHSS) *(465)*
Gateways *(491)*
GigE *(459)*
Local Area Network (LAN) *(424)*

Key Term Quiz   *LAN — page 424*

1. The __LAN__ is a sharing of resources that is bounded by distances.

2. To make the connection on the network, a __NIC-Card__ is installed in each PC.

3. __Ethernet__ runs at 10 Mbps, 100 Mbps, and 1,000 Mbps.

4. Each PC card has a unique __MAC-Address__ that consists of 48 bits (6 bytes).

5. The IEEE set the standards for Ethernet, naming it the __802.3__ standard.

6. To handle contention and possible collisions on the network, Ethernet uses __NIC-__. *(full duplex)*

7. Wireless LANs conform to the IEEE __802.11 X__ standard.

8. __fast-ethernet__ is another name for 100Base-T.

9. IBM created the __Token Ring__ network as a competitor to Ethernet. *infrared or radio frequency*

10. Wireless LANs can use __Infrared__ to achieve higher data rates of up to 54 Mbps.

11. A __Switch__ operates at layer 2 of the OSI and links two network segments together by filtering and forwarding across the segment.

12. __Routers__ work at layer 3 of the OSI model and, typically, forward packets to networks across the WAN.

Multiple-Choice Quiz

1. What is the main reason for installing a LAN?

   a. Making a network

   b. Sharing resources

   c. Because everyone else is doing it

   d. It is cheap

2. When the first LANs were used, they were both _____ and _____ laid out.

   a. Physically and topology

   b. Physiological and topological

   c. Physically and logically

   d. Physically and mentally

3. The three basic forms of a LAN are:

   a. Ring, bus, and star

   b. Ring, star, and hub

   c. Star, spoke, and wheel

   d. Physical, logical, and topological

4. The perceived need for a LAN began in _____.

   a. 1990

   b. 1980

   c. 1996

   d. 1974

5. Data switches, or data PBXs, were alternatives, but they could only support:

   a. IBM data

   b. Lower speeds

   c. Higher speeds

   d. Dial-up connections

6. One of the less obvious characteristics of a LAN is that all devices on it are viewed and function as being _____.

   a. Equals

   b. Subservient

   c. Adjacent

   d. Tangent

7. Ethernet is, in fact, a _____ medium.

   a. Duplex

   b. Half-duplex

   c. Simplex

   d. Bus

8. Every keystroke on terminals connected to a main computer generates a _____.

   a. Letter

   b. Interrupt

   c. Symbol

   d. Flag

9. Each node is connected to only two other nodes, which implies we are looking at a _____.

   a. Bus

   b. Star

   c. Spoke

   d. Ring

10. The use of a _____ server helps to share documents.

   a. File

   b. Print

   c. Application

   d. Communications

11. The card placed inside the PC is called _____.

   a. The LAN card

   b. The Network Interface Card (NIC)

   c. The Server Card

   d. A token

12. Routers are sophisticated and, therefore, more complex to _____.

   a. Design

   b. Install

   c. Purchase

   d. Manage

13. The NIC provides a unique LAN address called the _____.

   a. MAC node

   b. Apple Interface

   c. LAN address

   d. MAC address

14. LAN switches operate at layer _____ of the OSI model.

   a. 1

   b. 2

   c. 3

   d. 6

15. The device that spans the upper layers of the OSI model on a LAN is called a _____.

   a. Bridge

   b. Router

   c. Repeater

   d. Gateway

16. What three companies originally formed the Ethernet standard?

   a. IBM, DEC, and Xerox

   b. Intel, DEC, and IBM

c. Intel, Xerox, and DEC

d. Intel, DEC, and IEEE

17. The original speed for Ethernet was designed at _____.

   a. 1 Mbps

   b. 10 Mbps

   c. 100 Mbps

   d. 1,000 Mbps

18. The use of a _____ was the first Ethernet cabling system used.

   a. Thick wire fiber

   b. Thin wire coax

   c. Thick wire coax

   d. Thin fiber

19. The Ethernet specification that used thin coax is called _____.

   a. 10Base5

   b. 10Base2

   c. 100Base10

   d. 10Base-F

20. The 10Broad 36 standard is used by which other industry?

   a. The telephone companies

   b. The cable TV companies

   c. Corporations

   d. The ISPs

21. Regular 10-Mbps Ethernet will deliver approximately what throughput?

   a. 10 Mbps

   b. 6–8 Mbps

   c. 3.3–4 Mbps

   d. 5–6 Mbps

22. The Ethernet contention standard is called _____.

   a. CSMA/CA

   b. CSMA/DC

   c. CSMA/CDR

   d. CSMA/CD

23. The Ethernet standard is called _____.

   a. 802.1

   b. 802.5

   c. 802.11

   d. 802.3

24. The 802.11 series of wireless standards will deliver between _____ Mbps.

   a. 1 and 10

   b. 2 and 11

   c. 1 and 54

   d. 1–10–100

25. The minimum size frame in an Ethernet network is _____ bytes.

   a. 46

   b. 64

   c. 128

   d. 1,500

26. The Ethernet frame carries a payload of between _____ and ___ bytes.

   a. 64 and 1,518

   b. 46 and 1,500

   c. 64 and 1,500

   d. 46 and 1,518

27. Wireless LANs use the following contention algorithm:

    a. CSMA/CD

    b. CSMA/CC

    c. CSMA/CA

    d. TRS/CTS

Lab Projects

1. Most PCs come with a built-in NIC. Connect two devices together with a cable using RJ-45 jacks on both ends and set up a communication between them. Will it work? (Did the student use a cross-over cable or a straight-through cable?) Use a cross-over cable and connect these two PCs together. Set the IP to get a DHCP address. Now can they connect?

2. Using two PCs with built-in wireless NICs, do the same thing. Link the two together and let the system autodetect the speed and assign the IP address. Can they connect? Is the system set for ad-hoc mode?

3. Log on to the Internet with a wired and a wireless connection simultaneously. Download a file from the Internet that is at least 5 MB large and time the two. Which one delivers the fastest speed? Why? (Depending on the wired or wireless interface, the answer could be either device performs better. The WAN link is probably the same and slower than either the wired or wireless connection, so the interface in wired or wireless may make no difference.)

Chapter 11

Packets, Frames, and Cell-Switching Concepts

LEARNING OBJECTIVES:

Once you complete this chapter, you will be able to:

Understanding the concept of packet switching.

Identify the components of the packet-switching networks.

Discuss the process of switched virtual circuits.

Describe frame relay.

Understand the rationale for using frame relay services.

Describe the addressing techniques of frame relay.

Discuss the concept of cell relay.

Understand why the cells are so important.

Describe the broadband concept with ATM.

Understand how ATM is a precursor to B-ISDN.

Discuss the benefits of using Cell relay.

We spent a considerable amount of time in past chapters covering the pros and cons of the dial-up telephone network for voice and data communications. Remember, when the network was originally fashioned, it was designed as an analog voice telephone network.

In the late 1950s, the thought of carrying data communication blossomed. This was not a major problem because many other systems (Telex, TWX, and so forth) were already in place to carry low-speed data communications. Dial-up modem communications on the telephone network were moving data across the network at relatively low speeds, such as 1,200 bits per second or less. Data transfers and host-access applications being used on the network were rudimentary.

A problem existed, however, with data transfer. Earlier, we discussed the problems that could be experienced on the dial-up telephone network. The use of a modem implies that an analog data transmission is used, so all the problems inherent in analog communications were present. For voice, the analog systems posed no major problem. If a human does not understand part of a conversation, the problem is easily rectified. We merely shout, "What?" into the phone, and the conversation is immediately retransmitted—that is, the person on the other end repeats what was just said. If the line is too bad (full of static, snap, crackle, and other noises), then the two humans agree to hang up and remake the call, hoping for a better connection.

Data Communications Problems

In the data-communications world, things were different. Back in the early days of data transmission, transmission protocols were not as sophisticated as they are today. Consequently, if a data transfer was attempted, the overhead was significant. Refer to Chapter 8 on data communications and you will see that in the case of an asynchronous transmission, employing an ASCII code sent over the dial-up telephone network used approximately 40 percent overhead. This was a tremendous burden in data transfer. When you apply a 2,400-bit-per-second transmit mode with 40 percent overhead, the net data rate is only around 1,440 bits per second.

The Data Communications Review

This scenario was more the norm than the exception. Users were easily frustrated with the data communications system and dreaded using a modem. Clearly, the industry had to do something about the problem. In the late 1960s, the CCITT, now called the International Telecommunication Union (ITU), commissioned a study group to look for a resolution to this and many other problems. The study group arrived at several initial findings:

- The network was unreliable. Further, the use of data transmission across the analog network was at risk.

- The rollout of digital services was still limited, and the service was primarily a carrier service.

- Other systems, such as message store and forward, although more reliable than straight dial-up connections, still became congested delivering messages at customer demand. Therefore, the network could delay delivery for hours, if not days, because of the congestion factor.

- Other services did not offer any reliability, regardless of the delay.

The response to this whole study was the recommendation to use a packet-switching transport system, which would guarantee the reliable delivery of data, break the data down into more manageable pieces, deliver the data at the convenience of the network, sequentially deliver the information, and recover from any failures that might occur on the link without requiring retransmission of the entire file.

Line Check 11-1

Test what you learned and see what you have retained by filling in the blanks.

The data networks at the time were discovered to be _____.

The rollout of digital services was _____.

Other systems, such as message store and forward, were more _____ than dial-up data.

Other services did not offer any reliability, regardless of the _____.

Packet Switching Defined

Packet switching was born to accomplish these goals. To define packet switching, then, we will use the following guidelines:

Packet switching is a means of taking a large file (data) and delivering it to a processing device (either hardware or software). The hardware or software breaks the information down into smaller, more manageable pieces. As these pieces are broken down, additional overhead is applied to the original piece of data. This added overhead is used for control purposes. Because the information is segmented (broken into packets), the packet service inserts a unique destination address (like the telephone number of the addressee), along with the segment number (that is, packet #1, packet #2, packet #3, and so forth), so the data can be reassembled at the receiving end. Once the overhead is attached to the segmented data (now called a packet), the packet is transmitted across a physical link to a switching system that reads the address information (telephone number) and routes the packet accordingly. This establishes a virtual circuit to the distant end, and each packet is sent along the same route as the first packet (though for successful data transmission, different packets could even take different routes to the destination, as long as all packets arrived). A **virtual circuit** is a connection-oriented network service that is implemented on top of a network, which may be either connection-oriented or connectionless (packet switching).

Packet switching is a layer 3 protocol when compared to the OSI model. The system uses a connection-oriented transport based on a virtual circuit. This is quite a definition to work from. With this as a starting point, the rest should be easy to break down and discuss. We can "packetize" the definition and work at explaining it piece by piece.

❓ Line Check 11-2

Define packet switching.

What Is Packet Switching?

As already mentioned, packet switching is a means of breaking down the larger data files into more manageable pieces. Here's an example using the X.25 protocol that might make the whole concept a little easier to comprehend.

The Packet Concept

If an organization has large amounts of data to send, then the data can be delivered to a device called a packet assembler/disassembler (PAD). The **PAD** acts as the originating mail clerk in that the originating PAD receives the data and breaks it down into manageable pieces or packets. In the data-communications arena, a packet can be a variable length of information, usually up to 128 bytes of data (one page in the example). Other implementers of X.25 services have created packets up to 512 bytes, but the average is 128 bytes. The 128-byte capability is also referred to as a fast select. The **fast select** allows the packet-switching system to immediately route the packet to a distant end and pass data of up to 128 bytes (1,024 bits).

Overhead

To this packet, the PAD then applies some overhead as follows:

- An opening flag that is made up of 8 bits of information. Using a standard **High-Level Data Link Control (HDLC)** framing format covered in the chapters on data and LANs, the opening flag is a sequence of 8 bits that should not be construed as real data.

- A 16-bit address sequence, which is a binary description of the end points (the "from" address).

Control information consists of 8 bits of data describing the type of HDLC frame traversing the network (this is a notation on the envelope that describes the information inside). These can be supervisory, unnumbered, or information fields. To be more specific, these break down as follows:

- Information (I) is used to transfer data across the link at a rate determined by the receiver and with error detection and correction.

- Supervisory (S) is used to determine the ready state of the devices—receiver is ready (RR), receiver is not ready (RNR), or reject (REJ).

- Unnumbered is used to dictate parameters, such as set modes, disconnect, and so on.

Packet-specific information follows the HDLC information. The packet information consists of the following information:

- **General format identifier (GFI)**—4 bits of information that describe how the data in the packet is being used: from/to an end user, from/to a device controlling the end user device, and so on.

- **Logical channel group number (LGN)**—4 bits that describe the grouping of channels. Because only 4 bits are available, only eight combinations are used.

- **Logical channel number (LCN)**—an 8-bit description of the actual channel being used. The theoretical number of channels (ports) available is 2,048. The logical channels are broken down by channel groups, so the numbers play out (Table 11-1). Although the number of logical channels can be 2,048, most organizations implement significantly fewer ports or channels.

Type	Logical Group	Logical Channel	Number of Channels
PVC	0	1–255	0–255
PVC	1	256–511	0–255
Incoming-only	2	512–767	0–255
SVC	3	768–1,023	0–255
Two-way	4	1,024–1,279	0–255
SVC	5	1,280–1,535	0–255
Outgoing-only	6	1,536–1,791	0–255
SVC	7	1,792–2,047	0–255

Table 11-1 Summary of Logical Groups and Channel Numbers.

- **Packet type identifier (PTI)**—an 8-bit sequence that describes the type of packet being sent across the network. Six different packet types are used in an X.25 switching network. These packet types define what is expected of the devices across the network. The packet types are shown in Table 11-2. Note that the packet types have different uses, so their binary equivalent is shown for purposes of differentiation.

Packet Type	Description	Packet Type Identifier
Incoming call	Call request	00001011
Call connected	Call accepted	00001111
Clear indication	Clear request	00010011
Clear confirmed		00010111
Data		xxxxxxx0
Receiver ready		xxx00001
Receiver not ready		xxx00101
Reject		xxx01001
Interrupt indication	Interrupt request	00100011
Interrupt confirmation		00100111
Reset indication	Reset request	00011011
Reset confirmation		00011111
Restart indication	Restart request	11111011
Restart confirmation		11111111

Table 11-2 Summary of the Packet Types and Identifiers.

The variable data field is now inserted. This is where the 128 bytes of information are contained in the packet. The 128-byte field is the standard implementation, but as mentioned, it can be larger (as much as 512 bytes).

Following the information field is the CRC, a 16-bit sequence that will be used for error detection and/or correction. Using a CRC-16, the error-detection capability will be approximately 99.999995 percent. This is to ensure the integrity of the data. Rather than having to deliver information over and over again, the concept is to deliver reliable data to the far end.

The closure of the packet is the end of the frame flag. In the HDLC frame format, this denotes the end of the frame, so the switches and related equipment know that nothing follows. The switches then calculate all the error detection and accept or reject the packet on the basis of the data integrity.

Summary of Packet Format

Figure 11-1 is the actual HDLC frame format used for the packet of information. In this case, you can look at the fields and recheck through the sequencing information of what each field represents. Users who are intimidated by this process can relax. This will be done by the equipment that generates the packets across the network.

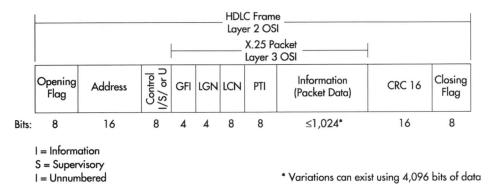

I = Information
S = Supervisory
I = Unnumbered   * Variations can exist using 4,096 bits of data

Figure 11-1 The HDLC framed format is used in the packet-switching mode.

？Line Check 11-3

Fill in the frame for the HDLC format:

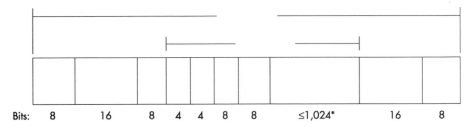

Bits: 8   16   8   4   4   8   8   ≤1,024*   16   8

Data Packet Info, Opening Flag, HDLC Frame Layer 2 OSI, Closing Flag, LGN, CRC, PTI, LCN, GFI, Control, Address, X.25 Layer 3 Packet

The Packet Network

Figure 11-2 shows a typical network layout. Here, the cloud in the center of the drawing represents the network provided by one of the carriers. From discussions in earlier chapters, the obvious network configuration is that each of the designated carriers has its own cloud. Actually, each cloud interconnects to the clouds provided by other carriers, so transparent communications can take place. Once the cloud is established, the next step is to provide the packet-switching systems, called packet switching exchanges (PSE). **PSEs** are nothing more than computers that are capable of reading the address and framing information. The PSEs then route the packet to an appropriate outgoing port to the next downstream neighbor. In many cases, these PSEs are connected to several other PSEs. The two most important pieces of equipment, therefore, are the PAD and the PSE.

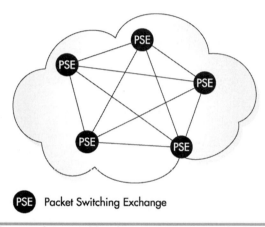

PSE Packet Switching Exchange

Figure 11-2 A meshed network is used by the carriers to provide the necessary connections throughout the network. The PSEs are all interconnected as necessary and dictated by the traffic.

A meshed network is, thus, provided by the carrier. The packet switches can select the outbound route to the next downstream neighbor on the basis of several variables. The selection process can be the circuit used least, the most direct, the most reliable, or some other predefined variable. Again, this is the magic that takes place inside the cloud. Now that the network cloud and the packet exchanges are in place, the next step is to connect a user.

? Line Check 11-4

The two main pieces of equipment are the _____ and the _____.

The User Connection

Users sign up with the carrier of choice and let the carrier worry about the physical connection. As shown in Figure 11-3, the user connection into the cloud is through a dedicated or leased line. The carrier notifies the LEC and orders a leased line at the appropriate speed (in the leased line, this can be up to 64 Kbps on digital circuits). The original network connections back in the initial rollout of X.25 services were on analog lines at up to 9.6 Kbps. A modem was provided by the carrier at the customer end or the customer purchased and provided it. Now that the modem is attached at the customer end, the circuit is terminated in a port on the computer (PSE). This is the incoming port that can be used as a permanent virtual connection or as an incoming-only channel. This is part of the addressing mechanism inside the packet where the PSE reads the packets' originating address. The incoming-only channels are the channel numbers assigned to each customer.

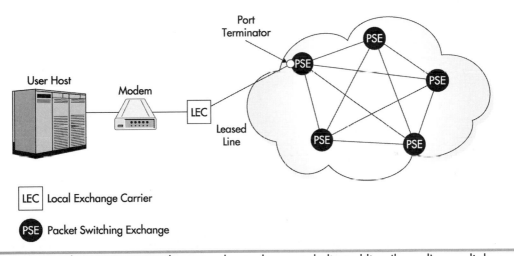

Figure 11-3 The connection to the network may be on a dedicated line (leased) or a dial-up connection. Regardless of the connection, the methodology is the same.

The next step follows the connection where the customer must initiate the PAD function, as shown in Figure 11-4. Remember that the PAD is the hardware or software installed to break the data into smaller pieces, attach the overhead, and forward the packetized data to the network. In the reverse order, the PAD is responsible for receiving the packets, peeling off the overhead, and reassembling the data into a serial data stream to the data terminal equipment, whether it is a terminal or a host computer. So, the PAD function is crucial. If a software package is performing the PAD function, then it is the customer who must purchase (or license) the software and install it. If the solution is a piece of hardware, the options are different. The customer might buy the PAD and install it, or the carrier might provide and install it. This hardware can be rented, leased, or sold by the carrier. Now the connection exists on one end of the cloud.

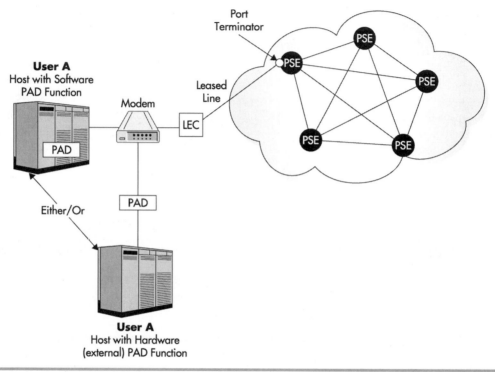

Figure 11-4 The PAD is now used to create the packets and forward them along the network.

In Figure 11-5, another device is attached on the other end of the cloud. What happens now is the magic of the packet-switching world. As packets are generated through the network from user *A* to user *B* across the network, several things happen, as shown in Figure 11-6.

● The data is sent serially from the DTE to the PAD (which acts as the DCE for the computer terminal).

● The PAD will break the data down into smaller pieces and add the necessary overhead for delivery.

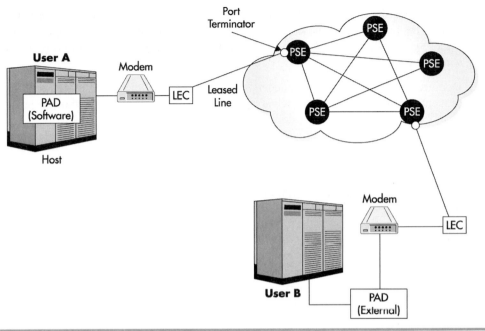

Figure 11-5 Another device is used on the receiving end of the network (another PAD) in this example.

- The PAD then routes the packets to the network PSE.

- The receiving PSE (PSE 1) sees the packet coming in on a logical channel, so it remembers where the packets are coming from. After analyzing the data (performing a CRC on the packet) and verifying that it is all right, the PSE will send back an acknowledgment to the originating device (which is the DCE).

- The PSE then sends the packet out across an outgoing channel to the next downstream neighbor (PSE 2). This establishes a logical connection between the two devices (PSEs) from the out channel to an in channel at the other end. The logical channel is already there; it is used for the transfer of these specific packets. A virtual connection is also created, allocating the time slots for the packets from *A* to *B* to run on the virtual circuit.

- Back at PSE 1, the next packet is sent down from the originating PAD. This again is analyzed and acknowledged, and then passed along. At the same time this is happening, PSE 2 is sending the first packet to PSE 3. Again, at each step of the way, the packets are opened and a CRC is performed before a packet is accepted.

● At each PSE along the way, the packet is buffered (at PSE 1) until the next receiving PSE accepts the packet and acknowledges it (PSE 2). Only after the packet is acknowledged does PSE 1 flush it away. Prior to that, the network node (PSE 1) stored it, just in case something went wrong.

● Don't forget what happens at the receiving end (device *B*), where the packets arrive in sequential order and then are checked and acknowledged. Then, the overhead is peeled away, so a serial data stream is delivered to the receiving DTE.

● This process continues from device *A* through the network to device *B,* until all data packets are received. Every packet along every step of the link is sent, accepted, acknowledged, and forwarded until all get through. Here is the guaranteed delivery of reliable data properly sequenced. The logical link established between devices *A* and *B* is full duplex. The two devices can be sending and receiving simultaneously.

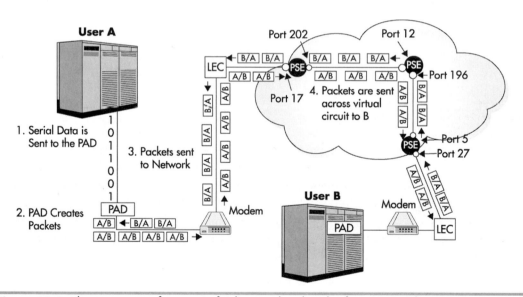

Figure 11-6 The sequence of events is fairly complex, but the function is what is important. Every step along the route, packets are received, error-checked, buffered, and forwarded to the next node.

You can see from the packet-delivery process that there is a benefit to the packet-switching process. However, nothing is perfect. The overhead on the packet, the buffering of multiple packets along the route, the CRC performance at each node along the network, and the final sequenced data delivery all combine to present the risk of serious delays. What you receive in integrity and reliability can be offset in delays across the network. You must always weigh the possibilities and choose the best service.

? Line Check 11-5

Every step along the route, the packets are:

1.

2.

3.

4.

5.

?

Benefits of Packets

The real benefit to this method of data delivery ties into the scenario presented at the beginning of this chapter. Remember the problems with the dial-up telephone network and the risk of sending three-quarters of a file transfer only to have a glitch in the transfer? Using the packetized effort, if a glitch occurs, the network might have from 7 to 128 outstanding packets traversing the links. Therefore, instead of scrapping the entire file, the network automatically recovers and resends the packets that were lost or corrupted. This means the users will save time and money on an error-prone network. Again, the risk of congestion and delay on the network might cause others to look for alternative solutions.

Other Benefits

Beyond these benefits, other benefits can be achieved from the use of the dedicated link into the network. As Figure 11-7 shows, the link is neither solely for one user at a time nor for one specific source-destination pair. When the organization uses a packet-switching network, the users might need to have multiple simultaneous connections up and running. Therefore, the PAD will act similarly to a statistical time division multiplexer (STDM). The **STDM** capability allows multiple connections into the single device and will sample each of the ports in a sequential mode to determine whether the port has anything to send. If a packet has been prepared, the STDM will generate the call request (initiate a call) to the network. The connection will be created and the data will flow. This assumes no problems are being experienced on the network.

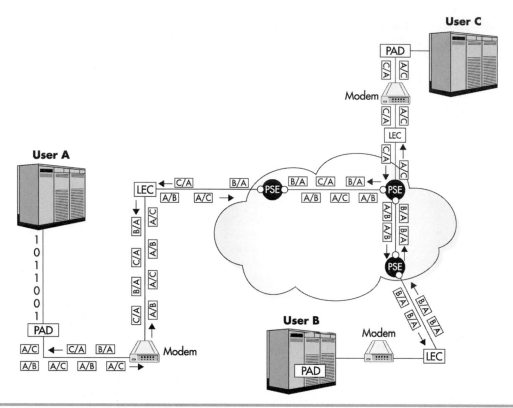

Figure 11-7 Using a STDM, packets can be sent between or among two or more users and/or two or more sites across a single interface.

As a new user logs on and generates a request to send data, the PAD will then set up this connection. Next, packets will be interleaved across the physical link among the various users. You can imagine that not all devices will transmit at the same rate of speed or have the same amount of two-way interactive traffic. Therefore, the STDM function of the PAD interleaves the packets based on an algorithm that allows each device to appear as though a dedicated link is available to it. The use of a STDM will be a benefit because it will enable users to employ the expensive leased link to the maximum benefit of the organization. This requires fewer physical links, takes advantage of the dead time between transmissions, and so on.

Figure 11-8 shows a series of sessions running on a single link, all interleaved. This also shows that packets are not specifically interleaved in the order of A, B, C. . . . Instead, they can be interleaved on the basis of the flow or delivery method used, such as A, B, A, B, C, B, A. . . . Herein lies the added benefit of packet switching—the user achieves the data throughput necessary without having a dedicated resource that is only periodically used.

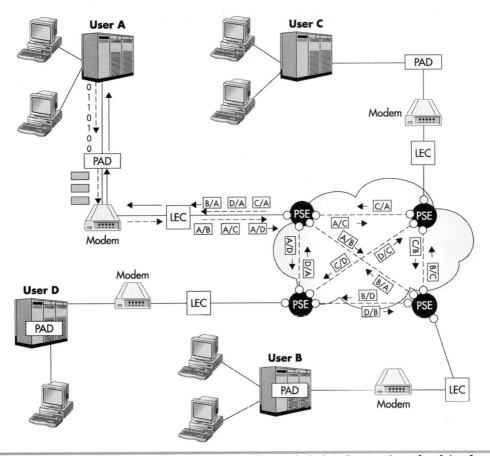

Figure 11-8 A series of connections running on the single link is the true benefit of this form of packet switching. Interleaving the packets on a single link eliminates much of the necessary circuitry.

Other Components of Packet Switching

Although the primary components of packet switching have already been discussed, there are others. As the evolution of the X.25 standard continued in the early 1970s, several different implementations were enhanced. This could include devices or access methods that you should understand. These are summarized so you can gain an appreciation of how these pieces all work together. Some of these added pieces include:

1. The capability to dial into the packet-switching network from an asynchronous modem communication. Although packet switching (a la X.25) is a synchronous transfer system, the need for remote dial-up communications exists. Therefore, the standards bodies included this capability in one of the enhanced versions of the network. As shown in Figure 11-9, a dial-up connection can be made from a user. In this case, the asynchronous communication will be a serial data transfer to a network-based PAD. The PAD will accept the serial asynchronous data, collect it, segment it into packets, and establish the connection to the remote host desired. In this case, the connection is now across the X.25 world, synchronously moving packets across the network. This uses an X.28 protocol to establish the connection between the asynchronous terminal and the PAD.

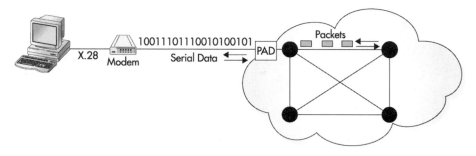

Figure 11-9 A dial-up connection can be made by a user into the X.25 network PAD. Asynchronous data can be accepted by the PAD and shipped as synchronous packets across the network.

2. The PAD-to-host arrangement is controlled by the X.29 protocol. Control information is exchanged between a PAD (X.3) and a packet mode DTE or another PAD (X.3). This is shown in Figure 11-10. In this case, as the communication is established between these devices, the X.3 PAD will set the parameters of the remote device. This could be the speed, format, control parameters, or anything that would be appropriate in the file transfer. The X.29 parameters can also provide keyboard conversion into network-usable information.

3. The internetworking capability of an X.25 network uses a protocol called X.75. Although this should be user-transparent, the network needs the X.75 parameters to provide a gateway between two different packet networks or between networks in different countries. In each case, the gateway function is something that should only concern the network carrier. However, as more organizations install their own private network switching systems, the need to interconnect to the public data networks rises. Therefore, the internetworking capability is moving closer to the end user's door. A representation of an X.75 interconnection is shown in Figure 11-11.

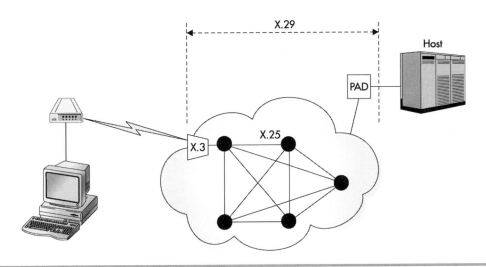

Figure 11-10 PAD-to-host communications is managed by the X.29 protocol.

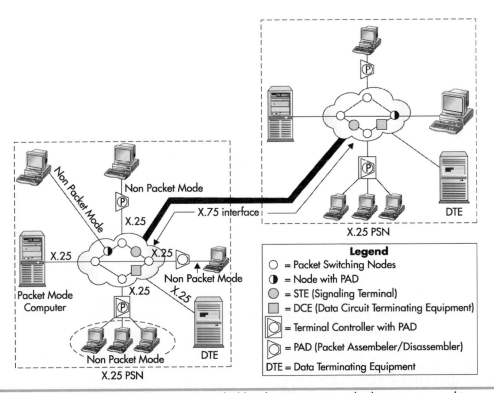

Figure 11-11 The internetworking is provided by the X.75 protocol. This internetworking capability is the essence of the packet network.

❓ Line Check 11-6

List some of the advantages of packet switching:

1.

2.

3.

4.

5.

6.

The X.25 Numbering Plan

The X.25 numbering plan takes advantage of the worldwide numbering plan designed by the CCITT International Telecommunications Union-Telephony Standardization Sector (ITU-TSS). This is known as the X.121 worldwide network numbering plan for the public data networks and was a design to allow for public networks only. However, in most of the world, this is acceptable because there is only one public network that is controlled and operated by the Post, Telephone, Telegraph (PTT) organizations.

In the United States, however, the proliferation of both public and private networks is completely different. Looking at all the players involved today in the carrier community, you can see that easily 300 networks could exist publicly. Couple that with the private organizations that can add packet switching to their networks and that want to access public networks, and the number can expand exponentially.

Other Forms of Packets

As an industry-accepted standard, X.25 was the most widely installed and accepted form of data transmission. This is a worldwide standard, and the interconnectivity solutions defined have created a usable form and format throughout the world. The most common form of packet switching to replace the X.25 standard is the use of the Internet Protocol (IP).

The Internet Protocol (IP)

The IP was developed to provide internetworking. Individual machines are first connected to a LAN. **TCP/IP** shares the LAN with other uses depending on the need (for example, Novell's initial use of IPX/SPX protocol or Apple's Appletalk). A router provides the TCP/IP connection between the LAN and the rest of the world. To ensure that all types of systems from all vendors can communicate, TCP/IP is absolutely standardized on the LAN. IP is a layer 3 protocol, whereas TCP is a layer 4 protocol using the OSI model for comparative purposes.

Larger networks based on long distances and phone lines are more volatile. Many organizations wanted to reuse large internal networks based on IBM's SNA. In Europe, the national phone companies traditionally standardized on X.25, which addresses layer 3 of the OSI model. However, the explosion of high-speed microprocessors, fiber optics, and digital phone systems created a burst of new options, such as ISDN, frame relay, and ATM. New technologies come and go in a few years. With cable TV and phone companies competing to build the national information superhighway, no single standard can govern nationwide or worldwide communications.

The original design of TCP/IP fits nicely within the current technological uncertainty. TCP/IP data can be sent across a LAN, carried within an internal corporate SNA network, or piggyback on the cable TV. Furthermore, machines connected to any of these networks can communicate to any other network through gateways supplied by the network vendor.

Various Platform Connectivity

The major reason for TCP/IP's success is the ability to port it across multiple platforms. Where other protocol stacks are typically used in a LAN or a WAN environment, TCP/IP works on all aspects of the internetwork. A typical network may involve the integration of the following:

- The local area network (LAN) operating on Ethernet.

- The campus area network (CAN) using Fiber Distributed Data Interface (FDDI) within a campus or high-rise office building.

- The metropolitan area network (MAN) linking networks with either a leased line (such as T1, T3) or SONET.

- The wide area network (WAN) using frame relay, ISDN, or ATM.

- A mainframe using the UNIX operating system uses TCP/IP as its core protocols.

Regardless of the topologies, TCP/IP is robust enough to link all the various systems together without any proprietary protocols. Figure 11-12 incorporates all the topologies discussed, using TCP/IP as the core set of protocols. These protocols sit on top of any of the subnet (layer 1 and layer 2) protocols in a stack.

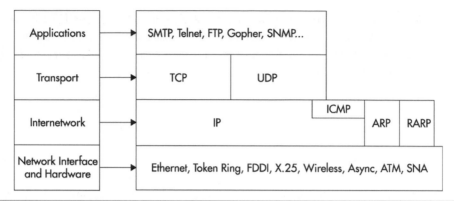

Figure 11-12 TCP/IP sits on top of nearly any subnet protocols as the suite that is preferred over all others.

NOTE

As you can see in the figure, X.25 also falls into the subnet category, which means IP can run on X.25.

Internet Protocol (IP)

IP uses several different ways of handling the data transmission across a network. Unlike the circuit-switched or leased-line networks where a connection is established between the two end points, IP uses a nonconnection-oriented, or connectionless, protocol. As a **connectionless service**, IP does not establish a true connection with the far end receiving the data.

IP sends packets into the network with a best attempt to deliver to the receiving end. IP does not know if the device exists or if it is online. IP makes no guarantees that the data will ever be delivered and does not concern itself with the integrity of the data. In X.25, every node-processing packet checked the data integrity and the sequencing. IP does not. It will deliver bad or corrupted data to the far end, if the datagram is deliverable at all.

IP does manage to route data through, and to, dissimilar networks. Whether the user is running a mainframe with SNA or a UNIX platform, IP does not get involved with the data differentiation. Another difference between IP and other protocols is that IP does not directly deal with the correct sequencing of the **datagrams**. Every datagram in the IP world is its own entity. Datagrams are not numbered 1, 2, 3, and so forth, as you will find in the X.25 packet-handling mechanisms and protocols. IP uses TCP as the connection-oriented protocol that confirms delivery and sequencing of data, which is why the two protocols exist together as the TCP/IP protocol suite.

Essentially, IP is referred to as a dumb protocol because it does nothing except attempt to deliver the data. TCP sends its segments to IP. All TCP tells IP about the data is the address. IP does not consider content. Its job is simply to get the information to the far end. IP does add some overhead to the datagrams as it passes the data onto the network.

IP Addressing

When IP was first standardized in September 1981, the specification required that each system attached to an IP-based Internet be assigned a unique 32-bit Internet address value. Some systems, such as routers, which have interfaces to more than one network, must be assigned a unique IP address for each network interface. The first part of an Internet address identifies the network on which the host resides, while the second part identifies the particular host on the given network. This created the two-level addressing hierarchy.

Each address assigned to a network is given an IP address consisting of a 4-byte address. The addressing mechanisms are controlled by an organization authorized by the IANA. Every Internet address is composed of a network and a host address. The class of network address is broken down into the following classes:

- Class *A* addresses use the first 8 bits (the first bit is set to a 0, leaving 7 bits for the network number) of the address for the network number, followed by a 24-bit address for the host.

- Class *B* addresses use a 16-bit network number (the first 2 bits are reserved and set to 10) leaving a 14-bit network number and a 16-bit host address.

- Class *C* addresses use a 24-bit address for the network number (the first 3 bits are set to 110, leaving the network address field at 21 bits long) followed by an 8-bit host address.

- Class *D* addresses are used for a multicast-addressing mechanism using a 4-bit network address (set to 1110) and a 28-bit multicast address for the host address.

- Class *E* addresses are special projects addresses reserved by the InterNIC using a 4-bit network address (set to 1111) and a 28-bit address for the host address.

These addresses are shown in Figure 11-13. The blocks of address space show the network and host space allotted for each class.

Like anything else in a network so widely deployed worldwide, a problem looms in the future. We are running out of address numbers! In the newest version of IP (called IP New Generation or IP Version 6), the address field will be expanded to a 128-bit address field for every source and destination node on the network.

11

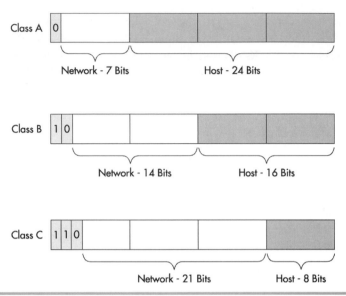

Figure 11-13 The IP addresses using a classful address designation use the 32-bit numbering plan divided into network number and host number. Shown here are the most common addresses in the *A*, *B*, and *C* classes.

👁 Line Check 11-7

The most commonly used network addresses are the:

A uses _____ bits for the network and _____ bits for the host number.

B uses _____ bits for the network number and _____ for the host number.

C uses _____ bits for the network number and _____ for the host number.

Unforeseen Limitations to Classful Addressing

The original designers of the Internet never envisioned that it would grow into the commercially available worldwide network we have seen. Many of the problems facing the Internet today can be traced back to the early decisions that were made during its formative years.

● During the early days of the Internet, the seemingly unlimited address space allowed IP addresses to be allocated to an organization based on its request, rather than its actual need. As a result, addresses were freely assigned to those who asked for them without concerns about the eventual depletion of the IP address space. We like to joke that when the address space was being allocated, anyone at the meeting that day was given a Class *A* address.

11

- The decision to standardize on a 32-bit address space meant only 2^{32} (4,294,967,296) IPv4 addresses were available. A decision to support a slightly larger address space would have exponentially increased the number of addresses, thus eliminating the current address-shortage problem. However, back then, even the wildest imagination would never have anticipated that we would ever need a larger number of addresses because we had over 4 billion of them.

- The classful *A*, *B*, and *C* octet boundaries were easy to understand and implement, but they did not foster the efficient allocation of a finite address space. Problems resulted from the lack of a network class that was designed to support medium-size organizations. A /24, which supports 254 hosts, is too small, while a /16, which supports 65,534 hosts, is too large. In the past, the Internet assigned sites with several hundred hosts a single /16 address instead of a couple of /24s addresses. Unfortunately, this has resulted in a premature depletion of the /16 network address space. The only readily available addresses for medium-size organizations are /24s, which have the potentially negative impact of increasing the size of the global Internet's routing table.

NOTE

In May 1996, 100 percent Class *A* addresses were either allocated or assigned, as well as 62 percent of Class *B* and 36.5 percent of Class *C* IP network addresses. This was just as the Internet and the IP protocols were becoming popularized and commercialized.

Even though we have 4,294,967,296 addresses available, we are concerned about running out of numbers because of poor initial management of the numbering plan.

Subnetting

Because of the explosive growth of the Internet, the principle of assigned IP addresses became too inflexible to allow easy changes to local network configurations. Those changes might occur when:

- A new type of physical network is installed at a location.

- Growth of the number of hosts requires splitting the local network into two or more separate networks.

- Growing distances require splitting a network into smaller networks, with gateways between them.

To avoid having to request additional IP network addresses, the concept of IP subnetting was introduced. The assignment of subnets is done locally. The entire network still appears as one IP network to the outside world.

The host number part of the IP address is subdivided into a second network number and a host number. This second network is termed a **subnetwork** or a **subnet**. The main network now consists of a number of subnets. The IP address is interpreted as shown in Figure 11-14. This can be done in various ways, but the easiest way to show it is a before and after view.

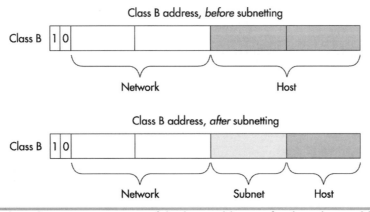

Figure 11-14 The subnet uses a portion of the host addresses for the subnet address numbers.

The combination of subnet number and host number is often termed the local address or the local portion of the IP address. Subnetting is implemented in a way that is transparent to remote networks. A host within a network that has subnets is aware of the subnetting structure. A host in a different network is not. This remote host still regards the local part of the IP address as a host number.

In 1985, RFC 950 defined a standard procedure to support the subnetting, or division, of a single Class A, B, or C network number into smaller pieces. Subnetting was introduced to overcome some of the problems that parts of the Internet were beginning to experience with the classful two-level addressing hierarchy:

● Internet routing tables were beginning to grow.

● Local administrators had to request another network number from the Internet before a new network could be installed at their site.

The division of the local part of the IP address into a subnet number and a host number is chosen by the local administrator. Any bits in the local portion can be used to form the subnet. The division is done using a 32-bit subnet mask.

The **subnet mask** is the network address plus the bits reserved for identifying the subnetwork. (By convention, the bits for the network address are all set to 1, though it would also work if the bits were set exactly as in the network address.) In this case, therefore, the subnet mask would be 11111111.11111111.11110000.00000000. It's called a mask because it can be used to identify the subnet to which an IP address belongs by performing a bitwise AND operation on the mask and the IP address. If your station is using the wrong subnet mask for the network to which you are attached, then it will not be able to correctly identify all users on that subnet and many users could be unreachable by your computer.

Bits with a value of 0 bits in the subnet mask indicate positions ascribed to the host number. Bits with a value of 1 indicate positions ascribed to the subnet number. The bit positions in the subnet mask belonging to the original network number are set to 1's, but are not used (in some platform configurations, this value was specified with 0's instead of 1's, but either way, it is not used). Like IP addresses, subnet masks are usually written in dotted decimal form.

The special treatment of all bits 0 and all bits 1 applies to each of the three parts of a subnetted IP address, just as it does to both parts of an IP address that has not been subnetted. For example, subnetting a Class *B* network could use one of the following schemes:

- The first octet is the subnet number; the second octet is the host number. This gives $2^8 - 2$ (254) possible subnets, each having up to $2^8 - 2$ (254) hosts. Recall that you subtract two from the possibilities to account for the cases of all ones and all zeros. The subnet mask is 255.255.255.0.

- The first 12 bits are used for the subnet number, and the last 4 bits for the host number. This gives $2^{12} - 2$ (4,094) possible subnets, but only $2^4 - 2$ (14) hosts per subnet. The subnet mask is 255.255.255.240.

NOTE

Subnetting was introduced to overcome some of the problems that parts of the Internet were beginning to experience with the classful two-level addressing hierarchy.

Subnetting attacked the expanding routing table problem by ensuring that the subnet structure of a network is never visible outside the organization's private network. The route from the Internet to any subnet of a given IP address is the same, no matter which subnet the destination host is on. This is because all subnets of a given network number use the same network prefix, but different subnet numbers. The routers within the private organization need to differentiate between the individual subnets, but as far as the Internet routers are concerned, all the subnets in the organization are collected into a single routing table entry. This allows the local administrator to introduce arbitrary complexity into the private network without affecting the size of the Internet's routing tables.

Subnetting overcame the registered number issue by assigning each organization one (or, at most, a few) network number(s) from the IPv4 address space. The organization was then free to assign a distinct subnetwork number for each of its internal networks. This allows the organization to deploy additional subnets without needing to obtain a new network number from the Internet.

In Figure 11-15, a site with several logical networks uses subnet addressing to cover them with a single /16 (Class *B*) network address. The router accepts all traffic from the Internet addressed to network 132.7.0.0, and forwards traffic to the interior subnetworks based on the third octet of the classful address. The deployment of subnetting within the private network provides several benefits:

- The size of the global Internet routing table does not grow because the site administrator does not need to obtain additional address space and the routing advertisements for all the subnets are combined into a single routing-table entry.

- The local administrator has the flexibility to deploy additional subnets without obtaining a new network number from the Internet.

- **Route flapping** (that is, the rapid changing of routes) within the private network does not affect the Internet routing table because Internet routers do not know about the reachability of the individual subnets—they just know about the reachability of the parent network number.

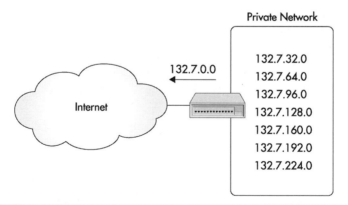

Figure 11-15 A single Class *B* network is used and subnetted to accommodate several logical networks.

Extended-Network-Prefix

Internet routers use only the network prefix of the destination address to route traffic to the subnetted environment. Routers within the subnetted environment use the extended network prefix to route traffic between the individual subnets. The extended-network prefix, shown in Figure 11-16, is composed of the classful network prefix and the subnet number.

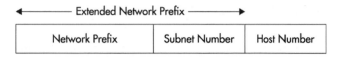

Figure 11-16 The extended network prefix includes the network number, plus the subnet number.

The extended-network-prefix has traditionally been identified by the subnet mask. For example, if you have the network address of 132.7.0.0, its default network mask will be 255.255.0.0. If you want to use the entire third octet to represent the subnet number, you need to specify a subnet mask of 255.255.255.0. The bits in the subnet mask and the Internet address have a one-to-one correspondence. The bits of the subnet mask are set to 1 if the system examining the address should treat the corresponding bit in the IP address as part of the extended network prefix. The bits in the mask are set to 0 if the system should treat the bit as part of the host number. Figure 11-17 illustrates this.

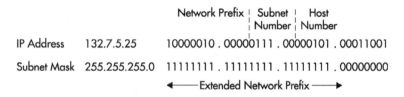

Figure 11-17 If the bit is part of the extended network prefix, the bits of the subnet mask are set to 1. If the bits are part of the host number, the bits of the mask are set to 0.

The standards describing modern routing protocols often refer to the extended network prefix length, rather than the subnet mask. The prefix length is equal to the number of contiguous 1 bits in the traditional subnet mask. This means that specifying the network address 132.7.5.25 with a subnet mask of 255.255.255.0 can also be expressed as 132.7.5.25/24. The /<prefix-length> notation is more compact and easier to understand than writing out the mask in its traditional dotted-decimal format.

However, it is important to note that some routing protocols still carry the subnet mask. No Internet-standard routing protocols have a 1-byte field in their header that contains the number of bits in the extended network prefix. Rather, each routing protocol is still required to carry the complete 4-octet subnet mask.

Subnet Design Considerations

The deployment of an addressing plan requires careful thought on the part of the network administrator. Four key questions must be answered before any design should be undertaken:

1. How many total subnets does the organization need today?

2. How many total subnets will the organization need in the future?

3. How many hosts are on the organization's largest subnet today?

4. How many hosts will be on the organization's largest subnet in the future?

The first step in the planning process is to take the maximum number of subnets required and round up to the nearest power of two. For example, if a organization needs 9 subnets, 2^3 (or 8) will not provide enough subnet addressing space, so the network administrator will need to round up to 2^4 (or 16). When performing this assessment, it is critical that the network administrator always allow adequate room for future growth.

For example, if 14 subnets are required today, then 16 subnets might not be enough in two years, when the 17th subnet needs to be deployed. In this case, it might be wise to allow for more growth and select 2^5 (or 32) as the maximum number of subnets. The second step is to make sure enough host addresses are available for the organization's largest subnet. If the largest subnet needs to support 50 host addresses today, 2^5 (or 32) will not provide enough host address space, so the network administrator will need to round up to 2^6 (or 64).

The final step is to make sure the organization's address allocation provides enough bits to deploy the required subnet addressing plan. For example, if the organization has a single /16, it could easily deploy 4 bits for the subnet number and 6 bits for the host number. However, if the organization has several /24s, and it needs to deploy 9 subnets, it may be required to subnet each of its /24s into four subnets (using 2 bits), and then build the Internet by combining the subnets of three different /24 network numbers. An alternative solution would be to deploy network numbers from the private address space (RFC 1918) for internal connectivity and use a Network Address Translator (NAT) to provide external Internet access.

❓ Line Check 11-8

Some of the key questions you need to ask for subnetting include:

1.

2.

3.

4.

Types of Subnetting

There are two types of subnetting: static and variable length. Variable-length subnetting is more flexible than static. Router devices use their own software, known as routing protocols, to manage IP routing. Older routing protocols, such as native IP routing and Routing Information Protocol (RIP) Version 1, support only static subnetting. Newer protocols such as RIP Version 2 and Open Shortest Path First (OSPF) support variable-length subnetting.

Static Subnetting

Static subnetting implies that all subnets obtained from the same network use the same subnet mask. While this is simple to implement and easy to maintain, it may waste address space in small networks. Consider a network of four hosts using a subnet mask of 255.255.255.0. This allocation wastes 250 IP addresses. All hosts and routers are required to support static subnetting.

Variable-Length Subnetting

When variable-length subnetting is used, allocated subnets within the same network can use different subnet masks. A small subnet with only a few hosts can use a mask that accommodates this need. A subnet with many hosts requires a different subnet mask. The capability to assign subnet masks according to the needs of the individual subnets helps conserve network addresses. Variable-length subnetting divides the network, so each subnet contains sufficient addresses to support the required number of hosts.

An existing subnet can be split into two parts by adding another bit to the subnet portion of the subnet mask. Other subnets in the network are unaffected by the change.

Mixing Static and Variable-Length Subnetting

Not every IP device includes support for variable-length subnetting. Initially, it would appear that the presence of a host that only supports static subnetting prevents the use of variable-length subnetting. This is not the case. Routers interconnecting the subnets are used to hide the different masks from hosts. Hosts continue to use basic IP routing. This offloads subnetting complexities to dedicated routers.

❔ Line Check 11-9

What are the two types of subnetting we use?

❔

IP Routing

Routing devices in the Internet have traditionally been called gateways, an unfortunate term because elsewhere in the industry, the term applies to a device with somewhat different functionality. Gateways (which we will call **routers** from this point on) within the Internet are organized hierarchically. Some routers are used to move information through one particular group of networks under the same administrative authority and control (such an entity is called an **autonomous system**). Routers used for information exchange within autonomous systems are called **interior routers**, and they use a variety of interior gateway protocols (IGPs) to accomplish this purpose. Routers that move information between autonomous systems are called **exterior routers**, and they use an exterior gateway protocol for this purpose.

When sending data to a remote destination, a host passes datagrams to a local router. The router forwards the datagrams toward the final destination. The datagrams travel from one router to another until they reach a router connected to the destination's LAN segment. Each router along the end-to-end path selects the next hop device used to reach the destination. The **next hop** represents the next device along the path to reach the destination, and it is located on a physical network connected to this intermediate system. Because this physical network differs from the one on which the system originally received the datagram, the intermediate host has forwarded (that is, routed) the IP datagram from one physical network to another.

The IP routing table in each device is used to forward packets between network segments. The basic table contains information about a router's locally connected networks. The configuration of the device can be extended to contain information detailing remote networks. This information provides a more complete view of the overall environment.

A robust routing protocol provides the capability to dynamically build and manage the information in the IP routing table. As network topology changes occur, the routing tables are updated with minimal or no manual intervention.

IP routing protocols are dynamic. Dynamic routing calls for routes to be calculated at regular intervals by software in the routing devices. This contrasts with static routing, where routes are established by the network administrator and do not change until the network administrator changes them. An IP routing table consists of destination address/next hop pairs. A sample entry is interpreted as meaning "to get to network 34.1.0.0 (subnet 1 on network 34), the next stop is the node at address 54.34.23.12."

An important function of the IP layer is **IP routing**, which provides the basic mechanism for routers to interconnect different physical networks. A device can simultaneously function as both a normal host and a router. A router of this type is referred to as a router with partial routing information.

The router only has information about four kinds of destinations:

- Hosts that are directly attached to one of the physical networks to which the router is attached.

- Hosts or networks for which the router has been given explicit definitions.

- Hosts or networks for which the router has received an ICMP redirect message.

- A default for all other destinations.

Additional protocols are needed to implement a full-function router. These types of routers are essential in most networks because they can exchange information with other routers in the environment. There are two types of IP routing: direct and indirect.

Direct Routing

If the destination host is attached to the same physical network as the source host, IP datagrams can be directly exchanged. This is done by encapsulating the IP datagram in the physical network frame. This is called **direct delivery** and is referred to as **direct routing**.

Indirect Routing

Indirect routing occurs when the destination host is not connected to a network directly attached to the source host. The only way to reach the destination is via one or more IP gateways. (Note that in TCP/IP terminology, the terms "gateway" and "router" are used interchangeably. This describes a system that performs the duties of a router.) The address of the first gateway (the first hop) is called an indirect route in the IP routing algorithm. The address of the first gateway is the only information needed by the source host to send a packet to the destination host.

In some cases, multiple subnets may be defined on the same physical network. If the source and destination hosts connect to the same physical network but are defined in different subnets, indirect routing is used to communicate between the pair of devices. A router is needed to forward traffic between subnets.

❓ Line Check 11-10

Early IP routing documentation often referred to an IP router as a(n) _____.

Two types of routing are _____ and _____.

❓

IP Datagram

The unit of transfer in an IP network is called an **IP datagram**, which consists of an IP header and data relevant to higher-level protocols. IP can provide fragmentation and reassembly of datagrams. The maximum length of an IP datagram is 65,535 octets. All IP hosts must support 576 octet datagrams without fragmentation. Fragmentation of a datagram is permitted if the original datagram size is larger than the size permitted in the layer 2 protocol used to transport IP (as may happen in Internet connections where multiple layer 2 protocols may be used in the different communication segments). Fragments of a datagram each have a header, and the header is copied from the original datagram. Fragments are treated as normal IP datagrams while being transported to their destination. If one of the fragments gets lost, though, the complete datagram is considered lost. Because IP does not provide any acknowledgment mechanism, the remaining fragments are discarded by the destination host.

The IP Header

The IP header is attached to the datagram to get the information to the destination address, as shown in Figure 11-18. The advantages of the robustness of the TCP/IP world are based on the IP's capability to deliver the data across a wide area of disparate systems and platforms. By using the header containing the addressing and other pieces of critical information, no trailer is needed to move the information.

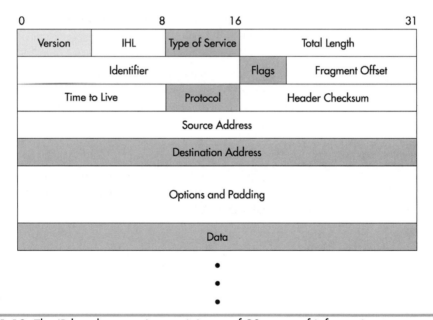

Figure 11-18 The IP header contains a minimum of 20 octets of information.

The header consists of the following pieces of information (not all are covered in this chapter):

● The IP version number of the IP datagram.

- The header length specifying the datagram header length in units of 32-bit words; the most common is 20 octets.

- The type of service covers the quality of service (QoS) and is used when different algorithms are used for routing the datagrams across the network. Unfortunately, the entire industry uses this field differently, so a standard is not defined.

- The total length defines the length of the entire datagram and overhead.

- The identification, flags, and offsets control the fragmentation of the datagrams, and they are used for the reassembly portion of the process.

- The Time to Live (TTL) is a hop counter that uses a decrementing counter for the delivery of the datagram. How many devices may the datagram pass through before being either delivered or discarded?

- The protocol field is used to define the higher-level protocol used (TCP or UDP).

- The header checksum is a CRC on the header for error detection of any problems with the datagram.

- Next, the source and destination addresses will show.

- Options include any special features allowed on the network.

- Padding is filler used to align the datagram and header to a 32-bit alignment.

Classless Interdomain Routing (CIDR)

By 1992, the exponential growth of the Internet was beginning to raise serious concerns among members of the IETF about the capability of the Internet's routing system to scale and support future growth. These problems were related to:

- The near-term exhaustion of the Class *B* network address space

- The rapid growth in the size of the global Internet's routing tables

- The eventual exhaustion of the 32-bit IPv4 address space

Projected Internet growth figures made it clear that the first two problems were likely to become critical by 1994 or 1995, especially when the commercialization of the Internet became reality. The response to these immediate challenges was the development of the concept of supernetting or **classless interdomain routing (CIDR)**.

The third problem, which is of a more long-term nature, can be accomplished with IPv6. However, we can only estimate this will be implemented within a few years because of the cost and workload of implementing such a scheme.

CIDR was officially documented in September 1993 in RFC 1517, 1518, 1519, and 1520. CIDR supports two important features that benefit the global Internet routing system:

- CIDR eliminated the traditional concept of Class *A*, Class *B*, and Class *C* network addresses. This enables the efficient allocation of the IPv4 address space, which allows the continued growth of the Internet until IPv6 is fully deployed.

- CIDR supports route aggregation where a single routing table entry can represent the address space of perhaps thousands of traditional classful routes. This allows a single routing table entry to specify how to route traffic to many individual network addresses. Route aggregation helps control the amount of routing information in the Internet's backbone routers, reduces route flapping, and eases the local administrative burden of updating external routing information.

Without the rapid deployment of CIDR in 1994 and 1995, the Internet routing tables would have exceeded 70,000 routes (instead of 30,000+). Today's Internet backbone routers store in excess of 100,000 networks. If CIDR had not been deployed, the Internet would probably not be functioning today! In early 1994, routers also processed 200,000 packets per second. Today, they must be fast and powerful enough to process more than 1 million packets per second. The older technologies had less computing power (circa 1993 to 1994) and limited memory. The technology today is handled in ASICs and DSPs that are much faster and more efficient than old router technologies. Constraints on these older routers made the use of CIDR that much more necessary.

CIDR Promotes the Efficient Allocation of the IPv4 Address Space

CIDR eliminates the traditional concept of Class *A*, Class *B*, and Class *C* network addresses and replaces them with the generalized concept of a "network prefix." Routers use the network prefix, rather than the first 3 bits of the IP address, to determine the dividing point between the network number and the host number. As a result, CIDR supports the deployment of arbitrarily sized networks rather than the standard 8-bit, 16-bit, or 24-bit network numbers associated with classful addressing.

In the CIDR model, each piece of routing information is advertised with a bit mask (or prefix length). The prefix length is a way of specifying the number of leftmost contiguous bits in the network portion of each routing table entry. For example, a network with 20 bits of network number and 12 bits of host number would be advertised with a 20-bit prefix length (a /20). The clever thing is that the IP address advertised with the /20 prefix could be a former Class *A*, Class *B*, or Class *C*. Routers that support CIDR do *not* make assumptions based on the first 3 bits of the address. They rely on the prefix-length information provided with the route.

In a classless environment, prefixes are viewed as bitwise contiguous blocks of the IP address space. For example, all prefixes with a /20 prefix represent the same amount of address space (2^{12}, or 4,096, host addresses). Furthermore, a /20 prefix can be assigned to a traditional Class *A*, Class *B*, or Class *C* network number. Figure 11-19 shows how each of the following /20 blocks represents 4,096 host addresses—10.23.64.0/20, 130.5.0.0/20, and 200.7.128.0/20.

Traditional A	10.23.64.0/20	00001010 . 00010111 . 01000000 . 00000000
Traditional B	130.5.0.0/20	10000010 . 00000101 . 00000000 . 00000000
Traditional C	200.7.128.0/20	11001000 . 00000111 . 10000000 . 00000000

Figure 11-19 The traditional classful addresses are shown here in a bitwise contiguous block.

Table 11-3 provides information about the most commonly deployed CIDR address blocks. Referring to this table, you can see that a /15 allocation can also be specified using the traditional dotted-decimal mask notation of 255.254.0.0. Also, a /15 allocation contains a bitwise contiguous block of 128K (131,072) IP addresses, which can be classfully interpreted as 2 Class *B* networks or 512 Class *C* networks.

Host Implications for CIDR Deployment

Note that severe host implications may exist when you deploy CIDR-based networks. Because some hosts are classful, their user interface will not permit them to be configured with a mask that is shorter than the "natural" mask for a traditional classful address. For example, potential problems could exist if you wanted to deploy 200.25.16.0 as a /20 to define a network capable of supporting 4,094 ($2^{12} - 2$) hosts. The software executing on each end station might not allow a traditional Class *C* (200.25.16.0) to be configured with a 20-bit mask because the natural mask for a Class *C* network is a 24-bit mask. If the host software supports CIDR, it will permit shorter masks to be configured.

However, there will be no host problems if you were to deploy the 200.25.16.0/20 (a traditional Class *C*) allocation as a block of 16 /24s because non-CIDR hosts will interpret their local /24 as a Class *C*. Likewise, 130.14.0.0/16 (a traditional Class *B*) could be deployed as a block of 255 /24s because the hosts will interpret the /24s as subnets of a /16.

CIDR Prefix Length	Dot Decimal Notation	Number of Individual Addresses	Number of Classful Networks	
			Bs	Cs
/13	255.248.0.0	512 K	8	2,048
/14	255.252.0.0	256 K	4	1,024
/15	255.254.0.0	128 K	2	512
/16	255.255.0.0	64 K	1	256
/17	255.255.128.0	32 K		128
/18	255.255.192.0	16 K		64
/19	255.255.224.0	8 K		32
/20	255.255.240.0	4 K		16
/21	255.255.248.0	2 K		8
/22	255.255.252.0	1 K		4
/23	255.255.254.0	512		2
/24	255.255.255.0	256		1
/25	255.255.255.128	128		½
/26	255.255.255.192	64		¼
/27	255.255.255.224	32		1/8

Table 11-3 Using the CIDR Prefix Lengths, the Following Numbers of Networks and Addresses Are Achieved.

If host software supports the configuration of shorter than expected masks, the network manager has tremendous flexibility in network design and address allocation.

CIDR Is Similar to VLSM

CIDR and VLSM are about the same thing because they both allow a portion of the IP address space to be repetitively divided into subsequently smaller pieces. With Variable Length Subnet Masking (VLSM), the repetition is performed on the address space previously assigned to an organization and is invisible to the global Internet. CIDR, on the other hand, permits the recursive allocation of an address block by an Internet Registry to a high-level ISP, to a mid-level ISP, to a low-level ISP, and, finally, to a private organization's network.

Reserved IP Addresses

A component of an IP address with a value all bits 0 or all bits 1 has a special meaning:

- All bits 0: An address with all bits 0 in the host number portion is interpreted as any host (as in the network 192.168.1.0). All bits 0 in the network number portion is *any* network (IP address with <network address> = 0). When a host wants to communicate over a network, but does not yet know its own IP address, it may send packets with <network address> = 0 and <host address> = 0 (written as 0.0.0.0). When specifying a route from a given host network to the Internet, the router will point to the Internet as the default network gateway of network 0.0.0.0.

- All bits 1: An address with all bits 1 is interpreted as *all* networks or *all* hosts. For example, the following means all hosts on network 128.2 (Class *B* address):

  128.2.255.255

  This is called a *directed broadcast address* because it contains both a valid <network address> and a broadcast <host address>. A pure IP broadcast address (255.255.255.255) will propagate in any local network and be received by all hosts, but it will not be routed to other networks.

- Loopback: The Class *A* network 127.0.0.0 is defined as the loopback network. Addresses from the *loopback* network are assigned to interfaces that process data within the local system. These loopback interfaces do not access a physical network.

- Private IP addresses. RFC 1918 defines certain address ranges as Private IP addresses. These addresses will not be routed across the Internet backbone, though they may be used and routed within an internal autonomous system. The private networks were defined as:

  - Class *A*: 10.0.0.0/8
  - Class *B*: 172.16.0.0 through 172.31.0.0 (172.16.0.0/12)
  - Class *C*: 192.168.0.0 through 192.168.255.0 (192.168.0.0/16)

Frame Relay-Frames

One of the data-transport systems developed in the mid-1980s and commercially implemented in 1992 is a higher-speed packet-switching technique called frame relay. Frames of information are generated by nearly all the data communications processes today. Although we call them by different names, such as packets, frames, or **cells**, they all are just a means of transmitting a specific amount of information across a network. Frame relay operates at layer 2 of the OSI with some modifications. Much of the overhead of layer 2 (such as error checking, sequencing, and ACK/NAK) is eliminated or compressed, as shown in the following illustration.

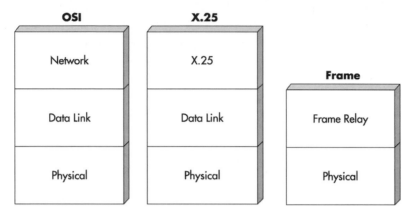

Frame relay operates at layer 2 of the OSI model, but is modified to eliminate much of the overhead.

When first introduced, frame relay was met with mild enthusiasm. We hear all the time that frame relay is now dead (we hear the same thing about X.25). Not so, yet. Many enterprise networks and carrier networks are still using frame as their means of carrying their data. Yes, IP-enabled frame relay is an alternative, but that means we use the IP address shown in the previous section of this chapter, and we encapsulate the datagrams inside frames. So frame will be around for a while to come.

What Is Frame Relay?

Frame relay is a high-performance, cost-efficient means of connecting an organization's multiple LANs and other data. Like the older X.25 packet-switching services, frame relay uses the transmission links only when they are needed. Essentially, the virtual-circuit concept applies here as much as in any other network service.

The customer rents or leases a physical circuit into the cloud, as shown in Figure 11-20. This circuit is terminated onto a port in a computer system. The switch recognizes where the connecting ends of the wires are located and uses the full set of wires when the customer has traffic to pass into the network. Thus, a virtual-circuit connection is established into the cloud for future use, as the customer's needs dictate. Because the connection is not always **nailed up** (a line that is always on and connected), other customers connected to the same network supplier can also transmit traffic across the same physical pairs of wires within the cloud. Additionally, like private-line connections, frame relay transports data quickly, with only a limited amount of delay for network processing to take place.

When comparing frame relay to the X.25 services, much less processing is required inside the switches. Frame relay eliminated the layer 2 error checking between switching devices that had been used in X.25. Therefore, the reduced processing allows the transport of data much more quickly. By eliminating the overhead in each of the processors, the network merely looks at an address in the frame and passes the frame along to the next node in the network.

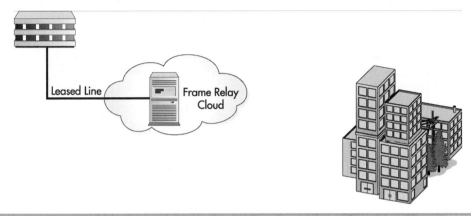

Figure 11-20 The nailed-up connection (leased line) from the customer site to the frame relay switch is the more common way this connection is used.

Why Was Frame Relay Developed?

Major trends in the industry led to the development of frame-relay services. These can be categorized into four major trends as follows:

The increased need for speed across the network platforms within the end user and the carrier networks. The need for higher speeds is driven by the move away from the original text-based services to graphics-oriented services and the bursty, time-sensitive data needs of the user. The proliferation of high-speed LANs being deployed has shifted the paradigm of computing platforms. The demands of these services will exceed by hundreds to thousands of times the data transport needs of the older text-based services. Users demand connectivity and speed to assure quick and reliable communications between systems. Fortunately, the bursty way we conduct business allows the sharing of resources among many users who, thereby, share the bandwidth available. To accommodate this connectivity, some changes had to be made to the overhead intensity. One way to accommodate the reduced overhead is to eliminate some of the processing, mainly in the error detection and correction schemes.

Increasing intelligence of the devices attached to the network. The use of data transfer between and among devices on the network has moved many of the processing functions to the desktop. The capacity to move the information around the network must meet the demands of each attached device. Increased functionality must be met with increases in the bandwidth allocation for these devices.

Improved transmission facilities. The days of "dirty" or poor-quality transmission lines required the use of overcorrecting protocols, such as X.25 and SNA. Because the network now performs better, a newer transmission capability is needed.

The need to connect LANs to WANs and the internetworking capabilities. Today's users want to connect LANs across the boundaries of the wide area. Users demand and expect the same speed and accuracy across the WAN that they get on the local networks. Therefore, a newer transport system to support the higher-speed connections across a wider area was needed.

NOTE

Frame relay was an evolutionary product to speed data transmission and improve the flow of the data. It will use the network and end-system intelligence to move data more efficiently and allow connections from the LAN to the WAN. For these reasons, frame relay was popular the instant it was available.

The Significance of Frame Relay

As an analog transmission system, the old network was extremely noisy, producing many network errors and corrupting data. When data errors were introduced, a retransmission was required. The more retransmissions were necessary, the less effective throughput was on the network. Frame relay was designed to take advantage of the low-error, high-performance digital network and to meet the needs of the intelligent, synchronous use of the newer and more sophisticated user applications.

Compared to private leased lines, frame relay makes network design much simpler. In Figure 11-21, a single frame relay access from each site is provided into the network cloud. Data transported across the network will be interleaved on a frame-by-frame basis. Multiple sessions can run on the same link concurrently. Communications from a single site to any other site can be handled using the predefined network connections of the virtual circuits. In frame relay, these connections use **permanent logical links (PLL)**, more commonly referred to as **permanent virtual circuits (PVCs)**. Each of the PVCs connects two sites just as a private line would, but in this case, the bandwidth is shared among multiple users rather than being dedicated to the one site for access to a single site.

Because the PVCs are predefined for each pair of end-to-end connections, a network path is always available for the customer's application to transport data. This eliminates the call setup time associated with the dial-up lines and the X.25 packet arrangements. The connection is always ready for the devices to ship data in a framed format.

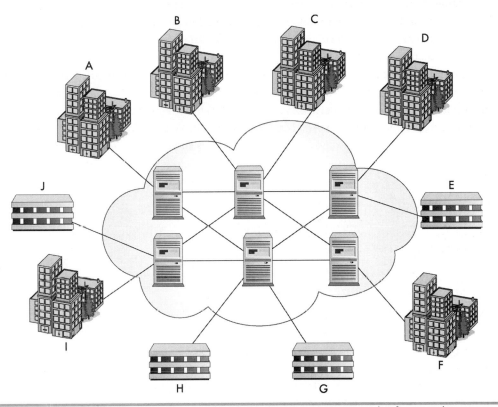

Figure 11-21 A single access link is needed from the customer site to the frame relay network, which allows a connection to any of the other sites.

Frame Relay Speeds

Frame relay was designed initially to start from 64 Kbps up to 1.544 Mbps in North America. Speeds of 2.048 Mbps were approved in the rest of the world. This speed is based on using T1 or E1 access links. Speeds of up to 50 Mbps are possible, but not widely deployed.

The customer must be aware of this need and select a specified delivery rate. There are various ways of assigning the speed from both an access and a pricing perspective. For small locations, such as branch offices with little predictable traffic, the customer might consider the lowest possible access speed. The frame relay suppliers offer speeds that are flat rate, usage-sensitive, and flat/usage-sensitive combined. Carriers now offer burstable frame relay. The customer selects a committed information rate (CIR). The **committed information rate** is a guaranteed rate of throughput when using frame relay. The CIR is assigned to each PVC. Because frame relay is a duplex service, a different CIR can be assigned in each direction. This produces an asymmetrical throughput based on demand.

Because the nature of LANs is that of bursty traffic, however, the CIR can be burst over and above the fixed rate for two seconds at a time in some carriers' networks. This committed burst rate (Bc) can be up to the link rate, but many of the carriers limit the burst rate to the speed of the CIR. When the network is not busy, the customer can still burst data onto the network at an even higher rate. The burst excess rate (Be) can be an additional speed of up to the channel capacity, or in some carriers' networks, it can be 50 percent above the committed burst rate, but only for one-second increments. Combining these rates, an example can be drawn as follows:

$$CIR + Bc + Be = Total\ throughput$$

128 Kbps + 128 Kbps + 64 Kbps = 320 Kbps total

Some carriers will not allow any bursts across the network. Rather, they require the maximum throughput be limited to the committed information rate.

Line Check 11-11

1. What are the normal link speeds associated with frame relay, both domestically and internationally?

2. How do we calculate the information throughput rates?

Guaranteed Delivery

When a committed information rate is used, the guarantee is that the network will make all efforts to deliver traffic (frames) at the CIR, but bursts are another situation. As you send data frames into the network, they will follow the same logical connection in sequence. Therefore, there should be neither out-of-sequencing nor loss of frames. Unfortunately, there is no real guarantee! Frames can be lost, discarded, or delayed while en route. When using the burst rate or the burst excess rate, the network will make its best attempt to deliver the frames; but no guarantees are made. As each frame bursts out through the network, it is marked within its overhead with a discard eligibility bit. This means as the network nodes attempt to serve higher rates of throughput, the frames are given a designator by the end-user equipment. This designator lets the other hops on the network know that if the network suddenly begins to get congested, the frames riding the network beyond the CIR can be discarded and other customer frames within the CIR will have priority. In essence, the network provides some breathing room for users by expanding and contracting based on how busy it is. The less busy the network, the higher a customer can burst without risk.

What Do You Think?

Discard eligibility is something new in the data communications industry. How do you feel about a network option that can selectively throw away your data and not tell you it is doing so?

Because the network will only make its best attempt to deliver the data, the end-user equipment must be intelligent enough to recognize that frames have been discarded. In Figure 11-22, the frame format is shown with the setup of the bytes in the header information, creating the discard eligibility setting. In this framed overhead, other pieces of information are also contained. These are shown in the framing overhead:

- The data-link connection identifier (DLCI). This identifier uses up to 1,024 LCNs.

- The command/response (C/R) bit. This is not used in frame relay.

- The extended address (EA) bit. When set to 0, it extends the DLCI address.

- Forward explicit congestion notification (FECN). This is set in the frames going out into the network toward the destination address.

- Backward explicit congestion notification (BECN). This is set in frames returning from the network to the source address.

- Discard eligibility (DE) bit. The DE bit is used by the source equipment to denote whether the frame is eligible to be discarded by the network if the network gets congested. When set to 1, it indicates the frame is eligible to be discarded during the congestion period.

- Extended address (EA) bit. When set to 1, the *EA bit* is used to end the DLCI.

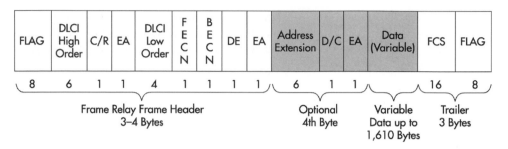

Figure 11-22 The format of the frame in a frame relay is a modified HDLC frame.

Encapsulated in the frame after the header is the *user data,* a variable-length frame of user information that can carry up to 1,610 bytes. When Cascade introduced a frame-relay switch, payloads of up to 4,096 bytes were sufficient to satisfy the data needs for IBM systems. The initial 1,610-byte payload can carry a full Ethernet frame with some overhead. The IBM token ring uses a frame of up to 4,048 bytes.

The bytes are not important at this point, but the variable length is. Because this is a variable, some inherent delays are in the processing of the data across the network. For this reason, the packet-switching networks have received a negative image.

Along with the variable-length data frames, the trailer represents the overhead associated with the error checking (frame check sequence). However, when transmitting data across the network, buffers must be allocated to receive the frames. Because the data are variable, the full-size buffer must be allocated to receive a frame. This happens even if the frame is only half-full. The switch cannot process the data until the beginning flag and the ending flag are received, and the CRC is calculated on what is in between. Therefore, added buffering is required for this system to work. Variable works in some cases, but in others, it introduces extra overhead and latency.

However, the frame-relay nodes across the network only perform the error checking of the addressing; they don't check the user data contained inside. Each node on the network only checks the address and passes the frame along the predefined path (the PVC) to the next node. Nowhere is the data verified. Data integrity is the responsibility of the end devices to perform error checking and retransmission requests. When the frame-relay system emerged in the network, the digital world was already well in place. Because you can expect fewer errors from the transmission medium, the intense error checking at each step along the network can be eliminated and save valuable transport time.

Advantages of Frame-Relay Services

The benefits and advantages of frame-relay services are many. At a minimum, these will include the following:

Increased Utilization and Efficiency

The network uses frame-relay services to allow the user network to "breathe" when necessary and dynamically allocates the bandwidth in real time. The support of multiple connections simultaneously allows multiple sessions to be online concurrently. The nature of the bursty data transmissions on our applications does not require the full-time allocation of bandwidth. This allows shared resources on corporate LANs in remote sites.

Savings Through Network Consolidations

Data from various sources can be applied to the network in various ways, such as SNA traffic from the host, LAN bursty traffic from the desktop devices, and traffic from other application-specific devices. The use of a single connection to support all these connections at various speeds and at variable times allows the end user to consolidate services and, therefore, save money. Frame relay enables the user to save on transmission and switching costs.

Improved Network Uptime

"Network downtime" is a term that will make even the most staunch data-processing person shudder. The use of a frame-relay service in the virtual cloud allows the reestablishment of the network connections within the cloud automatically. The only single point of failure that remains is in the local loop or the last mile. Uptime can achieve 99.9 percent availability on a network of this sort. Furthermore, only a single connection is required. The customer can reduce the equipment costs for the interface equipment [that is, DSU/CSU, routers, multiplexer (MUX) ports, and so forth] because the number and type of interfaces can be limited to one.

Improvements in Response Time

With direct logical connectivity to the multiple locations on the network, a single interface improves the response times. Limiting the number of hops the frames will traverse through, along with eliminating call setup time, vastly improves response times. Allocation of bandwidth to support the bursty data needs also improves the response times, especially when a burst rate can be accommodated. Frame relay is a reliable transport protocol for high-performance and fast-response interconnection of intelligent end-user devices, providing the highest ubiquitous speed and the lowest-overhead protocol standard available for the WAN.

Easily Modifiable and Fast Growth

The logically connected PVCs can be adjusted easily through the network administration group of the carrier. New PVCs can quickly be assigned on a single link or existing PVCs can be increased in capacity up to the access-channel capacity needed to support the dynamics of the organization's transport needs. With the PVC concept, a virtual connection is created quickly and without major modifications to the network.

Interface Signaling for Control

When frame relay was first proposed to the standards bodies, the concept was fairly straightforward: keep the network protocols simple and let the higher-layer protocols at the other end of the link deal with any problems. The networks would need to have a signaling mechanism to address several areas:

- Allowing the network to notify devices when congestion exists and becoming aware of the status of the permanent virtual circuits (PVCs)

- Guaranteeing throughput and equality for all users on the network, so a single user would not occupy the network and deny others their just access

- Creating the opportunity to expand the services and features of the network in the future

Unfortunately, these mechanisms add to the complexity of the frame relay network, so the actual use of the signaling mechanisms is optional. However, if a vendor chooses not to implement the signaling, other complications can arise. The effective throughput of the network, the expected vs. actual response times on the network, and the efficiencies gained from frame relay might all be lost.

Internal Networking

All the standards and modifications define what is supposed to happen at the frame relay interface, normally called the **user-to-network interface (UNI)**. How well the network performs is also determined by what happens inside the cloud; unfortunately, the standards do not attempt to specify how to determine this. Some of the functions that occur within the cloud include:

- Determining the path for the PVCs in use

- Estimating when congestion is building up and deciding what to do to stop it

- Responding quickly to mitigate the congestion when it does occur

- Deciding which frames to discard when this becomes necessary

- Providing guaranteed rates or quality of service levels to users

- Establishing or permitting multiple levels of priority traffic

- Providing the correct throughput levels of service

- Monitoring performance and producing reports effectively on statistics, routes, and so on

IP over Frame Relay

Internet Protocol (IP) datagrams sent over a frame relay network conform to the encapsulation described previously. Within this context, IP could be encapsulated in two different ways: NLPID value—indicating IP—or NLPID value—indicating SNAP.

Although both of these encapsulations are supported under the given definitions, it is advantageous to select only one method as the appropriate mechanism for encapsulating IP data. Therefore, IP data should be encapsulated using the NLPID value of 0xcc, indicating an IP packet. This option is more efficient, because it transmits 48 fewer bits without the SNAP header and is consistent with the encapsulation of IP in an X.25 network.

ATM

In early 1992, the industry adopted another fast packet or "cell relay" concept that uses a short (53-byte) fixed-length cell to transmit information across both private and public networks. This cell-relay technique was introduced as ATM. **Asynchronous transfer mode (ATM)** is one of a class of packet-switching technologies that relay traffic via an address contained within the packet. Packet-switching techniques are not new; some have been around since the late 1960s. However, when packet switching was first developed, the packets used variable lengths of information. This variable nature of each packet caused some latency within a network because the processing equipment used special timers and delimiters to ensure that all the data was enclosed in the packet. To overcome this overhead and latency, a fixed cell size was introduced.

ATM operates at layer 2 of the OSI model. At the bottom-half of layer 2 is ATM. The upper-half is what they call the ATM Adaptation Layer (AAL). This is shown in the following illustration.

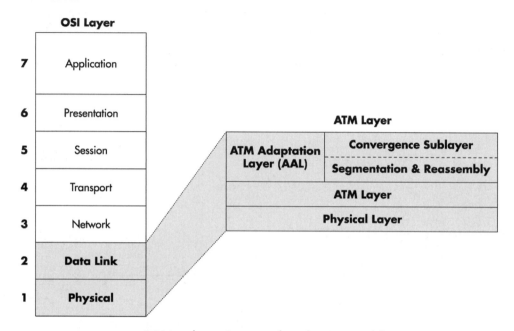

ATM is a layer 2 protocol on the OSI model.

ATM is defined as a transport-and-switching method in which information does not occur periodically with some time reference, such as a frame pattern. All other techniques used a fixed-timing reference, but ATM does not. Hence, the name "asynchronous." With ATM, data arrives and is processed across the network randomly. No specific timing is associated with ATM traffic, so the cells are generated as data needs to be transmitted. When no traffic exists, idle cells may be present on the network or cells carrying other payloads will be present.

What Is ATM?

ATM is a telecommunications concept for the transport of a broad range of user information including voice, data, and video communication on any user-to-network interface (UNI). Because the ATM concept covers these services, it might well be positioned as the high-speed networking tool of the 1990s and beyond. ATM can be used to aggregate user traffic from multiple existing applications onto a single UNI. The current version of the UNI is 3.1, which specifies the rates of speed and the agreed to throughput at the user interface. As shown in Figure 11-23, the ATM concept aggregates a myriad of services onto a single-access arrangement.

All these services can be combined at aggregate rates of up to 622 Mbps today for user traffic. However, the end-user future rates of speed will be OC-48 (2.4 Gbps). Most of the carriers are using speeds of 622 Mbps across their backbone networks, but they can scale up to 2.4 Gbps. In the future, the carriers will step up to the 10 Gbps and higher rates. End users will also be able to handle 1-Gbps packet rates for their Ethernet and Metro services.

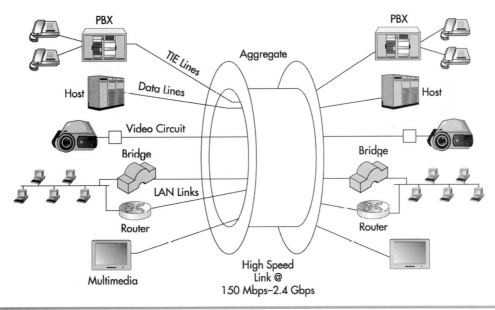

Figure 11-23 ATM allows aggregation of voice, data, LAN, and video services on a high-speed link, ranging from 150 Mbps to 2.4 Gbps.

The Cell Concept

Looking at user demands and the suppliers' own financial picture, a new concept emerged: rather than forcing the user to adapt to the constraints of the network, why not let the network adapt to the needs of the user? ATM gets around the inefficiency of the fixed timeslot, rates, and formats of the TDM world by allocating whatever is necessary to the user whenever the user wants it. To do this, the network suppliers looked to the packet-switching world and settled on a service that mimics packet switching. Differences exist, however. Instead of using the processor-intensive slow-speed services of X.25 packet switching (which tops out at 64 Kbps) or the speedier frame relay (2 Mbps), a mix of packet/frame technology evolved using a fixed-size cell that offers higher throughput because of efficient use of bandwidth without the overhead of X.25 and frame relay. The cell is fixed at 53 bytes.

These cells can get around the waste of frame relay or other frame concepts. In frame relay, the frames are larger, but variable in length. If a frame size is set to accommodate LAN traffic, such as an Ethernet frame of 1,500 bytes, the network deals with a frame of the same size. Consequently, the 1,500-byte frame is used, even if only 150 bytes are to be transmitted. In many implementations, a pad function (filler) is used to fill the frame for transmission. The network has been used for a much longer period to send an insignificant amount of data. The use of this frame was only 10 percent efficient.

While the network was handling this partially empty frame, other users who wanted to transmit were delayed. Moreover, when a variable frame size is used, the buffers across the network have to work accordingly. In many cases, the buffers in the frame-relay switches are set to expect a full frame of 1,610 bytes (plus the associated overhead). If a switch has a nearly full buffer and a frame arrives, the switch must allocate the full-size buffer for the receipt of the frame. If a full-frame buffer cannot be allocated, the switch throws the frame away. Although the frame may have been partially filled, the maximum buffer cannot be allocated. Therefore, the network is inefficiently used because the data is discarded when it did not have to be.

On the other hand, a much smaller cell allows the transmitter to break down large blocks of information into more manageable pieces. If the frame used (in this example) is only partially filled, the network need not be concerned. It will only be required to send the 150 bytes of information, plus any associated overhead in a couple of cells. Thus, the network performs more efficiently. The processor speed can be used to maximize the throughput and minimize delays across the network. Cells can now be processed quickly in silicon (chipsets). Many of the ATM switch manufacturers are now using application-specific integrated circuits (ASICs) in the systems to process the cells efficiently and quickly.

Deriving Bandwidth

When these fixed cells are used, another benefit is achieved. Users who needed to transmit 8 Mbps were stuck. Either they would have to settle for a T1 (1.544 Mbps) transmission, which would ultimately cause congestion, or they would have to lease a T3 (44.736 Mbps), which would be too expensive and mostly unused. Again, the fixed timeslot arrangement of the TDM world got in the way.

Using a cell concept, the user would transparently send cells interleaved across the network, regardless of the amount of bandwidth needed and, consequently, get an effective throughput of 8 Mbps.

NOTE

When a user needs to send data, the cell concept enables the user to send as fast as necessary and derive the bandwidth from the passing of the cells.

Cell Sizes and Formats

The standard-fixed cell size for ATM is 53 bytes (octets). This comprises 5 bytes of overhead for addressing and 48 bytes of payload. The cell is shown in Figure 11-24. The 48-byte payload will be a variable, depending on the information and control necessary. Several types of cells are used that could take 4 bytes of the 48 away for control, leaving the user 44 bytes of effective data. Another option gives the user all 48 bytes of payload for data. It depends on the implementation and the service run on ATM. Either way, the cell is still fixed at 53 bytes long.

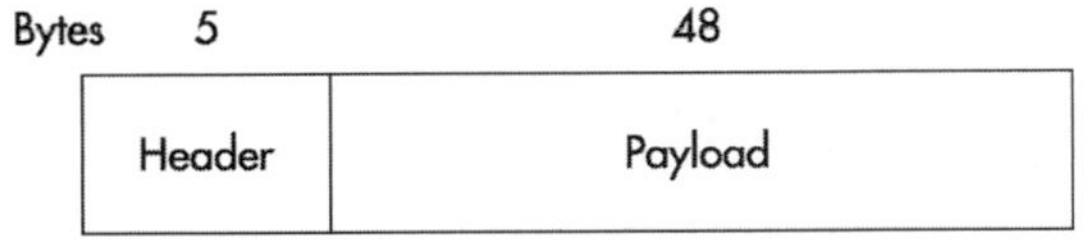

Bytes   5   48

Header	Payload

Figure 11-24 The cell uses 53 bytes, as shown here. The header always uses 5 bytes (addressing), and the remaining 48 bytes are the payload.

See Figure 11-25 for a more detailed look at the header information, as discussed in the following paragraphs. The description explains the fields in the header and the function they must serve.

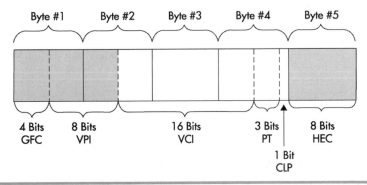

Figure 11-25 The header is broken down here to clarify the framing format of the cell.

General Flow Control Identifier

The first 4 bits of byte number 1 contain what is known as a general flow control (GFC) identifier. The **GFC identifier** is used to control the flow of traffic across the user-to-network interface (UNI) out to the network. Remember, this is only used at the user interface because, once the cell goes on to the **network-to-network interface (NNI)** that is between network nodes, these extra 4 bits will be reassigned for network addressing. The GFC is only used at the entry to the ATM backbone network between the user device and the rest of the network.

Virtual Path Identifier

The next 8 bits of the header are called the virtual path identifier (VPI). A **VPI** is part of the network address. A virtual path is a grouping of channels between network nodes.

Virtual Channel Identifier

The **virtual channel identifier (VCI)** is a pointer on which channel (virtual) the system is using on the path. The combination of the virtual path and virtual channel makes up the data link running between two network nodes. The VCI is 16 bits long, using the second 4 bits of byte 2, all 8 bits of byte 3, and the first 4 bits of byte 4.

Payload Type

A total of 3 bits in byte 4 are allocated to define the payload type (PT), which indicates the type of information contained in the cell. Because these cells will be used for transporting different types of information, the network equipment might have to handle them differently.

Cell-Loss Priority

Bit number 8 of byte number 4 is a cell-loss priority (CLP) bit. The user can define whether or not to discard the cell if congestion occurs on the network. If congestion occurs and the bit is set to 1 by the user, the network can discard the cell. If the bit is set to 0, then the cell may not be discarded.

Header Error Control

The 5th byte of the overhead is used as a header error control (HEC). This is an error-correcting byte that is conducted on the first 4 bytes of the header. HEC is used to correct single-bit errors and detect multiple errors in the header information. If a single-bit error occurs, the HEC will correct it. However, if multiple errors occur in the header, HEC will discard the cell, so cells will not be routed to the wrong address because of errors occurring on the network. The HEC only looks at the header information; it does not concern itself with the user data contained in the next 48 bytes.

Line Check 11-12

The cell is always _____ bytes long. This is made up of a header of _____ bytes and a payload of _____ bytes.

The Cell Format for User Data

Once the header is completed, the user information is then inserted. As already mentioned, the user field is either 44 or 48 bytes of information, depending on the process used. Here's how this works.

The Adaptation Layer

Called the ATM adaptation layer (AAL), this is probably the most significant part of ATM. The **AAL** provides the flexibility of a single communications process to carry multiple types of traffic, such as data, voice, video, and multimedia.

Each type of traffic has varying needs. Voice needs constant data traffic, LAN is bursty in nature, video is time-sensitive, and data transfers from host-to-host can be delayed without a problem. In this adaptation process, the network can deal freely with varying types of information and only route cells on the basis of the routing information in the header.

Just about any type of transmission will require more than a single cell of information (48 bytes), so the ATM adaptation layer divides the information into smaller segments that are capable of being inserted into cells for transport between two end nodes. Depending on the type of traffic, the adaptation layer functions in one of five ways. These are shown in Table 11-4, with various types of information and adaptation layers involved.

The Adaptation Layer Process

The AAL is broken down into two sublayers: the first is the convergence sublayer, and the second is the segmentation and reassembly sublayer (SAR). The purpose of the **SAR** is to break the data down into the 48-byte payloads, yet maintain data integrity and pointers for ID purposes.

Type	Name	Description
1.	Constant–bit rate (CBR) services	Allows ATM to handle voice services at DS0, DS1, and DS3 levels. Recovers timing and clocking for voice services.
2.	Variable–bit rate (VBR) time-sensitive services	Not finalized, but reserved for data transmissions that are synchronized. Also will address packet-mode video in a compressed mode using bursty data transmission.
3.	Connection-oriented VBR data transfer	Bursty data generated across the network between two users on a prearranged connection. Large file transfers fall into this category.
4.	Connectionless VBR transfer	Transmission of data without a prearranged connection. Suitable for LAN traffic that is bursty and short. Same reasoning as X.25, where dial-up connection and setup take longer than data transfer.
5.	Simple and efficient adaptation layer (SEAL)	Improved type 3 for data transfer where higher-level protocols can handle data and error recovery. Uses all 48 bytes as data transmission and handles message transfer as sequenced packets.

Table 11-4 Each of the Five Different Forms of AAL Addresses a Different Type of Service.

This process of two sublayers produces a **protocol data unit (PDU)**. The convergence sublayer PDU is of a variable length that is determined by the AAL type and the length of the higher-layer data passed to it. The SAR-PDU is always kept at 48 bytes to fill an ATM cell data stream. This is shown in Figure 11-26 as it goes through the process.

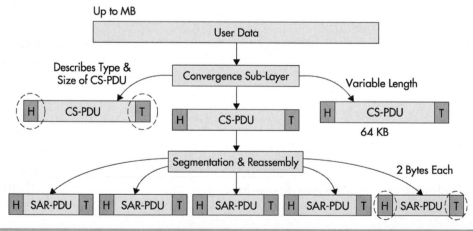

Figure 11-26 The process of creating the ATM cell includes the CS and SAR processes.

As the user data, which can be multimegabyte files, is passed down to the convergence sublayer (CS) process, the data is broken down into variable block lengths. A maximum of 64 KB is used in this process. The large user file is broken down into the 64-KB segments. A header and trailer describing the type and size of the CS-PDU are added. This is then passed on to the next sublayer process.

The SAR then receives the CS-PDU and breaks it down into 44-byte cells (if less than 44 bytes, the rest is padded). Additional overhead (2 bytes of header and 2 bytes of trailer) is added to the SAR-PDU. Instead, the simple and efficient adaptation layer (SEAL) uses all 48 bytes for user information and, therefore, uses the bandwidth more efficiently.

Finally, the PDU is inserted into an ATM cell with the 5-byte header. Following this, the cell is handed down to the physical cable system.

ATM Forum

The ATM Forum is an international consortium of members that is chartered to accelerate the acceptance of ATM products and services in local, metropolitan, and wide area networks. Although it is not an official standards body, the forum works with the official ATM standards groups to ensure interoperability among ATM systems. The consortium accelerates ATM adoption through the development of common implementation specifications. The forum's first specification on the ATM user network interface (UNI) provides an important platform on which vendors can design and build equipment. The UNI defines the interface between a router or a workstation and a private ATM switch, or between the private ATM switch and a public ATM switch.

Switches

ATM switches come in a variety of flavors, speeds, and access ports. At the heart of the switch is a dual-bus architecture with throughput starting at 622 Mbps on up to 2.4 Gbps and more, as shown in Figure 11-27. Several inputs from 4 to 16 in the user environment will match across a matrix of outputs (ranging from 4, 10, or 16 Mbps, and more). The ATM switch will process the AAL 3-, 4-, and 5-level services in the enterprise network.

The local switch handles the switching and routing of cells in a building or department. This local switch connects to a network backbone switch via an OC-3 (155 Mbps) or less service to start. Faster, higher throughput becomes available through upgrades at the backplane level and the number and speed of ports attached. This requires that the switch be scalable and migrate to the gigabit ranges. Cell switching breaks up data streams into small units that are independently routed through the switch. The routing occurs mostly in hardware through the

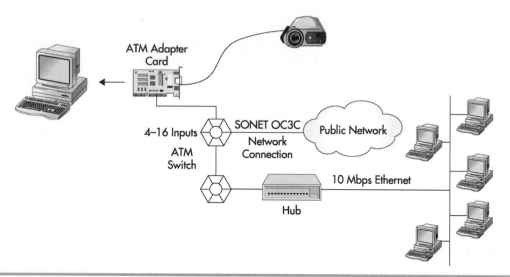

Figure 11-27 The switches can handle multiple inputs to multiple outputs. From 4 to 16 inputs can handle a variety of speeds through these switches.

switching fabric. The combination of cell switching and scalable switching fabrics is a key ingredient of ATM.

Public Switches

The public network ATM switch is a larger, more intelligent version of the customer premises switch. A public switch is capable of handling hundreds of thousands of cells per second, and it has thousands of switch ports, each operating at rates of 622 Mbps to 2.4 Gbps. All cell-processing functions are performed by the input controllers, the switch fabric, and the output controllers. In an ATM switch, cell arrivals are not scheduled. The control processor resolves contention when it occurs, as well as call setup and teardown, bandwidth reservation, maintenance, and management. The input controllers are synchronized, so cells arrive at the switch fabric with their headers aligned.

The resulting traffic is said to be slotted, and the time to transmit a cell across the switch fabric is called a **timeslot**. All VCIs are translated in the input controllers. Each incoming VCI is funneled into the proper output port, as defined in a routing table. At the output controllers, the cells are formatted in the proper transmission format.

Chapter 11 Review

Chapter Summary

Regardless of the means or the format, you can send data in several different ways. X.25 packet switching was developed in 1974 as a means of replacing older data-transfer modes (X.25 was developed to replace the IP method of packet switching). X.25 is a WAN protocol that is connection-oriented.

When packets are prepared, they are formatted into an HDLC frame. Then the packets are sent to the closest switch, where the packet headers are analyzed for the connection needed. The packet is buffered at the switch, error-checked, and forwarded on to the next hop. All packets are either acknowledged or nonacknowledged (ACK/NAK). Only after a packet is ACK, does the switch flush it from its buffer.

Packet switching is efficient, but in today's world, the original X.25 protocol is considered too slow for most applications. The data rate achieved by the standards group is 56 to 64 Kbps. This is much too little for the demands of networks today.

The Internet Protocol (IP) was originally designed to carry small amounts of data between computers. This was mail- and text-oriented. Later, as things evolved, the network demanded much higher data rates and more graphic-intense information. IP is connectionless-oriented, and it neither sequences the data (count) nor does an ACK or NAK. IP is considered a dumb protocol. IP works in nearly all our space (LAN, MAN, CAN, WAN) and is a robust set of protocols. There are no speed limitations on IP.

IP addressing is becoming a problem as we face the exhaustion of the current addressing scheme. We do not have 4 billion users, but the early developers and managers of the addresses were somewhat careless in the administration of the finite resource. We can forestall the inevitable number crunch through a series of tools, such as CIDR, subnetting, and NAT. Other tools can also help as things progress.

Frame relay was designed to overcome some of the pitfalls of the packet-switching world. Frames are larger than packets. Frames are not ACK or NAK across the network. The frame operates on a higher speed, has more-reliable circuits, and can be more bandwidth-efficient. Frame relay also depends on the bursty nature of data in that it allocates a committed information rate, and then allows for a burst rate and an excess burst rate, if the network is underutilized. Frame relay operates at speeds of up to 2 Mbps and carries 1,610 bytes of data in the frame. Frames are variable in length, which causes some inefficiency and latency.

ATM is another fast packet-switching technique. Cells use a 5-byte header and a 48-byte payload. The cells are fixed, which allows for a fast processing, yet the 5-byte header on a 48-byte payload causes many to complain about the overhead being too great. ATM operates at speeds of 155 Mbps or 622 Mbps, and scales up to 2.4 Gbps, or in fractional rated, below 155 Mbps.

Key Terms for Chapter 11

Asynchronous Transfer Mode (ATM) *(551)*
ATM Adaptation Layer (AAL) *(557)*
Autonomous System *(534)*
Cells *(541)*
Classless Interdomain Routing (CIDR) *(537)*
Committed Information Rate (CIR) *(546)*
Connectionless Service *(524)*
Datagrams *(524)*
Direct Delivery *(535)*
Direct Routing *(535)*
Exterior Routers *(534)*
Fast Select *(508)*
Frame Relay *(542)*
General Flow Control (GFC) Identifier *(556)*
General Format Identifier (GFI) *(509)*
High-Level Data Link Control (HDLC) *(508)*
Indirect Routing *(535)*
Interior Routers *(534)*
IP Datagram *(535)*
IP Routing *(534)*
Logical Channel Group Number (LGN) *(509)*
Logical Channel Number (LCN) *(509)*
Nailed Up *(542)*
Network-to-Network Interface (NNI) *(556)*
Next Hop *(534)*
Packet Assembler/Disassembler (PAD) *(508)*
Packet Switching *(507)*
Packet Switching Exchanges (PSEs) *(512)*
Packet Type Identifier (PTI) *(510)*
Permanent Logical Links (PLL) *(544)*
Permanent Virtual Circuits (PVCs) *(544)*
Protocol Data Unit (PDU) *(558)*
Route Flapping *(530)*
Routers *(534)*
Segmentation and Reassembly Sublayer (SAR) *(557)*
Statistical Time Division Multiplexer (STDM) *(517)*
Subnet *(528)*
Subnet Mask *(529)*
Subnetwork *(528)*
TCP/IP *(522)*

Timeslot *(560)*
User-to-Network Interface (UNI) *(550)*
Virtual Channel Identifier (VCI) *(556)*
Virtual Circuit *(508)*
Virtual Path Identifier (VPI) *(556)*

Key Term Quiz

1. The process of taking large files and breaking them down into smaller pieces for transmission is called _packet Switching_

2. The _____ is responsible for breaking the data into smaller segments and putting the data segments back together.

3. Using the OSI model and layer 2 to encapsulate the data, we create a _____ frame.

4. The most common form of packet switching today employs a protocol suite called _____.

5. IP uses a _____ protocol.

6. The addresses used in IP were frivolously handed out early in the development. This led to a new form of addressing called _____ to overcome the limitations of classful addresses.

7. When an address space needs to be spread across multiple departments of sites, the use of a _____ will aid in controlling the addresses.

8. The layer 2 protocol that replaced X.25 is called _____.

9. A fixed-size cell is used for _____ transmissions.

10. The _____ size is always made up of 53 bytes.

Multiple-Choice Quiz

1. What is the purpose of packet switching?

   a. To break the packets down for the heck of it

   b. To gain more reliable data transfers

   c. To get more revenue because the rates are charged on a packet-by-packet basis

   d. Because everyone else is doing it

2. What is the designated protocol name for packet switching?

   a. X.75

   b. X.29

   c. X.25

   d. X.400

3. The organization responsible for creating the packet switching protocol is _____ .

   a. Internet Engineering Task Force (IETF)

   b. Institute of Electrical and Electronic Engineers (IEEE)

   c. International Telecommunications Union (ITU)

   d. Internet service providers (ISP)

4. When the carriers offer X.25 packet switching, they are typically called ____ .

   a. PDN

   b. VAN

   c. WAN

   d. PSTN

5. The sharing of the circuit is done through a technique called _____ .

   a. Packet switching

   b. Frequency Division Multiplexing

   c. Statistical Time Division Multiplexing

   d. Time Division Multiplexing

6. The highest rated speed for X.25 packet switching is _____ .

   a. 56 Kbps

   b. 2 Mbps

   c. 128 Kbps

   d. 64 Kbps

7. The X.25 packets are encapsulated inside a _____ frame for transmission.

   a. SDLC

   b. HDLC

   c. PPP

   d. BDLC

8. Whenever a packet in X.25 gets transmitted, it is either _____ or _____ along the way.

   a. ACK or NAK

   b. Sent or received

   c. Held or discarded

   d. ACK or RAK

9. X.25 uses a _____ transmission mode.

   a. Half- duplex

   b. Simplex

   c. Redirection

   d. Duplex

10. Benefits of packet switching include (choose all that apply) _____.

   a. Less expensive data

   b. More reliable data

   c. Faster date transfers

   d. Reduced delay

   e. Guaranteed delivery

11. Frame relay is included as a member of the _____.

   a. Fast packet-switching family

   b. Cell relay family

   c. Circuit relay family

   d. Djal-up telephone network

12. When using a frame relay service, users select the _____ that they need for speed.

   a. Bc

   b. CIR

   c. Br

   d. Be

13. Frame relay was introduced in what year?

    a. 1990

    b. 1991

    c. 1992

    d. 1993

14. When using the CIR, a customer then specifies the locations where the _____ is logically connected.

    a. SVC

    b. PVC

    c. SNA

    d. TCP

15. The frame relay address is called the _____.

    a. IP address

    b. SNA address

    c. Data link connection identifier

    d. Logical channel number

16. The traffic congestion notifications are called the _____.

    a. FECE and BECE

    b. FEBC and REBC

    c. FEA and BEA

    d. FECN and BECN

17. What are the typical access link speeds used in North America? (choose all that apply)

    a. 2.048 Mbps

    b. 56 Kbps

    c. 64 Kbps

    d. 1.544 Mbps

18. When the variable payload was initially introduced, it contained up to _____ bytes.

    a. 2,096

    b. 1,610

    c. 1,518

    d. 4,048

19. Frame relay was designed to operate in the _____.

    a. LAN

    b. MAN

    c. WAN

    d. CAN

20. What does ATM stand for?

    a. Automated Teller Machine

    b. Adobe Type Manager

    c. Asynchronous Transfer Mode

    d. Asymmetrical Transfer Mode

21. What organization created the demand for ATM and ensured its acceptance?

    a. ITU

    b. ATM Forum

    c. ANSI

    d. CCITT

22. The layer sitting on top of ATM that provides for convergence of the data is called _____.

    a. IP

    b. ATMCS

    c. ACP

    d. AAL

23. One of the ATM speeds supported is _____.

    a. 175 Mbps

    b. 622 Mbps

    c. 1.9 Gbps

    d. 2.048 Gbps

24. ATM uses a cell payload that is____.

    a. 53 bytes

    b. 44 bytes

c. 46 bytes

d. 48 bytes

25. The cell header is _____ bytes long.

    a. 4

    b. 5

    c. 7

    d. 8

26. The complete address of a cell is called the _____.

    a. VPP/VCI

    b. VPI/VCC

    c. VPI/VCI

    d. VPP/VCI

27. There are _____ different forms of AAL.

    a. Three

    b. Four

    c. Five

    d. Six

28. ATM was invented in ____.

    a. 1992

    b. 1994

    c. 1996

    d. 1998

Essay Quiz

1. The use of X.25 guarantees delivery, integrity, and sequencing. Why, then, would anyone want to us the Internet Protocol when IP guarantees nothing?

2. Explain why the industry wants to move from a slow X.25 to the benefits of ATM.

3. List the four primary categories of packets we use in the WAN and assess why the evolution has taken place.

4. What is the benefit of frame relay over the previous network standards, such as X.25 and IP?

5. Which technology seems to be the front-runner in all aspects of our data-switching standards and why? Can you estimate what the next big movement will be using these protocols?

Exercises

1. Change the following IP addresses from binary notation to decimal dot notations:

   a. 01111111 11110000 01100111 01111101

   b. 10101111 11000000 11110000 00011101

   c. 11011111 10110000 00011111 01011101

2. Write the following masks in binary notation.

   a. 255.255.192.0

   b. 255.255.224.0

   c. 255.255.255.240

3. A frame relay router receives a 2-MB file to be transferred. Using full frames, how many frames will be transmitted?

4. An AAL1 layer receives data at 2 Mbps. How many cells are created per second by the ATM layer?

5. Using the OSI model, fill in the following chart with the X.25 layers (use only those which apply).

6. Using the same graph, plot the frame-relay model and the OSI model (use all that apply).

7. Using the following chart, fill in the header and the body of the ATM cell.

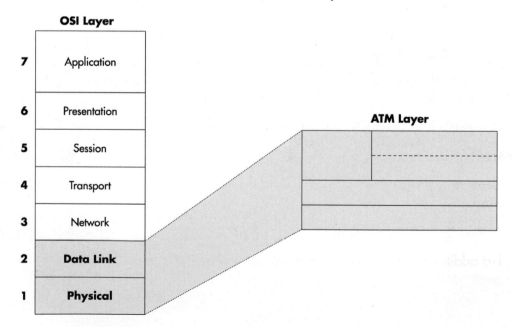

Chapter 12

xDSL

Introduction

One of the major problems facing the Incumbent Local Exchange Carriers (ILECs) is the capability to maintain and preserve their installed base. Ever since the Telecommunications Act of 1996, there has been mounting pressure on the ILECs to provide faster Internet access. To provide the higher-speed communications capability, these carriers have continually looked for new means of providing the service.

However, the ILECs have an installed base of unshielded twisted pair in the local loop that cannot be ignored or abandoned. Therefore, a new form of communications was needed to work over the existing copper cable plant. One of the technologies selected was the use of xDSL. The digital subscriber line (DSL) family includes several variations of what is known as digital subscriber line. The lowercase *x* in front of the DSL stands for the many variations. These include:

- ISDN (like) Digital Subscriber Line (IDSL)

- Asymmetrical Digital Subscriber Line (ADSL)

- High Data Rate Digital Subscriber Line (HDSL)

- Consumer Digital Subscriber Line (CDSL)

- Rate-Adaptive Digital Subscriber Line (RADSL)

- Single or Symmetric Digital Subscriber Line (SDSL)

Enhancements to the DSL family:

- Very High-Speed Digital Subscriber Line (VDSL)

- Symmetrical High-Bit Rate DSL (SHDSL)

- Universal DSL (UDSL)

As you can see, the variations on DSL are many. Each DSL capability carries with it differences in speed, throughput, and facilities used. At the same time, the ILEC can also support POTS for voice or fax communications on the same line. What this means is the ILEC does not have to install all new cabling to support high-speed communications access to the Internet.

The most popular member of this family under today's technology is the use of Asymmetrical Digital Subscriber Line (ADSL). ADSL is a technology being provided primarily by the ILECs because the existing cable plant can be supported and the speed throughput can vary depending on the quality of the copper. However, the most important and critical factor in dealing with ADSL technology is the capability to support speeds of 1.5 Mbps up to 8.192 Mbps.

Modem Technologies

Before proceeding too far in this discussion, we will review the basics of modem technology. **Modems**, or modulators/demodulators, were designed to provide for data communications across the voice–dial-up communication network. Modem technology was originally introduced back in the 1960s, enabling users to transmit data across the voice networks at speeds varying between 300 bps and 33,600 bps. This was introduced in Chapter 8.

Although the speeds seemed like high-speed communication (at the time), the demands and needs for faster communications quickly exceeded the capabilities of the then current modem services. Higher-speed modems could be produced, but the economics and variations in the delivery-wiring system proved this to be an impractical approach. Instead, the providers looked for a better way to provide data communications that mimic the digital transmission speeds we have grown accustomed to.

To utilize a modem for data access, using the telephone companies' voice services, the end user installed a modem on the local loop. The modem is the Data Circuit-Terminating Equipment (DCE) for the link. As shown in Figure 12-1, a modem is used on the ILEC's wires to communicate across the wide area networks (WANs), such as the long-distance voice networks. This figure shows the modem is the interface to the telephone network; its transmission quality is limited to the quality of the local loop. The ILEC installs a voice-grade line on the local copper-cable plant and allows the end user to connect the modem. The modem converts the data from a computer terminal into a voice equivalent analog signal. Data compression and other multi-modulation techniques allowed the data rates to increase from 300 bps to 33.6 Kbps.

In 1997, the introduction of the 56-Kbps (V.90) modem was touted to revolutionize the market and speed data transmission to meet the demands of the consumers. These newer modems are touted to handle data at speeds of up to 56 Kbps, but few get data across the network at these rates. The reality of the system has the consumer operating at speeds of approximately 33.6 Kbps.

NOTE

Manufacturers of 56K modems promise download speeds of up to 56 Kbps. However, these modems are limited in their upload speed to only 48 Kbps (V.92). This is the asymmetrical part of the dial-up modem technology. In reality, this modem is 53.6 Kbps download (maximum) and 48 Kbps (maximum) upload. Because line conditions on the Public Switched Telephone Network (PSTN) (static, noise, and hiss) affect signal quality, the modem responds by slowing down. Therefore, your connection that logged on at 56K is usually slowing down during your session.

However, even at 56 Kbps, users almost immediately wanted higher speeds. The modems did not satisfy the demands for higher-speed Internet access and video demands. Therefore, newer techniques to provide faster data communications across the local voice telephone networks were needed. The DSL modem was created to meet this need.

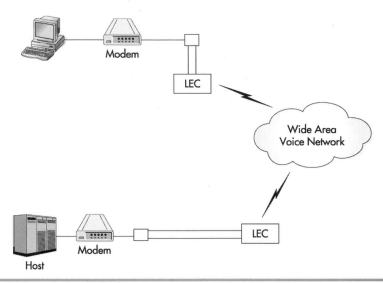

Figure 12-1 Modems are installed at the customer's location and use the existing telephone wires to transmit data across the voice network.

What Is Digital Subscriber Line (DSL)?

A **digital subscriber line (DSL)** is a means of utilizing the existing local loop provisioned for telephony to access the Internet at higher speeds than through dial-up access. DSL, in its most basic form, splits the transmission line into different signals: one an analog signal for voice and the other a digital signal for data access. To make this division of the transmission line, several pieces of equipment must be added. On the customer side is a DSL transceiver (a DSL modem), and a line splitter may also be required. On the carrier side is a **DSL Access Multiplexor (DSLAM)**.

The **DSL transceiver** acts in a similar manner as a traditional modem, sending and receiving bits of information over the access line. In the case of DSL, however, these signals are provided in a digital form.

A line splitter is used in some deployments of DSL. A **Plain Old Telephone Service (POTS) line splitter** is a device that divides the telephone signal into two or more signals, in different frequencies. In ADSL, the splitter provides two frequency ranges: a low range to provide signal flow for voice devices and a high-frequency range for data transmission. The POTS splitter allows the simultaneous access to telephony applications and high-speed data access to the Internet over the same pair of wires.

The DSLAM is the technology that makes DSL work. As its name implies, the DSLAM (which resides in the CO or in newer implementations on the curb) is responsible for managing multiple-access connections and then routing the information transmitted to the Internet. You should recall that a **multiplexor** is any device that combines multiple transmission paths over a single connection (to the Internet). The DSLAM sometimes is also responsible for routing or providing IP addresses to the customer's machine.

By adding this hardware to the existing copper plant, two signals can share the same transmission path at the same time because they are occurring at different frequencies on the same line, a form of frequency-division multiplexing (FDM). This is one of DSL's major benefits—allowing the same line to be connected to a phone and a computer. Both devices may be used simultaneously.

The process of adding data onto the line is accomplished with a coding technique. Several techniques were developed, but we will cover the most popular of them in the following sections.

NOTE

Newer advancements in DSLAM technology are allowing DSL to be deployed further than the 15,000-feet current reach. These remote DSLAMs support ADSL services at 3 Mbps, at distances of up to 60,000 feet. This type of solution utilizes existing line power to run the remote DSLAM, meaning it can be installed nearly anywhere on the loop.

xDSL Coding Techniques

Many approaches were developed as a means of encoding the data onto the xDSL circuits. The more common are carrierless amplitude phase modulation (CAP) and discrete multitone modulation (DMT). The industry, as a rule, selected DMT, but several developers and providers have used CAP, so it is appropriate to summarize both of these techniques.

Carrierless Amplitude Phase Modulation (CAP)

Carrierless amplitude phase modulation (CAP) is a single-carrier signaling technique. The data rate is divided and modulated onto two different orthogonal carriers before being combined and transmitted. CAP generates its two orthogonal signals and executes them digitally. Using two digital-transversal bandpass filters with equal amplitude characteristics and a p/2 difference in phase response, the signals are combined and fed into a digital-to-analog converter. Then the data is transmitted.

CAP was one of the original proposals for use with ADSL technology. Unfortunately, it was a proprietary solution offered by a single vendor, which prevented its widespread acceptance. Figure 12-2 shows CAP in its use of the frequency spectrum of the line. Most industry vendors agree that CAP has some benefits over DMT, but also that DMT has more benefits over CAP. The point here is this: two differing technologies were initially rolled out for ADSL (and the other family members) that contradict each other in their implementation.

CAP uses the entire loop bandwidth (excluding the 4-kHz analog voice channel) to send the bits all at once. There are no subchannels, as found in the DMT technique. The lack of subchannels removes the concern about the individual channel transmission and problems.

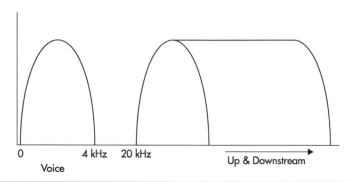

Figure 12-2 The spectral use of CAP.

To achieve the simultaneous send and receive capability, frequency division multiplexing is used (as is echo cancellation). Many of the Regional Bell Operating Companies (RBOCs) have used or tried CAP in their installations but have moved away from CAP to a uniform use of DMT.

Discrete Multitone Modulation (DMT)

Discrete Multitone Modulation (DMT) uses multiple narrow-band carriers, all transmitting simultaneously in a parallel transmission mode. Each of these carriers carries a portion of the information being transmitted. These multiple discrete bands, or in the world of frequency division multiplexing, **subchannels**, are modulated independently of each other, using a carrier frequency located in the center of the frequency being used. These carriers are then processed in parallel form.

To process the multicarrier frequencies at the same time, a lot of digital processing is required. In the past, this was not economically feasible, but integrated circuitry has made it more feasible.

The American National Standards Institute (ANSI) selected DMT with the use of 256 subcarriers, each with the standard 4.3125-kHz bandwidth. These subcarriers can be independently modulated with a maximum of 15 bits/second/Hz. This allows up to 60 Kbps per tone used. Figure 12-3 shows the use of the frequency spectrum for the combination of voice and two-way data transmission.

In this representation, voice is used in the normal 0–4 kHz band on the lower end of the spectrum (although the lower 20 kHz are provided). Separation is allowed between the voice channel and the upstream data communications, which operates between 20 kHz and 130 kHz. Then, a separation is allowed between the upstream and the downstream channels. The downstream flow uses between 140 kHz and 1 MHz. As shown in this drawing, the separation allows for the simultaneous up and down streams and the concurrent voice channel. The data rates are sustained on this spectrum. Each of the subchannels operates at approximately 4.3125 kHz, and a separation of 4.3125 kHz between channels is allocated.

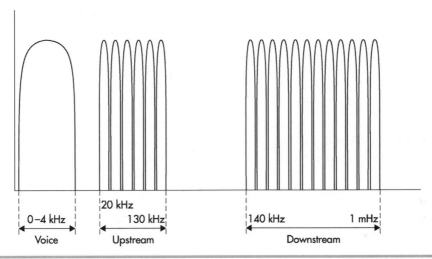

Figure 12-3 The ANSI DMT specification.

⍰ Line Check 12-1

1. If the voice channel of a phone call is only 4 KHz wide, why was so much room left between the voice channel and the upstream channel (which starts at 20 Khz)?

2. Would the signals interfere anyway because one is analog and the others are digital?

TYPES of DSL

The Asymmetrical Digital Subscriber Line (ADSL) Defined

Asymmetrical digital subscriber line (ADSL) is the new modem technology to converge the existing twisted-pair telephone lines into the high-speed communications access capability for various services. Most people consider ADSL a transmission system instead of a modification to the existing transmission facilities. However, ADSL is asymmetrical, meaning the upload speeds and download speeds differ. Typically, upload speeds for sending files range from 16 Kbps to 640 Kbps, and downloading speed receives information between 1.5 Mbps and 6 Mbps. The decision to provide faster download speeds is because of the nature of web browsing the Internet.

Most Internet users look at far more information on the Net than they send. ADSL takes advantage of this habit and maximizes efficiency.

Some say ADSL will support speeds about 8.192 Mbps. This definition of the higher range of ADSL speeds is yet to be proved; however, with changes in today's technology, it is highly likely these speeds will be achievable. We cover the newer standards of ADSL2 and ADSL2+ in the section "ADSL2 Standardization."

Some of the many capabilities being considered through the use of the DSL family are the services for converging voice, data, multimedia, video, and Internet-streaming-protocols services. The carriers see their future rollout of products and services to the general consuming public in these services. Table 12-1 shows various theoretical speed and distances of ADSL technologies.

Remember, the speeds and distances shown here are the theoretical limits based on good copper. If the copper wire has been damaged or impaired in any way, then the speed and distances will change accordingly (downward). The theoretical limits are what most engineers and providers have been claiming their technologies can support.

Reality is another thing, and the actual distances and speeds likely will be less than shown here. What is most important is to assume these speeds can be established and maintained on the installed base of unshielded twisted pairs (UTP) of wire. As long as the ILEC can approximate these speeds today, the consumer will not have much to complain about.

Current Data Rate	Wire Gauge	Distance in K Feet	Distance in Kilometers
1.5–2.048 Mbps	24	18	5.5
1.5–2.048 Mbps	26	15	4.6
6.3 Mbps	24	12	3.7
6.3 Mbps	26	9	2.7

Table 12-1 Data Rates for ADSL, Based on Installed Wiring at Varying Gauges.

To Split or Not to Split

Another issue in using ADSL is the use of splitters on the line. In normal ADSL and rate-adaptive DSL (covered in following sections), the local provider uses a splitter on the line. ADSL modems usually include a POTS splitter, which allows simultaneous access to telephony applications and high-speed data access. All splitters are not equal, but some vendors provision the service with an active POTS splitter device, allowing simultaneous telephone and data access. Unfortunately, with an active device, if the power or the modem fails, then the telephone also fails. This is problematic because we are accustomed to having lifeline services with our telephone systems that are always available, even if the power fails. The splitter is shown in Figure 12-4 as it is installed.

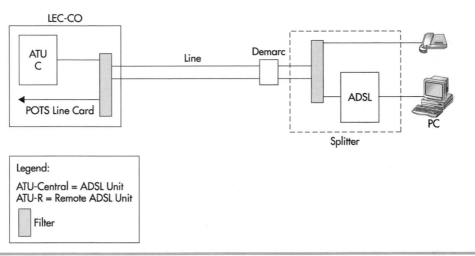

Figure 12-4 ADSL service with splitter and line filters attached.

A passive POTS splitter is a better alternative because it maintains the lifeline service of telephony, even if the modem fails. This is important because the telephone line is powered from the line instead of an external power source. Telephony service will be available as much as you have always expected from the normal service you have always received.

A POTS splitter is a three-pronged device, allowing telephony and simultaneous up-and-down loading data access on the same copper loop (see Figure 12-5). As shown in the previous figures, the POTS service operates at the low end of the frequency spectrum. All the data signals are

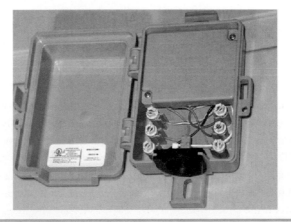

Figure 12-5 A picture of a POTS line splitter.

located in the higher frequencies. These signals start between 20 to 25 kHz and above. The splitter provides a low-pass filter between the copper line and the ADSL point on the modem.

One of the primary concerns is to allow a filter to block any transient noise coming from the POTS side of the line from crossing over into the ADSL side of the line. Ringing voltages can cause significant impulse noise across the line, destroying the data traversing at that moment. ADSL modem signals are also blocked from passing onto the POTS side of the line by the filters.

Most of the POTS splitters are passive. Passive filters provide higher degrees of reliability because they don't require power. They can isolate the equipment from surges on the line and can arrest lightning that may be coupled on the line. Active filters require power and are less adapted to suppress the surges. In many countries around the world, active filters are a requirement.

The G.Lite specification uses a splitterless device to facilitate the installation of low-speed DSL services. This is shown in Figure 12-6 for implementation. Without the splitter, the provider has less cost and the issues of active vs. passive splitters are eliminated.

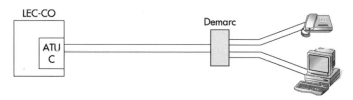

Figure 12-6   The splitterless G.Lite installation.

ADSL G.lite

Provisions for the high-speed data rates of full ADSL are good, but not every consumer is looking for the high data rates afforded on ADSL. Therefore, the Universal ADSL Working Group decided to reevaluate the need of the end user. What it determined is that many consumers need download speeds of up to 1.5 Mbps and upload speeds between 9.6 and 500 Kbps. As a result, the **ADSL Lite (ADSL G.lite)** specification was designed to accommodate these speeds, as a logical stepping stone to the higher speed needs for the future. Initially introduced in early 1998, the specification was ratified in late 1999 to facilitate the lower throughput needs of the average consumer. DMT is the preferred method of delivering the G.Lite specification and service, as it is now known. This involves a slightly different method of delivering the service, but it does accommodate the providers with a less expensive solution to provide full-rate ADSL.

There is no way to know if the network providers can support hundreds of multimegabit ADSL up- and download speeds on the existing infrastructure. But using the G.Lite specification can support lower-demand users more efficiently. Similar to the DMT used in the ANSI specification, the carriers are divided as shown in Figure 12-7. Note, in this case, the high end of the frequency spectrum tops out at approximately 550 kHz instead of the 1-MHz range with ADSL.

12

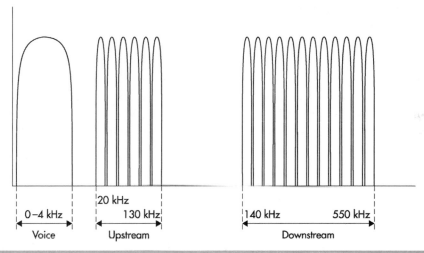

Figure 12-7 The DMT used in the ANSI specification. The carriers are divided as shown.

ISDN Digital Subscriber Line (IDSL)

The IDSL technique is an all-digital signal, operating two channels of 64 Kbps for voice or non-voice operation and a 16 Kbps data channel for signaling, control, and data packets (see Figure 12-8). The bandwidth used is from 0 to 80 kHz, as opposed to the arbitrarily limited 0 to 3,300 Hz on a voice line.

IDSL is an ISDN digital subscriber line used to deliver ISDN services (covered in Chapter 6). As the deployment of IDSL was speeding up on the local loop, the providers developed a new twist, called "always on ISDN," mimicking a leased set of channels that are always connected. By bonding the channels together, Internet users can "surf the Net" at speeds of 128 Kbps in each direction. Note that this is a symmetrical digital subscriber line.

IDSL delivers service at ISDN speeds. Many users have higher bandwidth needs, so IDSL is not a good fit for their usage. However, IDSL has the capability to run over fiber-optic trunks, which is a benefit to the carriers and people in remote areas where DSL service was previously lacking. Fiber can carry the IDSL signal over larger distances, and the DSLAM can be provided

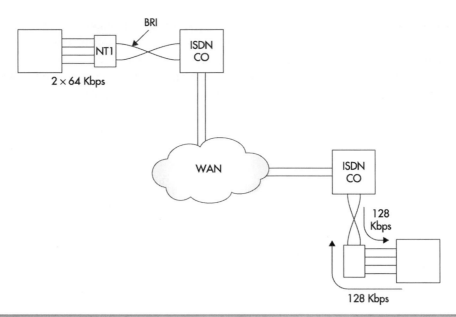

Figure 12-8 The IDSL line connection allows 128 Kbps in total simultaneously.

remotely. This enables users in smaller towns to have their copper pair interface to long-haul fiber, and then arrive at the remote DSLAM. IDSL is not an extremely popular service today because more and more COs have added local DSLAM access, but IDSL does fill a certain market niche.

NOTE

In certain markets, IDSL utilizes the *D* channel in conjunction with both *B* channels for bandwidth. This configuration allows 144-Kbps data transmission over the IDSL circuit but it is not a universal service offering among all carriers.

High-Data-Rate Digital Subscriber Line (HDSL)

In 1958, the Bell Laboratories developed a voice multiplexing system that used a 64-Kbps voice modulation technique called pulse code modulation (PCM). Using the PCM techniques, voice calls were sampled 8,000 times per second and coded using an 8-bit encoding. These samples were then organized into a framed format using 24 timeslots to bundle and multiplex 24 simultaneous conversations onto a single four-wire circuit. Each frame carries 24 samples of 8 bits, plus 1 framing bit (making the frame 193 bits long), 8,000 times a second. This produces a data rate of 1.544 Mbps or what we know as a T1 (for further discussions on T1 see Chapter 5). We now refer to this as a Digital Signal Level 1 (DS–1) at the framed data rate. This rate of data transfer is used in the U.S., Canada, and Japan.

Throughout the rest of the world, standards were set to operate using an E1 with a signaling rate of 2.048 Mbps. The differences between the two services (T1 and E1) are significant enough to prevent the seamless integration of the two services.

In the digital arena, T1 required the provider to install the circuits to the customer's premises on copper (other technologies can be used, but the UTP is easiest because it is already there). The local provider could install the circuit by using a four-wire circuit with repeaters spaced at 3,000 feet from the Central Office (CO) and 3,000 feet from the customer's entrance point. In between these two points, repeaters are used every 5,000 to 6,000 feet. When installing the T1 on the copper local loop, limitations of the delivery mechanism get in the way. T1 (and E1) uses alternate mark inversion (AMI), which demands all the bandwidth and corrupts the cable spectrum quickly. As a result, the providers can only use a single T1 in a 50-pair cable and could not install another in adjacent cables because of the corruption. Figure 12-9 is a representation of this cable layout. This is an inefficient use of the wiring to the door, making it impractical to install T1s in small office/home office and residential locations. Further limitations required the providers to remove bridge taps, clean up splices, and remove load coils from the wires to get the T1 to work.

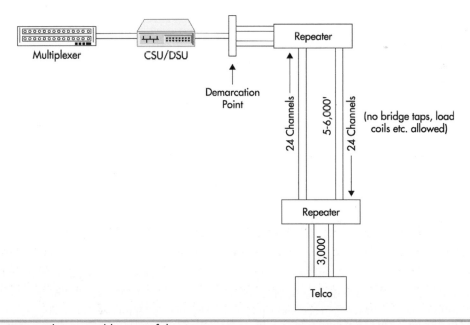

Figure 12-9 The typical layout of the T1.

To circumvent these cabling problems, High-data-rate Digital Subscriber Line (HDSL) was developed as a more efficient way of transmitting T1 (and E1) over the existing copper wires. HDSL does not require the repeaters on a local loop of up to 12,000 feet long. Bridge taps that may already be present will not bother the service, and the splices are left in place. This means the provider can offer HDSL as a more efficient delivery of 1.544 Mbps.

The modulation technique used in the HDSL service is more advanced than other offerings—it splits the T1 over two wire pairs. It sends 768 Kbps on the first pair of wires and another 768 Kbps on the second pair. This is shown in Figure 12-10.

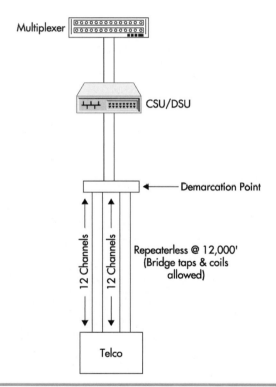

Figure 12-10 HDSL is impervious to the bridge and splices. The T1 is split onto two pairs.

Both speeds are **symmetric** (simultaneous in both directions). Originally, HDSL used two-wire pairs at distances of up to 15,000 feet. HDSL at 2.048 Mbps (E1 service) uses three pairs of wire for the same distances. Since the introduction of HDSL service, improvements now allow one pair of wires to accomplish its goal. This newer deployment is gaining acceptance by the providers. Today, almost all providers deliver T1 capabilities on some form of HDSL.

Symmetric DSL (SDSL)

Symmetric DSL (SDSL) was developed to provide high-speed communications on that single cable pair, but at distances no greater than 10,000 feet. Because a single cable pair is the standard line terminating at the customer site, SDSL was designed to deliver speeds of 1.544 Mbps on this pair. Typically, however, the providers provision SDSL at 768 Kbps. This creates a dilemma for the carriers because HDSL can do the same things as SDSL. Therefore, the carriers remain split as to their product offering between the two products.

Rate-Adaptive DSL (RADSL)

Typically with equipment, installed assumptions are made based on minimum-performance characteristics and speeds. In some cases, special equipment is used to condition the circuit to achieve those speeds. If the line conditions vary, however, the speed will be dependent on the sensitivity of the equipment. To achieve variations in the throughput and be sensitive to the line conditions, **rate-adaptive DSL (RADSL)** was developed.

This technology gives the flexibility to adapt to the changing conditions and adjust the speeds in each direction to potentially maximize the throughput on each line. Additionally, as line conditions change, you can see the speeds changing in each direction during the transmission. Many of the ILECs have installed RADSL as their choice, given the local-loop conditions. Speeds of up to 768 Kbps are the preferred rates offered by the incumbent providers.

Consumer DSL (CDSL)

Most consumers are not looking for symmetrical high-speed communication to achieve Internet access. For most Internet users, the majority of use comes through receiving information from web sites and, thus, requires a high downlink speed. Because most people do not send large files, the uplink speeds can be considerably less without causing too much user frustration. The speeds of ADSL technology are typically more than the average consumer can utilize.

As a result, the lower-speed communications capability was developed by using **Consumer DSL (CDSL)** as the model. With other forms of DSL (such as ADSL and RADSL), splitters are used on the line to separate the voice and the data communications. CDSL neither uses nor needs a splitter on the line. Speeds of up to 1 Mbps in the download direction and 160 Kbps in the upward direction are provided.

Enhancements to the DSL Family

DSL has several versions that offer improved enhancements and flexibility of services. These newer deployments have been slow to roll out as regular DSL penetrations remain slim. The future promises DSL with higher operating speeds and support for emerging applications.

Symmetric High-Bit Rate DSL (SHDSL)

Symmetric high-bit rate DSL (SHDSL) is an improvement over the previously mentioned forms of DSL. The ITU published a series of recommendations specified by G.991.2 to leverage the best capabilities of previously deployed products. One of the most significant improvements SHDSL brings to the business market is increased reach—at least 30 percent greater than any earlier symmetric DSL technology. SHDSL also supports repeaters, which further increase the reaching capability of this technology.

Another critical advantage of SHDSL is its increase in symmetric bandwidth. In a typical installation, up to 2.3 Mbps will be available on a single copper pair. For greater bandwidth needs in the future, a four-wire model that can provide up to 4.6 Mbps is also supported by the new standard.

SHDSL is also rate-adaptive, allowing flexible revenue-generation models and enabling service providers to offer service-level agreements that ensure businesses get the service they want, when they want it.

G.SHDSL is the acronym for symmetric high-bit rate digital subscriber loop defined by the ITU Global Standard G991.2 as of February 2001. This service delivers voice and data services based on highly innovative communication technologies and, thus, will be able to replace older communication technologies, such as T1, E1, HDSL, HDSL2, SDSL, ISDN, and IDSL in the future.

SHDSL provides high symmetric data rates with guaranteed bandwidth and low interference with other services. By supporting equal upstream and downstream data rates, G.SHDSL better fits the needs of:

- Remote LAN access
- Web hosting
- Application sharing
- Video conferencing

G.SHDSL targets the small business market. Multiple telephone and data channels, videoconferencing, remote LAN access, and leased lines with customer-specific data rates are among its many exciting characteristics. Spectrally friendly with other DSLs, it supports symmetric data rates varying from 192 kbps to 2.320 Mbps across greater distances than other technologies.

In an ATM-based network on the customer side, an **Integrated Access Device (IAD)** is installed to convert voice and data into ATM cells. An IAD can also contain some routing functionality. Data is converted using AAL5 (ATM Adaptation Layer), while voice requires AAL1 (without compression) or AAL2 (with compression and micro cells). These cells are mapped together in the SHDSL frame and recovered later on in the DSLAM. An ATM switch routes the cells either to an Internet service provider (ISP) or to a voice gateway that translates the voice cells back into the TDM world.

The voice part of the SHDSL frame will be treated in a similar fashion to normal ISDN or POTS services. However, the data needs to be converted into ATM. This can be done either in an IAD, resulting in a mix of TDM and ATM on the SHDSL line, or at the CO side. In the second case, it is necessary to protect the data on the line. This can be easily done by an HDLC protocol. The division between voice and data should be done in the loop carrier, so the ATM cells can be sent directly to the ATM backbone, so they do not congest the PSTN network. This approach has the advantage of being more bandwidth-efficient because the HDLC overhead is smaller than the ATM overhead. Additionally, the segmentation and reassembly (SAR) functionality can be centralized in the DLC. However, because an IAD normally uses Ethernet to connect to a LAN, some intelligence is required at the subscriber side to process the Ethernet MAC and also have SAR functionality.

ADSL2 Standardization

ADSL has undergone further modification since its inception. In 2002, the ITU completed work on two "new" ADSL standards: ADSL2 (G.992.3) and ADSL2+ (G.992.5). The **ADSL2** standard allowed for a download speed of 12 Mbps with an upload of 1 Mbps. Based on feedback from the original ADSL deployment, improvements in signaling, power usage, error detection, and diagnostics have allowed ADSL2 to operate more efficiently.

ADSL2plus (ITU G.992.5) is not a stand-alone offering. It works with ADSL2. Through the ATM data interface, two DSL lines can be bonded. **Bonding** is a process defined through the ATM forum (af-phy-0086.001) that doubles the maximum data rates for upstream/downstream transmission for ADSL2 (2 Mbps/20 Mbps, respectively) at distances up to 5,000 feet.

The ADSL2, ADSL2+ standards are now over three years old, and manufacturers have incorporated these into their product offerings. It will only be a matter of time until these products appear locally as users demand higher bandwidths to support newer applications.

Very High-Speed DSL (VDSL)

Clearly, changes will always occur as we demand faster and more reliable communications capabilities. It was only a matter of time until some users demanded higher-speed communications than were offered by any of the current DSL technologies. As a result, **very-high-rate DSL (VDSL)** was introduced to achieve the higher speeds.

If users are demanding speeds of up to 50 Mbps, then the distance limitations of the local cable plant will be a factor. VDSL will only support 50 Mbps over 1,000 to 2,000 feet; therefore, fiber must be used.

This technique will most likely carry ATM traffic (cells) as its primary payload. The pilot program of Qwest Communications in Arizona plans **fiber to the home (FTTH)** to provide voice, data, video, and multimedia communications to the consumer. Although this pilot is still emerging, a lot of excitement has been generated by the possibilities.

NOTE

FTTH is often referred to as fiber to the curb (FTTC). FTTH can be misleading to those unfamiliar with the term. FTTH does not mean fiber will terminate in your home. It means fiber will terminate at an interface point on the curb, and then it will be converted into an electrical signal and delivered on the existing copper pair.

Table 12-2 summarizes the speeds and characteristics of the DSL technologies discussed. These are the typical installation and operational characteristics; others will certainly exist in variations of installation and implementation.

Service	Explanation	Download	Upload	Mode of Operation
ADSL	Asymmetric DSL	1.5–8.192 Mbps	16–640 Kbps	Different up and down speeds. One-pair wire.
RADSL	Rate-Adaptive DSL	64 Kbps–8.192 Mbps	16–768 Kbps speeds.	Different up and down. Many common operations use 768 Kbps. One-pair wire.
CDSL	Consumer DSL	1 Mbps	16–160 Kbps	Now ratified as DSL-lite (G.lite). No splitters. One-pair wire.
HDSL	High-data rate DSL	1.544 Mbps in North America 2.048 Mbps in rest of world	1.544 Mbps 2.048 Mbps	Symmetrical services. Two pairs of wire.
IDSL	ISDN DSL	144 Kbps (64 + 64 + 16) as BRI	144 Kbps (64 + 64 + 16) as BRI	Symmetrical operation.One pair of wire. ISDN BRI
SDSL	Single DSL	1.544 Mbps 2.048 Mbps	1.544 Mbps 2.048 Mbps	Uses only one pair, but typically provisioned at 768 Kbps. One-pair wire.
VDSL	Very High data rate DSL	13–52 +/- Mbps	1.5–6.0 Mbps	Fiber needed and ATM probably used.
SHDSL (G.SHDSL)	Single High-speed DSL	192 Kbps—2.360 Mbps or 384 Kbps—4.720 Mbps	192 Kbps—2.360 Mbps or 384 Kbps—4.720 Mbps	Using one pair. Using one pair.

Table 12-2 Summary of DSL Speeds and Operations Using Current Methods.

Universal DSL (UDSL)

The latest promise for the DSL family is the idea of **Universal DSL (UDSL)**. Several companies have taken the best features of ADSL, ADSL2, and VDSL and incorporated them into a newer offering. This UDSL is not yet a standard, so it will likely undergo several changes before being accepted. UDSL holds great promise by providing a triple-data rate for voice and video services yielding 200-Mbps speed. ADSL is touted to be backward-compatible with the current DSL infrastructure that is already deployed.

Lately, many innovations have occurred in the DSL product line. UDSL is a proprietary product offering from Texas Instruments that incorporates ADSL/ADSL2 and VDSL technologies. The main driving forces behind UDSL are HDTV, VoIP, and quality of service (QoS) support.

Provisioning xDSL

The following figures show the various architectures of the xDSL implementations. The point to remember here is the goal of xDSL is to use the existing copper infrastructure, and improve the speed and throughput on the installed base of wires. Consequently, the installation process attempts to minimize the added equipment (particularly at the customer's premises) and the labor required to get the equipment installed.

Figure 12-11 shows the design of an ADSL model and the model components. The intent of the model is to show the infrastructure of the network from the customer's premises to the network provider. This model also shows the splitters in place to facilitate the ADSL model.

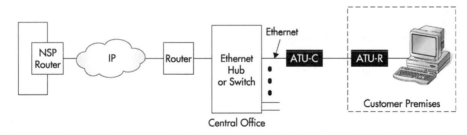

Figure 12-11 The ADSL model, as it is laid out from the customer's premises to the service provider.

Figure 12-12 demonstrates the connection from the service provider to the rest of the world. In many cases, ADSL access to the local network access (LAN) provider (the ILEC or other local loop provider) is then passed on to the ISP. This is designed to run over an ATM backbone, but this is not a firm requirement. Therefore, the NAP will assign a DSLAM card and assign an ATM VPI and a VCI as a default to carry the data into the Internet service provider (ISP) or other Network service provider (NSP).

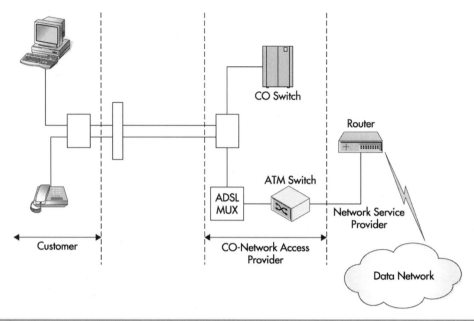

Figure 12-12 Access from the NAP to the NSP.

The application most commonly used is to gain high-speed access to the Internet. Many of the LSPs install the ADSL service into a single PC at the end-user location, as shown in Figure 12-13. The LSPs offer the customer a packaged deal with the following components:

● LAN NIC card operating at 10 Mbps

● DSL modem

● Splitter

● Management cables

The local provider will normally advise the customer that the termination must be to a single PC equipped with the NIC card. In the U.S., the customer owns the package when the installation is completed because of some of the regulatory constraints and the Public Utility Commission rulings. This places the burden of maintenance and diagnostics on the end user, rather than the LSP. In the case of a LAN attachment described previously, the ADSL modem is set to bridge from the LAN to the ATM network interfaces rather than route.

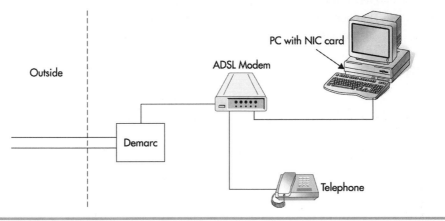

Figure 12-13 The typical local installation.

In other cases when a LAN is present at the customer location, and the end user wants to connect all the LAN devices to the high-speed outside network for Internet access or private network access, the local carrier may suggest that a proxy server is a requirement. The proxy server (PC dedicated to act in this function) will then act as the gateway to the outside world for all devices attached to the LAN (see Figure 12-14).

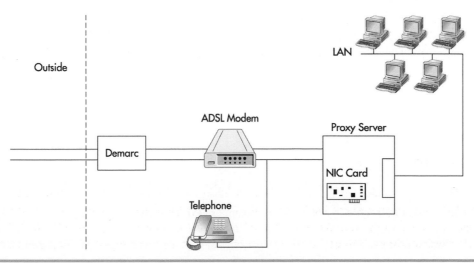

Figure 12-14 The proxy server, in lieu of a single attached PC.

An alternative to this approach is the direct connection to a LAN hub, such as that found in the telephone closet. Keeping the connection active, the carrier will normally assign an IP address, using DHCP for a contracted period of time. Normally, this is a lease period of four hours, and then the network server (outside) will renegotiate and assign a new IP address for the end user. This protects the end-user network from becoming visible on the Internet and helps prevent some of the normal security risks associated with a hard connection to the Net (see Figure 12-15).

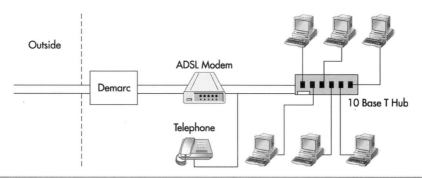

Figure 12-15 Connecting the ADSL service to a hub.

Many of the hubs located in customer locations are 10 Base T, or 10 Mbps Ethernet hubs. Occasionally, a customer may have a 10/100 autosensing hub or a 100 Base T hub. The local providers have been known to tell customers this arrangement will not work. Specific networks are already attached with direct attachment of 10/100 and 100 Base hubs with no impact, as shown in Figure 12-16. The connection allows for a specific number of simultaneous connections onto the ADSL service. The local providers will always try to configure the network connections in ways they can guarantee will work and with a standard way to troubleshoot problems. By working with the previous variations, the local providers still need to get up to speed on the way the data networks perform.

⏀ Line Check 12-2

1. Is it possible to get DSL service on a line that does not have dial tone on it?

2. Can you get in trouble if you hook up consumer DSL to multiple computers?

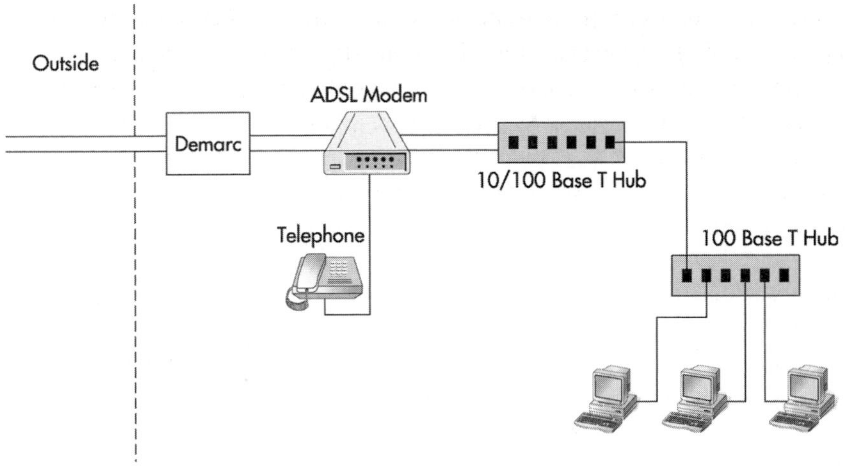

Figure 12-16 Connecting the ADSL modem directly through a 10/100 or a 100 Base T hub.

Final Comment on Deployment

The use of ADSL service is catching on. However, the local providers (ILECs and CLECs) are still dragging their feet. As of 2004, about 10,000,000 DSL modem pairs were installed in the U.S. In contrast, over 17,000,000 cable modems were installed in residences and businesses across the country. The local owners of the copper loop have to take a more aggressive approach to delivering the high-speed services or the consumer will go somewhere else.

As the market continues to mature and standards continue to develop, the local providers must preserve their infrastructure. Consumers (small and large alike) are demanding the higher-speed services. As a stepping stone for residential- and home-based businesses, the acceptance and standardization of the G.Lite specification will provide suitable transmission rates until the carriers can complete their data strategies. 1-Mbps modems, for example, giving the end user a 1-Mbps download speed and a lower 160-Kbps upload speed, will suffice for many today and into the next decade.

For the larger consumers, a full-rate ADSL may be just what is needed, bringing 1.544- to 8-Mbps downloads and 768-Kbps uploads to the forefront of Internet access.

Where the consumer is reluctant to proceed with ADSL, the HDSL or the SDSL services are still attractive alternatives, offering up to 1.544- to 2.048-Mbps symmetrical speeds or some variation as already discussed.

In the future, when high-speed media is installed to the door or to the curb, the logical stepping stone becomes the VDSL service, possibly in the year 2006. Although trials are already underway, too much time passes until the results are compiled and analyzed. Therefore, the reality of VDSL for the masses is still a long way off.

What Do You Think?

Given all of the types of DSL (and speeds) available, do you think that DSL is poised to bypass cable as the primary means of high-speed Internet access? What might be some other up-and-coming technologies that might give both DSL and cable a run for their money? Discuss the pros and cons of the technologies and then discuss the reasons you believe them to be true.

Additional DSL Applications

Voice over DSL (VoDSL)

Voice can be provisioned over DSL **(VoDSL)** lines in a number of ways: from station-to-station voice communications using computer software programs to private PBX systems using VoIP, with DSL as the carrier. Those differ, however, from a VoDSL system in that VoDSL systems are designed to pull the voice links off the system as part of their architecture (rather than the DSL being "ignorant" of the fact that it is carrying voice signals).

In general, a VoDSL system functions as an overlay solution to a DSL broadband access network, enabling a CLEC to extend multiline local telephone service off a centralized voice switch. For example, Jetstream's VoDSL solution allows up to 16 telephone lines and high-speed continuous data service to be provided over a single DSL connection, as shown in Figure 12-17. A VoDSL solution typically consists of three components.

- First, a carrier-class voice gateway resides in the regional switching center (RSC) and serves as a bridge between the circuit-based voice switch and the packet-based DSL access network.

- Second, an IAD resides at each subscriber premises and connects to a DSL circuit. It also serves as a circuit/packet gateway and provides the subscriber with standard telephone service via up to 16 analog POTS ports and Internet service via an Ethernet connection.

- The third component is the management system.

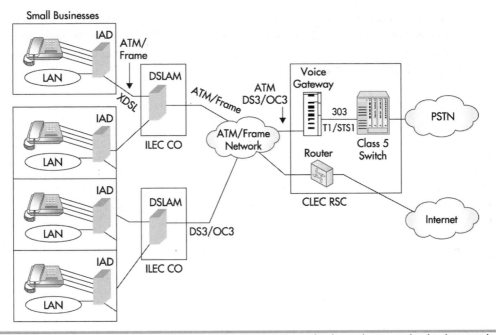

Figure 12-17 Jetstream's VoDSL solution allows up to 16 telephone lines and a high-speed continuous data service to be provided over a single DSL connection.

    With VoDSL solutions, DSL broadband-access networks now have the coverage, capacity, and cost attributes to enable CLECs to deliver local telephone services, as well as data services, to the small and mid-size business markets. It has already been established that DSL access networks have the right bandwidth to serve the data needs of small and mid-size businesses.

    With VoDSL access solutions, this is also true for serving the local telephone service needs of those subscribers. Some VoDSL solutions are capable of delivering 16 telephone lines over a DSL circuit along with standard data traffic. Because 95 percent of small businesses use 12 or fewer telephone lines, a single DSL circuit provides sufficient bandwidth to serve the voice needs of the vast majority of the market. In addition, if more than 16 lines are required, most VoDSL solutions enable a provider to scale service by provisioning additional DSL connections.

    In addition to providing the right capacity for providing local telephone service, DSL broadband access networks are efficient in the way they deliver service. TDM-based transport services, such as a T1 line, require the bandwidth of the line to be channelized and portions dedicated to certain services, such as a telephone line. Even if a call is not active on that line, the bandwidth allocated to that line cannot be used for other purposes. DSL access networks are packet-based, enabling VoDSL solutions to use the bandwidth of a DSL connection dynamically. VoDSL solutions only consume bandwidth on a DSL connection when a call is active on a line. If a call is not active, then that bandwidth is available for other services, such as Internet access. This dynamic bandwidth usage enables providers to maximize the potential of each DSL connection, delivering to subscribers the greatest number of telephone lines and the highest possible data speeds.

Because telephony traffic is more sensitive to latency than data traffic, VoDSL solutions guarantee the quality of telephone service by giving telephony packets priority over data packets onto a DSL connection. In other words, telephony traffic always receives the bandwidth it requires and data traffic uses the remaining bandwidth. Fortunately, telephony traffic tends to be bursty over the course of a typical business day, so the average amount of bandwidth consumed is minimal. For example, over a single 768-Kbps symmetric DSL connection, a CLEC could provide eight telephone lines (serving a PBX/KTS with 32 extensions) and still deliver data service with an average speed of 550 Kbps.

VoATM over DSL

Voice over ATM (VoATM) over DSL unites ATM and DSL technologies to deliver on the promise of fully integrated voice and data services. VoATM meets all requirements in terms of QoS, flexibility, and reliability because the underlying technology is ATM, a highly effective network architecture developed specifically to carry simultaneous voice and data traffic.

ATM Suitability for Voice Traffic

Sometimes mistakenly associated with VoIP, VoATM is a completely separate technology that predates VoIP. In contrast to IP and frame relay, ATM uses small, fixed-length data packets of 53 bytes each that fill more quickly, are sent immediately, and are much less susceptible to network delays. (Delays experienced by voice in a frame relay or an IP packet network can typically be ten times higher than for ATM and increase on slower links.)

ATM's packet characteristics make it by far the best-suited packet technology for guaranteeing the same QoS found in toll-quality voice connections.

The ATM Adaptation Layer (AAL), the part of ATM responsible for converting voice and data into ATM cells, enables various traffic types to have data converted to and from the ATM cell and translates high-layer services (such as TCP/IP) into the size and format of the ATM protocol layer. A number of AAL definitions exist to accommodate the various types of network traffic. The AAL types most commonly used for voice traffic are AAL1, AAL2, and AAL5.

VoATM with AAL1 is the traditional approach for constant bit rate (CBR), time-dependent traffic, such as voice and video, and provides circuit emulation for trunking applications. ATM with AAL1 is still suitable for voice traffic, but it is not the ideal solution for voice services in the local loop because its design for fixed bandwidth allocation means network resources are consumed, even when no voice traffic is present. Some equipment manufacturers use AAL5 to provide VoATM and support for variable bit rate (VBR) applications. They also use AAL5 because, in terms of bandwidth used, it is a better choice than AAL1. However, the means for carrying voice traffic over AAL5 is not yet fully standardized or widely deployed, and implementations are usually proprietary.

ATM with AAL2 is the newest approach to VoATM. Figure 12-18 shows how AAL2 provides a number of important improvements over AAL1 and AAL5, including support for CBR and VBR applications, dynamic bandwidth allocation, and support for multiple voice calls over a single ATM permanent virtual circuit (PVC). An additional and significant advantage of AAL2 is that cells carry content information. This feature provides traffic prioritization for packets (cells) and is the key to dynamic bandwidth allocation and efficient network use.

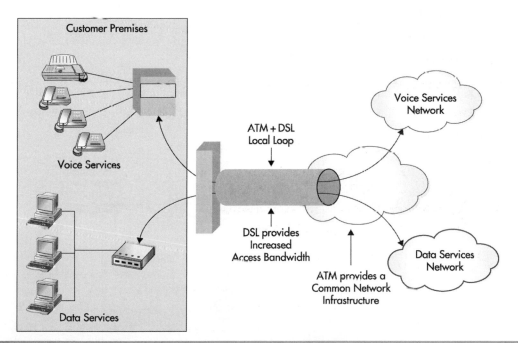

Figure 12-18 Important improvements over AAL1 and AAL5 include support for CBR and VBR applications, dynamic bandwidth allocation, and support for multiple voice calls over a single ATM permanent virtual circuit (PVC).

Because DSL links are ready-made for voice and data, and ATM excels at carrying varied traffic, using VoATM over DSL over the local loop to the customer is a natural extension of these services. To enable the combination, equipment that supports VoATM is needed at each end of the local loop: a **next-generation integrated access device (NG-IAD)** at the customer premises and a voice gateway at the CO. The integrated access device concept is shown in Figure 12-19. The integrated devices can use many applications, as shown in Figure 12-20.

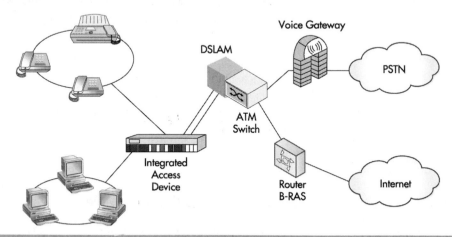

Figure 12-19 The IAD allows support of many different applications.

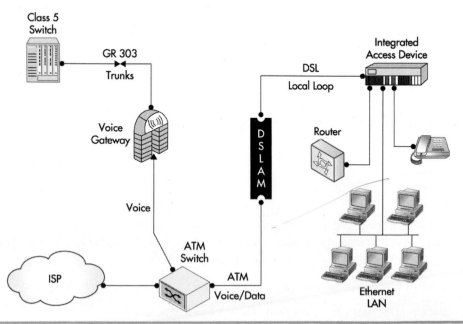

Figure 12-20 Through the use of an NG-IAD, the data protocols (IP) allow the multiplexing of several (16) conversations at once, provide Internet access on the higher bandwidth, and still have the lower end (0 to 4 kHz) available as a full-time fax line.

The real benefit is the telephone line that once carried a single phone call for voice, data, or fax traffic can now be expanded to carry data and voice simultaneously on the same pair of wires. Because we use the data protocols (IP), we can multiplex several (16) conversations and Internet access on the higher bandwidth, and still have the lower end (0 to 4 kHz) available as a full-time fax line. The use of the bandwidth that was once arbitrarily curtailed is now a reality.

Chapter 12 Review

Chapter Summary

Describe What DSL Is and List the Reasons Behind Its Development

- Since the birth of modem technology and the invention of the Internet, users have found a need to have greater access speeds for their web-browsing experience.

- Modems were the first solution to provide dial-up access over the PSTN. However, this service was slow, and did not allow for simultaneous voice and data communication.

- The xDSL family was created to provide services that allowed for voice and data transmission on the existing lines.

- Several forms of DSL are available, each with a slightly different speed and access method.

Identify What the Critical Components of DSL Are

- On the customer side it is a DSL transceiver (a DSL modem).

- A line splitter is often required for some DSL deployments.

- On the carrier side, a DSL Access Multiplexor (DSLAM) provides interface for the DSL modem to the Internet.

- Data is encoded onto the xDSL circuits either by carrierless amplitude phase modulation (CAP) or by discrete multitone modulation (DMT).

- CAP uses the entire loop bandwidth (excluding the 4-kHz baseband analog voice channel) to send the bits all at once. Frequency division multiplexing is used (as is echo cancellation).

- DMT uses multiple narrow-band carriers, all transmitting simultaneously in a parallel transmission mode.

● In DMT, voice is used in the normal 0–4 kHz band on the lower end of the spectrum (although the lower 20 kHz are provided). Separation is allowed between the voice channel and the upstream data communications, which operates between 20 kHz and 130 kHz. Then, a separation is allowed between the upstream and the downstream channels. The downstream flow uses between 140 kHz and 1 MHz.

State the Different Types of DSL Available, the Speeds They Operate at, and the Medium Used

ADSL

● ADSL is asymmetrical, meaning the upload speeds and download speeds differ. Typically, upload speeds for sending files range from 16 Kbps to 640 Kbps, and downloading speed receives information between 1.5 Mbps and 6 Mbps.

● ADSL modems usually include a Plain Old Telephone Service (POTS) splitter, which allows the simultaneous access to telephony applications and high-speed data access.

● The POTS service operates at the low end of the frequency spectrum. All the data signals are located in the higher frequencies. These signals start between 20 and 25 kHz and above.

ADSL G.Lite

● The ADSL G.Lite specification uses a splitterless device to facilitate the installation of low-speed DSL services.

● The ITU determined that many consumers need download speeds of up to 1.5 Mbps and upload speeds between 9.6 and 640 Kbps.

● DMT is the preferred method of delivering the G.Lite specification and service, as it is now known.

● Note that in this case, the high end of the frequency spectrum tops out at approximately 550 kHz instead of the 1-MHz range with ADSL.

IDSL

● The term IDSL is new, but it is a digital subscriber line that is used to deliver ISDN services.

● The IDSL technique is an all-digital signal, operating two channels of 64 Kbps for voice or nonvoice operation and a 16-Kbps data channel for signaling, control, and data packets.

● However, IDSL has the capability to run over fiber-optic trunks, which is a benefit to the carriers and people in remote areas where DSL service was previously lacking. Fiber can carry the IDSL signal over larger distances, and the DSLAM can be provided remotely.

- This enables users in smaller towns to have their copper-pair interface to long-haul fiber and then arrive at the remote DSLAM.

- IDSL is not an extremely popular service today because more and more COs have added local DSLAM access, but IDSL does fill a certain market niche.

HDSL

- High-data-rate Digital Subscriber Line (HDSL) was developed as a more efficient way of transmitting T1 (and E1) over the existing copper wires.

- HDSL does not require the repeaters on a local loop of up to 12,000 feet long. Bridge taps that may already be present will not bother the service, and the splices are left in place.

- The modulation technique used in the HDSL service is more advanced than other offerings. It splits the T1 bandwidth symmetrically over two wire pairs. (It sends 768 Kbps on the first pair of wires and another 768 Kbps on the second pair.)

- Since the introduction of HDSL service, improvements now allow one pair of wire to accomplish its goal.

Symmetric DSL (SDSL)

- SDSL was developed to provide high-speed communications on that single cable pair, but at distances no greater than 10,000 feet.

- Because a single cable pair is the standard line terminating at the customer site, SDSL was designed to deliver speeds of 1.544 Mbps on this pair. (768K is common.)

Rate-Adaptive DSL (RADSL)

- In some cases, special equipment is used to condition the circuit to achieve those speeds. If the line conditions vary, however, the speed will be dependent on the sensitivity of the equipment.

- To achieve variations in the throughput and be sensitive to the line conditions, rate adaptive DSL (RADSL) was developed.

- Speeds of up to 768 Kbps are the preferred rates offered by the incumbent providers.

Consumer DSL (CDSL)

- Because most people do not send large files, the uplink speeds can be considerably less without causing too much user frustration.

- CDSL neither uses nor needs a splitter on the line.

- Speeds of up to 1 Mbps in the download direction and 160 Kbps in the upward direction are provided.

Symmetric High-Bit Rate DSL (SHDSL)

- One of the most significant improvements SHDSL brings to the business market is increased reach—at least 30 percent greater than any earlier symmetric DSL technology. SHDSL also supports repeaters, which further increase the reaching capability of this technology.

- Another critical advantage of SHDSL is its increase in symmetric bandwidth, up to 2.3 Mbps will be available on a single copper pair.

- For greater bandwidth needs in the future, a four-wire model that can provide up to 4.6 Mbps is also supported by the new standard.

- SHDSL is also rate-adaptive, allowing flexible service-level agreements that ensure businesses get the service they want, when they want it.

- G.SHDSL targets the small business market. Multiple telephone and data channels, videoconferencing, remote LAN access, and leased lines with customer-specific data rates are among its many exciting characteristics.

- The voice part of the SHDSL frame will be treated in a similar fashion to normal ISDN or POTS services.

- Data needs to be converted into ATM; this can be done either in an Integrated Access Device (IAD), resulting in a mix of TDM and ATM on the SHDSL line, or at the CO side.

Very High-Speed DSL (VDSL)

- If users are demanding speeds of up to 50 Mbps, then the distance limitations of the local cable plant will be a factor.

- To deliver 50 Mbps, a fiber feed will be used to deliver VDSL and negate problems because of distance sensitivity and interference created by copper.

- This technique will most likely carry ATM traffic (cells) as its primary payload.

UDSL

- Universal DSL (UDSL) is a proprietary product offering from Texas Instruments that incorporates ADSL/ADSL2 and VDSL technologies.

- The main benefit of UDSL is providing triple data-rate voice and video services at up to 200-Mbps (aggregate) speeds.

Explain Step-by-Step How DSL Is Provisioned

- The ADSL line is ordered and connections at the CO are cross-connected with a DSLAM.

- ADSL access to the local network access provider (the ILEC or other local loop provider) is then passed on to the ISP.

- The NAP assigns a DSL Access Multiplexer card (DSLAM) and also assigns an ATM VPI and a VCI as a default to carry the data into the Internet service provider (ISP) or other network service provider (NSP).

- The local provider normally advises the customer that the termination must be to a single PC equipped with the NIC card.

- In other cases, when a LAN is present at the customer location, the local carrier may suggest that a proxy server or NAT server is a requirement.

- Keeping the connection active, the carrier normally assigns an IP address, using DHCP for a contracted period of time. Multiuser systems may expand the number of stations using the supplied IP address(es) by using NAT or proxy servers in their network.

List Additional Applications That Are Driving Future DSL Deployment

VoDSL

- Some Voice over DSL (VoDSL) solutions are capable of delivering 16 telephone lines over a DSL circuit, along with standard data traffic.

- VoDSL solutions only consume bandwidth on a DSL connection when a call is active on a line. If a call is not active, that bandwidth is available for other services, such as Internet access.

- VoDSL solutions guarantee the quality of telephone service by giving telephony packets priority over data packets onto a DSL connection.

VoATM over DSL

- Voice over ATM (VoATM) unites ATM and DSL technologies to deliver on the promise of fully integrated voice and data services.

- ATM's packet characteristics make it by far the best-suited packet technology for guaranteeing the same QoS found in toll-quality voice connections.

- Because you use the data protocols (IP), you can multiplex several (16) conversations and Internet access on the higher bandwidth and still have the lower end (0 to 4 kHz) available as a full-time fax line.

Key Terms for Chapter 12

ADSL2 *(587)*
ADSL2plus *(587)*
ADSL Lite (ADSL G.lite) *(580)*
Asymmetrical Digital Subscriber Line (ADSL) *(577)*
Bonding *(587)*
Carrierless Amplitude Phase Modulation (CAP) *(575)*
Consumer DSL (CDSL) *(585)*
Digital Subscriber Line (DSL) *(574)*
Discrete Multitone Modulation (DMT) *(576)*
DSL Access Multiplexor (DSLAM) *(574)*
DSL Transceiver *(574)*
Fiber to the Home (FTTH) *(587)*
High Data-Rate Digital Subscriber Line (HDSL) *(605)*
Integrated Access Device (IAD) *(586)*
ISDN Digital Subscriber Line (IDSL) *(581)*
Modems *(573)*
Multiplexor *(575)*
Next-Generation Integrated Access Device (NG-IAD) *(598)*
Plain Old Telephone Service (POTS) Line Splitter *(574)*
Rate-Adaptive DSL (RADSL) *(585)*
Subchannels *(576)*
Symmetric *(584)*
Symmetric DSL (SDSL) *(585)*
Symmetric High-Bit Rate DSL (SHDSL) *(586)*
Universal DSL (UDSL) *(589)*
Very-High-Rate DSL (VDSL) *(587)*
Voice over ATM (VoATM) over DSL *(596)*
Voice over DSL (VoDSL) *(594)*

Key Term Quiz

1. _____ is a high-speed DSL with data rates at 50 Mbps.

2. A _____ is used to divide the line into voice and data frequencies.

3. _____ is a type of DSL with equivalent upload and download speeds.

4. Some lines are conditioned to give optimum performance. As the line quality changes, _____ allows its bandwidth to adjust to the line conditions.

5. _____ delivers a signal to consumers on both fiber and copper.

6. The _____ modulation technique utilized the entire loop bandwidth (except the voice portion) to send all bits at once.

7. An _____ is used to convert voice and data into ATM cells.

8. Some _____ solutions are capable of delivering 16 telephone lines over a DSL circuit along with standard data traffic.

9. Which standard allows for a download speed of 12 Mbps with an upload of 1 Mbps? _____.

10. A DSL modem is also called a _____.

11. A _____ is responsible for managing multiple-access connections and then routing the information transmitted over them to the Internet.

12. Today, almost all providers deliver T1 capabilities on _____.

Multiple-Choice Quiz

1. What does DSL stand for?

   a. Direct subscriber link

   b. Digital subscriber loop

   c. Digital speed lines

   d. Digital subscriber line

2. The *x* in xDSL stands for _____.

   a. The speed of the DSL line

   b. The carrier that provides the DSL

   c. The type of DSL

   d. Extreme DSL service

3. ADSL can support download speeds up to _____.

   a. 6 Mbps

   b. 8 Mbps

    c. 52 Mbps

    d. 26 Mbps

4. RADSL is usually installed with an upload speed of _____.

    a. 1.544 Mbps

    b. 1.0 Mbps

    c. 768 Kbps

    d. 160 Kbps

5. What is the maximum distance ADSL can run on a 26 AWG cable?

    a. 8,000 feet

    b. 12,000 feet

    c. 15,000 feet

    d. 18,000 feet

6. Which member of the DSL family is not standardized?

    a. UDSL

    b. SHDSL

    c. CDSL

    d. VDSL

7. The upload speed of a G.lite service is limited to _____.

    a. One-half a megabit

    b. One megabit

    c. Two megabits

    d. Three megabits

8. VDSL will bring us download speed of up to _____.

    a. 20 Mbps

    b. 50 Mbps

    c. 75 Mbps

    d. 100 Mbps Ethernet

9. The two main types of modulation used today are _____.

   a. CAP, TMD

   b. CAP, MDT

   c. CAP, DMT

   d. CAP, TDM

10. The use of _____ is required to run xDSL on the copper cable pairs.

   a. Repeaters

   b. Splitters

   c. DSLAMs

   d. Fiber

11. The main types of xDSL use _____ wires.

   a. Two pairs of

   b. One pair of

   c. Special grade cable

   d. Fiber and copper wires

12. The IDSL service is primarily designed for _____.

   a. People who don't need T-1 speeds

   b. People who don't want to pay for ADSL

   c. People who are too far from a DSLAM to get ADSL

   d. People who are too close to the CO

Essay Quiz

   1. What are the three components of DSL? State the function of each component.

   2. What factors limit DSL speeds?

   3. What is the difference between IDSL and other forms of DSL?

   4. Why was rate-adaptive DSL developed?

   5. What characteristic of web browsing makes ADSL suitable for most users?

Lab Projects

Lab 12.1 Finding the Distance to the CO

For this lab, students will need a computer with Internet access and a web browser.

1. Visit the web site www.dslreports.com.

2. On the left side of the page is a menu with toolbars. Locate the Find Service section and click on it.

3. Under the popular functions section, select Broadband Qualification (what can I get) and click on it.

4. The next page asks you for your ZIP code, address, and phone number. Fill in the appropriate information. Select residential for the type of service. Then click Next.

5. If you want further information from marketers, enter your e-mail address on the next screen. If you do not, press Next.

6. Once the search finishes, click the indicator titled Ok! Click Here.

7. The next page will tell you if your CO is wired for DSL. If it is, in the center of the window it will tell you your address, the distance to the wire center, and the name of the wire center.

8. Below this window is a listing of quality ISPs that provide the best available service in your area. Look at these listings.

9. Slightly below the quality ISPs are listings of other ISPs that provide service to your wiring center. Click on them and then compare the service offerings and price.

10. If there are no DSL ISPs available, farther down on the page are two more options: cable ISPs and satellite ISPs. Compare pricing between the cable ISPs and the DSL ISPs for approximately the same speeds. Which is cheaper? Which service best suits your needs?

Lab 12.2

Running a speed test on your DSL connection.

For this lab, students need a computer with DSL access and a web browser loaded with Sun Microsystems JAVA Runtime Environment (JRE). If you do not have the JRE, it is available for download free from the Sun Microsystems web site located at http://www.java.com/en/index.jsp. Once you are on the Sun web site, click Get it now Java software for the desktop. Follow the instructions for loading this software.

Once you have purchased your DSL, how do you know it is running at the speeds promised to you by the vendor? Note, in many instances, the DSL provider makes no promise for basic service. It simply says speeds up to XXX Mbps. However, if your DSL is running at extremely slow speeds, this tool can be useful in diagnosing problems and reporting them to the ISP.

1. Visit the web site www.dslreports.com.

2. On the left toolbar, click the Test and Tools button.

3. An expansion of the Test and Tools button will show several buttons. Select the link titled Speed Tests.

4. Follow the four-step instructions on the page.

5. After selecting the server that will run the speed test, click the Start button in the window.

6. Do not visit any web sites or send any e-mail while the tests are running. The test works by sending several fixed-size files to the server and receiving the same. Time is measured between the start of the test and when the final packet arrives. Then this is converted into a speed by dividing the time by the total size of information sent.

7. Record your results.

8. Repeat the test from a different server.

9. Record your results and compare them with the previous tests. Are they the same? Why might they be different?

10. If you notice your service falls significantly below the threshold, call your ISP and open a trouble ticket. The ISP can then send a technician to determine if problems are on the line.

Chapter 13

Cable Modem Systems and Technology

LEARNING OBJECTIVES:

Once you complete this chapter, you will be able to:

Discuss why the CATV vendors jumped into the data business.

Describe the cable systems they use for data.

Understand the speeds that they offer.

Describe the technique they use to link users on their networks.

Discuss what DOCSIS means.

n the late 1970s, a major battle arose in the communications and computer industries. Convergence of the two industries was happening as a result of the implementation of local area networks (LANs). In the local networking arena, users began to implement solutions to their data connectivity needs within a localized environment. Two major choices were available for their installation of wiring: baseband coaxial (coax) cable and broadband coaxial cable. Other issues emerged as the industry began competing between the CATV companies and the telephone companies. In this chapter the goal is to address who are the players, what are the goals of their services, and finally what is the incentive for the customer to use the CATV companies over any other provider.

The Ethernet Cable

The baseband cable was based on Ethernet development, using a 20-MHz, 50-Ω coax. Designed as a half-duplex operation, Ethernet allowed the end user to transmit digital data on the cable at speeds of up to 10 Mbps. Clearly, 10 Mbps was the maximum throughput, but it was attractive in comparison to the technology of twisted pair at the time (telephone wires were capable of less than 1 Mbps of bursty data). Moreover, the use of the baseband technology allowed the data to be digitally applied directly onto the cable system. No analog modulation was necessary to apply the data. It was DC input placed directly onto the cable. The signal propagates to both ends of the cable before another device can transmit. This is shown as a quick review in Figure 13-1. To control the cable access, the attached devices used carrier-sense, multiple access with collision detection (CSMA/CD) as the access control. **CSMA/CD** allowed for the

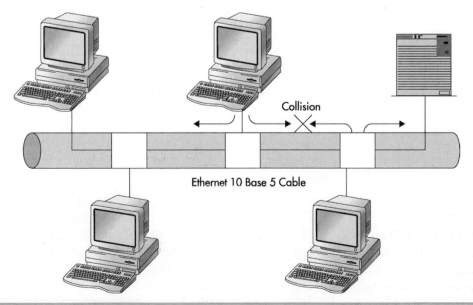

Figure 13-1 The Ethernet device propagates the signal in both directions to the ends of the cable.

possibility that two devices may attempt to transmit on the cable at the same time, causing a collision and corruption of the actual data. Consequently, use of the cable had to be controlled.

A second alternative at the time was to use the **broadband coaxial cable**, operating with a bandwidth of approximately 350 MHz on a 75-Ω cable. Broadband systems were well known because this is the same as CATV, which had surfaced in the early 1960s. Therefore, the technology was well deployed and commodity-priced. Moreover, the 350-MHz capacity was attractive to the computer industry and the communications industry partisans. The issues began to surface quickly regarding the benefits and losses of using each technique. This is shown in Figure 13-2.

13

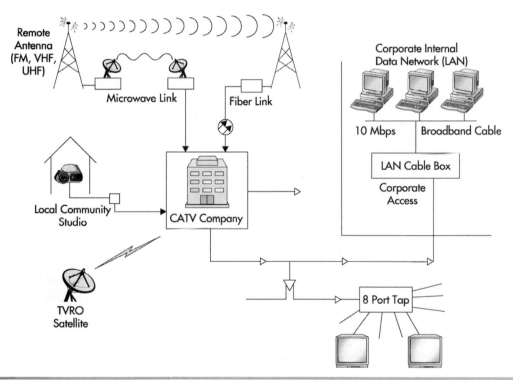

Figure 13-2 The broadband coaxial cable is an alternative to the Ethernet cable.

What the issue boiled down to was one of analog versus digital and the baseband versus broadband implementations to achieve this goal. This was a hot issue throughout both industries. The issue included using a broadband cable under the control of the voice communications departments, whereas the **baseband cables** were under the primary control of the data-processing departments. If one technology was chosen over another, the lines in the sand would be washed away, and the convergence of voice and data would force the convergence of the two groups.

The issue was, therefore, not whether to use a cable but what type of cable to use so the LAN would fall under the correct jurisdictional authority within the organization. Unfortunately, control is not the goal of organizations, but access and profitability are. As an industry, too much time was wasted over semantics. What ultimately rolled out of the bandwidth argument, though, was the baseband cable systems were better for the LAN. This was the decision of the 1980s, when all traffic on the LAN was geared to data only at speeds of 10 Mbps and less.

Cable TV Technology

Cable television (CATV) has been around since the early 1960s and is proven technology. In the early days of Ethernet, Digital Equipment Corporation (DEC) rolled out many systems using baseband (Ethernet) cable. However, some organizations needed more than just data on a large localized network. They worked with two major providers at the time to develop the interfaces for the broadband cable systems to attach an Ethernet to the CATV cable.

DEC developed several working arrangements with various suppliers to provide a **frequency-agile modem (FAM)** to work on the cable TV systems. A FAM is a modem that has the capability to tune to any of the various analog frequencies traversing the coaxial cable. The CATV companies did not necessarily own the broadband cable. Instead, this cable was locally owned in a high-rise office or a campus complex by the end user. The cable system provided a high bandwidth, but it was very complex for the data and LAN departments to understand. The reason is obvious: the broadband coax operated using frequency-division multiplexing (FDM) (analog techniques), which was beyond the scope of the LAN administrators and the data-processing departments. The voice people knew of analog transmission, but they had a hard time with digital transmission in those days. A silent department was at the crux of all the arguments—the video departments within many organizations stayed out of the fight.

As DEC began to roll out various choices, the average user had to justify the connection of the analog technologies (used as a carrier) with the digital-data demands of the LAN. What many organizations did on a campus was to consolidate voice, data, LAN, and video on a single cable infrastructure. What the industry came up with was a specification for 10Broad36 to satisfy the LAN needs over a coax cable. **10Broad36** stands for 10 Mbps on a broadband cable up to 3600 meters long. A classic representation of the combined services on 10Broad36 is shown in Figure 13-3.

The data industry was distraught because this encouraged the use of an analog carrier system to move digital data. Over the years, however, this has been revisited several times. Wang Computer Company developed a proprietary cable system for connecting Wang systems by using two broadband coax cables. Technologically, the system was sound, but the high price and proprietary nature of the Wang system forced its demise.

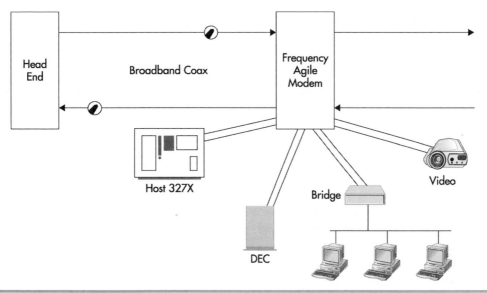

Figure 13-3 The CATV services are represented here on the broadband cable.

Later in the evolution of this service, the term "broadband LAN" became popularized. Ethernet grew to 100 Mbps, and then on to the gigabit range. A **broadband LAN** is any LAN connected with a multichannel network or a network that can support high-speed modulated data. Recall that modulation is the process of applying the data through some change, such as AM or FM. Therefore, the inherent nature of coaxial cable popularized this term and provided it with data rates in excess than those of Ethernet. Ethernet uses a baseband cable in which the transmitter (a network card) sends a pulse, using the entire bandwidth of the cable (digital), instead of modulating any data on a carrier signal on the cable. Justifying this high-speed communication met with resistance until the use of the various fiber and coaxial systems emerged. By taking a quantum leap in the industry, the data and voice departments saw both the benefit and the need to converge services to the desktop by offering voice and video over the LAN. The 10-Mbps Ethernet and coaxial cables could not handle this offering. Moreover, access to the Internet continued with demands to add speed and capacity (voice and video on the Internet). The industry began to seek a new method of bypassing the telephone companies' local loops. A technology already at the door, of course, was CATV. So, a new idea emerged: use CATV to support high-speed Internet access and bypass the local loop from telephone companies. Hence, cable-modem technology changed the way we will do business in the future.

❓ Line Check 13-1

1. What is the difference between baseband coaxial cable and broadband coaxial cable?

The New Market

The cable television companies are in the midst of a transition from their traditional core business of one-way entertainment video programming to a position as a full-service provider of video, voice, and data-telecommunications services. Among the elements that have made this transition possible are technologies such as the cable data modem. These companies have historically carried a number of data services. These have ranged from news and weather feeds—presented in alphanumeric form on single channels or as scrolling captions—to one-way transmission of data over classic cable systems. Often, the cable companies were carrying data feeds in the nonimage portions of the video signal (such as during flyback or the black sync bar between video frames) in an out-of-band channel. Today, these carriers bring closed captioning and secondary audio signals to augment conventional video images.

Information providers are targeting the upgraded cable network architecture as the delivery mechanism of choice for advanced high-speed data services. These changes stem from the commercial and residential data communications markets. The PC and LAN explosions in the early 1980s were rapidly followed by leaps in computer networking technology. More people now work from home and depend on connectivity from commercial online services (AOL, CompuServe, and Prodigy) to the global Internet.

Increased awareness has led to increasing demand for data service and for higher speeds and enhanced levels of service. Cable is in a unique position to meet these demands. There appear to be no serious barriers to cable deployment of high-speed data transmission.

System Upgrades

The cable platform is steadily evolving into a hybrid digital and analog transmission system. Cable television systems were originally designed to optimize the one-way analog transmission of television programming to the home. The underlying coaxial cable, however, has enough bandwidth to support two-way transport of signals. The hybrid network is shown in Figure 13-4.

Growth in demand for Internet access and other two-way services has dovetailed with the trend within the industry to enhance existing cable systems with fiber-optic technology. The resultant product of this pairing is called **hybrid fiber coax (HFC)**. Many cable companies are in the midst of upgrading the HFC plant to improve the existing cable services and support

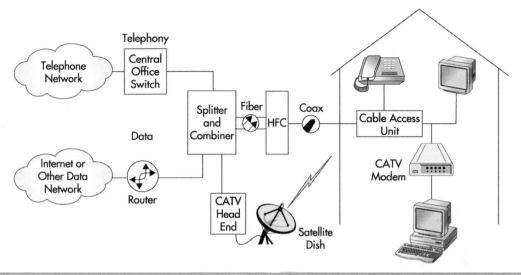

Figure 13-4 The combination of coaxial cable and fiber optics creates new opportunities for the CATV companies to offer high-speed data access and telephony services.

data and other new services. Companies are taking different approaches to online service access. For some applications, customers may be accessing information stored locally at or near the cable headend or regional hub. This may be temporary until wide-area cable interconnections and expanded Internet backbone networks are in place to allow information access from any remote site. Regardless, the CATV companies are striving for what the industry terms the "triple play." The triple play means that the CATV company offers voice, data, and video services bundled on a single interface via the cable infrastructure already connected to homes and businesses.

Cable Modems

Digital data signals are carried over **radio frequency (RF) carrier signals** on a cable system. Digital data utilizes cable modems, devices that convert digital information into a modulated RF signal and convert RF signals back to digital information. The conversion is performed by a modem at the subscriber's premises, and again by headend equipment handling multiple subscribers. See Figure 13-5 for a block diagram of the cable modem.

A single CATV channel can support multiple data streams or multiple users using shared LAN protocols, such as Ethernet, commonly in use in business-office LANs today. This is where Ethernet networks can be applied to the broadband coaxial networks. Different

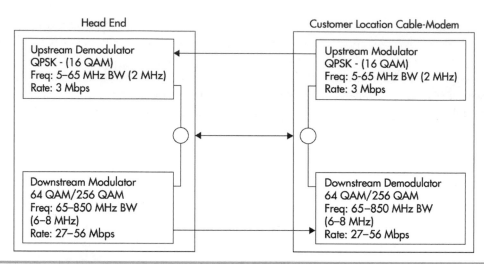

Figure 13-5 The diagram of a cable modem is fairly straightforward, but note that the upstream and downstream speeds are different.

modulation techniques are being tried to maximize the data speed that can be transmitted through a 6-MHz channel. Comparing the data traffic rates for different types of modems shows why the cable modem is so popular in today's environment. Table 13-1 shows a comparison of a file download of 500 KB using different techniques.

Method	Rate	Time
Telephone modem	28.8 Kbps	6–8 min.
ISDN	128 Kbps	1–1.5 min.
Cable modem	10 Mbps	Approximately 1 second

Source: CableLabs.

Table 13-1 A Comparison of the Speeds Available and the Download Times for a 500-KB File.

Careful traffic engineering is being performed on cable systems, so data speeds are maximized as customers are added. Just as office LANs are routinely subdivided to provide faster service for each individual user, cable data networks can also be custom tailored within each fiber node to meet customer demand. Multiple 6-MHz channels can be allocated to expand capacity as well.

Some manufacturers have designed modems providing asymmetrical capabilities, using less bandwidth for outgoing signals from the subscriber. CATV companies in some locations may not have completed system upgrades. Therefore, manufacturers have built migration strategies into such modems to allow for eventual transmission of broadband return signals when the systems are ready to provide such service and customers demand it. A representative sample of the way data speeds are provided on cable modems is shown in Table 13-2.

Manufacturer	Upstream	Downstream
General Instrument	1.5 Mbps	30 Mbps
Hybrid/Intel	96 Kbps	30 Mbps
LANcity	10 Mbps	10 Mbps
Motorola	768 Kbps	30 Mbps

Table 13-2 Comparative Capabilities of a Few Vendors Show Differences.

What Does a Cable Modem Do?

The cable modem performs the following functions:

● Transports subscriber IP traffic across the HFC system.

The cable modem receives traffic on its Ethernet port from the subscriber's equipment and forwards the appropriate IP packets on upstream RF channels to the cable router, as shown in Figure 13-6. The subscriber's equipment is any device that supports the TCP/IP protocol. It receives IP packets destined for its attached subscriber's equipment on downstream channels and transmits them across the Ethernet interface.

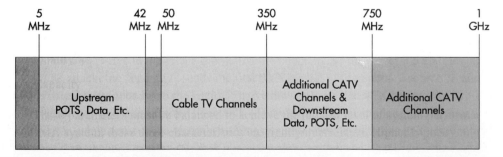

Figure 13-6 The cable modem handles all the RF management and the assignment of the channels on the cable for upstream and downstream services.

- Provides monitoring information to the cable router—The cable modem monitors the performance of the downstream channel and its internal operations, and it forwards the downstream channel statistics to the cable router when queried.

- Indicates connectivity status—The front panel LEDs indicate connectivity status and act as a diagnostic aid. See Figure 13-7 for a connectivity scheme using a cable modem. Figure 13-8 is a drawing of the rear of the cable modem with the various connections in place.

- Participates in encryption sessions with the cable router when passing upstream and downstream data.

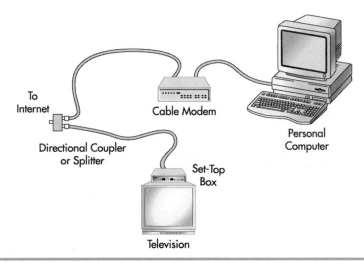

Figure 13-7 The cable modem is attached to the incoming cable splitter on one side and the PC on the other.

Figure 13-9 shows the upstream and the downstream traffic between the cable router and cable modems, and between the cable modems and subscriber's equipment.

What Does the Cable Router Do?

The cable router interfaces the HFC system to local and remote IP networks. The cable router is located at the headend and performs various functions.

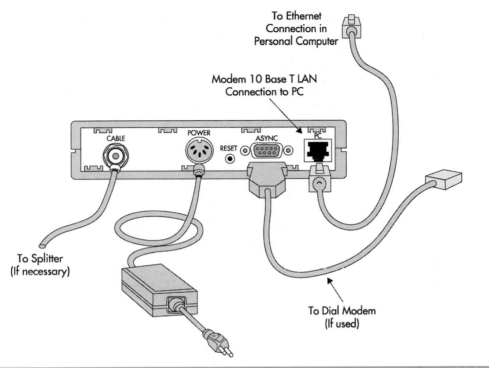

Figure 13-8 A rear-view look at the connections on the cable modem indicates the connections are fairly straightforward.

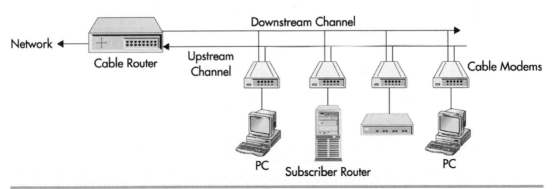

Figure 13-9 Upstream and downstream connections are connected to the cable in a bus topology. All devices share the same bandwidth on the cable.

Table 13-3 gives more detail on the functions of the router.

Feature	Function
Routing	• Performs IP routing. It uses the standard Routing Information Protocol (RIP) to advertise its routes to other routers in the IP network. • Routes traffic from cable subscribers to the Internet, cable subscribers, and service provider applications. • Filters upstream packets according to the rules you configure. • Controls group access for IP multicast. • Routes traffic to subscriber premise routers connected to cable modems located on the HFC subnet.
Spectrum Management	• Maximizes data-passing efficiency with its management of upstream and downstream channels. • Performs load balancing on upstream and downstream channels by managing the bandwidth allocation to the cable modems. • Performs forward error correction (FEC) to overcome transient ingress (impulse) noise. • Provides automatic congestion control for the upstream channels. • Performs upstream frequency agility to avoid ingress noise.
Variable Length Subnet Mask (VLSM)	• Allows configuration of subnets other than the Class C subnets supported in the past.
Dial Upstream	• Provides an alternate return path for passing data. • Provides secure communication.
Service Levels	• Enables each modem in an HFC subnet to have a configured level of service. • Prevents users from experiencing extreme performance variations across different loading conditions. • Protects bandwidth by preventing any one user from monopolizing all the bandwidth.
/4 DQPSK Modulation	• Provides 768 Kbps data signaling rate in the upstream data path. • Encodes two bits as one of four possible phase shifts.
16 QAM Modulation	• Doubles the data rate by encoding four bits per symbol as 1 of 16 possible amplitude and phase combinations. • Provides 1.5-Mbps data-signaling rate in the upstream path.

Table 13-3 A Summary of Cable Modem Activities and Features.

Network Management	• Configures and controls all cable modems.
	• Acts as software download server for the cable modem.
	• Stores usage statistics for cable modems, including information on following:
	   • Upstream and downstream HFC channels
	   • Receivers and transmitters
	   • IP traffic
	   • Automatically discovers modems

Trap Management	• Filters and forwards traps, based on configuration.
Security	• Provides secure communications between each registered modem and the cable router using special data-encryption techniques. • Provides management security by filtering unauthorized SNMP, Telnet, or FTP packets. The cable router accepts management traffic from trusted IP hosts only. • Provides firewall protection of the headend server complex from the HFC side of the network.

Table 13-3 A Summary of Cable Modem Activities and Features.(*Continued*)

Network Ports

The network ports on the cable router connect to standard Internet routers and remote devices for the purpose of transporting IP traffic. Each **network port** contains a processor for distributed IP routing and handles both input and output. Traffic received on each of these ports is routed by its local processor to the appropriate port of the cable router for transmission. No routing is done between network ports.

Network Port Types

The maximum number of network ports on the cable router is two, excluding the controller Ethernet port, unless you are using an ATM Network Port Card, and then you can have only one network port.

The types of network ports are:

• 100BaseT Ethernet

• Asynchronous transfer mode (ATM)

• Fiber Distributed Data Interface (FDDI)

The HFC ports on the cable router transmit data to and receive data from the subscriber. These ports handle the upstream and downstream channels on the receivers and transmitters. Modems are assigned to the upstream and downstream channels by the cable router.

Cable Frequency Spectrum Allocation

Figure 13-10 shows the division of cable frequency in a typical HFC system. Functionally, there are two frequency bands of operation. The upstream communications occur in the 5- to 42-MHz range. The downstream communications occur in the 65-MHz to 1-GHz range. Channel plans map channel assignments to specific frequencies. There are variations in the way the allocations work, but these are beyond the scope of this book.

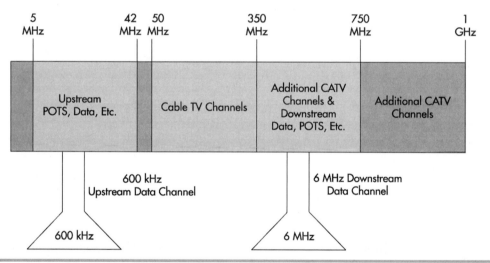

Figure 13-10 The spectrum is managed at the router, so all the data streams are kept up to speed.

Upstream channel assignments also follow these channel plans. Each upstream channel occupies 600 kHz of bandwidth and supports 1.5 Mbps. Upstream channels use encryption for security of subscriber data flows and Forward Error Correction (FEC) for robust throughput in hostile noise environments. As its name implies, **FEC** is an error-checking technique that includes some added data to correct single-bit errors at the receiving end. In traditional error-checking, an ACK or a NAK was transmitted to the originating end. Using FEC, the receiver attempts to correct any data errors that occurred during transmission across the network. Under high-noise condition, the cable modem can dynamically reduce speed to 768 Kbps to continue to pass data. A single upstream channel is shared by multiple cable modems, and each modem transmits on one channel at a time. Many of the CATV companies will limit the upstream from their residential customers to 128 or 256 Kbps. Commercial customers can pay for a higher uplink speed, such as 512 to 768 Kbps or more.

The cable router assigns upstream channels to the receivers. It selects the upstream channel from a list of possible upstream channels available in the cable router. The range of upstream channels is from 1 through 60. Because a receiver is dedicated to one serving group, the cable router assigns the best acceptable channel to that receiver. If it cannot assign an acceptable channel to a receiver, and if that is the only receiver in the serving group, then it operates on an unacceptable channel to maintain the subscriber service. Figure 13-11 looks at the cable router in the overall scheme of the network.

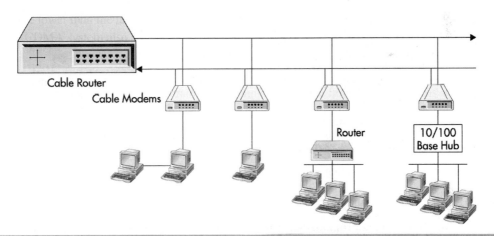

Figure 13-11 The cable router services the upstream and downstream of data, along with the management of the ancillary equipment at the customer location.

Each downstream channel occupies 6 MHz of bandwidth and supports 30 Mbps. Encryption and FEC are also included on all downstream data channels. Subscriber modems receive downstream data at a 30-Mbps burst rate. However, the maximum sustainable downstream throughput is 10 Mbps. In reality, the CATV companies use Ethernet switches and offer between 3 and 6 Mbps. This is a limitation of the Ethernet port on the cable modem. A downstream channel is assigned to the transmitter during configuration, and the range of downstream channels is 3 through 116. The list of possibilities of up and down speeds is as extensive as the number of manufacturers of cable modems and CATV companies.

Hybrid Fiber Coax (HFC) System

Before discussing how the cable router manages its physical resources that support data transmission over the HFC system, it is important to review the HFC system topology. We now have to consider:

● A review of a typical HFC system

● Graphics showing how the cable router and the cable modem fit into an HFC system

The **super headend** is the main signal reception, origination, and modulation point for the cable system. It performs the following functions:

● Receives satellite programming using the Television Receive Only (TVRO) sites

● Receives off-air broadcasts of television and radio

● Receives distant signals by frequency modulated link (FML) microwave or return band cable

● Modulates programming onto channel assignments for distribution

● FM modulates video for the distribution hub

● Performs local advertising insertion

● Inserts channels into trunk system

A distribution hub or **remote headend** is a scaled-down version of the super headend, which is a subdistribution point. A distribution hub does not perform all the functions of the super headend and may only process part of the cable spectrum. The **distribution hub** performs the following functions:

● Receives satellite programming

● Receives off-air programming

● Demodulates FM signals from the super headend

● Modulates programming onto the cable channels

● Inserts channels into the trunk system

● Inserts channels into the return path of the super trunk to the super headend

A fiber node is the location in an HFC system where the fiber cable ends and the coaxial cable begins. At the fiber node, the signal is converted from optics to electrical pulses. A service area is the area that includes all the homes served by the fiber node.

Example of Service Area

Figure 13-12 shows the details of the service area. The fiber comes into the fiber node, which is located in the neighborhood. From there, the coaxial cable branches off and is dropped to different homes. Amplifiers are required to boost the signal along the way. The fiber nodes, if upgraded to support HFC data communications, typically house the return laser.

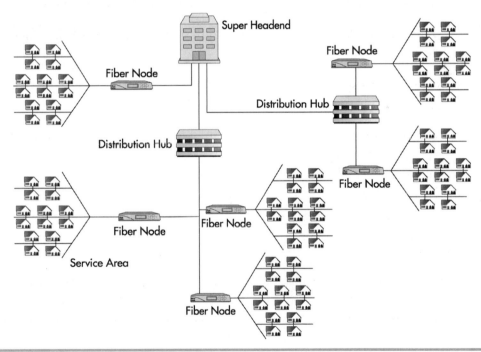

Figure 13-12 This is a typical layout of a service area using a CATV system.

Adding the Cable Data System to the HFC System

Figure 13-13 shows the cable router and the cable modem, components of the Cable Data System, fit into the HFC system. The **Cable Data System** defines a **serving group** as a

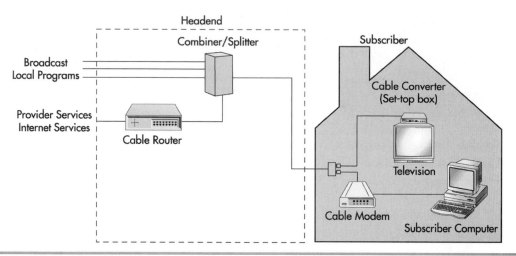

Figure 13-13 The cable router is used from the super headend to at least one receiver and one transmitter.

collection of fiber nodes (service areas) connected to transmitters and receivers on the cable router. A serving group has:

- At least one receiver
- At least one downstream transmitter
- Channels allocated to it
- Modems associated with it
- Upstream fiber nodes physically isolated from other fiber nodes

When you create multiple serving groups, you can reuse upstream channel assignments. This means cable-router receivers in different serving groups can be tuned to the same channel. You can assign the same set of upstream channels to more than one serving group. You can also reuse downstream channels provided the transmitters are in different serving groups. This is an extension of the network, as shown in Figure 13-14.

Once the cable router determines that a minimal level of service is not being met on the upstream channels because of congestion, it performs congestion control and reassigns specific

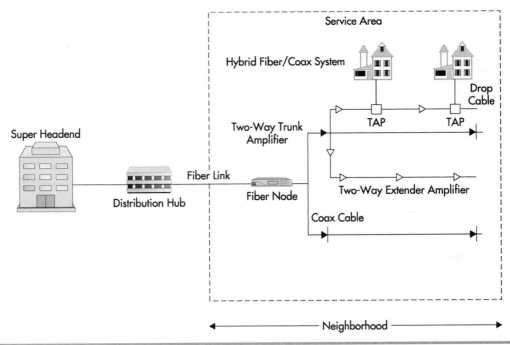

Figure 13-14 The cable-router network is used as an extended two-way service to deliver access to the high-speed cable by TV customers.

modems to other channels, if available. When the cable router dynamically learns about channel impairments (the channel error rate exceeds an internal error threshold), it determines a new channel to which to tune. Table 13-4 is an example of the allocations of the upstream and downstream channels. This is also shown in Figure 13-15.

Serving Group	Transmitter Allocation	Downstream	Receiver Allocation	Upstream	Modems
1	TX1	103	RX1	41, 43	Each modem has a unique serial number, for example, 12880600
2	TX2	103	RX2, RX3	41, 42, 43	

Source: Motorola.

Table 13-4 Cable Routers Use the Channel Allocations for Transmit and Receive.

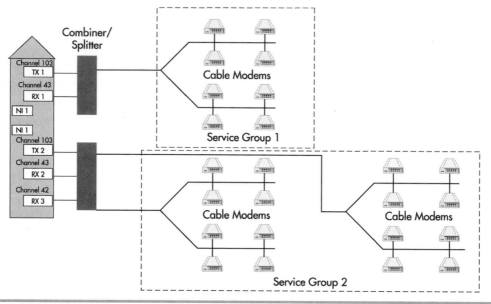

Figure 13-15 The cable router is fluid and assigns channels based on load and congestion, as well as traffic conditions.

Channel Allocation

Each serving group requires you to allocate spectrum for downstream and upstream data channels. The cable router uses this spectrum allocation to automatically and dynamically reassign upstream data channels when it detects noise that requires a change in channel frequency.

Downstream

You allocate downstream spectrum in 6-MHz blocks by specifying the **Standard Channel Plan**, IRC, or HRC channel number available for downstream assignment. Downstream channels are assigned per transmitter. The following describes these plans.

RF-TV Channel Frequencies—Channel Plans

Multiple TV-RF channels are being broadcast to an antenna or are available on a cable television system. For multiple TV-RF channels to exist, each must occupy a specific 6-MHz channel or frequency band.

TV stations and cable systems are assigned 6-MHz wide frequency bands by the Federal Communications Commission (FCC) in which TV-RF signals can be transmitted or transported. Channel numbers are assigned to these frequency bands for identification.

For example; Channel 2 is assigned a frequency range of 54 to 60 MHz, Channel 3 a range of 60 to 66 MHz, and Channel 4 a range of 66 to 72 MHz. Each channel has an audio or sound carrier with modulated audio. For most FCC-assigned channel frequency bands, channels are directly above or below the channel. The channel directly below the channel is called the lower adjacent channel, and the channel above it is the upper adjacent channel. For example, Channel 2 is the lower adjacent channel for Channel 3. The upper adjacent channel is Channel 4.

A TV receiver tuned to Channel 3 must provide adequate filtering of the adjacent channel signals to produce a good picture. Strong signal levels on the adjacent channels or improper TV receiver operation and rejection of adjacent channel signals may cause picture lines or interference.

Television broadcast stations are assigned transmitter channels in the VHF (very high frequency) and UHF (ultrahigh frequency) bands, as shown in Table 13-5.

Channel	Frequency Range
2–6	54–86 MHz
7–13	174–216 MHz
14–69	470–806 MHz

Table 13-5 The Channel Assignments in the Frequency Bands, as Allocated by the FCC.

Low-band VHF Channels 2 to 6 range from 54 to 86 MHz. High-band VHF Channels 7 to 13 range from 174 to 216 MHz. FM broadcast, aviation, and public service bands occupy the frequencies between Channel 6 and Channel 7. UHF channels 14 to 69 occupy channel frequencies from 470 MHz to 806 MHz. Take special notice of the gap in the frequency spectrum between VHF Channel 13 and Channel 14.

Cable television systems provide a conduit to transport signals from point-to-point. Because the conduit is like a water pipe and all the signals are held securely inside, the full-frequency spectrum range can be used to transport RF-TV signal channels.

When tuning a television to a channel number, you must consider if the channel is an off-air transmitted VHF/UHF TV channel or a cable TV channel number. While the channel numbers 2 to 13 designate the same channel frequency, channels above 13 designate different channel frequencies. For this reason, television receivers all have tuning modes that select between cable- and antenna-tuning channel plans.

HRC and ICC Offset Cable Channel Plans

Some cable systems purposefully shift the video and audio carrier frequencies of some or most channels. Two common carrier shift schemes are the **harmonically related carrier (HRC)** and **incremental coherent carrier (ICC)** or **incremental related carrier (IRC)**.

The HRC system shifts all the cable channels 2 to 125 down in frequency, –1.25 MHz from the FCC assigned or standard cable frequency, except Channels 4 and 5. Channels 4 and 5 are shifted up in frequency +0.75 MHz. An additional channel, designated Channel 1, is created between Channel 4 and Channel 5, with a carrier frequency of 72 MHz.

The IRC or ICC system shifts Channels 4 and 5 up in frequency +2.0 MHz from the FCC assigned or standard cable frequency. An additional channel, designated Channel 1, is created between Channels 4 and 5 with a carrier frequency of 73.25 MHz.

While an HRC or ICC system gains an extra cable channel, the main advantage of an HRC or ICC system is to reduce a form of interference called triple beat.

Triple beat is a cable-amplifier distortion in which an interference frequency results from the combination of three cable carriers. For example, Channel 2 frequency, plus Channel 3 frequency, plus Channel 4 frequency equals 183.75 MHz. This mixing or triple beat falls in the video of Channel 8. Multiple triple-beat combinations exist in cable systems; however, with proper design and signal levels these beat products usually do not cause picture interference.

HRC systems use a stable reference oscillator at 6.000300 MHz to derive all the video carriers on the cable system. The reference oscillator is multiplied by various multipliers to derive each channel's video-carrier frequency. For example, the reference oscillator is multiplied by 9 to produce the carrier for Channel 2. Because all the video carriers are in phase and direct multiples, any triple beat falls directly on another carrier frequency, masking the interference that may be seen on the picture.

Although HRC and ICC systems improved picture quality, few cable systems adopted these channel plans. Only about 10 percent of the cable systems use an HRC or ICC system. The local cable operator or engineer can confirm the use of an HRC or ICC cable system in your area.

When tuning a television, you may need to consider if an HRC or ICC cable channel plan is being used. Most modern-day televisions have versatile electronic tuning in the cable mode. Electronic tuning searches for a valid video carrier up to 2 MHz above and below the normal assigned FCC cable channel frequency. With this search, HRC or ICC carrier frequencies are found and tuned. Some television and VCR tuners are not automatic, so you may need to select FCC, HRC, or ICC on a rear panel switch or on the electronic on-screen menu to enable proper tuning to the cable channel plan being used. The channel shifts are shown in Table 13-6.

Upstream

You allocate upstream spectrum in 600-kHz blocks by specifying channel numbers available for upstream assignment. Upstream channels do not require contiguous assignment. For example, you may assign upstream Channels 41, 43, and 45 for use by the Cable Data System. In fact, spreading the channels out provides better noise immunity. Upstream channels are assigned per serving group.

Channel	HRC Shift MHz	IRC Shift MHz
2	–1.25	0
3	–1.25	0
4	–1.25	0
5	+0.75	+2.0
6	+0.75	+2.0
7	–1.25	0
All others	Shifted at –1.25 MHz	Not shifted

Table 13-6 Channel Shifts in Frequency Using HRC and IRC Channel Plans.

Transmitters

You assign each transmitter in a cable router to one or multiple serving groups. A serving group can have multiple transmitters. These transmitters may be shared with other serving groups. When multiple transmitters are used, the cable router automatically ensures that each transmitter uses a unique downstream channel within each serving group.

NOTE

If multiple transmitters are in a serving group and you disable one of the transmitters or alter the configuration file so the transmitter is unavailable, the cable router automatically tells the modems to retune their receivers to a channel on another transmitter within the serving group.

Receivers

You assign each receiver in the cable router to a single serving group. When and if detected noise becomes sufficient, the cable router may reassign a receiver (and all attached modems) to a new upstream data channel allocated in the serving group that is not currently in use by another receiver in that serving group. A serving group can also have multiple receivers. In configuration, you dedicate each receiver to a single serving group. The cable router dynamically tunes receivers to upstream channels that you allocated in the Cable Data System. The cable router ensures that each receiver in a serving group is tuned to a unique upstream channel.

Modems

You provision each cable modem by assigning it to a single serving group. You can also have the cable router automatically provision cable modems by enabling autodiscovery. Once provisioned, the Cable Data System automatically assigns cable modems to downstream and upstream data channels. The cable router initially assigns the channels to the cable modems during modem registration. The cable router also manages subsequent upstream channel assignments that may be triggered by detection of noise or congestion within the Cable Data System.

Line Check 13-2

1. What three channel types are available for downstream assignment?

2. What is the difference between these channel types?

Spectrum Management

The cable router manages the spectrum by performing the following tasks:

- Manages resources configured for each serving group.

- Assigns the modems to channels and manages the resource usage once allocated.

- Performs load balancing on the upstream channels.

- Performs frequency agility in these ways:

  - Controls upstream congestion by moving modems from one upstream channel to another.

  - Responds to noise by changing the channel assignment (frequency) of a receiver if the upstream channel quality is poor. Modems assigned to this channel are also instructed to transmit on the new channel assignment.

  - Frequency agility is transparent to the subscribers and requires no operator intervention.

- Performs FEC on upstream and downstream channels.

Figure 13-16 shows two serving groups. The cable router selects upstream channels from the configured list. It tunes the receivers to the upstream channels and instructs the modems to transmit on these specific channels. The downstream channel (103) is fixed as specified in the configuration file.

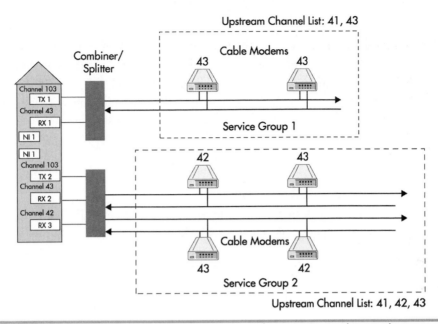

Figure 13-16 The cable modem is using channel 103 for transmit and tunes the receivers to accept the data from this channel.

Upstream Channel Assignment

The cable router assigns upstream channels to the receivers. It selects the upstream channel from a list of upstream channels that you configured in the cable router. The range of upstream channels is 1 through 60. Because a receiver is dedicated to one serving group, the cable router assigns the best acceptable channel to that receiver in the serving group. If it cannot assign an acceptable channel to a receiver, and if that is the only receiver in the serving group, the cable router operates on an impaired channel to maintain subscriber service. In this situation, the cable router periodically scans the allocated spectrum to determine if any other channel's quality is within an acceptable range. If it finds an acceptable channel, the cable router uses that channel.

Downstream Channel Assignment

You assign a downstream channel to the transmitter during configuration. The range of downstream channels is 3 through 116.

Upstream Channel Management

The cable router manages the set of upstream channels assigned to each of the serving groups. The assignment of an upstream channel to a receiver is not permanent. It may change as the cable router performs frequency agility, if there are multiple channels assigned.

What Do You Think?

Given all that you have learned about DSL from Chapter 12, which technology do you think is more proficient for gaining high-speed access? Cable outsold DSL by a ratio of 2 to 1 from 2000 to 2003. Which technology do you think will become the predominant access method in the future? Why? State your reasons and discuss them with other students in the classroom.

Address and Subnet Mask

The IP routing model consists of hosts that are connected to networks. Each network is assigned an IP network number. This number is an 8- to 30-bit number that is globally assigned by the Internet Assigned Number Authority (IANA). IP hosts are assigned 32-bit host IP addresses. The first 8 to 30 bits of the address represent the subnetwork on which the host is attached; the remaining bits represent its host number on that subnetwork. The subnet mask is a 32-bit number with 1 bit in each of the subnetwork bits.

Network Connection

Networks are interconnected by routers. Both hosts and routers have an IP route table. This table provides the IP address of the next router, so it can send an IP packet based on the IP address of the destination network. Hosts typically have only a default route in their route table. The default route gives the IP address of a default router, or default gateway, on the host's attached network, which the host uses as an outlet to send messages existing on an IP network other than its own. Routers typically have hundreds or thousands of routes, based on the number of IP subnetworks. IP routing protocols are used to distribute information about getting to different IP networks.

Subscriber PCs attach to a cable modem through an Ethernet LAN. The PC uses the Internet Engineering Task Force (IETF) protocols specified for IP communication over Ethernet. The PC is considered a host. In the IP model, the cable modem appears to the PC as its default router when it uses the cable router's IP address as the default gateway. A host computer must always know the following information so it can communicate using IP on a LAN:

- Its own IP host address

- The subnetwork mask of its attached LAN

- The IP address of its default router, which must be directly connected on the same IP subnet as the host

The following is an example of how a host forwards IP packets. In this example:

- Host IP address is 150.20.53.43

- Subnet mask is 255.255.255.0

- Default router, or gateway, is 150.20.53.1

Building the MAC Layer Header

All hosts and routers keep an Address Resolution Protocol (ARP) table, which maps local subnet IP addresses to MAC addresses. In the following table, which describes how the host or router obtains the MAC address, the term-requesting device is used for the requesting host or router.

To support the learning of IP addresses for devices in the HFC network that do not send IP packets, a downstream ARP capability exists on the cable router. If a packet comes into the cable router, destined for a device in the HFC network whose MAC address has not been learned, the cable router broadcasts an ARP request downstream to all cable modems in an attempt to resolve the MAC address.

Example of HFC Subnet

Figure 13-17 shows that the cable router supports up to 20 HFC subnets, which are 156.20.128.0 through 156.20.147.0 in this example. It also highlights one HFC subnet: 156.20.128.0. The HFC host address for this subnet is 156.20.128.1. Addresses from 156.20.128.2 through 156.20.128.254 are assigned to subscriber PCs. The address of each PC's default gateway for this subnet is 156.20.144.1.

Example of IP Logical Subnets

When traditional LANs are assigned a single IP network number, all devices on the LAN must have a host address from within that network address. As mentioned previously, the cable router does not require all subscribers on the same subnet to be physically connected. Figure 13-18 shows that PC 2 and PC 3 have different subnet addresses, although they are on the same physical network. PCs 3 and 4, although on physically different networks, may have the same subnet addresses. This flexibility is possible because the cable router treats HFC subnets as logical, not physical, networks.

Variable Length Subnet Masking

The Variable Length Subnet Masking (VLSM) feature lets you assign a subnet mask to your HFC network. If you have multiple subnets on the HFC side, each subnet mask can be different or of variable length. This means you can more efficiently use your assigned IP

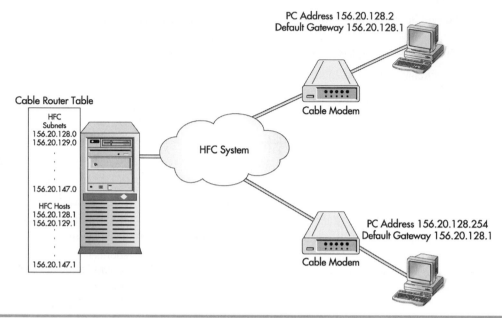

PC Address 156.20.128.2
Default Gateway 156.20.128.1

Cable Modem

Cable Router Table

HFC Subnets
156.20.128.0
156.20.129.0
.
.
.
156.20.147.0

HFC Hosts
156.20.128.1
156.20.129.1
.
.
.
156.20.147.1

HFC System

PC Address 156.20.128.254
Default Gateway 156.20.128.1

Cable Modem

Figure 13-17 The cable router will handle multiple addresses and subnets to accommodate the number of customers as the demands grow.

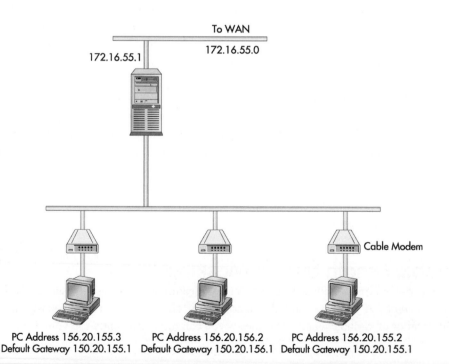

To WAN

172.16.55.1   172.16.55.0

Cable Modem

PC Address 156.20.155.3   PC Address 156.20.156.2   PC Address 156.20.155.2
Default Gateway 150.20.155.1   Default Gateway 150.20.156.1   Default Gateway 150.20.155.1

Figure 13-18 The IP subnets are shown here with different PCs on different subnets.

address space because you can effectively divide your address space. VSLM eases the burden caused by IP address resource limitations and improves the use of IP host addresses. The cable router now supports up to 256 HFC subnets. The total number of users supported is 5,060.

Cable Router Implementation

Subnet masks are typically expressed using the notation /number, where the *number* is the number of contiguous 1's. Before the implementation of VLSM in the cable router, you were required to use a Class C HFC subnet mask or a /24 mask, that is, 255.255.255.0. This meant you were locked into fixed-sized subnets. With VSLM, you can have subnet masks of different lengths, for example, a /24 mask, which is 255.255.255.0, a /19 mask, which is 255.255.224.0, or a /26 mask, which is 255.255.255.192. The cable router supports a range of /2 to /30 subnet masks.

Subnet Example

An organization receives an address of 172.20.0.0/16 (mask of 255.255.0.0) from the IANA. The address needs to be divided to accommodate four regions. Each region has five cities: three cities (potentially 4,000 subscribers) and two cities (potentially 2,000 subscribers). First, the address space is divided into four regions. This means there are 4/18 networks (mask of 255.255.192.0), as shown in Figure 13-19.

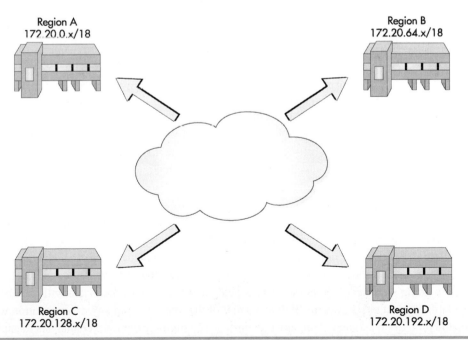

Region A
172.20.0.x/18

Region B
172.20.64.x/18

Region C
172.20.128.x/18

Region D
172.20.192.x/18

Figure 13-19 Four regions are created from the address space to serve the different city needs.

13

Standards

Modems are available today from a variety of vendors, each with their own unique technical approach. These modems are now making it possible for cable companies to enter the data communications market. In the longer term, modem costs must drop and greater interoperability is desirable. Customers who buy modems that work in their current cable system need assurance that the modem will work if they move to a different geographic location served by a different cable company. Further, agreement on a standard set of specifications allows the market to enjoy economies of scale and drives down the price of each individual modem. Ultimately, these modems will be available as standard peripheral devices offered as an option to customers buying new personal computers at retail stores. The cable companies and manufacturers came together formally in December 1995 to begin working toward an open standard.

Leading U.S. and Canadian cable companies were involved in this development toward an open-cable modem standard. Specifications were to be developed in three phases, and then be presented to standards-setting bodies for approval as standards. Individual vendors were free to offer their own implementations with a variety of additional, competitive features and future improvements. A data interoperability specification will comprise a number of interfaces. The resultant specification is called the **Data over Cable Service Interface Specification (DOCSIS)**.

Some interfaces reside within the cable network. Several of these system-level interfaces also will be specified to ensure interoperability.

Return Path

The portion of bandwidth reserved for return signals (from the customer to the cable network) is usually in the 5- to 40-MHz portion of the spectrum. This portion of the spectrum can be subject to ingress and other types of interference, so cable systems offering two-way data services have been designed to operate in this environment.

Industry engineers have assembled a set of alternative strategies for return-path operation. **Dynamic frequency agility** (shifting data from one channel to another when needed) may be designed into modems, so data signals may avoid unwanted interference as it arises. Other approaches utilize a "gate" that keeps the return path from an individual subscriber closed, except for those times when the subscriber sends a return signal. Demarcation filters, different return laser types, and reduced node size are among the other approaches, each involving tradeoffs between capital cost and maintenance effort and cost.

Return-path transmission issues have already been the subject of two years of lab and field-testing and product development. The full, two-way capability of the coaxial cable already going past most U.S. homes is now being utilized in many areas and will soon be available in most cable systems. Full activation of the return path in any given location will depend on individual cable company circumstances, ranging from market analysis to capital availability.

Applications

Cable modems open the door for customers to enjoy a range of high-speed data services, all at speeds hundreds of times faster than telephone modem calls. Subscribers can be fully connected, 24 hours a day, to services without interfering with cable television service or phone service. Among these services are:

- Information services—access to shopping, weather maps, household bill paying, and so forth.

- Internet access—electronic mail, discussion groups, and the World Wide Web.

- Business applications—interconnecting LANs or supporting collaborative work.

- Cable commuting—enabling the already popular notion of working from home.

- Education—allowing students to continue to access educational resources from home.

13

The promises of advanced telecommunications networks, once more hype than fact, are now within reach. Cable modems and other technology are being deployed to make this happen. Regardless of the technology selected, the main goal is to get the high-speed data communications on the cable adjacent to the TV and entertainment. This gives the CATV companies the leverage to act in an arbitrage situation, competing with the local telephone companies that have dragged their feet in moving high-speed services to the consumer's door.

Security on CATV

When CATV systems are used, they use shared high-speed Ethernet (albeit 10Broad36) backbone access to the Internet or other connections. You must be aware that on a shared cable, the PC is a peer to all others on the same cable, although they are in physically different locations. With 500 connections, many people will acquire the service from the CATV suppliers. The CATV company installs according to the appropriate technology, not according to security parameters. This is okay because it is merely providing the bandwidth to gain access. The end user is responsible for turning off all the leaks in the local system (the PC). By default, when you run the Microsoft Windows environment and the appropriate networking software, the shares on the PC are turned on, so the end user must go in and turn them off. This means that if the shared services are not turned off, any user on the same IP subnet can double-click on the "network neighborhood" icon and see all the other PCs connected to the cable. Not only can the users see the devices, they can double-click on the PC and see the resources available on that PC. From there, when a remote device has double-clicked on your PC, they may be able to open your drives and see your files. Unless some provisions have been taken to block this access, the intruder (used as a method of entry only) could read, write, edit, or delete your files. Worse yet, while intruders are on your system, you do not even know they are there.

Many users who have cable modem service from the cable companies are not aware of the risks. Worse, the installation personnel on these systems either do not totally understand or forget to point out the risks. Therefore, the user leaves the PC on 100 percent of the time, day and night, leaving access to the computer totally available. The cable modem is available 100 percent of the time, making the computer a target for hackers and the mischievous, without the permission or the knowledge of the penetrated computer owner. This is why newer-generation cable modems use firewalls to reduce the risks associated with connecting to cable networks.

Be aware that the risk is there and find out how to shut these open doors before leaving your computer on the network. Do not assume you are secure just because you shut your system off when you are not using it. When you do log on, you are exposed, and the perpetrator can also get on your system while you are on it.

Chapter 13 Review

Chapter Summary

CATV systems offer high-speed, RF frequency agile communications. Although they were initially installed using a one way entertainment system, newer cable modems and routers now allow bandwidth sharing on a two-way cable. As the CATV companies have evolved, they now offer the triple play of voice, data, and video services on a bundled service to the subscriber. Given the convenience and some of the pricing mechanisms, CATV access to the Internet has outsold the RBOCs' service offerings (xDSL) by a ratio of 2:1. This has changed the way we perceive the lifeline services of voice. Now we also see that the CATV companies using a 6-MHz channel can use an offset to prevent interchannel interference (a problem typically associated with radio-based systems). Moreover, the networks are proliferating at such an escalating rate, the CATV industry has introduced DOCSIS-based modems and routers that will increase channel capacity, increase up and down speeds, and make the service more ubiquitously available to the masses. You can expect to see many new battle lines drawn in the communications sand of time. Who will win is a matter of time; historically, the RBOCs have had a wait and see attitude. However, the RBOCs have now become far more aggressive in attacking the CATV suppliers with offerings that equal or surpass that of the cable company.

Key Terms for Chapter 13

10Broad36 *(614)*
Baseband Cables *(613)*
Broadband Coaxial Cable *(613)*
Broadband LAN *(615)*

Key Term Quiz

1. _____ is the open-system cable modem standard that allows off-the-shelf modems to work on any cable network.

2. _____ is a cable that operates at 10 Mbps over a maximum distance of 3,600 meters.

3. _____ defines a serving group as a collection of fiber nodes (service areas) connected to transmitters and receivers on the cable router.

4. A _____ is also called the remote headend.

5. Shifting data from one channel to another when needed is called _____.

6. A _____ is the location in an HFC system where the fiber cable ends and the coaxial cable begins.

7. The _____ on the cable router connect to standard Internet routers and remote devices for the purpose of transporting IP traffic.

8. The _____ is the main signal reception, origination, and modulation point for the cable system.

9. Cable modems use encryption for security of subscriber data flows in upstream channels, as well as _____ for robust throughput in hostile noise environments.

10. The acronym for cable TV is _____.

Multiple-Choice Quiz

1. In the late 1970s, a major battle arose in the _____ and computer industries.

   a. Cable TV

   b. Data

   c. Internet

   d. Communications

2. The traditional Ethernet ran on a _____ cable.

   a. Broadband coax

   b. Thin broadband

   c. Baseband coax

   d. Thick broadband

3. The CATV companies used a _____ as their primary means of carrying their traffic.

   a. Baseband coax

   b. Unshielded twisted pair

   c. Broadband coax

   d. Twinax coax

4. DEC developed several working arrangements with various suppliers to provide a _____ to work on the cable TV systems.

   a. MUX

   b. FAM

   c. TAP

   d. AMP

5. Wang Computer Company developed a proprietary cable system for connecting Wang systems using ____cables.

   a. Twin

   b. Single

   c. Three

   d. Mid-split

6. A new idea emerged to use _____ for Internet access and bypass the local loop.

   a. UTP

   b. Coax

   c. STP

   d. CATV

7. Digital data signals are carried over _____ signals on a cable system.

   a. CSMA/CD

   b. RF

   c. DOCSIS

   d. CSMA/CA

8. The CATV channel uses _____ of bandwidth used to transmit Ethernet.

   a. 10 MHz

   b. 24 MHz

   c. 350 MHz

   d. 6 MHz

9. The upload speed offered by the CATV cable is up to _____.

   a. 256 Kbps

   b. 100 Mbps

   c. 10 Mbps

   d. 1.5 Mbps

10. Download speeds on the Internet using CATV will yield somewhere around _____.

   a. 10 Mbps

   b. 5 Mbps

   c. 2 Mbps

   d. 1 Mbps

11. The portion of bandwidth reserved for _____ is usually in the 5- to 40-MHz portion of the spectrum.

    a. Ethernet

    b. Return Path

    c. Forward Path

    d. Multiuser Path

Chapter 14

Overview of Cellular Communications

1-2-3-4th Generation Cellular Services

Mobile communications transmission is one of the latest and greatest fronts in the industry. Although many people believe cellular transmission is a recent development, few realize it is a mature technology over 50 years old.

Cellular communications has undergone radical changes since its inception. In this chapter, we cover the various progression the industry has gone through, the technologies involved, and the applications supported, as well as what the future holds. The progression in service is described by the term "generation": a **generation** is an evolution or advancement in technology. In the cellular world, the term is abbreviated with a G. These are now buzz words in the industry: 3G and 4G services.

There has been great debate over what the milestone generations are. If two different sources are consulted, two different answers will be received. For the purposes of this book, we will define generations as follows:

Pre-first-generation services were mobile telecommunications service (MTS) and improved mobile telephone services (IMTS). We define these as pre-first-generation services because they were not cellular.

First-generation service was advanced mobile phone service (AMPS) or analog cellular.

Second-generation services are Digital Cellular Services—TDMA, CDMA, and GSM.

Two-and-a-half (2.5)-generation services are GPRS and EDGE.

Third-generation services are now being introduced. UMTS/WCDMA is 3G.

The reason for this distinction is the definition of 3G. According to the UMTS forum, the 3G forum, and several other standards bodies, 3G is the UMTS/WCDMA technology. Because GPRS and EDGE do not meet this standard, we are classifying them as 2.5G services. An argument can be made that these are the third versions of the original mobile phone network, but not achieving the standard 3G rates does not qualify them as such.

With that said, where did it all come from?

Before 1G—Mobile Telecommunications Service (MTS) and Improved Mobile Telecommunications Service (IMTS)

In 1946, the Illinois Bell Telephone Company introduced a **mobile telecommunications service (MTS)** (using a radio-to-telephone interface) that would enable users driving in and around the

St. Louis, Missouri, area to communicate directly to and from their vehicles. The telephone company's goal was trying to provide coverage in a 25-mile radius from the downtown area. The telephone company mounted a powerful high-gain antenna on top of the tallest high-rise buildings. It broadcast a powerful 250-watt signal from this antenna to get the best possible coverage.

All calls within the city had to be routed through the centralized tower because of the limited amount of channels. In this particular network, 12 channels were available. Each channel was used on a high-powered radio transmitter to provide the required coverage.

Further, the system operated on a half-duplex basis. Only one side of the call could speak at a given time. This was analogous to the older two-way, push-to-talk radio systems.

Unfortunately, getting this service was not as simple as driving up to the telephone company and setting up an account. Many areas of the country had a two-year wait as the service rolled out.

What was the reason for long delays in the roll-out phase? The Federal Communications Commission (FCC) had issued a limited number of frequencies for use in the MTS and IMTS networks.

Problems with the MTS/IMTS

Radio-based communications will travel greater distances as a function of the frequency used and the power output. This means if a second radio system was set up in the nearby area using the same frequencies, it could (and, most likely, would) cause interference with the first system. As shown in Figure 14-1, radio signals travel another 50 to 75 miles beyond the intended signal area, causing overlap areas. This means the radio-based system could only reuse the same frequencies every 100 miles apart. The buffer zone areas around the area of intended radio coverage exist to prevent interference between signals. In the discussion on bandwidth earlier in this book, we stated sidebands and frequency band-pass filters are used in the wired telephone world. Essentially the same holds true in the wireless world, where the telephone company allocated the buffer zones, so two conversations would not occur on the same channel. The figure shows the signal was used in the center (thicker) core, but the overlap areas are shown in the lighter core.

This arrangement worked for short periods, but as newer demands were placed on the system, channel capacity was limited. The limited number of channels (frequencies assigned by the FCC for this service) led to the need for frequency reuse planning by the telephone companies. **IMTS**, introduced in 1965, made the problem even more acute by using two channels simultaneously to provide full-duplex telephony (eliminating the push-to-talk of the MTS system).

Prior to the introduction of an improved telephony service through radio-based systems, the industry standards bodies faced a dilemma. They wanted to meet the demand for more

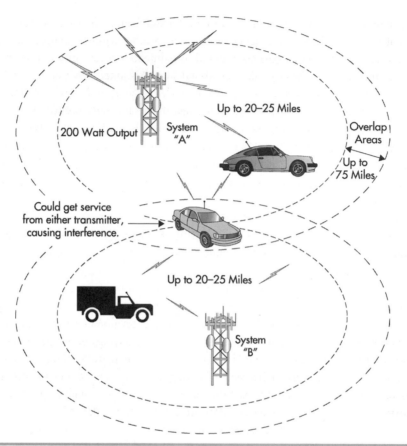

Figure 14-1 At 250 watts, radio signals exceed the 25-mile usable coverage area and still travel an additional 50 to 75 miles.

services, but they did not have the frequencies available. Therefore, the engineers went back to the drawing board and created a new technique called cellular communications. In **cellular communications**, coverage isn't achieved by massive towers transmitting at high power but by creating many small, low-power transmitters. This way, frequency reuse can be designed into a local system to allow the same frequency to be used multiple times by multiple phones in a single metropolitan area, relieving the channel congestion and limitations of MTS and IMTS.

1G Cellular Communications

Around the same time as the AT&T divestiture, developers of radio-telephone interconnection were experimenting with new cellular communications. In actuality, cellular communications were designed and ready to go in 1974. But not until 1981 did the U.S. FCC finally set aside

666 radio channels for cellular use in the United States. These frequencies were assigned to two separate carriers. The lower frequencies were reserved for wireline companies, the regulated providers (local telcos). The higher frequencies were reserved for nonwireline carriers, the competitors to the telcos. Both groups of carriers (wireline and nonwireline) are licensed to operate in a specific **metropolitan service area (MSA)** or **rural service area (RSA)**.

A lower-power cellular telephony market was invented in the 1980s. This newer implementation was called **advanced mobile phone service (AMPS)**. AMPS utilizes **frequency division multiple access (FDMA)**. FDMA means each user gets one entire 30-kHz subchannel or portion of an allocated channel for transmit and one 30-kHz subchannel for receive. Although this is a reliable form of communication, it is extremely wasteful (in terms of limited radio frequencies).

Cellular transmission overcomes the limitations of conventional mobile systems. Areas of coverage are divided into small honeycomb cells that overlap at the outer boundaries.

Frequencies can be divided into bands or cells with a protection zone established to prevent interference and jamming. The transmitter uses 3 watts of output at the radio, so frequencies can be reused much more often and can be closer to one another. The average cell is three to five miles across, with the distance depending on the expected number of users in a geographical area. Because the power output can be reduced to 3 watts for mobile phones and 0.6 watts or less for portable cellular sets, interference is limited. Each carrier uses approximately 312 frequencies for voice and data communication and 21 frequencies for control channels.

Controlled supervision and switching of calls is particularly critical in a mobile environment. Without the dynamic switching and control necessary to facilitate a seamless shift as the vehicle moves from one cell to another, all communication could be terminated.

2G—Digital Cellular Communications, TDMA, CDMA

The goal of cellular was to make more service available to vehicular users. Figure 14-2 shows the breakdown of the 666 radio channels for cellular service. These frequencies were assigned or set aside for two separate carriers in the 800- to 850-MHz range for transmit and 870 to 890 for receive frequencies. The upper half of each frequency allocation was reserved for the wireline companies. Wireline companies are the regulated providers (the local telcos, also known as the B [baby Bell] providers). The lower portion of each frequency allocation was assigned or reserved for nonwireline carriers, which are the competitors to the telephone carriers (known as the A [alternate] providers). Both operating carriers (the wireline and nonwireline) are licensed to operate in a specific geographic area. The areas are classified as the metropolitan service areas (MSAs) and rural service areas (RSAs). Each carrier used approximately 312 frequencies for voice/data communication and 21 channels for control channels.

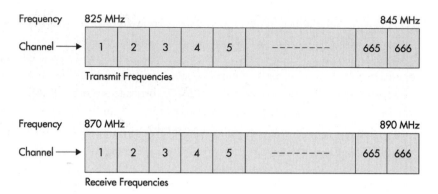

Figure 14-2 The 666 channels for cellular fall in the 800- to 850-MHz range. Channels in the middle of this band are used for paging and control, as well as a guard band between transmit and receive frequencies.

Cellular communications involve the following components:

- A cell—Using a frequency pattern from radio transmitters, the cellular concept produces a honeycomb pattern of overlapping cells of communication. A **cell** is a coverage area of an antenna or a cell tower. These cells can be minimal in size, making it possible to reuse the frequencies repeatedly. The idea of frequency reuse is what enables the cellular system to provide coverage for a greater number of subscribers. Although we draw them as symmetrical hexagonal shapes, in reality, they can be nearly any shape that can produce coverage.

- The MTSO—The cell towers are "dumb" antennas that connect back to a **mobile telephone switching office (MTSO)**. The MTSO is the equivalent of a Class 5 switch in the PSTN world. All intelligent decisions for the routing of calls take place in the MTSO, as well as new concepts required for cellular telephony, such as handoffs from one cell tower to another to maintain a call while moving.

- A handset—the handset is the end-user connection to the cellular network. A **handset** is a complex device incorporating a transmitter, a receiver, and a dial pad.

NOTE

Given that more and more users are utilizing cell phones, coverage becomes a big issue. Users want coverage everywhere, but many home-owner associations, municipalities, and parks have issued legislation to prevent "eyesore" cellular towers in the neighborhoods. Communities have taken the "Not in my backyard" approach, wanting service, but not wanting towers in the neighborhood. Several companies have addressed this issue by creating neighborhood-friendly cell towers. These include towers that look like flag poles, pine trees, or even palm trees. These towers meet the need without detracting from the natural beauty of the area. See Figure 14-3 and Figure 14-4 for examples of these cell sites.

Figure 14-3 In certain desert/tropical climates, a cell tower can be disguised as a palm tree, so its presence is less of an eyesore.

Figure 14-4 A cell tower is disguised as a pine tree.

The major difference between AMPS and Personal Communications Services (PCS)* is the use of control supervision and switching of calls to serve the cellular user adequately.

This is particularly true in a mobile environment when the vehicle moves from one cell to another. Dynamic switching and control are necessary to facilitate smooth and seamless handoff from one cell to another.

If this does not work properly, all communication may be terminated. The signal on conventional mobile radio telephones degrades as the vehicle moves farther away from the base station. This degradation frustrates both the caller and the called party. As the user goes beyond an area of coverage, the call is cut off, frustrating the calling and the called parties.

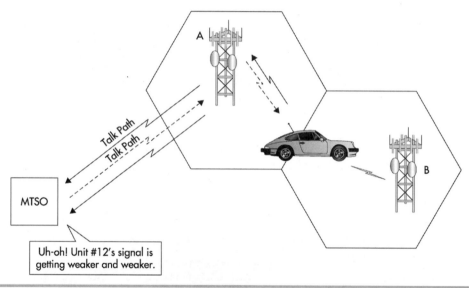

Figure 14-5 As the signal fades, the MTSO begins the handoff process.

With cellular communications, when a call is in progress and the caller moves away from the cell site toward a new cell, the call is handed off from one cell to another. Here is how **handoff** works: once a call is in progress and the handoff from cell-to-cell becomes necessary to keep it that way, the system initiates a change. As the cellular telephone approaches the imaginary boundary line, the signal strength transmitted back to the cell site starts to fall. The cell-site equipment sends a form of distress message to the mobile telephone switching office (MTSO)**, indicating the signal is getting weaker. The MTSO then orchestrates the passing of the call from one cell site to another. In Figure 14-5, the initial sequence begins as a cell site

---

*2G is PCS, but it should not be confused with Sprint PCS service.

**MTSO is an earlier term used to describe the central switching functions. Later, the term was replaced with MSC (mobile switching center) as the preferred embodiment.

senses the fading signal, sends out the distress message, and notifies the MTSO that something is going on.

Immediately after receiving the message from the cell site, the MTSO sends out a broadcast to the other cell sites in the area. The MTSO requests a determination of which site is receiving the cellular user's signal most strongly. This is called a **quality of service (QoS) measurement**. Each site responds accordingly. In Figure 14-6, the MTSO's initial broadcast goes out across the network.

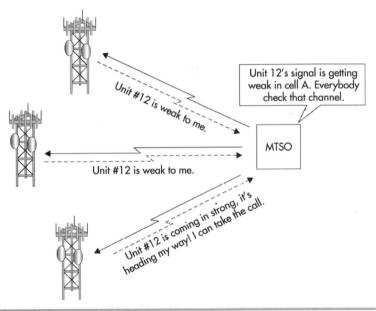

14

Figure 14-6 The distress call is sent from the MTSO to all cell sites in the network.

As the responses come back to the MTSO, the particular cell receiving the signal the strongest is then selected to accept the call (as long as it also has available capacity). The MTSO directs the targeted cell site to set up a voice path in parallel to the site losing the signal. When this is ready, the MTSO sends a command to the cellular set to resynthesize or go to the new frequency. The cellular set then retunes itself to the new frequency assigned to the receiving cell site, and the handoff takes place. This means the cell phone breaks the old connection, and then makes a new one, or what we refer to as "break before make." This takes approximately 100 to 200 milliseconds to enact. Figure 14-7 shows the handoff.

This might sound a little more complicated than it is. The designers recognized the original radio systems put out far too much power. Therefore, frequency reuse was not possible in a 100-mile radius. Using a lower-power output device, the radius of the radio transmission system is smaller. In fact, the cellular system was designed to operate in a range of an approximate

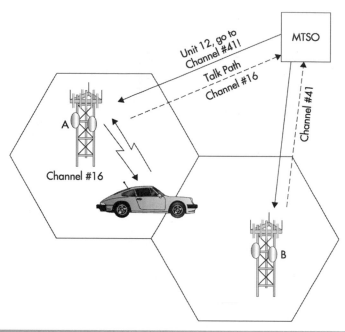

Figure 14-7 After the QoS measurements are received, the MTSO tells the handset to resynthesize and the handoff takes place.

three- to five-mile radius. If the power output is reduced to 10 to 15 watts, the radio transmission will travel a shorter distance. Therefore, the user must be closer to the equipment to receive the call. To accommodate this, the cellular cells include equipment placed (typically) in the center of each of these overlapping cells. The distance from the radio equipment to the user will be approximately one to two miles. Therefore, the system works more efficiently. In fact, in cellular systems, capacity is increased by reducing power, because it enables additional cell towers and increased frequency reuse.

With only a 10-watt output, the frequencies used in each of the cells can be reused repeatedly. A separation of at least two cells must exist, but that was taken into account. Figure 14-8 is a representation of a cell network with the honeycomb pattern, which is referred to as **N = 7** because seven different cells are in the pattern.

The carriers have been getting better at providing this coverage as the years have gone by. Many of the cellular suppliers now have provided for a seamless transition from cell-to-cell anywhere in the country. To do this, they have developed an interface into another telephone- or landline-based technique called signaling system 7 (SS7). SS7 was covered in depth in Chapter 4. Using SS7, the carriers can now hand a call off across the country without user involvement. It happens transparently. Figure 14-9 shows the SS7 linkage, where the MTSO

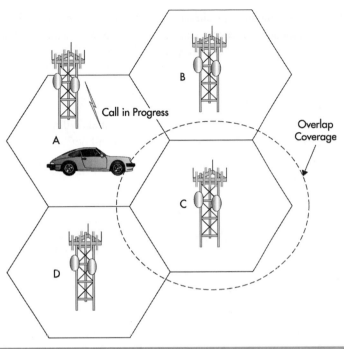

Figure 14-8 Cellular networks offer coverage in a honeycomb pattern in which a two-cell separation is used between sites for frequency reuse.

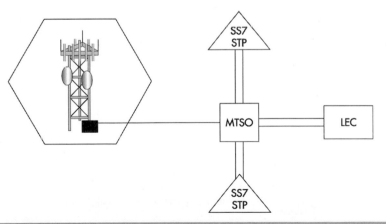

Figure 14-9 MTSOs utilize SS7 technology to ensure handoff without user involvement. SS7 also allows additional services and features to be added to cell service.

equipment is tied into a computer system called a **Signal Transfer Point (STP)**. In this figure, the MTSOs are tied to duplicate STPs as a means of providing redundancy in the network. With this interconnection, additional features were also provided in the cellular networks similar to the telephone networks.

The Telephone (Mobile) Set

The set houses a transceiver capable of tuning to all channels within an area. These are frequency-agile units capable of receiving/transmitting on all 666 frequencies, as opposed to the fixed-frequency units of old. The mobile set is shown in Figure 14-10. The major components of the unit are:

- Handset

- **Number assignment module (NAM)**—a chipset that holds an electronic fingerprint (a 32-bit binary sequence) and a 34-bit binary representation of the telephone number

- Logic unit

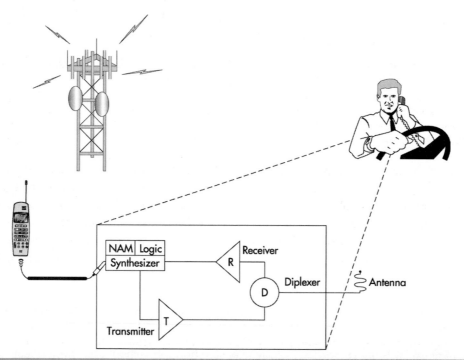

Figure 14-10 The modern mobile set with all the features indicated.

- Transmitter

- Receiver

- Frequency synthesizer (generation of frequencies under control of the logic unit)

- Diplexer—separates transmitter/receiver functions

- Antenna

Cellular's Success and Loss

In 1984, cellular communications became the hot button in the industry. This was the original attempt to add capacity to several systems around the country. In the preceding years, the mobile phone services and the IMTS were limited. An analog radio system will use analog input, such as voice communications. Because these systems were designed around voice applications, no one had any thought of the future transmission of data, fax, or packetized data from a vehicle or a mobile phone.

When cellular was first introduced, the industry experts were predicting that by the year 2000, approximately 900,000 users would be on the network conducting voice telephone calls. After all, it was a voice network designed to carry dial-up telephone calls. No one was sure what the acceptance rate would be of cellular radio/telephone services.

14

NOTE

Current estimates are 2 billion wireless subscribers worldwide by 2007! As of 2004, there were 1.1 billion GSM users, 140 to 150 million CDMA users, and 150 million TDMA subscribers (worldwide).

In 2004, the U.S. had approximately 200 million cellular users. This was a surprise to the industry experts, who had no idea of the pent-up demand. Approximately 150,000 new users sign up monthly. The problem is not one of acceptance and signing up new users but a problem of retaining users and encouraging them to use the service more. The churn ratio has been as high as 15 to 30 percent (**churn** is what happens when users change providers). This is a costly process for the providers and one they are trying to overcome. User frustration exists on three counts:

- **The high cost of the service** Depending on the location, the basic monthly service will range from $20 to $50 for 200 to 500 "anytime minutes." The per-minute charge for excess incoming or outgoing calls is $0.25 to $0.70. Roaming charges can also be $.65 to $.75/min if they are not included in the calling plan.

- **The possibility of getting poor transmission or reception on the network** This is a design problem that can be fixed.

- **The lack of available service** The network can get congested quickly, and if you are paying for the service, you obviously want it available constantly. Users typically don't want to hear about the providers' problems. To overcome this problem, many carriers have repeatedly split their cells into half and more, just to be able to use the frequencies repeatedly. Figure 14-11 shows where cell splitting has been performed. The graphic shows multiple smaller cells inside a normal cell. This might be overaccentuated, but it is primarily a means of showing how this can be accomplished.

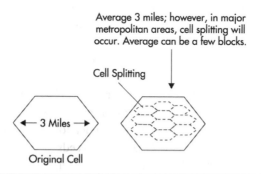

Figure 14-11 When the amount of subscribers within a cell begins to exceed the number of users supported, cells are split into smaller cells.

The capital costs of building the network are fixed and must be recuperated through usage. The worldwide marketplace is working in the carriers' favor—more and more people are utilizing cellular service as their primary (if not their only) voice communications service. Today, even children in elementary schools are utilizing these services to stay in touch with family and friends. The carriers are still trying to figure out how they can:

- Accommodate more users

- Encourage subscribers to use more price-sensitive services

- Generate new revenue

    We face a quandary in the industry:

- The carriers need more users to generate higher revenues to pay off the investment.

- The carriers must continue the evolution from analog to digital systems that will enable more efficient use of bandwidth (frequency spectrum).

- The need for security and protection against theft is putting pressure on carriers and users alike.

- Regulatory requirements [such as Local Number Portability (LNP) and enhanced 911] support increase costs without increasing revenues.

Analog systems do nothing for these three needs per se. Using either amplitude modulation or frequency modulation techniques, which were discussed in the data communications section of this book, to transmit voice on the radio signal uses all the available bandwidth (or most of it). Distance, noise, and other interference demand power, amplification, and bandwidth to deliver a quality service. This means the analog cellular carriers can support a single call on a single frequency (specific frequency). As such, the limitations of the systems are in channel availability on a given set of technologies.

If you consider the noisy nature of analog signals, you can also determine that quality is a matter of multiple factors, not the least of which will be congestion and atmospheric conditions.

Other concerns with analog systems rise from both security and fraud issues. The systems using a single frequency are subject to monitoring, but this is no different from the situation with any other airborne technique.

Furthermore, when the analog network can be penetrated fraudulently, we must be concerned. This is not strictly a problem with analog systems. As previously mentioned, the analog system was designed to provide the benefit of quick communications while on the road. Because this is considered a service that would meet the telephone needs of users on the go, the thought of heavy penetration was minimally addressed. However, as the MSAs began expanding, the carriers realized the analog systems were limited. With only a single user on a frequency, congestion in the MSA began to be a tremendous problem.

To ease congestion, many carriers began splitting their cells and making them into a tiered layout. By creating smaller cells, the network can support more users, but a limit exists to how far we can "shrink" a cell. When cell splitting takes place, other issues become problematic for the carriers. The more cells in use (because of splitting), the more critical is the arrangement of frequencies available to use. Furthermore, as smaller cells are created through splitting, other issues (shown in Table 14-1) become problematic.

Issue	Problem/Symptom
More equipment	Cost issues associated with buying the equipment. A cell site costs in the range of $650,000 to $800,000.
Real estate	Getting the space to mount added equipment plus local ordinances in the area. Consumer pressures leading to the not-in-my-backyard syndrome.
Power	Remote generation equipment required that is a cost and a security problem.
Logistical problems	Managing the new sites, new frequencies, and other ancillary services for a much larger equipment base.

Table 14-1 Issues Surrounding Cell-Site Splitting.

Because these problems have plagued the industry for some time, this puts an additional financial burden on the carriers as they attempt to match need with return on investment. As the industry began to search for new solutions, other uses of cellular communications began to crop up, putting an additional load on the service.

The cellular systems were designed for the road warrior driving around with a vehicular telephone. Initial installations were handled in cars and trucks. However, as the technology improved, transportable telephones became a requirement for cellular users. Why should they be required to remain in the vehicle to use the service? Units could be mounted in the vehicle, and when the user got out, the set could be removed and used for several hours of standby operation and one hour of online operation. This opened a whole new avenue for service opportunities. The transportables were initially expensive, but prices dropped to far more reasonable rates (in the range of $300 to $600), and now they are routinely provided at no charge with a service plan. Mobility became more flexible for the cellular user, who was no longer relegated to the vehicle. Figure 14-12 shows the transportable unit. This is still popular with contractors doing construction, landscaping, and remote facilities work when they roam outside their normal geographic coverage areas. In many cases, these phones are used when a contractor is on the periphery of a cell.

Figure 14-12 The transportable unit was an improvement over the car phone. These units allowed mobility for contractors working in remote areas.

As prices were dropping for the vehicle telephone, so, too, were those for the hand-held telephones. Recently, ads in the trade magazines and local newspapers around the U.S. have been offering the hand-held devices for a mere $0 to $15 with a two-year subscription to the carrier's network. The retail value of these telephones is as low as $360 or as high as $600. To entice people to buy the phones and use the service, the providers offer the sets at less than retail (loss leader). This has come a long way from the initial days of the cellular networks in 1984.

Features exploded also with the introduction of:

- Voice messaging
- Redial
- Display
- Call forwarding
- Memory
- Hands-free operation

Subcompact or shirt-pocket flip telephones caught on. Users became enamored with the technology, and the price was almost too good to pass up. These latest and greatest models have between 0.3 and 0.6 watts of power output; they are totally portable and accessible.

These evolutions in the analog arena were all driving forces in the use and acceptance of cellular communications. As the congestion problem continued to go unsolved, however, the carriers entered a new era. The whole world has been evolving to digital transmission systems on the local and long-distance scene. This evolution to digital has many benefits for the standard wire-based carriers, which include

- Higher usage
- Better quality
- Multiple techniques
- Digital speeds

Digital Cellular Evolution

Each move to digital requires newer equipment, which means capital investments for the PCS carriers. Moreover, as these carriers compete for radio frequency spectrum, they have to make significant investments during an auction from the FCC. This places an immense financial burden on the carriers before they even begin the construction of their networks.

Digital

Digital transmission delivers better multiplexing schemes, so the carriers can get more users on an already-strained radio-frequency spectrum. Additional possibilities for enhancing security and reducing fraud are also addressed with digital cellular. Again, this appears to be a win-win situation for the carriers. Table 14-2 provides a summary of the key benefits for the cellular carriers' migration to digital communications.

Key Benefits of Digital

Lower costs overall. Initially conversion will be expensive, but longer range will be less.

More users on the same or fewer frequencies and spectrum.

Better security than offered by the analog transport systems.

Less risk of theft and fraud.

Table 14-2 Benefits of Migrating to Digital Services.

NOTE

According to the Federal Communications Commission's (FCC) 8th Annual State of Competition Report on the wireless industry, as of 2003, 97 percent of the U.S. population lived in counties where digital mobile telephone services were offered. The cellular industry states that 92 percent of subscribers are for digital service.

This statistic can be somewhat misleading as large parts of those counties are rural areas served only by analog service. The FCC requires carriers to continue operating analog networks until February 18, 2008. This was done to allow analog users to extend the life of their analog devices. After 2008, it is expected that all networks in the U.S. will complete the transition to digital. This rural evolution will be a slow transition because of the number of cell sites affected and the cost of upgrading each site. Note that analog subscribers should not count on service for their analog phones after that date.

In 2005, there were still 35 million analog users, and many digital users "roamed" onto analog networks.

The digital techniques available to the carriers for PCS are:

- TDMA
- GSM
- CDMA

The two choices we typically saw in this arena were the use of digital cellular and PCS. Digital cellular uses the 800- to 900-MHz frequency bands, whereas PCS was introduced in the 1,900-MHz frequency bands, which became available in the mid-1990s as a reaction by the FCC to the need for additional services and carriers. Carriers and manufacturers are using a mix of these systems. The various means of implementing these systems have brought about several discussions regarding the benefits and losses of each choice. The real issue is that both exist and can be used differently.

Time Division Multiple Access (TDMA)

Time Division Multiple Access (TDMA) uses a time division-multiplexing scheme where time slices are allocated to multiple conversations. Multiple users share a single radio frequency without interfering with each other because they are kept separate by using fixed-timeslots. The current standard for **North American TDMA (NA-TDMA)** divides a single channel into six timeslots. Then, three different conversations use the timeslots by allocating two slots per conversation. This provides a threefold increase in the number of users on the same radio-frequency spectrum. Although TDMA deals typically with an analog to digital conversion using a typical pulse-code modulation technique, it performs differently in a radio transmission.

Pulse Coded Modulation (PCM) is translated into a quadrature phase-shift keying (QPSK) technique, thereby producing a four-phased shift, doubling the rate for data transmission. Figure 14-13 shows the typical timeslotting mechanism or TDMA.

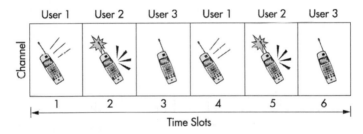

Figure 14-13 North American TDMA splits the 30-kHz channel into six timeslots. Each user gets two timeslots for his or her conversation. The pairing arrangements of timeslots are (1,4), (2,5), and (3,6).

The wireless industry began to deploy TDMA back in 1995 when the scarce radio-frequency spectrum problem became most noticeable. The intent was to improve the quality of radio transmission, as well as the efficiency usage of the limited spectrum available. TDMA can correctly increase the number of users on the RF by three times. We can see why it is so popular.

What Is a Microcell?

MICROCELLS

Microcells are used for densely populated areas. By splitting the existing areas into smaller cells, the number of channels available is increased, as is the capacity of the cells. The power level of the transmitters used in these cells is then decreased, reducing the possibility of interference among neighboring cells. Some of the microcells may be as small as .1 to 1 km, depending on the need. The cell splitting will often use the reduced power and the greater coverage to satisfy hot spots or dead spots in the network.

PICOCELLS

Picocells are nothing more than smaller versions of microcells. A **picocell** covers a 50- to 200-foot radius, allowing more frequencies to be reused in a smaller geographic area.

TDMA has another advantage over the older analog (FDMA) techniques. Here the analog transmission across the 800-MHz frequency band (in North America, it is 800 MHz; in much of the world, it is 900 MHz) supports the primary service, that being voice. The TDMA architecture uses a PCM input to the RF spectrum. Therefore, TDMA can also support digital services or data in increments of 64 Kbps. For now, many users are happy with the 64-Kbps options.

This is an attractive opportunity for the carriers that are developing PCS and digital cellular using the industry standards. The two standards still in use today include *IS-54,* which is the first evolution to TDMA from FDMA for digital cellular, and *IS-136,* the latest and greatest technology for 1,900-MHz PCS service. When the IS-136 service was introduced, it allowed the addition of data and other services. These include the short message service (SMS), caller-ID display, data transmission, and other service levels.

Using a TDMA approach, carriers feel they can meet the needs for voice, data, and video integration for the future.

The CDMA Cellular Standard

In cellular telephony, CDMA is a digital multiple-access technique specified by the Telecommunications Industry Association (TIA) as IS-95 (also called cdmaOne). Back in March 1992, the TIA created the TR-45.5 subcommittee. This committee's charter was to develop a spread-spectrum digital cellular standard. In July of 1993, the TIA gave its approval of the CDMA IS-95 standard.

IS-95 systems divide the radio spectrum into 1.25-MHz-wide carriers. One of the unique aspects of CDMA is that although the number of phone calls a carrier can handle is certainly limited, it is not fixed as it is with AMPS and TDMA. Instead, a variable number of calls can be handled at the same time in the same frequency carrier. The capacity will depend on many other factors.

Code Division Multiple Access (CDMA), unique digital codes known as Walsh codes, rather than separate radio frequencies or channels, are used to differentiate subscribers. The codes are shared by both the mobile station (cellular phone) and the base station, and they are called **pseudorandom code sequences**. Multiple users can share the same range of radio spectrum.

CDMA-PCS   What is CDMA? **CdmaOne (IS-95)** is a spread-spectrum technology, which means it spreads the information contained in a particular signal over a much greater bandwidth (in this case, 1.25 MHz). Figure 14-14 shows direct-sequence spread spectrum (DSSS) CDMA. IS-95 uses a multiple-access spectrum-spreading technique called direct-sequence (DS) CDMA.

During a conversation (a cellular call), each user is assigned a binary, direct-sequence

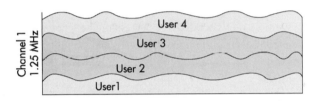

Figure 14-14 CDMA places multiple users on a single 1.25-MHz channel. Multiple conversations are "stacked" on top of other conversations through the use of the Walsh code.

64-bit Walsh code. The **DS code** is a signal generated by linear modulation with wideband pseudorandom noise (PN) sequences. Consequently, DS CDMA needs to use a much wider signal than other technologies. Wideband signals reduce interference and enable one-cell frequency reuse. No time division occurs; all users use the entire carrier all the time. CDMA cell coverage is contingent on the way the system is designed.

The three primary system characteristics include:

- Coverage
- Quality
- Capacity

These parameters must be balanced to achieve the highest level of system performance. In a CDMA system, these three characteristics are tightly interrelated. Higher capacity might be achieved through some degree of degradation in coverage and/or quality. Because these parameters are all intertwined, operators cannot have the best of all worlds—3 times wider coverage, 40 times capacity, and CD-quality sound.

Qualcomm engineered the use of both 8- and 13-Kbps vocoders (sound effects that can make a human voice sound synthetic). The best balance point may differ from one cell to another. Sites in dense downtown areas may trade off coverage for increased capacity. However, at the outer edges of a system where we expect fewer users, capacity might be sacrificed for the size of the coverage area.

Voice activity detection is another variable that helps increase the capacity of a CDMA system. IS-95 takes advantage of voice activity gain through the use of variable rate vocoders. We must understand that in a typical phone conversation, a person is actively talking only about 25 to 35 percent of the time. The difference is spent listening to the other party or is quiet time when neither party is speaking. The principle behind the variable rate vocoder is to have it run at high speed, providing the best speech quality, only when voice activity is detected.

When no speech is detected, the vocoder will drop its encoding rate because no reason exists to have high-speed encoding for silence. The encoded rate can drop from 13 or 8 to 4, 2 or even 1 Kbps. The variable-rate vocoder frees up channel capacity in this case and only uses the higher rates as needed. Because the level of interference created by all the users directly determines system capacity, and voice activity detection reduces the noise level in the system, capacity can be maximized.

Capacity Improvements   **Capacity** is a function of the number of channels installed in a specific coverage area. Using an example of what we have already seen in an AMPS environment, let's look at the possibilities of the use of CDMA in the same geographic area. Earlier in this chapter, we discussed how carriers tried to alleviate congestion in the AMPS network by cell splitting. This cell-splitting configuration could support upward of 300 channels in the same physical area of a cell. Although cell splitting alleviates some congestion, it comes at a premium price: the network also has to be planned carefully to avoid interference from neighboring cells. The carriers were looking for alternative means of providing coverage.

One CDMA carrier requires 1.25 MHz of bandwidth. Because three-sector AMPS uses a seven-cell reuse pattern, this example will spread the 1.25 MHz across seven cell sites. Each cell site would then lose 180 kHz of spectrum (1.25 MHz/7 = 0.180 MHz).Thus, a total of six AMPS channels must be removed from each cell site (180 kHz/30 kHz/AMPS channel = 6). The result means that 42 AMPS channels must be removed to support one CDMA carrier.

Unlike AMPS, CDMA can use the same 1.25 MHz in all three sectors in each of the seven cells, because the Walsh code and PN technologies can allow the same frequency to be broadcast from overlapping towers without degrading reception from the cellular phone. Many of the system designs from Motorola, for example, support 18 effective traffic channels per sector in a three-sector system. This provides 54 effective channels per cell. Given the seven cells, CDMA supports 378 channels. Hence, in this example, CDMA achieves capacity gains of nine times that of AMPS (378/42 = 9).We continually hear of eightfold to tenfold increases with CDMA. This example clearly points this out.

CDMA Benefits   When implemented in a cellular telephone system, CDMA technology provides many additional benefits to cellular operators and their subscribers.
Table 14-3 summarizes the benefits of CDMA.

Description	Benefit Goes To
1. Capacity increases of 8 to 10 times that of an AMPS analog system	Cellular provider: The increased revenues and the same radio frequencies, helping service providers increase their profitability. CDMA spread-spectrum technology can provide up to 10 times the capacity of analog equipment and more than 3 times the capacity of other digital platforms such as TDMA. With dual-mode phones, CDMA is also compatible with other technologies for seamless widespread roaming coverage.
2. Improved call quality, with better and more consistent sound as compared to AMPS system	Cellular provider and user: Improved overall performance and quality of voice communications. CDMA filters out background noise, crosstalk, and interference, delivering improved voice quality, greater privacy, and enhanced call quality. The CDMA variable rate vocoder engineered by Qualcomm translates voice into 0's and 1's. These vocoders operate at the highest translation rates possible (8 Kbps or 13 Kbps). This creates crystal-clear voice and also maximizes your system capacity. Many of the compression schemes in use today operate at 5.3 to 6.3 Kbps, have a tendency of distorting the voice conversation, and have trouble passing data communications. CDMA combines multiple signals and improves signal strength. This nearly eliminates interference and fading. Electrical noise (computer noise) and acoustic noise (conversations) are filtered out. This is possible by using narrow bandwidth corresponding to the frequency of the human voice.
3. Simplified system planning through the use of the same frequency in every sector of every cell	Cellular provider: Ease of design and installation. Less frequency coordination required and less interference inside cells and/or between cells. CDMA systems can be deployed and expanded faster and more cost-effectively. Because they require fewer cell sites, CDMA networks can be deployed faster.
4. Enhanced privacy	Cellular provider and user: Enhanced security means less worry. Less reluctance to use the system. CDMA uses a digitally encoded, spread-spectrum transmission that resists eavesdropping. Designed with about 4.4 trillion codes, CDMA virtually eliminates cloning and other types of fraud.

Table 14-3 CDMA Benefits Are Many. *(Continued)*

14

Description	Benefit Goes To
5. Improved coverage characteristics, creating the possibility of fewer cell sites	Cellular provider: More coverage and less cost all at the same time, fewer calls dropped during handoff because fewer handoff conditions will be present. CDMA-patented soft handoff method of passing calls between cells sharply reduces the risk of disruption or dropped calls during a handoff. The process of soft handoff leads to fewer drooped calls as two or three cells are monitoring a call at any given time. CDMA spread-spectrum signal also provides the greatest coverage, allowing networks to be built with fewer cell sites than other wireless technologies. Fewer cell sites reduce operating expenses, which results in savings to both operators and consumers.
6. Increased talk time for portables	User has fewer hassles and less battery replacement/charging. Fewer calls will drop due to lack of power. Users can leave their phone on with CDMA. CDMA uses power control to monitor the power your system and handset need at any time. CDMA handsets typically transmit at the lowest power levels in the industry, enabling longer battery life, which results in longer talk time and standby time. CDMA handsets can also incorporate smaller batteries, resulting in smaller, lighter-weight phones. They are therefore easier to carry and easier to use.
7. Bandwidth on demand	User: Growing access and more useful bandwidth utilization in CDMA technology enable users to access a wide range of new services, including caller identification, short messaging services, and Internet connections. Simultaneous voice and data calls are also possible using CDMA technology. A wideband CDMA channel provides a common resource that all mobiles in a system utilize based on their own specific needs, whether they are transmitting voice, data, facsimile, or other applications.
8. Packetized data	CDMA networks are built with standard IP packet data protocols. Other networks require costly upgrades to add new packet data equipment in the network and will require new packet data phones. Standard CDMA phones already have TCP/IP and PPP protocols built into them.

Table 14-3 ICDMA Benefits Are Many.

CDMA Today   CDMA is the fastest-growing wireless communications technology today throughout the world. Currently, CDMA offers the fastest data rates for wireless data applications with up to 144 Kbps and the promise of up to 2 Mbps in CDMA2000-EVDO. This is a given, whereas the use of General Packet Radio Service (covered in the following section) currently only offers 28.8 Kbps and promises 170 Kbps for the future, and EDGE is promising data rates of 384 Kbps. CDMA is also the technology of choice for many of the 3G products and services. A single CDMA standard with three modes provides flexibility for all operators to meet the growing demand for advanced voice and data services. Probably the most important concept to any cellular telephone system is **multiple access**, or how many simultaneous users can be supported. In other words, a large number of users share a common pool of radio channels and any user can gain access to any channel. (No user is permanently assigned to the same channel; instead they compete for the right to use the first available channel.) A channel can be thought of as a slice of the limited radio-frequency spectrum, temporarily allocated to someone's phone call. Multiple access defines how the radio spectrum is divided into channels and how channels are allocated to the users of the system.

Soft versus Hard Handoff   Traditional cellular systems use a **hard handoff**, whereby the mobile drops a channel before picking up the next channel; as we described earlier this is a break before make handoff. A **soft handoff** occurs when two or more cell sites monitor a mobile user and the transcoder circuitry compares the quality of the frames from the two receiving cell sites frame-by-frame. The system can take advantage of the moment-by-moment changes in signal strength at each of the two cells to pick out the best signal.

To make sure the best possible frame is used in the decoding process, the transcoder can toggle back and forth between the cell sites involved in a soft handoff on a frame-by-frame basis (if that is what is required to select the best quality of conversation).

These soft handoffs also contribute to high call quality by providing a "make before break" connection. How many times have we used the older systems and gotten cut off in the handoff process? This dropped call is a result of when the RF connection breaks from one cell to establish the call at the destination cell during a handoff. We hear this as a short disruption of speech with non-CDMA technologies. Narrow-band technologies compete for the signal. When cell *B* wins out over cell *A,* the user is dropped by cell *A* (hard handoff). With CDMA, the cells work together as a team to achieve the best possible information stream, even if it is shared among the cells. Eventually, cell *A* will no longer receive a strong enough signal from the mobile, and the transcoder will only be obtaining frames from cell *B*. The handoff will have been completed, undetected by the user. CDMA handoffs do not create the hole in speech that is heard in other technologies.

Some cellular systems also suffer from the ping-pong effect of a call being repetitively switched back and forth between two cells when the subscriber unit is moving along a cell border. At worst, such a situation increases the chance of a call getting dropped during one of the handoffs, and at a minimum, it causes noisier handoffs. CDMA is a soft handoff and avoids this problem entirely. Finally, because a CDMA call can be in a soft handoff condition among three cells at the same time, the chances of a dropped call are greatly reduced. CDMA also provides for softer handoffs. A **softer handoff** occurs when a subscriber is simultaneously communicating with more than one sector of the same cell.

14

Over-the-Air Activation   **Over-the-Air Activation (OTA)** is a feature that is key to the future business plans of many wireless operators. *OTA*, developed by the CDMA Development Group, enables a potential cellular-service subscriber to activate new cellular service without the intervention of a third party, such as an authorized dealer. A cellular user can activate a user-controlled feature and service. One of the primary objectives of OTA is to provide a secure authentication key to a mobile station to facilitate the authentication process. **Authentication** is the process by which information is exchanged between a mobile station and the network for the purpose of confirming and validating the identity of the mobile device. A successful outcome to the authentication process occurs only when it is demonstrated that the mobile station and the network possess identical sets of shared secret data (keys).

The OTA feature consists of over-the-air programming of the number assignment modules (NAMs), which are used to authorize cellular telecommunications service with a specific service provider. The feature incorporates an authentication key-exchange agreement algorithm. This algorithm allows the network to exchange authentication key parameters with a mobile station. These parameters are used to generate the authentication key used to generate the shared secret data. The authentication key-exchange agreement algorithm enhances security for the subscriber and reduces the potential for fraudulent use of cellular telecommunications service. This is similar to an encryption key used between computer systems. If you have the correct code (key), you can access information. If you do not have the appropriate key, you cannot read the data.

This feature alone has done much to substantially reduce distribution and activation costs for the providers and reduce frustration for the users. Other features can be activated by these specifications. For example, subscribers could gain easy access to other CDMA systems through automatic updates of roaming information or a new feature can be turned on, without the user ever having to go to the cellular provider's location.

What About Data?   CDMA circuit-switched services provide asynchronous data and facsimile transmission using an **Interworking Unit (IWU).** The IWU provides the functions needed for the mobile equipment to communicate with fixed-end equipment in a public network. This architecture adapts the air interface and landlines by providing retransmission protocols unique to the CDMA air interface, called the Radio Link Protocol (RLP), and rate adaptation to the landline modems.

Various data services are initiated as service options during call setup or any time during a call. The service option negotiation process specifies whether the service option will be used for the primary or secondary traffic. Therefore, the user can switch among voice, data, and fax service simply by initiating and terminating the appropriate service options.

This has led to innovations by Motorola and others in the CDG to develop and support the *L* interface, TIA standard IS-687 PN3473. The *L* interface allows both IWUs and Data Gateways to communicate with any infrastructure equipment that also uses this interface.

Circuit Mode Asynchronous Data/Fax Rates   CDMA systems support synchronous and asynchronous data services that emulate a traditional dial-up modem connection to the PSTN. In the CDMA system, the modem is not in the subscriber unit, but in the network. This enables direct digital communications over the radio channel. It preserves the advantages of true digital transmission, eliminating the need to convert from digital to analog and then back to digital. Using this approach enables a subscriber unit to transparently communicate with any landline modem.

The landline-user modem can support any existing V-Series modulation techniques. Typically, a data rate of 9.6 Kbps is supported with the 8-Kbps vocoder and 14.4 Kbps with the 13-Kbps vocoder. Higher speeds have been endorsed and designed to support 64 Kbps. Any of the transmission rates in the CDMA system can be used for data.

To support efficient transmission, flow control is an integral part of the CDMA system. Thus, the air interface transmission rate need not match the landline rate. For example, the air interface rate can be higher than the landline rate to reduce delay. Similarly, the air interface rate can be lower than the landline rate to support more users having simultaneous traffic demands. The CDMA system also supports Group III fax standards, which operate from 9.6 to 14.4 Kbps.

14

Simultaneous Voice and Data   CDMA systems support the simultaneous transmission of voice and data. The two digital streams will be multiplexed on a frame-by-frame basis with voice being given priority over data to maintain voice quality. As higher data-rate channels are introduced later, data throughput will increase. Several modes of operation, including turning on and off voice service during a data call or adding data to a voice call in progress, will be supported.

Packet Data Services   CDMA is defined as a lower-level protocol. The CDMA system will support higher-level protocols commonly used for data communications, such as TCP/IP. As the layers 1 and 2 of the OSI model, CDMA will carry the traditional IP packets. All CDMA sets today support the inherent passing of IP datagrams onto the channel. Simultaneous voice and data will be available in the case of packet data applications. Using a PCMCIA card in a PDA or laptop, we can access an "always on" packet-switching network at data rates of 144 to 300 Kbps (averaging about 100 to 200 Kbps) using CdmaOne and cdma2000. Newer 1X EV technologies can now support data rates of 400 to 500 Kbps and soon will approach 2-Mbps data transfer rates.

GSM

In 1982, to overcome the incompatibility problems associated with different international cellular networks, the Conference of European Posts and Telecommunications (CEPT) formed the Groupe Spécial Mobile (GSM) study group. GSM's charter was to develop a standardized pan-European mobile cellular radio system [the GSM acronym later became **Global System for Mobile Communications (GSM)**].

The standardized system had to meet certain criteria. The goals were that the new systems would provide:

- Improved spectrum efficiency

- International roaming capability

- Low-cost mobile sets and base stations

- Good speech quality

- Compatibility with other systems such as ISDN (Integrated Services Digital Network)*

- Capability to support new services

Unlike the existing cellular systems of the period that were developed using an analog technology, the GSM system was developed using a digital technology.

GSM Architecture

A GSM network is composed of several functional entities whose functions and interfaces are defined. The GSM network can be divided into three broad parts. The subscriber carries the **Mobile Station (MS)** (also called a handset); the **Base Station Subsystem (BSS)** controls the radio link with the MS; and the Network Subsystem, the main part of which is the **mobile services switching center (MSC)**, performs the switching of calls between the mobile and other fixed or mobile network users, as well as management of mobile services, such as authentication.

The MS and the BSS communicate across the U_m interface, also known as the air interface or radio link. The BSS communicates with the network service switching center across the *A* interface. The GSM architecture also houses several databases for billing and providing value-added services, such as SMS, wireless web access, e-mail, roaming, and others.

The Mobile Set   The mobile phone consists of two separate components, each having its own specific role. The two components include the:

1. Mobile Equipment—a cellular phone, which at the time was to be owned by the telephone company or the cellular provider, not the end user. That all changed after the privatization of these entities.

2. **Subscriber Identity Module (or SIM card)**—a smart card that was a value-added feature of GSM. Although the SIM is not required, it was built into international GSM as a means of providing the ubiquitous service that the GSM study group was trying to accomplish.

---

*ISDN was heavily deployed in Europe and other parts of the world, whereas in the U.S., it was barely deployed.

SIM   The SIM provides personal mobility, so the user can have access to all subscribed services, irrespective of both the location of the terminal and the use of a specific terminal. By inserting the SIM card into another GSM cellular phone, the user can receive calls at that phone, make calls from that phone, or receive other subscribed services. See Figure 14-15 for a representation of the SIM.

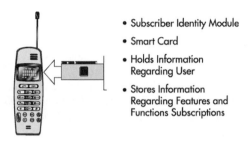

- Subscriber Identity Module
- Smart Card
- Holds Information Regarding User
- Stores Information Regarding Features and Functions Subscriptions

Figure 14-15 The mobile set can use an intelligent chip called a SIM card to make it work. The SIM stores user information, as well as the phone-book feature of the phone.

The mobile equipment is uniquely identified by the **International Mobile Equipment Identity (IMEI)**. The SIM card contains the **International Mobile Subscriber Identity (IMSI)**, identifying the subscriber, a secret key for authentication, and other user information. The IMEI and the IMSI are independent, thereby providing personal mobility. The SIM card may be protected against unauthorized use by a password or personal identity number (PIN).

Frequencies Allocated   In principle, the GSM system can be implemented in any frequency band. However, the GSM terminals are available in several bands. Furthermore, GSM terminals may incorporate one or more of the GSM frequency bands listed in the following to facilitate roaming on a global basis.

- **GSM 900**—Initially, the 890- to 915-MHz frequencies paired with the 935- to 960-MHz were used in GSM Primary. Later, additional channel capacity was added to be 880 to 915 MHz paired with 925- to 960-MHz bands. This added 10 MHz to the overall spectrum.

- **GSM 1900** (also called PCS in the U.S.)—1850 to 1910 MHz paired with 1930 to 1990 MHz. In the previous bands, mobile stations transmit in the lower-frequency sub-band and base stations transmit in the higher-frequency sub-band.

CAUTION

Although GSM in the U.S. operates at 800 and 1900 MHz, in the rest of the world, the European version of GSM (EGSM) operates in the 900- and 1800-MHz frequencies. The main reason for this difference was the frequencies available to the carriers. In the U.S., the 900-MHz band had been given as an open frequency in which many cordless phones transmitted. In 178 countries worldwide, GSM operates in the European configuration at the following frequencies.

GSM 900—880 to 915 MHz paired with 925 to 960 MHz.

GSM 1800 (also called DCS 1800) —1710 to 1785 MHz paired with 1805 to 1880 MHz.

To overcome the frequency problems associated with traveling between the EGSM and GSM standard, newer GSM phones operate in the following bands: EGSM 900, GSM 1800, and GSM 1900. This configuration allows the phones to be utilized worldwide, until the U.S. reclaims the 900-MHz frequency band.

Frequency Pairing

The pairing is shown as the way of handling the 45-MHz separations. Remember, Channel 0 was not used. It was reserved as a guard band from the lower frequencies to prevent interference.

Extended GSM   Once the added channels were implemented, the additional channels were still paired at 45-MHz separation. Because Channel 974 was not used, it became the guard band for the lower frequencies below 880 MHz and 925 MHz The initial Channel 0 in the primary GSM band is now used because of this shift.

DCS-1800 Frequency Pairing

In the 1800-MHz range, the channels are numbered from 512 to 885 and paired at 95-MHz spacing. Channel 512 is not used in both directions; it acts as a guard band from the lower frequencies and prevents interference.

U.S. Division of 1900 MHz

In the U.S., things are done differently. The FCC has allocated the 1900-MHz frequencies to PCS. Moreover, to distribute the frequencies to a multitude of suppliers, the FCC set aside the following blocks of capacity:

The U.S. was broken into 51 Major Trading Areas (MTAs). In each of these are three blocks of 15 MHz allocated for the operators. In addition, 493 Basic Trading Areas (BTAs) were assigned, and in each of the 493 BTAs, three blocks of 5-MHz spectrum were assigned.

FCC assigned the licenses over a ten-year period. In general, two operators are in each of the MTAs and a minimum of four operators are in each of the BTAs.

TDMA Frames   In GSM, the 25 MHz of spectrum is divided into 124 carrier channels that are 200 kHz wide. Normally a 25-MHz frequency band can provide 125 channels, but the first carrier frequency is used as a guard band between GSM and other services working on lower frequencies. Each carrier frequency is then divided in time, using a TDMA scheme. This scheme splits the 200-kHz radio channel into eight timeslots.

A **burst** is the unit of time in a TDMA system, and it lasts approximately 0.577 ms. A **TDMA frame** made up of eight bursts lasts 4.615 ms. Each of the eight timeslots that form a TDMA frame are then assigned to a user.

CAUTION

14

Although GSM utilizes TDMA, it uses an eight-timeslot-burst arrangement. This differs from North American TDMA, where six timeslots are used. In GSM, each 200-kHz channel is shared by eight users and each user gets 25 kHz in each direction.

GSM FDMA/TDMA Combination   To enable multiple access, GSM utilizes a blending of FDMA and TDMA. This combination is used to overcome the problems introduced in each individual scheme. In the case of FDMA, frequencies are divided into smaller ranges of frequency slots and each of these slots is assigned to a user during a call. Although this method will result in an increase of the number of users, it is not efficient in the case of high user demand. On the other hand, TDMA assigns a timeslot to each user for utilizing the entire frequency. Similarly, this will become easily overloaded when encountering high user demand. Hence, GSM uses a two-dimensional access scheme.

GSM uses the combined FDMA and TDMA architecture to provide the most efficient operation within the scope of price and reasonable data. The Physical Channels are TDMA timeslots, and the Radio Channels are frequencies. This scheme divides the entire frequency bandwidth into several smaller pieces, as in FDMA, and each of these frequency slots is to be divided into eight timeslots in a full-rate configuration. Figure 14-16 shows the breakdown of 200-kHz channels into the eight timeslot arrangement.

The Mobile Switching Center Service Areas   GSM utilizes a slightly different configuration for the service areas over traditional cellular service. The MTSO in cellular is configured as a MSC with access to the databases to decide if a user requires service. The MSC service area is further broken down into **Location Areas (LAs)**. Several LAs are within the MSC's jurisdiction.

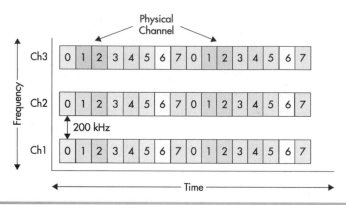

Figure 14-16 GSM utilizes TDMA and FDMA with 200-kHz radio channels with eight timeslots.

Location Areas   The LAs are then broken down into the cells. A cell is an identity served by one BTS. The MS distinguishes between cells by using the Base Station Identification Code (BSIC) that the cell site broadcasts over the air.

Location Updates   The purpose of a location update in any network is to let the network know the subscriber's approximate location. This allows the network to operate more efficiently, especially as it pertains to the paging capability. A subscriber is only paged in the last known (registered) network LA rather than across an entire network.

An LA within the GSM network is a unique area that normally consists of anywhere from one to a number of cells.

The Multiframe

Each group of eight timeslots is called a TDMA frame, which is transmitted every 4.615 ms. TDMA frames are further grouped into multiframes to carry control signals. There are two types of multiframe, containing 26 or 51 TDMA frames. The 26-frame multiframe contains 24 Traffic Channels (TCH) and two Slow Associated Control Channels (SACCH), which supervise each call in progress. The SACCH in Frame 12 contains eight channels, one for each of the eight connections carried by the TCHs. The SACCH in Frame 25 is not currently used but will carry eight additional SACCH channels when half-rate (half the speech rate) traffic is implemented. A **Fast Associated Control Channel (FACCH)** works by stealing slots from a traffic channel to transmit power control and hand over signaling messages. Setting one of the control bits in the timeslot burst controls the channel stealing.

In addition to the Associated Control Channels, there are several other control channels, which (except for the Stand-Alone Dedicated Control Channel) are implemented in timeslot 0 of specified TDMA frames in a 51-frame multiframe, implemented on a nonhopping carrier frequency in each cell. The control channels include:

- Broadcast Control Channel (BCCH). Continually broadcasts—on the downlink—information including base station identity, frequency allocations, and frequency hopping sequences.

- Stand-Alone Dedicated Control Channel (SDCCH). Used for registration, authentication, call setup, and location updating. Implemented on a timeslot, together with its SACCH, selected by the system operator.

- Common Control Channel (CCCH). Composed of three control channels used during call origination and call paging.

- Random Access Channel (RACH). A slotted Aloha channel to request access to the network.

- Paging Channel (PCH). Used to alert the mobile station of an incoming call.

- Access Grant Channel (AGCH). Used to allocate an SDCCH to a mobile for signaling, following a request on the RACH.

14

Control Channels

Control Channels do not carry user data (voice, data, or fax). Control channels carry data used by the network such as radio system alignment, efficiency, and timing. There are four classes of Control Channels:

- Broadcast Control Channels

- Common Control Channels

- Dedicated Control Channels

- Associated Control Channels

Only the base station transmits Broadcast Channels. These are intended to provide sufficient information to the mobile station to synchronize with the network.

The BCCH informs the mobile about specific parameters to identify the network and gain access to the network. The parameters include the

- Location Area Code

- MNC

- Frequencies to use from adjacent cells

Frequency Correction Channel (FCCH)

The Frequency Correction Channel (FCCH) provides frequency synchronization information in a burst, is used on the downlink, and is mapped onto the frequency correction burst for control procedures.

Synchronization Channel (SCH)

The Synchronization Channel (SCH) is a downlink broadcast that follows the FCCH burst (8 bits later). It provides a reference to all slots on a given frequency. The SCH is mapped onto a synchronization burst.

FCCH and SCH are used to synchronize the mobile to the timeslot structure of a cell by defining the boundaries of burst periods and the timeslot numbering. Every cell in a GSM network broadcasts exactly one FCCH and one SCH, which are, by definition, on timeslot number 0 (within a TDMA frame).

Common Control Channels

The Paging Channel (PCH) is used for the transmission of paging information, requesting the setup of a call to an MS. This is a downlink function.

The Random Access Channel (RACH) is an uplink channel used by the MS to request connections from the ground network. Because users of the network use this for the first access attempt, a random-access scheme is used to aid in avoiding collisions. This is an uplink function.

The Access Grant Channel (AGCH) is used by the base station to inform the mobile station about which channel it should use. This channel is the answer of a base station to an RACH from the mobile station and is a downlink function.

Dedicated Control Channels (DCCH)

The Dedicated Control Channels (DCCH) are used for message exchange among several mobiles or a mobile and the network. Two different types of DCCH can be defined:

- The Standalone Dedicated Control Channel (SDCCH), which is used to exchange signaling information in the downlink and uplink directions.

- The Slow Associated Control Channel (SACCH), which is used for channel maintenance and channel control.

Fast Associated Control Channel

The Fast Associated Control Channel (FACCH) replaces all or part of a traffic channel when urgent signaling information must be transmitted. The FACCH channels carry the same information as the SDCCH channels.

The Driving Force for 3G

Just as the industry was wrestling with the choices between the use of analog and digital networks and the use of the type of digital (TDMA, CDMA, or GSM), another phenomenon started to occur. The use of data transmission began to grow in use and in demand. Users wanted to move away from the circuit-switched data transmission to support packet-switched data because of all the hype of the Internet and the use of packet-switching technologies.

Why not have the same efficiencies available on wireless networks? Therefore, the movement was toward data transmission, which was

- Better

- Faster

- Cheaper

To solve this problem, the evolution to 3G wireless standards set the stage to move from circuit data (dial-up) to packet data (IP or X.25). The trend is shown in Figure 14-17 as the movement toward packet-switched data evolved the industry even more. The packets of data are

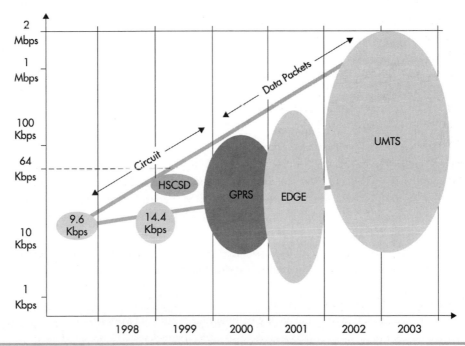

Figure 14-17 3G wireless standard supports packet-switched data services at speeds greater than any other wireless standard (up to 2 Mbps both ways). This is the result of the best practices of the industry, coupled with technological innovations from previous deployments.

destined to move us beyond basic voice calls and slow-speed data transfers. In fact, multimedia applications are where the industry is taking us. Packet data can handle a variety of data streams and formats, so it is determined to be the best solution on the road to 3G wireless solutions.

What to Call the Data Systems of the Future

Not long ago, everyone was surrounded by a single set of terms and definitions. The telecommunications industry was rife with different three-letter acronyms (TLAs) that no one understood. Just when we thought it was safe to come out of the telephone closets and use some terms, the industry began creating all new ones for the wireless industry. In Figure 14-18, the evolving data standards on the road to 3G created some unique data words and new data standards. These are shown in the figure and explained in this section. The data speeds for the late 1990s operated somewhere between 9.6 and 14.4 Kbps (if you were lucky). Later, the industry wanted to raise the bar for data transmission, so it created the means of transmitting high-speed circuit-switched data (HSCSD) to operate at speeds up to 64 Kbps.

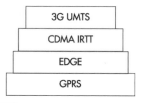

Figure 14-18 Standard evolution to 3G.

Voice to Data

Until recently, wireless data was also essentially a niche market, largely confined to vertical applications within large companies. For example, IBM, Federal Express, and UPS built successful private wireless data networks to enable their field service personnel to operate more efficiently. The explosion of the Internet, that of corporate intranets, and the convergence of the computing and communications industries are creating new opportunities. Shortly after the interest built for data communications, we saw that wireless data could be moved in various forms, including:

- Circuit-switched data over the analog cellular and digital networks

- Cellular Digital Packet Data (CDPD) over spare channels or dedicated channels on the existing networks

- Short Message Services (SMS) using the GSM standard

- Wireless Internet

Even these service offerings were not enough. Consequently, IP networking across a wireless network became the hot button. General Packet Radio Service (GPRS) was developed to sustain a packet data network over GSM at speeds of up to 170 Kbps.

Session (Circuit) versus Packet Transmission

Circuit-switched (or session-based) communications assign users a discrete line or radio channel dedicated to the users until the session is completed. Just as two cans and one string can only handle one conversation between two people, the circuit for the data exchange is tied up until the communication is complete. Using a wireline model, modem speeds began at 300 bits per second and rapidly progressed to support 1.2 to 33.6 Kbps. Current state-of-the-art speed is 33.6 or 56 Kbps. With compression, this rate can be driven to 115 to 230 Kbps when everything is working perfectly. Wireless data speeds are slower, but they're improving.

The goal of a wireless data product is to replicate the following elements of the circuit-switched wireline modems:

- Functionality

- Connectivity

- Reliability

- Speed

In the past, users complained about the ability to connect over a cellular modem. To solve the complaints, cellular modems were tested for performance using a cellular modem connected to a landline modem of the same brand and protocol. This happened in a lab without actual radios in the circuit. Sure, the devices could pass the connectivity test, but under real-world conditions, the results were much worse.

Normally, we need to try this under random cellular conditions, random landline conditions, random cellular locations, random landline locations, and random landline modem types. These conditions are designed to emulate the real world and must be checked. Moreover, the data throughput is another form of testing condition that must be used in this environment to see the rated speed of the modem, compared to the actual speed and throughput of the same modem under different conditions.

The randomness of the cellular conditions and locations can be achieved by testing the modem nationwide at different times of the day. Note that the dial-up circuit-switched networks use mostly analog connections, such as the modem.

14

Things are different, however, for wireless data transmission using a cellular modem. In fact, for the dial-up connection, the average you can expect to see is approximately 9.6 to 14.4 Kbps, assuming you have a good connection. In many cases, these are not assured speeds and may drop to a lower speed, depending on the distance from the cell site, the surrounding area, and the signal-to-noise (S/N) ratio. The modem on the cellular side is provided to accommodate the end user, whereas the standard landline modem is provided to ensure operability and connectivity in the PSTN. This connection may include modems at different speeds and services. Regardless of the modem type or the service dialed, the modem pool provides a form of connection from end-to-end into the PSTN. Once again, the speeds and throughput are conditioned on the link, distance, and S/N ratio.

Cellular Digital Packet Data (CDPD)

IBM and a consortium of large cellular suppliers in North America developed Cellular Digital Packet Data (CDPD). CDPD was built with the promise of 19.2 Kbps among the North American cellular providers, and most U.S. cellular operators support it. CDPD was designed to take advantage of unused space in the analog talk path but later evolved to use unassigned voice channels to connect to web-based services. CDPD devices search for unused voice channels using a channel-hopping approach, which allows the data to be transmitted over multiple available channels.

Circuit-Switched CDPD

Circuit-Switched CDPD (CS-CDPD) enables a modem to disconnect when no data activity is present, and then automatically reconnects on data flow in either direction. The short connect time makes this disconnection and reconnection transparent to the user. In effect, analog cellular communications can emulate a connectionless-oriented protocol such as CDPD while using the connection-oriented dial-up network. CS-CDPD will automatically reconnect when a call is dropped while driving through a tunnel.

Packet-Switched CDPD

CDPD is a packet technology that sends small packets (usually up to about 1,500 bytes) of information for small bursts of time. It is an overlay on the AMPS networks. Although, technically, files of virtually any length may be sent, the network is optimized for fast, low-cost transmission of smaller files. Because the data (such as a message) is often sent in small amounts, users aren't as concerned with throughput as they would be with circuit-switched data (where you are paying for time, not data).

Comparing the CDPD layer to a common architecture, such as the OSI model or the TCP/IP protocol stack, helps you understand how the CDPD network operates. The stacks are shown with standard OSI layers on the left, the TCP/IP stack in the middle, and the local area network (LAN) device driver at the data/network layer. Using a mobile CDPD stack shows that few changes are needed to operate over the CDPD network. The CDPD device driver is in place of the LAN driver. This is essential to the transparency CDPD offers. The application does not need to concern itself with the fact that the network card is a wireless communications device.

CDPD is designed as an IP network. It does not use telephone numbers directly; instead, it uses addresses for everyone on the network. As such, you would send a message to an address, which could go through a gateway to your LAN, and then to your desktop as another node on the network. CDPD uses Gaussian Minimum Shift Keying (GMSK) to modulate the carrier in a full-duplex mode (forward and reverse channels). It also uses Reed Solomon coding, a forward error-correction technique. Packet-switched CDPD is advertised as a 19.2-Kbps data networking system.

Packet Data Communications Are More Efficient

Packets from a number of different conversations or data messages can traverse the same channel. Packets are mixed on the channel but are reassembled correctly at the receiving end. This interleaving enables the increased capacities to serve the mass market but also provides the broadband communications as needed. With a GPRS network, the user can link eight TDMA timeslots on the uplink and eight TDMA timeslots on the downlink to create a speed of 170-Kbps packet data transmission. This requires Phase 2 of GPRS. In Phase 1, the mobile can only use three timeslots. This, of course, depends on the distance from the GSM cell, the interference in the area, and the S/N ratios being achieved. The use of a packet transmission generally uses the IP packets (also called datagrams) to achieve the data throughput.

2.5 G—GPRS and EDGE

In 2000, the industry began to test and deploy commercial data speeds as overlays to GSM (internationally and U.S.-based, such as VoiceStream) and TDMA (AT&T Wireless) networks, using a technique called **General Packet Radio Services (GPRS).** GPRS uses empty GSM timeslots or certain timeslots allocated specifically for data services to deliver packet-switched data over the GSM network. GPRS initially supported 22 Kbps, but it ultimately should support speeds of up to 170 Kbps. GPRS was a logical stepping stone as it was an overlay to the GSM network, taking advantage of the unused bandwidth to deliver the data.

As soon as the GPRS implementation is completed, the movement of the industry will take us to a newer form of data transmission called **Enhanced Data for GSM Evolution (EDGE).** *EDGE* is a newer standard that works similarly to GPRS but achieves higher data rates. EDGE is going to ultimately take the speeds up to 384-Kbps packet-switched IP or X.25 data.*

---

*X.25 is still used in some data networks around the world.

The next step in the 3G of wireless communications is to use what is called **universal mobile telecommunications services (UMTS)**. This is true 3G. UMTS is a set of standards designed to carry data at speeds of up to 2 Mbps. The bulk of these standards are designed around the GSM and TDMA architectures because of the proliferation of the technologies (85 percent worldwide use GSM). UMTS is one of the major new 3G mobile communications systems being developed within the framework, which has been defined by the ITU and is known as IMT-2000.

As the subject of intense worldwide efforts on research and development throughout the present decade, UMTS has the support of many major telecommunications operators and manufacturers. This is because UMTS represents a unique opportunity to create a mass market for highly personalized and user-friendly mobile access to tomorrow's information society.

UMTS will deliver pictures, graphics, video communications, and other wideband information, as well as voice and data, directly to people who are on the move. UMTS will build on and extend the capability of today's mobile technologies by providing increased capacity, data capability, and a far greater range of services using an innovative radio-access scheme and an enhanced, evolving core network. The full launch of UMTS services in the U.S., by 2005, was expected to see the evolution of a new, open communications universe, with players from many sectors (including providers of information and entertainment services) coming together harmoniously to deliver new communications services characterized by mobility and advanced multimedia capabilities. The successful deployment of UMTS will require new technologies, new partnerships, and the addressing of many commercial and regulatory issues. UMTS will use wideband CDMA (W-CDMA) in the core network, but it will provide integration to older GSM/GPRS/EDGE services.

What About the CDMA Folks?

We covered data over the CDMA interface in the preceding section. The first commercial launch of a cdmaOne network was in Hong Kong in September 1995. Today, cdmaOne has more than 50 million subscribers worldwide. Currently, the cdmaOne product portfolio has maximized the advantages of CDMA digital wireless technology while incorporating the efficiencies of IP—supporting packet data at rates of up to 14.4 Kbps.

The original IS-95-A air interface standard was supplemented with the IS-95-B standard, which includes several improvements for hard-handoff algorithms in multicarrier environments and in parameters that affect the control of soft handoffs. Nonetheless, the primary change in the standard had to do with higher data rates for packet- and circuit-switched CDMA data. Data rates of up to 115 Kbps can now be supported by bundling up to eight 14.4- or 9.6-Kbps data channels (14.4 Kbps × 8 = 115.2 Kbps). The term "1X," derived from **1XRTT** (radio transmission technology), is used to signify that the standard carrier on the air interface is 1.25 MHz—the same as for IS-95-A and IS-95-B.

The standard also paves the way for the next phase of 3G networks: cdma2000 3X (IS-2000-A).

IS-2000-A/cdma2000 3X

The cdma2000 3X standard was scheduled for completion in 2000. The term "3X," derived from **3XRTT**, is used to signify three times 1.25 MHz, or approximately 3.75 MHz. The cdma2000 3X multicarrier approach, or wideband cdmaOne, is an important part of the evolution of IS-95-based standards. In all likelihood, IS-2000-A will be followed by supplemental standards that offer additional functionality as the industry evolves. In short, cdma2000 3X:

- Offers greater capacity than 1X

- Supports data rates of up to 2 Mbps

- Is backward-compatible with 1X and cdmaOne deployments

- Enhances performance even more

14

Third-Generation (3G) Wireless

3G systems will provide access, by means of one or more radio links, to a wide range of telecommunication services supported by the fixed telecommunication networks and to other services that are specific to mobile users.

A range of mobile terminal types will be encompassed, linking to terrestrial and/or satellite-based networks, and the terminals may be designed for mobile or fixed use.

Key features of 3G systems are a high-degree of commonality of design worldwide, compatibility of services, use of small pocket terminals with worldwide roaming capability, Internet and other multimedia applications, and a wide range of services and terminals. According to the International Telecommunication Union (ITU) International Mobile Telecommunications 2000 initiative (IMT-2000), 3G mobile system services are beginning to appear, subject to market considerations.

3G wireless technology combines two powerful innovations: wireless communications and the Internet. Older wireless devices were designed to transmit voice and brief text messages and cannot handle digital multimedia and other high-bandwidth Internet content. 3G devices, by contrast, provide high-speed mobile connections to the Internet and other communications networks, giving users full access to the rich content and commercial possibilities of the information superhighway.

Mobile phones and other wireless devices, such as personal digital assistants (PDAs) equipped with 3G technologies, enable users to surf the Internet at high speeds. The immediate goal is to raise transmission speeds from approximately 9.6 Kbps to 2 Mbps.

Many critics feel that 3G is overhyped, comparing the rollout of 3G to the difficulties involved with creating standards for high-definition TV. Currently, the Internet is not totally friendly to mobile devices, but, over time, it will become more adaptable to mobility.

One of the biggest challenges facing 3G and one that slowed work on the proposed standard was negotiation among hardware makers and carriers that had vested interests in W-CDMA and TDMA/FDMA technologies. This appears to have been overcome with the introduction in late 1999 of a new radio-access technology called universal terrestrial radio access (UTRA), which was proposed by the 3G Partnership Project (3GPP) and combines elements of all three techniques. The problem with the UTRA specification is this: it appears to give service providers choices for how to implement multiplexing on their systems—and that could mean incompatibility. Currently, five different standards can be selected from to implement a 3G solution from the carriers' perspective. These include UMTS, CDMA 2000, WCDMA, TD/CDMA, and UWC-136, although indications are that the UWC-136 (a spin-off of IS-136) appears to be declining in its support.

Applications for 3G

Possible 3G applications are even more impressive. According to the International Telecommunication Union (ITU), 3G devices will be compact enough to fit into a pocket or handbag and will integrate the functions of a range of existing devices. The ITU suggests that the 3G device will function as a:

- Phone
- Computer
- PDA
- Television
- Pager
- Videoconferencing center
- Newspaper
- Diary
- Credit card

The 3G device will support not only voice communications but also real-time video and full-scale multimedia via a screen that can be pulled out of the device. It will also function as a portable address book and agenda, containing all the information about meetings and contacts, and it will be able to remind you automatically before an important appointment or automatically connect to an audio- or videoconference at a specified time. The new mobile handset will also automatically search the Internet for relevant news and information on preselected subjects, book your next holiday for you online, and download a bedtime story for your child, complete with moving pictures. It will even be able to pay for goods when you shop via wireless electronic funds transfer. In short, the new mobile handset will become the single, indispensable life tool, carried everywhere by everyone, just like a wallet or purse is today.*

Although some applications are already on the market, others are still developing. An example of this is the use of the 3G phones for TV reception. Figure 14-19 shows a TV included in a telephone. Can you imagine? Think of a person driving down the road today. Everyone is out to deny you access to your cell phones because it distracts you from your duty as a driver. Now, instead of being distracted by a phone call, the risk is you will be watching your favorite sports teams or soap operas on the TV (oops, I mean phone), while attempting to drive to and from work. This is a possibility.

Figure 14-19 TV streamed to a telephone is possible with 3G bandwidth.

What about the road warrior who is on the go all week long and needs to conduct business? Once again, the 3G phones can be used as a videoconferencing device. Now, not only can you call your office, you can host a meeting while driving down the road. You can see the party

---

*International Telecommunication Union, "The Next Generation of Mobile Communications." October 10, 2000.

(parties) you are having a meeting with. Figure 14-20 shows the videoconferencing capability. This adds a new dimension to the overall risk of using cellular phones. First, we were told they cause cancer (a claim that has never been truly proved). Then we could use the phone to download our e-mails (hopefully not reading them and responding while driving).

Figure 14-20 3G will also support real-time video conferencing.

The WAP-enabled phone enabled you to access your e-mail and web sites, as seen in Figure 14-21. **Wireless Access Protocol (WAP)** is a small-scale web browser that can utilize the phone to surf the Net. What can you do besides make a phone call? 3G architectures were built to handle high-speed data access and all the personalized communications needs, making the network and the provider a one-stop shopping environment.

What Does It All Mean?

The sum of all the pieces is that much work still remains to be done before you see a true 3G architecture, handset, and application working together. Like all other services, the piece parts are forming and being introduced as fast as the vendors can develop them. Many proprietary solutions are creeping into the business (even though 3G is supposed to be an open standard).

The applications and the speed are what everyone seems to be concentrating on. However, 3G was supposed to be a universal standard for all vendors to build to in order to ensure compatibility and interoperability. This is yet to happen, but there may be hope in the future.

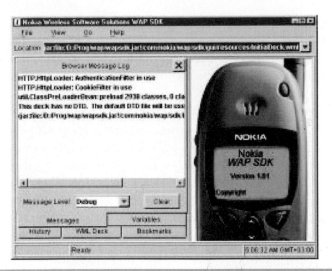

Figure 14-21 Wireless Access Protocol (WAP) can be used to retrieve e-mail.

More than 80 percent of all the wireless Internet users in the world are in Asia. Once 3G services are fully deployed in Japan, Korea, China, Hong Kong, and Malaysia, Internet penetration in the Asian region is expected to soar—making China, not the U.S.—the largest wireless and Internet market in the world. Moreover, within the next two years, Asia as a whole may far surpass the U.S. with respect to the number of Internet and wireless users.

China could have more Internet and wireless users than any other nation, and when combined with other Asian countries such as Japan and Korea, it will become a major force in the two revolutions shaping the new economy: the Internet and wireless technologies.

Currently, the U.S. is still reviewing the requirements for additional spectrum for 3G and is far from offering the types of services on the scale that will be offered abroad.

What About Nextel and Push to Talk Phones?

Integrated Dispatch Enhanced Network (iDEN)

Integrated Dispatch Enhanced Network (iDEN) is an atypical mobile communication system that is not a cellular phone. Although *iDEN* is a mobile communication system, the FCC does not allow it to be referred to as a cellular phone. This is, in fact, due to the FCC's lack of anticipation of a mobile service provider outside of cellular. Motorola's iDEN technology is a classification of **Specialized Mobile Radio (SMR)** based on a variety of proven RF technologies. The technology offers increased spectral efficiency and full-service integration, two of the main benefits of digital communications. The iDEN is also the basis for the SMR system operated by Nextel, a competitor in the wireless business that now touts it has better services and coverage than most of the PCS suppliers. Note that only Nextel provides SMR services in the Americas.

Improved Spectral Efficiency

The capacity to accommodate crowded markets and worldwide growth is a critical component of iDEN. The development of this spectrally efficient technology allows multiple communications to occur over a single analog channel. This expansion of the network gives users greater access to the network, and it provides space for new and expanded services to be added without rebuilding the infrastructure.

Motorola used a combination of technologies to create the increased capacities and the combination of services. Many of the enhancements and increased capacities come from Motorola's VSELP vocoding technique and Quadrature Amplitude Modulation (QAM) modulation process, as well as the TDMA channel-splitting process.

Motorola's VSELP-Coding Signals for Efficient Transmission

The key to the expanded capacity is the reduced transmission rate needed to send information. Motorola has developed a vocoder technology that handles the process. This vocoder, known as Vector Sum Excited Linear Predictor (VSELP), compresses the voice signals to reduce the transmission rate needed to send information. Moreover, *VSELP* provides for clear voice transmission by digitizing the voice and providing high-quality audio under conditions that normally will result in a distorted analog voice. Using speech extrapolation, the VSELP decoder can "repair" the loss of a speech segment over the radio channel.

The result is less distortion and interference (for example, breakup, static, and fading) as users move toward the periphery of the coverage area, enhancing the clarity and quality of voice communications at the outskirts of a cell.

iDEN is a high-capacity digital trunked radio system providing integrated voice and data services to its users. The iDEN system uses M16-QAM digital modulation and VSELP speech-coding techniques coupled with Time Division Multiple Access (TDMA) channel-access methodology to enhance channel capacity and system services.

QAM Modulation

While the VSELP compresses the signal and reduces the transmission rate, *QAM* increases the density of the information. QAM modulation technology was specifically designed to support the digital requirements of the iDEN network. Motorola's unique QAM technology transmits information at a 64-Kbps rate. No other existing modulation technology transmits as much information in a narrow band channel.

Multiplied Channel Capacity

Another essential element is TDMA, which is a technique for dividing the wireless radio channel into multiple communication pathways. In the iDEN system, each 25-kHz radio channel is divided into six timeslots. During transmission, voice and data are divided into packets. Each packet is assigned a timeslot and transmitted over the network. At the receiving end, the packets are reassembled according to their time assignments into the original information sequence.

The Advantage of Integration

More than ever before, users are demanding multifunction devices that are simple to use. With the iDEN network, users need only one telephone to access voice dispatch, two-way telephony, short message service, and future data transmission. This integration provides business users with flexible communications that enable users to access information in the most efficient and convenient way, no matter where they are in the system.

The SMR systems are part of a larger family of products that are classified as trunked radio systems. Trunked radio involves a combination of wired and wireless communication typically found in an emergency service operation, such as fire, police, and road maintenance operations. Exactly what is trunked radio?

M16-QAM Digital Modulation

The iDEN system uses M16-QAM modulation, a Motorola proprietary digital format utilizing M16-QAM modulation on four subcarriers. This format involves both amplitude and phase modulation.

Audio Digitization and Compression

Because iDEN is a digital trunking system, the audio coming from a user's microphone is digitized to produce a digital bit stream that becomes the modulating signal for the RF carrier. To make more efficient use of the channel, the digitized audio is compressed using a VSELP vocoder prior to being fed to the modulator.

iDEN Mobile Operations Control Channel Acquisition

When first powered up, an iDEN mobile radio scans selected iDEN frequencies and locks on to the designated control channel. The control channel carries information continuously broadcast by the fixed end system regarding system identification and timing parameters for the mobile radio to use when it operates on the system. The control channel also defines the maximum transmit power that radios on the system may use.

14

Mobile Synchronization

In its operational mode, the mobile radio aligns its frequency and transmit timing to the outbound signal received from the fixed end system.

Mobile Registration

Each mobile radio in an iDEN system is identified by an IMSI, which is assigned to it when it is first placed in service and performs an initial registration with the fixed end system. When making its registration request, the mobile radio supplies its IMEI to the fixed end system. After determining the validity of the IMEI, the fixed end station assigns an IMSI to the subscriber radio.

Innovation and Integration

Motorola's integrated digital-enhanced network technology and protocols combine dispatch radio, full-duplex telephone interconnect, short message service, and data transmission into a single integrated business-communications solution. The digital technology was the result of studies indicating that a high percentage of dispatch users carried cellular telephones and 30 percent of cellular users carried pagers, along with an increasing demand for data communications. For network design efficiency, iDEN uses a standard seven-cell, three-sector reuse pattern.

The technology is also designed to work around many SMR spectrum limitations. You can take individual channels and group them to work together as a single capacity. In cellular communications, the spectrum must be contiguous. Enhanced voice places iDEN-based services more on par with TDMA, GSM, and code-division multiple-access vocoders.

Although dispatch mode is simplex and not full-duplex, connections are quick. It's efficient and it's fast. A typical cellular call with speed call would take seven to ten seconds for a path to be established. With Motorola's product it takes about a second. Add in 140-character alphanumeric displays (for short message capability) and direct, circuit-switched data support, and you get innovation and integration in one neat little package.

Does Two-Way Radio Still Have a Benefit?

Frankly, yes! Any business with personnel in the field or any business where efficient use of resources can reduce operating costs and increase profits will benefit from two-way radio or an equivalent service as provided with Nextel's iDEN. Now that doesn't leave out too many businesses, does it? In fact, hundreds of businesses—of all sizes and types—have mobile radios in use, and the list grows with each year.

Police departments, delivery services, realtors, school systems, industrial plants, farmers, repair services, construction companies, contractors, vending companies, and many more organizations save time and money through the continued use of two-way radios.

Clearly, some cellular operators offer unlimited local calling services or local-to-local calling plans. These offer some attractive benefits, but they are cellular calls requiring a call setup and teardown, different from the instant on, two-way mobile radio operation. Moreover, the cellular caller may experience congestion or busy tones that would not be the case with the two-way radio option. Many operators are now looking to add the "Push to Talk" service offering on the cellular/PCS offering.

NOTE

Motorola and Nextel were first with this "Push to Talk" technology (PTT); however, it is now being emulated in other systems.

A two-way radio system generally consists of three types of units: a base station at a central dispatching location, mobile stations used in vehicles, and hand-held portables utilizing battery power. In today's business, conventional radio typically will not provide the wide-area communications that most businesses require. The cost for a business to construct its own radio system consisting of multiple tower sites can be too expensive. That's why a Specialized Mobile Radio (SMR) system provider is used. Customers pay a monthly fee to use the service, similar to cellular service, and the two-way PTT service is now available in national, and even international, coverage areas.

NOTE

Cellular is one of the more popular forms of wireless communications. Its inherent weakness comes from the coverage area of cellular towers. Newer technologies and the miniaturization of hardware have allowed a "new" set of players to overcome this weakness: satellite phone companies. Because much of the world lies outside of cellular coverage, satellite provides a worldwide footprint. When you decide to scale Mt. Everest or sail around the world, satellite phones provide the comfort of a wireless phone with unprecedented coverage. It is important to realize that worldwide coverage comes at a premium, though. Satellite phone calls vary from $.27/a minute to $2.99 a minute, depending on your service plan. Visit

www.iridium.com

www.globalstar.com

www.teledesic.com

for further information on satellite services.

Chapter 14 Review

Chapter Summary

MTS and IMTS

- Mobile phone service was provided in large metropolitan cities. Vehicles were equipped with a telephone that connected to transmitters located atop the highest buildings.

- Output power was 250 watts on 12 channels providing coverage in a 25-mile area.

- Although the signal was only usable within the 25-mile radius, it traveled up to 100 miles.

- Signals outside coverage areas could cause interference in adjacent metropolitan areas.

- With only 12 channels, the network became filled quickly. Inventors found that if transmission power was lowered, signals would travel less distance and could be reused more frequently.

Cellular Communications (AMPS)

- In 1981, the FCC finally set aside 666 radio channels for cellular use. These frequencies were assigned or set aside for two separate carriers

- Using a frequency pattern from radio transmitters, the cellular concept produces a honeycomb pattern of overlapping cells of communication. A cell is a coverage area of an antenna or cell tower.

- Frequencies could be reused with a two-cell separation, thereby enabling more users to be supported. This reuse pattern was standardized in a pattern known as N = 7.

- The components of the cellular network are the cell, the MTSO, and the handset.

- The U.S. frequencies used for analog cellular are 800 to 850 MHz. Thirty-kHz channels are used in an FDMA arrangement (one send and one receive, and one shared control channel) A .3-watt signal is used, and the cell site is up to 25 miles or more in diameter.

- Analog cellular worked, but the limited spectrum became an issue as the cost of equipment and service became more affordable to larger groups of people.

TDMA

- To overcome the spectrum issue, TDMA was deployed in 1990. TDMA breaks the 30-kHz channel up into six timeslots; each user gets two of the six slots, so TDMA provides a 300 percent spectrum efficiency increase over analog cellular.

- TDMA can correctly increase the number of users on the RF by three times. However, as more enhanced RF techniques such as microcells and picocells are used, the numbers can grow to as much as a 40-fold increase in the number of users per tower that can be supported when compared to the original analog cellular transmission patterns.

- TDMA, as a digital transmission system, can support in increments of 64 Kbps in addition to voice transmission.

- TDMA operates in the 800/1900-MHz bands in the U.S.

CDMA

- Unique digital codes, rather than separate radio frequencies or channels, are used to enable multiple transmissions over the available assigned bandwidth.

- The codes are shared by both the mobile station (cellular phone) and the base station and are called pseudorandom code sequences. All users share the same 1.25-MHz range of radio spectrum at 1900 MHz.

- Voice activity detection is another variable that helps increase the capacity of a CDMA system

- Unlike AMPS, CDMA can use the same 1.25 MHz in directly adjoining towers, eliminating the need for N = 7 frequency reuse patterns in cellular transmission engineering.

- A single CDMA standard with three modes provides flexibility for all operators to meet the growing demand for advanced voice and data services.

- CDMA circuit-switched services provide asynchronous data and facsimile transmission using an Interworking Unit (IWU) supporting Group III fax standards, which operate from 9.6 to 14.4 Kbps.

GSM

- The GSM network can be divided into three broad parts. The subscriber carries the Mobile Station, the Base Station Subsystem, and the Mobile Services Switching Center (MSC).

- The mobile phone supports dividing the cell phone into two separate components: the Mobile Equipment and the Subscriber Identity Module (or SIM card).

- GSM uses the combined FDMA and TDMA architecture to provide the most efficient operation within the scope of price and reasonable data.

- A 200-kHz channel is divided into eight timeslots.

GPRS

- GPRS is still evolving and being tested to support speeds initially at 28.8 Kbps, but it now supports speeds up to 170 Kbps.

- The evolution to 3G wireless standards set the stage to move from circuit data to packet data.

- GPRS is an overlay to the GSM network, utilizing either specifically set aside or vacant timeslots in the channel to deliver data.

- GPRS was deployed in 2000.

- No sooner will GPRS be installed than the movement will take us to a newer form of data transmission called Enhanced Data for GSM Evolution (EDGE).

EDGE

- EDGE is going to ultimately take the speeds up to 384 Kbps packet-switched IP or X.25 data.

- EDGE is deployed over GSM just as GPRS is.

UMTS-3G

- UMTS is one of the major new 3G mobile communications systems being developed within the framework, which has been defined by the ITU and is known as IMT-2000.

- UMTS is a set of standards designed to carry data at speeds of up to 2 Mbps. UMTS is also deployed over GSM and utilizes newer modulation techniques.

- 3G wireless technology combines two powerful innovations: wireless communications and the Internet.

- One of the biggest challenges facing 3G, and one that slowed work on the proposed standard, was negotiation among hardware makers and carriers that had vested interests in wideband CDMA and TDMA/FDMA technologies.

- In 1999, a new radio access technology was introduced called universal terrestrial radio access (UTRA). UTRA was proposed by the 3G Partnership Project and combines elements of all three techniques.

- Currently, five different standards can be selected from to implement a 3G solution from the carriers' perspective. These include UMTS, CDMA 2000, WCDMA, TD/CDMA, and UWC-136.

iDEN

- Motorola's iDEN technology is a classification of Specialized Mobile Radio (SMR) based on a variety of proven RF technologies. The technology offers increased spectral efficiency and full-service integration, two of the main benefits of digital communications.

- The iDEN is also the basis for the SMR system operated by Nextel, a competitor in the wireless business that now claims it has better services and coverage than most of the PCS suppliers.

- Motorola used a combination of technologies to create the increased capacities and the combination of services. Many of the enhancements and increased capacities come from Motorola's VSELP vocoding technique and QAM modulation process, as well as the TDMA channel-splitting process.

- Using speech extrapolation, the VSELP decoder can "repair" the loss of a speech segment over the radio channel. The result is less distortion and interference (for example, breakup, static, and fading) as users move toward the periphery of the coverage area, enhancing the clarity and quality of voice communications at the outskirts of a cell.

- Because iDEN is a digital trunking system, the audio coming from a user's microphone is digitized to produce a digital bit stream that becomes the modulating signal for the RF carrier.

Key Terms for Chapter 14

1XRTT *(686)*
3XRTT *(687)*
Advanced Mobile Phonc Services (AMPS) *(651)*
Authentication *(672)*
Base Station Subsystem (BSS) *(674)*
Burst *(677)*
Capacity *(668)*
CdmaOne (IS-95) *(667)*
Cell *(652)*
Cellular Communications *(650)*
Churn *(659)*
Code Division Multiple Access (CDMA) *(667)*
DS Code *(667)*
Enhanced Data for GSM Evolution (EDGE) *(685)*
Fast Associated Control Channel (FACCH) *(678)*
Frequency Division Multiple Access (FDMA) *(651)*
General Packet Radio Services (GPRS) *(685)*
Generation (G) *(648)*

14

REVIEW

Global System for Mobile Communications (GSM) *(673)*
Handoff *(654)*
Handset *(652)*
Hard Handoff *(671)*
Improved Mobile Telephone Services (IMTS) *(649)*
Integrated Dispatch Enhanced Network (iDEN) *(691)*
International Mobile Equipment Identity (IMEI) *(675)*
International Mobile Subscriber Identity (IMSI) *(675)*
Interworking Unit (IWU) *(672)*
Location Areas (LAs) *(677)*
Metropolitan Service Area (MSA) *(651)*
Microcells *(666)*
Mobile Services Switching Center (MSC) *(674)*
Mobile Station (MS) *(674)*
Mobile Telecommunications Service (MTS) *(648)*
Mobile Telephone Switching Office (MTSO) *(652)*
Multiple Access *(671)*
$N = 7$ *(656)*
North American TDMA (NA-TDMA) *(665)*
Number Assignment Module (NAM) *(658)*
Over-the-Air Activation (OTA) *(672)*
Picocells *(666)*
Pulse Coded Modulation (PCM) *(665)*
Pseudorandom Code Sequences *(667)*
Quality of Service (QoS) Measurement *(655)*
Rural Service Area (RSA) *(651)*
Signal Transfer Point (STP) *(658)*
SIM Card *(674)*
Soft Handoff *(671)*
Softer Handoff *(671)*
Specialized Mobile Radio (SMR) *(691)*
TDMA frame *(677)*
Time Division Multiple Access (TDMA) *(665)*
Universal Mobile Telecommunications Services (UMTS) *(686)*
Wireless Access Protocol (WAP) *(690)*

Key Term Quiz

1. A _____ in the cellular network is the equivalent of a Class 5 switch in the PSTN.

2. The process of being transferred from one cell to another is called _____.

3. The _____ access method provides a user one subchannel for transmit and a separate subchannel for receive.

4. The network operator Nextel in the U.S. utilizes _____ instead of cellular to carry its calls.

5. The _____ access method is a digital transmission system that provides a three times gain over analog cellular.

6. The process by which information is exchanged between a mobile station and the network for the purpose of confirming and validating the identity of the mobile device is called _____.

7. As a cell signal fades, the MTSO sends a _____ to all the cell towers to see which one has the strongest signal to the handset.

8. The two components of a mobile phone (in GSM) are _____.

9. An enhancement that is an overlay to GSM is _____, which produces data access of up to 170 Kbps.

10. The _____ wireless standard provides data access at 2-Mbps speed.

Multiple-Choice Quiz

1. What year was cellular first introduced?   *I Lin Bell → 1946*

   a. 1978

   b. 1984

   c. 1990

   d. 1994

2. The cellular network was used to replace the _____ networks.

   a. AMPS

   b. Two-way radio

   c. IMTS   *→ AMPS*

   d. Walkie-talkie

3. Cell sites operated at up to approximately _____ miles across.

   a. 10

   b. 7

   c. 12

   d. 25

4. The first cellular phones were made to operate in _____.

   a. Vehicles

   b. Shirt pockets

   c. Briefcases

   d. Wristwatches

5. The AMPS used what technology?

   a. Digital

   b. TDMA

   c. CDMA

   d. Analog

6. Cellular handoff occurs when the user is on the periphery of the cell.

   a. True

   b. False

7. As congestion occurred, one of the first steps to get more utilization is to:

   a. Allow fewer users

   b. Build more networks

   c. Perform cell splitting

   d. Use less bandwidth

8. The choices of digital were selected between two competing technologies:

   a. TDMA and FDMA

   b. ETDMA and N-AMPS

   c. IMTS and AMPS

   d. TDMA and CDMA

9. TDMA helps to achieve a _____ increase in number of users.

   a. Tenfold

   b. Twentyfold

   c. Fivefold

   d. Threefold

10. What does 3G stand for?

   a. Third goal

   b. TDMA generation

   c. TDMA global

   d. Third generation

11. What does GPRS mean?

   a. General packet data services

   b. General packet radio system

   c. Generic pocket radio system

   d. General packet radio service

12. For what technology is EDGE suited?

   a. TDMA

   b. FDMA

   c. GSM

   d. CDMA

13. Which technology utilizes a 1.25-MHz channel?

   a. TDMA

   b. CDMA

   c. GSM

   d. EDGE

14. Which is the only provider of iDEN services in the U.S.?

    a. Iridium

    b. AT&T wireless

    c. Verizon

    d. Nextel

Essay Quiz

1. What were the problems with AMPS service? How were these problems overcome?

2. What has been the problem in the U.S. in getting to 3G?

Chapter 15

Security and Virtual Private Networks (VPN)

LEARNING OBJECTIVES:

Once you complete this chapter, you will be able to:

Understand why security is important in telecommunications networks.

Describe what a security procedure entails.

Describe the crime triangle.

Discuss the means and motivations of the intruders.

Discuss the purpose of a VPN to secure data.

Describe the various forms of attack that may be launched against our networks.

Up to now, we have been describing the technologies of voice and data communications. More specifically, we have described the technologies, what they are, how they work, and why we use them. In every network, however, a different set of problems emerges that cannot be ignored. Instead of a technology, we need a process to protect the networks we have been discussing. To get there, yes, we do use various technologies, but the more important issue is to develop and design a set of policies and procedures to keep out the "bad guys." These policies and procedures will constitute the security necessary to protect the company's or the individual's private information. We use the following goals in creating our data networks:

- Confidentiality

- Integrity

- Availability

- Nonrepudiation

Many different approaches were developed over the years, but we keep hearing about security breaches. What constitutes a breach? Everyone has a slightly different definition of a breach, but for the most part, we can categorize breaches as follows:

- Hacking and penetration into our networks or systems

- Denial of service (DoS) attacks

- Virus infections

- Manipulation or changing our data

- Loss of confidentiality

Most people define a breach as a hacking event and, possibly, the manipulation of our data. As you can see, there is more to it than these two issues. Thus, we must design and implement tools and techniques to minimize these risks.

NOTE:

You cannot eliminate risk, but you certainly can minimize it by practicing safe networking!

There are at least four primary reasons for network security threats:

- **Technology weaknesses**—Each network and computing technology has inherent security problems.

- **Configuration weaknesses**—Even the most secure technology can be misconfigured or misused, exposing security problems.

- **Policy weaknesses**—A poorly defined or improperly implemented and managed security policy can make the best security and network technology ripe for security abuse.

- **Human weaknesses**—Issues related to social engineering (outsiders gaining access by obtaining access information by manipulating people), failure to follow accepted policies and practices, and insider intentional actions.

There are people who are eager, willing, qualified, and sometimes compensated to take advantage of each security weakness and to discover and exploit new weaknesses.

However, the reality is we cannot pay more to protect the data or assets than they are worth. It would never do to pay $1,000,000 to secure $1,000,000 worth of assets. Thus, we get caught up in the cost and the associated risks in our planning. We must make tradeoffs based on the degree of risk associated with our particular network or data. Moreover, planning for security is usually an afterthought.

The Crime Triangle

Security specialists and industry pundits all agree that to effectively launch an attack, three basic ingredients are needed. This is called the crime triangle, as shown in Figure 15-1. The three ingredients include:

- Motive—the perpetrator needs a reason to attack your network. This can come from various angles, such as a disgruntled employee seeking revenge, a competitor seeking confidential or proprietary information, people who do it for the thrill of conquest, and so forth.

- Opportunity—somehow the door needs to be left open, so the opportunity avails itself. People will test the defenses of a network or system to see how and where they might penetrate it.

- Means—the mechanism necessary to penetrate or disrupt our networks and services, such as DoS generation software, buffer overrun code, and more.

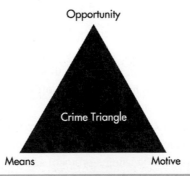

Figure 15-1 The crime triangle includes these three ingredients necessary to formulate an attack.

Assuming the crime triangle avails all three components to a perpetrator, then the attacks will begin.

How Attackers Think

Understanding how typical attackers think is useful to grasp how they come up with the various ways of attacking computers and gaining unauthorized access to those systems. First, like any burglar or other criminal, they usually look for the easiest way in. In many cases, that involves people, not technology. Either attackers have someone on the inside to help them or they become insiders.

Attackers think creatively to invent new ways to gain access to a system. They tend to think outside the box. Rather than thinking "How does this work?" they think "What happens if I do . . .?" By trying unexpected things, they can find a hole where the administrator didn't consider all the possibilities.

NOTE:

A good analogy is that of a rat that climbs over the walls of the maze to get to the cheese, rather than following the pathways in the maze. The hacker bypasses all the normal stops and finds new ways into a system.

Usually, the first thing an attacker does before breaking into a computer is to gather information. An attacker can use several useful techniques to gather information.

Dumpster Diving

Dumpster diving is searching through an organization's trash to find items such as company directories, old Post-It notes with passwords scribbled on them, organizational charts that show names of staff who can be impersonated in a social engineering attack, and so forth. You may recall the movie where this was done effectively and compromised many an organization.

Shoulder Surfing

Shoulder surfing is looking over another's shoulder to watch as a calling card or credit card number or access code is typed into a keypad. This is most often done in a busy location, for example, in an airport or a train station. How many times have you sat next to someone at an airport and seen that person log in to his or her home office computer system?

Sniffing

Sniffing, named after a commercial product from Network Associates, Inc. (www.nai.com), is the process of reading network traffic using a protocol analyzer. Many products do not encrypt sensitive data, making this a viable information-gathering tool. Although many sites protect their networks from unauthorized physical access, the attacker need only penetrate a host from anywhere on a network path and either run frequently available protocol analysis there or download one of his or her own. Packet sniffing is shown as a concept in Figure 15-2. Packet sniffing can be considered as a sort of wiretap device, a device that can "plug" into computer networks and eavesdrop on the network traffic.

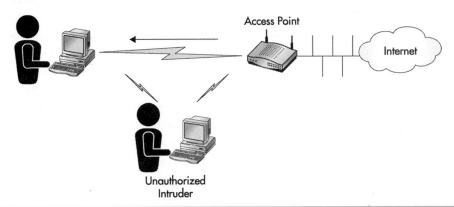

Figure 15-2 Packet sniffing can be done either on a wired or a wireless network. The perpetrator need only gain access from anywhere on the network and use a sniffer to capture and decode the packets.

15

Social Engineering

Social engineering is more psychology than engineering, and it is the least technical of the attack methods discussed here. Social engineering is the process of gaining information or opening security holes by talking to people. It depends on skills in conversation, a self-confident sound, and a certain amount of bravado or bluster.

The attacker calls someone in your organization, pretending to be someone in a position of trust. The attacker attempts to gain the person's confidence (sounds like a con artist, doesn't it?) and get that person to perform some action that violates your security policy. Because people are basically helpful and trusting by nature, this type of attack often succeeds.

The best defense against this type of attack is for people in your organization to verify a stranger's identity and authority before taking any action that might compromise security. Although you want people to be alert and aware, having everyone paranoid is inefficient, so this kind of defense requires a large educational effort.

Solution: Authenticate

—Call the person back at a phone number you can verify.

—Ask for identification.

Scanning and Version Information

Scanning is the process of attempting to connect to a range of port numbers or Internet Protocol (IP) addresses to discover what services or computers exist and are turned on. This is one of the methods probably most used by attackers to discover information about their next potential victims. A number of automated tools are available to aid an attacker. Ping is often used to find IP addresses. Some of the programs that scan port numbers are WinStrobe, nmap, and UltraScan. This type of tool is usually easy to detect, but attackers have developed ways (called stealth scanning and slow scanning) to make detection more difficult.

What Do You Think?

Log on to www.sandstorm.net and view products such as Phonesweep and sandtrap. Also look at the information contained in LanWatch. How secure do you think the average network is today?

Wardialing is the scanning of phone numbers in an attempt to find ones with modems on them, in the hope that the attacker can break in via the computer attached to the modem. Often, these lines are set up without the knowledge or approval of an organization's information technology (IT) or security group, and they frequently are poorly secured, making the attacker's job easier. Several hacking tools have been developed to perform this type of scanning, and a commercial product called Phonesweep is available from SandStorm (http://www.sandstorm.net).

NOTE:

In the movie *War Games*, the main character used wardialing to break into a defense network computer. Although the movie was fiction, the main plot revolved around hacking by a teenager who penetrated a computer and nearly caused world annihilation.

Wardriving is the process of scanning for available wireless 802.11 networks that an attacker may be able to attach to for network access. Wardriving gets its name from the first attacks, which were done by driving around an area with a laptop equipped with a wireless network card and an antenna to improve signal reception. Every year, a coordinated war drive is held, whereby participants drive up and down the streets of major cities. Equipped with a laptop and GPS, a wireless local area network (LAN) card, and a high-gain antenna, these people discover all the local wireless LANs and whether or not they are using security methods to keep intruders out.

DO THIS:

Log on to www.netstumbler.org and peruse this site regarding the wardriving and packet capture utilities on this site. The tools being discussed in this chapter are to let you know how easy and they are to obtain and use.

Version information is typically the next item that an attacker looks for. When an attacker connects to an available, open port number, the service running on that port can output a banner message containing the version number of the service. An older version may indicate an unpatched system that is vulnerable to a particular security hole.

Scanning, wardialing, and wardriving can also be useful tools for the security or network administrator to help find unauthorized hosts or services before an attacker does.

15

NOTE:

The best solution here is to limit exposure by blocking or turning off any IP addresses, port numbers, or modems that are not necessary. For version information, it helps to turn this off via administration of the service. Always ensure that the latest security patches have been applied. For wardriving, turn on the available security measures.

Unauthorized Access

Unauthorized access to computers usually follows the information gathering. Some of the ways attackers gain unauthorized access can be prevented by careful administration, but others can only be fixed by installing patches from vendors once a bug has been reported.

The list below is roughly in the order of the likelihood of occurrence. Most successful attacks happen in poorly administered systems. Few attacks via session hijacking have ever been perpetrated because of the level of sophistication required.

- Misadministration
  - User Accounts
  - Passwords

- Software Bugs
- Buffer Overflows
- Malicious Code
- Session Hijacking

Passwords

Simplistic passwords picked by users are the easiest method used by attackers to gain unauthorized access to systems. Most users pick passwords that are easy for them to remember. An attacker will start by trying trivial passwords, no password, a password the same as the user account name, some variation of the user's real name, or something related to the user, such as a relative's name or birth date. Available services that allow multiple attempts without reporting an error or delaying bad attempts make the attacker's job easier.

From there, the attacker will try dictionary attacks or move to brute force, trying all possible character combinations. A dictionary-attack program that attempts relentlessly to guess a correct username-password pair is a serious threat. A **dictionary attack** consists of trying "every word in the dictionary" as a possible password for an encrypted message. A dictionary attack is generally more efficient than a brute force attack, because users typically choose poor passwords.

Brute force (also known as brute-force cracking) is a trial-and-error method used by application programs to decode encrypted data, such as passwords or **data encryption standard (DES) keys**, through exhaustive effort (using brute force), rather than employing intellectual strategies. These types of attacks are almost always done using automated tools (such as Crack, L0phtcrack, John the Ripper, and so forth), and they are usually aided by the attacker gaining a copy of the password file from the victim system. Although the password files on most operating systems (OSs) are encrypted, a copy of them makes it easy for attackers to work offline, on their own systems, testing possible guesses against the encrypted value to see if they are correct.

NOTE:

The solution to this type of attack is to educate users to select complex passwords, to use some method of strong authentication, to protect the password files from remote access, and to change passwords regularly.

Log on to http://www.ftponline.com/vsm/2003_12/magazine/features/mccaffrey/default_pf.aspx and read an article about the complexities and opportunities of dictionary attacks.

Defaults Left On

The default installations of many OSs and applications provide many ways for attackers to gain unauthorized access to systems. First among these are default service accounts or special backdoor accesses built in by the vendor for remote maintenance or to ease customer support (for example, "I forgot my password").

Providers assume that most network-service applications on modern OSs will be installed in trusted environments, and thus, most avenues of access are turned on. This makes systems work better when they're first installed without a lot of administrative effort, but it leaves many holes open for an attacker to exploit. Things such as shared resource access (NFS on UNIX or File and Print Sharing on Microsoft Windows) are notoriously lax when first installed. Firewall appliances typically come with a default configuration, which should still be modified to match an organization's security policy before installing. Most of them allow all outbound connections by default. This might allow a **Trojan horse** that some user opened to originate a connection back to the attacker's site. In today's computer world, a Trojan horse is defined as a "malicious, security-breaking program that is disguised as something benign." For example, you download what appears to be a movie or a music file, but when you click on it, you unleash a dangerous program that erases your disk, sends your credit card numbers and passwords to a stranger, or lets that stranger hijack your computer to commit illegal DoS attacks like those that have virtually crippled the network for months on end.

15

SUGGESTION:

Shut down every service or avenue of access that is not needed and be careful to secure any access routes that are left enabled. Any default accounts should be turned off or have the passwords changed. The better an administrator understands how a service operates, the easier it is to secure.

Buffer Overflows

This exploit, also called "smashing the stack," is used to crash a system or gain access to the system. It is a highly technical attack and requires a great deal of skill on the part of the attacker code writer (though, unfortunately, it can be performed by almost anyone once the attack code has become available on the Internet). Buffer overflows count on variables in an application not being tested or bound for length. The attacker's code sends an input sting that is larger than the buffer space allotted by the program, and it overwrites the next bytes in memory, which often contain the stack pointer values. These values tell the program where to jump to execute its next instructions. By carefully crafting the bytes of information, the attacker can redirect the program to execute instructions embedded earlier in the input sting.

In this way, the attacker gets the program to run his or her own code. This creates truly malicious data.

For this type of attack to work, the attacker must craft the specific computer-language instructions and know how memory and computer architecture work in detail. The attack must be targeted at a specific variable, in a specific program, and on a specific hardware and operating system (OS) platform. Usually the attacker has the same setup available to experiment on to get this attack to work. Even if the attacker cannot get his or her own code to be run, many attacks based on this principle can cause the victim's computer to lock up or reboot.

Despite the amount of technical expertise needed to complete this attack, it is being reported regularly on security advisory sites and mailing lists. It appears that few programmers test the length of input information to ensure that the buffer cannot overflow.

SUGGESTION:

The solution is to test the length of all input variables. More details about buffer overflow are available in "Phrack," issue 49 (http://www.phrack.org), and from http://www.l0pht.org (the 0 is a zero).

Malicious Code

A newer term, **malicious code** (also known as malware, hostile active code, or hostile applet), has been coined to describe an expanded class of attacks, formerly known as viruses.

Previously, any executable content that a user downloaded (.exe file) was a potential source of attack, wherein the executable file would cause harm to the user's system, usually by replicating and, perhaps, propagating to other systems. Now, the Internet and the latest operating systems and applications are including features that allow many types of data to be input and processed by a computer system. This type of data is known generically as active code.

The various forms of active code have different capabilities and dangers. Some, like Java, have security models that restrict what the active code can do. Others digitally sign the code, making it easy for the user to know who the code is from before deciding to execute it. Some of it runs automatically.

When this active code or executable content contains instructions that cause harm to a victim's system, the code is considered hostile. A number of attacks have been perpetrated in this manner, causing considerable damage. These new methods of attack are similar to viruses, but they use new features as avenues into computers. Few users realize how much programming capability exists in their applications, making it easier for an attacker to get a victim to unknowingly run a script or applet that can compromise the victim's computer.

NOTE:

The solutions to the problem of malicious code include educating users to the dangers, screening all incoming executable content, constraining the environment the code runs in, and blocking active code altogether. The only way to know if a piece of active code is safe to run is to examine it or control its environment Many people don't want to make that effort, and the only other choice is not to run it at all.

Denial of Service (DoS)

DoS (denial of service) attacks cause a user to lose access to a resource rather than allow the attacker to gain unauthorized access to that resource. Causing this type of attack usually involves overloading a resource, be it disk space, network bandwidth, internal tables, or memory, or input buffers (buffer overflow). This overload then causes the host or particular service to be unavailable for legitimate use. Effects range from simply blocking access to a service to causing a host to crash. By way of example, let's look at two typical DoS attacks: the TCP SYN flood and the distributed DoS attack. A DoS attack is shown in Figure 15-3.

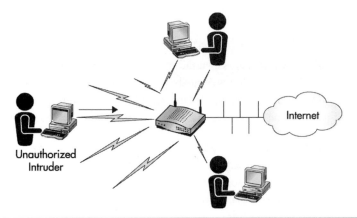

Internet

Unauthorized
Intruder

Figure 15-3 DoS attacks can bottle up an entire network. Although it's shown here in a wireless LAN environment, this kind of attack works equally well on wired networks.

TCP SYN Floods

TCP SYN flooding is a DoS attack that can block a service on a host with a small number of packets sent every couple of minutes. This attack uses the TCP three-step handshake as part of its exploit. Normally, a TCP session is started by the client sending a SYN packet to the server. The server responds by sending a reply packet that ACKs (acknowledges) the first packet and also sends a SYN flag to the client. Normally, the client ACKs the server's SYN message.

In the attack, the "bad guy" sends the first SYN packet with a spoofed source IP address of a nonexistent host (nobody) to the victim. The victim sends a SYN/ACK back to the non-existent host—nobody—and waits for the final ACK. The waiting can take as long as 75 seconds in many cases, while a slot in the victim's backlog queue is taken up with this half-open connection. This backlog queue is limited to about six to ten slots per port number, depending on the vendor. If the attacker sends enough of these forged packets to fill the backlog queue on the victim, the victim can no longer accept connection requests for the service that is under attack (http in this example). As long as the attacker—the bad guy—sends six to ten of these forged packets every minute or so, no one can connect to the web server or victim. Nothing shows up in any log on the victim host. Typically, the only indicator of an attack is the inability to connect to the targeted service.

Security and protocol experts are still debating how best to defend against this type of attack. Some vendors have written code to shorten that 75-second timer or increase the size of the backlog queue, but even then, the attacker just needs to send more packets in a shorter time. Some intrusion-detection software can watch for this type of attack and send RST (reset) packets to the victim host to clear its backlog queue. A good defense is still to be found.

Distributed Denial of Service (DDoS)

Distributed denial of service (DDoS) is a variation on the simple DoS attack where a sophisticated tool infects a large quantity of vulnerable hosts with an agent or daemon, which, in turn (under command of a few master programs), sends large quantities of packets to a victim host, thereby massively flooding it with an incredible volume of traffic. There are several things to note about how these types of attacks work:

- The tools that infect the vulnerable systems typically find those systems through an automated process, making it simple for an attacker to enlist many of these unwitting dupes to perform the attack. The automated process looks for hosts with certain known, unpatched security vulnerabilities and infects them with the agent or daemons.

- Some versions of the tools encrypt communications between the client, master, and daemons to make detection difficult, if not impossible. The daemons make efforts to hide their existence on the hosting site by running with common command names.

- The actual packets sent have been mostly SYN floods, pings, or User Datagram Protocol (UDP) floods. These packets often spoof their source IP addresses to foil tracking efforts.

- The volume of traffic that can be generated by one of these distributed systems was measured in one instance at 1 gigabit per second. This volume can be achieved with a quantity of agent daemons in the tens to the low hundreds.

NOTE:

Solutions to DDoS attacks are not simple. If every network on the Internet blocked outbound spoofed IP addresses, this would help. Of course, if every network on the Internet patched all its known security holes, that would help, too. But in the current real world, this is unlikely to occur anytime soon.

Data Manipulation

A network intruder can capture, manipulate, and replay data sent over a communication channel by using data manipulation. Data manipulation is also used with impersonation. Impersonation occurs when the actual identity of the individual is suspect. Manipulation can take the form of IP address spoofing, session replay and hijacking, rerouting, and repudiation. Data manipulation can also include graffiti—vandalizing a web site by accessing the web server and altering web pages. Data manipulation is made possible by vulnerabilities in the IP protocol and associated services and applications. Data manipulation attacks are also known as **man-in-the-middle attacks** because the attack usually involves a person in the middle exploiting IP session susceptibilities between two TCP/IP hosts. The typical name here is now man-in-the-middle attack, as shown in Figure 15-4.

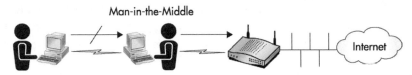

Man-in-the-Middle

Figure 15-4 The man-in-the-middle allows the attacker to launch an attack by capturing real packets and manipulating them. Next, the hacker will launch the changed packets as real data.

15

IP Spoofing

A network intruder can use IP spoofing to impersonate the identity of a host for applications or services that use source or destination addresses for authentication. An **IP spoofing** attack occurs when a network intruder outside your network pretends to be a trusted computer inside or outside your network. The spoof uses an IP address within the range of IP addresses for your network or uses an authorized external IP address that you trust and to which you want to provide access to specified resources on your network. Spoofing usually includes manipulating TCP/IP packets to falsify IP addresses, thereby appearing to be another host. For example, the intruder could use IP address spoofing to assume the identity of a valid or trusted host and to gain the host's access privileges by falsifying the source address of a trusted host. Spoofing is also known as a masquerade attack. An attacker can specify an arbitrary source address for a packet in an attempt to bypass address-based authentication mechanisms. This is especially effective if the arbitrary source address is that of a host behind a perimeter router or a firewall.

Normally, an IP spoofing attack, as shown in Figure 15-5, is limited to the injection of data or commands into an existing stream of data passed between a client and a server application or a peer-to-peer network connection. Attackers using IP spoofing might be able to bypass authentication mechanisms, and if they are improperly implemented, they might subvert filters on packet-filtering routers. Countermeasures against IP spoofing include filtering packets at the perimeter router that come from outside but claim to be from the inside.

Figure 15-5 The IP spoofing attack is similar to session replay or session hijacking.

Session Replay and Hijacking

Session replay is an attack in which a network intruder intercepts and captures a sequence of packets or application commands, manipulates the captured data (such as by altering the dollar amount of a transaction), and then replays the data to cause an unauthorized action. Session replay exploits weaknesses in authentication of data traffic.

Session hijacking is an attack in which a network intruder takes over an IP session and inserts falsified IP data packets after session establishment. Session-hijacking methods include IP spoofing, source and/or destination address manipulation over TCP/IP, and sequence number prediction and alteration. The network intruder uses a protocol analyzer or utility program to observe, predict, and then alter and retransmit TCP/IP packet-sequence numbers. An example of a documented session-hijacking attack is the use of a tool that redirects X-terminal output to an intruder's terminal instead of the intended terminal.

One exploit that is a session replay attack involves the use of JavaScript to allow a network intruder to exploit a hole in Hotmail and other web-based e-mail systems. The hole lets the malicious hacker create a piece of incriminating e-mail that can be falsely traced to another person's computer. The user is exposed to this attack by being lured to a seemingly innocent web page into which the hacker has inserted the malicious JavaScript code.

Session replay and hijacking attacks can only be carried out by skilled programmers, so there have been few documented attacks. One session hijacking tool is the hunt-1.0 program that runs on Linux systems.

NOTE:

Countermeasures for session replay and hijacking include the following methods and technologies:

Adjust the web browser's security setting to prevent downloads of applets or make the browser notify you for permission to execute mobile code when it is encountered.

Block corporate access to public e-mail sites to limit the risk of infection or disclosure of confidential data.

Use access control features in the perimeter.

Use authentication, such as Remote Access Dial-In User Service (RADIUS) or Secure Sockets Layer (SSL).

Use encryption technologies to protect the integrity and privacy of data.

Use digital signatures offered by certification authorities for nonrepudiation.

Rerouting

Network intruders can manipulate IP routing by using source routing, by gaining unauthorized access to routers and altering the routing configuration, or by spoofing the identity of routers or hosts along a network path. The consequence of **rerouting** is that it can allow a connection stream to be misrouted to an alternate destination and/or permit a remote host to pose as a local host on your network. Services that rely on IP addresses as authentication might be compromised as a result.

The countermeasures for rerouting attacks are to limit access to routers to prevent reconfiguration of routes, to filter source-routed packets at the router, to use route authentication features, and to disable source routing on all hosts.

Repudiation

If one or more parties involved in a communication, such as a secure financial transaction, can deny participation, that can jeopardize electronic transactions and contractual agreements. This would prevent a third party from being able to prove that a communication between two other parties ever took place. This is a desirable quality if you do not want your communications to be traceable. Nonrepudiation is the opposite quality—a third party can prove that a communication between two other parties took place. Nonrepudiation is desirable if you want to be able to trace your communications and prove that they occurred.

Some of the top web sites are as follows:

CERT: http://www.cert.org

TruSecure: http://www.trusecure.com

Security Wire Digest: http://infosecuritymag.techtarget.com

SANS NewsBites: http://www.sans.org/sansnews

It only takes one security hole to compromise a host and, consequently, an entire network. The attackers are like bugs trying to get into your house. You have to plug every hole; they only have to find one. Plugging security holes needs to be a continual process, not a one-time effort.

- Security is rarely designed up front. It is almost always an afterthought, at which point it becomes expensive and typically involves patching security holes after they are found. It is best to plan at the beginning.

- As more applications have features added to couple them together, more unintended security flaws appear. The complexity of all these feature interactions makes them much more difficult to understand, let alone secure.

Security Intelligence

Security intelligence is the process of staying informed about new vulnerabilities and attacks as they happen. Several resources are available to help you stay current, ranging from subscription services to free e-mail newsletters.

Virtual Private Networks (VPN)

Virtual private networks (VPNs) are becoming an increasingly popular means for organizations to provide wide area connectivity to remote users, branch offices, telecommuters, and business partners. A **VPN** is an extension of an organization's private intranet across a public network (that is, the Internet), creating a secure connection essentially through a tunnel. These private connections over shared public networks, such as the Internet, offer substantial cost savings compared with dedicated point-to-point connections, such as 800 numbers or leased lines, and they're faster than dial-up networks.

One might say that data VPNs are the same as voice VPNs, but different at the same time. The philosophical point is that a dedicated network will be overbuilt in some areas and underbuilt in others. A shared network offers the hope that we can spread the overall cost out while getting the benefits of a private network. Historically, this accounts for the popularity of shared data networks beginning with X.25, frame relay, ATM, and, now, the Internet. The Internet has become a popular, low-cost backbone infrastructure.

Because of its ubiquity, many companies now want to use a secure private network (VPN) over the public Internet. The challenge in designing a VPN is to exploit the technologies for both intracompany and intercompany communication, while still providing security. Of course, the rule of thumb we now use in an IP network is "IP on everything." VPNs securely convey information across the Internet, connecting remote users, branch offices, and business partners into the corporate network. Figure 15-6 is a graphic depiction of an Internet-based VPN.

VPNs are owned by the carriers but used by corporate customers, as if the customers owned them. A VPN is a secure connection that offers the privacy and management controls of a dedicated point-to-point leased line but operates over a shared routed network.

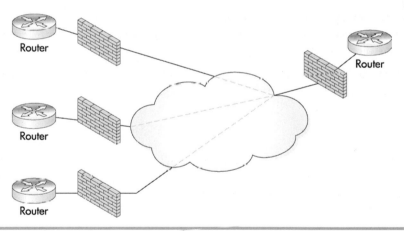

Figure 15-6 Tunnels provide secure access for VPNs.

In the past, organizations built networks for their own data only—that is, they built private networks. Private networks consisted of the physical segments (wire) and host computers that are owned and operated by a single company. Usually, these networks were composed of one large computer (a mainframe) and several peripherals (terminals and printers), and they were referred to as centralized computing.

15

The distributed computing model gave networking a new look and a new name. LANs (the new name) were made up of smaller server systems and desktop computers. These systems were eventually connected to or replaced the mainframe. As companies grew into several geographic locations and needed to share data among various locations, metropolitan area networks (MANs) and wide area networks (WANs) were developed.

Regardless of the number of locations or geographic topologies that the network spanned, however, they were all still owned or leased by a single company for its private use. Since the advent of the Internet, organizations have been finding that transmitting data over shared networks can achieve almost the same response time at possibly greater bandwidths with substantial cost savings. This is what VPNs are intended to achieve. With companies beholden to shareholders and, therefore, closely watching profits and losses, the benefits of VPNs are obvious.

In the past, we saw traditional networks being built as part of a leased line, point-to-point network. This was expensive and risky. A single link error brought the network down. Later, a virtual networking scenario emerged using a packet-switching technology called frame relay. This demanded that presubscribed links be established by being premapped in logic.

VPNs are created using encryption, authentication, and tunneling, (tunneling is a method by which data packets are encapsulated in another packet).

It is easy to jump to the conclusion that the Internet is free and, therefore, that tremendous cost savings can be had from this "free" shared network. Later, we explore some cost comparisons, but as you might guess, the relative cost benefit depends greatly on each network's geography and traffic volume.

NOTE:

VPNs are created using encryption, authentication, and tunneling.

Goals

In general, the challenges should be addressed in whole or in part for nearly all VPN implementations to be successful. Certainly, some implementations stress one or more over the other challenges and other implementations require all to be addressed equally. However, if we accept the definition of transmitting private data over public networks, as in the term VPN, then all should be addressed in some fashion or another.

- Providing data integrity—Ensuring the data remains intact during transmission

- Providing message privacy—Ensuring the data is not disclosed to nonparticipating parties

- Providing authentication—Ensuring only the appropriate parties participate in the transmissions

- Providing access controls—Ensuring the participating parties have access only to data to which they are authorized

- Audit and logging—Ensuring the proper accountability and recover capabilities

- Providing class/quality of service (QoS)—Ensuring there is not an unacceptable degradation in transmission speeds

REMEMBER

A VPN provides the following:

1. Data integrity

2. Message privacy

3. Authentication

4. Access controls

5. Audit and logging

6. Class of service and QoS

The goal of any network is to support users in a flexible, reliable, secure, and inexpensive manner.

- Network managers want the network to be flexible.

- Users want the network to be reliable and secure.

- Management wants the network to be inexpensive.

A balance of these often-competing goals can be achieved, provided a good dialog is maintained among the participants. Table 15-1 shows the network goals in terms of applications, users, potential network solutions, and access to the network. It is an exercise left to the reader to select from the list those applications and users who are to be served. The network list indicates these users and applications could be interconnected by any of these network technologies. As indicated previously, dedicated networks are expensive and rarely fit the need perfectly. Frame relay and ATM are shared network technologies that can be cost-effective, depending on the geography and traffic volume. Dial-up telephony can be a networking technology for highly mobile, low-volume users. Normally, we would like to have a backbone network with direct access for various users and dial-up remote access for infrequent users. We discuss these alternatives in following sections.

15

Access	Network	Users	Application
Dial-Up	Dial-Up	Road Warriors	E-Mail
ISP	Dedicated	Tele-Commuters	db Access
XDSL	X.25	Branch Office	Sales Support
Cable Modem	Frame Relay	Customer	Customer Service
ISDN	Internet	Partners	e-Commerce
Dedicated	ATM		Order Entry

Table 15-1 Mix of Methods to Pick From.

Shared Networks

The advantage of shared networks is that organizations do not have to incur the entire cost of the infrastructure. For that reason, frame relay has been extremely popular. Because frame relay (like X.25 before it) is virtual circuit-based, there is little concern about misdirected or intercepted traffic. Still, frame relay service is not universally available and access charges to a POP can be expensive. However, compared to the cost of dedicated networks, shared networks offer equivalent performance and a much lower cost.

Internet

The next logical step is to use the Internet as the private network. It is almost universally accessible, minimizing access charges. From our discussion of the Internet, two things are clear:

1. No one is watching the traffic or the performance of the Net as a whole.

2. The path our data takes across the network is quite unpredictable.

This leads to the conclusion that performance will be unpredictable and our precious corporate data may pass through a router on the campus of "Den-of-Hackers University." (The intent here is not to malign university students, but only to offer the observation that they are bright, curious, love a challenge, and may have time on their hands and access opportunity to do a little extra curricular research on the vulnerability of data on the Internet.)

There are then two problems: performance and security.

Performance

The performance issue poses the problem of sizing the bandwidth on each link, which becomes a major task as the network grows. Unfortunately, few network managers have a good handle on the amount of traffic flowing between any given pair of locations. Typically, they are too busy handling moves and additions to the network, which frequently leads to performance problems. Because the network grew without the benefit of a design plan, invariably this means portions of the network, including servers, become overloaded.

A dedicated-line network is expensive, requires maintenance, and necessitates a backup plan should a line or two fail. Using a shared network does not alleviate the problem of traffic analysis. On the contrary, we now have to worry about the capability of the Internet to provide the bandwidth we need when we need it. Selecting our ISP to provide the performance we need becomes an important issue.

Outsourcing

One solution is to outsource the network to a network provider (the analogy to a voice VPN here is strong). The most popular previous solution was to lease frame relay service. The benefit was that the network provider took care of the management of the network and even provided levels of redundancy (for which you paid) within its network. Unfortunately, to make the most efficient use of this service, you still need to have a handle on traffic volumes. For example, a Committed Information Rate (CIR) that was too low resulted in lost data and retransmission, while a CIR set too high was a waste of money.

A national or international carrier with its own Internet backbone then becomes a good choice as a VPN provider. One negotiates Service Level Agreements (SLA), which include QoS guarantees. Some ISPs even provide Virtual IP Routing (VIPR), in which they permit you to use an internally used, unregistered IP address [with the ISP providing Network Address Translation (NAT) to facilitate Internet access].

If you build a completely independent, internal (intranet) network, you can use any set of IP addresses you choose. This alternative is attractive to large corporations that are constrained to using Class C addresses. If these private addresses were to get out onto the Internet, chaos would quickly ensue. VIPR permits the flexibility to continue to use this "unregistered" set of addresses transparently across the Internet. This is strongly analogous to having your own dialing plan on a voice VPN.

Many possibilities and choices are here. We can outsource the whole network, including the VPN equipment on each site, or we can outsource pieces.

Network Address Translation (NAT)

Globally unique IP addresses are a scarce resource. A company simply may want to keep the IP addresses of the machines in its intranet secret. Both of these situations can be addressed with Network Address Translation (NAT), which is usually implemented in a machine that resides at the boundary of a company's intranet, at the point where there is a link to the public Internet. In most cases, this machine will be a firewall or router. NAT sets up and maintains a mapping between internal IP addresses and external public (globally unique) IP addresses. Because the internal addresses are not advertised outside of the intranet, NAT can be used when they are private addresses or when they are public addresses that a company wants to keep secret.

The weakness of NAT in comparison to VPNs is this: by definition, the NAT-enabled machine will change some or all of the address information in an IP packet. When end-to-end **IP Security (IPSec)** authentication is used, a packet whose address has been changed will fail its integrity check under the Authentication Header (AH) protocol because any change to any bit in the datagram will invalidate the integrity check value generated by the source.

Because NAT makes it impossible to authenticate a packet using IPSec's AH protocol, NAT is considered a temporary measure at best, but not be pursued as a long-term solution to the addressing problem when dealing with secure VPNs. IPSec protocols offer some solutions to the addressing issues previously handled with NAT. There is no need for NAT when all the hosts that constitute a given VPN use public IP addresses. Address hiding can be achieved using IPSec's tunnel mode. If a company uses private addresses within its intranet, IPSec's tunnel mode can keep them from ever appearing in cleartext form in the public Internet, which eliminates the need for NAT.

NOTE:

Be careful about NAT issues in conjunction with VPNs. If you are using private IP addresses and have a need to access public resources on the Internet, you are likely to have a need for NAT. If you are going to deploy an IPSec-based VPN, there are scenarios where using NAT would be detrimental to what you are trying to achieve.

Standard Outsourcing Issues

A few points are worth making about outsourcing. You must take a realistic look at the task at hand.

1. If the internal staff possesses the capability to implement the VPN, do they have the time?

2. If you outsource the whole network, how permanent will the relationship be?

3. To what extent will the internal staff become involved in the design and maintenance of the VPN?

Choose your vendor carefully. Evaluate responsiveness in the areas of presale support, project management, and postsales support. As in any procurement process, writing a system specification and Request for Proposal (RFP) is essential. Also, make up the evaluation criteria ahead of time. You may (or may not) choose to publish the evaluation criteria in the RFP. Select the vendor who is most responsive to your requirements. Here is a good opportunity for the vendor to do the traffic analysis, so a traffic baseline for design can be established. Always include growth in the RFP.

Ongoing support will be critical. If the network spans multiple time zones, specify the minimum support requirements. For example, 9 A.M. to 5 P.M. CST is of little use to offices located in Taiwan. What training is offered as part of the package? The more knowledgeable the internal staff can be, the better they will be able to support the VPN—even when they are outsourcing support.

Having a coordinated security plan is important, so you have an integrated and consistent view across your firewalls, proxy servers, and VPN equipment.

Tunnel switching is a means of increasing VPN security and flexibility by making it possible to extend tunnels inside firewalls and terminate them at any location. Tunnel switching also improves manageability by shielding remote tunnel users from changes in the internal network, boosts VPN performance by reducing tunnel setup and teardown overhead, and increases scalability by allowing multiple tunneling components to be cascaded as VPN demand grows.

What Is Tunnel Switching?

Tunnel switching is a technology that increases the security, manageability, performance, and scalability of VPNs. It provides these benefits by allowing organizations to bring multiple VPNs into the network through a single edge device, efficiently aggregate them for internal delivery, and flexibly locate their end points anywhere in the enterprise.

As stated, a VPN is a secure connection that offers the privacy and management controls of a dedicated point-to-point link but actually occurs over a shared, routed network. VPNs are enabling enterprises to use the Internet and other public networks as their own private wide area network (WAN), connecting remote users and, in some cases, branch offices, with enterprise resources at a fraction of the cost of 800 number dial-in, leased lines, or frame relay.

VPNs are created using encryption, authentication, and tunneling—a method by which data packets are encapsulated in another packet. Tunneling enables traffic from multiple enterprises to travel across the same network unaware of each other, as if enclosed in their own private pipes (something like pulling serial cables across a WAN cloud). It can also enable packets to travel across incompatible networks (for example, IPX or SNA packets across an IP network). At the destination point (tunnel termination), packets are unwrapped, returning them to their underlying protocol format.

While tunnels are generally terminated at the enterprise network edge, tunnel switching allows them to be extended safely across firewalls to specific tunnel termination points within LAN administrative domains. In this way, all tunneled traffic can be addressed to the tunnel

15

switch, with its single publicly known address, while being terminated at any number of internal destinations, whose addresses and security measures are hidden from the Internet. Realize, however, the trade-off between convenience and security: packets that are tunneled through a firewall are not checked by the firewall and may introduce vulnerabilities into the network.

Regardless of the section of the network (internal or external) the data traverses over, common points exist where the VPN begins and ends. The beginning and end points of the VPN are determined by where its functions (for example, integrity, privacy, authentication, access controls, auditing, and performance maintenance) occur. These functions may begin with the originator and end with the endpoint. They may be provided by some intermediate systems. They may also begin with an originator and end with an intermediate to the final endpoint.

NOTE:

Tunnel switching increases VPN:

1. Security

2. Manageability

3. Performance

4. Scalability

Security

The basic concept of a VPN is to provide a secure, point-to-point connection across the network between communicating entities. Several more words about security are important to keep our paranoia in check.

The first question is "How much security is enough?"

To answer that question, you must consider the impact on your business if the data you are sending is:

1. Simply lost. Is there a backup mechanism for sending or recovering the data?

2. Found by a benign entity (not a competitor).

3. Found by a competitor.

4. Actively pursued by a competitor, as shown in Figure 15-7.

5. Found by a hostile entity (hacker, criminal, and so forth).

Figure 15-7 Competitors may actively pursue your data.

In the case of the competitor or the criminal, you must ask "How much effort is the person willing to invest to get my data?"

The answer to these questions can help you decided how much security is enough.

What About Security Issues?

Turning back to security, remote access to a system must have integral security to protect the network and users from unauthorized access and penetration. You have heard about the teenage hackers who have been creating havoc in the data processing and Internet business. These young hackers break into systems for the sheer pleasure of challenging the system and showing their prowess with the modem, as shown in Figure 15-8. And it works, because they do it every day, so we have to consider these issues before opening a door.

Figure 15-8 Hackers break in just to prove their prowess.

We must start with different techniques, such as VPNs, encryption, authenticating servers, and secure firewalls. The key technologies that constitute the security component of a VPN are:

● Access control to guarantee the security of network connections

● Encryption to protect the privacy of data

● Authentication to verify the user's identity, as well as the integrity of the data

What Can We Do to Secure the Site?

Remote access for users sitting in a distant site requires that they know how to use the system, so training is important. Check the pieces of the puzzle, as shown in Figure 15-9, to make sure you have a good solution provider to handle your needs. A company with salespersons who travel frequently would provide 800 number access or access through a public broadband connection as is found in hotels, airports, and Internet cafes, or provide other means. Hardware considerations vary depending on what networking you're using, the number of users, and whether the users need desktops or laptops at the remote location. Standardization is essential—you don't want three or four different platforms, and you don't want to have to support 47 varieties of software. We want to leave the variety of flavors to the ice cream manufacturers!

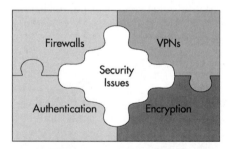

Figure 15-9 Many pieces must be considered for security.

Additionally, a firewall service will offer a bastion router capability to filter the packet, the protocol, or the user ID and address. These systems will help keep out unwanted guests. The firewall can be in different places, as you will see. They can also be integrated or CPE solutions.

Security must also be ensured while the data is in transit, which means you need to use a form of encryption so an eavesdropper cannot listen in on your data and intercept it. By using IPSec techniques, you introduce up to five different forms of encryption and digital signatures.

These will be sufficient to delay any access to the data, and by the time the code could be broken, the data will have little value.

Authentication is also an effective tool that challenges the caller and requests a "key" coded response. In a security dynamics environment, a challenge and a response can be issued by default every 30 seconds or whatever variable the user chooses to manage the logged-on users.

Implementing a VPN brings increased security by potentially inhibiting:

- Intermediate interference

  - Cryptography can nearly eliminate the possibility of system and service inundation attacks, such as SYN flood, by requiring users to authenticate themselves during the startup process. Authentication prior to the establishment of a session is a step in forming a VPN session, and it is true that failure to authenticate will make SYN floods impossible.

  - Cryptography can nearly eliminate the possibility of an intruder interfering with or hijacking a user session. It could be difficult computationally for someone to crack the encryption used in a session while it is running.

- Eavesdropping/sniffing

  - Cryptography can nearly eliminate all fears associated with password or data sniffing via transitioning the data from cleartext to ciphertext and back.

- Forgery/manipulation

  - With the use of advanced authentication processes, cryptography can nearly eliminate the possibility of intruders posing as trusted users or hosts via IP address/DNS name/user ID spoofing.

  - VPNs could significantly improve the integrity validation of transmitted data by implementing the use of one-way hash or message-digest calculations.

What Are the Risks?

You can better protect your network if you know your intruder. The people who steal from you can be relentless. They are probably intelligent and are likely to find ways around static security implementations. For effective long-term security, you need to invest in a robust security architecture and a continuous, multistep security process.

Who are network intruders? They are an extremely diverse lot who defy categorization. Yet we attempt to help you know your enemy. Network intruder motivations are complex

15

and numerous. The network intruder may fall under either the internal or the external threat category, as seen in Figure 15-10.

- Hacker—A hacker is a person who investigates the integrity and security of an OS or network. Usually a programmer, the person uses advanced knowledge of hardware and software to hack systems in innovative ways. The hacker then often freely shares his knowledge with others, usually over the Internet, which can be embarrassing to the victim. The hacker usually does not have malicious intent; he maintains his efforts to offer a service to the Internet community. Hackers are also known as "ethical hackers" or "white hat" hackers, though less scrupulous people can exploit weaknesses found by these ethical hackers.

- Cracker—A cracker is a person who uses advanced knowledge of the Internet or networks to probe or compromise network security without authorization. The cracker usually has malicious intent.

- Salami Attacker—A salami attacker is someone who breaks into the network and only takes small slices of the data at a time, usually hiding it somewhere on a casual user's system.

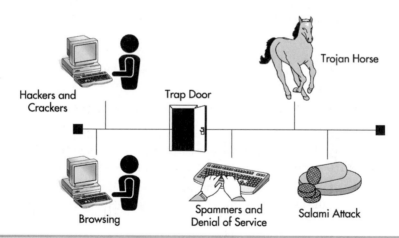

Figure 15-10 Hackers, crackers, and salami attackers are but some of the risks you must defend against.

Internal Threats

Internal threats are perpetrated by those inside an organization through intentional or unintentional activities, such as the following:

- **Current employees with less-than-honorable intentions**—Employees who might want to test security vulnerabilities or who might even have malicious intent, hoping to exploit their employer's trust for profit or theft (these are called browsers and are shown in Figure 15-10).

- **Current employees pursuing unintentional activities**—Employees who accidentally download a virus or another harmful program or who accidentally access a sensitive internal network or host.

- **Employees who mismanage the environment**—Employees who do not use safe passwords or who misconfigure network equipment out of ignorance.

External Threats

External threats are carried out by those outside an organization through intentional or unintentional activities such as the following:

- **Thrill seekers**—Many intruders do their work for excitement or to impress peers.

- **Competitors**—Your competition might enlist the help of a competitive analysis group to gain access to sensitive competitive information.

- **Enemies**—Many governments are concerned about information warfare from friendly or hostile countries motivated by nationalism, zealotry, or ideology. For example, during the Kosovo conflict, the NATO web site experienced increased hacker activity.

- **Thieves**—Intruders might seek specific valuable information for profit or some other purpose.

- **Spies**—Industrial espionage is on the increase.

- **Hostile former employees**—Employees with inside knowledge seeking revenge, thrills, or profit.

- **Others**—People might perform network intrusions for sport or for the challenge of it, to learn, or out of boredom, curiosity, or the need for acceptance from peers.

15

NOTE:

Having seen this list of enemies, both internal and external, can you ever feel secure?

Creating the VPN

There are five possible types of endpoints in a VPN, as the following shows. VPNs can be, and routinely are, established between desktop/laptop workstations and routers or VPN concentrators. The result is the end devices need not be the same to successfully create a VPN.

1. Between desktops

2. Between routers

3. Between firewalls

4. Between VPN specific boxes

5. Inside integrated boxes

Although not normally considered a VPN, someone can certainly use desktop PCs to encrypt data and send it across the Internet securely. Additionally, software is available that runs on a desktop capable of creating a VPN to a firewall or a stand-alone VPN device. Most VPN equipment vendors offer corresponding software that runs on a laptop or desktop to provide a secure path to the home office over the Internet. Most of the discussion then involves creating a VPN among business locations, branch offices, and road warriors.

Cryptography

Cryptography is the science of keeping your data and communications secure. To achieve this goal, techniques such as encryption, decryption, and authentication are used. With the recent advances in this field, the frontiers of cryptography have become blurred.

Every procedure consisting of transforming data based on methods that are difficult to reverse can be considered cryptography. The key factor to strong cryptography is the difficulty of reverse engineering. Strong cryptography means the computational effort needed to retrieve your cleartext messages without knowing the proper procedure makes the retrieval infeasible. The process of retrieval is called cryptanalysis. An attempted cryptanalysis is an attack.

Encryption

Encryption is the transformation of a cleartext message into an unreadable form to hide its meaning. The opposite transformation, which retrieves the original cleartext, is the decryption. The mathematical function used for encryption and decryption is the cryptographic algorithm or cipher.

The currently used algorithms are keyed; that is, the encryption and decryption makes use of a parameter, the key. The key can be chosen from a set of possible values called the keyspace. The keyspace usually is huge—the bigger, the better. The security of these algorithms relies entirely on the key, not on their internal secrets. In fact, the algorithms themselves are public and are extensively analyzed for possible weaknesses.

Symmetric or Secret-Key Algorithms

Symmetric algorithms are keyed algorithms where the decryption key is the same as the encryption key. These are the conventional cryptographic algorithms where the sender and the receiver must agree on the key before any secured communication can take place between them.

There are two types of symmetric algorithms: block algorithms, which operate on the cleartext in blocks of bits, and stream algorithms, which operate on a single bit (or byte) of cleartext at a time. Block ciphers are used in several modes.

The algorithms often make use of initialization vectors (IVs). IVs are variables independent of the keys, and they are good for setting up the initial state of the algorithms.

A well-known block algorithm is DES, a worldwide standard cipher developed by IBM.

An example of a stream algorithm is A5, which is used to encrypt digital cellular telephony traffic in the worldwide GSM standard. The advantage of the symmetric algorithms is their efficiency. They can be easily implemented in hardware. A major disadvantage is the difficulty of key management. A secure way of exchanging the keys must exist, which is often hard to implement.

Asymmetric or Public-Key Algorithms

These algorithms address the major drawback of the symmetric ones, the requirement of the secure key-exchange channel. The idea is this: two different keys should be used—a public key, which, as the name implies, is known to everyone, and a private key, which is to be kept in tight security by the owner.

The private key cannot be determined from the public key. A cleartext encrypted with the public key can only be decrypted with the corresponding private key, and vice versa. A cleartext encrypted with the private key can only be decrypted with the corresponding public key. Thus, if someone sends a message encrypted with the recipient's public key, it can be read by the intended recipient only. Because the public key is available to anyone, privacy is assured without the need for a secure key-exchange channel. Parties who want to communicate retrieve each other's public key.

The basic rule is: the more secure it is, the less convenient it is to use and the greater impact (negative) it will have on overall system performance. The strength of an encryption mechanism is dependent on the complexity of the calculation and the length of the key. The most readily available encryption standard is DES, developed by IBM and now standardized. The DES algorithm is the most widely used encryption algorithm in the world. For many years, and among many people, "secret code making" and DES have been synonymous. The basic key is 56 bits long. Triple DES (3DES) involves simply running the algorithm with an effective 168-bit key (by applying three different 56-bit keys). Given a plaintext message, the first key is used to DES-encrypt the message. A second key is used to DES-decrypt the encrypted message. (Because the second key is not the correct key for decryption, this decryption just scrambles the data further.) The twice-scrambled message is then encrypted again with a third key to yield the final ciphertext. This three-step procedure is called **3DES**. (Some less-secure forms of 3DES reuse the first key in the third key, weakening the algorithm.)

15

The question here is, as always, "How secure do you need to be?" The more secure, the larger the key used (or the more times the algorithm is run with different keys). This all takes time to encode and decode. Much has been made lately of the fact that by using thousands of computers, a DES-encoded message can be broken in less than three days.

Remember, this is for one key. If you change keys, it would take the crackers and hackers another three days. Are they (hackers and competitors) motivated to do this? The previously mentioned method used the brute force attack of guessing keys. Changing keys often means the attackers must start all over again. Because increased computing power had made DES vulnerable, a federal competition was conducted in the late 1990s and a new standard known as **Advanced Encryption Standard (AES)** has been approved for adoption. AES uses **Rijndael Encryption** at 128 bits, 192 bits, or 256 bits. Other encryption algorithms, such as Blowfish and **International Data Encryption Algorithm (IDEA)**, also exist, but they do not meet U.S. government requirements for adoption.

The second basic rule is that encryption performed in hardware is much faster than in software.

Key Handling

Modern encryption systems publish how their encryption algorithms work. System security is not provided by the privacy of the encryption algorithm but by the privacy of the encryption keys. Therefore, the most important part of an encryption is the mechanism used to manage keys. Here again, security is the inverse of convenience. True, keys can be sent in an e-mail. They can also be sent by snail mail or given over the telephone (not secure). The problem with this private key system is that both communicating parties must have the same key, and none of the previously discussed methods ensures the keys will not be compromised. If all locations are talking to the home office, they all must have the same key or the CO must keep separate key pairs for each location.

This key management nightmare can be handled using a different type of encryption system—public key cryptography—as a means of sharing symmetric encryption keys to securely exchange keys from the encrypter to the decrypter. X.509 digital certificate system and public key repositories are two common implementations of this technology.

Public Key Cryptography (RSA)

RSA is an Internet encryption and authentication system that uses an algorithm developed in 1977 by Ron **R**ivest, Adi **S**hamir, and Leonard **A**dleman. The RSA algorithm is the most commonly used encryption and authentication algorithm, and it is included as part of the web browsers from Microsoft and Netscape. The layman's version (don't try this at home because it won't work as described here) is that each of us thinks up a couple of prime numbers (the bigger, the better). You use one number to create a private key, which you keep for yourself, and the other number is used to create a public key, which you publish for others to use when initiating encrypted sessions with you. Anyone who wants to send you something will use the public key to encrypt, and only you can decrypt the message with your private key. Because this type of encryption is much more CPU-intensive than shared-key encryption, most implementations use public key cryptography as a means for securely transferring shared keys, which are then used to transfer the data using shared key encryption.

A common example is in the use of HTTPS (HTTP secure) in web browsers. When an end user connects to an HTTPS site, the site provides its public key to the requesting machine. That machine randomly generates shared keys for the symmetric encryption method chosen for use. That randomly generated shared key value (which will only be used for one data transfer session) is then encrypted with the public key. Because only the private key can now decipher the encrypted shared key, the key can travel across the Internet without concern for being compromised. Once the encryption of the shared key reaches the web server, the shared key is decrypted by the private key of the web server to gain access to the shared key generated by the remote computer. Because both the remote machine and the web server now have a shared key, the data transfer between the two machines can be conducted using shared key encryption.

You can also authenticate the source if the sender used his private key to encrypt his signature because only his public key will decrypt his signature. This process is shown in Figure 15-11, but it depends on trusting that when you receive Alice's public key, you can verify it *is* Alice's public key. If a third party gave you a key and convinced you it was Alice's key, you'd be encrypting the information to the third party rather than to Alice. This is where certificate authorities (CAs) come into play: they can verify the authenticity of someone's public key to you.

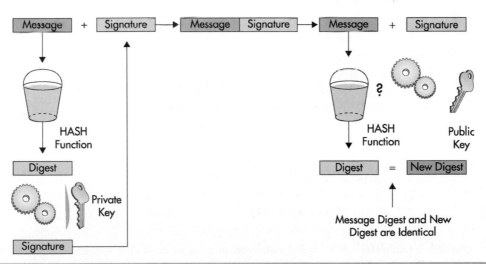

Figure 15-11 Security key management is used for IPSec.

This system is secure because of the tremendous amount of processing power it takes to factor large prime numbers. (For example, if you could factor the product, you could determine the private key.) Unfortunately, performing the encryption and decryption is also processor-intensive (read "slow"). But it sure solves the key distribution problem. Therefore, you could use public key cryptography to encrypt and distribute the keys to all your VPN boxes.

Authentication

Authentication is the process of verifying that "this is the party to whom I am speaking" and that this party has authorized access. You can do this in several ways, but the most common way is to provide an authentication server that passes out authenticated certificates based on something the user has or knows.

User level authentication   The user has or knows his or her account code (name) and password. User names are public and passwords can be compromised. The Internet commonly uses a set of layer 2 protocols called the Point-to-Point Protocol (PPP) or PPPoE (PPP over Ethernet), In PPP, the basic security methods used are Password Authentication Procedure (PAP) and Challenge Handshake Authentication Protocol (CHAP), with CHAP being much more secure than PAP.

PAP provides a simple method for the peer to establish its identity by using a two-way handshake. This is done only on initial link establishment. After the link establishment phase is complete, an ID/password pair is repeatedly sent by the peer to the authenticator until authentication is acknowledged or the connection is terminated. PAP is not a strong authentication method. Passwords are sent over the circuit "in the clear," and there is no protection from playback or repeated trial-and-error attacks. The peer is in control of the frequency and timing of the attempts.

CHAP is a type of authentication in which the authentication agent (typically a network server) sends the client program a random value, which is used only once, and an ID value. Both the sender and the peer share a predefined secret.

In fact, as part of the basic PPP protocol suite, PAP and CHAP fall short in providing a true security procedure. These schemes do not address issues of ironclad authentication and integrity or eavesdropping. PAP and CHAP are rudimentary procedures used to log on to a network, but hackers and crackers can easily defeat both.

More secure systems use a type of secure ID card or biometric information (in other words, something you have or something you are rather than merely something you know, such as a password). The credit card-sized devices use a number of possible systems for storing complex passkeys or generating one-time passwords. Biometric systems may use a fingerprint, a handprint, retinal scans, voice recognition, or even your unique typing pattern to confirm your identity.

Layer 2 Tunnel Protocol (L2TP) and Point-to-Point Protocol (PPTP) are two variations of PPP used to provide encapsulated authentication of remote layer 2 connections over layer 3 networks (as shown in Figure 15-12). An L2TP or PPTP tunnel is created by encapsulating a layer 2 authentication request frame inside a UDP packet, which, in turn, is encapsulated inside an IP packet, whose source and destination addresses define the tunnel's ends. The layer 2 authentication request can then be authenticated remotely, allowing a corporate network to challenge and authenticate a user at the network perimeter before allowing any IP traffic to be permitted into the corporate network.

Because the outer encapsulating protocol is IP, IPSec protocols can clearly be applied to this composite IP packet, thus protecting the data that flows within the L2TP or the PPTP tunnel. Layer 2 tunnel protocols are an excellent way of providing cost-effective remote access, multiprotocol transport, and remote LAN access. L2TP does not provide encryption (while Microsoft-proprietary PPTP uses Microsoft-proprietary encryption automatically). L2TP should, therefore, be used in conjunction with IPSec for providing secure remote access. L2TP supports both host-created and ISP-created tunnels. A remote host that implements L2TP should use IPSec to protect any protocol that can be carried within a PPP packet.

15

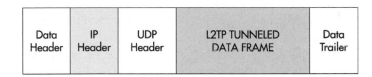

Figure 15-12 The L2TP packet tunnels the data to help protect it from eavesdropping and manipulation.

Integrated at the VPN point of access, user authentication establishes the identity of the person using the VPN node. This is because an encrypted session is established between the two locations. The user authentication mechanism allows the authorized user of the VPN system access to the system, while preventing the attacker from accessing the system.

Some of the common user-authentication schemes are:

- Operating system user name/password

- S/Key (one-time) password

- RADIUS authentication scheme

- Strong two-factor, token-based scheme

The strongest user authentication schemes available on the market are two-factor authentication schemes. These require two elements to verify a user's identity, a physical element in their possession (a hardware electronic token) and a memorized code (a PIN number).

Some cutting-edge solutions are beginning to use biometrics mechanisms, such as fingerprints, voiceprints, and retinal scans. However, these are still relatively unproven.

When evaluating VPN solutions, it is important to consider a solution that has both data-authentication and user-authentication mechanisms. Currently, VPN solutions provide only one form of authentication.

Because of this, VPN solution providers that only support one of the two authentication mechanisms typically refer to authentication generically, without qualification of whether it supports data authentication, user authentication, or both. A complete VPN solution will support both data authentication (also known as the digital signature process or data integrity) as well as user authentication (the process of verifying VPN user identity).

Packet-level authentication   The IPSec standard provides for packet-level authentication to prevent man-in-the-middle attacks. IPSec is a layer 3 protocol that enhances the use of the layer 2 underlying protocols. An authentication header is created for each packet. The layman's version of this is that a checksum is calculated and encrypted with the data. If the checksum calculated by the recipient doesn't match the one sent by the originator, someone has tampered with the data. The IPSec standard specifies two different algorithms for doing this: MD-5 and SHA=1. If your vendor's equipment supports both algorithms, it improves the chances for intervendor compatibility. The other alternative is simply not to use packet-level authentication.

To guarantee authenticity of the packets, a digital signature is required to authenticate the devices to one another. IPSec has included the X.509 digital certificate standard. Essentially, the X.509 certificate server keeps a list of certificates for each user. When you want to receive data from another device, you first ask for the certificate from the certificate server. The sender stamps all data with that certificate. Because this process is secure, you can be sure these packets are authentic.

Your vendor ideally supports both authentication algorithms and X.509. In any case, it is essential that someone in your organization understands in detail how each vendor supports the various levels of security you intend to use. These authentication and encryption systems all have to work together flawlessly. If the vendors you choose stick to the standards, this improves the chances of, but does not guarantee, an integrated working environment.

IPSec Offers a Variety of Advantages
The chief among those are:

- IPSec is widely supported by the industry, including Cisco, Microsoft, Nortel Networks, and so forth.

- This universal presence ensures interoperability and availability of secure solutions for types and kinds of end users. In addition, all IPSec-compliant products from different vendors are required to be compatible.

- IPSec provides for transparent security, irrespective of the applications used.

- IPSec is not limited to OS-specific solutions. It will be ubiquitous with IP. IPSec will also be a mandatory part of the forthcoming IPv6 standard.

- IPSec offers a variety of strong encryption standards. The key-design decision to support an open architecture allows for easy adaptability of newer, stronger cryptographic algorithms.

- IPSec includes a secure key-management solution with digital certificate support. IPSec guarantees the ease of management and use. This reduces deployment costs in large-scale corporate networks.

IPSec used in conjunction with L2TP provides secure remote-access client to server communication. L2TP alone cannot provide for a totally secure communication channel because of its failure to provide per packet integrity, its inability to encrypt the user datagram, and the limited security coverage only at the ends of the established tunnel. The major drawback to packet-filtering techniques is they require access to clear text, both in packet headers and in the packet payloads.

IPSec has two major modes: Tunnel mode and Transport mode. It also has two encapsulation schemes: Authentication Header (AH) and Encapsulated Security Payload (ESP). All four combinations of Tunnel/Transport and AH/ESP can be used. They are defined as follows:

- **Transport mode** is used when communication is to occur between a tunnel device and a defined endpoint (such as talking directly to the tunnel device). Transport mode is the least common method.

- **Tunnel mode** is when two tunnel devices create the tunnel that will carry data sent from a device behind the tunnel to a destination device beyond the tunnel device. This can be used between two tunnel-creation devices to create a tunnel between one location and another. This is usually used even when one end of the tunnel is a workstation: the workstation creates a tunnel "virtual device" to act as a tunnel endpoint that the workstation uses to introduce data into the tunnel for carrying through to the other end of the tunnel.

- **Authentication Header (AH)** is used to provide connectionless integrity and data origin authentication for an entire IP datagram, including the source and destination IP addresses (hereafter referred to as authentication).

- **Encapsulated Security Payload (ESP)** provides authentication and encryption for IP datagrams with the encryption algorithm used determined by the user. In ESP authentication, the actual message digest is now inserted at the end of the packet (whereas in AH, the digest is inside the authentication). ESP also creates a second IP source and destination header, as the entire original datagram (including the original source and destination IP address) are encrypted and unavailable for routing the packet. The IP addresses used for the second IP header are addresses of the two tunnel devices which encapsulate and deencapsulate the tunnel payload.

15

AH provides data integrity only, and ESP, formerly encryption only, now provides both encryption and data integrity. The difference between AH data integrity and ESP data integrity is the scope of the data being authenticated.

AH authenticates the entire packet, while ESP doesn't authenticate the outer IP header. In ESP authentication, the actual message digest is now inserted at the end of the packet, whereas in AH, the digest is inside the authentication header.

The IPSec standard dictates that prior to any data transfer occurring, a Security Association (SA) must be negotiated between the two VPN nodes (gateways or clients). The SA contains all the information required for execution of various network security services, such as the IP layer services (header authentication and payload encapsulation), transport or application layer services, and self-protection of negotiation traffic.

These formats provide a consistent framework for transferring key and authentication data that is independent of the key generation technique, encryption algorithm, and authentication mechanism.

One of the major benefits of the IPSec efforts is that the standardized packet structure and security association within the IPSec standard will facilitate third-party VPN solutions that interoperate at the data transmission level. However, IPSec does not provide an automatic mechanism to exchange the encryption and data authentication keys needed to establish the encrypted session, which introduces the second major benefit of the IPSec standard: key management infrastructure or Public Key Infrastructure (PKI).

The IPSec working group is in the development and adoption stages of a standardized key-management mechanism that enables safe and secure negotiation and distribution and storage of encryption and authentication keys. A standardized packet structure and key-management mechanism will facilitate *fully* interoperable third-party VPN solutions.

Other VPN technologies being proposed or implemented as alternatives to the IPSec standard are not true IP security standards. Instead, they are encapsulation protocols that "tunnel" higher-level protocols into link-layer protocols. When encryption is applied, some or all of the information needed by the packet filters may no longer be available. Many different forms of IPSec packets exist, as shown in Figure 15-13. For example:

- In Transport mode, ESP will encrypt the payload of the IP datagram. In Tunnel mode, ESP will encrypt the entire original datagram, both header and payload.

- In most IPSec-based VPNs, packet filtering will no longer be the principal method for enforcing access control. IPSec's AH protocol, which is cryptographically robust, will fill that role, thereby reducing the role of packet filtering for further refining after IPSec has encrypted the packet.

Moreover, because IPSec's authentication and encryption protocols can be applied simultaneously to a given packet, strong access control can be enforced, even when the data itself is encrypted.

Another issue in selection and engineering of VPNs is the presence or absence of Network Address Translation (NAT) in the route from source to destination. AH protocols generally "break" when used in VPNs passing through NAT because AH packets authenticate the entire packet, including IP addresses in the header, and NAT changes the IP addresses in the header, breaking the authentication.

The issue is especially problematic when remote users connect because many end-user broadband connections use NAT and this is not under the user's control. Main offices also often use NAT to increase security by obscuring addresses of stations in the main office. The two main options for connectivity are terminating the VPN tunnel before entering a NAT device, or using ESP, rather than AH, as the tunnel encapsulation method.

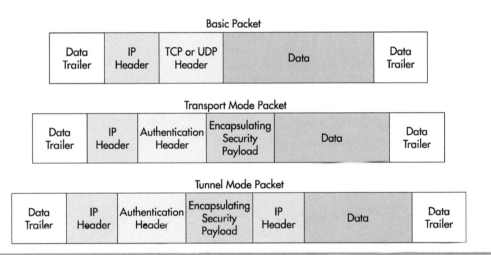

Figure 15-13 Various forms of IP packets are used to provide the encapsulation and encryption and to protect the data enroute across the network.

Router-Based VPN

Several router vendors offer VPN products based on the capability of the router to perform the requisite security functions. If your VPN is relatively small and the traffic volume not too heavy, then you might consider this option as a cost-effective approach. You need to have compatible routers at each location, as Figure 15-14 shows. If there are individuals (for example, laptop users or telecommuters) who don't have routers, they must have software that is compatible with that provided on the router. Make sure your vendor provides the compatible software that provides the level of security you require for your VPN. The absence of a firewall in Figure 15-14 may be taken to mean that in this low-cost approach, we are doing firewall functions on the router. In this case, the network would logically appear as shown in Figure 15-15.

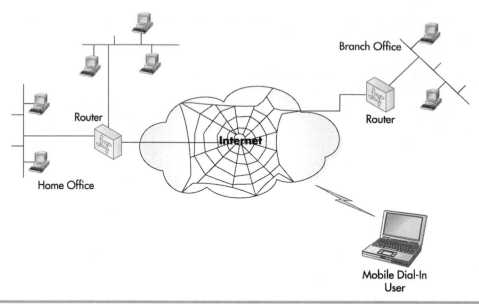

Figure 15-14 Compatible routers are used at each location for VPN services.

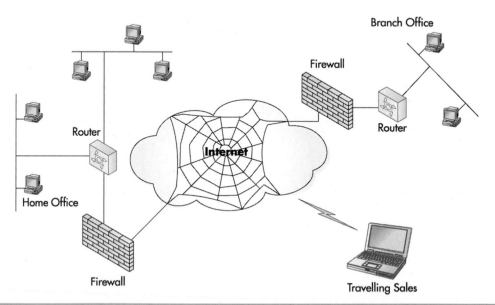

Figure 15-15 A stand-alone firewall can also be used to protect our network.

The general admonition here is you may be creating a bottleneck in the router. For large networks, let routers route.

Firewall-Based VPN

The same issues exist here as with routers. You need to have compatible (preferably from the same vendor) firewalls at each location. Mobile users or telecommuters must have compatible VPN software. Firewalls are always potential bottlenecks, so asking them to perform VPN encryption can adversely affect all other access to your network. Here again, there is no substitute for traffic analysis. We only recommend this solution for small networks where the traffic through the firewall can easily be handled by the firewall hardware.

Figure 15-15 shows a stand-alone firewall hardware that filters all traffic into our network, in addition to VPN functionality.

VPN-Specific Boxes

VPN-specific boxes are the recommended solution for high-volume large networks. Several vendors offer these solutions in both hardware and software incarnations. The general rule is this: hardware boxes will outperform software boxes and are theoretically more secure because they are based on proprietary technology that is harder to hack than publicly available OSs. (A hardened UNIX-based system is also extremely difficult to hack.) Traffic volume and feature support for remote terminals and industry compatibility will guide your decision here.

These boxes set up secure tunneling by using IPSec encryption and certificates, as described previously. They are typically installed in parallel with your firewall. The firewall handles web (HTTP) requests, while the VPN box handles access to your internal database. Figure 15-16 shows the firewall and the VPN box in parallel, reinforcing the division of labor between the two boxes. Because we now have two "holes" into our network, it is imperative that we have the permissions and access rights set up correctly. The firewall should not let users in who would be required to authenticate via the VPN box.

The integrated solution that some vendors are offering is an integrated custom box that does routing, firewall, and VPN all under one roof. This is an attractive option where traffic volume and performance is not going to be an issue. Again, Figures 15-14 and 15-15 might be used to depict this configuration.

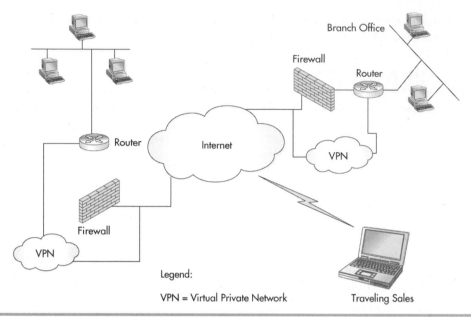

Figure 15-16 The firewall and VPN box can work in parallel to add dimension to the security needs.

Throughput Comparison

Unfortunately, while there is compatibility testing, there are no consistent performance criteria across the industry, so it becomes difficult to compare the performance of different vendor offerings. Vendor claims tend to be exaggerated. They will measure their products in the best possible light (for example, maximum-sized packets and data compression turned on, using the simplest encryption algorithm). Our recommendation is, as a starting point, to search the periodical literature for tests on the vendors you are considering.

Then, in your RFP, specify a test sequence. With encryption and authentication, there is a lot of end-of-packet processing. This causes a significant performance hit when packet sizes are small.

The number of simultaneous sessions also affects performance. Vendors claim thousands of simultaneous sessions, but ask them how many they can set up or tear down at a time, and the number drops to fewer than 100. Notice also that during this peak-processing load of session setup, overall throughput will be affected.

Here again, having knowledge of how your users use the system when the peak sign-on demand occurs, when the peak traffic occurs, and what kinds of response time you consider reasonable influences your product selection. By the way, being able to set up 100 sessions/second is plenty in a 1,000-user network. (How many of these users are using the VPN?) Worst case (which, statistically, never occurs) means the last user might have to wait ten seconds to get a session setup. Most likely, no one except the network manager with the sniffer will ever notice a delay.

NOTE:

The old saying "Pay me now or pay me later" shines through here. If you add the security of a VPN and the encryption of the packets, then performance and throughput will suffer.

Remote Management of VPN Components

If you have only two locations on your VPN, remote management of policy is probably not an issue. For a large network, visiting each site to install policy rules becomes a burden. For larger networks, look for the capability to provide secure remote policy management of not only your VPN devices but also your firewalls and routers.

15

Proprietary Protocols

Most VPN products are designed strictly around IP. They will often handle other protocols, such as AppleTalk and IPX, by tunneling them inside IP packets. This introduces both overhead and delay. If the amount of "foreign" protocol traffic is small, then this is not significant. If the bulk of your network is IPX or Apple talk, we recommend you investigate VPN vendors that will support these protocols in native mode.

Voice over the Internet Protocol (VoIP) VPN

The justification for doing Voice over the Internet Protocol (VoIP) on a VPN is primarily security, along with the reduced cost of VoIP. Depending on usage, voice generates relatively large amounts of traffic. Be sure to include this additional traffic in your sizing estimates.

Our discussion of VoIP applies whether or not we have a VPN. With a VPN, the delays because of encryption are larger, and therefore, we would expect that the performance of voice over the VPN would be worse than voice over IP. If we have chosen a network provider that will offer an SLA with QoS, there is a better chance for success, but the delays because of encryption and basic packet switching will still be there. With the exception of international calling, you must have a large calling volume to make it worthwhile to put voice over the Internet and suffer the attendant quality reduction.

VPN, the End Station, and Security

The last issue with VPNs concerns the problems with connecting devices external to your network into your network. Extending a network beyond your secure borders introduces a number of new security issues, including:

- Connecting unmanaged home workstations to the network that may have viruses or other problems that would be introduced into the corporate network via the VPN.

- Workstations connected to the Internet while connected to the VPN. If anything unauthorized occurs through the Internet to the workstation, someone taking control of the workstation could access the corporate network through the VPN.

- A lack of physical security in either remote sites or remote user facilities can introduce network compromise through unauthorized users accessing the physical workstation or VPN equipment at the remote site. This could enable unauthorized access to the corporate network through the VPN.

Chapter 15 Review

Chapter Summary

Security is not a given in a network. As a matter of fact, security has traditionally been considered last when designing a network. You cannot eliminate the risks, but you can minimize them. You can, however, get carried away and run the risk of spending more to protect a network or its assets than what the network is worth, so common sense must be applied.

When looking at the risks, you must understand many different attacks can be launched against your network. These might include dictionary attacks, brute force efforts, denial of service, SYN floods, or distributed DoS. Moreover the amounts of viruses, Trojans, spoofing tools, and other tools used by the "bad guys" are increasing daily. This means we must plan to secure the network as best we can within budgetary constraints.

VPNs can provide a cost-effective solution to having secure communications across the Internet. Performance can be improved by utilizing a national/international ISP that will offer SLAs and QoS. Choosing hardware-based over software-based VPN equipment will generally provide better performance. Choosing VPN vendors that embrace standards and support multiple standards increases your flexibility in your vendor/equipment choices. Knowing your current and anticipated traffic volumes permits you to make improved cost-performance studies.

Key Terms for Chapter 15

3DES *(735)*
Advanced Encryption Standard (AES) *(736)*
Authentication *(738)*
Authentication Header (AH) *(741)*
Brute Force *(712)*
Challenge Handshake Authentication Protocol (CHAP) *(738)*
Data Encryption Standard (DES) Keys *(712)*
Denial of Service (DoS) *(715)*
Dictionary Attack *(712)*
Distributed Denial of Service (DDoS) *(716)*
Encapsulated Security Payload (ESP) *(741)*
International Data Encryption Algorithm (IDEA) *(736)*
IP Security (IPSec) *(726)*
IP Spoofing *(717)*
Layer 2 Tunnel Protocol (L2TP) *(739)*
Malicious Code *(714)*
Man-in-the-Middle Attacks *(717)*
Password Authentication Procedure (PAP) *(738)*
Rerouting *(719)*
Rijndael Encryption *(736)*
RSA *(736)*
Session Hijacking *(718)*
Session Replay *(718)*
Sniffing *(708)*
TCP SYN Flooding *(715)*
Transport Mode *(741)*
Triple Data Encryption Standard (3DES) *(735)*
Trojan Horse *(713)*
Tunnel Mode *(741)*
Tunnel Switching *(727)*
Virtual Private Network (VPN) *(720)*
Wardialing *(710)*
Wardriving *(711)*

Key Term Quiz

1. The process of reading network traffic using a protocol analyzer is called _____.

2. Using a technique known as _____, you need only create lists of modems by scanning blocks of 10,000 numbers.

3. _____ is the act of passively collecting information about wireless networks using a laptop with a high-gain antenna connected to a wireless NIC and GPS.

4. Three basic ingredients, motive, _____, and means, create the crime triangle.

5. When an attacker tries to link user ID and passwords, this is called a _____.

6. _____ is an exhaustive trial-and-error method used by application programs to decode encrypted data, such as passwords or Data Encryption Standard (DES) keys.

7. With a _____, you download what appears to be a movie or music file, but you unleash a dangerous program that erases your disk, sends your credit card numbers and passwords to a stranger, or lets that stranger hijack your computer.

8. Also known as malware, hostile active code, or hostile applet, _____ is also known as an expanded class of attacks, formerly known as viruses.

9. This _____ attack usually involves overloading a resource, be it disk space, network bandwidth, internal tables or memory, or input buffers (buffer overflow).

10. When a "bad guy" sends a SYN packet with a spoofed source IP address of a nonexistent host (nobody) to a victim, this is considered a _____.

11. This sophisticated tool, called a _____, infects a large quantity of vulnerable hosts.

12. Data manipulation attacks during data transport are also known as _____.

13. A network intruder outside your network, pretending to be a trusted computer inside or outside your network, is called a _____.

14. Exploiting the weaknesses in authentication of data traffic is called _____.

15. The _____ methods include IP spoofing, source and/or destination address manipulation (MAC) spoofing over TCP/IP, and sequence number prediction and alteration.

16. The consequence of _____ is it can allow a remote host to pose as a local host on your network.

17. A _____ is an extension of an organization's private intranet across a public network.

18. To increase the security, manageability, performance, and scalability of virtual private networks, you can use a _____ technology.

19. The most popular encryption mechanism for which hardware is readily available is _____, developed by IBM and now standardized.

20. A three-step procedure to protect and secure your data is called _____.

21. A different encryption standard (not widely accepted or implemented) that uses 128-bit encryption keys is called _____.

22. _____ and _____ are part of the basic PPP protocol suite and fall short in providing a true security procedure.

23. A _____ tunnel is created by encapsulating a layer 2 frame inside a UDP packet, which, in turn, is encapsulated inside an IP packet.

24. A layer 3 protocol that encrypts data received from upper-layer protocols is called _____.

25. When dealing with layer 3 VPNs, _____ provides data integrity only and authenticates the entire packet.

26. In _____ authentication, the actual message digest is inserted at the end of the packet.

Multiple-Choice Quiz

1. In securing a network, you cannot eliminate_____. (Choose the best answer.)

a. Money

b. Risk

c. Management

d. Fun

2. The three pieces needed to form a _____ include means, motive, and opportunity.

a. Puzzle

b. Network attack

   c. Crime triangle

   d. Security system

3. The three forms of weaknesses that create network threats include technology, _____, and policy.

   a. Encryption

   b. Procedures

   c. Management

   d. Configuration

4. One form of data gathering, which involves sorting through several sources of information available on calendars, note pads, Post-Its, and company directories, is called _____.

   a. Honeypots

   b. Dumpster diving

   c. Scanning

   d. Social engineering

5. Say an imposter calls the help desk. He says he is the VP of Finance, and he has forgotten his user ID and password. He demands this information be given to him. What is this called?

   a. Social engineering

   b. Executive privilege

   c. Pulling rank

   d. Normal operations

6. What program is used to find users' IP addresses on a network?

   a. Version information

   b. Trace route

   c. IP configuration

   d. Scanning

7. NetStumbler is a program used to discover wireless networks while doing _____.

   a. Wardialing

   b. Port scanning

    c. Wardriving

    d. Packet capture

8. When an attacker connects to an open available port, the service running on that port can output a banner message containing _____.

    a. User ID and password

    b. Version number

    c. Protocols

    d. Host ID

9. A _____ attack is one where the attacker relentlessly guesses at all the possible combinations of names, passwords, and encryption keys.

    a. Dictionary

    b. Password

    c. Account

    d. Brute force

10. Smashing the stack is another name for _____.

    a. Buffer overruns

    b. DDoS

    c. DoS

    d. Breaking the code

11. A _____ is a popular means of providing secure access across the WAN.

    a. Security policy

    b. Router

    c. Firewall

    d. VPN

12. A _____ provides secure access for the VPN.

    a. Radius

    b. Firewall

    c. Tunnel

    d. Sniffer

13. Two critical issues that must be considered when considering network security are_____.

    a. Performance and price

    b. Performance and policies

    c. Performance and security

    d. Encryption and VPNs

14. _____ increases security, manageability, performance, and scalability in a virtual network.

    a. Tunnel switching

    b. VPN paranoia

    c. Firewall

    d. Virtual IP routing

15. The basic concept of this mechanism is to provide secure end-to-end communications:

    a. WAN

    b. IPSec

    c. VPN

    d. Encryption

16. This type of attacker will steal small amounts of information over a period of time, usually hiding the information until he or she has enough to remove from the network.

    a. Hacker

    b. Cracker

    c. Trojan horse

    d. Salami

17. Two somewhat inefficient forms of protection are _____.

    a. PAP and CHAP

    b. DES and triple DES

    c. L2TP and PPP

    d. AH and ESP

18. L2TP packets are protected from _____ and _____.

    a. Corruption and man in the middle

    b. PAP and CHAP

    c. DES and RSA

    d. Eavesdropping and manipulation

19. _____ is widely supported by the industry, including Cisco, Nortel, Microsoft, and others.

    a. PPTP

    b. PPP

    c. IPSec

    d. RSA

20. Two reasons for providing VoIP on a VPN are _____.

    a. Security and technology

    b. Price and performance

    c. Price and security

    d. Performance and encryption

15

REVIEW

Case Study

Early Adopters See Real Business Benefits to VPNs

Some companies are reluctant to use virtual private networks (VPNs) because they're concerned about Internet outages and poor performance. But that doesn't have to be the case.

FastPrint Corp., which sells electronic forms to automation and enterprise workflow systems, tore out a 14-node frame-relay network that connected 13 offices in North America and Europe to corporate headquarters in Canada and replaced it with an international VPN. FastPrint now uses a VPN gateway in each site, as well as a single international service provider for the VPN IP backbone and Internet access.

The move is reaping huge cost savings in telecommunications charges and, surprisingly, a significant reduction in response times on the network. Using the frame relay network, FastPrint had response times between Canada and California of about 300 to 400 milliseconds. In the VPN configuration, the company's typical response times are less than 200 milliseconds.

In fact, the network has been so adept at handling FastPrint's data traffic that the company hopes to move about one-third of its internal voice traffic over to the network. The first two keys to the VPN's performance are the traffic stays on one provider's backbone the entire way and the VPN uses higher-speed access lines at lower cost.

In the frame relay configuration, FastPrint paid about $2,500 USD per site per month for 56/64-Kbps connections. Now, the company uses 128-Kbps Internet access links for each site, at a monthly cost of about $1,500 USD.

In addition to the higher-capacity access lines, a third key influenced network performance: the network architecture that FastPrint used before and after the conversion. Utilizing a frame relay network, anyone surfing the Web had to go through the network to headquarters and out to the Internet through a dedicated link. All Internet traffic, including all downloaded web pages, had to cross two frame relay connections—the one linking the corporate headquarters and the one linking that user's site.

Moving to the VPN connections, when someone in a branch office surfs the Web, that user goes directly to the Internet rather than through the corporate network to headquarters.

Another important architectural difference is that with the frame relay network, traffic between branch offices had to pass through headquarters. Direct links between each site required multiple permanent virtual circuits (PVCs), which can be cost-prohibitive. With the VPN, FastPrint gets a fully meshed topology without paying for all the PVCs, because VPN tunnels can dynamically be established between any two sites.

How Do Service Providers Fit in the VPN World?

IT managers need to decide what role a service provider is going to play in their virtual private network implementation. What makes the decision difficult is that the provider's role can range from simply supplying Internet access to one where the provider offers a turnkey system that includes access, equipment, and management of the equipment and administration of VPN services.

Between these two extremes, countless variations are available to IT managers, with pluses and minuses to every approach. One strategy is to keep the role of the provider to a minimum. An IT manager purchases a VPN tunnel termination device for headquarters, sets up remote users with VPN client software, and then puts VPN equipment in branch offices. In this scenario, the provider is simply there for access. The IT staff must manage the equipment and VPN services, such as user authentication and encryption key distribution. The provider is not involved in managing the VPN.

This approach is generally regarded as an economical one. A company pays for an Internet access line to headquarters and branch offices. Users, in turn, each get an unlimited access and a flat-rate monthly ISP account, or if the carrier is charging on a per-minute basis, they get a usage-sensitive account.

One potential problem with this approach is that with a normal ISP account, there is no distinction between a VPN user dialing into the service provider for business and a teenager surfing the Web and chatting with friends. That's why some IT managers opt for a higher level of service from their ISPs. An alternative gaining popularity is to subscribe to premium access services for VPN applications.

In contrast to the normal service, a premium service provides performance guarantees. These guarantees typically come with some financial incentive for the user organization. If the provider fails to meet promised service level agreements (SLAs) for latency across its backbone or network availability, the customer gets a credit on the monthly bill. One thing to look for with SLAs is how the process works. Does the provider give the IT manager a tool to measure performance? And are user organization accounts credited automatically in the event of a network outage or a performance problem? Remember, the SLAs go out the door when traffic does not stay on a provider's network.

With SLAs in hand, some providers are offering premium usage-based user accounts that deliver much better performance than flat-rate monthly ISP accounts. Such services cost more than a flat-rate service but deliver the performance that would be required for business applications (typically, in North America, a manager can expect to pay anywhere from $2 to $5 per hour for these services). The cost, while frequently more than a flat-rate, $20-per-month ISP account, typically makes a VPN a less-expensive alternative than either direct-dial access utilizing an 800 service or paying for long-distance phone calls.

15

Applications Aplenty

Several distinct VPN applications are emerging. Each application has its own performance requirements, dictating a set of equipment and service requirements. The emerging application areas are remote access, site-to-site connectivity, extranets, and an all-encompassing "other" category.

When it comes to remote-access VPNs, the basic concept is to give telecommuters and mobile workers a way to get back to a corporate network over the Internet or a service provider's backbone. In a remote access VPN, a user dials into a service provider's point of presence, establishes a tunnel back to headquarters over that provider's network or the Internet, and authenticates herself to gain access to the corporate network. That is in contrast to the traditional dial-access approach, whereby a user dials into a bank of modems, a remote access server, or a concentrator located within the corporate headquarters.

There are a number of reasons to use a VPN for remote access. First is the cost savings on the calls. Rather than having users make a long-distance phone call or use an 800 service to dial directly into the company, the VPN approach lets the user make a local phone call to the provider's POP.

The cost savings can be substantial. Some companies say they cut their remote users' telecommunications charges by as much as 90 percent or more per month per person with dial access. Further savings can come from reducing the operational costs associated with supporting remote users. For example, when using a VPN, companies can get rid of their modem pools and remote-access servers.

Additionally, companies may be able to save other communications charges. For example, before using a VPN, a company may have a dedicated link to an ISP for Internet access and a channelized T1/E1 line into a remote access server to support dial-in users. A complete cutover to a VPN would eliminate the need for the T1/E1 line for dial access. The traffic from these users would be rolled over onto the existing Internet access line. Thus, the monthly cost of a T1/E1 line to support dial access could be cut out.

Branching Out

The next general application of VPNs is for site-to-site connectivity. As in the remote-access scenario, branch offices are connected to corporate headquarters through tunnels that transport traffic over the Internet or via a provider's backbone. Again, as in the case of remote access, a company might be able to reduce communications costs by paying only for the access line from a branch office to the service provider's POP, rather than paying for a long-distance link to headquarters.

In some cases, the cost of using a VPN link is not significantly less than that of frame relay because, essentially, the only cost is for a local connection at each end. But there are a number of other ways a VPN site-to-site connection can cut down on communications costs. For instance, many sites have multiple access lines: one to carry data back to headquarters and a second for Internet access. In fact, some industry studies have found that as many as 72 percent of sites have multiple access lines.

Using VPN technology for site-to-site connectivity would let a branch office with multiple links get rid of the data line and move traffic over the existing Internet access connection. Additionally, site-to-site VPNs can cut communications costs significantly if a company has many international sites. Typically, the cost to link a European site or a North American site to an Asian headquarters office can be quite high when using leased lines or data services, such as frame relay. A VPN built around a service provider with points of presence in countries where there are branch offices would allow the international sites to pay only for dedicated Internet access to that point of presence. This would be much less expensive than paying for a long-distance link among the United States, European, and Asian locations.

In both dial access and site-to-site connectivity VPNs, some other economic differences exist between a VPN and traditional access. With VPNs, there is flexibility. Most data services require long-term contracts. That's typically not the case with Internet services. This flexibility allows companies to quickly move to a lower-priced service if they so desire. Another area where VPNs can have an impact on a company's finances is the time to establish a connection. Although not always the case, companies can usually get a high-speed Internet connection established in a much shorter time frame—on the order of weeks—than it takes to get high-speed data services. This is particularly true if you are talking about using a VPN instead of a leased line, where it can take several months to a year for the connection to be installed in foreign countries. In industries such as construction and insurance where temporary styles are set up, this time difference can be the deciding factor in completing a project or not.

15

Does Your Organization Need Onsite, Instructor-Led Training?
1-800-322-2202—www.tcic.com

TCIC specializes in technology training on the following topics:
(These are just some of the titles)

- **Data Communications**

- **Voice Communications**

- **LAN/WAN Networking**

- **Wireless Communications**

- **Introduction to GSM**

- **GPRS Overview**

- **Understanding ATM**

- **Frame Relay**

- **Signaling System 7 (SS7)**

- **Voice over IP**

Don't have the time to spend days away from your job? We now offer some of the best computer-based training (multimedia) in the industry:

- Voice Communications Demystified

- Data Communications Demystified

- LAN/WAN Networking

  - Module I

  - Module II

  - Module III

- **T1 Networking**

  - Module I

  - Module II

- **xDSL**

- **SS7**

Available soon on CD: SONET and SDH, ATM, cable modems, and frame relay
(These titles are also available for your intranet in HTML format.)

Keynote Speeches

Hire the author for your next keynote! Bates is knowledgeable, and at the same time, animated, motivational, and engaging! He has ignited and charged audiences around the globe!

Call now 1-800-322-2202 or visit our web site at www.tcic.com.

Photo Credits

Chapter 1

National Museum of American History and the U.S. Patent Office, p. 3

100 Years of Radio (http://www.alpcom.it/hamradio/, p. 4

Courtesy of Bud Bates, p. 6

National Museum of American History and the U.S. Patent Office, p. 7

Chapter 2

Courtesy of Bud Bates, p. 31

Property of AT&T Archives. Reprinted with permission of AT&T, p. 32

Courtesy of Bud Bates, p. 33

Courtesy of Bud Bates, p. 35

Courtesy of Bud Bates, p. 36

Courtesy of David Massey, p. 39

Courtesy of David Massey, p. 40

Courtesy of David Massey, p. 42

Courtesy of Bud Bates, p. 45

Courtesy of Bud Bates, p. 50

Courtesy of Bud Bates, p. 52

Courtesy of Bud Bates, p. 57

Courtesy of Bud Bates, p. 58

Chapter 6

National Museum of American History and the U.S. Patent Office, p. 234

National Museum of American History and the U.S. Patent Office, p. 235

Chapter 9

Screen Capture - Xten, p. 420

Chapter 12

Courtesy of Bud Bates, p. 579

Chapter 14

Courtesy of Bud Bates, p. 653

Courtesy of Bud Bates, p. 653

From "Understanding and Implementing Wireless" ©1992- Courtesy of Bud Bates, p. 662

Samsung Corporation, p. 689

Nokia Corporation, p. 690

Nokia Corporation, p. 691

Index

Private branch exchanges (PBX)
  components of, 56
  digital, 58
  explanation of, 44, 54–55, 57
  peripheral devices for, 62
Private IP enabled networks, 383–384
Private-line services, 84
Protocol data unit (PDU), 558–559
Protocols. *See also specific protocols*
  explanation of, 334
  Internet, 384–389
Pseudorandom code sequences, 667
PSTN. *See* Public-switched telephone network (PSTN)
Public key cryptography (RSA), 736–739
Public key repositories, 736
Public-switched telephone network (PSTN)
  area code and, 85–86
  data communications over, 235
  exchange code and, 86–87
  explanation of, 8–9, 74, 84
  as lifeline service, 10
  subscriber extension and, 87–88
Public switches, 560
Public Utilities Commissions, 97
Pulse coded modulation (PCM), 202–203, 582, 665
Pulse stuffing, 212

Q

QAM modulation, 692
Quadrature with amplitude modulation (QAM), 368
Quality of service (QoS)
  explanation of, 411–413
  measurement of, 655
Quasi-associated signaling links, 131
Quasi-route, 134
Quick connect, 371–372

R

Radio, 4
Radio Act of 1927, 79
Radio frequency (RF) carrier signals, 617
RADIUS server, 370–371
Rate-Adaptive Digital Subscriber Line (RADSL), 103–104, 572, 585
RBOC. *See* Regional Bell operating companies (RBOC)
Real-Time Transport Control Protocol (RTCP), 155

Receivers
  cable television, 633
  explanation of, 34–35
  function of, 333–334
Regional Bell operating companies (RBOC)
  CAP and, 576
  emerging areas of business for, 103–104
  explanation of, 61, 92, 93
Regional center, 90
Registration, Admission and Status Protocol (RAS), 155
Regulation. *See* Telecommunications
Remote headend, 626
Remote switching modules (RSM), 248
Repeaters, 192, 194, 195, 489–490
Repudiation, 719
Rerouting, 719
Reverse Address Resolution Protocol (RARP), 484–487
RF transmission methods, 464–465
RF-TV channels, 630–631
Rijndael Encryption, 736
Ringers, 40
Rivest, Ron, 736
RJ-11C, 36
Rotary dialing, 40–41
Route flapping, 530
Router-based VPN, 743–745
Routers
  cable, 620–621, 625, 639
  explanation of, 490–491
  exterior, 534
  interior, 534
  Internet, 533–534
  within subnetted environment, 530–531
Routes, 133–135
Routesets, 133–135
RSA. *See* Public key cryptography (RSA)
Run-length encoding, 355–356
Rural service area (RSA), 651

S

Salami attackers, 732
Sampling, 189–190
Sanders, Thomas, 75
SandStorm, 710
Sandtrap (SandStorm), 710
Satellite communications, 4
SBC, 405
Scalability, 434
Scanning, 710, 711